Discovering Meanings in
Elementary School Mathematics

Discovering Meanings in Elementary School Mathematics

SEVENTH EDITION

Foster E. Grossnickle

Professor Emeritus, Jersey City State College

John Reckzeh

Professor Emeritus, Jersey City State College

Leland M. Perry

Professor of Teacher Education
California State University at Long Beach

Noreen S. Ganoe

Teacher Education Consultant

Holt, Rinehart and Winston
New York *Chicago* *San Francisco* *Philadelphia*
Montreal *Toronto* *London* *Sydney*
Tokyo *Mexico City* *Rio di Janeiro* *Madrid*

Library of Congress Cataloging in Publication Data
Main entry under title:

Discovering meanings in elementary school mathematics.

   Rev. ed. of: Discovering meanings in elementary
school mathematics / Foster E. Grossnickle, John Reckzeh.
6th ed. [1973]
   Includes bibliographies and index.
   1. Mathematics—Study and teaching (Elementary)
I. Grossnickle, Foster E. (Foster Earl), 1896–
II. Grossnickle, Foster E. (Foster Earl), 1896–
Discovering meanings in elementary school mathematics.
QA135.5.D59   1983   372.7   82-21335

ISBN 0-03-059933-4

Address correspondence to:
383 Madison Avenue
New York, N.Y. 10017

CBS COLLEGE PUBLISHING
Holt, Rinehart and Winston
The Dryden Press
Saunders College Publishing

Preface

This edition of *Discovering Meanings in Elementary School Mathematics* is the seventh in the series. The first three editions, published in 1947, 1953, and 1959, emphasized teaching arithmetic meaningfully. The meaning theory of learning implies that pupils should understand what they learn and should be able to use number in situations having social significance.

The Soviet Union launched Sputnik I in 1957, the first manmade satellite to orbit the Earth. This achievement demonstrated that Russia was ahead of the United States in space technology, the basis of which is a knowledge of mathematics and science. Consequently, great pressures were brought on schools to improve their mathematics and science programs. The mathematics program that was developed and implemented in elementary schools was popularly known as the "New Math," which emphasized mathematical structure, set terminology and symbolism, and included topics from algebra, geometry, and statistics. The fourth, fifth, and sixth editions of *Discovering Meanings in Elementary School Mathematics*, published in 1963, 1968, and 1973, all emphasized features of the New Math program.

Since 1973 the mathematics program in the elementary school has changed due to a number of factors. One of these has been the great increase in school costs caused by inflation. Another has been the lower achievement of pupils enrolled in the New Math program compared with the achievement on standard tests made by pupils enrolled in the more traditional program. These factors and others resulted in sharp criticism of the New Math by the media and others. The critics of the program took as their slogan, "back to basics," which meant a return to a program of arithmetic designed to teach pupils how to compute and solve verbal problems.

The Back to Basics movement brought with it a heated debate among leaders in mathematics education on the question, "What is *basic* in school mathematics?" The National Council of Teachers of Mathematics proposed new objectives for school mathematics in a brochure entitled *An*

Agenda for Action: Recommendations for School Mathematics for the 1980s. The first two of eight recommendations made by the Council were: (1) Problem solving should be the focus of school mathematics in the 1980s; and (2) "basic skills" should be defined as more than computational ability.

Because the objectives of mathematical programs for the elementary school have changed drastically since the publication of the sixth edition in 1973, a seventh edition became a necessity.

The first six editions had a thread of continuity that is continued in the seventh edition. The common elements in all editions include: (1) emphasis on meaning and understanding; (2) stress given to learning by discovery instead of by telling; (3) use of manipulative and visual aids to introduce a new topic; and (4) step-by-step development of a topic so the learner can discover a pattern to follow.

Each of the six editions had its own distinctive features. The following characteristics differentiate the seventh edition from its immediate predecessor.

1. *This edition is geared to teaching problem solving.* The former edition has problems to be solved at the end of each chapter dealing with a basic operation. The present edition retains that feature and includes Chapter 10, which gives the result of research on problem solving as well as the long experiences of the authors in instructing teachers on how to teach problem solving.

2. *This edition discusses the role of calculators and computers in the mathematics classroom.* In this age of automation and electronic wizardy, business no longer depends upon mental computation. A small handheld calculator can be purchased for less than five dollars and a computer for less than a thousand dollars. The widespread use of these instruments is certain to affect the mathematics curriculum in the elementary school. Chapter 11 deals with the use of these instruments in the classroom.

3. *This edition shows the teacher how to deal with the metric system of measure.* In 1975 President Ford signed the Metrication Act, which established a national policy for the United States to convert to the metric system of measures. The conversion should be completed in about ten years. Chapter 16 gives a short history of both the English and metric systems of measures and shows the teacher how to present the metric system so that the pupils will experience a minimum of difficulty in learning metric measures.

4. *This edition shows the teacher how to instruct pupils to read and understand the textbook.* A number of research studies show that many pupils in the elementary school are not able to read and understand mathematics textbooks. Satisfactory achievement in problem solving is impossible for the pupil who cannot read the textbook. A section of Chapter 3 deals with procedures for the teacher to follow to enable the pupil to read and understand the textbook.

Several aids to the student that were not provided in the previous editions are included in the seventh. Each chapter contains a list of achievement goals to be attained, and new words or concepts the reader may not know are presented at the beginning of a chapter and then defined in the glossary. Chapters conclude with summaries of the main points presented.

5. *Some of the topics dealing with the New Math that proved difficult for many pupils in the elementary school either have been deleted or abridged in this edition.* This edition does not include set terminology and symbolism and nondecimal bases, and gives less emphasis to nonmetric geometry than in the previous edition. The treatment of probability has been moved from the body of the text and is dealt with in Appendix B, because in very many school districts this topic is not introduced below the level of the junior high school. The topic is optional for the class that is using this book as a basic text.

This edition retains the term *set* as used in common parlance, as a set of golf clubs, but not in its technical meaning. The writers do not make a fine distinction between numeral and number as was done in the sixth edition. This edition retains the concept of *structure*, which implies there is a set of laws or properties of number governing the four basic operations of addition, subtraction, multiplication, and division.

6. *This edition has added new authorship.* Two new authors have been added to this edition, Dr. Leland M. Perry and Ms. Noreen S. Ganoe, who are both active teachers in the field.

Dr. Perry is Professor of Teacher Education at California State University, Long Beach, and has a long and distinguished career in preparing elementary teachers in mathematics. He has had extensive experience as an educational consultant and as a teacher of elementary mathematics, methods of teaching mathematics, and educational research. He has a comprehensive personal library of important publications dealing with research in elementary mathematics. His knowledge in this field is reflected in this edition. Ms. Ganoe is a Teacher Education Consultant in Florida. She has served as an elementary teacher and administrator in Florida for many years. Governor Graham appointed her to a special committee of teachers and administrators to work with districts in Florida to improve education for pupils in the primary grades. Her practical experience in the field of elementary education is reflected in this edition.

The senior writer has coauthored all six previous editions. The second writer in seniority coauthored the fifth and sixth editions. Their participation in this edition gives assurance the tested features of former editions that popularized this text for more than three decades are retained in this edition.

Organization of the Text

The nineteen chapters in the text may be divided into two groups. One group consists of Chapters 4, 11, and 12; the other consists of the remaining chapters. Chapters 4, 11, and 12 are a review of subject matter for the teacher and do not include teaching of the subject. With the exception of Chapter 1, the remaining fifteen chapters deal with the teaching of mathematics in the elementary school.

Chapter 1 provides a brief historical overview of the curriculum in mathematics during this century and gives an introduction to a modern program for the 1980s and beyond.

Chapter 2 considers the latest findings in the psychology of learning, with applications to learning elementary mathematics. As in previous editions of the book, this edition presents three levels of learning, namely, *exploratory, symbolic,* and *mastery.*

Chapter 3 provides a complete discussion of classroom organization, instructional materials, and learning activities.

Chapter 4 introduces many of the concepts of modern mathematics for the student to review our decimal system of numeration and the essential features of structure.

Chapter 5 is concerned with presenting number experiences for children in preschool and in the kindergarten.

Chapter 6–9 deal with introducing the basic facts in the four operations and the algorisms for these operations.

Chapter 10 gives an exhaustive treatment of problem solving. The suggestions given for teaching problem solving are verified by research and tested by the experience of the authors.

Chapter 11 deals with calculators and is evaluated in item 2.

Chapter 12 gives a review of subject matter dealing with primes, composites, and integers. In some schools, negative numbers are introduced before the level of the junior high school, a procedure that justifies a brief treatment of signed numbers.

Chapters 13, 14, and 15 deal with rational numbers expressed as common fractions, decimals, and percents. The text emphasizes the relationship between the set of fractional numbers and the set of whole numbers.

Chapters 16 and 17 are devoted to metric and other measurements and to geometry. The geometry pertains to learning experiences involving concepts that are appropriate for children of elementary school age.

Chapter 18 provides a comprehensive treatment of evaluation and diagnosis of strength and weakness of learnings. Oral work is stressed in diagnosis.

The concluding chapter deals with provision for individual differences within the framework of the classroom.

This edition of *Discovering Meanings in Elementary School Mathematics* not only shows how to teach elementary mathematics but also takes the teacher through the process of learning and discovery of the subject matter to be taught. The student acquires the psychology of learning elementary mathematics as well as its methodology.

Acknowledgments

The writers express their gratitude for the intangible contributions of the late Leo J. Brueckner through the first five editions of this text. His insight into how pupils learn and his knowledge of the curriculum has been reflected in his writings and has enriched each of the editions.

The writers also are grateful to the following educators who critically read the manuscript and made valuable suggestions for its improvement: Ernest Duncan, Emeritus Professor of Education, Rutgers University; James l. Fejfar, University of Nebraska; John Kerrigan, Ohio University; Charles Lamb, University of Texas; Philip Peak, Emeritus Professor of Education, Indiana University; and Charles W. Smith, Jr., Ohio University. The writers, however, assume full responsibility for the content of this text.

F. E. G.
J.R.
L. M. P.
N. S. G.

Contents

Chapter 1

Mathematics for Today's Elementary Schools 1

Chapter 2

Principles of Teaching and Learning Mathematics 14

Chapter 3

The Classroom as a Learning Laboratory 28

Chapter 8

Patterns for Teaching Basic Facts in Multiplication and Division 132

Chapter 9

The Algorisms for Multiplication and Division 155

Chapter 10

Problem Solving 176

Chapter 11

Calculators and Computers 193

Chapter 12

Primes, Composites, and Integers 206

Chapter 13

Addition and Subtraction with Fractions 220

Chapter 14

Multiplication and Division of Fractions 243

Chapter 15

Decimal Fractions and Percent 257

Chapter 16

Measurement: Metric and English Systems 285

Chapter 17

Geometry 307

Chapter 18

Evaluation and Diagnosis 329

Chapter 19

Accommodating Individual Differences 349

Chapter 1

Mathematics for Today's Elementary Schools

"The basic fact of today is the tremendous pace of change in human life."[1]

Introduction

Progress is the result of change, but change does not always result in progress. When teachers are unclear about major changes in curriculum or procedures, the result is often failure and dissatisfaction. As teachers, our greatest challenge is to glean and retain the successful elements of earlier programs and include them in a modern program in elementary mathematics.

Achievement Goals

After studying this chapter, you should be able to:

1. Describe three approaches to teaching arithmetic that were practiced from 1900 to 1960.
2. Identify four basic features of meaningful arithmetic.
3. Distinguish between New Math and meaningful programs.
4. Discuss some of the factors that contributed to the Back to Basics movement.
5. Summarize the results of Back to Basics.
6. Give several reasons why it is important for pupils to study mathematics.
7. Describe the four components of a good elementary mathematics program.

Vocabulary

A review of the following key terms will help you to understand the chapter. Each term is defined or illustrated in the Glossary at the end of the book.

Accountability	Mathematical
Approximation	sentence
Discovery method	Mathematical
of learning	structure
Exploratory level	Place value
of learning	Quantitative
Expository method	thinking
Inequalities	Social promotion
Mastery level of	
maturity	

1. From *Credo*, reprinted in the *New York Times*, Sept. 7, 1958.

1

Approaches to Teaching and Learning Arithmetic: 1900–1960

The Drill Approach

Between 1900 and 1920, the most common method of teaching arithmetic was the drill approach. A major aim of this approach was to develop skills of computation, which was accomplished by having pupils memorize combinations and computational steps by means of repetitive drill. Learning was viewed essentially as the formation of connections, or bonds, which were strengthened by exercise or repetition. Drill programs did not stress meaning and understanding.

The Social Approach

The focus of the social approach was the applications of arithmetic to real-life situations. Arithmetic experiences were carefully planned and included in the activities of "experience units." The immediate goal was problem solving in simulated real-life situations, in which several subject matter areas were treated together as an integrated whole. Typically, teachers created experience units such as "The Garden," "Our Post Office," or "The Grocery Store." Children participated in the activities of these units with much enthusiasm. Problems in measuring and reading scale drawings provided opportunities for children to see arithmetic in action.

The social approach was used widely during the 1930s. However, many prominent educators were very critical of selecting mathematical content solely on the basis of social utility. They claimed that the social approach neglected the systematic study of our number system; that it deemphasized the understanding of meaning in arithmetic; and that it paid too little attention to the development of computational skills.[2] And so, despite its many strengths, the social approach gave way to a new method of teaching arithmetic.

The Meaningful Approach

The basis for the meaningful approach was an article written by William A. Brownell in 1935.[3] Thereafter, until the early 1960s, the meaningful approach was popular and successful and greatly improved the teaching of this subject.

What were the essential features of the meaningful approach? In 1938 the National Council's Committee on Arithmetic described the meaning theory in detail.[4] Briefly, the meaningful approach recognized both the *mathematical* and *social* aims of arithmetic as interdependent and interrelated. In mathematical terms, arithmetic was described as a closely knit system of understandable ideas, principles, processes, and number relations. The social aim of teaching and learning arithmetic was the use of arithmetic knowledge and skills to deal with situations in everyday life.

In 1959 the National Council of Teachers of Mathematics reaffirmed their support of the meaningful approach. They adopted the following two basic principles:

1. "The best learning is that in which the learned facts and processes are meaningful to and understood by the learner. . . ."

2. National Society for the Study of Education, *The Report of the Society's Committee on Arithmetic*, Twenty-Ninth Yearbook (Chicago: University of Chicago Press, 1930), p. 685.

3. W. A. Brownell, "Psychological Considerations in the Learning and Teaching of Arithmetic," *The Teaching of Arithmetic*, Tenth Yearbook (Reston, VA: The National Council of Teachers of Mathematics, 1935), pp. 1–31.

4. R. L. Morton, "The National Council Committee on Arithmetic," *The Mathematics Teacher*, October 1938, 31:267.

2. "Understanding and meaningfulness are rarely, if ever, 'all or none' insights in either the sense of being achieved instantaneously or in the sense of embracing the whole of a concept and its implications at any one time. . . ."[5]

Arithmetic programs that took the meaningful approach centered on having students fulfill several basic criteria essential for successful learning of arithmetic.

1. *Experience with concrete materials.* The meaningful approach recognized that many pupils need experience with concrete materials and semiabstract visual representations before they can work with abstract symbols. Learning experiences involving objects, pictures, and drawings became known as the *exploratory level* of learning.

2. *Understanding our number system and number operations.* The development of a meaningful understanding of our number system and number operations was stressed. Understanding basic mathematical ideas was emphasized, such as "base ten," "place value," "properties of number operations," and "relationships of the four fundamental operations."

3. *Use of mathematics in social situations.* The social applications of arithmetic in everyday life were emphasized in situations involving problem solving and measurement. This technique became known as teaching arithmetic for *social significance.*

4. *Learning by guided discovery.* Learning by guided discovery became the central method of the meaningful approach. In 1960 the National Council defined this method as ". . . a program that emphasizes exploration and discovery in problem solv-

ing and aims at acquiring mathematical understanding."[6]

It should be noted that the meaningful approach was a sound and workable program for teaching *arithmetic* to children. However, in the view of leading mathematics educators, it was not enough for elementary school children to learn arithmetic. What children needed for a correct start at quantitative thinking was an early study of different topics in *mathematics.*

The "New Math" of the 1960s

Sputnik I in 1957

The successful 1957 launching of Sputnik, the first satellite, by the Soviet Union prompted large-scale, coordinated efforts to improve curriculums in mathematics and science. The effort was aimed at an American victory over the Soviet Union in the space race, which would be run and won by mathematicians and scientists. Thus another revolution in school mathematics was begun.[7]

Even before Sputnik I, the vast improvements in elementary arithmetic programs created by the meaningful approach generated professional interest in improving high school mathematics programs. The University of Illinois Committee on School Mathematics (UICSM), founded in 1951 under the direction of Max Beberman, had a profound influence on post-Sputnik mathematics programs. In addition, the National Science Foundation sponsored institutes designed to strengthen the background of mathematics teachers. After Sputnik, dozens of insti-

---

5. Phillip S. Jones, "The Growth and Development of Mathematical Ideas in Children," *The Growth of Mathematical Ideas, Grades K–12* (Reston, VA: The National Council of Teachers of Mathematics, 1959), p. 1.

6. Lee E. Boyder et al., "Definitions in Arithmetic," *Instruction in Arithmetic* (Reston, VA: The National Council of Teachers of Mathematics, 1960), p. 257.

7. See *The Revolution in School Mathematics* (Reston, VA: The National Council of Teachers of Mathematics, 1961).

tutes and organizations were created to improve the mathematics curriculum.

The School Study Mathematics Group

In 1958, when high school teachers and mathematicians gathered at Yale University to form the School Mathematics Study Group (SMSG), a project of national scope was started. The group functioned under the leadership of Dr. Edward G. Begle, and received more than $4 million from the National Science Foundation. When it became evident that initial efforts should be concentrated on grades seven through twelve, SMSG produced a series of textbooks and detailed teacher's manuals for these grades that were made available to schools for experimental use. Later SMSG produced materials applicable to the elementary grades.

SMSG was neither the first nor the only group that set out to improve mathematics teaching in the schools. But it was the largest and best-financed operation, receiving the support of the three largest mathematics organizations in the United States: The National Council of Teachers of Mathematics, The Mathematics Association of America, and The American Mathematical Society. Through a series of grants, the National Science Foundation continued to provide SMSG with large sums of money to conduct research, write textbooks, and produce instructional materials for experimental use in centers across the nation.

Differences between SMSG and the Meaningful Programs

The work of SMSG can be considered the basis of "modern mathematics," which is often misnamed New Math. The SMSG program differed from the meaningful approach in three respects.

1. *SMSG emphasized mathematical structure.* The SMSG program accepted the meaningful theory of teaching elementary mathematics, but extended the program to include *structure.* Structure implies that a limited list of number properties can be used to explain the steps involved in performing the two basic operations of addition and multiplication. Subtraction and division are the inverse operations of addition and multiplication, respectively. We discuss these number properties in Chapter 4.

2. *A mathematics curriculum replaced the arithmetic program.* Meaningful arithmetic was aimed at teaching a topic so that pupils could understand the work and apply what they had learned to solving daily problems. SMSG provided an elementary mathematics program that included a precise vocabulary of mathematical terminology and introduced many new mathematical topics, such as *sets, mathematical sentences,* and *geometry,* and many *properties of number* and set operations.

At that time the term *set* was new to almost every teacher of elementary mathematics. Previously, set operations of *union* and *intersection* had never been included in elementary programs. These ideas involve many other terms that we shall not discuss at this point.

The new mathematics curriculum expanded the subject matter to include various aspects of *algebra.* Although the pupils did not encounter the term *algebra,* they worked with equations, inequalities, and number sentences of the type $n + 3 = 7$ and $n + 1 < 6$.

The *geometry* of SMSG included both metric and nonmetric geometry. Geometry was included in the conventional curriculum only in the measurement of properties of various geometric shapes and in finding the areas of familiar figures, such as triangles and rectangles. Very few courses in the conventional program treated nonmetric topics such as points, segments, lines, rays, and one- or two-dimensional figures.

3. *SMSG introduced topics earlier in the*

program. The third curricular change was in the grade placement of topics. The New Math program introduced many topics at least one grade level earlier than they were in the conventional program. In the new program, the 100 facts of addition and subtraction were presented in the first and second grades rather than in the second and third grades. However, programs of this type were found to be very difficult for many average pupils and most slow learners.[8]

Typically, innovations in education take a hiatus, and then acquire the proper perspective. In the context of a national emergency, New Math programs were introduced into the elementary schools, and "crash" in-service programs were set up for teachers and parents. Consequently, there was a great deal of confusion and controversy over both the mathematical content of the new program and the methods of teaching that were advocated.

Factors Contributing to "Back to Basics"

Anti-New Math Forces

The essence of the almost universal revolt against the New Math programs of the 1960s was articulated most clearly in a *Time* magazine article. The article decried New Math as a "faddish theory (that) swept through the profession, changing standards, techniques, procedures (that were introduced) without adequate tryout, and poorly understood by teachers and parents (with the result of) lowered basic skills and test scores in elementary mathematics."[9]

8. For a historical account of the workings of SMSG see William Wooton, *SMSG: The Making of a Curriculum* (New Haven: Yale University Press, 1965).

9. "Help! Teacher Can't Teach," *Time,* June 16, 1980, 115:59.

The pressures exerted by many social influences during the 1970s resulted in a general revolt against New Math, especially as it was implemented in the primary grades. The panic for superiority in space that arose from Sputnik I finally disappeared when the United States landed men on the moon. And the major forces responsible for the development of New Math were succeeded by various social, professional, and technological pressures for a renewed emphasis on changing: (a) what we teach children in elementary mathematics and (b) how we help children learn elementary mathematics.

Research on Cognitive Development

The proponents of New Math held that if the subject is sequentially ordered around basic unifying structural properties, such as number, number operations, equations, and geometric designs, children should be able to learn faster, remember longer, and better understand many topics in elementary mathematics. Furthermore, new topics in mathematics could be introduced at a very early age.

But the foundations of New Math were undermined by research on cognitive development conducted by noted psychologists, such as Piaget and Brownell. Their findings showed that most children do not adequately understand the "structural properties" of mathematics before age seven and, until age eleven, depend on physical objects to shape their thinking.

Logic alone is not a sufficient basis for selecting the content of mathematics and ordering it for teaching. The evidence on cognitive development was largely disregarded in the development and implementation of many New Math programs. As Glennon observed, "Eminent cognitive/developmental psychologists such as William A. Brownell in this country and Jean Piaget in Switzerland were like voices crying in the wilderness, despite the fact that they had earlier produced the major theories and research on cognitive development."[10]

Teacher Concerns

Many elementary school teachers found New Math difficult both to understand and to teach to children. Teachers claimed that most of the topics were introduced too early and too abstractly, at a level beyond what most young children can understand. Little of the new content could actually be applied to real-life situations—a requirement for learning to be meaningful to children. Parents became concerned when they had trouble helping their children with homework. There was a clamor to return to the "good old days" of solving real-life problems with good, old-fashioned computation![11]

Increased Cost of Schools

In addition to the anti-New Math forces, research on cognitive development, and teacher concerns, several other factors led to the Back to Basics movement of the 1970s. School costs rose very rapidly during the first part of the decade. Boards of education found it difficult to get school budgets approved. In many communities, the student population shrank while school costs increased. Naturally, citizens began to ask why public education had become so costly; and to avoid more tax increases, they began to pressure the schools to concentrate on teaching children only the basics.

Reported Low Academic Achievement

Another factor that tended to support the Back to Basics movement was the reported low academic achievement—that is, declining test scores—of school graduates. When many of these graduates applied for jobs, they proved to be deficient in computational ability and in reading skills. In a climate of mounting costs and low achievement, foes of public education called for an investigation of the causes.

Surveys revealed a wide range of causes of poor achievement. Some of those cited most frequently were *lack of discipline, limited time for recitation, lack of homework, social promotions,* and a *grading system* that nonprofessionals could not interpret.[12]

Lack of Discipline

Since 1969, Phi Delta Kappa has sponsored the Annual George Gallup Poll on the Public's Attitude Toward Education.[13] In all but one survey, the most serious obstacle to education, in the view of both parents and teachers, was lack of discipline. Typically, parents and teachers would respond to this finding by demanding stricter standards of behavior. Schools were called on to "clamp down," with punishments for misbehaving to include the use of corporal punishment.

In the name of better discipline, the Back to Basics movement in many cases brought back drill-type programs using abstract materials to teach computational skills in a quiet, routinized manner. As a result of the new "quiet" classroom atmosphere, many valuable teaching techniques, such as the use of learning centers, small group discussions, and exploratory experiences with manipulatives, were cut from school programs

10. Vincent J. Glennon, "Mathematics: How Firm the Foundations?" *Phi Delta Kappan,* January 1976, 57:303.

11. David Rappaport, "The New Math and Its Aftermath," *School Science and Mathematics,* November 1976, 76:563–570.

12. Ben Brodinsky, "Back to the Basics: The Movement and Its Meaning," *Phi Delta Kappan,* March 1977, 58:522–527, and Ben Brodinsky, "Something Happened: Education and the Seventies," *Phi Delta Kappan,* December 1979, 61:238.

13. See "Annual Gallup Poll on the Public's Attitude Toward Teaching," *Phi Delta Kappan,* published each September since 1969.

because these activities caused children to make too much noise.

Consequences of the "Back to Basics" Movement

Narrow Curriculum in Mathematics

Many of the topics introduced in the 1960s to emphasize the *structural* aspects of mathematics were dropped from the Back to Basics curriculum. As a result, the program tended to stress computational skills. This narrow view of elementary mathematics produced serious deficiencies in problem-solving abilities and in mathematical applications skills. (See Chapter 10, Problem Solving, and Chapter 16, Measurement: Metric and English Systems.)

Increased Testing

With the Back to Basics movement came an increase in testing, as a result of efforts to

use standardized tests to indicate mastery in elementary mathematics.[14]

use competency tests to determine promotion to the next grade and to determine who would qualify for a diploma.

use state and national assessment tests to monitor the success and failure, in terms of test scores, of schools and school districts.

Minimum Competency Tests Used to Prove Accountability

By 1978 thirty-six states had laws requiring that some type of test be used to demonstrate that students had in fact achieved essential learning. Five states required competency in "computational skills." Two

states required tests in "arithmetic." Seventeen states had minimum competency tests in "mathematics."[15]

Low Teacher Morale

Throughout the Back to Basics movement, teacher morale was low. Many factors contributed to lack of job satisfaction, which in turn hampered teacher effectiveness. Inflation, and the ensuing taxpayers' revolt, strained school budgets. Boards of education found it increasingly difficult to fund teachers' pay raises and to purchase needed books and supplies. Inevitably, teacher contract negotiations were rife with conflict among teachers, administrators, and boards of education over many issues, leading to further frustration and dissatisfaction among teachers. An opinion poll conducted in early 1980 by the National Education Association revealed that:

less than 50 percent of the teachers planned to teach until retirement age.

35 percent indicated dissatisfaction with their current positions.

9 percent said that they would leave teaching as soon as possible.

Declining SAT Scores

Back to Basics was supposed to reverse the trend of declining test scores. However, an analysis of test results for the twelve years from 1967 to 1979 revealed a continuing decline in Scholastic Aptitude Test scores of college-bound high school seniors.[16]

14. These types of tests, their strengths, and their weaknesses are discussed in Chapter 18, Evaluation and Diagnosis.

15. For a more detailed discussion of minimum competency testing, see Chris Pipho, "Minimum Competency Testing 1978: A Look at State Standards," *Phi Delta Kappan*, May 1978, 59:585, and Henry S. Dyer, *Parents Can Understand Testing* (Columbia, MD: The National Committee for Citizens in Education, 1980).

16. *Admissions Testing Program of the College Board, National Report, College Bound Seniors* (Princeton, NJ: College Entrance Examination Board, 1979), p. 5.

Declining National Assessment of Educational Progress Scores

In response to the continuing decline of college admissions scores, the public established various state and national testing programs to monitor the progress of students through elementary and secondary schools. The National Assessment of Educational Progress was established to determine the extent to which the students in American schools were achieving educational goals in the areas of reading, writing, citizenship, social studies, science, mathematics, music, literature, art, and career/occupational development.[17]

When the results of the 1973 and the 1978 Assessments in Mathematics were compared for nine-, thirteen-, and seventeen-year-olds in the four major areas tested, no improvements were noted for any age group in any major area of mathematics. In fact, there were *declines* in three areas:

- mathematics skills for 13- and 17-year-olds
- mathematics understanding for 13- and 17-year-olds (9-year-olds were not tested in this area)
- mathematical applications and problem solving: serious declines for all three age groups tested

The Back to Basics movement, with its demands for teaching the three R's and strict discipline, did not enhance the learning of elementary mathematics. Concerted efforts to prepare children for tests in basic skills denied them necessary experiences in the learning cycle, such as working with concrete materials and applying their knowledge to real-life problem situations.

Hechinger summed up the impact of the Back to Basics movement as follows:

> [The movement confused] . . . a necessary effort to wipe out widespread and severely debilitating deficiencies in basic skills with a counter-productive drive to "restore" the schools to the philosophy that learning should be unpleasant medicine. [We need to] give education a structure that draws its strength from an inherent sense of accomplishment rather than from the negative restrictions of autocratic discipline or the drab concentration on skills. Basic and essential as they are, skills remain only tools with which to manage the multifaceted business of learning, living, and striving.[18]

From the Past to the Future— Elementary Mathematics Programs for the 1980s and Beyond

Each of the movements discussed in this chapter was a valid attempt to improve the teaching and learning of elementary mathematics. Each movement emphasized certain objectives and approaches; however, because of the dynamic nature and the diversity of American public education, it cannot be assumed that these principles were fully accepted or implemented by teachers. Future elementary mathematics programs will continue to change to meet the challenges of the changing times.

The teacher is the key to improvements. Improvements in elementary mathematics programs will result from the efforts of competent, well-informed, skillful, and caring teachers who

- understand mathematics, are skillful in working with number and operations, and can put mathematics to use in problem-solving activities.
- understand children and how they learn,

17. Information about the National Assessment of Educational Progress can be obtained from the Education Commission of the States, 1960 Lincoln, Suite 700, Denver, CO 80203.

18. Fred M. Hechinger, "The Back-to-Basics Impact," *Today's Education,* February/March 1978, 67:32.

grow, and develop, and are skillful in dealing with students in the teaching–learning process.

understand the teaching–learning process and can apply psychological principles in bringing mathematics to the children's level of mental development.

Problem solving is the central goal of mathematics instruction. The National Council of Teachers of Mathematics has established as a first priority the teaching of problem solving. They state that "problem solving must be the focus of school mathematics in the 1980s."[19] It is important to recognize that although problem solving will be the central focus of elementary mathematics programs through the 1980s, many other learning objectives must be considered and kept in proper balance.

Clear goals and objectives are the basis of a comprehensive, balanced mathematics program. In 1978 leaders of eighteen professional organizations reviewed *The Essentials of Education* and concluded that knowledge and skills in mathematics were among the essential attributes of an educated person. Specifically, these attributes included the ability

"to use mathematical knowledge and methods to solve problems";

"to reason logically";

"to use abstractions and symbols with power and ease";

"to understand spatial relationships . . ."; and

"to prepare to go on learning for a lifetime"[20]

19. *An Agenda for Action—Recommendations for School Mathematics of the 1980s* (Reston, VA: The National Council of Teachers of Mathematics, 1980).

20. See *The Essentials of Education* (Urbana, IL: Organization for the Essentials of Education, 1980, p. 3). Copies can be obtained by writing to Organization for the Essentials of Education, 1111 Kenyon Road, Urbana, IL 61801.

By listing the essentials as broad goals, one can begin to construct more specific program objectives for today's mathematics. Generally, children are expected to develop

an intelligent system of *quantitative thinking* in *problem-solving* situations.

a functional knowledge of the *language* and *structure* of mathematics, including techniques of *approximating* and *estimating*, as well as *determining the reasonableness of the results of problem solving.*

a sensitivity to a wide variety of *quantitative situations* in society and the ability to *apply* mathematics in everyday situations.

an *intelligent mastery of computational skills,* with an emphasis on working with single-digit number facts for the operations of addition, subtraction, multiplication, and division with whole numbers, rationals, decimals, and percents *as a prerequisite for* mastering the use of the *hand-held calculator* for multidigit number operations. We use the term *intelligent mastery* of computation to emphasize the fact that children must *understand the meanings* of number, number symbols and signs, number operations and their relationships to each other, properties of number and number operations, and the like. Intelligent mastery also means that children learn computation as one important phase of the *problem-solving* process.

an appreciation of the *use and importance of mathematics* in modern society, including

an understanding of and skills in *measuring* in metric as well as English units.

the ability to *read mathematical* content in written problems, tables, maps, charts, and graphs.

beginning concepts and use of *probability* to predict the likelihood of future events.

an awareness of the role of the electronic *computer* in our modern society.

a *healthy, favorable attitude* toward learning and inquiry in mathematics.[21]

Automation and the Study of Mathematics

The growing commercial use of electronic computational devices has nearly eliminated the need for workers to have highly developed computational skills. As a result, students may ask why they need to learn mathematics. This question stems from the erroneous idea that computation is the essence of mathematics. Here are some of the reasons why students need to study mathematics.

1. A computational instrument can do only mechanical operations that do not require thought. The operator of the device and the person who design the program must have a substantial knowledge of mathematics.

2. To enter most of the major professions, students need a strong mathematical background. Many students complete junior and senior high school, and even college, without choosing their life's work. With a limited background in mathematics, their options are severely limited. Indeed, President Reagan commented to the press that pages of want ads in the Sunday paper offer jobs that cannot be filled because the unemployed are not qualified. Many of the jobs now available demand a knowledge of mathematics. Even though unemployment is high, the number of available jobs is also high.

21. "Ten Basic Skill Areas," *Arithmetic Teacher,* October 1977, 25:20.

3. Because mathematics is systematic and sequential, it is vital to have a good foundation so that one can continue to study. The basic facts of addition, subtraction, multiplication, and division are the building blocks for later study. Students who know and understand these facts and the basic concepts associated with them will have background needed to continue working in this field.

4. Teachers should encourage and motivate pupils to study mathematics. Often, pupils' attitudes toward a subject are a reflection of their teachers' attitude. Teachers should emphasize the enjoyment of acquiring a knowledge of mathematics and the satisfaction gained from using it. It follows, then, that students will not fear mathematics and dread studying it.

5. As long as they live in the United States, people who cannot read or write English face serious economic and social problems. Likewise, people who are illiterate in mathematics face burdensome economic problems. Mathematics is a language. Students must learn this language to become literate in the use of number just as they must learn to use their mother tongue.

It is a known fact that careers in engineering and the sciences require a strong background in mathematics. Students who avoid studying mathematics today will find that they are limiting their options for successful careers tomorrow.

Four Components of Elementary Mathematics Programs

The four essential features of a good, comprehensive, elementary mathematics program are:

1. A component designed to assist children in *discovering* meanings, through the use of manipulative materials.

The computer is changing how mathematics is learned. *(Photo by Leland Perry)*

A mathematics laboratory stocked with carefully selected instructional materials provides children with many opportunities to explore basic number ideas.

2. A component designed to assist children in developing an understanding of *mathematical structure*, through the use of pictures, drawings, structural aids, mathematical notations, and the like. Emphasis is on using number patterns created at the concrete level and recorded at the picture and symbolic levels of learning. The knowledge that children acquire encompasses ideas from arithmetic, geometry, algebra, and metrics.

3. A component designed to assist children in developing an intelligent mastery of *computational skills*. This is a different type of knowledge from that of components 1 and 2, though it stems from experiences provided by these two components.

4. A component designed to assist children in developing *problem-solving skills*, as well as an understanding and appreciation of the *applications* and uses of mathematics in various real-life problem settings, including *measurement.*

The four components need to be kept in the proper *balance* because the learning that takes place as a result of component 1 is a readiness and prerequisite for the learning due to component 2; this component in turn serves to make the skills developed by component 3 more meaningful, which in turn enables children to use mathematics more efficiently in problem-solving and measurement situations.

Throughout the 1980s and 1990s, there will be many changes in mathematics in the elementary schools. There will be advancements in many areas. Several questions will need to be addressed:

1. Will the emphasis on problem solving generate a new kind of quantitative thinking by students?

2. Will laboratory approaches become a stronger component of the learning environment?

3. Will the increased use of minicalculators lead educators to reevaluate the process of teaching students to calculate with multi-digit numbers?

4. As metric measurement is introduced, will there be a trend to teach decimals early in the learning sequence, leaving the treatment of common fractions to the later grades?

> The 1980s will be more demanding, present more challenges, bring about more change (in society and schools), and place more emphasis on mathematics, than either of the last two decades.[22]

The seventh edition of *Discovering Meanings in Elementary School Mathematics* is a blueprint for teaching mathematics in the elementary school for the 1980s and be-

22. James W. Wilson, "Aren't We Doing Something Right?" *Arithmetic Teacher*, March 1980, 27:5.

yond. Use of this text should enable the teacher to understand and implement an effective program of modern mathematics.

Summary

Between 1900 and 1980 there were five major movements that changed mathematics programs in the elementary schools. Each movement had a major theme, and each had deficiencies. Elements of each approach still appeal to today's elementary school teachers, so one can find evidence of each movement in some classrooms.

The *drill approach* was designed to develop the "faculties of the mind" through repetitive drill on computational skills. But it lacked meaning and did not apply computational skills to problem-solving situations. The *social approach* attempted to make arithmetic more useful and practical. But it neglected the systematic development of the content and skills of arithmetic. The *meaningful approach* merged the fundamental concepts and skills of arithmetic with social utility. But the meaningful approach emphasized only arithmetic.

New Math brought major changes in the content of mathematics in the elementary schools, emphasizing structure and including new topics in mathematics. However, New Math introduced too much content into the curriculum too fast and expected pupils to learn it too soon. The *Back to Basics* movement prompted a reexamination of the mathematics curriculum in order to determine the most essential content to be taught in the elementary schools. It resulted in several changes in elementary mathematics textbooks that in turn produced changes in what was taught to pupils. Many New Math topics were either reduced or dropped from the curriculum, and more pages of the textbook were devoted to drill exercises. In response to Back to Basics, many leading mathematics educators feared a return to the overemphasis on learning computational skills through rote drill. They hastened to advocate a broader interpretation of the "basics." The National Council of Teachers of Mathematics identified *ten basic skill areas* and adopted *An Agenda for Action,* which is designed to serve as a blueprint for future programs. The key factor in this program is problem solving.

Exercises

1. In what ways did New Math differ from the meaningful approach?

2. What are the essential features of a "modern approach" to the teaching of elementary school mathematics?

3. Identify two desirable features and two undesirable features of (1) the drill approach, (2) the social approach, (3) the meaningful approach, (4) the New Math approach, and (5) the Back to Basics approach.

4. Why are improvements in mathematics education so heavily dependent on the actions of teachers?

5. Discuss: "The computer: Why is it essential to the future of American education?"

Selected Readings

Goodlad, John I. *What Schools Are For.* Bloomington, IN: Phi Delta Kappa Educational Foundation, 1979.

Heddens, James W. *Today's Mathematics,* Fourth Edition. Chicago: Science Research Associates, 1980, pp. 1–6.

Kramer, Klaas. *Teaching Elementary School Mathematics,* Third Edition. Boston, MA: Allyn and Bacon, 1975, pp. 13–25.

Lindquist, Mary Montgomery (Ed.). *Selected Issues in Mathematics Education,* 1981 Yearbook of the National Society for the Study of Education. Berkeley, CA: McCutchan Publishing Company, 1980.

Priorities in School Mathematics. Reston, VA: The National Council of Teachers of Mathematics, 1981, p. 32.

Riedesel, C. Alan. *Teaching Elementary School Mathematics,* Third Edition. Englewood Cliffs, NJ: Prentice-Hall, 1980, pp. 31–41.

Chapter 2

Principles of Teaching and Learning Mathematics

Educational psychologists are concerned with both the nature of the learner and the learning process. Their research has yielded many useful insights about children and how they learn. The many applications of the research findings and writings of pioneers such as Piaget, Brownell, Bruner, and Gagné have led to major improvements in mathematics education. Their findings have also been valuable in the selection and placement of mathematical content at each grade level and in establishing the sequence of topics to give optimum learning. Today's mathematics programs are based on both the structure of the subject and the nature of the learner's needs, interests, and abilities.

There are many ways to learn mathematics. Consequently, there are many ways to teach mathematics. Ultimately, it is the teacher's responsibility to organize and create for each student the most favorable environment for learning.

Achievement Goals

After studying this chapter, you should be able to:

1. Identify three broad areas of *learning objectives* and list at least two specific objectives within each.
2. Explain the meaning and importance of three *levels of learning* mathematics.
3. Describe *readiness* in terms of two major aspects of growth.
4. Illustrate several ways to enhance the *motivation* of pupils to learn mathematics.
5. Defend *guided discovery* as an effective approach to teaching certain aspects of mathematics.
6. Name two factors that are part of the *discovery approach*.
7. Summarize the role of *number properties and patterns* in learning mathematics.
8. Discuss two types of *practice* and the purposes of each.
9. Analyze a mathematics lesson in terms of seven principles of learning.

Vocabulary

Knowing the meanings of the following key terms will help you to understand the chapter. Each term is defined or illustrated in the Glossary at the end of the book.

Brain hemispheres
Exploratory level
  of learning
Mastery level of
  learning
Number patterns
Number properties
Overload a place

Place value
Quantitative
  thinking
Reinforcement
Regroup
Rename
Symbolic level of
  learning

Establishing Learning Objectives

PRINCIPLE 1: *Both the teacher and the pupils should clearly understand* what *is to be learned and* how to go about *the learning process.* Children are expected to achieve the goals and objectives of elementary mathematics through a series of planned learning experiences. Learning activities should be determined by the educational goals and objectives established for the program.

The major goal of elementary mathematics is to provide pupils with a *system of quantitative thinking* that arises from understanding fundamental concepts and skills. A meaningful program must go beyond rote memorization. Children should understand and see sense in what they learn. As a result, they will remember longer and be able to use more efficiently the *cognitive* aspects of mathematics.

Behavioral objectives should emphasize understanding mathematics, developing intellectual skills, proficiency in problem solving, applying mathematics, and fostering a positive attitude toward the subject. These objectives can be classified as *cognitive, skillful,* and *affective* areas.

Cognitive Objectives

Understanding mathematical concepts and principles is a major goal of instruction. *Cognition* is the act or process of knowing, which includes both awareness and judgment.[1] Here is a list of some cognitive objectives.

to remember facts and definitions in mathematics

to discover patterns and number relationships

to reason logically from what is known to what is to be found

to understand the meanings of concepts such as place value, the four fundamental operations, and familiar geometric figures

to draw conclusions and make judgments based on mathematical thinking

Skillful Objectives

Included in modern mathematics programs are a wide variety of skills that children need to acquire. The following items are some skillful objectives.

mastery of the basic facts in the four fundamental operations

ability to perform the four fundamental operations using algorisms

ability to solve a number sentence with a missing number that has been replaced with a frame, such as: $8 + \square = 12$; $13 - \square = 9$; $4 \times \square = 12$; and $21 \div \square = 7$.

Affective Objectives

Affective objectives involve the students' level of interest and their attitudes and val-

---

1. See Benjamin S. Bloom et al., *Taxonomy of Educational Objectives: The Classification of Educational Goals: Handbook I: Cognitive Domain* (New York: McKay, 1956).

ues toward the self, others, learning in general, and mathematics in particular. A child who is developing a positive attitude toward mathematics and sees it as worthwhile will behave essentially as described here for the following levels:[2]

Level 1: Receiving/Attending

Attention is directed toward the learning activity, and the child is aware of what is happening.
Child willingly listens and receives stimuli from the activity.
Child seeks out ideas, facts, procedures, and is alert and attentive.

Level 2: Responding

Because of a new inner compulsion, the child becomes willing to respond and to participate.
Emotional satisfaction is gained from responding; there is enjoyment.

Level 3: Valuing

The child recognizes that learning mathematics has value and importance in society.
The child shows a preference for mathematics activities over other activities.
The child realizes a knowledge of mathematics is valuable and desires further study.

Fostering the Growth of Concepts and Skills

PRINCIPLE 2: *Learning is a growth process that has three stages: exploratory, symbolic, and mastery.* Two facts are central to the acquisition of mathematical concepts and skills. These are that mathematics is sequential, and that learning is a growth process. To foster the acquisition of mathematical concepts, one must recognize that there

are levels of cognitive development. Piaget identified four stages of cognitive development between birth and the age of twelve: (1) sensorimotor stage, (2) preoperational stage, (3) concrete operations stage, and (4) formal operations stage.[3] Bruner built upon Piaget's four stages of cognitive development, and formulated the following three levels of learning:

At the first level, the child manipulates objects or things.

At the second level, the child deals with pictures or images of objects, but does not manipulate the objects.

At the third level, the child deals with symbols or numerals and no longer deals with tangible or concrete objects.[4]

Throughout this text, we will stress the following three levels of learning.

1. *Exploratory:* the same as Bruner's first level.

2. *Symbolic:* a combination of Bruner's second and third levels.

3. *Mastery:* the level attained when a student understands the work and can perform the skill required for an operation in a habitual manner. Computational errors will occur by chance and will not be constant.

Meaningful learning involves manipulative materials that give meaning to symbols and numerals and make possible a gradual transition from the concrete to the abstract level of thinking. The teacher must diagnose each child's level of learning to discern the appropriate activities for the most effective learning. (In Chapter 18 we will describe appropriate diagnostic methods.)

2. D. R. Krathwohl, B. S. Bloom, and B. B. Masia, *Taxonomy of Educational Objectives: Handbook II: Affective Domain* (New York: McKay, 1964).

3. Ved P. Varma and Phillip Williams (Eds.), *Piaget, Psychology and Education* (Itasca, IL: Peacock, 1976).

4. Jerome S. Bruner, Rose R. Oliver, and Patricia M. Greenfield, *Studies in Cognitive Growth* (New York: Wiley, 1966), p. 12.

Determining and Developing Readiness

PRINCIPLE 3: *Readiness is essential for learning.* Teachers should introduce each new topic in mathematics in simple and easily understood terms and foster a sequential understanding of the topic at various levels of learning. Children will grow aware of the need for a new idea or skill before they are asked to learn it. *Readiness for any progression means that there must be an optimum set of conditions that enable the child to get the maximum value from instruction.*

Readiness to learn a particular topic in mathematics is directly related to two major aspects of growth.

1. Each pupil has achieved sufficient learning and maturity to deal with the new topic. Pupils who are still counting objects to determine the sum of $6 + 9 = \square$ are not ready to solve addition examples of the type $27 + 18 = \square$.

2. Each pupil has acquired prerequisite skills. Mathematics is a subject that proceeds sequentially, from simple concepts and skills to more complex ones. Pupils who do not adequately master the prerequisites to a new topic will have difficulty.

It is often possible for a teacher to start the whole class on the same topic, such as the addition of whole numbers. After making an initial class presentation, the teacher is better able to diagnose the learning needs of each child. For subsequent lessons, the teacher can then divide the class into groups according to special needs on the topic; for example, one group may deal with objects in the joining process, while another group works with the properties of addition; or both groups may be working on the same problems, but at two different levels of abstraction.

Pupils who are deficient in the prerequisite concepts and/or skills should be grouped together for special relearning activities. Many times special remedial work needs to be highly individualized to each pupil's needs. For example, a pupil who has not mastered the multiplication facts by the beginning of the fifth grade cannot solve multiplication in an example of the type 24×36. However, it would not be appropriate to place this pupil in a group with second-graders learning the beginning concepts of multiplication by counting objects. Each child's degree of mastery must be monitored. Pupils must be given appropriate relearning to remove deficiencies.

Providing Motivation

PRINCIPLE 4: *Learning is most economical when it is highly motivated by advantageous psychological and social conditions.* Children should be appropriately motivated to learn. A person's inner motivation determines and directs his or her behavior and performance. But behavior is complex and caused by many factors, so no one factor can explain the diversity of behavior that even one person displays.

Every teacher has a degree of control over some factors that tend to motivate learning. Teachers can use the following techniques to increase motivation:

relating learning to its usefulness

making clear what the child is expected to learn, explaining why and how to go about the learning task

providing for readiness and background experiences

using a variety of learning materials

making sure each child experiences a degree of success

using positive reinforcement

making learning fun and interesting

varying the teaching–learning methods

using guided discovery methods

keeping the child informed of progress

helping each child set reasonable and attainable goals

Motivation is an emotional state that provides the driving force to cause an individual to learn and make the effort to achieve.

Pupils are motivated when they are able to apply what they have learned in measurement and problem-solving situations. Thus, teachers should include a study of problem-solving and measurement content in every phase of mathematics instruction. Studying these areas deepens mathematical meanings, broadens the appreciation of mathematics as part of our culture, and improves skill at estimation, computation, and drawing conclusions.

Guiding Discovery from the Concrete to the Abstract Level

PRINCIPLE 5: *The opportunity to discover promotes better learning.* Leading educators have long recognized the importance of discovery in teaching and learning mathematics. Discovery teaching means that the learning situation is structured so that *the child participates actively in the learning process* and is not simply told everything by the teacher. For some children, however, independent self-discovery is not easy and teachers, pressed for time, sometimes resort to "telling approaches," which are the least effective.

Pulaski reports that ". . . Piaget [felt] that many teachers are using archaic educational methods . . . their students who are not actively alienated are sitting passively in classes which they find meaningless and irrelevant . . ."[5]

Jerome Bruner is a leading advocate of learning by discovery. Although the discovery method of teaching number was known before it was advocated by Bruner, it was

not widely considered in the United States until 1960, with the publication of Bruner's *The Process of Education.*[6]

A pupil learns by discovery when he or she finds or uncovers a pattern or answer to a quantitative situation. According to Piaget, students will manipulate concrete objects or materials in order to reorganize their thinking until they see a pattern that applies to a given situation. The opposite of pupil discovery is the telling approach, whereby the teacher tells students how to proceed in a certain situation or gives them a rule to follow.

Different Kinds of Discovery Learning

There is no clear-cut definition of learning by discovery. Biggs[7] describes five different types of discovery learning.

1. *Impromptu learning* occurs when a situation stimulates a pupil to find an answer. The teacher neither presents the problem nor aids in the solution.

2. *Free exploratory discovery* is different from impromptu learning in that the teacher initiates the discovery by providing materials that are effective in creating a situation for discovery.

3. *Guided discovery* also originates with the teacher, who supplies the necessary materials or asks the questions that direct the learning.

4. *Directed discovery* is more structured or controlled than guided discovery in that the materials and questions are planned in advance by the teacher and are usually in the form of worksheets.

5. *Programmed learning* leads students step by step through an activity to its conclu-

5. Mary Ann Spencer Pulaski, *Understanding Piaget* (New York: Harper & Row, 1980), p. 202.

6. Jerome S. Bruner, *The Process of Education* (Cambridge: Harvard University Press, 1960).

7. Edith E. Biggs, "The Role of Experience in the Learning of Mathematics," *The Arithmetic Teacher,* May 1971, 18:278–285.

sion. The work is highly structured and offers little opportunity for free-ranging discovery.

As these five classifications admit, discovery learning has many different connotations that describe learning that takes place under certain conditions.

Discovery Is Not Spontaneous

Except in very limited situations, discovery of a number relationship does not occur spontaneously when a pupil experiences a quantitative situation. The teacher may find it necessary to ask pointed questions so as to enable a pupil to make a desired discovery. When the work is introduced properly, most pupils will discover that the order of adding two numbers does not affect the sum.

$$2 + 3 = 5 \qquad 3 + 2 = 5$$

For example, a teacher might write these number sentences on the chalkboard and ask the class what the sentences show about addition. Asking this type of open-ended question is usually enough to enable most pupils to discover that the order of adding two numbers does not affect the sum. In most cases, however, there will be learners who will not make this discovery. Then pointed and detailed questions must supplement the open-ended question. Questions such as the following are certain to elicit the discovery of how changing the order of numbers will affect the sum:

Are the sums equal or unequal?

Are the numbers named the same in each sentence?

How does the order of adding the two numbers affect the sum?

Students can verify their discovery by adding other pairs of numbers to show that this generalization is true. By asking incisive questions, teachers can enable students to apply the inductive approach so as to discover a pattern or relationship between a pair of numbers. The questions asked or the materials used enable the pupil to make the desired discovery. This form of teaching is known as the *guided discovery method*.

During the learning process, children should be given an opportunity to *discover* new ideas, patterns, structure, and processes. Teachers can use the following techniques:

1. *Use instructional materials* so that children are encouraged to think for themselves at various levels of abstractness.

2. *Give encouragement and suggestions.* No child is expected to discover independently essential meanings in mathematics. Mathematics content must follow a developmental sequence that is conducive to discovery in learning.

3. *Provide guidance when necessary.* The skillful teacher will create several different situations involving the new topic. Some children may need to use manipulative materials, while others will profit from pictures, drawings, and diagrams, self-made or otherwise.

Children learning mathematics cannot be expected to advance on their own without special help on difficult topics. Thus, for children to master logically organized subject matter, *instruction must include teacher direction, guidance, and assistance.*

Teachers must plan experiences carefully so that one experience leads logically to the next, and each is guided so that desirable learning results. In a good textbook series, the important mathematical topics are arranged according to levels of difficulty. But no textbook can possibly provide the variety of experiences needed by children working at different levels of abstraction and at different levels of maturity. The teacher can help by asking the right questions, provoking new lines of thought, giving praise when deserved, and giving encouragement when needed. The teacher can provide hints or clues when a child is discouraged and progress is temporarily blocked.

Factors Leading to Effective Learning

In the past few decades, leading mathematics educators have advocated a discovery-type learning situation for children. The belief that a discovery approach would enhance pupil achievement was based on the research of Piaget, Bruner, Dienes, Brownell, and many others. In general, these researchers concluded that, as part of the discovery approach, children would learn better if the following factors were taken into consideration:

1. Learning should be directed toward attainment of known *goals and objectives* that are considered desirable by society.

2. Children should *participate actively in discovery* learning experiences with materials designed to produce desired responses. Children should explore patterns, operations, and the like with teacher guidance.

3. Each child needs to be *ready*, in terms of prerequisites and levels of abstractness, to learn any new topic. This readiness should be a planned aspect of the teaching–learning process.

4. Learning is most economical when it is highly *motivated*.

5. Children are most likely to transfer what they have learned in mathematics if they participate actively in *solving real-life problems* as a regular part of the program.

6. Each child needs to know *how well he or she is doing* in achieving the learning objectives. Teachers need to be prepared to give positive feedback for successful learning, and to point out what needs further study.

Discovery Is Not the Only Technique

Giving children *an opportunity* to explore and discover *does not mean* that the teacher

may not *tell* the children anything—that everything they learn must be of their own creation. The *discovery approach* is not a complete method of instruction for all the components of a comprehensive elementary mathematics program. Discovery learning is more of a point of view about children—that they seek active, purposeful, meaningful participation in learning.

The intent of the discovery approach is that the learning environment be arranged to include learning materials and activities designed to create situations that give children opportunities to make certain discoveries. Without completely individualized instruction, all members of a class are usually not able to make the desired discoveries, but *all students must be given the opportunity to explore*.

The teacher must provide guidance and encouragement or, even for those pupils who did not make the discovery on their own, a rational explanation of the situation so that they can progress with the rest of the class. This type of *telling*, if done in a meaningful way—with the active attention and participation of the children—is a very acceptable part of the teaching–learning process.

Brain Hemispheres and Learning Mathematics

Recent brain research has implications for the discovery approach to learning. Research has shown that at birth the human brain consists of a left and a right hemisphere connected·by a bridge called the corpus callosum, which is not fully developed. The right hemisphere is dominant until about the age of two; its development continues to precede that of the left hemisphere for some time. From the ages of five to ten the brain remains relatively flexible. Even though the right side is dominant and the two hemispheres develop independently, brain functions occur holistically. Special kinds of learning situations provide optimum brain development. Leslie A. Hart suggests several guidelines to effect *brain-compatible teaching.*[8]

1. Pupils must talk in order to learn. They need to verbalize about learning situations. Often when pupils stop talking they stop learning.

2. Pupils need to use manipulative materials as they learn mathematics. They need to work at their own pace and in their own way.

3. Pupils need to work with real objects and with real problems rather than with contrived ones. Learning to cope with reality is a complex process that is not explained in textbooks.

4. Pupils must be given the challenge to use their brains in creative and pattern-detecting ways.

Using Number Properties and Patterns

PRINCIPLE 6: *Number properties and patterns should be used to help children discover the structural aspects of mathematics.* The structural aspects of mathematics are the basic unifying properties of number and number operations that show relationships of number and number operations to one another. Students can discover mathematical structure by exploring number patterns. (See Chapter 4.)

Contemporary programs include structural models, pictures, and drawings done specially to assist children in taking what they discover with objects in the real world and making a record of these findings. Children take what they discover at the *exploratory* level to the *symbolic* level by creating patterns with signs and symbols. Patterns

can be used to assist each child in discovering some of the most important structural aspects of mathematics.

When pupils understand the structure of a subject, they learn how the different elements of that subject are related. Structure does not consist of learning a new skill or fact. Rather, it involves recognizing a pattern or a property that can be applied to a new situation. Many number patterns are based on structure, or they are a consequence of structure. Therefore the discovery of patterns and the identification of structure and relationships supplement each other and are interwoven in meaningful learning. According to Bruner: ". . . teaching and learning of structure rather than simply the mastery of facts and techniques is at the center of the classic problem of transfer."[9]

Piaget made a very insightful remark with regard to teaching structure:

> The question comes up whether to teach the structure, or to present the child with situations where he is active and creates the structure himself. . . . The goal in education is not to increase the amount of knowledge, but to create the possibilities for a child to invent and discover. When we teach too fast, we keep the child from inventing and discovering himself. . . . Teaching means creating situations where structure can be discovered; it does not mean transmitting structure which may be assimilated at nothing other than a verbal level.[10]

Mastering Concepts and Skills

PRINCIPLE 7: *Reinforcement through practice and applications is essential for mastery.* It is a well-known fact that in teaching and

---

8. Leslie A. Hart, "Brain-Compatible Teaching," *Today's Education*, November–December 1978, 67:45.

9. Jerome S. Bruner, *The Process of Education* (Cambridge: Harvard University Press, 1960), p. 12.

10. Eleanor Duckworth, *Piaget Rediscovered: A Report of the Conference on Cognitive Studies and Curriculum Development* (Ithaca: School of Education, Cornell University, 1964), p. 3.

learning elementary mathematics, *fixation* of concepts and skills is essential for *mastery*-level achievement. Reinforcement is delivered via practice activities and by the child's participating in a variety of applications in measurement and problem-solving situations.

Types of Practice

There are two different kinds of practice: varied *purposeful practice* and *repetitive practices*, also called drill. Varied purposeful practice is designed to increase mathematical understanding and to move the learner toward more mature, economical abstract thinking at the symbolic level of learning. Repetitive drill is necessary to fix a desired skill and to increase the proficiency of using the skills taught.

Both types of practice must involve thinking, and both are necessary in a modern program. Each type of practice needs to be given with a specific objective in mind. Special attention must be paid to the time and the amount of practice needed by each learner.

Principles Applied to a Sample Lesson

The following paragraphs describe a third-grade lesson in addition of two two-digit numbers with *regrouping*. The teaching–learning approaches that were used exemplify the principles of learning that we identified.

Illustrative Lesson

A problem arose in connection with a shopping experience when a third-grade class had to find the answer to the addition example $37 + 15 = \square$. The class had not yet learned the *renaming* step that was involved. The teacher first stated the problem as follows: "If you went to the store and bought two items, a tablet priced at 37¢ and a pencil for 15¢, how much did both items cost?" The teacher then wrote example (a) in vertical form on the chalkboard to focus the attention of the class to the new step.

(a)   37
       + 15

The teacher asked the children to think of a way to find the answer using what they already knew about number.

One boy suggested that we take 37 pennies and 15 pennies and count them to find the total, but this would take too long. Another child suggested that a shorter way would be to use dimes and pennies. Several pupils suggested that *base-ten blocks* could be used to solve the problem. Each pupil had a kit of base-ten blocks. The teacher asked each child to represent 37 in terms of 3 tens and 7 ones (3 longs and 7 cubes), and 15 as 1 ten and 5 ones (1 long and 5 cubes). The children had no difficulty in representing these two numbers with the base-ten blocks.

The teacher then directed the pupils to *join* the objects used to represent the two numbers and find out how many tens and how many ones there would be. The pupils concluded that the answer was 3 longs and 12 cubes (3 tens and 12 ones). The pupils were then asked if the answer 3 tens 12 ones helped them to find the total cost of the two articles. One pupil suggested that the 12 ones could be changed to 1 ten 2 ones. The teacher asked the other pupils to perform the *regrouping* with their materials so that the result was a sum of 5 tens 2 ones, or 52.

The teacher now felt that the class was ready to learn the new step for regrouping

Pupils explore regrouping with an abacus. *(Photo by Leland Perry)*

in addition. To make sure that the new step was understood, the teacher had a pupil use an 18-bead abacus to demonstrate the procedure, as shown in Figure 2.1.

First the pupil showed 15 on the abacus by moving one bead to the tens-rod and by moving 5 beads to the ones-rod. Then he showed 37 by moving 3 beads to the tens place and 7 beads to the ones place. The two sets of beads were separated by a clothespin. Next he joined the ones-place beads and the tens-place beads by removing the clothespin; the result was 4 beads in the tens place and 12 beads in the ones place. Because there were "too many ones" (the ones place was *overloaded*), he then regrouped the 12 ones by exchanging 10 beads in the ones place for 1 bead in the tens place. This exchange left only 2 beads in the ones place, while 5 beads had been moved to the tens place.

One girl volunteered to write out her

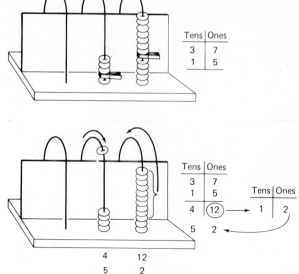

Represent 3 tens 7 ones
and 1 ten 5 ones
on the abacus.

Join beads at the tens-
place and at the ones-
place = 4 tens 12 ones.

The ones place is now
overloaded, so regrouping
will be necessary.

Regroup the 12 ones to
1 ten 2 ones by removing
ten beads from the
ones place in exchange
for one bead at the
tens place.

Answer: 5 tens 2 ones = 52.

Figure 2.1

Use of the Abacus in Showing Regrouping in Addition

steps on the chalkboard and give a reason for each step:

A. 3 tens 7 ones First, we added the number
  1 ten 5 ones of tens, then the number
  4 tens 12 ones of ones and got 4 tens
     and 12 ones.

B. 12 ones = Then we noticed we had
  1 ten 2 ones 12 ones and changed that to
     1 ten 2 ones.

C. 3 tens 7 ones
  1 ten 5 ones So that made our
  4 tens 12 ones answer 5 Tens 2 ones.
  1 ten 2 ones
  5 Tens 2 ones

Principles of Learning Implicit in the Lesson

In the following sections, we analyze the principles of learning that underlie the procedures used in the preceding lesson.

1. *Learning experiences should be purposeful and realistic.* The need to learn the new step in addition arose in a realistic problem situation. The teacher believed that learning is most effective when its basis is problem solving. The purpose for the lesson was to solve a problem that required a new step in addition—that is, regrouping when the sum of the one-place numbers is ten or more.

2. *Learning is a growth process involving three stages—exploratory, symbolic, and mastery.* The three levels of learning were used in this lesson to foster the acquisition of the mathematical concepts and skills involved in the addition, with regrouping of two two-digit numbers. Pupils were given the opportunity to explore with materials and to perform at the symbolic level. Most of these pupils cannot be expected to achieve mastery of this topic until some later point.

3. *Readiness is essential for learning.* Before this lesson, the pupils already had considerable experience with basic addition situations and had used a variety of instructional materials. Each pupil was ready for the types of experiences involved in this lesson.

4. *Learning requires a high level of motivation.* In this lesson, motivation resulted from the need to solve a real-life problem and the opportunity for each pupil to participate actively in learning activities. The teacher did not do all the telling; children were asked to share their thoughts with the class.

Next the teacher had the children read the presentation in their textbook, which used the same example. The class explained each step in the presentation.

Now the teacher was ready to discuss how to handle the ones when the sum is 10 or more, as illustrated in (a) and (b).

The class told why the 1 ten from the sum in (a) is written above the 3 tens in (b).

The class used the pattern in (b) to add in further examples. The pupil uses the pattern in (c) after he or she is able to think the 1 ten without writing it in the tens place. When students reach this stage, they are approaching the mastery level of learning.

5. *Opportunities for discovery promote better learning.* Discovery played an important role in the lesson. Using symbolic notations and a variety of activities with manipulative materials, the teacher led the children to discover the answer to the problem in several ways. These methods were meaningful to the children, and easy to understand. The teacher made sure that each child had an opportunity to discover the steps that were necessary to understand the written record. The regrouping step was demonstrated on an abacus and with written notations. The

pupils' discoveries with manipulative materials enabled them to follow the teacher's demonstration so that later they will be able to understand regrouping in addition.

6. *Number patterns should be used to help children discover the structural aspects of mathematics.* The emphasis in this lesson was on regrouping in addition. The number patterns used were related to the structural properties of place value and regrouping. The technique of writing 37 as 3 tens and 7 ones was used to help children understand the meaning of place value. When 12 ones was regrouped, the structural property of naming a number in different *equal* forms was emphasized. That is, the fact that 12 ones is *regrouped* as 1 ten 2 ones was an important insight in mathematics.

The pupils used manipulative materials to find solutions to the problem. The class explained the different steps in a solution, thereby demonstrating that they had understood the work and would be able to interpret the printed page. Then the teacher had the class read the presentation of the same problem in the textbook. The initial presentation of a basic operation is never complete until the pupil is able to read and interpret the textbook presentation.

7. *Reinforcement through practice and application is essential for mastery.* In this lesson the teacher did not assign practice exercises to "fix" the steps being learned until the children understood them. The assigned practice followed naturally from the class discussion. The children were encouraged to use a variety of approaches to find solutions to the examples assigned. Drill was not appropriate at this stage of learning.

Summary

Research in learning theory and in mathematics education has resulted in the formulation of seven essential principles of teaching and learning mathematics.

1. Both the teacher and the students should understand clearly what is to be learned and how to go about the learning process.

2. Learning is a growth process that has three stages—exploratory, symbolic, and mastery.

3. Readiness is essential for learning.

4. Learning is most economical when it is highly motivated by desirable psychological and social conditions.

5. The opportunity to discover promotes favorable learning.

6. Number properties and patterns should be used to help children discover the structural aspects of mathematics.

7. Reinforcement through practice and applications is essential for mastery.

Teachers should make every effort to implement the principles of teaching and learning discussed in previous sections of this chapter and elaborated in later chapters. Traditional rote methods that stress repetitive drill as the basis of learning should be discarded in favor of approaches that emphasize the discovery of meanings in elementary mathematics. These approaches are the keys to the successful teaching and learning of elementary mathematics. The teacher plays an important role in a program of this kind.

Exercises

1. Examine and criticize the objectives listed in the teacher's edition of a recently published textbook on elementary mathematics for a particular grade level.

2. Examine Piaget's and Bruner's levels of learning and suggest appropriate readiness activities for a topic in elementary mathematics.

3. You are working with a group of third-graders who are not interested in learning mathematics. What techniques can you use to motivate these children?

4. Illustrate a number pattern not discussed in this chapter, and show how that pattern can be used in a new learning situation.

5. Under what conditions, if any, would you tell a pupil the procedure to follow for a mathematical solution? When would you insist that he discover it?

6. What are the implications, for teaching elementary mathematics, of recent research findings on the hemispheres of the brain?

7. What was Piaget's chief contribution to the teaching of elementary school mathematics in this country?

8. What are some objections to a rote drill program without mathematical meanings?

9. The concepts of meaning and understanding convey different things to different people. State what meaning conveys to you and why you hold your interpretation.

10. Using the sample lesson to introduce regrouping in addition, write a lesson plan to introduce regrouping in subtraction.

Selected Readings

Bell, Frederick H. *Teaching Elementary School Mathematics: Methods and Content for Grades K–8*, Unit 3—How Children Learn Mathematics. Dubuque, IA: Wm C. Brown, 1980, pp. 59–95.

Collis, K. F. "Mathematical Thinking in Children," in *Piaget, Psychology and Education*. Itasca, IL: F. E. Peacock, 1976, pp. 144–154.

Gagné, Robert M. "Designing Instruction for Learning," in *The Conditions of Learning*, Third Edition. New York: Holt, Rinehart and Winston, 1977, Chapter 12, pp. 283–313.

Reisman, Fredricka K. *Diagnostic Teaching of Elementary School Mathematics, Methods and Content*. Chicago: Rand McNally, 1977, Chapter 3, How Children Learn Basic Concepts of Mathematics, pp. 1149–1176.

Riedesel, C. Alan. *Teaching Elementary School Mathematics*, Third Edition. Englewood Cliffs, NJ: Prentice-Hall, 1980, Chapter 2, Principles of Teaching, Learning and Organizing for Teaching, pp. 27–60.

Stevenson, Harold W. "Learning and Cognition," in *Mathematics Learning in Early Childhood*, Thirty-Seventh Yearbook. Reston, VA: The National Council of Teachers of Mathematics, 1975, pp. 1–14.

Chapter 3
The Classroom as a Learning Laboratory

In order to meet the needs of learners, teachers must provide activities for introducing new concepts, for the mastery of concepts already taught, and for remediation when necessary. The well-equipped classroom contains materials and aids to serve all these purposes. Because teachers must juggle many variables, such as time, space, instructional materials, student needs, and teaching methods, a planning process is vital so that good instruction can be provided. This process involves scouting for and selecting appropriate teaching materials and thinking through, step-by-step, the procedures that promote effective learning.

Achievement Goals

After studying this chapter, you should be able to:

1. Understand the elements and activities involved in planning a mathematical program.
2. Understand how the strands, scope, and sequence of a mathematical program are related.
3. Organize classroom furniture, materials, and procedures.
4. Know what materials are needed to implement an effective program in the classroom.
5. Teach the students to read and understand the textbook.
6. Discover what research has shown about the use of manipulatives.
7. Select instructional materials.
8. Classify types of learning centers and describe their functions.
9. Identify different types of projection materials and their functions.
10. Select kinds of materials to include in a pupil's kit.

Vocabulary

Mastery of the following key terms will help you to understand this chapter. Each term is defined or illustrated in the Glossary at the end of the book.

Abacus
Associative picture
Attribute blocks
Base-ten blocks
Complex numbers
Diagnostic testing
Expressive
  vocabulary
Frame
Functional picture
Geoboard
Interpretative
  vocabulary
Irrational number

Learning
  laboratory
Manipulative
  material
Overload
Pattern blocks
Rational number
Real number
Scope and
  sequence
Seriation
Strand
Unifix cubes
Venn diagrams

Planning for Instruction

The process of planning for instruction enables you to become clear about what you are seeking to have the children learn. Thorough, consistent, and persistent planning is the key to a good mathematics program.

Effective planning includes both long-range and short-range projections. It includes broad goals and involves organizing numerous details into smooth sequences of learning activities. The teacher must keep the design flexible to allow for variations in children's responses and abilities, time limits, learning conditions, and access to materials and equipment. Planning is a creative paper-and-pencil process. Although plans may take shape on paper, there never is really a finished product. The creativity of planning must extend into the teaching process itself.

Organizing Strands, Objectives, and Skills

Words such as *strands, objectives,* and *skills* can be confusing because in the literature these terms take on various meanings. We use the word *strand* to refer to the content

of mathematics that is to be taught. Organizing strands, objectives, and skills helps a teacher to decide what to teach. Should a teacher begin the first day of school by introducing geometry or one of the basic operations? A teacher must use resources, such as state and local community guidelines, instructor's manuals, and a knowledge of the structure of mathematics, as guides to answer this question. Once a strand is chosen, many additional decisions must be made.

After choosing a strand, one must consider what long-term goals are to be attained. To select broad goals, one must choose definite objectives as guides in long-range planning. For example, a teacher might say, "In the first three months of school, my children are going to work on these fifteen objectives." After making this decision, a teacher then decides what to teach in each daily lesson to ensure that the class will master the chosen objectives. Skills are the necessary steps toward mastery of an objective; since they are acquired by practice, skills are taught on a daily basis. Look at Figure 3.1. Why are there more boxes to represent skills than to represent objectives?

An illustration of strand is found in the Holt mathematics textbook series published

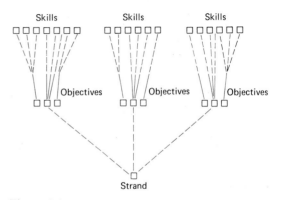

Figure 3.1

in 1981. This series lists the major strands as:

Problem solving

Real-life applications/Reasoning

Reasonableness of results

Estimation/Approximation

Numeration/Computation

Geometry

Measurement

Graphs/Tables

Predicting

Calculators/Flow charts/Computer appreciation

There are three stages to teaching a strand. First is an introductory phase consisting of exploratory activities, then the development of structural aspects by means of reinforcement and extension experiences, and, finally, the mastery and maintenance level. Most children take several years to progress through a given strand, and during this time they are in various stages of other strands. Some strands, such as applications and estimation, become part of the teaching–learning process. Other strands, such as geometry and measurement, are cognitive subdivisions of the curriculum.

Certain strands, such as problem solving and predicting, can be presented in any order, whereas others must be presented in a specific sequence. For example, in order to learn to multiply and divide correctly, a student must have mastered numeration, addition, and subtraction. These three strands are taught before multiplication and division.

Strands such as geometry, time, and graphing do not require basic instruction in other strands and can be thought of as "floating" since they can be taught independently. Appropriate interweaving of strands helps pupils gain confidence in applying mathematics and practice skills in a variety of situations.

Every strand is important for continuous mathematical growth, and each should be taught yearly at each grade level. Strands should be taught in a *spiral* manner—that is, by first introducing a concept informally and intuitively, followed by reteaching the concept with greater depth until mastery is achieved. Readiness for strands such as probability and statistics should occur in the lower grades. Providing readiness activities for concepts that will be mastered at a higher grade level ensures continuous student growth.

Objectives

Objectives are guidelines that involve teaching and learning goals, sometimes stated in terms of desired student behavior. An example might be "Given ten addition problems that require regrouping, students will solve 80 percent of the problems correctly." Some texts state objectives in the imperative form, such as "Identify congruent line segments." Regardless of the way in which objectives are stated, teachers should use them in lesson planning since they provide definite direction.

Skills

Students must acquire many skills before they can master an objective. For example, students must know the meaning of plus (+) and equals (=) before beginning an objective in addition. Some skills are generic, and, once learned, can be applied to several areas of mathematics. Daily lessons often cover only one or two skills that are a part of a large plan—teaching aimed at mastery of a specific objective.

Scope and Sequence

Schools today generally determine the *scope*—how much is to be covered—and the *sequence*—the order in which the material is presented—of the mathematics program. Scope and sequence refer to a plan that includes strands, objectives, and skills to be taught at each grade level. A district may simply choose a textbook and follow the scope and sequence given by the textbook authors. Or a district may prepare its own mathematics curriculum guide. Such guides develop a framework for teaching mathematics and in general use various textbooks by "keying" or noting appropriate pages that relate to objectives and skills. Although teachers are often asked to assist in choosing a text or in developing curriculum guides, rarely does an individual teacher solely determine what is to be taught. Teachers are expected to follow as closely as possible the plan developed by the school district.

Keying Resources

A major advantage of working from a comprehensive scope and sequence plan is that resources for each skill can be "keyed," or identified and noted. Resources include texts, commercial aids, manipulatives, games, and audiovisual materials, and can be classified as either (1) exploratory, or concrete, (2) symbolic, or semiconcrete, or (3) mastery, or abstract.

Table 3.1 (p. 32) highlights a typical grade 3 mathematics objective and illustrates a method for organizing materials according to strand, category, objective, and skill. This table illustrates "keying" for only one of the many mathematics objectives possible to highlight. The skills column on the left of the table lists the skills most students need to acquire before they can master the objective. What do the other columns show? The companion column lists resources that are useful in teaching that particular skill. The materials "keyed" to each are vehicles that can assist pupils in moving through the various strands, objectives, and skills, and from the exploratory through the symbolic to the mastery level of learning.

Placement Procedures to Determine Level of Instruction

Placement procedures, or the manner in which a teacher decides the approximate level of instruction for each pupil, are an essential part of planning for instruction. It is the teacher's task to see that each child is given instruction at the level that gives him or her the most benefit. A pupil may be at grade level, capable of advanced work, or in need of remedial instruction. Each child must be considered individually to determine proper placement.

Most textbook companies suggest procedures and offer tests designed to reveal a child's level of instruction. If a pupil is in the second year in one program, achievement records can be helpful in placement decisions. It is essential to use whatever information is available about a child when first assessing the level at which he or she will succeed. A placement test is then given to confirm the estimated level. After checking and recording the results, a teacher should note those children whose scores do not confirm the estimate. If the percentage of either correct or incorrect answers is much higher than predicted, then the original estimate was in error and additional placement testing is probably necessary. Testing services generally provide information regarding scores and how they relate to placement of pupils. In general, placement tests are short and cover a great many objectives. As a rule, these tests are not designed to provide in-depth information about a child's ability. Teachers acquire such information as they become familiar with actual classroom performance and through diagnostic testing.

Teaching Assistants

In many schools, resource personnel, such as Chapter I teachers and aides, volunteers, and specialists, assist teachers with instruction. Although the teacher is held accountable for the success of the program, these as-

Table 3.1. Multiplication and Division Strand, Grade 3

Objective: Completes Division Equations in Horizontal and Vertical Form with Products to 50

	Related Resources			
Skills	**Exploratory**	**Symbolic**	**Mastery**	**Other**
Divides sets into groups of equal number	Plastic toys Counters	Ginn: sheets 12, 26, 27, 28	Textbook pages 7, 9, 12, 16	Holt: drill tapes
Uses repeated subtraction to illustrate division	Counters	Number line Pictured examples	13, 15	Games: Heads Up Tuf
Knows and uses symbols		Symbols kit		Math Match
Uses terms factor, dividend, divisor, quotient, and product			Workbook pages 5, 6, 7	
Recognizes division as the inverse of multiplication	Arrays Pegboards Arithmaboard	Graph paper		
Demonstrates oral proficiency of facts				

sistants work part of the day with pupils and can use an organized scope and sequence with "keyed" resources. Ideally, teaching assistants work to complement the teacher's classroom instruction and to support the students in learning at their appropriate instruction levels. Assistants usually do not make independent decisions regarding material to be taught, but rely on the teacher's ability to "place" each child appropriately in the instructional program.

Organizing the Classroom Environment

Organizing the classroom environment involves:

1. Flexible arrangements for classroom furniture. (See Figure 3.2 for examples.)

2. Sorting and labeling materials in language the children can read and understand.

3. Preparing mathematics displays. Are bulletin boards to be for adult-made designs, for displaying student work, or for a combination of purposes?

4. Planning pick-up procedures for manipulatives.

5. Determining classroom rules for control of noise level.

6. Deciding how to use volunteers and/or teacher aides (if available).

7. Securing a sufficient number of textbooks and supplies.

8. Setting the emotional tone of the classroom atmosphere.

The classroom should be thought of as a flexible area capable of meeting student needs. Figure 3.2[1] suggests several general furniture arrangements, each of which has advantages and disadvantages. The teacher selects the classroom arrangement according to the planned learning activities. Changes in learning activities should be accompanied by appropriate changes in the floor plan. In plan A, there is open floor space and the possibility of nine learning-center areas. In B, the attention of the class is directed toward one or two people. This arrangement is useful for discussing and evaluating a recently completed activity. Section C is conducive to small-group activities and allows for a smooth flow of traffic between work areas. Plan D provides for both large-group and small-group work. An advantage of this arrangement is that the children in the large group are facing away from the small-group work areas.[2] An effective plan contains a balance between quiet and noisy work areas. Plans A, C, and D are conducive to the use of sufficient audiovi-

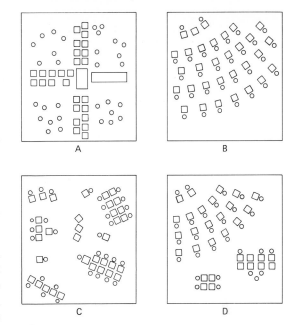

Figure 3.2

sual equipment to enable three to eight children to use headsets. Which plan is most appropriate for viewing films?

Many of the environmental organizing tasks can be handled early in the year, such as labeling materials, "keying" resources, determining classroom rules, and planning housekeeping procedures. Some tasks can be shared, such as bulletin board preparation and the ordering of materials.

In addition to the physical surroundings, the emotional atmosphere of the mathematics classroom is of utmost importance in enabling children to learn and to feel comfortable asking questions and expressing their thoughts. There is much research literature on this topic that could be explored by a teacher who wishes to create a warm, cooperative atmosphere that will enhance the child's development of a positive self-image. See the references by Purkey and Combs at the end of this chapter for recent publications that deal with the emotional atmosphere of a classroom.

1. Robert E. Reys and Thomas R. Post, *The Mathematics Laboratory* (Boston: Prindle, Weber & Schmidt, 1973).

2. Reys and Post, p. 59.

Kinds of Aids

The teacher of elementary school mathematics works with three basic types of materials:

1. Manipulative, or concrete

2. Visual, audio, and audiovisual

3. Symbolic, or abstract

The following sections contain a brief description of each type of material. A broader characterization appears later in the text.

Manipulative Materials

Manipulative materials are objects that the pupil can feel, touch, handle, and move. They can be real objects with social application in everyday life, or they can be objects that are used to represent an idea. They are commonly used in the classroom and/or laboratory setting when concepts that can be depicted concretely are introduced.

Visual, Audio, and Audiovisual Materials

Visual materials include pictures, diagrams, charts, films, filmstrips, and some electronic devices. Tape recordings and records are two common *audio materials* that are generally used after a concept has been introduced concretely. They are also effective motivators and are occasionally used to introduce or review a topic.

Symbolic Materials

Symbolic materials are represented by words, numerals, and mathematical symbols. Textbooks and ditto masters are common sources of symbolic/abstract materials. Tests are also symbolic materials. In some texts, the symbolic level is called the mastery level.

The Mathematics Textbook

The textbook is the most widely used instructional aid in mathematics classrooms. In this country, most mathematics classrooms use this book as the course of study for grades 3–6.

It is unfortunate that many pupils are unable to read and understand the content of this book. One of a teacher's top priorities is to assist students in learning to *read* the text intelligently. The following list of procedures and suggestions will help teachers to attain that goal.

Manipulatives as an Aid in Understanding Language Patterns in the Textbook

Teachers should use manipulatives to objectify most of the new quantitative situations a pupil encounters in studying mathematics. Learners should be encouraged to say what they think as they work with manipulatives. Teachers should guide the children to develop correct language patterns associated with mathematical concepts and procedures. Thus, when students read the words in the text, they can more easily form associations with their firsthand experiences. A child who reads "Allen had 10 marbles and lost 3 of them," can associate this printed problem to his experience with manipulatives.

Manipulatives are very helpful in solving problems, such as adding two two-place numbers with regrouping the sum, as in the sample lesson presented on page 24. A vital part of such lessons is developing meaningful verbal descriptions of the mathematical procedures that are used to solve the problem. Pupils using manipulatives are encouraged to discuss their procedures because discussion yields understanding of the verbal description of the operation. After the demonstration with manipulatives, the teacher has the pupils read the presentation in the textbook. Manipulatives help create a background to enable the pupil to interpret the printed page. The presentation of a new topic is never complete until the learner can read and understand the descriptive material in the textbook.

Building the Mathematics Vocabulary

Every pupil has two vocabularies: the expressive and the interpretative. The *expressive vocabulary* is the one used in speaking and writing; the *interpretative vocabulary* relates to listening and reading. Often a teacher will talk and hope that the children are listening. To promote effective learning, teachers should listen and have the pupils talk.

Any mathematics textbook contains some words that are unfamiliar to many children. The teacher should read each new word in a lesson and then write it on the chalkboard. The children should also read the word and say in their own words what the word means. A dictionary should be consulted if none of the children can define a term adequately. Some textbooks list the terms introduced in a chapter and indicate the page on which each term is presented. These lists are valuable aids for reviewing the vocabulary in that chapter. Each chapter in this text has a list of terms that may be unfamiliar to readers. These terms are defined in the Glossary to help readers understand the subject under discussion.

Teachers can use the chalkboard, a flannel board, or an overhead projector to help clarify the language of mathematics, such as a number sentence, by placing the elements of a number sentence in a jumbled order as shown in A, Figure 3.3. The class forms a true number sentence, such as in B and C, noting that the order of adding two numbers does not affect the sum.

The teacher has the class read the sen-

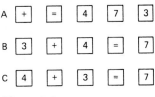

Figure 3.3

tences in B and C from *left to right* and from *right to left*. One major difference between number sentences and verbal sentences is that number sentences can be read correctly in either direction. This fact needs to be made clear to children.

Reading and Understanding Number Symbols

To read mathematics, one must learn certain words and symbols unique to the subject. Some symbols have more than one meaning; for example, the period (.) can represent a decimal point, as in 2.5, or a sign of multiplication, as in 2·5. Some pupils find the symbolism of mathematics an obstacle to reading the textbook. Consider the symbolism involved in designating a basic operation, such as multiplication.

$$3 \times 4 \qquad \begin{array}{r} 4 \\ \times\ 3 \\ \hline \end{array} \qquad 3 \cdot 4 \qquad 3\,(4) \qquad (3)(4)$$

The pupil must be able to interpret each of these designations. These and similar symbols raise the reading level of a mathematics textbook.

The list given here is the symbolic representation for multiplication. Have the class give the verbal representation. Some of the phrases or statements would be: "multiply," "find the product," "three times four," "three fours," "perform the operation," "write the number sentence," and so on. Challenge the fast learners to give the various ways to read the representation.

Some textbooks use *frames*, such as familiar geometric figures, to indicate a missing numeral. Frames are common in expendable materials. In this example, the frames in A are the same but different in B. Have the class tell why. A pupil must be able to answer this question in order to write the correct numerals in the frames.

A. $\dfrac{2}{3} \times \dfrac{\triangle}{\triangle} = \dfrac{4}{6}$

B. $\dfrac{2}{3} \times \dfrac{\triangle}{\square} = \dfrac{6}{8} = \square$

Improving Reading in Problem Solving

To solve verbal problems the first thing pupils must do is to identify the problem question. We shall not discuss here how to solve verbal problems, as this is covered in Chapter 10. Pupils who have difficulty in reading verbal problems need special assistance in this type of reading.

Poor readers should be grouped together during problem-solving activities and assisted in reading problems. The teacher should have a pupil who articulates well read a problem aloud. The special group should then read the problem aloud in unison. Each pupil should identify the problem question and then solve the problem. Further help may be needed at this point.

Using Pictures

All elementary school mathematics textbooks contain pictures that should be used as reading exercises. Nearly all these pictures can be classified as either associative or functional. An *associative picture* shows a scene connected with an activity or event, such as children at play on an outing. A *functional picture* contains data that are essential to the solution of the problem on that page or that enrich the meaning of a concept.

Have the class explain or describe a pic-

ture. When pupils tell what they see in the picture or how they interpret it, they exercise their expressive vocabularies. Have pupils make up one or more problems about a picture so as to exercise their interpretative vocabularies. The teacher can direct the activity by having the class make up a problem dealing with a particular operation, such as subtraction.

The text may have quantitative tables, such as height and weight charts. Teachers should make certain that students learn how to read and interpret the data in tabular form.

Conventional Reading versus Mathematical Reading

Reading a mathematics text is not like reading conventional material, in which a thread of continuity holds the interest of the reader, who seeks recreation or information. Most readers are curious to know the outcome of a story or news item, or wish to add to their knowledge of the subject at hand. In contrast, most of the reading in elementary mathematics textbooks constitutes verbal problems, among which there is no thread of continuity. In most cases pupils do not know what the outcome of the problem will be. The reader's chief source of interest in reading mathematics textbooks is the desire to excel and to get the correct answer. Often, readers require much extra time for reading a mathematics text so as to take in all the details, to read equations in two directions, to glance at tables or charts, and to translate symbols into words.

The adage that every teacher should be a teacher of English, both oral (spoken) and silent (reading), is very true for elementary mathematics. The teacher not only must give professional instruction in mathematics but also must be skillful in giving instruction in reading and interpreting the textbook.

Research on Manipulatives

The work of many researchers, including Piaget and Bruner, supports the view that the first stage of the learning cycle occurs at the exploratory level of maturity, when children must be given the opportunity to work with manipulative, hands-on materials in a laboratory-type approach. Since 1960, nearly 100 studies have reported on the effects of various manipulative-material models for arithmetic concepts and skills— an approach that emphasizes discovery as a result of pupil exploration with appropriate instructional aids.

Most researchers have concluded that it is essential for teachers to use manipulative materials when introducing new concepts, when working in student-directed learning centers that provide practice and independent drill, and in measurement situations. In order to offer hands-on instruction to all types of learners, teachers need to be able to answer the following questions:

1. What materials are most useful for different content and for various types of children?

2. What is the proper time to use manipulatives and for how long should they be used?

3. How can manipulatives be used wisely— that is, as demonstrated by teachers, in independent learning centers, in small groups, and so on?

4. For whom is the use of manipulatives most valuable?

The Importance of Being Familiar with Aids

Before using instructional devices with children, including that of textbooks, the teacher must spend time becoming thoroughly acquainted with the particular aid. Practice is vital to smooth, effective classroom use of manipulatives.

The companies that produce the manipulatives listed on the chart in Table 3.2 also provide helpful guide books to aid teachers in becoming acquainted with each manipulative.

Often, adults have more difficulty than children in working with concrete materials because adults have operated at the abstract level for so long. Sometimes adults need a few practice sessions to feel comfortable with concrete materials. When you practice, use actual examples from a student's textbook, verbalize as you would expect a child to, and, if possible, work with other teachers. The practice sessions will inspire confidence, promote creative ideas for extending the use of manipulatives, and assist you in understanding how children feel as they work.

How long a teacher will want a pupil to work with manipulatives will depend on the individual pupil and the topic being presented. Children need manipulatives until they can work with symbols. To use manipulatives when they are not needed is just as harmful as not using them when they are needed. Teaching is good when pupils operate at the highest level of abstraction of which they are capable.

Selecting Manipulatives

There is a wide variety of materials on the market today called manipulative devices. Cathcart[3] suggests that teachers follow five guidelines in selecting manipulatives.

1. The materials should be a true representation of the mathematical concept or idea being explored.

3. George W. Cathcart (Ed.), *The Mathematics Laboratory: Readings from the Arithmetic Teacher* (The National Council of Teachers of Mathematics, 1977), pp. 103–104.

Table 3.2 Manipulative Use Chart

Manipulative	Numeration									Geometry and Measurement							
	Counting	Discrimination	Sorting and ordering	Pattern relations	Place value	Addition/Subtraction	Multiplication/Division	Fractions	Decimals	Boundaries and regions	Geometric relationships	Symmetry	Linear	Volume	Weight	Graphing	Money
Abacus	X				X												
Attribute blocks	X	X	X	X		X				X	X	X					
Base-ten blocks	X	X	X			X	X	X	X				X	X	X		
Geoboards		X		X				X		X	X	X	X				
Pattern blocks	X	X	X	X		X	X	X		X	X	X				X	X
Unifix cubes	X	X	X	X	X	X	X	X				X	X			X	
Pocket place value chart					X				X								

2. The materials should stimulate the pupil's imagination and interest.

3. The materials should be appropriate for use on several grade levels as well as for different levels of concept formation.

4. The materials should provide a basis for abstraction.

5. The materials should be adopted for individual work. That is, each pupil should have ample opportunity to handle the materials physically.

Physical criteria are important. The following physical characteristics should be considered when selecting manipulative materials.

1. *Durability.* The device must be strong enough to withstand normal use and handling by children.

2. *Attractiveness.* The materials should appeal to the child's natural curiosity and desire for action.

3. *Simplicity.* Although the degree of complexity is a function of the concept being developed and the children involved, generally the materials should be simple to operate and manipulate.

4. *Physical qualities.* The materials should be designed to accommodate a child's small hands and not cause too much noise when in use. Size also determines how and where materials can be stored.

5. *Cost.* The estimated cost of manipulative materials should reflect the teacher-education phase as well as the expenditure for materials.

Table 3.2 suggests manipulatives that meet all the above criteria, and although the initial cost may be high, they are excellent purchases because of the multiple strands and grade levels at which they can be used. All the manipulatives on the chart can be purchased commercially and some can be constructed by hand.

Examples of Manipulatives

Abacus

The abacus is designed to help children understand base ten and place value. Before it is introduced, children need exploratory experiences using aids such as: ten–ten counting frames, sticks and rubber bands for grouping by tens, bean sticks, base-ten blocks, and money (pennies, dimes, and dollars).

The abacus comes in many forms. Figure 3.4 shows an abacus with a bridge that divides the vertical rods in half. A bead can be passed from one half to the other by forcing it past the bridge. When all the beads are above the bridge, the abacus is clear. The beads below the bridge in Figure 3.4 represent the number 4249.

Each rod contains nine beads of one color (such as red), and a tenth bead of a different color (green, for example), which is the color of the nine beads on the next rod to the left. In this case, the nine green beads would represent the digits from 1 to 9. The tenth bead *overloads* a place. When a rod is overloaded, regrouping is necessary, and so the ten beads on the rod are removed and a single bead is added to the next rod on the left. Beads are removed by pushing them from below the bridge to above it. There are two main advantages to this type of abacus:

1. It is clear when a place is filled and overloaded. The rod is filled when it contains nine beads of the same color. The rod is overloaded and regrouping is necessary when the bead of a different color appears.

2. It is easy to discover the relationship between consecutive places in a numeral.

An Open-Ended Abacus

Figure 3.5 shows an open-ended abacus. This device consists of a base, which is a block of wood or plastic with equally spaced holes in which dowels are inserted. Each dowel holds a place that corresponds to a place in a numeral. The number of dowels that are needed depends on the numeral to be represented.

Markers, usually disks with holes large enough for easy movement, are placed on the dowels or rods. What numeral is represented on the open-ended abacus in Figure 3.5? (1426)

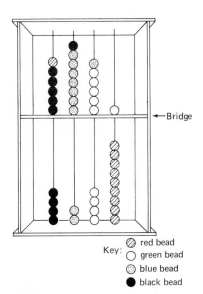

Key:
⊘ red bead
○ green bead
◎ blue bead
● black bead

Figure 3.4

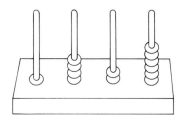

Figure 3.5

There are two main advantages to the open-ended abacus:

1. It is easy to make.

2. It is suitable for modeling addition and subtraction with regrouping because more than ten disks can be placed on a rod.

A simple, useful abacus can be made by inserting straight wires (cut from a clothes hanger) vertically in a wooden or plastic base. The markers can be made from heavy cardboard or by drilling holes in checkers or similar disks.

Figure 3.6 illustrates regrouping to find the sum of 29 and 16. The 15 ones shown in A and B must be regrouped as 1 ten and 5 ones, leading to the result of 4 tens and 5 ones shown in C.

Figure 3.7 shows a modified form of an open-ended abacus, sometimes called a U-bar abacus. A bent metal rod replaces the vertical dowel. Each rod extends over the back of the frame and contains about 18 markers that are not visible from the front of the abacus. A marker is moved from the back to the front to represent a digit. What numeral is represented on the abacus in Figure 3.7? (5156) It should be noted that the

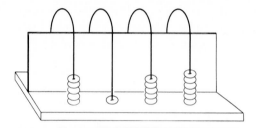

Figure 3.7

U-bar abacus with 18 beads or so per bar serves the same purpose as an open-ended abacus and has the advantage of no lost beads. Zero is represented by an empty rod on each abacus.

Attribute Blocks

Attribute blocks, also called logic or relationship blocks, come in sets that depict

1. five shapes (square, circle, rectangle, triangle, and hexagon).

2. two sizes (large and small).

3. three colors (red, blue, and yellow).

4. two thicknesses (thick and thin).

To stimulate thinking and to generate practice for reasoning, logic activities using blocks for all elementary school grade levels can be developed. One method involves "logic maps." A child must choose the appropriate area of a map that a block can enter as directed by pictured signs along the roadway. Logic maps can be made on large poster board. The entrance to each area on the "map" is marked with a picture of the block that may enter the area. Color, size, and shape are shown on the signs. Figure 3.8 presents examples of logic maps. Maps B and C are more difficult than map A because more decisions are required.

Logic can also be taught to young pupils with a Carroll diagram, as shown in Figure 3.9. Here very little reading is required. A dash through a word or symbol means "not." For example, blue and not blue are

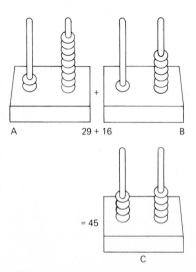

A   29 + 16   B

= 45

C

Figure 3.6

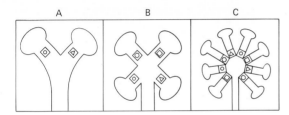

Figure 3.8

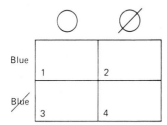

Figure 3.9

Base-Ten Blocks

The most durable base-ten block sets are made from natural hardwood and scored to indicate the number of units, or ones, in each piece. The design of some is metric, in which the smallest unit is a cubic centimeter. This type (scored in centimeter units) can be used for metric projects as well as base-ten numeration and activities in length, area, and volume. The base-ten set depicted in Figure 3.10 includes models of: one (a unit), ten (a rod), one hundred (a flat), and one thousand (a block).

Geoboards

Geoboards can be constructed by hand or purchased commercially. The commercial types range from the heavy-duty particle-

indicated along the left side of the diagram, and circle and not circle are indicated across the top. This diagram is read much like a multiplication table. In box 1, a pupil would place blue circles; in box 2, pieces that are blue but not circles; in box 3, circles that are not blue. What goes in box 4 (pieces that are neither blue nor circles)? More complicated Carroll diagrams can be designed to challenge older and more advanced pupils.

The "One Difference Game"[4] can be played by using all the pieces in an attribute block set. The game begins with one pupil choosing a block; the next player must choose a block that has all the attributes of the first block played, except for one. Play continues until all the blocks have been used in possible plays. Each player should state the one difference he or she has discovered. Other versions of the game include finding blocks that have two differences and three differences.

4. Adapted from Brevard Inservice Teaching Center materials, ESEA Title IV-C, State of Florida, 1973.

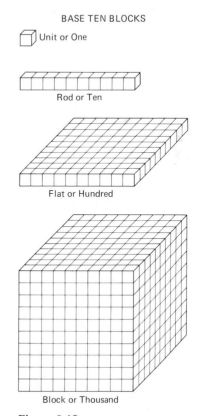

Figure 3.10

board style, featuring blackboard-like surfaces and nails with heads, to lightweight plastic models, many of which use plastic pegs instead of nails.

Although smaller and larger styles are available, a desk-size geoboard is usually 10″ × 10″ with a 5″ × 5″ nail array. Young children seem to have difficulty using the plastic varieties, which tend to slip and slide when the bands are being placed on the pegs.

Shape Relationships and the Geoboard

The following is a sample primary grade activity using geoboards to illustrate basic relationships of geometric shapes.

1. Ask students to use "geobands" (rubber bands) and make a small square near the center of their geoboard.

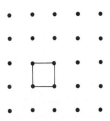

2. Next ask them to move one side of the square, thus changing the square into a rectangle.

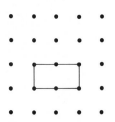

3. Now have them change the rectangle into a triangle.

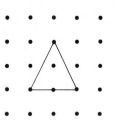

Geoboards are well known as an effective aid in teaching geometric concepts; they are also useful in teaching addition/subtraction, multiplication/division, and area and perimeter. We cannot explain all these uses in this text; however, several companies offer teacher's guides on how to use geoboards for many purposes.

Pattern Blocks

Pattern blocks (Figure 3.11) are usually made from hardwood and come in six different sizes and colors. Because each size has its own color, pupils who do not know the names of geometric shapes can do geometric work only by referring to the color of the block. These blocks are excellent for counting, sorting, matching, and linear plus area measurement. They can be used with older students (through junior high and senior high) for complicated pattern designs, and in the beginning study of functions.

In addition to the blocks themselves,

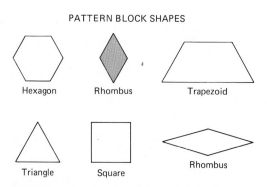

Figure 3.11

A pupil explores number patterns with the unifix
cubes. *(Photo by Leland Perry)*

posters, workbooks, and stickers are available that are useful as worksheets and for learning-center activities. Pattern-block activities range from cover tasks, used in the lower grades, to those that reinforce fractional concepts, useful in the intermediate grades. Depending on the creativity of the teacher and the needs of the students, many activities involving pattern blocks can be designed.

Unifix Cubes

Unifix cubes can be used to teach one-to-one correspondence, set membership, number and numeral matching, seriation, and in comparing amounts. All "families" for basic facts can be illustrated by using the appropriate number of cubes in two colors. A sample of this type of activity can be found in Chapter 6.

Unifix cubes differ from other manipulative materials in three major respects: First, the unit or single cube is the basic unit on which all higher values are constructed. Second, the cubes have an interlocking device so that one can build rods of any length from single cubes and take them apart just as readily. Thus, values can be increased or decreased by physical manipulation. And third, color has no intrinsic value or significance; cubes come in ten colors, but color value is purely arbitrary. Related materials include kits, tracks for ease in handling, and teacher's guides. These are available commercially.

Learning Centers

"A learning center is an area in the classroom which contains a collection of activities and materials to teach, reinforce, and/or enrich a skill or concept. For the student the learning center is used as: a self-selected activity for independent study, a follow-up for a teacher-taught lesson, an activity in the place of a regular assignment, or possibly as an enrichment activity. For teachers the learning center is used as: follow-up for a lesson taught, a small group instruction area, or an individualized assignment."[5] A teacher should collect all the learning tools needed to complete an activity and have them readily accessible so that a child can complete the task with a minimum of teacher direction. A teacher should clarify the rules regarding use of a center and provide a means of record keeping and evaluation so that both students and teacher can account for the time spent and the results produced at the center. The bibliography on page 50 includes several references to books useful for assisting teachers in designing learning-center activities.

The materials in a learning center include task cards, kits, manipulatives, audiovisual aids, posters, charts, worksheets, games, measuring instruments, and calculators. Before constructing activities or choosing materials for a learning center, the teacher must decide on the type and purpose of the center.

Types of Learning Centers

Several different types of learning centers can be developed. The following are the most popular.

1. Broad subject centers—these are general and can be classified under one title, such as "math." Activities suitable for this type have to do with the mathematics appropriate for a specific grade level.

2. Strand center—in which all activities relate to the same strand, such as a numeration center, an addition center, or a subtraction center. Each activity in each center deals with the same topic, and usually the instructions require that a child work part A before doing part B.

5. Sandra N. Kaplan, Jo Ann B. Kaplan, Madsen Shiliak, and Bette K. Taylor, *Change for Children* (Pacific Palisades, CA: Goodyear, 1973).

3. Learning process center—in which activities emphasize or provide experiences in one or more learning processes, such as discovery, observation, estimation, following directions, decision making, or creating, all of which can be applied to the process of learning mathematics.

Purpose of Centers

Teachers must also ask themselves, "What role will the center play in the instructional program in my classroom?" Several roles are possible.

1. Remediation
2. Enrichment
3. Motivation
4. Mini-course
5. Major instructional strategy
6. Testing
7. Drill
8. Concept introduction
9. A combination of several purposes

Evaluating Learning Centers

The work that children accomplish in learning centers must be monitored in some way by the teacher. Several evaluation techniques are possible. A teacher should choose the one most suitable for the group and the one that reveals, both to student and teacher, how much progress is being made. The following is a list of some *possible* evaluation techniques.

1. Teacher-made tests
2. Commercially produced tests
3. Reports
4. Tape recordings
5. Interviews
6. Observation
7. Checklists
8. Logs or diaries
9. Construction projects
10. Debates

Before gathering materials or designing activities, a teacher must choose the type of center, the purpose of the center, and the evaluation technique to be used. It is best to begin with one kind of center and then, as teacher and children become accustomed to this type of instruction, to expand the activities. Volunteers and teacher aides are often helpful in creating activities and monitoring students working at a center. Materials must be organized according to their purpose. The following list illustrates the kind of *organization* that is needed for ease in keeping "like" materials together. Perhaps the different types of aids can be color coded. Not all these aids will be found in a single classroom.

I. *Aids for Counting and Number Concepts*

Flannel board with various cutouts
Number lines—individual, walk on, demonstration
Hundred board
Sets of various objects with storage boxes
Counters, spinners, and various types of games

II. *Aids for Base and Place Value*

Base concepts (grouping by tens or by any other base)
Ten–ten counting frames
Sticks or straws and rubber bands for grouping by tens
Money, play money
Base blocks of different groupings
Games
Place-value concept
Place-value charts
Abacuses
Games, such as chip trading

III. *Aids for Basic Number Facts and Number Operations*

Flannel board with cutouts of objects, numerals, and signs
Number ladder
Balances of various types
Drill cards, flash cards, drill wheels, drill devices
Everybody show cards, individual chalkboards

Basic fact charts

Counters, spinners, and various types of games

IV.   *Aids for Fractional Numbers*

Fraction cutouts

Pupil's fraction kits

Practice charts of various types

Fraction equivalent aids

Fraction number lines

V.   *Geometric Devices and Measuring Instruments*

Geoboards with task cards

Tangrams with task cards

Models

Measuring instruments, both English and metric

Exploratory Materials Used in Measurement

Measuring instruments are particularly well suited for classroom laboratory and learning-center use. A pupil learns to use an instrument, such as a ruler, by making measurements. Similarly, he learns to read a scale, such as that on a thermometer, by observing and recording temperatures. Because of the great variety of measuring instruments, the teacher is faced with the problem of choosing those most appropriate to the classroom. The following is a list of some of the many different measuring instruments that would be available in the self-contained classroom.

1. *Quantity:* abacus, adding machine, calculators, number charts, tallying devices, street numbers, fact finders, counting blocks

2. *Lengths:* ruler, yardstick, tape measure, meter stick, standards for measuring heights, micrometer, protractor, speedometer, odometer

3. *Time:* calendar, clock (standard and digital face), watch, stopwatch, sundial, timetables for airlines, trains, and buses, minute timers, hour timers

4. *Value:* coins, bills, checks, food stamps, food coupons, tax schedules, postage meter, stamps (U.S. and food trading stamps), price tags

5. *Weight:* postal scales, balances, spring scales, pressure gauges, height/weight charts, pictures of scales for weighing large amounts, labels showing weights of common objects

6. *Volume:* pint, quart, gallon, metric containers, teaspoon, tablespoon, cooking measures, bushel measures, rainfall gauge, cubic and metric volume blocks

7. *Area:* square-inch cards, square-foot cards, maps

8. *Temperature:* thermometer, clinical thermometer, cooking thermometer

9. *Metric:* meter stick, liter containers, fraction of liter containers, metricized scales, metric weights, trundle wheel

Commerical Resources

Projection Materials

Today's mathematics teachers have a tremendous advantage over their predecessors in that a wide variety of audio, visual, and combination materials is available. Pupils today can see geometry in nature more readily through the camera magic of film producers such as Walt Disney than through conventional methods. Students in modern society have never known the world without motion pictures. They have been trained to absorb knowledge rapidly by watching television and films. Mathematics teachers can capitalize on this training by using projection materials, such as films, filmstrips, film loops, overhead projectors, and slides in their classrooms.

Reasons for Using Films

There are several reasons for using films and filmstrips in the mathematics classroom. These include:

1. increasing motivation.

2. providing experiences that would otherwise be unavailable, such as viewing a 16-mm film on weighing objects in outer space.

3. equalizing the experiences of all students. Perhaps only one or two students have actually seen the hexagonal shape of a honeycomb.

4. providing practice and drill on basic facts without teacher direction.

5. using materials that do not require a student to read.

Source Books for Aids

The thirty-fourth National Council of Teachers of Mathematics yearbook, titled *Instructional Aids in Mathematics*,[6] provides information regarding the growing number of available aids, suggestions for evaluating materials, and guidance in using them. Teachers will find this issue valuable.

Filmstrip Companies

Most textbook companies produce filmstrips that are specifically designed to complement their texts. For information, write to the company publishing your text. In many instances films are available for preview. The following companies are listed in the NCTM,[7] Thirty-fourth Yearbook, as major 35-mm filmstrip producers:

Central Scientific Co.
Cenco Center
2600 S. Kostner Ave.
Chicago, IL 60623

Educational Audio Visual, Inc.
29 Marble Ave.
Pleasantville, NY 10570

Jam Handy School Services
2821 East Grand Blvd.
Detroit, MI 48211

Filmstrip House
432 Park Ave. South
New York, NY 10016

Curriculum Materials Corp.
1319 Vine Street
Philadelphia, PA 19107

Film (16-mm) Companies

Of the great many distributors of educational films, the following seem to be *some* of the main sources of mathematical films, according to the NCTM.[8]

Coronet Films
65 East South Water Street
Chicago, IL 60601

Encyclopedia Britannica Educational Corporation
425 North Michigan Ave.
Chicago, IL 60611

Film Associates of California
11559 Santa Monica Blvd.
Los Angeles, CA 90025

Association Films, Inc.
600 Madison Ave.
New York, NY 10022

Bailey Films, Inc.
6509 DeLongpre Ave.
Hollywood, CA 90028

Individual Pupil Mathematics Kits

Ideally, a kit of materials should be made available to each child at each grade level. The contents of the kit should match the materials used in teacher demonstrations. Pupil-discovery materials need not be as large as teacher-demonstration materials,

6. *Instructional Aids in Mathematics*, Thirty-fourth Yearbook (Washington, D.C.: The National Council of Teachers of Mathematics, 1977).

7. NCTM, p. 229.

8. NCTM, pp. 228, 229.

since the teacher's materials in a class demonstration must be visible from all parts of the room.

The contents of the learner's kit will vary from grade to grade because of the strands that are introduced. For instance, pupils in kindergarten and grades one and two should have personal sets of small objects (counters) to use and group as they learn the meanings of numbers and basic facts. A fifth-grader's kit might contain a set of fractional parts to be used in studying processes with fractions.

The problem facing the teacher is to select a minimum number of materials for the individual kits and to organize the classroom so that pupils can use their kits freely without disrupting the rest of the class.

Primary Grade Kits

A typical kit of materials for pupils in the primary grades might contain:

1. Objects to be used in counting, grouping and representing sets (disks or small objects)

2. Materials to be used in showing place value (arrays of 100 squares, strips of 10 squares, and single squares, bundles of straws, pictures, etc.)

3. A ruler divided into standard or metric units. The ruler can be made of heavy cardboard, wood, plastic, or thin metal. The numerals do not have to be permanently inscribed on the ruler, as you may wish to introduce measuring first by using nonstandard units. When the pupils understand the value and meaning of standard units, the numerals can be inscribed with a fine-point, felt-tip marker.

Intermediate Grade Kits

A typical kit of materials for pupils in the intermediate grades might contain:

1. Materials for discovering products and quotients (for example, ten strips of groups of geometric patterns arranged by twos, threes, fours, and so on, up to nines)

2. A ruler showing fractional parts of an inch, including sixteenths; a metric rule

3. A fraction kit

4. Materials to show decimals

Commercial Mathematics Kits

In addition to producing manipulatives, filmstrips, workbooks, and worksheets to accompany their textbook series, many publishers also produce classroom mathematics kits that are "keyed" to the text. Additional companies that produce commercial kits are:

L. W. Singer Company, Inc.
Division of Random House
501 Madison Ave.
New York, NY 10022

Educational Teaching Aids
159 W. Kinzie Street
Chicago, IL 60610

Teaching Resource Corporation
100 Boylston Street
Boston, MA 02116

Spellbinder, Inc.
33 Bradford Street
Concord, MA 01742

S.V.E.
1345 Diversey Pkwy.
Chicago, IL 60614

Hoffman Information Systems
El Monte, CA 91734

We are not suggesting that schools should purchase commercial materials. For schools that prefer to make such purchases, the companies listed here provide that service.

Summary

In this chapter, we describe different kinds of learning and recommend guided discovery as the most effective type. The classroom should be equipped as a laboratory in order to implement this kind of learning. Long-range planning is needed to transform the classroom into a learning laboratory. The planning includes the selection of strands, or major mathematical topics, to be presented, formulation of broad and specific objectives to be accomplished, definite skills to be acquired, and the kinds of practice exercises needed to maintain them.

A mathematics classroom designed to function as a laboratory must include three types of materials. These are manipulatives, audiovisual, and symbolic. Manipulatives are objects that a child can move and handle and are designed to enable the learner to discover number relationships and patterns. Some of the most useful manipulatives are the abacus, place-value chart, and base-ten blocks. Audiovisual materials include pictures, maps, projection materials, and cassettes. Tests and textbooks are examples of symbolic materials.

Some of the major difficulties pupils encounter in dealing with symbolic materials result from their inability to read the text. Mathematics teachers must be able to give instruction in mathematical reading so that pupils can interpret the problems given and understand the presentation of the basic operations and procedures.

To create a classroom equipped with materials for both teacher demonstration and pupil kits, a teacher must understand the use and function of the materials. One of the best ways for programs of mathematics to be taught effectively in the elementary school is by means of competent teachers who use a limited number of well-chosen materials.

Exercises

1. Make a design that illustrates an arrangement of classroom furniture that includes areas for large- and small-group work. The design should include storage areas, a traffic flow plan, and provisions for quiet and noisy work areas.

2. Select a mathematical strand, such as problem solving. Examine a scope and sequence plan from a contemporary textbook company to determine how the concept is developed for a particular grade level. Write a summary of how the strand is taught at the selected grade level.

3. Choose a strand and an objective(s) related to the strand; list related resources to teach the strand for each level—that is, exploratory, symbolic, and mastery.

4. Name the tasks for organizing the classroom environment that a teacher can do before the pupils enter the classroom that will assist in establishing an efficient and welcoming atmosphere.

5. Write to a commercial source for a catalog of supplementary materials.

6. Reread the section on selecting manipulatives. Find examples of ma-

nipulatives that are not listed in this chapter and explain why or why not they should be considered for classroom use.

7. Choose one of the manipulatives listed on the chart in Table 3.2. Demonstrate how to use the manipulative for both a primary and an intermediate grade activity.

8. Select a lesson from a contemporary elementary mathematics textbook and write a plan that teaches the reading skills required for the lesson.

9. Design a learning center. Name the type and purpose, and describe the method of evaluating the pupils' work.

10. Discuss the importance of the following statement: The emotional tone of the mathematics classroom is of utmost importance in creating an environment in which children can learn and feel comfortable asking questions and expressing their thoughts.

Selected Readings

Berger, Emil J. (Ed.). *Instructional Aids in Mathematics,* 34th Yearbook. Reston, VA: National Council of Teachers of Mathematics, 1973.

Combs, A. W., D. L. Avila, and W. W. Purkey. *Helping Relationships: Basic Concepts for the Helping Professions.* Boston: Allyn and Bacon, 1978.

Crosswhite, F. Joe, and Robert E. Reys (Eds.). *Organizing for Mathematics Instruction, 1977 Yearbook.* Reston, VA: National Council of Teachers of Mathematics, 1977.

Earle, Richard A. *Teaching Reading and Mathematics.* Newark, DE: International Reading Association, 1976.

Higgins, John L., and Larry A. Sacks. *Mathematics Laboratories: 150 Activities and Games for Elementary Schools.* Columbus, OH: ERIC/SMEAC, Ohio State University, December 1974.

Kane, Robert B., Mary Ann Byrne, and Mary Ann Hater. *Helping Children Read Mathematics.* New York: American Book Co., 1974.

Purkey, W. William. *Inviting School Success.* Belmont, CA: Wadsworth, 1978.

Smith, Seaton C., and Carl A. Backman. *Teacher-Made Aids for Elementary School Mathematics: Readings for the Arithmetic Teacher.* Reston, VA: National Council of Teachers of Mathematics, 1974.

Vochko, Lee E. *Manipulative Activities and Games in the Mathematics Classroom.* Washington, D.C.: National Education Association, 1979.

Chapter 4

Systems of Numeration and of Number

Mathematics resists definition; it tends to be what mathematicians say it is. Elementary mathematics tends to be what is included in mathematics textbooks. Great thinkers through the ages have expressed diverse views on the nature of mathematics in different ways.

> Aristotle, who was as sure of everything as anyone can be of anything, thought mathematics the study of quantity; whereas Russell, in a less playful mood, thinks of it as the "class of all propositions of the type 'p implies q,' which seems to have little to do with quantity—or indeed (that is the point) with *any* special thing." Willard Gibbs thought of mathematics as a language. Hilbert thought of it as a meaningless game. For Benjamin Peirce it was "the science that draws necessary conclusions." G. H. Hardy joyfully stresses its uselessness; Lancelot Hogben joylessly stresses its practicality. J. S. Mill thought it an empirical science, like chemistry, only more general and more certain, whereas to J. W. N. Sullivan it was an art, and to the wonderful J. J. Sylvester it was "the music of reason." Finally, Spengler is sure that there is no such thing as mathe-

matics, but only mathematicses, differing absolutely with each culture.[1]

Achievement Goals

After studying this chapter, you should be able to:

1. Describe how number concepts were communicated in ancient civilizations.
2. Rename Egyptian and Roman numerals in Hindu-Arabic notation and rename Hindu-Arabic numerals in Egyptian and Roman notations.
3. Identify the characteristics of the Hindu-Arabic decimal system of notation.
4. Name five elements of an effective system of numeration.
5. Explain the contemporary view of sets and the number/numeral distinction.
6. List and discuss the special properties of zero and one.

---

1. Clifton Fadiman, "Meditations of a Mathematical Moron," in *Any Number Can Play* (Cleveland: World, 1957), p. 149.

7. Describe the properties of addition and multiplication and give the identities for these operations.

8. Distinguish between whole numbers and integers, and between whole numbers and rationals. Arrange the following sets of numbers in order of inclusiveness: whole numbers, integers, real numbers, counting numbers.

Vocabulary

Mastery of the following terms will help you to understand the chapter. Each term is defined or illustrated in the Glossary at the end of the book.

Addend	Factor
Array	Fraction
Associative property	Identity element
	Inequality
Base (system of numeration)	Integer
	Inverse operation
Binary operation	Natural number
Cardinal number	Negative number
Closure	Number line
Commutative property	Number period
	Open sentence
Complex number	Ordinal number
Counting numbers	Overloaded place
Decimal	Place value
Digit	Rational numbers
Distributive property	Real numbers
	Signed number
Equation	Total value (digit)

The Earliest Concepts of Number

Matching

Early civilizations used systems of matching to keep track of the number of items, such as the number of sheep in a flock. As each animal left the pen, a pebble was placed in a container. When the flock returned, a pebble was removed as each animal reentered the pen. If no pebbles remained after the last animal entered the pen, no sheep were missing. The set of pebbles *matched* the set of sheep. For each pebble there was one sheep, and for each sheep there was one pebble.

This type of one-to-one matching is still useful today. When you set a table, you don't count the napkins you need, but merely place a napkin at each place setting. Counting is related to the matching process, but requires names for numbers.

Early Number Concepts

Number was first used to communicate how many things were involved, such as how many animals, how many warriors, and the like. Fingers, pebbles, marks in the sand, and similar devices made symbolic communication possible before there were names for numbers, which enabled such information to be transmitted verbally. Historians of mathematics agree that humans clearly chose a base of ten for their system of communicating "how many" because of the ease of matching fingers with things. Soon it became expedient to name quantities represented by common groupings of things. In one early culture, the phrase "taking the thumb" indicated the quantity five. Historical records show other common names for small groupings.

Counting—A Major Invention

Counting requires that names be given to numbers. It is the basis of the ordinal concept of number as well as the cardinal concept.

Number is defined in two ways. An *ordinal* number denotes the position of a specific number in a set; a *cardinal* number indicates the size of a set or collection. For example, the ordinal number 4 describes an item as fourth in a group of at least 4 items. The cardinal number 4 indicates that there are 4 items in the collection. An ordinal number tells "which one" while a cardinal number tells "how many." Changing the position of an item in a set will change its ordinal number but will not change the cardinal number. Every set has a cardinal number.

Uses of Number in Measurement

During the Stone Age, people were involved in making, inventing, and developing ways to communicate in words, perhaps in written symbols, a limited number of quantitative ideas. The motivation to do this was probably a need to answer the questions "How many" and "Which one?"

Numbers soon took on an additional task—to measure, or describe "how much." For example, to talk and write about how many days had passed, a prehistoric person could merely use counting numbers. But to describe how far it was to the next village, the person had to use counting numbers in conjunction with a measurement unit, such as so many steps, so many pole lengths, or how many days it took to walk the distance. "Ten Sleeps," an Indian settlement in Wyoming, took its name from the process of applying number to measurement.

Symbolization of Numbers

Earlier civilizations developed number systems to suit their needs. The set of counting, or natural, numbers was the first set to be developed. The symbols (numerals) used to represent these numbers differed according to each culture. To some extent, the complexity of a civilization corresponds to the number of sets beyond the counting numbers that were used.

The Egyptian System of Notation

The culture that built the pyramids also produced a system of numeration and notation. It is likely that the Egyptian number system arose out of need. By about 3000 B.C. prosperous cities had grown up along the Nile River. Markets, businesses, and government activities demanded a system of records, and record keeping required numbers.

The ancient Egyptian system of numeration used a new symbol to represent each power of 10. Table 4.1 shows the different symbols used by the Egyptians and their corresponding values in our number system.

In the Egyptian system, ten strokes had the same value as one arch. Each new symbol, as we move from left to right in the table, represents a number ten times larger than the preceding symbol.

The number represented by a numeral is the sum of the numbers represented by its various symbols. For example, consider the numeral for 14,375:

Using Egyptian symbols, the number represented is the sum of 10,000, 4000, 300, 70, and 5, or 14,375.

Table 4.1 Egyptian Number Symbols and Their Values

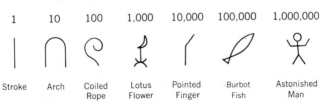

The symbols in this numeral are arranged in order of their value. The symbol of greatest value is on the left, and the symbol of least value is on the right. The symbols could have been in the reverse order or placed randomly. Therefore, the position or place of a symbol in a numeral did not affect the value of that symbol. The Egyptian system of numeration used neither order nor place value.

The Egyptian numeral for 14,375 contains 20 symbols. In contrast, our numeral for this amount would use only five symbols.

The Egyptian system is adequate to describe "how many," but it is not suited for computation. This is also true of the Roman system.

Exercises 4.1

1. What number is represented by each of these Egyptian numerals?

2. Use Egyptian numerals to represent the following numbers:
   (a) 32
   (b) 320
   (c) 203
   (d) 1560
   (e) 1,001,001
   (f) this year

The Roman System of Notation

One ancient number system that has lasted until modern times is the Roman system of notation, commonly called *Roman numerals*. The ancient Romans used the abacus to perform computations and Roman numerals to record the answers. Because it has no zero and is not a place-value system, the Roman system is very inefficient for computations with paper and pencil.

The Roman system uses a new symbol for each succeeding greater group. The symbols used in Roman notation are:

I	V	X	L	C	D	M
1	5	10	50	100	500	1000

A bar placed above a numeral multiplies the value of the number by 1000. Thus $\overline{C}$ represents 100,000, rather than 100.

The plan of counting by five, as in tallying votes, suggests how the symbols I, V, and X came to be used in Roman notation. Four vertical strokes and one cross stroke suggest V, to represent five. The representation for the numbers 5 through 10 would be as follows:

Tally	Ж∣	Ж∣	Ж∣∣	Ж∣∣∣	Ж∣∣∣∣	ЖЖ
Numeral	V	VI	VII	VIII	VIIII	X

The Roman system operates according to four principles:

Repetition: A symbol is repeated to indicate the number value.

Subtraction (not a part of early Roman usage): For the numbers 4, 40, 400 and 9, 90, 900, subtraction is done by writing a symbol representing a smaller value *to the left* of a symbol of greater value.

Multiplication: A bar drawn over any Roman numeral indicates that the value is to be multiplied by 1000.

Addition: All the values of the symbols written are added to get the total value of the number.

The Roman system used a "cycle of numerals" in a "times 5, times 2" sequence:

$$I \times 5 = V \quad X \times 5 = L \quad C \times 5 = D$$
$$V \times 2 = X \quad L \times 2 = C \quad D \times 2 = M$$

This cycle may have stemmed from thinking of fingers and arms, but it has no use today except perhaps as an aid in learning and remembering Roman numerals. The Roman numerals for numbers to one million are given in Table 4.2.

The value of a number represented in Roman numerals is the sum of the numbers represented by each symbol, except when subtraction is involved. Thus, the number represented by MMCCCXXVI is 2326, which is the sum of the numbers represented by each symbol:

MM   CCC   XX   V   I
2000 + 300 + 20 + 5 + 1 = 2326

Exercises 4.2

1. Find the number represented by these Roman numerals:
   - (a) CCXLV
   - (b) CDXL
   - (c) MMDCXLV
   - (d) $\overline{\text{M}}$ MDC
   - (e) DLXXXIV
   - (f) $\overline{\text{C}}$ CXLIX
   - (g) $\overline{\text{MM}}$
   - (h) DCCIV
   - (i) $\overline{\text{DC}}$
   - (j) $\overline{\text{DC}}$

2. Represent the following numbers in Roman numerals:
   - (a) 105
   - (b) 2250
   - (c) 1440
   - (d) 1001
   - (e) 1,000,000
   - (f) 200,000

The Hindu-Arabic System of Notation

During the Middle Ages, the Roman system was replaced by the Hindu-Arabic system in most major civilizations. Because it is a place-value system with zero, efficient paper-and-pencil computation in the Hindu-Arabic system is possible.

The Hindu-Arabic system was invented by Hindu priests in central India, and was spread to the West by the Arabs. Its distinctive feature is *place value*. The Hindus invented place value sometime between the sixth and seventh centuries A.D. Later, after the system reached the West, the Hindus discovered the digit zero, which could be used as a place holder for an empty groove on their clay counting boards, as shown in Figure 4.1. The system was complete with

Table 4.2 Numerals in the Roman Number System

1	I	6	VI	20	XX	100	C	10,000	$\overline{\text{X}}$
2	II	7	VII	40	XL	400	CD	50,000	$\overline{\text{L}}$
3	III	8	VIII	50	L	500	D	(1000	
								x	
4	IV	9	IX	60	LX	900	CM	1000)	$\overline{\text{M}}$
5	V	10	X	90	XC	1000	M		

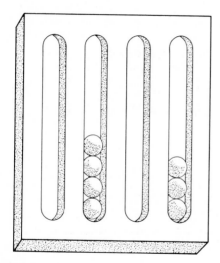

Figure 4.1
A Hindu Counting Board—An Abacus-like Device

the distinctive features of *place value* and *zero.*

We can illustrate the principle of *place value* with the aid of the counting board. Counting was accomplished by a one-to-one matching of pebbles with the items being counted. Before the invention of place value, when the "counter" reached ten, or the base of the system, the things being used to represent ones were exchanged for *one* object of *another type,* usually bigger in

size or at least visually different. In modern times, exchanging ten pennies for one dime is the same general idea.

The Hindus did not exchange a pebble or marker for a pebble or marker of a different size. With the aid of a counting board, when the first groove on the right had ten pebbles—usually all that would fit—the Hindus would exchange the ten pebbles for *one* of the *same kind,* and place that *one* pebble in the groove to the left of the first place. This groove then became the *tens place.* Any single pebble in that position represented ten pebbles in the *ones place.* The *position* of a pebble on the counting board determined its total numerical value!

Of the systems discussed in this chapter, only the Hindu-Arabic decimal, place-value system is convenient for paper-and-pencil computation. For just this reason it replaced the Roman system in Europe during the Middle Ages.

Complete Place Value

The English language abounds with words that have different meanings in different contexts. For example, the word "frog" represents an animal, part of a horse's hoof, a temporary obstruction in the throat, and a closing on a coat. To give more than one meaning to a numeral would seem to confound matters, but this is done in our Hindu-Arabic system. We give a value to the *place* occupied by the digit as well as to the value of the digit itself. For example, 3 in 234 is in the *tens place*, indicating that the place contains *3 tens* or 30 ones.

Place value is implicit in the column arrangement of the abacus. Again, the principle of place value, along with zero, sets the Hindu-Arabic system apart from all other previously developed systems, as by far superior.

Zero

Many historians regard the introduction of zero into the number system as an invention with as much importance as the wheel. The origins of both are equally obscure. According to Swiss-American mathematician Florian Cajori, the Egyptian astronomer, mathematician, and geographer Ptolemy (A.D. 100–170) used the Greek letter omicron (o) to represent blanks in the sexagesimal system about 130 A.D. But this o was not used exactly as zero is used today. The first modern use of zero probably occurred during the seventh century A.D.[2]

Characteristics of a Place-Value System

There are eight main characteristics of the decimal system of numeration for whole numbers. These are:

1. The base of the system is 10, as there are exactly 10 digits in the system.

2. The digits used are 1, 2, 3, 4, 5, 6, 7, 8, 9, 0.

3. Each digit in a numeral performs two functions: It holds a place, and it shows the frequency of that place.

2. Vera Sanford, "Hindu Arabic Numerals," *Arithmetic Teacher*, December 1955, 2:115.

4. Each digit in a two-or-more-place numeral that names a whole number has three values:

    a. *cardinal value*, sometimes called the *face value*
    b. *positional value*
    c. *total value*

The positional value is the value of the place the digit holds in a numeral. This value is a power of the base. The power is the same as the number of places the digit is to the left of the ones place. The total value is the product of the cardinal and the positional values.

We can illustrate the different values of a digit by considering the numeral 732. The *cardinal value:*

    of 7 is 7; of 3 is 3; of 2 is 2.

The *positional value:*

    of 7 is 100; of 3 is 10; of 2 is 1.

The *total value:*

    of 7 is 700; of 3 is 30; of 2 is 2.

The cardinal and total values of a digit are the same for each digit in the ones place. These two values are also the same for the digit 0, because the product of 0 and a number is 0.

5. The number is the sum of the total values of the digits in the different places.

6. Moving a digit to the left in a whole number multiplies its place value by a power of 10. If 3 is moved two places to the left, the value of the 3 has been multiplied by 10^2. We read the numeral 10^2 as "ten to the second power," or "ten squared."

7. Moving a digit to the right divides its place value by a power of 10. Since dividing by 10 is the same as multiplying by $\frac{1}{10}$, or 10^{-1}, moving a digit to the right in a numeral multiplies the value of that digit by a power of $\frac{1}{10}$. The power is the same as the number of places the digit is moved.

8. Every two-or-more-place numeral can be named in different ways. The *standard numeral* for three hundred forty-nine is 349. This number may be written as:

a. 349 = 3 hundreds, 4 tens, 9 ones = 34 tens, 9 ones = 349 ones
b. 349 = 300 + 40 + 9
c. 349 = $3 \times 10^2 + 4 \times 10^1 + 9 \times 10^0$.

Example (a) illustrates place value. Example (b) shows how to rename 349 to illustrate total values. The 3 in 349 represents 3 hundreds, or 3×100, the 4 represents 4 tens, or 4×10, while the 9 represents 9 ones, or 9×1. The total value of 3 is 300, of 4 is 40, and of 9 is 9. Example (c) illustrates the base-ten aspect of our system by using exponential notation.

Elements of a Numeration System

By examining the ancient Egyptian and Roman systems of numeration, we can see that they are deficient in many respects. If we compare these systems with the Hindu-Arabic, we can easily identify the essential elements of an effective system of numeration. Such a system must have the property of completeness so that it can function without the use of supplementary aids. The elements of a complete system include:

1. A base

2. Symbols or numerals

3. A fixed value for a place in a numeral

4. Zero

5. A decimal point

Man invented all five of these elements in order to deal effectively with numbers.

Ten is the base of the decimal system, and so ten symbols are needed. The base of most ancient numeration systems was a multiple of five—5, 10, or 20. The Babylonian numeration system used a base of sixty. We measure time on this scale today.

A symbol used in a numeration system must have a *name*, as well as a *design*, or *form*. The names of the digits, which vary in different languages, are used in enumeration. Table 4.3 gives the number names of the first ten counting numbers in three different languages.

Although different societies in the West have different names for the digits, the symbols used to represent numbers are the same, except for 7 and 1. Many Europeans write the numeral one as *1* and so must write the numeral seven as *7* to avoid confusion.

The third and fourth essential elements in a system of numeration are place value and zero, which we have already described. The fifth element is a point, such as the decimal point, used to locate the ones place. The use of a decimal point extends place value to the right of the ones place in the decimal system. Any digit, except 0, written to the right of that point has a value less than one but greater than zero.

Periods in Numerals

It is difficult to read the numeral 371495 as it is written here. To make it easier to read large numbers, we use *periods* in the

Table 4.3 Number Names in Different Languages

English	one	two	three	four	five	six	seven	eight	nine	ten
German	ein	zwei	drei	vier	fünf	sechs	sieben	acht	neun	zehn
Spanish	uno	dos	tres	cuatro	cinco	seis	siete	ocho	nueve	diez

numerals. Beginning on the right, three consecutive places constitute a period. A comma, or a single space, is used to separate periods in numerals containing five or more digits. The space is used in the metric system. A four-place numeral can be separated into two periods by a comma, or a space, provided that the numeral does not represent a date or a time interval.

The first period designates *units*. This period and each succeeding full period to the left contain three places, designated as ones, tens, and hundreds. Every period must contain three places except the first period on the left, as is seen in the third period of the numeral 8,371,495.

Table 4.4 lists the first four periods in grouping numerals. Each period to the left has a value 1000 times the value of the period to the right. There are 1000 thousands in a million and 1000 millions in a billion. It is possible, therefore, to represent a million as 1000 thousands. Similarly, 1000 millions represents a billion.

The value of a billion is not the same in all countries. In our country a billion is equal to 1000 millions, while in England a billion is equal to a million millions. A billion of this value is 1000 times as large as our billion.

There are other period names that can be used to designate a period to the left of the group for billions. For a numeral to represent a value greater than a numeral in the group or period for billions, that numeral must have at least thirteen places.

Overloading a Place

Efficient computation is possible in the Hindu-Arabic decimal, place-value system not only because each place can be calculated as easily as the ones place, but also because it is possible to *overload* a place as needed. A place is *overloaded* when the number at that place is greater than 9. Consequently, to subtract 23 from 71, the 71 could be renamed 6 tens 11 ones, so that subtraction can be done at both the ones place and the tens place.

Table 4.4 Use of Periods in Grouping Numerals

Billions	Millions	Thousands	Units
Hundreds-Tens-Ones	Hundreds-Tens-Ones	Hundreds-Tens-Ones	Hundreds-Tens-Ones

Exercises 4.3

1. Write the standard numeral for the following:
   (a) 7000 + 300 + 50 + 6
   (b) $(5 \times 10^3) + (1 \times 10^2) + (6 \times 10) + 5$
   (c) 7 hundreds 35 ones
   (d) 20 tens 9 ones
   (e) 3 thousands 26 ones

2. Write place-value names as shown in 1(a):
   (a) 3782   (b) 4025

3. Rename in terms of powers of ten:
   (a) 4730
   (b) 29,100

4. Rename 732 in three different ways so that every digit is used once in each numeral:

732 = 7 hundreds + ☐ tens + 2☐

☐ tens + 2 ones

☐ ones

5. Use the pattern in problem 4 to rename the following:
   (a) 378   (b) 2235

6. Give the value of the following:
   (a) 3×10^3 (c) 10^0
   (b) 5×10^2 (d) $(2 \times 10^2) + (3 \times 10^0)$

Properties of Number and Number Operations

Sets

Set concepts and notation were introduced into the elementary mathematics curriculum in the 1960s as New Math became popular. Unfortunately, too much emphasis was placed on many of the technical aspects of sets, especially the abstract notation of sets, subsets, union, intersection, Cartesian product, and the like. Both teachers and parents questioned the value of this emphasis, given that the mathematics curriculum was already overcrowded and children were unable to learn what many considered more important and more basic subject matter.

Set concepts are basic to mathematics. On advanced levels, set theory is very complex. Set ideas in elementary mathematics are useful in relating abstract number concepts to the world of objects. Collections of things occur naturally in our lives—for example, "sets of books," "a set of dishes," "a herd of cattle." This text uses "set" in the everyday sense.

Number and Numeral

A *number* is an abstract idea. It cannot be seen, touched, or erased. The number two is an idea common to all pairs of things.

A *numeral* is a written symbol that represents a number. It can be seen, touched, and erased. The numeral 2 is one of many symbols that can be used to represent the intangible number two.

The New Math programs of the 1960s placed great emphasis on having children learn the fine distinction between "number" and "numeral." In many cases, the language was overdetailed and confusing. The simplest solution is for a teacher to make this distinction when it comes up naturally in conversation and helps to clarify an idea. Otherwise, just keep in mind that we think with numbers and record with numerals.

Possibly the most useful concept associated with the number–numeral distinction is that each number has many names (numerals) and that renaming numbers is one of the most common mathematical activities. Renaming 23 as 20 + 3 or (2 × 10) + 3 sometimes makes it easier to understand arithmetic operations.

Equalities and Inequalities

The word *equal* means "names the same number." Forming an equality usually involves discovering another name for the same number. The equality 1 + 1 = 2 indicates that *1 + 1* and *2* are different symbols or names for the same number.

The statement $2 \neq 3$ indicates that the numerals name different numbers but gives no information as to which is larger. The inequalities $2 < 3$ and $3 > 2$ indicate that 2 is less than 3 and that 3 is greater than 2. These inequalities are equivalent to one another, since each can be read from right to left as well as from left to right, a characteristic of mathematical sentences. The tip of the arrow always points to the smaller number.

Properties of Number Operations

In the past, mathematics was taught largely by rote rules, such as "invert and multiply," with little or no effort to make the rules meaningful. In the 1950s and 1960s, there was concerted effort to use sound mathematical number properties in place of such rules.

Understanding certain properties of number reduces the task of learning the basic facts in addition and subtraction. Similarly, discovering certain properties or relationships between multiplication and division helps the pupil to work with these operations. In the following sections we discuss some of the most important properties of number, beginning with *zero*.

SPECIAL PROPERTIES OF ZERO

Zero has very special number properties:

1. $0 + 1 = 1 + 0 = 1$. Zero is the *additive identity*; the sum of zero and any number is that number.

2. $0 \times N = N \times 0$. The product of zero and any number is zero. A consequence of this is that for $N \neq 0$, $0 \div N = 0 \times 1/N = 0$.

3. $^+N + {}^-N = 0$. The sum of any number and its opposite is zero. This is the most fundamental fact of dealing with signed numbers. The word "opposite" is an everyday term for the technical term *additive inverse*.

4. Division by zero is impossible and is often described as undefined. If a nonzero number N divided by 0 equals K, as in $N \div 0 = K$, then it must follow that $N = 0 \times K$, which contradicts the statement $0 \times K = 0$.

SPECIAL PROPERTIES OF *One*

The number *one* has some very special properties:

1. Where N is a counting number, $N + 1$ is the next counting number.

2. $N \times 1 = N$. Any number multiplied by one equals that number. The equation $N \times 1 = N$ expresses the *identity* property for multiplication. Renaming 1 as $^2/_2$ is often useful in examples such as: $^3/_4 \times 1 = ^3/_4 \times ^2/_2 = ^6/_8$.

3. Where N is a nonzero number, $N \div N = 1$. Any nonzero number divided by itself equals *one*.

4. Any fractional number in the form of a/b, where a *and* b $\neq 0$, multiplied by its *reciprocal* equals *one*. The reciprocal of a/b is b/a or $^a/_b \times ^b/_a = 1$.

THE IDENTITY PROPERTY

The identity property can be introduced by tables of the following type:

(a) $1 + 0 = 1$ (b) $1 \times 1 = 1$
$2 + 0 = 2$ $2 \times 1 = 2$
$3 + 0 = 3$ $3 \times 1 = 3$
$4 + 0 = \square$ $4 \times 1 = \square$
$5 + \square = 5$ $5 \times \square = 5$

The pattern in (a) shows that 0 is the identity element for addition; the sum of any number and 0 is that number.

The pattern in (b) shows that 1 is the identity element for multiplication; the product of any number and 1 is that number.

Tables (a) and (b) illustrate that the number 0 in addition behaves just as 1 behaves in multiplication.

Elementary pupils should become familiar with the identity concept through the renaming process. They should learn to rename 2 as $2 + 0$ or $0 + 2$ and, when multiplication has been introduced, 2×1 and 1×2. Renaming 5 as $5 + 0$ can be useful in helping pupils to learn that $4 + 1 = 5$ and $3 + 2 = 5$. Renaming ½ as ½ × 1 is useful in helping pupils recognize that one-half and two-fourths name the same number.

THE INVERSE PROPERTY

The inverse property is probably the most complex number operation we will discuss. It can be illustrated by the following patterns:

(a) $0 + 0 = 0$ (b) $1 \times 1 = 1$
    $^-1 + 1 = 0$ $\dfrac{2}{1} \times \dfrac{1}{2} = 1$

    $^-2 + 2 = 0$ $\dfrac{3}{1} \times \dfrac{1}{3} = 1$

$$^-3 + 3 = 0 \qquad\qquad \frac{4}{1} \times \frac{1}{4} = 1$$

$$^-4 + 4 = 0$$

The pattern in (a) shows pairs of *inverse numbers* for addition. A pair of inverse numbers in addition has a sum of 0 (the identity element for addition). The pattern in (b) shows pairs of inverse numbers in multiplication. A pair of inverse numbers in multiplication has a product of 1 (the identity element for multiplication).

Our number system is said to have the *inverse property for addition* because for every number X in the system there is a number $^-$X, such that $^-X + X = X + {}^-X = 0$.

Our number system is said to have the *inverse property for multiplication* because for every number X there is a number $\dfrac{1}{X}$ such that: $\dfrac{X}{1} \times \dfrac{1}{X} = \dfrac{1}{X} \times \dfrac{X}{1} = \dfrac{X}{X} = 1$, where X cannot equal zero.

Exercises 4.4

1. A common property of 0 and 1 discussed in this chapter is the _____ property.

2. Show how the number one behaves in multiplication just as the number zero behaves in addition.

3. Rename 5 in four different ways, using the identity for addition and multiplication.

4. Use the equality $1 = \dfrac{2}{2}$ to show that $\dfrac{3}{4} = \dfrac{6}{8}$.

5. Illustrate that zero is not the identity element for subtraction.

6. Complete each of the sentences below by writing the correct numeral in the frame or frames.

(a) $\square + 3 = 3$.
(b) $4 \times \square = 4$.
(c) $\dfrac{2}{3} \times \dfrac{\square}{\square} = \dfrac{8}{12}$.
(d) $\dfrac{4}{5} \times \dfrac{2}{\square} = \dfrac{8}{\square}$.

(e) $0 + 3 = \square$.
(f) $5 + (3 - 3) = 8 - \square$.
(g) $5 - \square = 5$.
(h) $5 \div \triangle = 5$.

(i) $\dfrac{3}{3} \times \dfrac{2}{3} = 1 \times \dfrac{\triangle}{\square}$.

(j) $\dfrac{5}{6} + 0 = \square$.

(k) $\dfrac{2}{5} \times \square = \dfrac{2}{5}$.

(l) $3 \times \square = \square \times 3$.

THE COMMUTATIVE PROPERTY

Our number system is commutative for addition because the sum of any two numbers is the same regardless of the order in which they are added. This property can be stated more concisely in algebraic terms: For every x and y in our system of numbers:

$x + y = y + x$.

By comparing the two given statements, we see why properties of number systems are frequently stated with algebraic symbolism rather than in purely verbal form. Modern programs use more algebraic language than do traditional programs, although the difference between the newer and older programs is not as apparent at the elementary level as at the secondary level.

All the number systems of elementary mathematics are commutative for addition and multiplication but not for subtraction and division.

The commutative property of number systems is simple enough to be understood by pupils in the lower elementary grades and important enough to be referred to at all levels of mathematics. Pupils in the elementary grades should recognize the commutative property as a nonverbal pattern. The teacher may refer to it by name, but pupils should not be required to do so.

THE ASSOCIATIVE PROPERTY

The associative property of our number system for addition and multiplication can be stated as follows: For all x and y in our number system:

$(x + y) + z = x + (y + z)$
$x(yz) = (xy)z$

The associative property is important because of the *binary* nature of addition and multiplication.[3] These two operations are binary because each operation can be performed on only two numbers at a time.

When more than two numbers are to be added, the binary nature of addition requires that the operation first be performed on two numbers. The associative property of addition states that when three numbers are to be added, the result of adding the sum of the first and second numbers to the third number is the same as adding the first number to the sum of the second and third numbers. A similar statement can be made for multiplication.

---

3. Subtraction and division are also binary operations, but do not have the associative or commutative property, as illustrated by the following counterexamples:

$6 - 5 \neq 5 - 6$
$(6 - 3) - 2 \neq 6 - (3 - 2)$
$6 \div 2 \neq 2 \div 6$
$(8 \div 4) \div 2 \neq 8 \div (4 \div 2)$

Exercises 4.5

1. Rename $3 + 4$ using the commutative property.

2. Rename $3 + (4 - 1)$ using only the commutative property.

3. Rename $3 + (4 + 1)$ in two different ways by using only the commutative property.

4. How can understanding the commutative property reduce the memory load for addition and multiplication facts?

The associative property makes it easier to handle addition combinations with sums greater than ten. Using the associative property, we can rename the second addend so as to create an addend that, when added to the first number of the addition example, has a sum of ten. Then it is easy to find the sum of the combination.

1. Example: $7 + 5 = \square$

2. Question: $7 + \square = 10$; Answer 3

3. So rename the 5 as $3 + 2$

4. Now the example is: $7 + (3 + 2) = \square$

5. Apply the associative property: $7 + (3 + 2) = (7 + 3) + 2 = 10 + 3 = 13$.

ACTIVITIES

The following is a list of some useful activities involving the associative and commutative properties.

1. Ask students to rename $2 + 3$. A response of 5 is natural and correct at any grade level, but with teacher guidance the response of $3 + 2$ should be common as early as grade one. Answers of $(1 + 1) + 3$ and $2 + (2 + 1)$ should also be obtained by first-grade pupils.

Pupils should be able to rename $76 + 234$ as $234 + 76$ long before they can determine the sum of 310. Exercises of this nature help pupils learn the basic pattern of the commutative property long before a name is attached to it. When a pattern is understood, it is much easier to give it a name.

2. Ask the class to rename $4 + (6 + 1)$. Again, $4 + 7$ and 11 are correct, but examples of this type should be given often enough so that $(4 + 6) + 1$ will also be given. In a renaming activity any correct answer should be accepted, but pupils should be encouraged to give others until the name or numeral desired by the teacher is obtained. If the desired answer is not given in a reasonable time the teacher should give the answer and then immediately give several similar examples to see if the class understands the idea involved. Renaming sessions should be frquent and brief and should usually have a specific goal.

3. Both of the stated activities can be repeated with examples such as 3×4 and $4 \times (5 \times 3)$ when the multiplication concept has been introduced.

4. The following exercise involves pupil recognition of an equation as true or false. The correct answers are given in parentheses.

$5 - 3 = 3 - 5$	(False)
$3 \times 5 = 5 \times 3$	(True)
$3(4 + 5) = 3 \times 4 + 5$	(False)
$32 \times 25 = 8 \times (4 \times 25)$	(True)
$4 \times (7 \times 25) = (4 \times 25) \times 7$	(True)
$89 + 43 = (89 + 11) + 32$	(True)

A teacher should use examples similar to these and discuss why they are *true* or *false* in terms of the properties of the number systems under discussion.

Exercises 4.6

1. Which of the following words is frequently used to describe the application of the associative property?
   (a) Change   (b) Regroup   (c) Rearrange

2. Rename by applying the associative property: $2 + (8 + 7)$.

3. Give one property for each of the following statements: (A) Commutative (B) Associative (C) Commutative and associative:
   (a) $2 + 3 = 3 + 2$
   (b) $4 + (5 + 7) = 4 + (7 + 5)$

(c) $4 + (5 + 7) = (4 + 5) + 7$
(d) $4 + (5 + 7) = (7 + 5) + 4$
(e) $4 + (5 + 7) = (4 + 7) + 5$

4. Complete the sentences below by writing the correct answer in each of the frames. Indicate which property is illustrated in each sentence:

(a) $2 + (3 + 5) = 2 + (\square + 3)$ Property _____

(b) $3 + (4 + \triangle) = (4 + 0) + 3$ Property _____

(c) $(2 + 5) + \square = 2 + (5 + 3)$ Property _____

(d) $(2 + 7) + 8 = (2 + 8) + \square$ Property _____

The *commutative* property is probably learned most readily on a nonverbal level by most children. The *associative* property is more subtle and not learned as easily. Two words that are useful in dealing with these two properties are "rearrange" and "regroup." Rearranging can apply to only the commutative property (changing the order of the addends or factors) or both the commutative and associative properties (changing both the order and the grouping of the addends or factors). For example, if $2 + 3$ is rearranged as $3 + 2$, only the commutative property is involved. If $7 + 4 + 6$ is rearranged as $4 + 6 + 7$, then both the associative and the commutative properties are involved. Although this distinction can and should be made later in the elementary grades, possibly the most useful feature during the early stages of learning the associative and commutative properties is the combined effect that: *Addends (or factors) can be rearranged and regrouped in any manner without changing the sum (or product).*

Pupils should learn quickly that rearranging and regrouping *does* affect the answer in subtraction and division examples, as seen in the following examples:

$5 - 4$ is not equal to $4 - 5$
$6 \div 2$ is not equal to $2 \div 6$
$(6 - 4) - 2$ is not equal to $6 - (4 - 2)$
$(6 \div 4) \div 2$ is not equal to $6 \div (4 \div 2)$

The four operations are binary. As the following example illustrates, this fact is useful in dealing with the order of operations:

(1) $3 + 4 \times 2$
(2) $3 + 4 \div 2$

When no parentheses are used, many students solve (1) as $3 + 4 = 7, 7 \times 2 = 14$. This answer is incorrect because of the universal convention that in an expression involving both addition (or subtraction) and multiplication (or division), multiplication (or division) is done before addition (or subtraction).

Expressions with more than two operations rarely occur in the elementary textbooks. When they do, parentheses should be used to remove any ambiguity.

When dealing with expressions that involve more than two numbers, pupils should recognize that the choice of the numbers used to start the series of operations can affect the results.

THE DISTRIBUTIVE PROPERTY

The associative and commutative properties are defined in terms of a set of numbers and *one* binary operation. Our number system is commutative with respect to one binary operation (addition) and not for another (subtraction). The distributive property is defined in terms of a set of numbers and *two* operations. The distributive property is the only property discussed in this chapter that is defined in terms of two operations.

The distributive property—of multiplication over addition for our number system—can be defined as follows: For all x, y, and z in our number system, $x(y + z) = xy + xz$.

The distributive property indicates that $3(4 + 5)$ can be renamed as $(3 \times 4) + (3 \times 5)$. There are many other names for the number represented by $3(4 + 5)$, including 3×9. The distributive property indicates that if multiplication is to be performed before addition in $3(4 + 5)$, the *multiplication must be distributed over both addends*.

Pupils should be reminded periodically that in $(3 \times 4) + (3 \times 5)$ the multiplication is to be performed before the addition.

Multiplication is also distributive over subtraction, but this fact is not usually stated in the definition of the distributive property. It can be stated: for all x, y, and z in our number system, $x(y - z) = (xy) - (xz)$. For example:

$$3 \times (9 - 2) = (3 \times 9) - (3 \times 2)$$
$$= 27 - 6 = 21$$

Worked another way:

$$3 \times (9 - 2) = 3 \times 7 = 21$$

A very good visual way to show the distributive property of multiplication over addition is with an *array*. For example, the number fact $2 \times 3 = ?$ can be visualized in an array as:

• • •
• • •

Likewise, the number array 5×8 can be shown visually as:

Then 8 can be renamed as $4 + 4$ and the array for $5 (4 + 4)$ can be shown as:

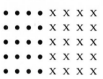

This technique enables one to take a difficult number combination and break it into two easier number facts; in this case, $(5 \times 4) + (5 \times 4) = 20 + 20 = 40$.

ACTIVITIES

The following are some typical activities that can help pupils obtain a better understanding of the distributive property.

1. Ask pupils to rename $4(5 + 10)$. Continue the activity until $(4 \times 5) + (4 \times 10)$ is obtained. If it is necessary to give the answer, use several other examples to be certain that the basic pattern is understood. Talk about multiplying each addend or distributing the multiplication over both addends.

2. The activity in Item 1 can be performed before pupils know the name of the distributive property. After pupils have learned this property by name, the following activity, and others like it, can be introduced. Ask pupils to rename the following using the distributive property. Correct answers are given in parentheses.

$4(10 + 7)$	$(4 \times 10) + (4 \times 7)$
4×23	$(4 \times 20) + (4 \times 3)$
Other answers possible.	
5×8	$(5 \times 5) + (5 \times 3)$
Other answers possible.	

3. When pupils learn that multiplication is also distributive with respect to subtraction, they can rename $7(30 - 2)$ as $7 \times 30 - 7 \times 2$. This can be done beneficially both before and after pupils have learned the meaning of the word "distributive."

4. Pupils should learn that the expression $7(3 + 7)$ can be solved most easily as 7×10, while for most people $7(20 - 1)$ can be solved most readily if renamed $(7 \times 20) - (7 \times 1)$. A list similar to the following can be given and pupils asked whether to add (subtract) or multiply first. Keep in mind that this is a subjective question and that different pupils may give different answers, as a result of their attitudes and skills. Pupil disagreements that provoke discussions should be encouraged.

$$10(8 + 9)$$

Adding first is easier (comparing two choices), but multiplying first is not much more difficult.

$$17(4 + 6)$$

Adding first is shorter.

$$11(40 - 1)$$

Multiplying first is probably easier for most pupils.

5. If $a = b$, then the renaming concept allows a to be renamed as b or b to be renamed as a. Therefore, since $3(4 + 5) = (3 \times 4) + (3 \times 5)$, the left-hand member of the equation can be renamed as $(3 \times 4) + (3 \times 5)$, or the right-hand member renamed as $3(4 + 5)$. Pupils will tend not to do the latter renaming without guidance. The following situations illustrate the advantage of this renaming:

$$(7 \times 12) + (7 \times 8)$$
Rename as $7(12 + 8)$ or 7×20

$$(\frac{1}{4} \times 49) + (\frac{1}{4} \times 51)$$

Rename as $\frac{1}{4}(49 + 51)$ or $\frac{1}{4} \times 100$

The value of this activity cannot be over-emphasized.

Closure

The final property to be discussed is closure. The whole numbers are closed with respect to addition because the sum of two whole numbers is always a whole number. The whole numbers are not closed with respect to subtraction because the difference $6 - 8$ is not a whole number.

The whole numbers are closed with respect to multiplication but not with respect to division since $2 \div 3$ is not a whole number. One counterexample is sufficient to prove that a class of number is not closed for a given operation.

The closure property has very few direct applications, but understanding this concept helps one gain a knowledge of the development of number systems.

Exercises 4.7

1. What is the most important and apparent difference between the distributive property and the associative and commutative properties?

2. Why is it not appropriate to say that the operation of addition is distributive?

3. Rename each of the following using the distributive property:
   (a) $3(4 + 5)$
   (b) $(4 \times 5) + (4 \times 15)$
   (c) $(2 \times \frac{1}{7}) + (3 \times \frac{1}{7})$
   (d) $2x + 3x$

4. Use the distributive property of multiplication over subtraction to re-name $(18 \times \frac{1}{7}) - (4 \times \frac{1}{7})$.

5. To illustrate the distributive property of multiplication over addition for the example $3(4 + 5)$, we multiply each of the terms in parentheses by 3 and then add the results. Use the expression $3 + 4 \times 5$ to show that addition is not distributive over multiplication.

6. Using the expressions $(8 - 4) \div 2$ and $2 \div (8 - 4)$, show that the right-hand distributive property of division over subtraction applies, but not the left-hand.

7. Complete the open sentences below by writing the correct numerals in the frames:
   (a) $(2 \times 3) + (2 \times 4) = 2(3 + \square)$.
   (b) $3(4 + 5) = 3 \times 4 + \triangle \times 5$.
   (c) $(8 \times \frac{1}{7}) - (5 \times \frac{1}{7}) = \square \times \frac{1}{7}$.

8. Just as the frame $\square$ holds a place for a numeral, the circle $\bigcirc$ is frequently used to hold a place for an operation. For example, the statement $2 \bigcirc 3 = 6$ becomes a true statement when the symbol for multiplication is placed in the circle. Write a symbol for multiplication, division, addition, or subtraction in each of the following circles so that the sentence will be true:
   (a) $2(3 + 4) = 2 \bigcirc (3 + 4)$.
   (b) $4(3 \bigcirc 5) = (4 \times 3) + (4 \times 5)$.
   (c) $5(3 + 6) = (5 \bigcirc 3) + (5 \bigcirc 6)$.
   (d) $7(8 - 5) = (7 \times 8) \bigcirc (7 \times 5)$.

9. The parentheses in $(2 \times 3) + (2 \times 5)$ are sometimes omitted because of the almost universal convention that multiplication and division are performed before addition and subtraction in expressions of this type. Place parentheses in each of the following expressions so that a person not familiar with the order of operations will not make an error:
   (a) $3 \times 5 + 2$
   (b) $4 + 3 \times 4$
   (c) $9 - 2 \times 3$
   (d) $8 \div 4 + 2$
   (e) $2 \times 3 + 2 \times 4$
   (f) $5 \times 7 - 5 \times 2$
   (g) $7 - 4 \div 2$
   (h) $6 \div 2 + 6 \div 3$
   (i) $6 \times 2 - 6 \div 3$
   (j) $12 \times 3 - 8 + 5$

Kinds of Numbers in the Real Number System

THE NATURAL NUMBERS

The natural numbers, also called the counting numbers, were the first to be discovered by any civilization. The natural numbers are 1, 2, 3, 4, 5, . . . Figure 4.2 presents a graph of the natural numbers.

The properties of natural numbers are such that addition and multiplication can always be performed with the set of natural numbers and yield a natural number answer but that subtraction and division cannot al-

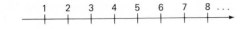

Figure 4.2
Counting Numbers

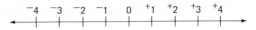

Figure 4.3

ways be performed. The difference 2 − 6 and the quotient 2 ÷ 6 do not exist in the set of natural numbers. In traditional programs pupils were frequently told that it was impossible to subtract 6 from 2. In a modern program pupils are told that 6 cannot be subtracted from 2 in the set of natural numbers (the subtraction is possible in the set of integers).

The natural numbers are more than adequate to meet the needs of a primitive civilization. These numbers even serve the everyday needs of somewhat advanced civilizations. The Roman system of numeration is a set of numerals representing the natural numbers, since 0 is not involved. This system met the needs of Roman merchants (with the help of an abacus or similar device).

When a civilization begins to advance technically the natural numbers quickly become inadequate. At this point a resourceful civilization extends the number system. The next logical developments are *whole numbers* and *integers*.

THE WHOLE NUMBERS

The *whole numbers* include the natural numbers plus *zero*. Zero was first introduced by the Hindus as a place holder in a numeral. Its name comes from the Arabic word *sifr*, which means "vacant." Later zero was considered a whole number.

THE INTEGERS

The *integers* are numbers as:

. . . ⁻3, ⁻2, ⁻1, 0, ⁺1, ⁺2, ⁺3, . . .

Figure 4.3 presents a graph of the integers.

Every integer has an inverse element for addition. Pairs of inverse numbers are shown on the graph in Figure 4.4.

The mathematical consequence of the existence of inverses for addition is that the integers are now closed with respect to subtraction. The difference 2 − 6 can be translated into the sum 2 + ⁻6 or ⁻4. The difference 2 − ⁻6 can be translated into the sum 2 + 6, or 8.

The integers are not much more useful for everyday purposes than are the natural numbers. Negative numbers have relatively few everyday applications. They are useful in business for representing profit and loss, and in reading temperature and changes in altitude.

From a mathematical standpoint, the major deficiency of the integers is that division cannot always be performed, since 2 ÷ 6 is not an integer. This fact provides the basis for the next logical progression: to the rational numbers.

THE RATIONAL NUMBERS

The set of rational numbers includes ⁻¾, ⁻½, 0, ⅔, 1, ¹⁷⁄₃, 203. Figure 4.5 presents a graph of the set of rational numbers.

It is not possible to define natural num-

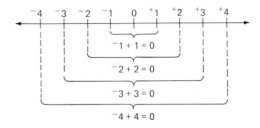

Figure 4.4

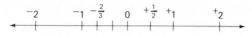

It is not possible to label all the points on the graph to make clear which numbers do and which do not belong to the graph.

Figure 4.5

Figure 4.7

bers or integers suitably for elementary pupils. A *rational number* can be defined as the quotient of two integers with the divisor not equal to 0. In everyday language, rational numbers are known as *fractions*.

Listing some typical rational numbers, as was done above, is somewhat misleading, in terms of suggesting the range of the set. For example, the number ¹⁷⁄₃ does not make it clear that ²³⁴⁄₄₁₈ is also a rational number.

As well, the graph of the rational numbers is deceptive. It appears to be a complete line because rational numbers are so "close" together (dense) that the physical points representing these numbers merge to make an apparently continuous line. The graph of the rational numbers is actually full of "holes." One "hole" is at the point $\sqrt{2}$. The proof that $\sqrt{2}$ is not rational is now included in many secondary textbooks, as well as in those designed for elementary school teachers.

Every rational number except 0 has an inverse for multiplication. Thus the rational numbers are closed with respect to division, except for division by 0. The graph in Figure 4.6 indicates some pairs of inverses for multiplication.

The rational numbers are adequate to

meet almost all the everyday needs of individuals and businesses in modern society, but these numbers do not suffice for many scientific and technical needs. Since $\sqrt{2}$ is not a rational number, it is not possible to find a rational number to describe the length of the hypotenuse of a right triangle whose other two sides are equal to 1, as shown in Figure 4.7. This fact leads to the next extension, *the real numbers*.

THE REAL NUMBERS

The *real numbers* include all the rational numbers (and therefore all the integers and natural numbers). A real number that is not rational, such as $\sqrt{2}$, is an *irrational number*. The real numbers consist of the *rational numbers* and the *irrational numbers*. Typical real numbers are ⁻3, ⁻$\sqrt{2}$, ⁻½, 0, 1, $\sqrt{2}$, 7, ¹⁸⁄₇.

The real numbers are closed with respect to addition, subtraction, multiplication, and division (except for division by 0). The operation of square root is possible for all *positive* reals. The operation of square root of a negative real does not yield a real number. Thus, some operations are still not possible in the reals.

The real numbers are adequate to meet most modern technical and industrial needs. For some scientific purposes, however, real numbers are insufficient.

The Complex Numbers

Complex numbers are of the form $a + bi$ where $i = \sqrt{-1}$ and a and b are real numbers. The graph of the complex num-

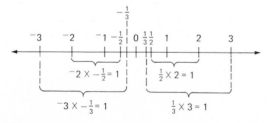

Figure 4.6

bers covers the entire plane. The complex numbers include the real numbers (and therefore the rationals, integers, and naturals). Typical complex numbers are -13, $\sqrt{-1}$, $2 + \sqrt{-1}$, 0, $\sqrt{7}$, $^-5$, $+ \sqrt{-13}$.

It is possible to find the square root of any complex number, but inequalities do not always make sense in this system. For example, it is not possible to decide consistently whether $3 - 2i$ is greater or less than $2 + 3i$.

The set of complex numbers is the most complete number system that has thus far been devised. Complex numbers have practical uses in describing the properties of electricity, as well as many important theoretical applications.

Exercises 4.8

1. Name each of the following number sets:
   (a) 0, 1, 2, 3, 4, . . .
   (b) 1, 2, 3, 4, . . .
   (c) . . . $^-2$, $^-1$, 0, $^+1$, $^+2$, . . .
   (d) The set of all numbers formed by the quotient of two integers (divisor $\neq$ 0).

2. The number 1 is a natural number, a cardinal (whole) number, an integer, a rational, and a real number. We can describe the sets of numbers to which 1 belongs by writing: 1, N, C, I, Ra, R. Similarly, we can indicate that $\sqrt{2}$ is irrational and real by writing: $\sqrt{2}$, Ir, R. Write the abbreviations indicating all the sets of numbers to which each of the following numbers belongs.
   (a) 3   (d) $^-3$
   (b) 0   (e) $\sqrt{9}$
   (c) $\dfrac{2}{3}$ (f) $\sqrt{3}$

Summary

Our number system evolved over many centuries. Today this system is part of our cultural heritage. We have developed the ability to add, subtract, multiply, and divide. These four ways of operating with number are known as the four basic operations.

Various civilizations invented different systems of numeration, but the Hindu-Arabic endured because place value, made possible by zero, enabled much more efficient computation. Stressing properties of our number system promotes understanding. The commutative and associative properties apply to addition and multiplication, and the distributive property applies to multiplication over addition. Subtraction is the inverse of addition, and division is the inverse of multiplication: the properties that apply to addition and multiplication do not apply to the inverse operations.

Number is not a tool to be learned in rote fashion. Rather, it is a cultural artifact intimately linked with quantity. Because the set of whole numbers is inadequate to record quantities such as the daily change in stock quotations, the integers were invented. Since it was impossible with whole numbers to record the length of a board of two units that is cut into three pieces of equal measure, rational (fractional) numbers were invented. But the rational numbers could not be used to record the length of the diagonal of a square, and so irrational numbers were invented. Taken together, the sets of rational and irrational numbers form the set of real numbers. This set includes the whole numbers and the integers. Elementary school pupils will not encounter numbers that are not in the set of real numbers. The teacher must be able to create the kind of experiences that will enable pupils to discover the distinguishing features of our number system. This system is the best means man has found to deal with quantitative situations.

Exercises 4.9

1. Identify the property used to rename each of the following numbers.
   (a) $3 + 6 = 6 + 3$
   (b) $4 = 4 + 0$
   (c) $5 \times 3 = 3 \times 5$
   (d) $3 = 3 \times 1$
   (e) $23 = 3 + 20$
   (f) $4 \times \dfrac{1}{4} = 1$
   (g) $3(30 + 2) = (3 \times 30) + (3 \times 2)$
   (h) $50 = 10 \times 5$
   (i) $99 + 18 = (99 + 1) + 17$
   (j) $28 \times 25 = 7(4 \times 25)$
   (k) $^-3 + 3 = 0$

2. Indicate which of the following statements are true of all replacements of the variable.
   (a) $\square + 3 = (\square + 2) + 1$
   (b) $3(1 + \square) = 3 + 3 \times \square$
   (c) $3 \times \square = \square + 2$
   (d) $8 \times \square = 2 \times (4 \times \square)$
   (e) $4 \div 2 = \square$
   (f) $\square \div 3 = 3 \div \square$
   (g) $4 + \square = 2 - \square$
   (h) $4 \times \square = \square \times 4$

3. List the property illustrated in each part of Problem 2 that is true for all replacements of the variable.

4. Complete each of the following statements by writing the correct numeral in each frame.
   (a) $2 \div 3 = 2 \times \square$
   (b) $3 \div \dfrac{3}{4} = 3 \times \square$
   (c) $4 \times \dfrac{1}{2} = 4 \div \square$
   (d) $3 + {}^-2 = 3 - \square$
   (e) $5 - 2 = 5 + \square$
   (f) $2 + \square = 0$

Selected Readings

Allendoerfer, Carl B. *Principles of Arithmetic and Geometry for Elementary School Teachers*. New York: Macmillan, 1971, Chapters 8–12.

Eves, Howard. *An Introduction to the History of Mathematics,* Fourth Edition. New York: Holt, Rinehart and Winston, 1976, pp. 7–43.

Frand, Jason L., and Evelyn B. Granville. *Theory and Applications of Mathematics for Teachers,* Second Edition. Belmont, CA: Wadsworth, 1978, Chapter 3, Base-Ten Arithmetic.

Miller, Charles D., and Vern E. Heeren. *Mathematical Ideas,* Third Edition. Glenview, IL: Scott, Foresman, 1978, Chapter 3, Numeration Systems.

Willerding, Margaret F. *Elementary Mathematics: Its Structure and Concepts,* Second Edition. New York: Wiley, 1970, Chapters 3 and 4.

Chapter 5
Approaches to Teaching Young Children

The early stages are always the most important. This statement is especially true about childhood, for it is then when character and attitudes are being formed. Teachers must acknowledge the important role they play in this process. To do so, teachers must be keenly aware of the interactions among the young child's *physical, social,* and *mental* development.

Thus, the activities that one chooses for instruction need to be appropriate to these three areas. Research on cognitive development suggests that concrete manipulatives be used to introduce new concepts, enabling children to make physical models of a number situation. Manipulatives bridge the gap from concrete to abstract. In this chapter we suggest numerous activities suitable for younger pupils.

Because children's preschool experiences and their physical abilities vary widely, the teacher should consider each child's capabilities individually before beginning instruction. At the kindergarten level, mathematics is often taught in conjunction with other subjects, such as physical education, art, and social skills. In grades one and two, class time is usually set aside for the teaching of mathematics.

Achievement Goals

After studying this chapter, you should be able to:

1. Identify the levels of physical and mental development of children of different ages.
2. Anticipate what number knowledge children have when they enter school.
3. Know the main topics in a typical program for K–2.
4. Teach rational counting.
5. Teach pupils how to write the numerals.
6. Use picture and bar graphs with beginning students.
7. Have pupils identify familiar geometric figures and shapes.
8. Use board games to introduce and strengthen knowledge of number.

Vocabulary

Mastery of the following terms will help you to understand this chapter. Each term is defined or illustrated in the Glossary at the end of the book.

Cognitive	Personal attributes
Congruency	Psychomotor
Egocentric	development
behavior	Sequence cards
Mappings	Sorting board
Matching	Tactile experiences
Number line	

Understanding the Young Learner

Cognitive Development

In the late 1950s and early 1960s, the results of considerable research on the cognitive, or mental, development of young children were published. These works had a profound and lasting impact on elementary education. The works of Piaget were among the landmark publications. Teachers should become familiar with these and other studies, and with their implications for teaching mathematics.

As we have learned in various writings by Piaget, he identified four basic stages of cognitive development.

Sensorimotor period. From birth until about age two, the child gradually develops control and coordination of body movements, through use. By age two, the child's bodily development enables him or her to move at will. For example, a child who wishes to reach for a toy will succeed.

Preoperational period. Between ages two and seven, the child learns to recognize symbols, to use language, and to draw, and has the ability to dream and imitate. Preoperational children are unable to consider more than one idea at a time.

Concrete operational period. Between ages seven and eleven, the child develops the ability to think logically and be-

gins to learn sequentially. Children at this stage can understand mathematical structure if it is introduced using appropriate manipulatives.

Formal operations period. From age eleven on, cognitive development involves a growing ability to reason from a hypothesis to all its conclusions, however theoretical. Concrete experiences are advantageous; however, operating from thoughts or theories is possible without firsthand experiences.

The Thirty-seventh Yearbook of the National Council of Teachers of Mathematics[1] states that most research has confirmed that these stages occur, and by and large in the order that Piaget has suggested. His studies suggest many ways to improve the teaching of elementary mathematics. For example, instead of chanting $2 + 2 = 4$, $4 + 2 = 6$, $6 + 2 = 8$, children use blocks or rods in games or activities to build models that show, in structural form, that whenever two is added to a number, the answer is not the next larger number, as in adding one, but the number beyond it: $3 + 2$ is not 4, but 5. By actively grouping objects and arranging them in serial order, children develop a strong, internal understanding of number. They also come to realize that numbers can be reversed by subtraction or combined by addition. When a child constructs models, he or she is constructing logic, mentally; logical operations grow out of simple activities, such as counting beads, classifying objects, and seriating by length or height.[2]

Teachers should rely on early childhood research and incorporate the results into daily teaching practices. The emphasis should be on creating experiences that help

1. Joseph N. Payne (Ed.), *Mathematics Learning in Early Childhood*, Thirty-seventh Yearbook of the National Council of Teachers of Mathematics (Reston, VA: NCTM, 1975), p. 47.

2. Mary Ann Spencer Pulaski, *Understanding Piaget* (New York: Harper & Row, 1971), p. 125.

to enlarge the child's understanding. Daily lessons should include concrete, firsthand experiences. Children *learn by doing,* and so they must be given opportunities to manipulate and handle devices that enhance their understanding of mental operations and mathematical relationships.

Social Development

The child's affective and social development is the cornerstone of his or her self-concept. The notions children have about themselves are reflected in the way they walk, talk, hold their head and eyes, and in their reactions to others. A skillful teacher observes how children do these things and so becomes aware of the positive and negative self-images they project.

Fostering the development of the child's positive self-image should be the paramount concern in the design of the entire curriculum. The child's attitudes toward mathematics are part of the total self-concept. Generally, positive attitudes enhance the entire self-concept. By carefully controlling the *language* they use, by avoiding biases and prejudices, and by projecting their own positive self-image, teachers influence their students' feelings about themselves, about school in general, and toward mathematics.

The teacher should have frequent private conversations with children and listen as they talk about their mathematics experiences. Help children "hear" what they are saying by occasionally paraphrasing their words. The child may react by giving added information, resulting in a deeper understanding between teacher and child. By asking the correct question at the correct time, a teacher will gain insight into a child's level of understanding of a mathematics problem. Project T.E.A.C.H.[3] offers specific suggestions for effective teaching practices.

3. Joe Hasenstab, *Project T.E.A.C.H. Training Manual* (Westwood, NJ: Performance Learning Systems, 1980), pp. 1–20.

Physical Development

The term *psychomotor* refers to the muscular activity that is directly related to mental processes. The following chart summarizes common characteristics of primary age children and their implications for teaching mathematics.

Characteristic	Implication
Lack of fine motor control	Provide materials that can be handled easily.
Difficulty in quickly shifting focus from close to distant work	Avoid rapid changes from desk to distant materials. Stand close to a small group when referring to pictures or charts.
Egocentric behavior	Have children work in small groups, as well as individually.
Very active and energetic but short attention spans	Devise learning activities that involve total body movements (for example, walking on number line). Change activities often.
Unaware of the "personal space" boundaries of others	Designate each child's floor or table work area with a round hoop, masking tape, or paint (unless children are working at individual desks).

The Preschool Child

Children bring to their first school experience a wide variety of mathematical knowledge and skills. The following is a list of the factors that help to determine how much learning takes place during a child's preschool years:

1. Attendance at nursery school
2. The level of education of the parents
3. Television programs viewed
4. Opportunities to see books and listen to stories
5. Travel experiences
6. Play opportunities
7. Family relationships

It is difficult to determine precisely what children know before they enter school. Suydam and Weaver[4] have summarized the available data on five-year-olds without prior schooling as follows:

1. Many children can count and find the number of objects to ten, and some are able to count as high as twenty.

2. Some can count by ten in order (that is, ten, twenty, thirty . . .), and a few can count by two and five.

3. Most know the meaning of "first," and many can identify ordinal positions through "fifth."

4. Many can recognize the numerals from 1 to 10, and some can write them.

5. Most can solve simple addition and subtraction problems presented verbally, either with or without manipulative aids.

6. Most have some knowledge about coins, time, and other measures, and about simple fractional concepts and geometric shapes.

A Mathematics Program, K–2

In this section, we outline a sample program with *broad* objectives for a K–2 mathemat-

ics program. Our aim is to give the reader a general idea of the type of mathematics to be introduced in these grades. Items 1 through 6 in the kindergarten experiences are adapted from a research study conducted by Kurtz.[5] The additional kindergarten experiences and the grade 1 and 2 lists were taken from a variety of sources—experimental program curriculum guides, current textbooks, and from procedures established in former editions of this text.

Number Experiences

Clearly Kindergarten

1. Rationally count to 20.

2. Recognize numerals to 10.

3. Identify groups of objects 0–10.

4. Write numerals 0–10 in order.

5. Identify a circle, square, rectangle, and triangle.

6. Identify the inside and outside of a circle.

Additional Kindergarten

7. Classify objects, order objects, and make patterns.

8. Write numerals in order to 20.

9. Identify groups of one more and one less.

10. Join two groups to form sums to 5.

11. Join two groups to form sums to 10.

12. Separate two sets to form differences from 5.

13. Add numbers to sums of 5.

14. Tell time on the hour.

15. Locate a day of the month on the calendar.

16. Use nonstandard units of measure.

4. Marilyn Suydam and Fred Weaver, "Research on Mathematics Learning." In *Mathematics Learning in Early Childhood,* Thirty-seventh Yearbook of the National Council of Teachers of Mathematics (Reston, VA: NCTM, 1975), pp. 44–67.

5. Ray V. Kurtz, "Kindergarten Mathematics—A Survey," *Arithmetic Teacher,* May 1978, pp. 51–53.

Grade 1

1. Read and write numerals to 100.

2. Add and subtract (sums to 10).

3. Make patterns (addition/subtraction pattern, families of facts).

4. Identify the fractional part of a figure, such as a circle or square or a group of objects, to show ½, ¼, and ⅓.

5. Use the centimeter and inch as standard units of measure.

6. Identify a circle, rectangle, square, and triangle.

7. Tell time on the hour and half-hour.

8. Find the value of a collection of pennies, nickels, and dimes to 25¢.

9. Summarize data from a bar graph.

10. Solve problems based on classroom number situations.

Grade 2

1. Complete the basic addition and subtraction facts.

2. Add and subtract numbers named by two-place numerals with regrouping. Example: 31
  − 17

3. Read and write numbers to 1000 forward from any starting point.

4. Recognize the fractional numbers ½, ⅓, and ¼ (no computation).

5. Use the centimeter, inch, yard, and meter as standard units of measure.

6. Select the clock face that shows a given time for five-minute intervals.

7. Find the value of coins to $1.00.

8. Read simple bar or picture graphs.

9. Add doubles or triples (premultiplication).

10. Subtract equal numbers (predivision).

11. Recognize, analyze, and compare familiar geometric figures, such as a square, circle, etc.

12. Apply the above experiences to problem-solving situations.

Beginning Number Activities

Children begin number activities such as classifying objects at about the same time as they begin to recognize objects. For example, an infant might have two classifications—things he recognizes and things he does not recognize. How, then, would a baby bottle be classified? Older toddlers may sort objects by big and little even before they can name these categories. When we say that a child can classify objects into sets, we mean that he or she can recognize an observable property about the object. Classifying also enables us to cope with large numbers of objects, by grouping them. Early experiences with classification, ordering, and patterning form the foundation of mathematical problem-solving skills. To solve a problem, a child must use given information to supply missing information. To classify an object, a child must put it where it belongs, based on observable information. Both processes involve similar skills. By creating experiences in these areas, you will help children make decisions and observations that will lead to problem-solving skills.

Classifying, Ordering, and Making Patterns

Beginning activities for understanding number include experiences with classifying, ordering, and identifying patterns. These activities can be accomplished by using common materials, such as crayons, keys, building blocks, collections of pegs, golf tees, buttons, small boxes, inch cubes, shells, small toys, coins, and other objects that children can handle safely. Informal situations offer a wealth of opportunities for classifying and sorting; one example would be giving directions such as "Put the

A pupil learns the meanings of number. (*Photo by Leland Perry.*)

wooden toys on the shelf and the metal toys in the box." Because many kindergartens have no formal mathematics classes, informal teaching is necessary. One way would be to have children separate a variety of objects by using their own classification systems. Doll furniture and plastic eating utensils could be used for sorting. You can then inquire into the child's system; tell the child to put all the furniture together and all the knives, forks, and spoons together. Or provide a box of ribbons and let the child sort them by length or color. When objects look very similar to a child, such as various kinds of pasta, the more difficult a sorting task becomes. Begin with simple, unlike objects. Children should be given time to play with the objects before using them for the specific mathematical purpose. This play time is important for two reasons. First, it satisfies a child's natural curiosity, and, second, through playing, children discover how an object feels, its shape, size, color, and how it might fit with other objects. Each time new materials are introduced, time for such exploration is necessary.

Classifying with Attribute Blocks

Attribute block sets usually contain pieces with the attributes, or features, of size, shape, color, and thickness. A beginning activity with young learners is to have each child select one block and tell the other children one feature of the block. Comments like "It is green" or "It is square" can be expected. You may then ask the child to give two features about a block. Expect replies such as "It is red and square" or "It is yellow and smooth."

Figure 5.1 shows the use of blocks in a classification activity involving a child's motor ability and logic skills. With young learners, select no more than twelve blocks that have one or two differences, and keep the activity simple. Designate two regions,

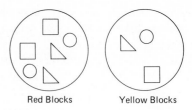

Red Blocks   Yellow Blocks

Figure 5.1

perhaps two yarn loops, for each child. Instruct them to place all the red blocks in one region and all the yellow blocks in another region. In this case, the difficult decision involves blocks that are neither red nor yellow. These can fit in neither region. Making this decision involves logic. You can repeat this activity several times by changing the rules as to the type of blocks that "fit" the loop. Children need practice in activities of similar difficulty before going on to more difficult ones.

With older pupils, the loops should be intersected and the pupils asked to place shapes that are both yellow and square in the overlapping area. Learners should be encouraged to verbalize as they work. The results should look like Figure 5.2

Classifying by Using Personal Attributes

An effective teaching strategy that combines classification skills with personal awareness is classifying children—for ex-

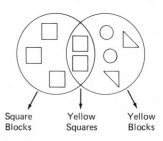

Square   Yellow   Yellow
Blocks   Squares   Blocks

Figure 5.2

ample, by the color of their hair or shoes, as bus riders or bike riders, and by other attributes that the entire group can identify. This can be done by simple commands such as "All the children who ride the bus to school make a line," and "Children who walk to school make a circle." Activities using personal attributes will not only teach classification, but will also help young learners to recognize how they are like other children and how they are different. This knowledge benefits a child socially, because the first step toward appreciating others is knowing about oneself.

Relationships

To help children identify the relationship of one object to another, have several of them sit in a circle. Roll a ball to one and say a word such as "comb." Ask the child to roll the ball back and name something that goes with comb. Answers can vary; for example, brush, mirror, and hair would all be correct replies. The teacher should accept answers as long as they have a relationship to the first word. When the children understand what is expected of them, begin to use number examples. For example, say "three" and have a child name three visible objects, such as "three books."

Using Patterns

Patterns are important in mathematics. Many mathematical patterns or models are related to the physical environment. Often, the patterns that scientists observe in the physical world are best described using a mathematical pattern. An early understanding of mathematical patterns is fundamental to the later discovery of basic ideas. For example, by arranging or matching objects in the early grades, children gain a foundation for understanding ratio later on.

Pattern construction can be taught using almost any material, provided that the ma-

terial can be moved about and is not part of or permanently attached to something else. Materials typically used in pattern activities include pattern blocks, unifix cubes, buttons, paper, and paste.

Instruction should begin by discussing patterns that are obvious in the pupil's surroundings—perhaps a pattern in the teacher's necklace or necktie, such as alternating blue and white beads or stripes. Allow time for children to find patterns around them and tell about their discovery. Children can be asked to give a "pattern report" along with the morning weather report. Patterns in wallpaper, desk arrangements, and carpet design can be discovered. Collect old wallpaper books and examine patterns to use as a base for discussion.

You might give learners a container of materials, such as styrofoam pieces, buttons, macaroni, paste, and construction paper, so that they can make a pattern using the various materials. Allow time for experimenting, then have them choose their favorite patterns and paste them on the paper. Go around the room and display each pattern, allowing the children to describe their own. Have the pupils use the objects that can be strung together to create a necklace, and ask them to describe its pattern.

Using Unifix Cubes to Make Patterns

Unifix cubes, described on page 44, are interlocking plastic cubes that are easy for young pupils to manage because they fasten together securely. Demonstrate patterns with unifix cubes, beginning with simple examples, such as red, white, red, white, etc. Help pupils understand the variations of patterns by introducing more complex designs, such as: two blue, three red, two blue, three red. Allow time for discussion of the pattern. After completing the activity, have pupils build patterns of their own design.

Snapping Patterns

Rhythm clapping and snapping fingers are patterns that pupils will enjoy repeating and making up. Use simple rhythm instruments and foot tapping for variation in music pattern making. Combine pattern identification with teaching music and physical education by including body movements.

Stickers

Patterns can be made from stickers, which can be purchased commercially. Stickers with pictures of flowers, animals, and the like can be used. Pattern-block stickers of the same size, shape, and color as pattern blocks are available. See Appendix A for directions on using pattern-block stickers.

One-to-One Matching

Two groups of objects are said to match in number if each object in one group corresponds to a member of the other group on a one-to-one basis. Often pupils carry out matching by saying "One for you, one for me." Objects that can be used for matching include milk cartons and straws, so that the child would place one straw in each carton and then answer the question, "Do you have the correct number of straws?" Children should learn that when sets match, they have the same number; when sets do not match, they have different numbers and the group with members without partners has the greatest number.

Children in kindergarten and grade 1 in some schools in Florida use a computer for recognition of numerals and to identify the number of objects in a group. For example, the screen of the computer may show the numeral 4. The pupil presses the key on the computer that contains the numeral 4. The screen may show two toys. The pupil selects the key on the computer to identify the number of toys. Activities of this kind help pupils become familiar with the keyboard of a computer. Also, these activities create great interest and motivation for learning about number.

More or Less

Children can acquire the idea of more than and less than during one-to-one matching activities when they experience groups with an unequal number. When a pupil states that one group has more objects than another, he or she recognizes that the cardinal number of one group is greater than the cardinal number of another. Sets of counters, flannel board cutouts, and magnetic cutouts are excellent materials for providing concrete experiences. Give directions, such as "Make a group that has more," "Make a group that has less," or "Make a group that is one more, one less."

Number Awareness

A child has acquired number awareness when he or she associates a correct number with a collection of objects or pictures. It is easier for children to give the correct number for groups containing up to four items than for larger groups; often counting is not needed. For groups of five or more, most children need to count. Children readily recognize two in a group because of the many natural models of the number 2, such as two eyes, ears, and legs, while there are fewer models of the number 3. With young learners, begin by displaying a group of two and assist pupils to make the association; then move on to groups of three and then four. Zero and 1 should also be taught. Many children are familiar with zero because of firsthand experiences such as "No more cookies." What they may be unfamiliar with is that when they are all gone, the word zero is used to describe the number remaining. Before young children can be expected to learn higher numbers, they must be taught the names for the numbers 0 through 4, with reinforcement of the concepts of these numbers and the recognition of the corresponding numeral.

Counting

When pupils are able to match groups, identify a number name, and give order to numbers, the background for counting has been established. Though some pupils might identify the number of things in a small group without counting, most must count to identify groups with more than four or five objects.

Counting is a method of describing quantity. In ancient times, men had to use groups of pebbles or sticks to represent the number of animals in their herds. One pebble or object corresponded to each animal. If people had known how to count, they would have paired each animal with a number. The basic concept conveyed by counting is pairing or matching an object with a number.

The counting numbers are ordered, beginning with 1 and continuing in sequence. It is significant that the number name of the last object counted in a group is the cardinal number of that group. The order in which the objects are counted does not affect the name of the number of the group. In every classroom there are opportunities for counting activities. Teachers should stress one-to-one correspondence as well as order and sequence.

Songs can aid pupils in rote counting. The song "One Little, Two Little, Three Little Indians" is one example. Songs of this type can be used to help pupils remember number names and order, but not what the number actually means. Counting to find "how many" involves knowing the order of the number names and matching names in a one-to-one correspondence with the ob-

jects counted. (For example, one would say, while counting the number of beads on a string, "One, two, three. I have three beads on my string.") Only groups of one to ten are used at this stage of learning.

"Step Along," the Counting Game

A counting game called "Step Along" can be devised using ten cards approximately 20 cm × 30 cm in size. On each card a large foot is drawn, and written on it is a numeral from 1 to 10, as shown in Figure 5.3. The cards should be placed on the floor and arranged in sequence. The position of the toes indicates the direction to proceed, but a starting point should be chosen. Make up a story that gives a reason to "step along" the cards; for example, crossing a stream or dodging puddles in a driveway. Pictures may be placed next to each foot to illustrate the story. Ask a pupil to step along the path as the story unfolds. Indicate the starting point and direction to move. Provide counting experiences by giving directions and asking questions, such as "Take three steps on the path"; "What step are you standing on?" "Take four steps"; "Where are you?" and "How many steps must you take to reach the house, or bridge?" Place the numeral cards in random order and have the pupils form the "path" in the correct sequence.

After playing "Step Along," which stresses sequence, move to a chalkboard line that has objects associated with each point, such as the books pictured in Figure 5.4 (p. 84). Use the objects associated with each number for counting activities. The children

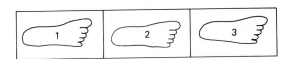

Figure 5.3

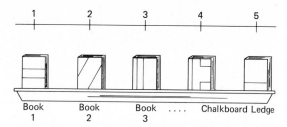

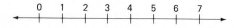

Figure 5.4

should be able to see the objects and the numerals at the same time. Then a *number line* such as the following can be used.

This number line is at a more abstract level than the two previously discussed. The starting point of this number line is zero.

Numerals—Names for Numbers

Pupils should learn the numerals by associating them with pictures having the corresponding numbers. They should not learn numerals by rote. A set of ten digits in flannel or magnetized cutouts can be arranged

on a flannel board or chalkboard. As a pupil identifies the number of a set verbally, he or she points to the numeral on the board.

Each pupil demonstrates the number of a set by arranging markers. The teacher then has the class make a representation of that set on paper.

Display cards that show the digits and corresponding pictures can be made or purchased for bulletin boards. These can aid pupils in associating the correct number with a pictured set. (See Figure 5.5.)

Everyday Counting Materials

Children greatly benefit from the practice of counting. A variety of common materials can be used to create counting centers. Children can use plastic utensils, paper plates, and cups to arrange place settings. They can arrange a place setting for each character in a story and count as they work to make sure that they have an adequate number of each item.

Young learners enjoy placing the correct number of objects in small containers such as juice cans. A set of cans for a counting center can be created by covering cans with contact paper to make them attractive and safe to handle. A numeral 0 through 9, writ-

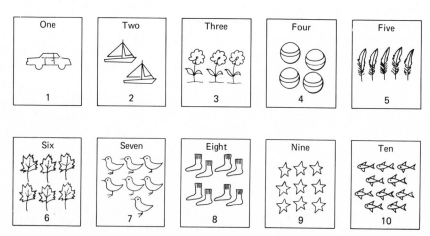

Figure 5.5

ten on each can, designates the number of objects to be placed in each one. Milk containers and small boxes can also be used.

Small plastic toys, such as animals, cars, boats, and airplanes are inexpensive, and provide ample opportunities for constructing counting devices. For example, they can be used with a mat that tells the number of toys to place on each mat. The mats can be decorated to represent such locations as garages, corrals, marinas, or airports. A child is to put a given number of horses in each "corral," or a specified number of airplanes at each "airport," and so on.

Sequence Cards

Sequence cards are large cards, individually numbered, which a pupil must arrange sequentially. Only the number series the teacher wishes to stress need be displayed at one time; for example:

Two children can play Number Guess, a guessing game using several numbered cards. First the children should arrange the cards face up in an orderly sequence. Both should agree that the sequence is correct. The child who is to guess first turns away while the other chooses one card and turns it face down:

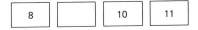

The child guessing must turn around, look at the blank space, and quickly name the missing numeral. Before the child proceeds, the card should be lifted and checked.

Learning to Write Numerals

Children need careful teaching and guidance when learning to write numerals. Success requires much practice from the children and a great deal of patience from the teacher. Large models of the ten digits are desirable because they can be used to analyze each digit for specific characteristics. Children learning to write numerals must note where to start and stop, in the manner shown in Figure 5.6, which demonstrates a widely accepted way to form the numerals.

Techniques such as making the numerals in salt, sand, clay, tempura paint, or with wet fingers on blackboard, or paintbrush and water on the sidewalk, can be used for practice. A kinesthetic approach is suggested to aid children who have difficulty in forming the numerals correctly. Obtain large numerals made of sandpaper or any rough-textured surface that children can trace with their fingers.

Tactile experiences include gluing materials such as dried beans, yarn, and macaroni to cardboard to form the numerals. The cardboard may or may not have a printed example to follow. Sewing cards and dot-to-dot cards are also effective.

Many children have difficulty in learning to write numerals. Some of the common difficulties are:

1. Distinguishing between 3 and 5.

2. Distinguishing between 6 and 9.

3. Writing 5 as a capital S.

Figure 5.6

4. Writing 8 as two unconnected circles.

5. Beginning a 7 or 9 on the baseline, then using an upward movement.

6. Constructing the 3 backward like a capital E.

Such difficulties are usually treated by making sure that the child's sense perception is correct. This is done by carefully analyzing the numeral and with guided tracing of the numeral made with tactile materials.

Going Beyond Nine

The fact that our number system has ten digits—0, 1, 2, 3, 4, 5, 6, 7, 8, 9—and place value makes it possible for us to express very large and small numbers. When first presented with a group of ten objects, children must learn the base concepts of grouping by tens and renaming before they can learn the concept of place value. Ten is the smallest two-digit numeral. The digit 1 stands for a set of ten and the digit 0 stands for no ones.

A teacher should develop the idea of base ten when introducing two-digit numbers. For instance, in demonstrating 11, show eleven sticks and then regroup the bundle to show ten and one more. Name the set as "one ten and one." Explain that numbers, like people, are often called by more than one name. The common name for one ten and one is eleven.

A difficulty is that, in the teens, the names of the units digit precede the name that identifies the decade, as in "sixteen," or six plus ten. Beyond 19, the name designating the decade precedes the name of the digit in ones place, as "twenty four" for the numeral 24.

Base-Ten Blocks

One of the most effective concrete manipulatives for teaching base-ten concepts is

that of base-ten blocks, such as those pictured on page 41 of Chapter 3. The pieces that make up a set are units (or ones), rods (or tens), flats (or hundreds), and a large block that represents one thousand.

When you introduce base-ten blocks, allow children to experiment freely. The children might build or make trains with them. They need the opportunity to discover how the blocks feel and to become aware of relationships; for example, they might discover the number of little blocks needed to make a length equal to a rod. Discussions should follow an exploration period, since verbalizing helps children organize their thoughts. As a result, clearer mental images are formed and the concept of base ten will be better understood. Some commercially produced base-ten blocks are made from hardwood, and the tens rod, hundred block, and thousand block are scored (indented) to show the number of ones each block equals. It is easier for young children to use and learn from scored blocks than from unscored blocks. "Bean sticks" are a teacher-made device on the order of base-ten blocks. See the Appendix for directions.

Work with the children and blocks in making numbers. Twenty-one would be 21 units, or 2 tens and 1 unit. Allow much time for practice. The next activity might include "show-me" cards such as the one pictured in Figure 5.7. Place numeral cards in the appropriate pockets and hold up the card. The children should use the blocks to make the numeral, or the teacher may show the amount with blocks and have the children insert the correct cards. Each pupil must have a holder and a set of nineteen cards. See Appendix A for directions on constructing show-me cards.

Graphing

Pupils can be taught to communicate ideas and information through graphical repre-

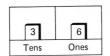

Figure 5.7

sentation. Pupils can learn to participate in making graphs and in summarizing data from them. Once a graph is made, it is important to give pupils time to discuss the details shown on the graph. It is also important to prepare a summary of the information found in a graph. Until a summary is discussed and written, a graph has not fulfilled its usefulness. Matching and ordering are skills that are developed through graphing.

Make a graph that enables the entire class to participate (see Figure 5.8). Prepare a chart, writing the names of the months across the top in twelve columns. Give to each pupil a one-inch wooden cube. Call out the name of each month and have a pupil whose birthday falls in that month place his or her cube in the column under the name of that month. When all have participated, comparisons can be drawn. Have the children name the month that has the most birthdays; see Figure 5.8. Write the findings on chart paper so that they can be consulted later. Use a similar technique to graph other information about the class. For example, use heights, first letter of names, bedtimes,

types of pets, favorite television shows, cereals, color of eyes, food preferences, and the like.

Two skills are valuable in beginning work with graphs—the ability to match groups of objects in a one-to-one correspondence and the ability to sort objects according to a given characteristic. For example, a set of clown faces could be sorted into two categories, those with hats and those without hats. Once sorted, each group can be put into rows and matched one-to-one to determine whether there is the same number of each type. It may be difficult for some children to organize into rows the faces that are to be compared. If so, give the child a large piece of paper that has large, premarked squares on it. The child should be taught to place one face in each square.

Mapping

Representing data by diagrams is sometimes called "mapping." Two basic types of mapping can be developed. One type is one-to-one mapping, which matches two words or objects that belong together; the other is many-to-one matching, which depicts several words or objects that belong in the same category. Examples are shown in Figure 5.9. Example B indicates that all the people named have birthdays during the month of October.

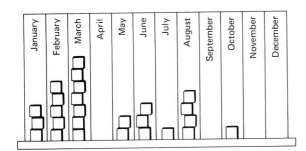

Figure 5.8

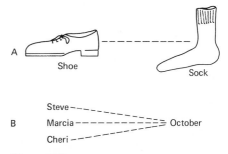

Figure 5.9

Children can be taught to look for the causes of a problem, such as litter on the classroom floor, by collecting the litter found there, sorting it, and attaching the findings to sheets of paper. The sheets should be labeled according to the types of litter collected—such as pencils, lunch bags, notebook paper, and other items. Discuss and generalize according to number of objects collected.

Money

The child's ability to recognize pennies, nickels, and dimes can be reinforced by providing opportunities to sort coins. If it is not appropriate to use real money, purchase rubber money stamps and make play coins by using the rubber stamp, ink, and construction paper. These should look real enough to provide a proper likeness, free of distortions.

You can construct a "sorting board," like that shown in Figure 5.10, with a definite area for pennies, nickels, and dimes. Pupils would be expected to sort the coins by placing one of each type in the appropriate area. Baby-food jars with slotted lids can also be used as sorting containers.

Beginning Geometry

It is important that you develop correct concepts when you introduce geometric shapes.

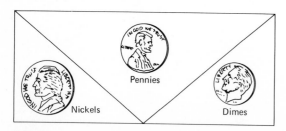

Figure 5.10

For example, pupils traditionally are asked to cut out a circle, when in fact a circular shape is desired. The boundary is the circle, not the circular disk. Primary teachers should strive for correctness of vocabulary, a somewhat difficult goal because of the child's limited ability for listening and speech. Some differentiations must be accomplished in later grades.

Properties that distinguish shapes should be discussed. Point out concepts such as:

1. A triangle has three sides and three corners.

2. A square has four sides and four corners.

One way to teach young learners to distinguish the properties of shapes is to provide large outline forms that are taped to the floor or painted on any large flat surface. Give directions such as "Walk around the path that makes a square," "Jump into the triangle," or "Sit inside the circle." Pupils benefit from gross motor activities because their entire body can become involved in the learning process. An additional benefit of such an activity is in teaching youngsters to follow directions.

The use of *geoboards* was introduced in Chapter 3. They can be used to teach the concepts of closed figures, parallel lines, three- and four-sided figures, and basic shape relationships. For example, children can experience making a triangle into a square in a smooth, fluid manner by stretching a geoband around the correct nails.

Shape Pictures

Teacher-made shape pictures can serve as models for children to imitate. They study the picture and then make one like it. Give the children pieces to work with that are the exact size and shape as the example. Some teachers use standard manila file folders and make the example on the left side of the folder, while placing on the right side a pocket containing the necessary pieces for the pupil to use. The pieces are put together like a puzzle or glued in place on a separate sheet of paper.

Children need to discover the various geometric shapes in their surroundings. Discussions of such discoveries are valuable. As a follow-up activity to these discussions, you might create a class "triangle book" containing a collection of pictures of triangular-shaped objects. Even though very little homework is assigned in the early grades, parents may enjoy helping children look through magazines and catalogs for appropriate pictures. Make a "square" and "circle" book also, in similar fashion.

Matching Shapes: Things That Fit

By matching objects that fit together, like the proper lid to a jar, and pieces to a puzzle, children come to develop the concept of *congruency*. Through trial and error, pupils become adept at deciding what will fit where. You can devise a learning center that features matching activities with a variety of materials for practice. Follow practice sessions by asking for estimations of what will fit where. Use materials that are similar, but not identical, to those that the children have been using in the matching center. As proof, ask a pupil to try what he or she thinks is correct. Teach similarity by "stacking tow-

ers." Pieces of a tower will stack correctly because they are comparable. Children appear to enjoy "stacking" objects.

Board Games

When using board games, either commercial or hand-made, choose those with sturdy backboards and large numerals. A game chosen for drill purposes should reinforce the mathematical skills taught by the teacher and should not require skills not previously taught. It is possible that a game that goes beyond the instructional level of the children will frustrate them so that they will not be able to play the game without constant teacher guidance.

Preparing games can be time consuming. One way to conserve construction time is to design game boards that can be used for many purposes. Figure 5.11 presents one example, a game board called Frog Pond, which requires a deck of cards that can contain any mathematical sentence or equation. For younger learners, each card may be a digit from 0 to 9, or simple addition or subtraction facts; for more advanced learners, multiplication or division facts can be used. As cards are answered correctly, moves can be made. If forward and reverse directions are desired (toward or away from the pond), code each card with a symbol that the children can identify as to the desired direction.

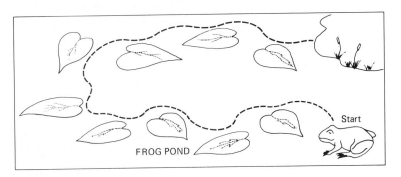

Figure 5.11

The only limitation to the open-ended game board design is the creativity of the teacher, as there is an endless choice of illustrations to use.

"I Can"

"I Can" is a game designed to teach numeral recognition and to instill in the pupils a feeling of accomplishment. Printed on the markers used to cover the numerals are the words "I Can." Give each pupil playing the game a board containing an array of numerals, each blocked off from the others as in Figure 5.12, and markers (I Can) large enough to cover the numeral.

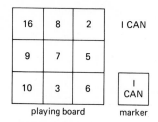

playing board   marker

Figure 5.12

To begin play, the teacher calls out a number by saying, "Who can find fourteen?" The child looks over her board and, if it is found, covers it with an "I Can" marker. Rules are similar to those of Bingo. The winner might be the first to cover a row, column or diagonal. When a child wins, she calls out "I CAN!"

Summary

Piaget identifies four stages of cognitive development. In order, these are the sensorimotor period, from birth to age two; the preoperational period, from age two to age seven; the concrete operations period, ages seven through eleven, and the formal operations period, from age eleven to adulthood. In this chapter we are concerned with the second and third periods of development. Instruction at these levels must include manipulatives to enable the learner to exercise both physical and mental development.

One of the first number activities the child experiences involves matching items to compare two sets. If the items match, the numbers of the sets are equal. Conversely, if one set has unmatched items, that set has more members than the other set. The next developmental step beyond matching is counting. To count, the pupil must have number names, a fixed sequence, and a base. When they enter kindergarten, children usually can count and recognize objects up to 5 and often can count to 10 by rote. In grade 1 the pupil learns to read and write numbers to 100 and learns the basic facts of addition with a sum of 10 or less and the corresponding facts in subtraction.

Pupils in grades K–2 learn to read and make picture graphs. They also learn to name the most familiar geometric figures, such as rectangles, triangles, and circles, and to reproduce them on a geoboard.

The key to successful instruction at the K–2 level is to be sure the learner participates in activities that include both muscular movement and intellectual responses. Children should verbalize what they do when they move an object and what the result is. Learning situations are optimum when the child physically moves materials, and thus becomes able to discover a pattern or procedure and then verbalize the activity.

Exercises

1. Discuss the place of the textbook or workbook in number activities in the kindergarten, and in grade 1.

2. Compare the contents of the curriculum for grades K–2 with several contemporary primary textbooks.

3. Discuss how a young child's physical, social, and mental development are interrelated.

4. Discuss the importance of permitting children to verbalize as they work.

5. Prepare a set of display cards to show the relationship of numerals to the number in a set of 1 through 10.

6. Evaluate the use of a picture line for teaching counting.

7. List the geometric and graphing concepts you would introduce in grade 1.

8. Prepare a board game to use in a second-grade classroom. Give the rules for playing, the necessary game pieces, and name the specific skill(s) the game reinforces.

Selected Readings

Baratta-Lorton, Mary. *Workjobs II: Number Activities for Early Childhood.* Menlo Park, CA: Addison-Wesley, 1979.

Cruikshank, Douglas E., David L. Fitzgerald, and Linda R. Jensen. *Young Children Learning Mathematics.* Boston: Allyn and Bacon, 1980, pp. 36–40, 342.

Matthias, Margaret, and Diane Thiessen. *Children's Mathematics Books: A Critical Bibliography.* Chicago: American Library Association, 1979.

Payne, Joseph N. (Ed.). *Mathematics Learning in Early Childhood,* Thirty-seventh Yearbook, Reston, VA: National Council of Teachers of Mathematics, 1975.

Piaget, Jean. *The Child and Reality.* New York: Penguin, 1976.

Pulaski, Mary Ann Spencer. *Understanding Piaget.* New York: Harper & Row, 1971, pp. 124–150.

Purkey, William Watson. *Inviting School Success.* Belmont, CA: Wadsworth, 1978, pp. 44–63.

Research on Mathematical Thinking of Young Children. Reston, VA: The National Council of Teachers of Mathematics, 1975.

Chapter 6

Patterns for Teaching Basic Facts in Addition and Subtraction

Mastery of the basic facts in addition and subtraction involves a combination of memorization and analytical skills. Pupils should be able to recall easily the facts they have memorized, and find the correct answer to a problem that has not been memorized by analyzing the operation and numbers involved. Children need ample practice with manipulatives to develop an understanding of number situations.

Achievement Goals

After studying this chapter, you should be able to:

1. Define a basic fact.
2. Teach the basic facts with sum less than 10.
3. Understand three types of basic facts.
4. Implement strategies for teaching basic facts.
5. Know how to teach fixation of facts.
6. Teach facts involving zero.
7. Teach the facts with sum greater than 10.
8. Apply the associative and commutative properties to learning facts.

9. Understand column addition.
10. Learn the different concepts of subtraction.
11. Discover the relationship between addition and subtraction.
12. Use basic facts to teach problem solving, emphasizing the importance of the exploratory, symbolic, and mastery levels of learning.

Vocabulary

Mastery of the following key terms will help you to understand this chapter. Each term is defined or illustrated in the Glossary at the end of the book.

Addend	Difference
Associative property (addition)	Error pattern
	Equation
	Identity element
Basic fact	Minuend
Commutative property (addition)	Number family
	Open sentence
	Strategy

Defining a Basic Fact

In addition and multiplication, a *basic fact* is a true equation that is formed by applying each of these operations to any pair of the single-digit numbers 0, 1, 2, 3, 4, 5, 6, 7, 8, and 9. The corresponding equations from the addition/subtraction and multiplication/division patterns are the basic facts in subtraction and division, provided that zero is not used as a divisor. Except for division, which contains 90 basic facts, there are 100 basic facts (10 × 10) in each operation, for a total of 390. Table 6.1 helps pupils to visualize concisely the basic facts in addition and subtraction.

Table 6.1 gives the sums of the pairs of one-digit numbers. To find the sum of a pair, such as (3, 5), locate the row headed by 3 and the column headed by 5 and read the numeral 8 found in both the row and column. The sum of 3 and 5 is 8, and so the basic fact is 3 + 5 = 8. When the order of the numbers is reversed, the fact is 5 + 3 = 8.

Since subtraction is the inverse of addition, the table is read in the reverse order to find the two subtraction facts derived from the number pair (3, 5). Begin with the sum 8 and one of the numbers, such as 3. Follow the row headed by 3 to 8. The solution is the numeral 5 at the head of the column containing 8. One of the basic facts in subtraction for the number pair (3, 5) is 8 − 5 = 3.

Pupils should not use this table before *all the facts have been introduced concretely.* To elicit discoveries of these patterns, questions and instructions such as the following can be used at the appropriate time:

1. Begin at the left of any row. How much larger is the next number in that row?

2. Begin at the top of any column. How much larger is the next number in that column?

3. What name is given to each horizontal and vertical number when it is used in a number sentence?

4. Using the table, find the sum of 3 + 2.

5. How can the table be used to show that the sum of 6 + 7 is the same as 7 + 6?

6. Find all the facts with the sum of 12. What are the related subtraction facts?

7. In how many of the number pairs are the two numbers the same? (Answer: 10.)

8. How many numbers in a row are even? What makes a number even?

9. How many numbers in a row are odd? What makes a number odd?

Grouping the Facts

Grouping the facts helps you make decisions about the order in which facts are introduced. Textbook authors incorporate "grouping the facts" into the scope and sequence plan for a given series. There are 45 number pairs that have sums of 10 or less. We will call this Set I, and locate it in the shaded area of Table 6.1. Set II contains the 19 facts in which at least one of the number pairs is zero, and is noted in the table in boldface type. Set III contains 36 number pairs with sums greater than 10, which are found in the unshaded area of the table. There are 100 facts, but when students are taught to apply some basic properties, they need to learn only 45 as separate entities.

Table 6.1

+	0	1	2	3	4	5	6	7	8	9
0	0	1	2	3	4	5	6	7	8	9
1	1	2	3	4	5	6	7	8	9	10
2	2	3	4	5	6	7	8	9	10	11
3	3	4	5	6	7	8	9	10	11	12
4	4	5	6	7	8	9	10	11	12	13
5	5	6	7	8	9	10	11	12	13	14
6	6	7	8	9	10	11	12	13	14	15
7	7	8	9	10	11	12	13	14	15	16
8	8	9	10	11	12	13	14	15	16	17
9	9	10	11	12	13	14	15	16	17	18

One way to group the facts is to view them as the *plus one facts, plus two facts, plus three* facts, and so on. This type of grouping may lead a child to perceive the addition process as a counting process. He or she may fall into the habit of counting to determine the answer. This habit is very unsatisfactory and should be avoided.

The *number family approach* is another way to group the facts. This method involves concentrating on a specific number, such as 7, and identifying the ways it can be renamed by using a number pair in *addition and subtraction*. All the pairs of digits that are correct for 7 are then designated as the "seven family." Most current texts do not present "number families" until the later stages of developing addition and subtraction facts individually. Most texts teach a few addition facts, perhaps to sums of 5 or 9; then a few subtraction facts, minuends to 5 or 9. The two operations are first related before the sums of 10 and more are introduced, followed by the subtraction facts. Most current texts emphasize that addition is the action of "putting together" and that subtraction relates to problems involving "take-away" situations. Many text materials become meaningful through problem settings and by instructing children to manipulate objects and use pictures to depict the operation.

There is a consensus—of tradition, the evaluations of teachers, and today's textbooks—that the facts formed from the number pairs in Set I of Table 6.1, sums of 10 or less, should be introduced first.

Grade Level

There is no one grade level at which the basic facts in addition and subtraction should be taught. By current practice, all 100 facts in both operations are introduced by the end of grade 2. The number of facts that are introduced in either grade 1 or 2 usually depends on the local curriculum policy as to grouping in class, and the level of pupil readiness for learning the facts. If a pupil has had meaningful number experiences in kindergarten, and these experiences are expanded in grade 1, he or she has the background to understand the work with the basic facts in addition and subtraction. At least some of the number pairs, such as those with sums not larger than 10, should be introduced in grade 1. In an ungraded school, pupils of ages six and seven usually correspond to those enrolled in grades 1 and 2.

Learning Situations

There are three phases of a learning situation: (1) the acquisition of new learning, (2) the search for a pattern, and (3) the application of the pattern. Learning the basic facts in all four operations also occurs in these three phases. It is important for the pupil to discover a pattern for finding an addition fact from a number pair as well as to derive the corresponding fact in subtraction.

Teach Simultaneously

Most mathematics textbooks present the facts in addition and subtraction together. This method is effective for two reasons. First, it guides the pupils' discovery of the relationship between the two operations; and second, the pattern for writing a fact in one operation enables the pupil to write the corresponding fact in the other operation. The addition/subtraction pattern is almost universally accepted in modern mathematics, and so the two operations must be presented simultaneously.

According to Bruner,[1] the two most difficult number ideas for the pupils to grasp are *invariance* and *reversibility*. Invariance refers to the idea that renaming or regrouping does not change the value of a number, as

1. Jerome Bruner, *The Process of Education* (Cambridge: Harvard University Press, 1960), p. 41.

in 5 = 2 + 3 and 34 = 20 + 14. Reversibility means that there is an inverse or undoing operation for a given operation. In mathematics we indicate reversibility when we say that addition and subtraction—and multiplication and division—are inverse operations. There should be opportunities in early number work for pupils to begin discovering that the operations in each of the two pairs are reversible.

Properties

Addition and subtraction are inverse, or undoing, operations. There are many cases, therefore, in which a property applies to addition but not to subtraction. Table 6.2 compares the two operations. The properties that apply to the addition facts are:

commutative property, as $a + b = b + a$

associative property, as $(a + b) + c = a + (b + c)$

identity elements, as $a + 0 = a$

closure

The set of whole numbers is closed for addition since the sum of any two numbers is a whole number.

Subtraction is neither commutative [$5 - 3 \neq 3 - 5$] nor associative [$(5 - 3) - 2 \neq 5 - (3 - 2)$]. There is no identity element for subtraction, although $a - 0 = a$ for all a; $0 - a \neq a$. When $a \geq b$—read as "equal to or greater than"—for the set of whole numbers, subtraction is possible only in such examples, $a - b = c$.

Table 6.2 Comparison of Addition and Subtraction of Whole Numbers

Addition	Subtraction
1. The order of adding two numbers does not affect the sum.	1. The order of subtracting two numbers affects the difference.
2. The way numbers are grouped or arranged does not affect the sum.	2. The way numbers are grouped or arranged affects the answer.
3. Zero is the identity element for addition.	3. There is no identity element for subtraction.
4. The sum of any two whole numbers is in the set of whole numbers.	4. The difference of any two whole numbers is not always in the set of whole numbers.
5. Addition is the inverse of subtraction.	5. Subtraction is the inverse of addition.
6. Addition describes a joining process.	6. Subtraction describes a separating process.
7. To find the sum $A + B$, start with A and count forward B more.	7. To find the difference $A - B$, start with A and count backward B less. $(A > B)$
8. Show addition on a number line working from left to right.	8. Show subtraction on a number line working from right to left.
9. Regroup, proceeding from right to left.	9. Regroup, proceeding from left to right.
10. Add and then regroup.	10. Regroup and then subtract.
11. If B is added to A, the larger the B, the larger the sum.	11. If B is subtracted from A, the larger the B, the smaller the difference. $(A \geq B)$
12. Begin with two addends and end with the sum.	12. Begin with the sum and one addend and end with the other addend.
13. In column addition the recommended procedure is to add downward.	13. In column form the recommended procedure is to subtract upward.

Program for Teaching the Facts

Readiness Activities

Readiness activities similar to those described in Chapter 5 provide the background for learning the basic facts in addition and subtraction. These include sorting, classifying, ordering, identifying patterns, counting, and reading and writing numerals. Children who have never had these experiences should be given this background before they can be expected to (1) depict the basic facts with pictures and objects, and (2) record the facts in the appropriate fashion.

Children are probably ready for in-depth experiences dealing with addition and subtraction concepts if readiness opportunities have included:

1. Matching groups of objects for a one-to-one correspondence.

2. Combining two groups of objects and orally giving the number of objects in the union.

3. Separating groups of objects and giving the number in each subgroup.

4. Writing the numeral that tells how many are in a group of objects with not more than 10 members.

5. Reading a numeral, between 0 and 10, and then demonstrating with counters the number of objects named by that numeral.

6. Comparing two groups of objects and telling orally how much larger or smaller one group is than the other.

Facts Involving Zero

Pupils are ready to deal with zero after they have become familiar with the number family pattern. The nineteen facts in addition involving zero are generally not introduced until at least all the number pairs with sums of 5 or less have been introduced in both addition and subtraction. A game in

which points can be scored is a good way to introduce an addition fact involving zero. A pupil may toss a bean bag or some other nonrolling object to a marked area on the floor. He or she may make three tosses and score on all three, but the next time may fail to score on any toss. The teacher keeps score in equation form. The written record is $3 + 0 = 3$ or $0 + 3 = 3$. After you write a few number sentences involving zero, have the class discuss how adding zero to a number affects the score.

All nineteen facts in Set II of Table 6.1 can be introduced at the symbolic level by noting that the sum of zero and a number is that number. Zero is the *identity element* for addition. The child is not expected to remember or use the technical term "identity element."

Teaching Related Facts

Some texts teach addition and subtraction as related facts, a practice favored by some teachers because it enables young learners to see the connection between the inverse operations of addition and subtraction. The teacher should begin by working with the addition facts. For example, the set of related facts for 7 is:

$$0 + 7 = 7 \qquad 7 + 0 = 7$$
$$1 + 6 = 7 \qquad 6 + 1 = 7$$
$$2 + 5 = 7 \qquad 5 + 2 = 7$$
$$3 + 4 = 7 \qquad 4 + 3 = 7$$

$$7 - 0 = 7 \qquad 7 - 7 = 0$$
$$7 - 1 = 6 \qquad 7 - 6 = 1$$
$$7 - 2 = 5 \qquad 7 - 5 = 2$$
$$7 - 3 = 4 \qquad 7 - 4 = 3$$

One way to teach the addition/subtraction relationship in the number sentences above is to place seven felt cutouts in a row on a flannel board. Use yarn to separate the cutouts so that there are some on both sides of the yarn. (See Figure 6.1.)

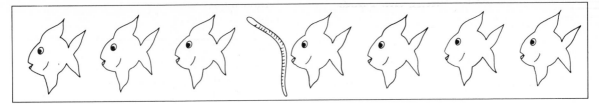

Figure 6.1

ASK: "How many are on each side of the yarn?" "What addition equation can I write that tells this?"

WRITE: 3 + 4 = 7

ASK: "If it were written as 4 + 3, would the answer also be 7?"

Reach an agreement that the answer would also be seven, and then write 4 + 3 = 7. Move the yarn so that it separates the felt cutouts in a different way and continue asking questions. Each time write the equation and the related equation. Explore all the number pairs for seven. Again, make the connection between addition and subtraction by displaying a given number of flannel cutouts in a row. This time, do not separate the set with yarn. Ask the class, "How many are there all together?" Then record the answer.

Place the yarn between some of the cutouts and determine the number on each side of the yarn. Cover part of the set and ask, "How many do you see now?" Describe what has taken place and write the subtraction equation. Continue helping the children discover other subtraction equations. Before children can begin to understand the related addition and subtraction facts, they need to practice with many activities of this sort.

Have on hand a variety of simple counters, such as dried beans, one-inch cubes, and plastic disks for the children to use at their desks to solve problems. Use as problem-solving examples any situations that

arise from classroom experiences; also use practice sheets.

The following equations, or open sentences, are typical of practice-sheet exercises included in some texts for second-grade pupils.

2 + ☐ = 8	8 − ☐ = 2
3 + ☐ = 8	8 − 5 = ☐
4 + ☐ = 8	8 − 4 = ☐
5 + ☐ = 8	8 − 3 = ☐
6 + ☐ = 8	8 − 2 = ☐
8 + ☐ = 8	8 − ☐ = 8

Sentences like these can be presented to a class so as to help pupils discover patterns related to thinking strategies. Lead them to understand that solutions to the equation △ + ☐ = 8 include the entire set of related facts in which the sum of each number pair is 8.

Discovering Patterns

Patterns play an important role in everyday life and are a large part of the way the world is organized and understood. Patterns and the perception of patterns are basic to learning.[2] Children who have discovered number patterns early in life are encouraged to develop the ability to move from recognizing a pattern in a series to predicting an outcome or formulating a more general rule.

2. Carol A. Thornton, "A Glance at the Power of Patterns," *Arithmetic Teacher*, February 1977, 24: 154–157.

If thinking habits of this sort are formed in the early learning years, it is likely that later, when a pupil is introduced to multiplication, fractions, decimals, the metric system, and other mathematical relationships, he or she will naturally look for patterns.

The following set of number sentences is an example of simple patterns formed from number groups. The first pattern uses the number 2, the second 5, and the third 3:

$2 + 3 = 5$	$2 + 5 = 7$	$3 + 2 = 5$
$2 + 4 = 6$	$3 + 5 = 8$	$3 + 3 = \square$
$2 + 5 = 7$	$4 + 5 = 9$	$3 + 4 = \square$
$2 + 6 = 8$	$5 + 5 = 10$	$3 + 5 = \square$

When pupils discover that they can derive a new fact from a given fact by using a pattern, their need to use counters drops measurably. After pupils know a fact in a set of related facts, such as $3 + 4 = 7$, they can write the corresponding equations that use multiples of 10 or 100 for the numbers 3, 4, and 7. The more able learners will make this transition more quickly than the slow learners.

By using number lines like those shown in Figure 6.2, pupils can see how multiples of 10 or 100 times the numbers 3, 4, and 7 make a pattern. More able students are challenged by work of this sort.

For practice, have the class read and write the equations listed on the number lines. Then give them open number sentences of the kind that follow. Have pupils complete each sentence.

$1 + 4 = \square$	$100 + 400 = \square$
$10 + 40 = \square$	$\square + 400 = 500$
$\square + 40 = 50$	$100 + \square = 500$
$10 + \square = 50$	$400 + 100 = \square$
$4 + 5 = \square$	$400 + 500 = \square$
$40 + 50 = \square$	$400 + \square = 500$

Discovering patterns leads naturally to discovering mathematical relationships, such as:

1. The order in which two numbers are added does not affect the sum.

2. Adding one to a number gives the next number.

3. Adding one to one member of a number pair and subtracting one from the other member does not change the sum. (Only one-digit numbers are used.)

4. In addition, only one true equation can be formed when the numbers in a pair are the same, but two true equations can be formed when the numbers are different.

5. For every equation that shows a number fact in addition, there is a corresponding fact in subtraction.

6. The sum of zero and a number is the same as that number.

7. When zero is subtracted from a number, the difference is that number.

8. In a set of related facts, the number of facts in either addition or subtraction is one more than the sum of each pair.

The number of discoveries that pupils will make depends on how much a teacher emphasizes the discovery of patterns and on the opportunities that pupils have to express these relationships and incorporate them into their personal thinking strategies.

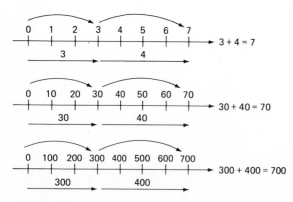

Figure 6.2

Reading and Writing Facts

The facts for addition can be recorded as equations written in horizontal form, such as $2 + 3 = 5$, or in vertical form, such as 2 using columns.

$$\begin{array}{r} 2 \\ +3 \\ \hline 5 \end{array}$$

Pupils should read the fact in the horizontal form as "2 plus 3 equals 5" and in the vertical form as "2 plus 3 equals 5" or "2 and 3 are 5."

There are many different ways to read a fact in subtraction. Note the following ways to read $5 - 2 = 3$ and

$$\begin{array}{r} 5 \\ -2 \\ \hline 3 \end{array}$$

1. "Two from 5 is 3."

2. "Five less 2 is 3."

3. "Five take away 2 is 3."

4. "Five minus 2 is 3."

5. "Five subtract 2 is 3."

The equation $a - b = c$ would be read as "a minus b is c" or "a minus b equals c." When a subtraction fact is written vertically, the preferred way of reading it is "b from a is c," since this phraseology is generally followed in performing the operation.

When children have concrete objects on hand to illustrate what is being said or written, it is easier for them to read and write the facts. One way to illustrate facts is by using clothespins and a card, as shown below.

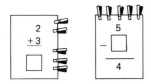

The child could add or remove the clothespins as he or she talks about the example on the card.

Helping Children Understand the Basic Facts

The Role of Manipulative Materials

Manipulative materials are used when one introduces an operation so that children can find the correct answer, develop appropriate language, and introduce thinking strategies.

When you use manipulatives, divide the class into small groups and work with only one group at a time. It is preferable to sit at a table or on the floor with the children. Give each child a set of objects, such as plastic disks, wooden blocks, dried beans, or small plastic toys. It is best to use simple but like objects in a single lesson.

The following sample activity, which is visualized in the photograph, is designed to have pupils discover the addition facts for 4, excluding zero pairs. Ask the pupils to take four objects and to place them on the paper mat on the table in front of them. The mat has a large triangle and a large square marked on it.

Proceed in this manner:

1. TEACHER: "How many objects [use real name of objects] do you have in front of you?" Expect a response.

2. TEACHER: "Put two of the objects in the triangle and two in the square."

3. TEACHER: "How many objects are there all together?"

4. Encourage correct language. "I have 2 + 2 and I have 4 all together."

5. Continue by asking the children to make the other addition facts for 4.

Optional:

6. TEACHER: "Use the numeral and sign cards to make an addition fact that shows $2 + 2 = 4$."

The numeral cards can be placed near the large triangle and large square to show the number of objects in each. The cards can

Pupils use objects to discover addition sentences. *(Photo by Leland Perry)*

also be used at a later time without the mat to show the addition facts for four. Before they do this, children need to practice extensively with concrete objects and discover combinations for other numbers. The *addend bead cards* shown in Figure 6.3 contain enough beads to solve the equations that are written on the cards. Children can use the bead cards to "practice" a variety of facts. If the cards are laminated, pupils can write on them with a grease pencil, and the answer can be erased. The beads are on a string and fastened to the card, eliminating the possibility of losing beads or handling

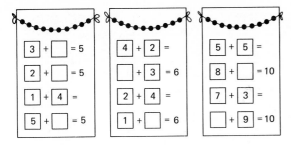

Figure 6.3

more than one device. Plastic caps with holes punched in them or other inexpensive (or free) materials can be used in place of beads.

The Role of Thinking Strategies

Teaching children thinking strategies will help them to develop efficiency and the ability to solve problems that are too difficult to solve simply by counting.

Very young children use counting methods successfully to solve addition problems involving concrete objects. Unfortunately, many children tend to continue to use counting even after this strategy has become cumbersome and time consuming. Some children invent "speedy" ways to count, such as by tapping their fingers, counting their fingers, touching their lips or cheek with their tongue, and by making pencil marks. Eventually such methods become obvious and the child becomes self-conscious, realizing that he or she is too slow at finding the answer without the aid of such methods. At this point, the child may develop a negative reaction to mathematics that is difficult to overcome.

Carol A. Thornton[3] has reviewed several research studies that emphasize the importance of teaching children thinking strategies as they learn basic number facts. When

children learn to think about the meanings of facts and develop thinking strategies for finding the answers, mastery is achieved more easily.

Common Thinking Strategies	Mathematical Examples
1. Mastery of the doubles.	1 + 1, 2 + 2, etc. Most pupils learn the doubles easily.
2. Relating harder facts to easier, known facts.	5 + 6 = ? 5 + 5 = 10; 6 is 1 more than 5; 5 + 6 = 11.
3. Sharing numbers.	Both addends are changed, one increased and one decreased to make a double (6 + 8 is 7 + 7).
4. Adding 9 when it is treated as one less than 10.	6 + 9 is thought of as 6 + 10 minus 1.
5. Counting on.	8 + 2 = ? is thought of as 8 and "counting on" 9, 10.
6. Making a ten.	Mentally changing one of the numbers to a 10, as in 8 + 5. Two from 5 added to 8 makes 10 plus the 3 that are left, for 13. 8 + 5 = (8 + 2) + 3 = 10 + 3 = 13

It takes time for children to develop thinking strategies that will work for them. Children may need to be reminded of a particular strategy that they used earlier. A good method is to discuss one strategy at a time and then apply it. Strive to assist chil-

3. Carol A. Thornton, "Emphasizing Thinking Strategies in Basic Fact Instruction," *Journal for Research in Mathematics Education*, May 1978, pp. 214–227.

dren in putting their thoughts into logical order and in discovering patterns and number relationships.

Regrouping Addends

Before you can introduce the basic number pairs with a sum greater than 10, the class must be able to regroup addends. Figure 6.4 shows how the numbers 3, 1, and 4 can be regrouped without affecting the sum. The figure represents an application of the associative property of addition. Pupils need many experiences involving the grouping of addends to understand that the way numbers are combined (order unchanged) does not affect the sum.

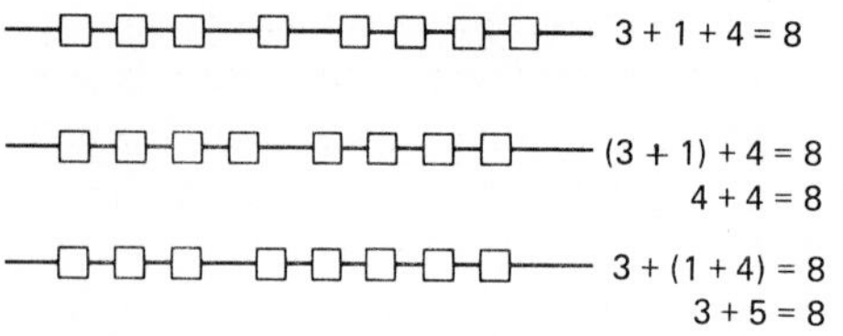

$$3 + 1 + 4 = 8$$

$$(3 + 1) + 4 = 8$$
$$4 + 4 = 8$$

$$3 + (1 + 4) = 8$$
$$3 + 5 = 8$$

Figure 6.4

Teaching Facts with the Sum Greater Than 10

The 20 number pairs in Set III of Table 6.1 can be used to form the 36 facts in addition and subtraction that have sums greater than 10. Using manipulatives, introduce the facts at the exploratory level. Base-ten blocks can be used effectively for modeling numbers. (It is assumed that pupils have had prior experience in using them.) The emphasis is on building models of the number and not on place-value concepts. We shall present two different plans for introducing a number pair in this group. The following problem uses the number pair (7, 5).

A. There are 7 boys in the class who plan to join the Cub Scouts and 5 girls who plan

Figure 6.5

to join the Brownie Scouts. How many pupils plan to join the Scouts?

1. Write the number sentence on the chalkboard: $7 + 5 = n$. Each pupil uses the base-ten blocks to find the sum of 10.

2. Next the teacher has the class show the sum on a number line (Figure 6.5).

3. Then each pupil writes the number sentence $7 + 5 = 12$ to state that there are 12 pupils who plan to be Scouts.

4. The class now writes the other addition fact $5 + 7 = 12$. In the next exercise, the pupils learn how to find the corresponding subtraction facts by dealing with facts whose sum is 10 or less. The four facts for the number pair (7, 5) are:

$$7 + 5 = 12 \qquad 12 - 7 = 5$$
$$5 + 7 = 12 \qquad 12 - 5 = 7$$

B. The second way to find the sum of the number pair (7, 5) is to rename one of the addends to have a sum of 10 and then apply the associative property.

1. Begin by having each pupil find the missing numerals in sentences of the following type:

$$5 + \square = 10 \qquad 7 + \square = 10$$
$$3 + \square = 10 \qquad 8 + \square = 10$$

Use base-ten blocks to make sure each sentence is correct.

2. Next have the class find the sum of 10 and a one-place number, as in the following:

$$10 + 2 = \square \qquad 10 + 3 = \square$$
$$10 + 5 = \square \qquad 10 + 1 = \square$$

Use the same problem as in Method A.

3. Write on the chalkboard the number sentence $7 + 5 = n$. What number, when added to 7, will make 10? (The answer is 3.) Have slow learners use base-ten blocks to show 3 is correct. How can we rename 5 so as to have a 3? Write 5 as $3 + 2$.

4. Now write the number sentence as $7 + (3 + 2) = n$.
$7 + (3 + 2) = (7 + 3) + 2$ Why? (The way numbers are grouped does not change the sum.)
$(7 + 3) + 2 = 10 + 2 = 12$
$7 + 5 = 12$ There are 12 pupils who plan to become Scouts.

5. Have each pupil write the other addition fact and the related subtraction facts as

$7 + 5 = 12$	$12 - 7 = 5$
$5 + 7 = 12$	$12 - 5 = 7$

Members of a Number Family

The class can derive other members of a number family by applying the strategy used above—that adding one to one member of a number pair and subtracting one from the other member does not affect the sum. Thus, the fact $7 + 5 = 12$ can be changed to $8 + 4 = 12$. This procedure enables the class to discover the remaining members of a number family when one member is known.

The two methods we described for dealing with number facts involved a number pair with the sum missing. The teacher can follow a different procedure by reversing the sequence—that is, the sum is given but the number pair is missing. Since the plans described facts with a sum of 12, we shall find one or more number pairs with sums of 12. For this exercise you will need an egg carton, twelve plastic eggs, and a grease pen.

EXPLORATORY LEVEL

Have a pupil put the twelve eggs into the carton. There are two rows, so he or she will put six eggs in each row. Have the class read aloud the fact $6 + 6 = 12$.

Next, have the demonstrator take away the eggs in one row to illustrate the subtraction fact, $12 - 6 = 6$, which the class now reads aloud.

Now have the class use a manipulative, such as base-ten blocks, to show the same facts. Then have each pupil make a drawing to show the facts by using circles or squares, such as ○ ○ ○ ○ ○ ○.
○ ○ ○ ○ ○ ○

SYMBOLIC LEVEL

After pupils see the demonstration, represent the facts with a manipulative and in a drawing; they may then write the facts $6 + 6 = 12$ and $12 - 6 = 6$.

In a later lesson the class learns another number fact that has a sum of 12. Begin by having a pupil put five eggs in the carton and then add seven more to fill it. It is very easy to write and erase markings on a plastic surface when the markings are made with a grease pen. Use this type of pen and mark the first five eggs with a symbol, such as X, and the other seven eggs with a different symbol. Then have the class read the two addition facts represented as "$5 + 7 = 12$" and "$7 + 5 = 12$."

Remove the eggs marked with X and read the subtraction facts. Put back the five eggs and remove the seven eggs marked with a different symbol. Again, have the class read the facts represented.

Follow the same pattern for the fact $6 + 6 = 12$. You can use this procedure to derive the seven facts in both addition and subtraction for which the sum is 12. As the class becomes more adept at deriving number pairs, individual work at the exploratory level can be decreased or eliminated.

The plastic eggs and the carton can be used to derive the number pairs in the set with sums of 11 but not for sets with sums greater than 12. An open-ended abacus and a clothespin can be used for these facts, as well as for all the facts whose sums exceed 10. The eggs and carton simply add variety to the class work.

The plan described here makes it possible for learning to take place at symbolic levels. Pupils reach the mastery level through drill activities, application problems, and various activities in and out of the classroom.

The Role of Drill Activities

For decades teachers have used drill activities to help pupils memorize the basic facts. Fifty years ago there was a large consensus for teaching predominantly by drill. Whether skills were understood or had meaning was secondary to the need to be able to recite tables correctly. Today's curriculum recognizes the importance of both. There is overwhelming agreement among researchers that drill activities are most relevant *after* concepts like number, addition, or subtraction have been developed for children in a *meaningful* way. For example, children should see the relationship between $5 + 6 = 11$ and $5 + 5 = 10$, or between $5 + 6 = 11$ and the corresponding subtraction fact, $11 - 6 = 5$.

Edward J. Davis[4] has suggested some points that a teacher should consider about each child before presenting drill activities. Using $5 + 4 = 9$ as an example, he stresses that the teacher should first look for a sign that the child understands what the fact says, such that:

1. The child can create or recognize embodiments of the fact—he or she can use a number line, rods, counters, or fingers to show $5 + 4 = 9$.

2. The child can understand the concepts

in the fact—he or she characterizes and describes the symbols denoted by 5, 4, 9, +, and =.

3. The child can use the fact in simple exercises, such as $5 + 4 + 1 = ?$

At the next level there are signs that the child understands *why* the fact is true:

4. The child can show the truth of the fact, using objects, models, or other facts. For example, starting with $4 + 4 = 8$, he or she can show that $5 + 4 = 9$ or can separate a set of 9 objects into a set of 5 objects and a set of 4 objects.

5. The child can complete related statements of the number fact, such as "What number makes $5 + \square = 9$ true?"

Examples of Drill Activities

Through drill activities, children become trained to respond to mathematical situations spontaneously and with assurance. Before you can do such activities, however, you must look carefully to see that pupils understand what they are doing, or else you could find them practicing incorrect procedures. By itself, extra drill cannot cure error *patterns.* It is the teacher's role to discover why pupils make errors, to teach them to avoid mistakes, and, finally, to provide suitable drill when it is apparent that each child understands (1) what to do, (2) why it is done, and (3) how to proceed. Under these conditions, drill will help children memorize the basic facts.

You can create interesting drill activities by using flash cards, games, calculators, *tachistoscopic* devices (electronic and self-powered), and by other means. An example of a self-powered tachistoscope is shown in Figure 6.6. This tachistoscope is easily constructed. Using any type of stiff paper, make a sleeve, with a "window" cut into it, that fits snugly over an appropriate list of basic pairs. The child simply pulls the list through the sleeve and gives the answer to

---

4. Edward J. Davis, "Suggestions for Teaching the Basic Facts of Arithmetic." In M. N. Suydam and R. E. Reys (Eds.), *Developing Computational Skills,* 1978 Yearbook of the National Council of Teachers of Mathematics (Reston, VA: NCTM, 1978).

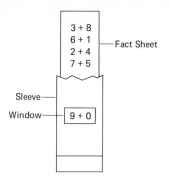

3 + 8
6 + 1
2 + 4
7 + 5 ———— Fact Sheet

Sleeve ——

Window —— 9 + 0

Figure 6.6

each pair as it appears in the window. Answers to the pairs can be written on the back of the list. A window can also be cut into the back of the sleeve to reveal the answers and make quick checking possible.

Electronic tachistoscopic devices that are programmed to display difficult or easy facts are also available. Many of these devices give immediate feedback, telling a child if a correct or incorrect answer has been given, by flashing a smile or frown.

Some devices tell the percentage of answers that are correct. Electronic devices have been shown to be strong motivators for some children.

The teacher should try to provide practice activities that use a fact in several settings. Progress records should be kept. When your intention is to help the children learn to memorize, drill sessions should be short.

The *addition crows* shown in Figure 6.7 assist pupils in adding 8 to other one-digit numbers. The crows are made of sturdy cardboard and are small enough to be held in a child's hand comfortably. The small circle (on the front, A) is cut to form an aperture through which numerals on a wheel, fastened to the back of the crow, will appear as the wheel is turned. The pupil adds to the number 8 the numeral that appears and then rotates the wheel until the next numeral appears. Write the answers on the back of the wheel (see B) for self-checking. Many variations of this design are possible.

Pupils solve *cross-number puzzles* (Figure 6.8) by writing in the missing numerals.

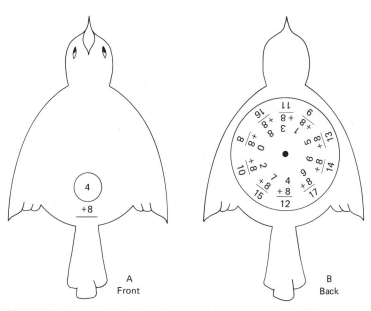

Figure 6.7

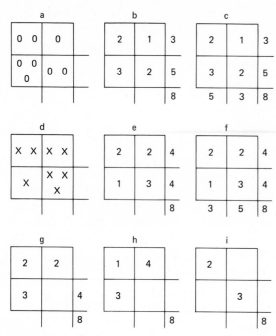

Figure 6.8

Figure 6.9

This type of puzzle can be used after teaching a given number pair, such as (2, 3), shown in puzzles a, b, and c. Pupils will not be able to fill in the squares in the sum until they have learned the sum of all number pairs given.

Cover-up is the name of a game in which each child has 13 markers and a copy of the activity sheet. (See Figure 6.9.) Two dice, or cubes with the numerals 1 through 6 on each cube, are needed for each group of children playing. The players take turns tossing the cubes and "cover up" on the activity sheet either the sum or the difference of the two numbers rolled in the toss. The other players should check the arithmetic. If there is no play (because the sum or difference is already covered), the cubes are passed to the next player. The first player to cover his or her activity sheet is the winner.

This activity can be extended to let the children record all the possible ways to make each number using the two cubes.

Charts could be used for pupils' record sheets. When completed, each chart should list all the ways to make each number.

A number *fact circle* has numerals around the outside and one numeral in the center. This device can be used in drills with the numbers on the outside of the circle in combination with the number on the inside of the circle to add or subtract. If a record of the answers is necessary, the child can write the fact and the answer on a sheet of paper.

Magic squares will challenge pupils who are able to create a 3 × 3 array of numbers in which all columns, rows, and diagonals have the same sum. Below is an example of a magic square.

8	1	6
3	5	7
4	9	2

"*Show Me*" cards, as shown in Figure 6.10, are useful for practicing the basic facts in each operation. Each pupil needs a card holder, a set of the digits 0 through 9, and an extra 1 card. To make "Show Me" cards

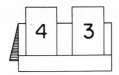

Figure 6.10

and holder, follow the directions given in Appendix A.

When the teacher calls out a fact, the pupil selects the digit card(s) that illustrates the answer, inserts the card(s) into the holder pocket, and holds it up so that the teacher can see the response. Response times will vary considerably. In drill, the response time is a good way to see whether a child is answering without counting. "Show Me" cards are also very valuable for place-value activities.

Many teachers make *tape recordings* of the facts. The pupils use headsets to listen to the tape and write sums or differences as the tape is played. The teacher may include the answers at the end of the tape for self-checking. Commercially produced tapes are also available, and several textbook publishers offer tapes compatible with their series. Let children make their own tapes and compete to find the answer.

Some drill activities can be effective learning-center situations. Each activity should be viewed as an "idea starter"—that is, teachers need to expand these ideas and prepare additional, and similar, activities. For example, give each pupil a set of ones. Have the pupils make a set of 6 objects and a set of 7 objects, representing the addends as 6 + 7 = □. Next bring the objects together, then count to show how many there are in both sets. The teacher should ask, "How many all together?" The desired answer is 13. Sometimes children need to figure out the number of tens they have and then the number of ones before being able to give the answer 13. In this case, let the child verbalize the number of tens and ones

before expecting the desired answer. Work many examples before going on to more difficult problems.

Column Addition

Columns of three or more addends require addition with unseen numerals. If the unseen numeral were visible, it could be either a one- or a two-place numeral. In (a) below, adding downward involves adding the unseen 8 to 7. Adding upward involves adding 12 to 3.

$$
\text{(a)} \quad
\begin{array}{r}
3 \\
5 \\
\underline{7} \\
15
\end{array}
\qquad
\text{(b)} \quad
\begin{array}{r}
2 \\
5 \\
\underline{3} \\
10
\end{array}
$$

The numeral for 12 has two places. For most first-graders, column addition should be limited to examples in which the unseen addend is a one-place numeral. Some pupils have difficulty in adding columns such as (b) because, when adding downward, they cannot think "seven" without seeing the numeral 7, or think "eight" without seeing the numeral 8.

Pupils who can find the sum in (c) but not in (b) are unable to deal with a number that is not named by a visible numeral.

$$
\text{(c)} \quad (3 + 2) + 4 =
$$
$$
5 + 4 = 9
$$
$$
\text{(d)} \quad
\begin{array}{r}
3 \\
2 \\
\underline{4}
\end{array}
$$

Two different procedures can be followed to remedy this deficiency. First, have the pupil write a different digit, such as 4, 2, 5, on separate lines of ruled paper. Next, dictate a number, perhaps 3, and have the pupil write the *sum* of the *dictated number* and the number named on each line of the sheet of paper. Second, have the pupil write the sum of the first number pair to the right of the column, as shown, for use as an aid in remembering the unnamed sum.

$$
\begin{array}{l}
2 \\
4 \quad (6) \\
\underline{3}
\end{array}
$$

For first- and second-graders being taught column addition, the unseen number being added to a seen number should never exceed nine. This enables the child to use only basic facts to find the sum.

Mastery of the Basic Facts

Most of the work with the basic facts is at the exploratory or symbolic level of maturity. Before pupils can reach the mastery level, they must understand how to deal with the facts at the other two levels. This can be accomplished by practicing and applying the facts. To master the basic facts in addition and subtraction, children should do the following:

1. Demonstrate the fact with markers, drawings, and on a number line.

2. Write the fact in both vertical and horizontal forms.

3. Verify the fact from other known facts.

4. Give the four facts for each pair of unequal numbers.

5. Show the pattern for each set of related facts in both addition and subtraction. For the sevens, the pupil can give all sixteen facts.

6. Identify addends and sum in an equation involving a basic fact, and find any missing term in an equation of this kind.

7. Show how addition and subtraction are related.

8. Give the answer to a number pair with assurance and without hesitation.

9. The pupil should be able to construct a verbal problem by using a number pair in either addition or subtraction.

As this list of activities demonstrates, mastery of a basic fact reveals increased power in dealing with number.

Teaching Verbal Problems Involving the Facts

Readiness

The teacher can create readiness to solve verbal problems by having the class solve number sentences that represent the three operations needed for problem solving: adding (joining), subtracting (separating), and comparing. The following situations illustrate how the operations can be taught.

1. Combine a group of four objects with a group of three objects to discover how many are in the union.

2. Remove four objects from a group of seven to discover how many remain.

3. Compare a group of six objects with a group of two objects to discover how many more are in the first group.

These situations are typical of those met in beginning work with verbal problems in addition and subtraction.

Teachers should keep in mind that primary children can often solve verbal problems if the problems are given orally. Their inability to read makes it difficult for young learners to solve problems on a printed page.

As Krulick[5] points out, the main difficulty in discussing problem solving is the lack of a clear-cut definition of a problem. He names the following criteria:

1. The student has a clear, consciously chosen goal; in other words, there is some personal involvement.

2. The student's path toward achieving this goal is blocked. The usual, habitual responses do not remove the block; he or she experiences a sense of frustration.

3. The student must deliberate carefully; he

5. Stephen Krulick, "Problem Solving: Some Considerations," *Arithmetic Teacher*, December 1977, 25:51.

or she must think about how to remove the block.

Notice that what constitutes a problem is not the posing of a question. Rather, a problem is what is accepted by the learner as a problem to be solved.

Judged by these criteria, many of the traditional exercises labeled "verbal problems" in many mathematics textbooks are not problems in the problem-solving sense. They resemble the three examples given as readiness for problem solving and are valuable for that purpose.

Children need to develop *attitudes, as well as skills,* in order to become successful problem solvers. These attitudes include:

1. A desire to explore all alternatives of a problem situation without hesitancy about suggesting solutions.

2. Willingness to examine and organize data before attempting to solve a word problem.

3. Willingness to see if there is more than one possible answer to a situation or route to the answer.

4. Calmness in taking whatever time is needed to think out a solution.

Educators have long recognized that developing the ability to solve problems is one of the main reasons for learning mathematics. In order to solve problems, young learners must be taught to use their skills effectively and with assurance. This process requires the teacher's patience and ability to match the learner with a problem situation familiar to his surroundings.

Personalizing Word Problems

Strive to create problem-solving situations from actual, everyday occurrences. The children can create their own opportunities to use numbers in solving problems. Many of today's elementary pupils bring money for lunch, milk, movies, and school supplies; they also plan special projects. Any of these activities can be turned into a personalized problem-solving situation if the teacher is aware of the possibilities. Muller and Kurtz offer specific suggestions for eliciting number word problems from home and school situations.

> Reading teachers have known for years that a child who has reading difficulties can read with ease a story the child and teacher developed together. This is due to (1) a high level of motivation resulting from pride of ownership and (2) the familiarity with the words used in the story. This same pride of ownership and familiarity with the vocabulary can be accomplished in developing mathematical word problems from pupil experiences.[6]

Translating from Words to Equations

Most pupils in the early grades vary widely in their ability to translate from words to equations. While some children are at the exploratory level, others are at the symbolic level, and there may be some who can operate at the mastery level.

The teacher should begin at the exploratory level and group the pupils according to their ability to solve verbal problems. The following problems illustrate a plan for introducing verbal problems that involve the addition and subtraction facts at the exploratory level:

1. Steve had 4 tennis balls and bought 3 more. How many tennis balls did he have? What is the problem question? (to find the number of tennis balls Steve had)
Show with counters the set of balls he had, the set of balls he bought:

6. Adelyn C. Muller and Ray Kurtz, "Students Like Personalized Word Problems," *Arithmetic Teacher,* May 1981, 28: 13–14.

Do we join or separate the sets to show the number Steve had in all? Why? (problem question)

Use counters to show the number in the two sets:

A set of 4 is joined with a set of 3. Write the number sentence 4 + 3 = n. What number would make this statement true? If necessary, count to discover the answer.

2. This problem asks the class to separate sets. Marcia had 8 marbles and lost 5 of them. How many marbles does she have now? What is the problem question?

Show with counters the set of marbles that Marcia had.

Did she add more to the set or take some away?

Remove the number of counters to show how many she lost or make a diagram to show the set that was left.

Mark off from right to left to represent subtraction. Taking away 5 from a set of 8 leaves a set of n. Write the number sentence for this statement. (8 − 5 = n) Find n to make the number sentence true. (8 − 5 = 3) Marcia had three marbles left.

3. Cheri has 7 seashells and Kim has 5 seashells. How many more seashells does Cheri have than Kim? What is the problem question?

Make a diagram to show the set of seashells Cheri has; the set Kim has:

Are we to join the sets? Why not?

Are we to compare the sets? Which set is larger?

We can compare the sets by matching the members in a diagram. Use a diagram to compare the two sets:

A set of 7 minus a set of 5 is a set of n. Write the number sentence for this statement. (7 − 5 = n) Find n to make the sentence true. (7 − 5 = 2)

Cheri has 2 more seashells than Kim has. To find how much larger one set is than another, match the members of the sets; to find how much larger one number is than another, subtract the numbers.

Summary

Use of calculators has reduced the number of mental computations that adults perform. Today's schoolchildren will probably make use of such devices on a regular basis. However, both to use machines successfully and to compute with pencil and paper, it is necessary to teach the basic facts. Children must know the facts to check answers and to determine whether an answer is reasonable.

Children need to develop thinking strategies to apply to problem situations. Simple strategies, perhaps counting to determine an answer, are efficient to use with sums up to 5, but not with sums larger than 10. For this, the strategy of "making a ten" or several others mentioned in this chapter are more efficient.

Manipulative materials are vital in giving children an opportunity to build concrete models of problem situations and to help them develop thinking strategies. Manipulatives should be used to introduce addition and subtraction facts. Children can also use them to practice the facts.

Drill activities can take many forms. They should be used after children have been introduced to the facts by means of manipulatives, and after it is clear that they understand the concepts of addition and subtraction. These activities should be chosen with the intent to help children memorize the basic facts. Progress records and listing the facts a child has memorized are necessary for planning activities and as an acknowledgment of the work a child has accomplished.

There are three basic types of verbal problems in addition and subtraction situations with young learners. These are joining, separating, and comparing activities, which are presented verbally to children. In these activities, children use manipulatives to clarify and guide them in solving a problem.

Exercises

1. Prepare a lesson that stresses a specific "thinking strategy."

2. Manipulative materials are used to help children find the correct answer, to develop appropriate language, and as a means of developing thinking strategies. Use a manipulative and demonstrate these three functions.

3. List six drill activities.

4. Explain how a teacher would determine whether a child is ready to experience drill activities on the basic facts.

5. Agree or disagree with each statement below and give reason(s) for your position.
   a. Calculators should be used in the primary grades to introduce the basic facts.
   b. Activities such as sorting, matching, and classifying provide readiness to learn the basic facts.
   c. The facts involving zero should be taught first.

6. Demonstrate a lesson designed to teach the relationship between addition and subtraction.

7. Design several "real-life" problems for a selected grade level that are to be solved with the aid of manipulatives.

8. Discuss this statement: Young learners need to develop attitudes as well as skills to become successful problem solvers.

9. A pupil knows the basic facts in addition but cannot add effectively when the numerals are written in a column. What remedial measures should be taken?

$$\begin{array}{r} 3 \\ 2 \\ \underline{6} \end{array}$$

10. A teacher remarked, "I teach all the addition facts and then all the subtraction facts." Evaluate this procedure.

11. Evaluate the plans on page 102 for teaching the basic facts when the number pairs are given but the sums are missing.

12. Evaluate the plan on page 102 for teaching the basic facts in addition when the sums are given but the number pairs are missing.

Selected Readings

Copeland, Richard W. *Mathematics and the Elementary Teacher,* Third Edition. Philadelphia: Saunders, 1976, pp. 110–114.

Cratty, Bryant J. *Active Learning Games to Enhance Academic Abilities.* Englewood Cliffs, NJ: Prentice-Hall, 1971, pp. 60–70.

Dumas, Enoch. *Math Activities for Child Involvement.* Boston: Allyn and Bacon, 1971, Chapter 3.

Schminke, Clarence W., Norbert Maertens, and William Arnold. *Teaching the Child Mathematics.* New York: Holt, Rinehart and Winston, 1978, pp. 78–89.

Suydam, Marilyn N., and Robert E. Reys (Eds.). *Developing Computational Skills.* 1978 Yearbook, National Council of Teachers of Mathematics. Reston, VA: National Council of Teachers of Mathematics, 1978, pp. 1–51.

Chapter 7

Algorisms for Addition and Subtraction of Whole Numbers

The word *algorism* comes from the name of a ninth-century Arabic mathematician, Al Kohowarizmi, who outlined specific steps to be followed in performing computations. Today, the term algorism (also spelled algorithm) refers to the sequence of steps involved in performing calculations in addition, subtraction, multiplication, and division.

Much of the early work on basic facts becomes meaningful when children begin to add and subtract "big numbers." Most children go through several learning stages before reaching the level of maturity that the "standard algorism" requires. This *development* gives the teacher an opportunity to use different algorisms that build *meaning*. Because their purpose is different, many of these *developmental algorisms* differ from the more mature "standard algorisms." Standard algorisms are used because they are *efficient*; often, they sacrifice meaning for ease of computing. Developmental algorisms are used to build a child's understanding of the operation before a more efficient algorism can be introduced.

In Chapter 6 we introduced the basic facts in addition and subtraction. The next step is to apply these basic facts in solving computation problems. Concrete materials—emphasizing the effect of positional value in the number system, the properties of mathematical operations, and knowledge of the basic facts—help children to understand exactly what takes place within the algorism. This is not to deny that, when they get older, children will use mechanical means to compute; but the foundation of the child's ability to solve problems is the understanding developed through use of the algorisms.

Achievement Goals

After studying this chapter, you should be able to:

1. Teach addition and subtraction without regrouping.
2. Teach addition and subtraction with regrouping.
3. Use the addition/subtraction pattern.
4. Deal with an overloaded place.

113

5. Teach higher-decade addition with and without bridging.

6. Teach higher-decade addition in column form.

7. Use problem-solving skills in both addition and subtraction at the exploratory, symbolic, and mastery levels.

8. Teach addition and subtraction with three-place numbers.

9. Make sure students can check addition and subtraction.

Vocabulary

Mastery of the following key terms will help you to understand this chapter. Each term is defined or illustrated in the Glossary at the end of the book.

Addend
Adding by endings
Algorism
  (algorithm)
Bridging the
  decade
Column impasse
Comparison
  subtraction
Decomposition
  method
Difference

Equal additions
  method of
  subtraction
Expanded form
Higher-decade
  addition
Minuend
Multiples
Regrouping
Renaming
Standard algorism
Subtrahend

Addition and Subtraction of Two Two-Digit Numbers without Renaming / Regrouping

Terms: Regrouping and Renaming

The terms "regrouping" and "renaming" are used interchangeably in many elementary mathematics texts. The process described by either term deals with a place in a numeral that is "overloaded"; that is, there are *more than* 9 at the place. The word "regrouping," when working with base-ten materials or place-value devices, is often associated with the physical exchange of objects. When ten single objects are changed into one group of ten, or a bundle of ten is

changed into ten ones, the materials have been "regrouped." At the symbolic level, however, the process of changing 32 ones into 3 tens 2 ones, or $\underline{\text{Tens} \mid \text{Ones}}$, is often $3 \mid 2$

called "renaming" numbers. Regrouping is often used to denote both meanings and even though it is not precise, it will be used throughout this chapter.

When pupils have learned the addition and subtraction facts to sums of 9, they can use the facts they know in examples involving numbers of two or more digits where regrouping is not encountered. This knowledge is based on the concept of place value. Within a place-value number system, it is possible to add or subtract the numbers named in like places in the numerals.

The teacher can use the following sequence of activities to introduce addition and subtraction of two-place numbers without regrouping. In general, examples would be presented to pupils in the following order:

(a) Addition of a one-place number to a two-place number:

$$
\begin{array}{ccc}
15 & 21 & 42 \\
+\ 2 & +\ 3 & +\ 4
\end{array}
$$

(b) Addition of two two-digit numbers that are multiples of ten:

$$
\begin{array}{ccc}
30 & 40 & 50 \\
+20 & +30 & +10
\end{array}
$$

(c) Addition of two two-digit numbers without renaming:

$$
\begin{array}{ccc}
31 & 14 & 50 \\
+24 & +82 & +53
\end{array}
$$

(d) Subtraction of a one-digit number from a two-digit number:

$$
\begin{array}{ccc}
26 & 35 & 44 \\
-\ 5 & -\ 2 & -\ 1
\end{array}
$$

(e) Subtraction of two two-digit numbers that are multiples of ten:

$$
\begin{array}{ccc}
50 & 40 & 60 \\
-20 & -10 & -30
\end{array}
$$

(f) Subtraction of two two-digit numbers without renaming:

$$\begin{array}{r} 35 \\ -14 \\ \hline \end{array} \qquad \begin{array}{r} 73 \\ -32 \\ \hline \end{array} \qquad \begin{array}{r} 65 \\ -13 \\ \hline \end{array}$$

In some elementary mathematics programs, addition and subtraction algorisms are presented more or less simultaneously for each level of difficulty. In this plan, the addition and subtraction examples in groups (a) and (d) would be presented simultaneously. Groups (b) and (e) would be taught together, as would (c) and (f). Some programs use the *sequential* approach of (a) through (f), as discussed briefly in the subsequent examples.

You can use word problems to introduce addition and subtraction of two-place numbers without regrouping in the sum. If the textbook introduces the topic with a problem, use that problem for demonstration. Otherwise, design a problem similar to the one that follows to demonstrate addition of a one-place number to a two-place number without regrouping.

There are 15 crayons in a box. Two more are on the table. How many crayons are there all together? To stress place-value concepts, instead of counting to solve this problem, take the 15 crayons out of the box. Tell the children they will add to find the answer.

Bundle 10 of the crayons together with a rubber band. Make sure that the children understand that there are 10 in the bundle. Place the bundle and the 5 loose crayons side by side, as shown. Write 10 + 5.

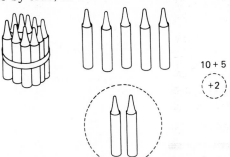

10 + 5
+2

Place the 2 crayons (from the table) under the 5 loose crayons and write +2 under the 10 + 5, as shown. Have the children determine the number of loose crayons by adding

$$\begin{array}{r} 5 \\ +2 \\ \hline \end{array}$$

. Discuss the idea that there are 7 "loose crayons" and a "bundle of 10." Ten must be added to the 7. The developmental algorism 10 + 5 is useful to help the children

$$\begin{array}{r} 10 + 5 \\ +\ 2 \\ \hline 10 + 7 = 17 \end{array}$$

understand the process. Follow this example with many similar ones, each time writing the developmental algorisms and using concrete materials, such as sticks, rods, or base-ten blocks, to illustrate the process. Use a tens and ones chart to teach addition of two two-digit numbers that are multiples of 10.

In the same manner, using bundles of ten, show that 30 + 20 = 50.

Tens	Ones

Then show the chart like this:

Tens	Ones

3 tens   30
+ 2 tens   + 20
5 tens   50

Help the children think "in tens." For example, just as 3 boys and 2 boys are 5 boys, so 3 tens and 2 tens are 5 tens, and 30 + 20 = 50. Follow with more examples.

Use the charts or base-ten materials as

shown to demonstrate an example such as
$$\begin{array}{r} 31 \\ +24 \\ \hline \end{array}$$
, which involves the addition of two
two-digit numbers without renaming. Problems from everyday situations are particularly illustrative.

You might, for example, tell the class that there are 31 pupils in one classroom and 24 pupils in another classroom. How many pupils are there in both classrooms? Write the number sentence 31 + 24 = □ on the chalkboard.

1. Show the numbers, using base-ten materials. (See Figure 7.1.)

2. Fill in the blanks:

31 = _____ tens _____ one

24 = _____ tens _____ ones

3. Find the sum:

Tens	Ones
3	1
+2	4
═══	═══

4. Find the sum in the example:
$$\begin{array}{r} 31 \\ +24 \\ \hline \end{array}$$

5. Have the class read the presentation in the textbook.

6. Give the class examples to add, such as:
$$\begin{array}{r} 26 \\ +21 \\ \hline \end{array} \qquad \begin{array}{r} 30 \\ +15 \\ \hline \end{array}$$

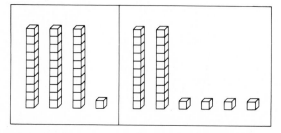

Figure 7.1

Subtraction problems should first involve a "taking-away" process, whereby ones are

taken from ones and tens are taken from tens. You should continue using concrete materials to demonstrate the process for the subtraction of a one-digit number from a two-digit number. For example, to demonstrate the problem
$$\begin{array}{r} 26 \\ -5 \\ \hline \end{array}$$
you might use dimes and pennies. Show 2 dimes and 6 pennies; then take away 5 pennies. Show the result as 2 dimes 1 penny.

Write:

2 tens	6 ones
	−5 ones
2 tens	1 one

In a similar fashion, demonstrate the subtraction of two two-digit numbers that are multiples of 10. For the example
$$\begin{array}{r} 50 \\ -20 \\ \hline \end{array}$$
first show 5 bundles of 10.

Take 2 bundles of 10 away from the 5 bundles. Three bundles of 10, or 30, remain.

The following problem could be used to introduce the subtraction of two two-digit numbers without grouping.

Billy had 35 baseball cards. If he gave John 14 of them, how many would he have left? You should write the number sentence 35 − 14 = □ on the chalkboard.

The pupils can solve the problem with base-ten blocks. First have each pupil represent the 35 baseball cards that Billy started with before he gave 14 to John. Pupils who have had previous experience in using base-ten materials will readily represent 35 with 3 longs 5 cubes. Those who do not do so should be given individual attention to help them understand this step.

Next have the pupils take 4 cubes and 1 long away from 3 longs 5 cubes. Then ask, "How many cards does Billy have left?" Figure 7.2 shows the sequence of the process used in solving this problem, with (a) representing the 35 Billy had to start with, (b) showing the 14 taken away from the 35 to give to John, and (c) showing how many Billy had left.

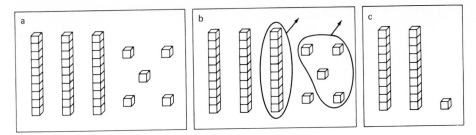

Figure 7.2

Place-Value Devices

After pupils have had experience using base-ten materials to perform addition and subtraction, the teacher should introduce the use of a place-value device. The two most useful place-value devices are (a) the place-value pocket chart, and (b) the 18-bead computing abacus, shown in Figure 7.3

The transition from visualizing numbers with base-ten materials to their representations on a place-value device is an important step in concept learning. When a pupil moves from base-ten materials to a place-value device, he or she begins to deal with a more abstract representation of a two-place number. The three tens represented by a bundle of sticks, for example, are shown on the place-value device as three sticks in the tens place. The position to the left of the ones place on the device gives *each stick* the value of one ten.

Pupils can use a place-value device to solve addition and subtraction problems involving two two-digit numbers in about the same way that they used base-ten materials. The concept emphasized on the place-value device is that numbers in the tens place are added and subtracted as if they were ones. For example, finding 5 tens + 3 tens is as simple as finding 5 + 3 except that the answer to the first problem must be recorded in the tens place.

Transition from Expanded to Compact Form

Most pupils make the transition from writing two-digit numbers in an expanded

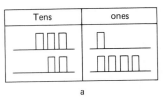

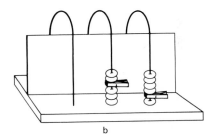

Figure 7.3

form, such as 34 = 3 tens 4 ones, to using compact two-place numbers, such as 34, with relative ease. The chart below shows the recommended way to write addition or subtraction examples using (a) expanded base-ten notation and (b) a place-value grid:

(a)				(b) Tens	Ones
3	tens	1	ones	3	1
+ 2	tens	4	ones	+ 2	4
	tens		ones		
				Tens	Ones
2	tens	5	ones	3	5
− 1	ten	4	ones	− 1	4

Expanded notations were first introduced as a form of record keeping useful when working with base-ten and place-value materials. Here the notations are used without reference to the manipulation of concrete materials. The idea is that these forms of notation should be presented at the time the different materials were used. Note that the ___ tens ___ ones notation form used in (a) emphasizes base ten, whereas the notation in (b) relates closely to place value.

The standard algorism is the most efficient way to record the steps in an operation. One or more longer approaches should precede the introduction of the standard algorism. The pupils should be given an opportunity to decide why the standard algorism is the most efficient in most cases. The standard algorisms for addition and subtraction of two two-digit numbers without regrouping are illustrated. Have the class find the missing numerals in the following example(s):

42	31	26	75	55	68
+35	+24	+42	−35	−24	−42
77	5		40	1	

At the mastery and symbolic levels, children work these examples and record the sums and differences without having to use manipulatives and counting techniques. At the mastery level, they should be able to respond immediately and accurately to each basic fact.

Terminology for Addition and Subtraction

Precise, formal mathematical terminology, which was emphasized in New Math programs, has given way to a more informal approach to describing mathematical concepts and processes. Rather than stress the ability to use precise terms for addition and subtraction, teachers now focus on having pupils understand how these terms relate to problem situations, for pupils need to be able to find sums and differences with

speed and accuracy. It is not hard to see how confusion arose. During the New Math era, subtraction was defined as the inverse of addition. The terms "addend" and "sum," which referred to the numbers in addition, were also used to designate the numbers in subtraction, such as:

addend	sum
+ addend	− addend
sum	addend

To complicate matters further, subtraction was defined as "seeking a missing addend" when a sum and one addend were given; that is, addend + □ = sum. Using the same terminology for both addition and subtraction caused some children to become confused when they first encountered subtraction as it relates to a "take-away" situation.

Pupils will encounter problem situations in which two numbers are to be *compared* to determine their difference. In this case, the meaning of the numbers and the process used to find the difference are not the same as in the take-away situation. Here the language would be as follows:

First, choose a number, such as 8. Show this as a measure on a number line.

Next, compare this number with another, perhaps 3. Show this as a measure on a second number line.

Third, determine the difference between 8 and 3 by *comparison*.

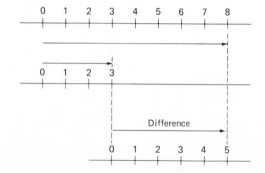

The symbols and signs traditionally used to write the subtraction fact are the same as those used in the comparison situation, namely: $8 - 3 = 5$. The same subtraction fact answers both questions raised in two different physical settings.

Some recent elementary textbooks now introduce the *more traditional terminology* for subtraction as:

> 48 *minuend,* the number from which a number is to be subtracted,
> −15 *subtrahend,* the number being subtracted,
> 23 *difference,* the answer to a subtraction example.

The terminology "sum minus addend equals addend" is acceptable after pupils understand subtraction but is not recommended at the introduction of the process.

Addition of Two Two-Digit Numbers with Regrouping

One of the greatest difficulties pupils have in adding multidigit numbers is with regrouping. Regrouping is necessary when the numbers at any place in the sum *overload* that place. In the example $38 + 16$, the sum in the ones place is 14 ones, as shown below in base-ten long form and in place-value form:

		Tens	Ones
3 tens	8 ones	3	8
+1 ten	6 ones	+1	6
4 tens	14 ones	4	14

To be in "standard form," the final answer to an addition example must have digits of 9 or less at each place. Consequently, the 14 ones must be renamed 1 ten 4 ones, resulting in a sum of 5 tens 4 ones, or 54.

Readiness for renaming involves:

1. A mastery of the addition facts to sums of 18.

2. Ability to regroup many single objects into bundles of tens and ones and to regroup with other types of base-ten materials.

3. Ability to regroup on a place-value device—that is, the ability to exchange ten in the ones place for one in the tens place.

4. A well-developed understanding of and proficiency in working with two two-digit numbers without regrouping.

Review of Demonstration Lesson

A demonstration lesson illustrating the principles of teaching and learning mathematics was included at the end of Chapter 2. Since it centered on the teaching and learning of addition of multidigit numbers with regrouping, we suggest that readers review that lesson, presented on page 24, before continuing with this chapter.

Summary of the Steps for Regrouping

We can summarize the steps used to develop the addition algorism for multidigit numbers with regrouping as follows:

1. Start with a problem setting. The problem must involve numbers that, when added, will "overload" the ones place. The following is a good example: Every weekday Dick delivers 25 morning papers and 48 evening papers. How many papers does he deliver each weekday? The pupils should be able to write one of the following addition examples for this problem:

(a) $25 + 48 = \Box$ (c) $\begin{array}{r} 25 \\ +48 \end{array}$

(b) $48 + 25 = \Box$ (d) $\begin{array}{r} 48 \\ +25 \end{array}$

These notations are at the most advanced symbolic level. A less abstract notation for (a) would be:

(2 tens 5 ones) + (4 tens 8 ones) = ____tens ____ones, a type of notation that can be developed by working with base-ten materials.

The following is another way to record example (c):

Tens	Ones
2	5
+4	8

a type of notation that can be developed by working with a place-value device.

2. Have pupils solve the problem at the exploratory level by using base-ten materials. The desired result of this activity is for the pupils to discover the need to regroup the 13 ones as 1 ten 3 ones. From their experience with base-ten materials, pupils can generalize that "ten ones can be regrouped into one ten." This concept can be shown by exchanging ten pennies for one dime, ten cubes for one long, or ten single sticks for one bundle of ten. Although various types of materials can be used, only one type should be used in each presentation.

3. Have the pupils write in long form the numerals for the addition example illustrated by the base-ten materials. Figure 7.4 shows how pictures can be used in place of the base-ten models.

4. Have pupils use a tens and ones chart to record the solution. Write the solution in long notation form. The result can be shown in two steps: (a) shows 6 tens 13 ones, and (b) shows addition of the 1 ten and 3 ones to make a total of 7 tens 3 ones.

(a)

Tens	Ones
2	5
+4	8
6	13 ←

13 = 1

Ten	Ones
	3

(b)

Tens	Ones
1	
2	5
+4	8
7	3

5. Discuss with the pupils the standard algorism for writing the problem in (b). Ask the pupils to use the standard form to solve the problem. If necessary, refer again to base-ten materials to clarify the operation.

(a)
$$\begin{array}{r} \overset{1}{25} \\ +48 \\ \hline 73 \end{array}$$

(b)
$$\begin{array}{r} 25 \\ +48 \\ \hline 73 \end{array}$$

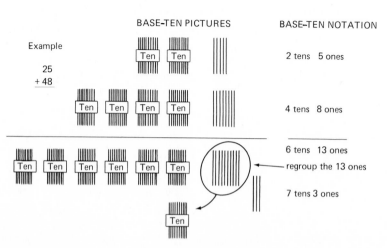

BASE-TEN PICTURES   BASE-TEN NOTATION

Example

25
+48

2 tens   5 ones

4 tens   8 ones

6 tens   13 ones

regroup the 13 ones

7 tens 3 ones

Figure 7.4

Three-Place Addends

When you teach addition involving re-naming, first deal with two-place addends, and then with three-place addends in which an overloaded place occurs (a) in the ones place only, (b) in the tens place only, (c) in both the ones place and the tens place, (d) in the hundreds place only, (e) in two or more places, and (f) in each place given.

(a) $\begin{array}{r} 248 \\ +327 \end{array}$ (b) $\begin{array}{r} 482 \\ +256 \end{array}$ (c) $\begin{array}{r} 567 \\ +384 \end{array}$

(d) $\begin{array}{r} 824 \\ +632 \end{array}$ (e) $\begin{array}{r} 869 \\ +356 \end{array}$ (f) $\begin{array}{r} 487 \\ +635 \end{array}$

By the time pupils are ready to work three-place addends with renaming in one or more places, they should be able to operate entirely at the symbolic level.

The major value of working with three-place addends with and without regrouping is to discover how to deal with an over-loaded place in a sum, regardless of the number of places in the addends.

Higher-Decade Addition

In *higher-decade addition*, also called add-ing by endings, the sum of a one-place num-ber added to a two-place addend is found in one mental operation. If a pupil thinks "18 + 5 = 23," he or she has used adding by endings. On the other hand, if the child thinks "8 + 5 = 13; 1 + 1 = 2," he or she has added by regrouping. The sum in higher-decade addition can be in the same decade as the two-place addend or in the next higher decade. Here are some examples of higher-decade addition:

(a) 23 + 5   (b) 17 + 3   (c) 28 + 5

Example (a) is relatively easy because the sum is in the same decade (same ten) as the two-place addend, and so there is no bridg-

ing of the decade. Examples (b) and (c) are more difficult because each sum is in the next decade, thus bridging the decade.

Higher-decade addition can also occur at any point in a column of digits where a sub-sum is a two-digit number. This is shown in example (d) below:

(d) $\begin{array}{r} 5 \\ 7 \\ 6 \\ \underline{3} \end{array}$ Adding downward:
5 + 7 = 12, a basic fact
12 + 6 = 18, *adding endings*, no bridging
18 + 3 = 21, *adding by end-ings, bridging*

Adding upward:
3 + 6 = 9, a basic fact
9 + 7 = 16, a basic fact with one addend unseen
16 + 5 = 21, *adding by end-ings, bridging*

Higher Decade Addition without Bridging

The most logical and easiest procedure to follow when there is no bridging is to "think forward" and find the sum in one mental re-sponse—from the tens place to the ones place. This technique of starting with the tens place in finding a sum violates a pre-viously learned rule for adding two two-place numbers. Pupils are instructed always to add the ones place first, because an over-loaded place in the sum is regrouped more easily if the ones-place addends are added first, then the tens place, and so on; how-ever, in column addition it is helpful to "think forward" by starting with the tens-place number. In doing so, the subsums of a column of numbers are thought and verbal-ized "forward"—in the same way that we say the number names.

In example (e), the subsums are verbal-ized in sequence downward as:

(e)   3
    9
    2
    3   *"Twelve, fourteen, seventeen, eigh-*
  <u> 1</u>   *teen"*
  18

Higher-decade addition is a less important topic today than it was before the use of calculators became widespread. Although mental addition of long columns of numbers is rare these days, this skill will assist children in learning multiplication and division.

Examples (f) through (h) show that a two-digit number ending in 6, when added to 5, always ends in 1; but in the next higher decade. Children should practice this form of addition on examples in which the sum is less than 50:

(f)   16   (g)   26   (h)   36
   <u>+ 5</u>   <u>+ 5</u>   <u>+ 5</u>

1. Have pupils give the sums when the examples are written:

(a) In sequence in vertical form:

  12   22   32
<u>+3</u>   <u>+3</u>   <u>+3</u>

The number pair 2 + 3 is the key fact in each example in the set.

(b) In sequence in equation form:

12 + 3 = □   22 + 3 = □
32 + 3 = □   42 + 3 = □

(c) Out of sequence, using the same key facts:

12 + 3 = □   32 + 3 = □
22 + 3 = □   42 + 3 = □

(d) Out of sequence, using different key facts:

11 + 4 = □   13 + 5 = □
25 + 2 = □   33 + 3 = □

(e) On a number line and bridging the decade, as shown in Figure 7.5:

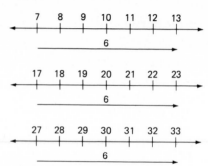
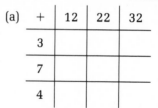
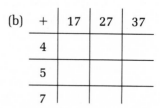

Figure 7.5

2. The following type of exercise helps pupils learn to bridge the decade:

8 + 4 = 10 + □   6 + 7 = □ + 3
18 + 4 = 20 + □   16 + 7 = □ + 3
28 + 4 = 30 + □   26 + 7 = □ + 3

3. Creating tables is an effective way to practice adding by endings. For example, the sum in Table (a) does not bridge the decade, but it does in Table (b):

(a)

+	12	22	32
3			
7			
4			

(b)

+	17	27	37
4			
5			
7			

4. A short oral exercise in which the class deals with dictated numbers is recommended. The teacher writes a numeral, such as 4, on the chalkboard and dictates numbers, such as 12, 28, or 35. The two-place numeral is unseen; hence the pupil must think this number and add it to the visible 4. The exercise can be varied so that all numerals are unseen. The pupil is directed to add a one-place number, such as 6, to each number dictated.

Practicing Higher-Decade Addition in Column Addition

When children first begin to use higher-decade addition in columns, the exercises should be limited to three addends with the sum of the first two ranging from 10 to 18. Write exercises in the fashion shown here, and leave a space between the second and third addends (downward) for pupils to write the two-digit subsum of the first two addends, if needed. The following sequence is recommended:

1. No bridging:

```
 8       7       5       9
 9       8       6       5
   (17)    (  )    (  )    (  )
 2       3       4       5
───     ───     ───     ───
19
```

2. Bridging in each example:

```
 7       8       7       5
 8       9       6       9
   (15)    (  )    (  )    (  )
 6       5       8       9
───     ───     ───     ───
21
```

3. Mixed examples, with some bridging, and some not bridging.

```
 7       8       9       8       8
 6       8       6       3       5
   (13)    (  )    (  )    (  )    (  )
 3       7       6       3       8
───     ───     ───     ───     ───
16
```

The first example in each group above can be solved with the suggested notations. Pupils should practice working other, similar examples.

After pupils become proficient in adding a column of three addends with and without bridging and understand the process, they can practice with four addends. Let the children write the subsums until they are no longer needed.

Mastery Level of Higher-Decade Addition

At the mastery level, pupils are able to add a column downward by *thinking* each subsum (forward) and without writing the subsums. Mastery is shown in the solution of example (k):

```
(k)   6       The pupil should think the
      8       following subsums: "Four-
      7       teen, twenty-one, twenty-five,
      4       thirty-four."
      9
     ──
     34
```

This approach is called the "direct method" of adding a column. The sum can be checked by adding the column upward, and thinking: "Thirteen, twenty, twenty-eight, thirty-four."

We recommend that column addition be taught first with the direct method. Later, you can use a search-for pattern as an alternative approach. Alternative approaches are presented at the end of this chapter.

Subtraction of Two Two-Digit Numbers with Regrouping

Young students have long been observed to have great difficulty in learning to subtract multidigit numbers with regrouping. The 1977–1978 *National Assessment of Educational Progress* in mathematics examined, among other things, how well students could compute. It was found that when asked to subtract one two-digit number from another two-digit number with one regrouping, only 66 percent of the nine-year-olds gave the correct answers. The performance of the third-grade pupils was further analyzed.

Why were 34 percent of the nine-year-olds unable to find the correct answer to this type of subtraction problem? The conclusion drawn from the analysis of the results that is included in the official report is

Pupils demonstrate the regrouping step in subtraction. *Photo by Leland Perry)*

that ". . . the most common error made by 9-year-olds was subtracting a smaller digit from a larger digit, regardless of whether or not the smaller digit was in the minuend. . . ."[1]

Much of the research on approaches to teaching multidigit subtraction with regrouping has compared approaches at the

symbolic level for dealing with *column impasse*—that is, subtraction at a particular place is not possible. For example, the National Assessment found that pupils often subtracted a smaller number from a larger number at a given place regardless of the order. Thus, when subtracting 17 from 53, a pupil might give an answer of 44.

Pupils need to understand that in a place-value system each place in an example represents a separate subtraction fact. Example (1) presents three different subtraction facts (moving from right to left):

(l)   682 $2 - 1 =$ ____
    -241 $8 - 4 =$ ____
              $6 - 4 =$ ____

The difficulty arises when the first number (minuend) in the subtraction fact at a particular place is less than the second number (subtrahend), as in example (m). In the ones place there is a *column impasse*, because $2 - 8$ has *no answer* in the set of whole numbers. When subtracting multidigit numbers, pupils must be able to recognize a column impasse, or else they will arrive at incorrect answers.

(m)

Hundreds Place	Tens Place	Ones Place
8	6	2
− 3	− 2	− 8
5	4	?

How do pupils deal with a column impasse? When pupils cannot solve a problem, such as $2 - 8$, they must ask themselves, "What can be done to make subtraction at the ones place possible?"

There are two basic approaches to overcome a column impasse in multidigit subtraction. These are (1) the *decomposition method* and (2) the *equal-addition approach*.

In the past, research has generally favored the decomposition method, which is easily understood and is accurate. More recent studies,[2] comparing the results of the two approaches, still favor the decomposition method for its ease in teaching and for the achievements it produces among pupils.

The Decomposition Method

In the decomposition method, the minuend is renamed so that there is a basic sub-

2. James M. Sherill, "Subtraction: Decomposition versus Equal Addends, *Arithmetic Teacher*, September 1979, 27:16–17.

traction fact at each place in the example. The traditional name for this technique is "borrowing."

1. Begin with a "take-away" problem having a column impasse in the ones place.

> Matthew has 3 dimes and 2 pennies. He goes to the store to buy a new metric ruler. The price of the ruler is 16¢. The sign on the cash register says MUST USE EXACT CHANGE. Matthew needs 1 dime and 6 pennies. What will Matthew have to do before he can buy the ruler?

Pupils might suggest the simple solution that Matthew *change* one of his dimes into 10 pennies. This solution gets at the heart of regrouping in subtraction. If still more ones are needed, the next logical solution would be to regroup one of the tens in the tens place as 10 ones. Pupils have little trouble seeing that 1 dime = 10 pennies and that 1 ten = 10 ones.

2. Have pupils explore regrouping 1 ten to 10 ones with dimes and pennies (real or models). See Figure 7.6 on page 126.

(a) Start with 3 dimes 2 pennies.
(b) Change 1 dime to 10 pennies.
(c) Now name the coins as 2 dimes 12 pennies.

3. Using the long form of place-value notation, provide practice exercises that involve renaming (that is, rename 1 ten to 10 ones). Ask pupils to show their work.

(a) 3 tens   4 ones =   2 tens   ___ ones

(b) 4 tens   2 ones = ___ tens   12 ones

(c) 5 tens   5 ones =   4 ___   ___ ones

4. Give pupils a practice sheet with several subtraction examples involving two two-digit numbers. Have some of the examples require no regrouping and some examples require regrouping as a first step in the solution. Ask the pupils to mark the examples in which the minuend must be regrouped

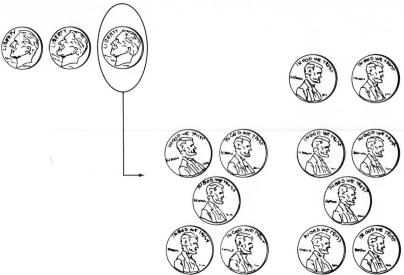

Figure 7.6

before subtracting. Ask the pupils to give their reasons for marking the examples they thought would need to be regrouped.

5. Give pupils several word problems to solve by using base-ten materials. Have them draw pictures of their solutions. Make a record of the solution with expanded notation. For example, give them the following problem:

> A second-grade class grew 62 carrots in their garden. They pulled 15 carrots for a school party. How many carrots were left in the garden? Have the children use base-ten or place-value materials to solve the problem; then draw the picture and record the notations.

6. Have the pupils study the presentation of this topic in their textbooks. Recent textbooks use a variety of pictures and notations to illustrate the process of regrouping and subtracting.

7. Give pupils practice exercises at the symbolic level, requiring both expanded notation and standard algorithm form.

After pupils understand how to regroup 1

ten to 10 ones with manipulative materials and can use this procedure to solve multi-digit subtraction with and without regrouping, they can be expected to work at the symbolic level without using manipulative materials. Table 7.1 illustrates the symbolic level of subtraction with regrouping.

Multiple Regrouping in Subtraction

After the pupils understand how to rename 1 ten to 10 ones and have had symbolic-level practice in regrouping for more ones, give them problems that require regrouping at the tens place, as in example (n):

(n)   825   528
    $-\,362$ $-\,365$

Special attention needs to be paid to examples involving zero in the tens place in the minuend, as in example (o):

(o)   302   More ones are
    $-\,186$ needed at the ones
                   place, but there are
                   zero tens. What can

Table 7.1 Subtraction with Regrouping at Symbolic Level

Example	Expanded Form Tens	Ones	Tens	Ones	Developmental Algorism	Standard Algorism
					(14)	
74 =	7	4 =	6	14	6̸ 4̸	74
− 26 =	− 2	6 =	− 2	6	− 2 6	− 26
			4	8	4 8	48

be done? The 3 hundreds can be viewed as 30 tens; after one of the 30 tens is changed to 10 ones, 29 tens are left in the minuend. Now we can subtract.

Tens	Ones
29	12
30	2
− 18	6

The thought pattern to subtract in example (o) by the decomposition method is "6 from 12, 6; 8 from 9, 1; 1 from 2, 1."

Checks for Addition and Subtraction

Children should be taught effective ways to check addition:

1. Find the sum by adding in the opposite direction.

2. If there are more than five or six addends, form two examples and find the sum of each. Then add the two sums.

3. Use a calculator.

Effective checks for subtraction are:

4. Add the difference and the subtrahend. This sum must equal the minuend. If $a − b = c$, then $a = b + c$.

5. Subtract the difference from the sum to find the subtrahend, such that $a − c = b$.

6. Use a calculator.

Solving Verbal Problems

Learning to solve problems will be the central focus of modern elementary mathematics programs throughout the 1980s. After pupils have learned the algorisms for addition and subtraction, they have the background to solve one-step equation problems. They should also be taught to solve problems with more than one step. The solution of a multistep problem usually follows the pattern for solving a one-step problem.

Addition Samples

Addition describes the process of combining things. As you read the following problems, stress to the class the fact that two or more sets or groups of things are being combined into a single collection.

1. Jane had 4 pencils in her box and added 5 more. How many does she have now?

2. Sam weighed 61 kilograms last month and has gained 2 kilograms since then. How much does he weigh now?

3. Jean earned $5 on Monday, $3 on Tuesday, $7 on Wednesday, $2 on Thursday, and $10 on Friday. What was her total for the week?

When you work with your class in the early stages of problem solving or with individuals or small groups, you may find it useful to have the pupils reword the first problem as follows:

Given: 4 pencils in the box; 5 more are added.

This rewording can be done orally or on the chalkboard, as the situation demands.

Here are two common methods for recording the solution to problem 1:

Solution A:
$$\begin{array}{r} 4 \\ +5 \\ \hline 9 \end{array}$$

Solution B: $N = 4 + 5$
$N = 9$

You can provide guidance for pupils who have difficulty rewording a problem by asking the following sequence of questions.

What is to be found?
What is given?
Can you reword the problem in easier or fewer words?

Encourage the pupils to check the computation by whatever means is available. It is important for pupils to determine whether their answers are sensible. In this case, they should clearly realize that the answer must be greater than 4. It is essential for pupils to show that they understand the problem by stating an appropriate interpretation.

Subtraction Samples

Subtraction describes the process of separation of sets. The following problems can be solved by visualizing part of a set being removed from a given set or separation of that set or quantity into two parts:

1. A man has $20 and spends $5. How much does he have now?

2. Susan begins a trip with 10 gallons of gasoline in her car and uses 7 gallons. How

much is left in the tank at the end of the trip?

3. A storekeeper starts the day with 50 bags of potatoes. He sells 32 bags. How many bags are left at the end of the day?

Here are two common methods for recording the solution to problem 1:

Solution A:
$$\begin{array}{r} 20 \\ -\ 5 \\ \hline 15 \end{array}$$
He now has $15.

Solution B: $N = 20 - 5$
$N = 15$
He now has $15.

Each of the above solutions used subtraction to describe the removal of a set of 5 from a set of 20 or to separate a set of 20 into a set of 5 and a set of 15. Using an equation or number sentence makes it possible to take another approach to solving this problem. The $20.00 is to be separated into a set of $5.00 and an amount to be determined, and so the sum must be $20.00. This reasoning leads to the following solution:

Solution C: $N + 5 = 20$
$N = 15$
He now has $15.

Solution C shows that a subtraction problem can be viewed as an addition problem in which the sum (20) and one addend (5) are known and the other addend is to be found. In purely mathematical terms, subtraction is defined as the inverse operation of addition. In other words, subtraction undoes addition. The addition of 5 to 15 to obtain a sum of 20 can be "undone" by subtracting 5 from 20.

The first solution of the equation $N + 3 = 10$ should follow from knowledge of the basic fact $3 + 7 = 10$. The students should later recognize that the unknown addend (N) can be determined by subtracting 3 from 10.

Comparison Subtraction

Subtraction is also used to compare two distinct sets to determine how much larger or smaller one set is than the other. For example, if Sue had 11 marbles and Jim had 14 marbles, subtraction would show that Jim had 3 more than Sue or that Sue had 3 fewer than Jim. It is often difficult to determine whether subtraction describes a separation or comparison problem. If one asks how many marbles must be added to Sue's collection to make it equal to Jim's, no such confusion will arise.

Alternative Approaches to Addition (Optional)

Fast learners often discover other ways to perform the basic operations. This practice should be encouraged. In this section we give examples showing alternative approaches that can be used for enrichment.

After pupils have mastered addition of two two-place numbers with and without regrouping the sum, alternative approaches to addition can be introduced. Osborne[3] describes an alternative algorism to renaming in multidigit addition, shown here in example (p):

(p)	238	This algorism is designed to
	+ 95	strengthen the understand-
	200	ing of place value and build
	120	a readiness for a better un-
	+ 13	derstanding of the renaming
	333	step in the standard algor-
		ism.

The two addends are combined by writing 200; adding 30 and 90; adding 8 and 5.

3. Alan R. Osborne, "Conditions for Algorithmic Imagination," in *Algorithmic Learning* (Columbus, OH: ERIC Science, Mathematics, and Environmental Education Clearinghouse, 1980), p. 18.

Another alternative approach to adding two or more numbers is to rename the addends so as not to change the sum. This can be done by the property of *compensation for addition:* when a number is added to or subtracted from one of the addends, the sum will not change as long as the opposite operation is performed on a second addend, as illustrated in the following example:

$$
\begin{array}{rrr}
36 & +4 = & 40 \\
\underline{+44} & -4 = & \underline{40} \\
 & & 80 \\
82 & -2 = & 80 \\
\underline{+96} & +2 = & \underline{98} \\
 & & 178
\end{array}
$$

Alternative Approaches to Subtraction with Regrouping (Optional)

After pupils have developed a meaningful understanding of the *decomposition method* of adjusting a column impasse, the teacher can introduce other alternative techniques. One of alternatives, described here, is based on the mathematical property of *compensation for subtraction*—that is, the same number can be added to both the minuend and the subtrahend without changing the difference. This technique is commonly referred to as the *equal additions* or the *equal addends* approach. The meaning of this method is best demonstrated with a comparison-type subtraction problem, in which two numbers or measures are compared to determine the difference. The idea is that if both lengths are increased by the same measure, the difference would remain the same.

8 cm	18 cm
− 5 cm	− 15 cm
3 cm	3 cm

If we started with a problem requiring regrouping, would adding 10 to both the minuend and subtrahend take care of the column impasse? In example (q) there is still a column impasse, even after adding 10 to both numbers. How does the property of compensation help?

(q) $\quad\begin{array}{r} 62 = 60 + 2 \\ -46 = 40 + 6 \end{array} \quad \rightarrow \quad \begin{array}{r} 60 + 12 \\ 50 + 6 \\ \hline 10 + 6 = 16 \end{array}$

In the solution of sample (q), 10 is added to the minuend in the form of *10 ones* and to the subtrahend in the form of *1 ten!* When this technique is applied to the example, the minuend and subtrahend both increase in value by 10. However, the minuend becomes 6 tens 12 ones, and the subtrahend becomes 5 tens 6 ones, a shift that eliminates the column impasse without changing the difference. The thought pattern to subtract in the example below by the equal additions method is "7 from 13, 6; 4 from 10, 6; 5 from 8, 3."

$\quad\begin{array}{r} 803 \\ -437 \\ \hline \end{array}$

Summary

Developmental algorisms often are written differently from the standard algorism because their purpose is different. Developmental algorisms are used to build a child's understanding of the operation, whereas the standard form is gradually taught after such an understanding has been developed.

Aids such as base-ten materials and place-value charts are valuable in demonstrating to children the operations of addition and subtraction. Place-value materials are usually introduced after base-ten materials, because they represent a number more abstractly.

Addition and subtraction without regrouping should be taught before addition and subtraction with regrouping. Texts differ on the specific sequence for each and also as to whether addition and subtraction algorisms should be presented simultaneously. A good technique is to introduce the algorism with a story as the problem situation. Have the children use concrete materials to demonstrate how they would go about solving the problem in the story and have them write the corresponding algorism as they work.

Teachers must keep in mind that before children can be expected to operate on numbers at a symbolic level they will need much practice with concrete materials and developmental algorisms. Some children will learn faster than others. Teachers will need to adjust their techniques to meet the needs of each child.

Children should be taught to add downward in column addition and to check their work by adding in the opposite direction. They should be taught to check subtraction by adding the difference to the subtrahend, so that the sum equals the minuend. Students should learn to use a calculator to check both addition and subtraction.

Exercises

1. Discuss the concept of place value as it relates to teaching addition and subtraction algorisms.

2. Design a sequence of activities for developing the algorism for the addition of multidigit numbers without regrouping.

3. Design a sequence of activities for developing the algorism for the subtraction of multidigit numbers without regrouping.

4. Complete a sequence of activities, for both addition and subtraction, in which regrouping is necessary.

5. Prepare a talk on the readiness activities for addition and subtraction. Indicate the nature of readiness and how it is achieved.

6. Distinguish between checking an answer for accuracy and checking for reasonableness.

7. Give the relevant thought pattern, discuss, and solve each of the following problems.

   a. Sandra gave the clerk $1.00 for a glass of orange juice and received 55¢ in change. What did the orange juice cost?
   b. Each weekday Jane delivers 25 morning papers and 42 evening papers. How many papers does she deliver each weekday?
   c. The larger of two numbers is 54, and their difference is 15. What is the smaller number?
   d. The sum of the measure of three sides of a triangle is 56 centimeters. The length of one side is 21 cm and the length of another side is 18 cm. What is the length of the third side?

8. Give the thought pattern to subtract in the example below by the decomposition method; by the equal additions method.

$$\begin{array}{r} 5002 \\ -1309 \\ \hline \end{array}$$

Selected Readings

Mahaffey, Michael L., and Alex F. Perrodin. *Teaching Elementary School Mathematics*. Itasca, IL: Peacock, 1973, Chapter 2, pp. 27–57.

Reidesel, C. Alan. *Teaching Elementary School Mathematics,* Third Edition. Englewood Cliffs, NJ: Prentice-Hall, 1980, Chapters 6 and 7, pp. 147–204.

Reisman, Fredricka K. *Teaching Mathematics: Methods and Content,* Second Edition. Boston: Houghton Mifflin, 1981, Chapter 5, pp. 88–98, and Chapter 9, pp. 158–174.

Schminke, C. W., Norbert Maertens, and William Arnold. *Teaching the Child Mathematics,* Second Edition. New York: Holt, Rinehart and Winston, 1978, Chapter 7, pp. 160–178.

Silbert, Jerry, Douglas Carnine, and Marcy Stein. *Direct Instruction Mathematics.* Columbus, OH: Charles E. Merrill, 1981, Chapters 7 and 8, pp. 108–160.

Chapter 8

Patterns for Teaching Basic Facts in Multiplication and Division

To perform multiplication and division, one must have a solid understanding of addition and subtraction. Historically, multiplication and division are relatively new to Western civilization. Francis J. Mueller relates the story of a fifteenth-century German merchant who wanted his son to attend a university where he would receive a good commercial education. The merchant asked a university professor to recommend a school. The professor advised that a German university would provide a good training in addition and subtraction, but if the son wanted to learn multiplication and division, he would have to attend a university in Italy, for only there could he study "those advanced arts."[1]

Achievement Goals

After studying this chapter, you should be able to:

1. Identify the sequence in which basic multiplication and division facts are learned at the exploratory level.
2. Describe different kinds of multiplication situations.
3. Illustrate the differences between measurement and partitive division situations.
4. Show children how to use manipulatives to solve multiplication and division problems.
5. Use drawings to demonstrate solutions to multiplication and division problems.
6. Disucss ways to bridge the gap from using objects to notation.
7. Illustrate the commutative, distributive, and associative properties for multiplication.
8. Summarize ways to help pupils master basic multiplication and division facts.
9. Explain how to make division with remainders meaningful to pupils.
10. Write different kinds of verbal problems involving multiplication and division situations and show how each could be solved (a) with objects, (b) with drawings, and (c) with numbers.

1. Francis J. Mueller, *Arithmetic, Its Structure and Concepts*, Second Edition (Englewood Cliffs, NJ: Prentice-Hall, 1964), p. 82.

Vocabulary

Mastery of the following key terms will help you to understand this chapter. Each term is defined or illustrated in the Glossary at the end of the book.

Array	Inverse operation
Associative property	Measurement division
Commutative property	Partitive division
Distributive property	Quotient
Factor	Rational numbers
Identity	Remainder
	Sequence

Relationships among the Fundamental Operations

Figure 8.1 shows how the four fundamental operations are related to one another. Addition describes the process of joining of two or more collections. When two or more groups are equal in number, the joining process can also be described by multiplica-tion. For example, the addition fact $6 + 6 = 12$ can be renamed as the multiplication fact $2 \times 6 = 12$. Subtraction describes the process of separating a collection into two parts. The process of separating a group of things into two or more smaller groups equal in number can also be described by division. Division can be performed by successive subtraction. The example $18 \div 6$ can be solved by subtracting 6 from 18 three times.

Sequence for Learning Basic Facts at the Exploratory Level

Children's first experiences with multiplication and division facts are with everyday situations in which they put things together and take them apart by *equals*. Long before children can understand the nature of these operations, they can solve real-life problems involving groups *equal* in number by manipulating physical objects and by counting. Teachers of primary grade children should look for various natural settings to illustrate

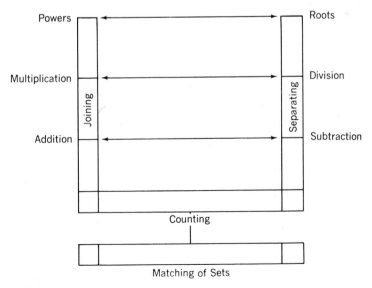

Figure 8.1
Relationships among the Fundamental Operations

common instances of groups of equal number. Introductory work should not include discussions of *zero* or *one*, because these are special cases.

By the end of the second grade and during the third grade, most children have developed an understanding of addition and subtraction, as a result of working with concrete materials, drawings, and abstract notation. These activities provide the readiness children need to understand the meanings of multiplication and division. Children in early stages of learning perceive multiplication and division as very different operations. Although the two operations are related mathematically, each needs to be emphasized in separate lessons. In grades 1 through 3, lessons should be presented at the exploratory level as follows:

1. Start with a simple verbal problem involving a basic fact in multiplication and/or division.

2. Give children manipulative materials to use and discuss in solving problems.

3. Guide each child in using and discussing drawings to represent the problem-solving process.

4. Emphasize how manipulatives and drawings relate to the way that multiplication and division are transcribed symbolically. Exploratory work without writing may be useless.

Multiplication and Division Problem Situations

Multiplication Situations

As a readiness for multiplication, children use counting to find answers to problem situations involving objects that naturally form the following groupings:

1. twos: shoes, eyes, ears, arms, legs, bicycle wheels

2. threes: tricycle wheels, clover leaves

3. fours: wheels on a car, wheels on a wagon

4. fives: fingers on each hand, cents in a nickel

Real-life situations should be used to introduce multiplication. For example, say to the class, "A box has 3 rows of doughnuts with 4 in each row. How many doughnuts are there in the box?" In early stages of learning, the children should be shown a real box of doughnuts. The problem should be stated to them verbally as above, then translated into the mathematical question, "How many are there in 3 fours?" Each child should be encouraged to work the problem in his or her own way.

Two Division Situations

At the exploratory level, division describes the process of *separating* a collection into two or more groups *equal* in number. Later, it can be described or defined as finding an unknown factor when the product and one factor are known. If introduced too early, the latter definition can be more confusing than helpful to young learners.

The division example $8 \div 2 = \square$ can be related to a situation requiring a solution to a problem of "sharing 8 equally," or "breaking 8 into 2 equal parts." In problem settings, the 8 can refer to anything, such as cents, candies, blocks, children, and so on. The 2 in the equation refers to the number of desired *parts*. The process of "sharing by equals" or "breaking into equal parts" is the core of a *partitive* type of division problem.

Here are some additional examples of partitive division problems:

1. Tom paid 20¢ for 4 candies. How much did each cost?

2. There are 2 cars and 8 children. The

same number of children ride in each car. How many will ride in each car?

3. You have 8 cookies to share equally with a friend. How many will each of you get?

4. You have 8 big blocks the same size to build 2 towers the same height. How many blocks will you use for each tower?

Young children do much *sharing by equals* before they recognize that these problems can be solved by division. In each situation above, the problem is to find the *number in each part* after a certain number of items have been separated into a specified number of parts.

The example $15 \div 3 = \square$ can be related to a situation in which 15 things are to be regrouped (separated) into groups of threes. Thus, 3 things at a time are identified or removed (measured) from a group of 15 things. The question is "How many groups of 3 are there in 15?" Problems of this type are relatively easy for children to solve with manipulative materials. This experience of "breaking into equal parts" is called a *measurement* type of division problem.

Here are some examples of *measurement* division problems:

1. At 3¢ each, how many candies could you buy for 15¢?

2. There are 15 children to play a game with 3 children on each team. How many teams of 3 will there be?

3. You have a candy bar 15 cm long and want to cut it in pieces 3 cm long. How many pieces will there be?

4. There are 15 roses in a bunch. It takes 3 roses to make a bouquet. How many bouquets can you make?

The solutions to these problems require a *measuring* process, in which one would ask, "How many *a*'s are there in *b*?"

1. Three cents measures 15¢ five times.

2. If we separated 15 children into groups of 3 children, we would have 5 groups.

3. Three centimeters measures 15 cm five times.

4. Fifteen roses can be separated into 5 bouquets of 3 roses each.

As a teacher, you must bear in mind that in spite of the difference between partitive and measurement division, you should be careful not to overemphasize the distinction. Once a pupil has found an equation to solve the problem, the solution is the same, whether the problem is a partitive or a measurement situation. Whether a problem is a partitive or measurement situation is relevant only when it is time to interpret the quotient.

Solving Problems with Manipulative Materials

The following discussion illustrates how problems can be solved at the exploratory level of learning by using manipulative materials.

Problem 1: You receive an allowance of $3.00 per week. How much will you receive in four weeks?

Young children should be encouraged to solve this problem by using dollar bills, or an appropriate substitute for dollar bills, as follows:

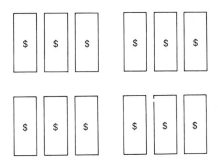

Once the materials are arranged to match the problem situation, the answer can be found by counting or regrouping by tens.

Problem 2: We are going to plant some pansies in a flat box. We have 4 rows and plant 3 pansies in each row. How many pansies will we need?

Because it is not convenient to have the children use real pansies to solve this problem, you should supply objects or drawings to serve as substitutes in the configuration below:

/ / /

/ / /

/ / /

/ / /

The physical or visual model then represents 4 threes, or 3 + 3 + 3 + 3, which equals 12.

Problem 3: Two boys want to share 8 doughnuts equally. How many will each boy get?

Eight is to be separated into two parts, equal in number. Eight counters can be used to represent the doughnuts. Then, using these counters, the children share the 8 things by separating them into two parts of equal number, by saying "One for you, one for me, etc. . . ." Some pupils may be able to see that the 8 can be distributed "two at a time," and a quick child may see immediately that 8 is made up of 2 fours. The physical array will show that when 8 is broken into two equal parts there will be 4 in each, or 8 ÷ 2 = 4.

Problem 4: The teacher has 10 cookies to be given as prizes for special work. Each prize is 2 cookies. How many children can be treated?

You can illustrate the process of separating the 10 cookies into groups of 2 by:

1. Using 10 cookies or appropriate objects to represent cookies.

2. Removing 2 cookies or objects at a time.

3. Counting the number of groups of 2 created.

4. Stating the result as the multiplication sentence "5 groups of 2 equals 10."

5. Stating the answer as "There can be 5 treats."

Showing Multiplication and Division Facts with Drawings

The children can be taught to make marks on paper to represent real objects in a problem situation and in its solution.

Problem: How many arms do five children have?

The problem situation and its solution are shown with drawings below:

5 Children:

Arms:

Five children each with 2 arms 10 arms all together

Problem: How many pieces of candy that cost 3¢ each can you buy for 12¢?

1. Draw 12 pennies.

○○○○○○○○○○○○

2. Mark off (measure) by 3s.

○○○ ○○○ ○○○ ○○○

3. Because each set of 3¢ equals one piece of candy, the number of candies is the number of sets of 3s, which is equal to 4.

Problem: You have 5 flowers in each of 2 vases. How many flowers are there in all?

An *array* is a type of drawing that is one of the best ways for children to gain an understanding of multiplication and division.

1. Represent 5 flowers with five dots.

2. Draw two sets of dots for 2 vases.

3. The array is a 2 by 5 figure, containing 10 dots in all. So there will be 10 flowers.

· · · · ·

· · · · ·

Problem: You pay 5¢ for one pencil. How many can you buy for 15¢?

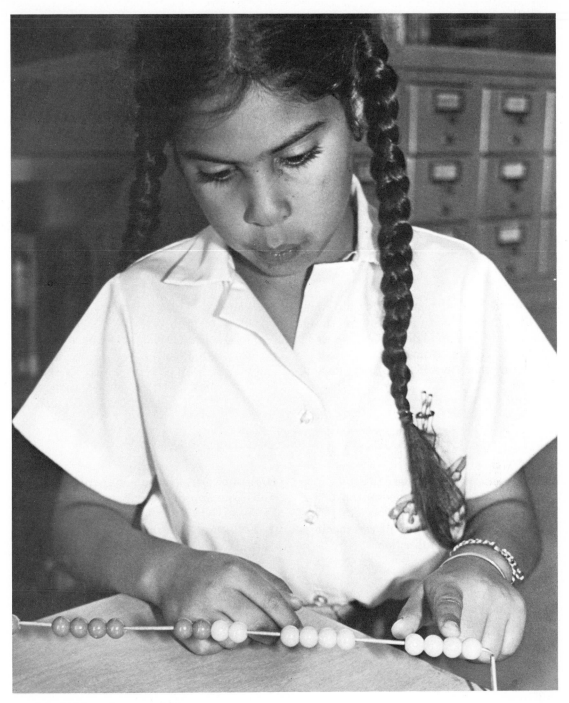

A pupil explores groups of fours. *(Photo by Leland Perry)*

Solution: Draw an array with dots as follows:

1. Represent 5¢ • • • • •   1 pencil
with five dots.

2. You have 10¢   • • • • •   2 pencils,
left. Draw another   for 10¢
set of five dots.

3. You have 5¢   • • • • •   3 pencils,
left. Draw another   for 15¢
five dots.

When complete, the array is 5 dots 3 times, for a 3 by 5 array. It contains 15 dots, showing that 3 × 15 = 15 and 15 ÷ 5 = 3. Thus 5¢ measures 15¢ three times.

The Number Line

Many elementary mathematics textbooks use the *number line* to illustrate the meanings of multiplication and division.

Problem: Three children have 5 marbles each. How many marbles do they have all together?

Solution with a number line:

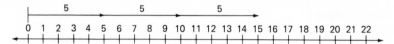

Five, taken 3 times, equals 15.

Problem: You have a wooden rod that is 12 cm long. You want to cut pegs that are 4 cm long. How many pegs will you have?

Solution with a number line:

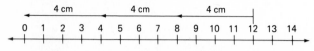

There will be 3 pegs 4 cm long.

Bridging the Gap from Objects to Notation

We recommend that you use the following activities to help children understand the patterns for learning the multiplication and

division facts with factors of 2 through 5.

1. *From counters to multiplication and division facts.* Use counters to show any multiplication example.

(a) For factors 2 and 3 show two arrangements with counters:

(b) Write as equal addends:
   3 + 3 = 6   2 + 2 + 2 = 6

(c) Relate to multiplication facts:
   "Two 3s equal 6."   2 × 3 = 6
   "Three 2s equal 6."   3 × 2 = 6

(d) Relate to division facts:
   "6 broken into 2 parts equals 3 in each part," or "How many 2s are there in 6?"   6 ÷ 2 = 3
   "6 broken into 3 parts equals 2 in each part," or "How many 3s are there in 6?"   6 ÷ 3 = 2

In situations like (a) above, each child should be able to *represent with objects,* draw an array, show on a number line, and *write appropriate number sentences.*

2. *From arrays to multiplication and division facts.* Draw two arrays, such as:

(a) Interpret the array with addends:
   4 + 4 + 4 = 12
   3 + 3 + 3 + 3 = 12

(b) Interpret the array as a multiplication fact:
   3 × 4 = 12   4 × 3 = 12

(c) Generalize: 3 × 4 = 4 × 3 (Illustrates the commutative property for multiplication.)

(d) Stress equal parts or equal numbers of parts.

Separate 12 into 3 parts of 4, or

"How many 3s are there in 12?" $12 \div 3 = 4$

"12 into 4 parts = 3 in each part," or

"How many 4s are there in 12?" $12 \div 4 = 3$

3. *From number lines to multiplication and division facts.* Draw a number line with 3 segments, each 4 cm long:

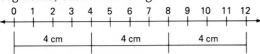

(a) Interpret with addends:
$4 + 4 + 4 = 12$

(b) Write as a multiplication fact:
$3 \times 4 = 12$

(c) State two division problems:
"12 divided into 3 equal parts gives how much in each part?" or
"How many 4s are there in 12?"

(d) Write two division facts:
$12 \div 3 = 4$ $12 \div 4 = 3$

4. Construct a multiplication/division table.

(a) Start with a table such as this, which lists factors from 2 to 5.

x	2	3	4	5
2				
3				
4				
5				

(b) Begin by filling in the "squared" numbers, such as 2^2, 3^2, 4^2, 5^2.

(c) Next fill in the 3×2 cell.

x	2	3	4	5
2	4			
3		9		
4			16	
5				25

(d) Find the 2×3 cell; this will have the same product as 3×2.

(e) Continue for other factors.

x	2	3	4	5
2	4	6	8	
3	6	9		
4	8		16	
5				25

etc.

Notation for Facts

There are two accepted ways of writing facts in multiplication: the vertical form and the equation form:

$$\begin{array}{r} 6 \\ \times\ 3 \\ \hline 18 \end{array} \qquad 3 \times 6 = 18$$

There are three different ways to represent a division fact:

$$3\overline{)18} \qquad 18 \div 3 = 6 \qquad \frac{18}{3} = 6$$

Elementary textbooks seldom use the third way to present the basic facts in division. Repeated use of this notation should help pupils change fractions to decimal notation. (See Chapters 14 and 15.)

An activity that will challenge the faster learners is to rename $18 \div 3$ in various ways, such as:

$$(18 \div 3) \times 1 \qquad 1 \times \frac{18}{3} \qquad (9 + 9) \div 3$$

$$(24 - 6) \div 3$$

Properties for Multiplication and Division of Whole Numbers

In this chapter we are concerned only with one-place whole numbers and their products. In teaching multiplication and division to beginning children, one should not stress mathematical properties. Rather, the emphasis should be on the exploratory-level solution with real objects and drawings.

The activities at the symbolic level enable the pupil to discover *patterns* and *relationships* among the multiplication and division facts. These discoveries should minimize the need for exploratory materials, and enrich the pupils' understanding of the facts so that they can easily be recalled in doing later work.

Exercises 8.1

1. Given a collection of objects represented by an array such as this:

   O O O O O

   O O O O O

   O O O O O

   (a) Write two addition facts with *unequal* addends.
   (b) Write two addition examples with *equal* addends.
   (c) Write two multiplication facts.
   (d) Write two division facts.
   (e) For each division fact:
       (1) Write a word problem illustrating a partitive division situation.
       (2) Write a word problem illustrating a measurement division situation.

2. In solving each of the following word problems, first identify the kind of problem situation (multiplication, partitive division, measurement division), then represent the solution with drawings, and, third, write an equation.
   (a) Jay bought 4 pencils at 8¢ each. How much did he spend on pencils?
   (b) Scott has 35¢ to spend on graph paper. Each sheet costs 5¢ How many sheets can he buy?
   (c) It takes Mary 8 minutes to walk to school each way. How long does it take her to walk to and from school each day?
   (d) Steve walks at the rate of 4 miles per hour. How long does it take him to walk 12 miles?
   (e) Lucy has $10 to spend on her five-day vacation. On the average, how much can she spend each day?
   (f) Mark has saved $25 for airplane models, and he wants to buy 5 models. On the average, how much can he spend on each one?

The Commutative Property

The commutative property for multiplication means that the order of the factors does not affect the product. We have already demonstrated this property by rotating the array 90° and by showing two ways of marking off on the number line. In symbolic-level activities, have the pupils rename a number pair to discover that the order of the factors does not affect the product:

$$2 \times 3 = 3 \times 2$$
$$2 \times 4 = \square \times 2$$
$$2 \times 5 = 5 \times \square$$

Relationship between Equal Addends and Multiplication

Equal addends can be related to multiplication; for example, $3 + 3$ can be renamed as 2×3, and conversely, 3×4 can be renamed with addends as $4 + 4 + 4$. At the symbolic level, pupils can be expected to write a number sentence using both equal addends and factors:

$2 \times 3 = 3 + \square$
$2 \times 5 = \square + \square$
$4 \times 2 = 2 + \square + \square + \square$

$4 + 4 = 2 \times \square$
$3 + 3 + 3 = \square \times \square$
$5 + 5 + 5 + 5 = \square \times 5$

Relationship between Subtraction and Division

At the symbolic level, pupils should be able to discover for themselves the relationship between subtraction and division. Give them examples in which equal numbers are subtracted from a given number and ask them to rename them into division examples:

$6 - 3 = 3; 3 - 3 = 0;$
How many 3s in 6, or $6 \div 3 = 2$
$8 - 4 = 4; 4 - 4 = 0;$
How many 4s in 8, or $8 \div 4 = 2$
$10 - 5 = 5; 5 - 5 = 0;$
How many 5s in 10, or $10 \div 5 = 2$

Relationship between Multiplication and Division

Each multiplication fact that involves two different nonzero factors can be renamed as two division facts; for example, $4 \times 5 = 20$ can be renamed as $20 \div 4 = 5$ and $20 \div 5 = 4$. The pupils should be able to complete these number sentences by writing the correct answers in the frames:

$2 \times 3 = \square$ $\square \div 3 = 2$
$2 \times \square = 8$ $8 \div \square = 2$
$\square \times 5 = 10$ $10 \div \square = 5$

SPECIAL PROPERTY OF ONE AS A FACTOR OR AS DIVISOR

Multiplying by a factor of one is the *identity property for multiplication* because the product of any factor and one equals the given factor $n \times 1 = n$. The earliest that you should introduce *one* as the identity element for multiplication is probably after the children have completely understood and mastered the multiplication facts for factors of 2 through 5.

SPECIAL PROPERTY OF ZERO AS A FACTOR OR DIVISOR

When zero is one of two factors, the product is always *zero*. You can illustrate this concept by using zero as addends, then relating it to multiplication:

$0 + 0 + 0 = 0$ $0 + 0 + 0 + 0 = 0$
$3 \times 0 = 0$ $4 \times 0 = 0$

Applying the commutative property, if $3 \times 0 = 0$, then $0 \times 3 = 0$. *When 0 is a factor, the product is 0. When 0 is a divisor, division is impossible.*

PRODUCTS OF FACTORS 2 THROUGH 9

Pupils should be encouraged to use exploratory materials in multiplying number pairs with products of 25 or less. But for number pairs having products greater than 25, manipulative materials should be used sparingly. Arrays can be helpful with these facts, especially in helping children to understand the distributive property of multiplication over addition.

The Distributive Property

Once pupils have mastered the multiplication facts to products of up to 25, they should learn the facts with products to 81 at the symbolic level by means of patterns and properties, rather than manipulative materials. A good visual approach to learn products greater than 25 is the *array*. For a problem with one factor greater than 5, students should be asked to rename that factor as the sum of two addends as follows:

Problem: Find the product of 5×8 by using the distributive property of multiplication over addition.

Solution with an array: Draw an array such that 8 is renamed as two different addends: 7 + 1, 6 + 2, 5 + 3, 4 + 4. Because the purpose of this activity is to find the product by using two known multiplication facts, the addends of 6 and 7 should not be used. Rename the 8 in the factors 5 × 8 as (5 + 3) so that the number sentence becomes 5 × (5 + 3) = □. The array for this number sentence is:

x x x x x ○ ○ ○
x x x x x ○ ○ ○
x x x x x ○ ○ ○
x x x x x ○ ○ ○
x x x x x ○ ○ ○

Pupils should now be able to see two multiplication facts in the array: the x-array forms a 5 by 5 array for 5 × 5 = 25, and the o-array forms a 5 by 3 array for 5 × 3 = 15. The product is then the sum of the numbers in the two arrays, or 25 + 15 = 40. So 5 × (5 + 3) = (5 × 5) + (5 × 3) = 25 + 15 = 40. Applying the commutative property, when we know that 5 × 8 = 40, we also know that 8 × 5 = 40.

In the same way, pupils can find the product of any pair of one-digit factors by renaming one factor and then applying the distributive property. The *double array* serves as a visual aid to demonstrate how the distributive property works.

The Associative Property of Multiplication

The *associative property of multiplication* is stated in symbolic form as $a \times (b \times c) = (a \times b) \times c$. In other words, in an example with three factors, the number b can be associated first with *either* c or a without changing the product. Sometimes this property is described as regrouping three factors without changing the order. With numbers, the associative property works as follows:

$$3 \times (2 \times 4) = (3 \times 2) \times 4$$
$$3 \times 8 \qquad = \qquad 6 \times 4$$
$$24 \qquad = \qquad 24$$

A useful application of the associative property of multiplication is to make new facts from old ones in the following manner:

1. Start with a two-factor example.
   4 × 6 = □
2. Rename the factor 6 as 2 × 3.
   4 × (2 × 3) = □
3. Associate the 2 with the 4.
   (4 × 2) × 3 = □
4. Multiply (4 × 2) = 8 and substitute.
   8 × 3 = □
5. Generalize that 4 × 6 = 8 × 3 = 24.

Mastering the Facts in Multiplication and Division

After pupils have come to understand the facts in multiplication and division, in problem settings and with patterns, you need to take different approaches so as to help them achieve mastery of these facts. One aspect of mastery is instant recall of number facts. The following activities at the symbolic and mastery levels should strengthen the learner's grasp of the facts and help fixate the learning of them so that pupils attain the mastery level.

1. Construct tables from which a product or factor is missing, and ask the pupil to write the missing numeral. Tables (a), (b), and (c) are short, but can be expanded to include all the facts for a given factor, such as 2 in table (a).

(a)

×	2	3	4
2	4	?	?

(b)

×	3	7	8
2	?	?	?

(c)

×	3	4	?	7	?
2	2 × 3	?	12	?	18

A vertical table, as shown in (d), illustrates the commutative property of multiplication:

(d)

×	2
3	3 × 2
?	8
5	?
6	?
?	18

2. Have pupils complete open sentences to discover the relationships between addition and multiplication and between multiplication and division:

$$3 + 3 = \square \qquad 3 \times 4 = \square$$
$$2 \times 3 = \square \qquad 4 + 4 + \triangle = \square$$
$$15 \div 3 = \square \qquad 21 \div 3 = \square$$
$$3 \times \square = 15 \qquad \square \times 3 = 21$$

Just as the squares and triangles in number sentences hold a plcae for a numeral, a circle is frequently used to hold a place for a sign of operation, such as +, ×, −, or ÷.

To complete each of the following numver sentences, pupils must replace the circle with the sign of operation that will make the sentence true:

$$2 \bigcirc 4 = 8 \qquad 8 \bigcirc 2 = 16$$
$$12 \bigcirc 4 = 3 \qquad 8 \bigcirc 4 = 2$$

3. Have pupils fill in the missing data in each category below. Follow the pattern established in the first row.

4. Write the products or quotients of the number pairs below:

$$\begin{array}{cccc} 5 & 6 & 3 & 9 \\ \times 3 & \times 4 & \times 7 & \times 5 \end{array}$$

$$4\overline{)20} \qquad 3\overline{)24} \qquad 9\overline{)0} \qquad 6\overline{)30}$$

5. Write the other number sentences when one of the related facts is given, as in 3 × 7 = 21:

$$7 \times 3 = 21 \quad 21 \div 3 = 7 \quad 21 \div 7 = 3$$

Array	Set Sentence	Abbreviated Set Sentence	Addition Equation	Multiplication Equation	Number Line
• • • • • •	Two sets of 3 books is a set of □ books	Two 3s are n	3 + 3 = □	2 × 3 = □	0 5 •••••• 3 3
? ?	? ?	Two 5s are n ?	? ?	? 2 × 6 = □	? ?

6. Give a product and have the class write all the basic multiplication facts that have that product. In initial work of this type, the teacher should supply the frames for an equation using a given product, such as 12:

(a) $\triangle \times \square = 12$ (b) $\triangle \times \square = 12$
$\square \times \triangle = 12$ $\square \times \triangle = 12$

The equations in (a) and (b) illustrate the commutative property. Tell the class that different pairs of numbers are used in (a) and (b), and have the class write the corresponding equations in division.

Pupils should learn to distinguish between the equations $\square \times \square = 16$ and $\triangle \times \square = 16$. When both frames are squares, the same number is represented twice; when a square and a triangle are used, the numbers can be the same or different. The equation $4 \times 4 = 16$ can be correct for both $\square \times \square = 16$ and $\triangle \times \square = 16$, but only the equation $2 \times 8 = 16$ is correct for the latter.

7. Give a set of whole numbers, such as 3, 4, 12, and have the class write the four basic facts that use these numbers.

The set may include a variable, such as [3, n, 15]. The equations formed from these numbers are $3 \times n = 15$, $n \times 3 = 15$, $15 \div n = 3$, and $15 \div 3 = n$.

8. Have pupils write in sequence the numerals for the numbers from 1 to 30 for the 3s, from 1 to 40 for the 4s, and so on. Then cross off each third numeral for the 3s and every fourth numeral for the 4s. As they cross off each numeral, the pupils write the number pair for that product. If they cross off 21, the number pair is 3 and 7. They would then write the following four facts derived from this number pair: $3 \times 7 = 21$, $7 \times 3 = 21$, $21 \div 3 = 7$, and $21 \div 7 = 3$.

9. Draw more complex tables than those in item 1, which should be used after a few facts have been introduced. Create and use tables of this type after many facts have been introduced.

Tables (c) and (d) show how pupils can

(c)

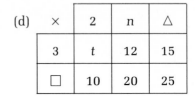

×	2	4
3	$\square$	$\triangle$
5	t	n

$3 \times 2 = \square$ $3 \times 4 = \triangle$
$5 \times 2 = t$ $5 \times 4 = n$

(d)

×	2	n	$\triangle$
3	t	12	15
$\square$	10	20	25

$3 \times 2 = t$ $\square \times 2 = 10$
$3 \times n = 12$ $\square \times n = 20$
$3 \times \triangle = 15$ $\square \times \triangle = 25$

(e)

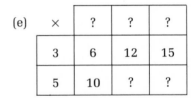

×	?	?	?
3	6	12	15
5	10	?	?

develop number sentences from given data. Table (e) can be used effectively to show the inverse relationship between multiplication and division.

10. Have pupils discover patterns by filling in the blanks with the numbers that belong in a series of this type:

(a) 1, 2, 3, 4, _____, _____, _____.
(b) 2, 4, 6, 8, _____, _____, _____.
(c) 3, 6, 9, 12, _____, _____, _____.
(d) 6, 12, 18, 24, _____, _____, _____.

Pupils do two things with the table. First, they write the three numerals that name the numbers for the blanks. Second, they rename each of the numbers in the series by writing a number pair whose product is equal to the given number. Renaming the numbers in series (a) involves the identity element. The first and fourth numbers in each series can be renamed as follows:

(a) $1 \times 1 = 1$ $4 \times 1 = 4$
(b) $1 \times 2 = 2$ $4 \times 2 = 8$
(c) $1 \times 3 = 3$ $4 \times 3 = 12$
(d) $1 \times 6 = 6$ $4 \times 6 = 24$

Formation of Tables

Table for the Facts in Multiplication and Division

As you introduce sets of facts, have pupils construct a table that includes these facts, for example, the set of facts for the 2s, 3s, and 4s. When you have introduced all the facts in multiplication, each pupil should make a composite table of these facts. Some of these tables can be displayed on the classroom bulletin board. A composite shows the orderly arrangement of a set of factors and products.

Table 8.1 is a composite tabke for all the facts in multiplication and division. The pupil must understand that division by 0 is not permissible. Each number set in bold-face type is a product. The numerals at the beginning of each row and at the top of each column name the factors of the product, which appears in both a column and a row.

There are two unequal factors for each product, except the products named along the diagonal that runs from the upper left-hand corner of the table to the lower right-hand corner. These products are the squares of the numbers from 0 through 9. The square of a number is the product of that number and itself. Each pair of unequal nonzero factors forms a set of four related facts, two in multiplication and two in division.

Interpreting a Composite Table

Each pupil's composite table of multiplication facts should be done on cross-ruled paper so that the products will be in rows and columns. Give the class some time to make discoveries about the table. Have pupils tell about or identify their discoveries. Write a table of the facts on the chalkboard, and have the class answer the following questions:

1. Each succeeding number in a row increases by what amount?

2. Each succeeding number in a column increases by what amount?

3. Any number in a row or column can be found by adding what number to the preceding number?

4. If a number in a row is divided by the factor (not 0) at the beginning of the row, what number will be the quotient?

5. Reverse the procedure in item 4.

6. When one factor is 0, what is the product?

7. When one factor is 1, what is the product?

8. What property does item 7 represent?

Table 8.1 Composite Table of Multiplication and Division Facts

X	0	1	2	3	4	5	6	7	8	9
0	0	0	0	0	0	0	0	0	0	0
1	0	1	2	3	4	5	6	7	8	9
2	0	2	4	6	8	10	12	14	16	18
3	0	3	6	9	12	15	18	21	24	27
4	0	4	8	12	16	20	24	28	32	36
5	0	5	10	15	20	25	30	35	40	45
6	0	6	12	18	24	30	36	42	48	54
7	0	7	14	21	28	35	42	49	56	63
8	0	8	16	24	32	40	48	56	64	72
9	0	9	18	27	36	45	54	63	72	81

9. Use the table to show the commutative property of multiplication.

10. Use the table to show the distributive property in the equation $3 \times 7 = \square$ by renaming 7 as $(2 + 5)$.

11. The numbers along the diagonal that runs from the upper left to lower right are the squares of the numbers from 0 to 9 inclusive. Are the factors of each product equal or unequal?

12. Are the squares even or odd?

13. In which rows or columns are all the products even numbers? Is the number at the head of each of these rows or columns odd or even?

14. In which row or column does an odd product follow an even product? Is the number at the head of each of these rows or columns odd or even?

15. From problems 13 and 14, complete the following:

(a) The product of two even numbers is

_____ .

(b) The product of two odd numbers is

_____ .

(c) The product of an even and an odd number is _____ .

16. Write the squares given along the diagonal. Find the difference between consecutive (next in order) squares. What name is given to the set of numbers of the differences? (The first 9 odd numbers.)

17. What is the sum of the first 3 odd numbers in problem 16? The first 5 odd numbers? The first 8 odd numbers? The first n odd numbers?

18. What is the sum of the numbers in the column headed by 1? by 2? by 3?

19. Write the sum of the numbers in the remaining columns in problem 18 without adding the numbers.

The list of questions about the table can be expanded to include the differences between consecutive products along imaginary lines drawn parallel to the diagonals.

The teacher need not have the class answer all the questions listed. It is important, however, for the pupils to make a table and discuss some of its characteristics. Use the principle of guided discovery to have the class explore the table.

Making a Table from Known Facts

All students in a class should make a table, such as the table of 4s. Certain facts involving the 4s are given. New facts are derived from the known facts. The teacher challenges each pupil to discover as many ways as possible to find a new fact. As each new fact or element in a table is verified, this fact can be used to discover other facts in a table. For example, to make a table of the 4s from known facts, assume that the following facts are known:

$$1 \times 4 = 4$$
$$2 \times 4 = 8$$
.
.
.
$$10 \times 4 = 40$$

The next step is to derive the fact $3 \times 4 = 12$. The class suggests all the possible ways to find the fact by using only the facts assumed to be known and also basic knowledge of multiplication. The class should be able to verify that $3 \times 4 = 12$ with the following discoveries:

"Since 1 four is 4 and 2 fours are 8, add 4 and 8 to find 3 fours." This method applies the distributive property.
"Add 3 fours."
"Add 4 threes."

The next step is to find the fact $4 \times 4 = 16$. The thought pattern may be as follows:

"Add 1 four to the product of 3 fours."
"Add 4 fours."

"Since 2 fours are 8, 4 fours will be twice as much, or 16."

"Since 10 fours are 40, 5 fours will be half as much, or 20. The 4 fours will be 1 less four, or $20 - 4 = 16$."

These answers are typical of those that pupils will give to express the relationships among multiplication facts in a table. The teacher should provide pupils with the opportunities to discover some of these relationships.

Applying the Distributive Property

Tables involving the 2s, 5s, and 10s are the easiest to learn. If pupils know these facts, they can find the facts in other tables by applying the distributive property.

Multiplication facts involving the 3s can be derived from a knowledge of the 2s by renaming 3 as $(2 + 1)$ and applying the distributive property:

$$2 \times (2 + 1) = 4 + 2 = 6$$
$$3 \times (2 + 1) = 6 + 3 = 9$$

The facts involving the 4s can be derived by two procedures. The first is by doubling each fact in the table of the 2s. Thus, $2 \times 2 = 4$; hence 2×4 will be $2 \times (2 \times 2)$, or 8. The second way is to rename 4 as $(5 - 1)$ and apply the distributive property.

The facts involving the 6s can be determined from a knowledge of the 5s. First rename 6 as $(5 + 1)$ and then apply the distributive property. Similarly, the facts involving the 7s can be found by renaming 7 as $(5 + 2)$, and then proceeding as described.

The facts involving the 8s can be found by two procedures, as we done for the 4s. The first double each fact in the table of the 4s. Second, rename 8 as $(10 - 2)$ and apply the distributive property. Finally, the facts involving the 9s can be derived from the 10s by renaming 9 as $(10 - 1)$, and proceeding as described.

The aim of these activities for deriving facts by new procedures is to supplement and deepen pupils' insight into number relationships among the multiplication facts.

Number Patterns

The 9s form some very interesting patterns in multiplication. You should encourage the calss to discover some of the patterns. Extending the table or the few facts given should enable the pupils to make the following two discoveries about the products:

$$9 \times 1 = 9$$
$$9 \times 2 = 18$$
$$9 \times 3 = 27$$

1. The sum of the numbers named by the digits in each product is 9.

2. The ones digit in each succeeding product decreases by 1 and the tens digit increases by 1.

Students can discover the truth of the second statement by renaming 9 as $(10 - 1)$ and applying the distributive property.

Since 9 is one less than the decimal base of our number system, and 11 one more than the base, these facts can be used to form a pattern for the tables of the 9s and 11s.

$$1 \times 9 = 10 - 1 \qquad 1 \times 11 = 10 + 1$$
$$2 \times 9 = 20 - 2 \qquad 2 \times 11 = 20 + 2$$
$$3 \times 9 = 30 - 3 \qquad 3 \times 11 = 30 + 3$$

An intriguing application of the 9s in multiplication enables us to find the difference between a two-place number and the number with the digits reversed:

$$\begin{array}{r} 21 \\ -12 \\ \hline 9 \end{array} \qquad\qquad \begin{array}{r} 31 \\ -13 \\ \hline 18 \end{array}$$

$$2 - 1 = \triangle \qquad 3 - 1 = \triangle$$
$$\triangle \times 9 = \square \qquad \triangle \times 9 = \square$$

After a few illustrations, the pupils should discover the pattern for finding the difference between any two-place number and the number with the digits reversed. Fast learners should be able to arrive at the generalization. Generalizing with regard to a pattern is much more difficult than discovering the pattern.

Changing Sequence of Factors

In a table of the multiplication facts, such as the 6s, one factor is 6 and the other factor consists of the 10 digits in order. An interesting pattern is formed by changing the sequence of the factors as shown in (a) and (b):

(a) $6 \times 6 = 36$ (b) $6 \times 5 = 30$
      $7 \times 5 = 35$ $7 \times 4 = 28$
      $8 \times 4 = 32$ $8 \times 3 = 24$
        .   .
        .   .
        .   .
   $11 \times 1 = 11$ $11 \times 0 = 0$

Supply the class with a few facts for a table, and ask the pupils to discover the pattern and supply the missing numerals. In the examples given, the pupils should be able to discover the pattern for writing missing numerals from the sequence of either the factors or the products. In (a) the difference of the products is the series of odd numbers; in (b) the difference is the series of even numbers.

Division with Remainders

Unfortunately, not all numbers of things can be regrouped into parts of equal number. For example, 16 cannot be distributed into groups of 5 without having one left over. After they have had a great deal of experience with problems having no remainders, children at the exploratory level should be given some problem situations that have remainders. The following problems and so-

lutions illustrate the ways to help children understand division with remainders.

Problem: How many teams of 5 girls each can be formed from 12 girls?

1. Use girls—have 12 girls line up, and have the girls get into groups of 5. Clearly, there are 2 groups and 2 girls left unassigned.

2. Make a drawing to show the formation of teams:

3. Write a number sentence:
   $12 \div 5 = 2 \text{ r } 2$.

4. State the solution, "From 12 girls, there can be 2 teams of 5 girls, with 2 girls remaining."

Problem: John's father wants to give each of his three children a weekly allowance of exactly $5. If he has 16 one-dollar bills, how much will each child get?

1. Lay out the 16 one-dollar bills, paper money, or markers.

2. Go through a "sharing process" and distribute the dollar bills to the three children. Remove $3 and give $1 to each child. Repeat this five times.

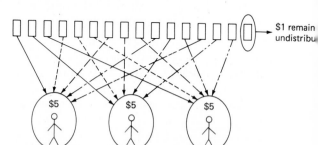

3. Show that after the sharing process, each child will have 5 one-dollar bills, with one bill left over.

4. Use the drawing in step 2 to write the number sentence
   $16 \div 3 = 5$, remainder 1. (5 r 1)

PRACTICING DIVISION WITH REMAINDERS
GREATER THAN ZERO

There is no whole number that will make the equations $3 \times \square = 7$ or $7 \div 3 = \square$ true. Although 7 is not a multiple of 3, division can be used to find the number that will make the sentence $7 \div 3 = \square$ true. When 7 is divided by 3, there is a remainder greater than zero.

At the symbolic level, there are three different procedures for finding a one-place quotient of a nonmultiple of a one-place divisor:

1. Number sequences

2. Open sentences

3. The division algorism

1. Pupils write the numbers in sequence up to 10 times the divisor, circling the multiples of the divisor 3 as shown:

$$0 \quad 1 \quad 2 \quad ③ \quad 4 \quad 5 \quad ⑥ \quad 7 \quad 8 \quad ⑨$$
$$10 \quad 11 \quad ⑫ \quad 13 \quad 14 \quad ⑮ \quad 16 \quad 17 \quad ⑱ \quad 19$$
$$20 \quad ㉑ \quad 22 \quad 23 \quad ㉔ \quad 25 \quad 26 \quad ㉗ \quad 28 \quad 29$$

Then they use both multiplication and division to express the nonmultiples of three in a number sequence. For example, the different ways to write the number pair $13 \div 3$ are:

$$13 = (3 \times 4) + 1 \qquad 13 \div 3 = 4 \, r \, 1$$

The two number sentences show the relationship between multiplication and division. The r in 4 r 1 stands for "remainder." An effective teaching technique is to have each pupil write a few number sentences that have been derived from sequences on a number line.

2. Have the class solve open sentences of the following type:

$$16 = 3 \times \square + 1 \qquad \square \div 6 = 3 \, r \, 4$$
$$21 \div 4 = \square \, r \, 1 \qquad 14 = \square \times 5 + 4$$
$$\square \div 3 = 4 \, r \, 2 \qquad 23 \div 3 = \square \, r \, 2$$
$$27 = 4 \times 6 + \square \qquad \square \div 5 = 2 \, r \, 4$$
$$15 \div 6 = 2 \, r \, \square \qquad 20 = 3 \times \square + 2$$

3. Have the class use the division algorism as shown in example (a).

$$\text{(a)} \quad 3 \overline{)17} \quad {}^{5 \, r \, 2}$$
$$\underline{15}$$
$$2$$

Have pupils who are unable to give the quotient and the remainder in the manner illustrated express the dividend as the sum of two addends and then apply the distributive property of division. For example, a pupil who does not know the largest multiple of 6 in 52 may rename 52 as $36 + 16$ or $30 + 22$. One of the addends should be a multiple of 6. The example can now be written as:

$$52 \div 6 = (36 + 16) \div 6$$
$$= (36 \div 6) + (16 \div 6)$$

The quotient of $36 \div 6$ is 6. Since 16 is not a multiple of 6, and 12 is the largest multiple of 6 that is less than 16, $16 \div 6 = (12 \div 6)$, with a remainder of 4. Therefore, $52 \div 6 = (36 + 12) \div 6$, with a remainder of 4. The quotient is 8, with a remainder of 4. The same answer can be found by using division, as shown in example (b). The pupil did not recall the largest multiple of 6 that is less than 52, but he knew that $6 \times 6 = 36$.

$$\text{(b)} \quad 6 \overline{)52}$$
$$\underline{36} \quad 6$$
$$16$$
$$\underline{12} \quad 2$$
$$4 \quad 8$$

$$52 = 6 \times 8 + 4$$

The pupil indicated this fact as shown in the first step. After the subtraction, there is a remainder of 16, which is divided as shown in the second step. The quotient is $6 + 2$, or 8, with a remainder of 4. The same answer can be found by repeated subtraction of 6 from 52. The short forms in (c) and (d) for (17, 3), q = 5 and r = 2, so that:

(c) $17 = 5 \times 3 + 2$, or $3\overline{)17}^{\,5\,r\,2}$

For (3, 17), q = 0 and r = 3, so that:

(d) $3 = 0 \times 17 + 3$, or $17\overline{)3}^{\,0\,r\,3}$

If the remainder is greater than the divisor, the division is not complete. It is true that $17 = 4 \times 3 + 5$, but 4 is not considered to be the quotient, since 5 is not less than the divisor 3.

EXPRESSING THE REMAINDER IN DIVISION

When division is performed on a number that is not a multiple of the divisor, the remainder will be greater than 0. The way to express that remainder depends on the kind of numbers on which the operation is performed and on the division situation. For whole numbers, the quotient can be expressed only as a whole number with a remainder. For rational numbers, the quotient can be expressed in fractional form, as shown here for $8 \div 3$:

$$\frac{8}{3} = \frac{6 + 2}{3} = \frac{6}{3} + \frac{2}{3} = 2 + \frac{2}{3}, \text{ or } 2\frac{2}{3}.$$

THE REMAINDER IN PROBLEM SITUATIONS

In division there are two situations that require different representations of the remainder. In one the remainder is expressed as part of the quotient, with the quotient expressed as a fractional number. An illustration of this situation is the following problem.

A piece of wire 9 feet long is cut into 4 pieces of equal length. What is the length of each piece?

The length of each piece is 2¼ feet. It makes no sense to give this answer as 2 with remainder 1. With rational numbers, it is possible to divide 9 by 4 and express the quotient as 2¼; with whole numbers this problem cannot be solved. The need to solve problems of this kind prompted the expansion of the number system to include rational numbers.

The other division situation requires that the remainder be expressed as a remainder and not as part of the quotient. This condition prevails in the set of whole numbers. An illustration of this situation is the following problem.

How many groups of 4 children can be formed from 9 children?

The answer is 2 with a remainder of 1. A quotient of 2¼ is meaningless in this situation.

The way to express quotients in division situations involving nonmultiples of the divisor depends on the situation. The pupils must be able to interpret the answer. The structure of the number system is such that the division process can be applied to any two whole numbers (divisor not 0). The quotient of $a \div b$ is q, with a remainder $r(r < b)$. If a is a multiple of b, r is 0.

MATHEMATICAL ANSWERS NOT ALWAYS APPLICABLE

Interpreting a remainder in division relies on social usage and the good judgment of the teacher. This is shown by the following two problems:

1. A grocer sells 3 oranges for 50¢. Find the cost of 1 orange.

2. If 91 pupils are to be transported and a bus will only hold 45 pupils, how many buses will be needed?

The mathematical answer to problem 1 is 16⅔¢. Since fractional parts of a cent do not exist, the cost of one orange is 17¢. In many stores the cost may be 20¢.

The conventional answer to problem 2 is 2 buses and 1 child remaining. In a real situation one child would not be left out of the group. Some means of transportation would be provided for that child. Realistically, the correct answer would be 2 buses, and not the mathematical answer that would be given in a textbook.

Verbal Problems Involving Multiplication and Division

Readiness

Most of the beginning work with verbal problems involving the facts in multiplication and division is at the exploratory level. This work should give the pupils a solid background for solving problems at the symbolic level.

Symbolic Level

Pupils at the symbolic level solve verbal problems by following a specific pattern. In sequence, the pattern consists of stating the number sentence, which is written as an equation, solving the equation, checking the computation for accuracy, and interpreting the answer.

Problem: A page of Nell's stamp album contains 4 rows of 5 stamps each. There are how many stamps on the page?

1. *State* the number sentence: Four rows of 5 stamps equals how many stamps?

2. *Write* an equation for the number sentence: $4 \times 5 = \square$.

3. *Solve* and *check*: $4 \times 5 = 20$; $5 + 5 + 5 + 5 = 20$; $5 \times 4 = 20$; $5 (2 + 2) = 10 + 10 = 20$.

4. *Interpret:* The page contains 20 stamps.

Problem: How many teams of 3 pupils can be formed from 15 pupils?

1. *State* the number sentence: How many groups of 3 pupils are there in 15 pupils?

2. *Write* an equation: 3s in 15; $15 \div 3 = \square$; $\square \times 3 = 15$; $3 n = 15$.

3. *Solve* and *check*: $15 \div 3 = \boxed{5}$; because $\boxed{5} \times 3 = 15$, $3 \times 5 = 15$ and $15 \div 5 = 3$.

4. *Interpret:* There are 5 teams.

Problem: If Dorothy puts 2 doughnuts in a package, how many packages can she make with 12 doughnuts?

1. *State* the number sentence: How many 2s are there in 12?

2. *Write* an equation: $12 \div 2 = \square$; $\square \times 2 = 12$; or $2 n = 12$.

3. *Solve* and *check*: $12 \div 2 = 6$, because $\boxed{6} \times 2 = 12$; $2 \times 6 = 12$; $12 \div 6 = 2$.

4. *Interpret:* Dorothy can make 6 packages.

Problem: You ride your bike at the average rate of 8 km per hour. How many hours will it take you to go 24 km?
Solution with a number line: The line segments between consecutive points will represent 1 km as a scale drawing.

1. Draw a number line showing 24 km.

2. Starting at zero, mark off segments 8 km long until 24 is reached.

3. Each 8 km represents 1 hour of time. Because there are three 8 km in 24 km, it will take 3 hours.

Some textbooks show *division* on the number line from right to left to emphasize the subtractions involved.

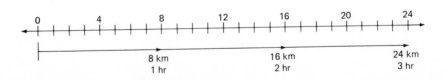

Problem: If each rubber ball costs $3, how many can you buy for $15?
Solution with a number line:

1. Draw a number line of 15 spaces to represent $15.

2. Starting at 15, mark off line segments by moving to the left 3 units at a time, with each move representing $3.

3. Make a record of the process, step by step.

These illustrations show that more than one equation can be written for a given problem. If a pupil writes an equation using multiplication, have him or her write the equation using the inverse operation.

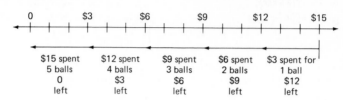

Summary

Once the pupils clearly understand the operations of addition and subtraction of whole numbers, the study of multiplication and division facts follows naturally. Pupils who understand addition as the operation that describes the combining of two groups of objects are ready to explore the process of combining two or more parts equal in number. This process can be described as either addition, as in $7 + 7 = 14$, or multiplication, $2 \times 7 = 14$. Likewise, pupils who are proficient at separating a collection into two parts and can describe this process as subtraction are ready to separate a group of objects into two or more parts equal in number and describe this process with division.

Pupils should be introduced to multiplication and division facts in problem situations. Experiences with manipulative materials serve to help pupils understand the meaning of these operations. Pupils should then learn to show multiplication and division facts with drawings and later with symbolic notations. The use of notations should flow from exploratory experiences with objects and drawings. Careful attention must be paid to bridging the gap from working with objects to solving problems at the symbolic level of thinking.

Pupils at the symbolic level are ready to study the properties of multiplication and division. The teacher must strive to help pupils discover the meanings of each property in terms of patterns and relationships. The relationship between multiplication and division can be stressed at the symbolic level of learning.

Mastery of the facts in multiplication and division requires (a) an ability to respond to each fact quickly and accurately, without using supplementary aids, (b) an understanding of the meaning of each operation and ability to show facts with drawings and with objects, and (c) an ability to solve word problems and verify the correctness of the solutions.

Exercises 8.2

The first six problems in this exercise use the facts in multiplication or division. Give the thought pattern you would use in teaching these problems to a class at the third-grade level:

1. If each team contains 5 players, how many players would there be on 4 teams?

2. There are 3 feet in a yard. What is the length in feet of a string 8 yards long?

3. One day, Jim rode his bicycle 18 km. He rode at an average rate of 6 km per hour. How many hours did he ride that day?

4. How many packages of 5 cookies each can be made with 35 cookies?

5. There are 8 trees in a row. How many trees are there in 5 rows?

6. How many 8¢ stamps can you buy with 48¢?

7. What properties of multiplication are common to addition?

8. Show how finding this product illustrates the distributive property:

$$\begin{array}{r} 32 \\ \times\ 3 \\ \hline \end{array}$$

9. Show why it is impossible to divide by 0.

10. Give four ways a pupil can discover the product of 3 × 8, or verify the product if he or she knows the 3s through the 5s.

11. Identify each of the following problems as either a *partitive* or a *measurement* situation:
    (a) How many yards are there in 15 feet?
    (b) How many quarts are there in 6 pints?
    (c) At 15 miles per gallon, how many gallons of gasoline are needed to travel 60 miles?
    (d) A car used 4 gallons of gasoline on a 60-mile trip. What was the average mileage per gallon?
    (e) There are 40 tulip bulbs in 5 rows of equal length. How many bulbs are there in a row?

12. Some pupils use the algorism shown in (a) to find the quotient of the example 53 ÷ 8. Other pupils use the one shown in (b). Evaluate these procedures

    (a) 53 ÷ 8 = 6 r 5   (b) $\begin{array}{r} 8)\overline{53} \\ \underline{40}\,\Big|\ 5 \\ 13 \\ \underline{\ 8}\,\Big|\ 1 \\ \overline{\ 5\ \ \ 6} \end{array}$

13. A teacher writes the following number sentences on the chalkboard and asks the class to fill in the table. One pupil asks why the numbers behave as they do. Give a satisfactory answer to this question.

    1 × 9 + 1 = 10
    2 × 9 + 2 = 20
    10 × 9 + △ = □

14. Write the set of tables for the 2s, 4s, and 8s. Identify at least three distinguishing featuers of the products or of the sequence of the digits in the products.

15. List the ways to show that multiplication and division are opposites.

16. State two word problems that fit each of the following:

(a) $n \div 4 = 5$ (b) $n \times 6 = 30$ (c) $\dfrac{16}{n} = 3 \; r \; 1$

Selected Readings

Adams, Sam, Leslie C. Ellis, and B. F. Beeson. *Teaching Mathematics with Emphasis on the Diagnostic Approach.* New York: Harper & Row, 1977, Chapter 9, pp. 87–107.

Heimer, Ralph T., and Cecil R. Trueblood. *Strategies for Teaching Young Children Mathematics.* Reading, MA: Addison-Wesley, 1977, Chapter 6, pp. 146–171.

Hlavaty, Julius H. (Ed.). *Mathematics for Elementary School Teachers.* Reston, VA: National Council of Teachers of Mathematics, 1966, Chapter 4, pp. 46–66.

Marks, John L., C. Richard Purdy, Lucien B. Kinney, and Arthur A. Hiatt. *Teaching Elementary School Mathematics for Understanding.* New York: McGraw-Hill, 1975, Chapter 5, pp. 103–132.

Reisman, Fredricka K. *Teaching Mathematics: Methods and Content,* Second Edition. Boston: Houghton Mifflin, 1981, Chapter 8, pp. 206–235.

Chapter 9

The Algorisms for Multiplication and Division

In Chapter 8, we described general methods enabling pupils to learn basic facts and associated concepts in multiplication and division. Pupils must master these facts if they are to perform and understand the algorisms for these operations.

Achievement Goals

After studying this chapter, you should be able to:

1. Understand the levels of difficulty for learning the multiplication algorism.
2. Understand the levels of difficulty for learning the division algorism.
3. Deal with individual differences by reinforcing learning at the exploratory, symbolic, and mastery levels.
4. Understand the procedures for checking algorisms.
5. Teach pupils how to use the basic number properties in learning the algorisms.
6. Know procedures and concepts that are useful in teaching problem solving.

Vocabulary

Mastery of the following key terms will help you to understand this chapter. Each term is defined or illustrated in the Glossary at the end of the book.

Adding by endings	Multiplier
Bridging a decade	Partial dividend
Composite number	Power of 10
Dividend	Product
Divisor	Quotient
Factor	Regroup
Multiple	Remainder
Multiplicand	Rename

Number of Digits

Those who advocate the use of calculators in the elementary schools also suggest limiting the number of digits in multipliers and divisors. Wheatley,[1] for example, would limit these to one-place numbers. The Na-

1. Grayson H. Wheatley, "Calculators in the Classroom: A Program for Curricular Change," *Arithmetic Teacher*, December 1980, 28:37–39.

tional Council of Teachers of Mathematics[2] recommends that divisors and most multipliers be limited to two-place numbers.

We agree with the National Council. The multiplicand, or the number multiplied, can contain three digits, but the multiplier should have no more than two digits, unless one of the digits is zero, in which case three-place numbers are acceptable. The dividend, or number divided, should not exceed four digits, but the divisor should be no larger than 100.

More important than the number of digits to be used, however, is that the students learn and understand the algorisms so that they can be applied in problem-solving situations. It is almost useless to learn these procedures without understanding them.

One-Digit Multipliers and Divisors without Regrouping

Example (a) illustrates multiplication by a one-digit number without regrouping. Example (b) is a corresponding example in division.

(a) $\begin{array}{r} 23 \\ \times\ 3 \\ \hline 69 \end{array}$ (b) $\begin{array}{r} 23 \\ 3\overline{)69} \end{array}$

Note that the apparent multiplication of 3×2 in (a) is actually 3×20 and the apparent division of $6 \div 3$ in (b) is actually $60 \div 3$.

2. *An Agenda for Action: Recommendations for School Mathematics for the 1980s* (Reston, VA: National Council of Teachers of Mathematics, 1980), p. 29.

Exploratory Level

The following exploratory activities provide readiness for later learning:

1. Counting by tens.

2. A double number line, such as that in Figure 9.1, to demonstrate 1×10, 2×10, 3×10, and so on.

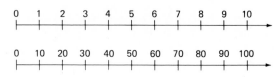

Figure 9.1

3. Consider the problem: How many cookies in 3 dozen?

    a. Use an abacus to find $12 + 12 + 12$.

    b. Use a number line to find 3×12. (See Figure 9.2 below).

4. Supplement or replace the previous activities with a pocket chart, base-ten blocks, or similar manipulatives.

Symbolic Level

1. Make tables showing multiplication by 10 as follows:

$10 \times 0 = 0$ $0 \times 10 = 0$
$10 \times 1 = 10$ $1 \times 10 = 10$
$10 \times 2 = 20$ $2 \times 10 = 20$
....

2. Ask pupils to create verbal problems that can be solved by the computation in example 1, such as How many cents are there in zero dimes? in 1 dime? in 2 dimes?

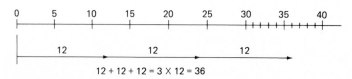

Figure 9.2

3. Construct a table showing multiplication by 100 as follows:

$100 \times 0 = 0$ $0 \times 100 = 0$
$100 \times 1 = 100$ $1 \times 100 = 100$
$100 \times 2 = 200$ $2 \times 100 = 200$

....

4. Rename multiples of 10 and 100 as follows:

$30 = \Box \times 10$ $300 = \Box \times 100$
$50 = \Box \times 10$ $500 = \Box \times 100$

5. Find the product of multiples of 10 and 100 with one-digit numbers, as follows:

$2 \times (3 \text{ tens}) = \Box \times \text{ten} = 60$
$3 \times (4 \text{ hundreds}) = 12 \times \text{one hundred} = \Box$
$2 \times 30 = 2 \times (3 \times 10) = (2 \times 3) \times 10 = \Box \times 10 = \triangle$
$3 \times 400 = 3 \times (4 \times 100) = 12 \times \Box = \triangle$

6. Mastery level for problem 5:

$2 \times (3 \text{ tens}) = \Box \text{ tens} = \triangle$
$3 \times (4 \text{ hundreds}) = \Box \text{ hundreds} = \triangle$
$2 \times 30 = \Box$
$3 \times 400 = \Box$

7. Rename, stressing place value:

$45 = 4 \times 10 + \Box = 40 + 5$
$37 = \Box \times 10 + 7 = 30 + 7$
$54 = \Box \times 10 + \triangle$
$234 = 2 \times \Box + 3 \times \triangle + 4$

Renaming $2 \times (3 \times 10)$ as $(2 \times 3) \times 10$ illustrates the associative property for multiplication, the property by which three factors are regrouped without changing the order of the factors. The associative property is involved in every multiplication of a single-digit number and a multiple of 10 or 100. The distributive property is also involved in some multiplications by a single-digit number that do not require regrouping, as in 2×34:

$2 \times 34 = 2 \times (30 + 4) = 2 \times 30 + 2 \times \Box = 68$

The general statement of the distributive property is:

$A \times (B + C) = A \times B + A \times C$

Pupils should recognize these properties as nonverbal patterns but should not be required to name the properties. Teachers should refer to the properties by name to help pupils gradually become familiar with the correct names.

After pupils have done sufficient work with the horizontal form, the vertical form can be introduced:

$$
\begin{array}{cc}
& 23 \\
\text{(c)} & \underline{\times\ 2} \\
& 6 \\
& \underline{40} \\
& 46
\end{array}
\qquad
\begin{array}{cc}
& 23 \\
\text{(d)} & \underline{\times\ 2} \\
& 46
\end{array}
$$

Example (c) presents a useful supplemental form, and example (d) illustrates the mastery level. Teachers must determine from their experience with each class how much time to spend on readiness and exploratory work. If too much time is spent on these activities, students can become bored; if coverage is brief, there can be a lack of understanding by students, who may then resort to rote learning. The 1978 Yearbook of the National Council offers additional ideas on the teaching of multiplication of whole numbers.[3]

Dividing by a One-Digit Number without Regrouping

Exploratory Level

1. Ask pupils how many 2s there are in 6. Use any six objects and remove objects in pairs. Have pupils complete the following sentence:

$6 \div 2 = \Box$

3. *Developing Computational Skills* (Reston, VA: National Council of Teachers of Mathematics, 1978), Chapter 7.

2. Ask pupils how many 2s there are in 2. Have them complete the sentence 2 ÷ 2 = □.

3. Ask the class how many 2s there are in 20. Remove pairs of objects from a set of 20 objects; have pupils complete the sentence 20 ÷ 2 = □.

4. Use the number line to show that 20 ÷ 2 = 10.

5. Have pupils write the answers to examples 4 and 5 in standard form:

$$\begin{array}{r} 10 \\ 2\overline{)20} \end{array}$$

6. Remove pairs of objects from a set of 8 objects to demonstrate 8 ÷ 2 = 4. Recombine the 4 pairs of 2 and record the result, 4 × 2 = 8. This activity should help reinforce the pupils' understanding of the relationship between multiplication and division and help to provide readiness for the "missing factor" definition of division.

Symbolic Level

From working with basic facts and exploratory work, pupils should be able to recognize that the statement 2 ÷ 2 = 1 implies that 20 ÷ 2 = 10, and that 6 ÷ 2 = 3 implies that 60 ÷ 2 = 30. Knowing that 2 × 34 = 2 × 30 + 2 × 4 should also help pupils to see that 68 ÷ 2 = 60 ÷ 2 + 8 ÷ 2. The notation in (e) emphasizes place value.

(e) $\begin{array}{r} 30 + 4 \\ 2\overline{)60 + 8} \end{array}$

The following notation is also helpful:

$$2\overline{)68} = \frac{60 + 8}{2} = \frac{60}{2} + \frac{8}{2} = 30 + 4 = 34$$

Example (f) shows the conventional algorism for division in examples of this type, but is not to be used until pupils understand place value.

(f) $\begin{array}{r} 34 \\ 2\overline{)68} \end{array}$

The pupil expresses the product 3 × 23 as shown in (g) and the division 3$\overline{)69}$ as shown in (h) and (i).

(g) $\begin{aligned} 3 \times 23 &= 3 \times 20 + 3 \times 3 \\ &= 60 + 9 \\ &= 69 \end{aligned}$

(h) $\begin{array}{r} 20 + 3 = 23 \\ 3\overline{)60 + 9} \end{array}$

(i) $3\overline{)69} = \dfrac{60 + 9}{3} = 20 + 3 = 23$

Multiplying by a One-Digit Number with Regrouping

Exploratory Level

The multiplication of a one-digit number by a two-digit number should be introduced to most pupils at the symbolic level. Pupils with inadequate background may benefit from performing multiplications such as 2 × 14 or 2 × 23 on the abacus, with base-ten blocks or pocket chart, or on a number line. The numbers used in exploratory work must be small enough so that the manipulatives are not unwieldy.

Symbolic Level

The student must do new work at the symbolic level when the first partial product overloads the ones place. For example, in 3 × 24, the 12 obtained from 3 × 4 overloads the ones place and must be regrouped as 1 ten and 2 ones. The same type of activities can be used as when no regrouping is involved. The sequence of steps to find the product of 3 × 24 is as follows:

1. Express 24 as 20 + 4 and multiply as shown in (a).

(a) $\begin{aligned} 3 \times 24 &= 3 \times (20 + 4) \\ &= 3 \times 20 + 3 \times 4 \\ &= 3 \times 20 + 12 = 72 \end{aligned}$

2. Use repeated addition, as shown in (b). Use only small multipliers for this type of activity.

(b) $3 \times 24 = 24 + 24 + 24 = 72$

$$
\begin{array}{r}
24 \\
24 \\
+\,24 \\
\hline
72
\end{array}
$$

3. Perform the multiplication in vertical form as in (c), (d), and (e).

(c)
$$
\begin{array}{r}
20 + \;4 \\
\times\;\;\; 3 \\
\hline
60 + 12 = 72
\end{array}
$$

(d)
$$
\begin{array}{l}
3 \times 20 = 60 \\
3 \times \;\;4 = 12 \\
\hline
3 \times 24 = 72
\end{array}
$$

(e)
$$
\begin{array}{r}
24 \\
\times 3 \\
\hline
12 \\
60 \\
\hline
72
\end{array}
$$

4. Examples (f) and (g) represent the mastery level.

(f)
$$
\begin{array}{r}
24 \\
\times 3 \\
\hline
72
\end{array}
$$

(g) $3 \times 24 = 72$

Adding by Endings in Multiplication

In Chapter 6, we showed how students can be taught to use adding by endings in column addition. Adding by endings is the process of adding a two-place number and a one-place number in one mental response. This form of addition is also found in multiplication, when a one-place number is added to a two-place product. The examples

$11 + 5 \qquad 19 + 6 \qquad 25 + 7 \qquad 30 + 8$

all involve addition but none would occur in multiplication. In the first two, the two-place numbers are not products; in the other two, the two-place numbers are products but multiplication is not involved in the addition of 7 to 25 and 8 to 30. Have the

class find the largest regrouped number to be added to a product by working the following examples.

$$
\begin{array}{cccc}
\begin{array}{r} 99 \\ \times 2 \\ \hline 198 \end{array} &
\begin{array}{r} 99 \\ \times 5 \\ \hline 495 \end{array} &
\begin{array}{r} 99 \\ \times 6 \\ \hline 594 \end{array} &
\begin{array}{r} 99 \\ \times 8 \\ \hline 792 \end{array}
\end{array}
$$

The class should discover that the largest regrouped number to add to a product is one less than the multiplier. Therefore, in multiplication by 7, the numbers 1 through 6 can be added to the multiples of 7, beginning with 14 and ending with 63.

Some examples in adding by endings involve bridging the decade, as in $36 + 7$. Bridging the decade occurs when the sum is in the next higher decade than the product. Bridging occurs almost exclusively in multiplication by 6, 7, 8, and 9. Generally, pupils find it more difficult to work problems with bridging than to work problems with the sum in the same decade as the product.

Teaching Adding by Endings in Multiplication

Several different procedures can be followed to teach pupils to add by endings in multiplication. One plan is to hand out practice sheets containing examples written horizontally and have the pupils write the sums. Remember to have the two-place number be the product and the one-place number not exceed one less than the largest one-place factor of the product. Here are some typical practice examples.

$16 + 4 \qquad 15 + 3 \qquad 24 + 6 \qquad 36 + 7$

How many of the above examples involve bridging the decade? To make sure that the pupils find the sum in one mental step, dictate the examples and have the pupils write the sums.

In example (a) the pupil would write the regrouped number as shown. When you introduce the topic, let pupils follow this procedure. Encourage pupils to solve the example without writing the regrouped numbers as soon as possible.

(a) 45
    579
    ×6
    ————
    3474

Example (b) shows the procedure for students who find it difficult to work with unseen numerals. Since each partial product is written, students are not required to add by endings.

(b) 579
    ×6
    ————
    54
    420
    3000
    ————
    3474

Pupils who can write the product as shown in (c) operate at the mastery level. They are able to complete the solution without using visual aids and demonstrate competence in multiplying by a one-place number.

(c) 579
    ×6
    ————
    3474

Enrichment with One-Place Factors

An effective program for teaching the basic operations in arithmetic has two characteristics. First, there is a minimally acceptable level of achievement for all pupils. Second, the program has room for superior pupils to master the operations and develop a level of insight into a meaning of the operations that most of the class will not attain. These pupils should discover unconventional ways to multiply a two-place factor by a one-place factor. For example:

1. To multiply by the composite number 6, multiply by 2 and then multiply by 3. A composite number has factors other than itself and 1.

$$6 \times 15 = 3 \times (2 \times 15) = 3 \times 30 = 90$$

2. To multiply by 9, rename 9 as $10 - 1$. Use distributive property.

$$67 \times 9 = 67 \times (10 - 1)$$
$$= 670 - 67 = 603$$

The pupil annexes 0 to 67 and then subtracts 67 from 670.

3. To multiply 7×48, rename 48 as $40 + 8$ or as $50 - 2$ and use the distributive property.

$$7 \times 48 = 7 \times (40 + 8)$$
$$= 280 + 56 = 336$$
$$= 7 \times (50 - 2)$$
$$= 350 - 14 = 336$$

4. To multiply 6×35, multiply the factor of 2 in 6 by the factor of 5 in 35.

$$6 \times 35 = (2 \times 3) \times (7 \times 5)$$
$$= (2 \times 5) \times (3 \times 7)$$
$$= 10 \times 21 = 210$$

5. To multiply 25×84, rename 84 as 4×21.

$$25 \times 84 = 25 \times (4 \times 21)$$
$$= 100 \times 21 = 2100$$

6. Multiplying a number by 4 and then dividing by 4 does not change the number. Thus, $25 \times n$, multiplied by 4, gives $100n$, which, divided by 4, gives $100 \times \frac{n}{4}$. This fact enables one to perform the multiplication in example 5 more efficiently: $25 \times 84 = 100 \times \frac{84}{4} = 2100$.

Dividing by a One-Digit Number with Regrouping

The solution of the example $3\overline{)72}$ involves regrouping. To solve this example, a pupil must:

1. Identify 6 as the largest multiple of 3 in 7.

2. Subtract 6 from 7 to get 1 and rename the 1 ten as 10 ones.

In general, pupils must be able to:

1. Select the largest multiple of the divisor in each partial dividend.

2. Subtract the largest multiple found in step 1 from the partial dividend and express this difference in terms of the place value of the digit one place to the right of the partial dividend. In the example 3)73, the partial dividend is 7 and the difference 7 − 6 = 1 is expressed as 10 ones—that is, in terms of the place value of the digit one place to the right of 7. Pupils must rely on their knowledge of multiplication facts to find the largest multiple of the divisor in the partial dividend. The pupil recognizes the largest multiple by knowing that the difference between it and the partial dividend is less than the divisor. In solving 3)252, the pupil notes that 25 − 21 is greater than 3, indicating that 21 is not the largest multiple of 3 in 25.

The Algorism for a One-Place Divisor

(a) $\begin{array}{r} 32 \\ 3\overline{)96} \end{array}$ (b) $\begin{array}{r} 93 \\ 4\overline{)372} \\ \underline{36} \\ 12 \\ \underline{12} \end{array}$

Example (a) shows the procedure for dividing by a one-place divisor when regrouping

is not involved. Each digit represents a number divisible by the divisor. Examples of this type are infrequent in everyday affairs.

Example (b) shows the procedure for dividing by a one-place divisor. Since each partial dividend is visible, the pupil need not find a quotient figure for an unseen number.

Teaching Division Involving Regrouping

To introduce division by a one-place number with regrouping, problems of the following type are useful:

A class of 72 pupils is to be separated into three groups of equal size. How many pupils will be in each group?

EXPLORATORY LEVEL

Have pupils use rectangular strips and squares to represent 72 and separate them into three equal groups, as shown in Figure 9.3. Each pupil places one strip in each of three groups and repeats the process, obtaining three groups of two strips with one strip left over. The remaining strip is exchanged for 10 squares, for a total of 12 squares. The pupils separate the 12 squares into three groups of four squares by placing one square at a time in each of the three groups. Each group now contains two strips (of 10 squares each) and four squares. Therefore, the quotient of 72 divided by 3 is 24.

When they are available, other types of manipulatives such as the pocket chart,

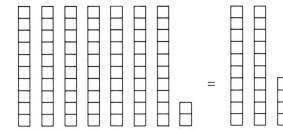

Figure 9.3

base-ten blocks, and the abacus, are equally useful. Regardless of what type of manipulative is used, the key step is changing 1 ten into 10 ones.

If the problem is reworded to require separating 72 cents into three equal groups, students can solve it by using dimes and pennies in the following sequence:

1. Start with 7 dimes and 2 pennies.

2. Regroup into 3 sets of 2 dimes, with one dime and 2 pennies left over.

3. Change the dime to 10 pennies to obtain a total of 12 pennies.

4. Distribute the 12 cents equally among the 3 groups to obtain 3 equal sets, each containing 2 dimes and 4 pennies, or 24 cents.

Symbolic Level

1. Rename 72 as 70 + 2. Since 70 is not a multiple of 3, it should be renamed as 60 + 10. Then 72 becomes 60 + 12. Now proceed as shown in (c) and (d).

(c) $3\overline{)72} = 3\overline{)70 + 2} = 3\overline{)60 + 12}$

(d) $\dfrac{72}{3} = \dfrac{70 + 2}{3}$

$\quad = \dfrac{60 + 12}{3} = \dfrac{60}{3} + \dfrac{12}{3} = 20 + 4$

$\quad = 24$

2. As can be shown by successive subtraction, there are four 3s in 12. It is too tedious and time consuming to use successive subtraction of 3s to solve the division of 72 ÷ 3. However, it is practical and useful to solve this division problem by successive subtraction of multiples of 3, as shown in (e).

(e)
```
     72
   − 30   (10 × 3)
     42
   − 30   (10 × 3)
     12
   − 12   (4 × 3)
```

We see, then, that there are 10 + 10 + 4,

or 24 3s in 72, so the quotient of 72 ÷ 3 = 24.

Subtractive Method

The successive subtraction in (e) can be written in the division format, as shown in (f).

(f)
```
3)72
  30   10
  42
  30   10
  12
  12    4
  24
```

We will refer to the method shown in (f) as the *subtractive method*, which is useful in introducing division involving regrouping for the following reasons:

1. It emphasizes the division algorism as repeated subtraction.

2. It is not necessary to find the largest multiple of the divisor in order to find the quotient.

Example (f) illustrates the procedure when the largest multiple of the divisor is not chosen. Example (g) shows that the procedure works equally well when the largest multiple is chosen. Example (h) illustrates the mastery level.

(g)
```
3)72
  60   20
  12
  12    4
  24
```

(h)
```
    24
 3)72
    60
    12
    12
```

The subtractive method, sometimes called the *Greenwood method*, has a variation called the *pyramid method*, which is illustrated in (i). The pyramid method is similar in procedure to the subtractive method. The difference is that the partial quotients are placed not on the side, as in (g), but above the dividend so as to indicate place value, the major advantage of this method. The pyramid method can take up a lot of vertical space.

(i)   24
     4

    20
3)72
    60
    12
    12

Division with a Remainder

Unfortunately, the dividend is not always a multiple of the divisor. When the dividend is not a multiple of the divisor, there is a remainder, as in (j), which illustrates the subtractive, pyramids and master-level solutions of the same division problem. What the students must learn in division with a remainder is that the remainder must be less than the divisor.

(j)   22 r1
     2
    10
    10   22   r 1
3)67   3)67   3)67
    30   30   10   60
    37   37   7
    30   30   10   6
     7   7   1
     6   6   2
     1   1   22 r1

$$67 = 3 \times 22 + 1$$

Checking Division

When the dividend is a multiple of the divisor, one uses the relationship between multiplication and division as a check. For a solution to check, the dividend must equal the product of the quotient and the divisor. Example (h) checks because 3×24 equals 72.

When a remainder is involved, pupils may discover the check by examining simple divisions, such as $7 \div 3 = 2$ r 1. The dividend 7 is obtained from $2 \times 3 + 1$. The check for division with a remainder can be stated as: *The dividend must equal the*

product of the divisor and quotient plus the remainder. Symbolically, this can be written as $D = d \times q + r$, where D is the dividend, d the divisor, q the quotient, and r the remainder.

Calculators may be of value in checking division when there is no remainder. If the dividend is not a multiple of the divisor, the calculator will not give a remainder in the form shown in (j), but will give the quotient 32.33333; the number of decimal places indicated will depend on the calculator. The remainder can be determined in this case by subtracting 32 from 32.33333 and multiplying by 3, although the product may need to be rounded to the nearest whole number because of round-off errors by the calculator. Pupils will not be able to understand this procedure until they recognize that 32 r 1 can be written as 32 $\frac{1}{3}$, and that the decimal equivalent of $\frac{1}{3}$ is .3333333 . . . , a nonterminating decimal. (See Chapter 15.)

Although it is desirable for all pupils to perform division at the mastery level, an ability to succeed using the pyramid or subtractive method will meet the requirements for minimum competency division. Calculators and computers are just beginning to have an effect in the elementary schools. If the recommendations of the National Council are followed, calculators will be used in most elementary classrooms by the end of the decade, and microcomputers will not be far behind, particularly for the upper grades. Wheatley[4] estimates that as much as three years of instructional time is used in teaching the division algorism. Effective use of calculators can reduce the instructional time spent on the algorism, leaving more time for stressing concepts and problem solving.

Paper-and-pencil computation of the division algorism is rare in business and industry today. It is far too time consuming to

4. Ibid.

be cost effective. A five-dollar calculator can perform a division problem in a few seconds that would take minutes for most people using paper and pencil.

The Standard Division Algorism

Pupils will make fewer errors in place value if they first determine the number of digits in the quotient. For the division $4\overline{)275}$, this can be done as:

1. Find the product $4 \times 10 = 40$ and note that 40 is less than the dividend 275.

2. Find the product $4 \times 100 = 400$ and note that 400 is greater than the dividend 275.

3. Because the dividend 275 is between 4×10 and 4×100, the quotient must be a two-digit number between 10 and 100.

As this procedure illustrates, the first step in division involving regrouping is to determine the number of digits in the quotient. The divisor is multiplied by 10, 100, and successive powers of 10 until the product is larger than the dividend. If 10 times the divisor is too large, the quotient is a one-digit number, and so on.

In (k) the dividend is between 10×28 and 100×28, so the quotient is a two-place number. The first digit in the quotient will be over the tens place in the dividend. In introductory work, especially with slow learners, encourage them to indicate the location of the quotient digits as illustrated.

(k)

$$\begin{array}{c|c|c} & T & O \\ \hline & & \\ \hline 28\overline{)6} & 4 & 7 \end{array}$$

In (1) the quotient is a three-place number because the dividend is between 100×28 and 1000×28. The first digit in a three-place quotient is placed over the hundreds place in the dividend. Without using the columns to identify the places in the quotient, a pupil may write 25 as the quotient instead of the true quotient 205.

(l)

$$\begin{array}{c|c|c|c} H & T & O \\ \hline & & & \\ \hline 28\overline{)5} & 7 & 4 & 0 \end{array}$$

Finding the Quotient Digit

After determining the number of digits in the quotient, pupils find each digit of the quotient by either of two procedures. In $4\overline{)275}$, the quotient contains two digits, as shown in the previous section. The pupils can use multiplication facts to determine that 275 is between 4×60 and 4×70, finding a partial quotient of 60, then writing the 6 in the tens place as indicated in (m).

(m)

$$\begin{array}{c|c} T & O \\ \hline 6 & \\ \hline 4\overline{)2} & 7 & 5 \end{array}$$

(n)

$$\begin{array}{c|c} & \\ \hline 2 & \\ \hline 3\overline{)7} & 2 \end{array}$$

In the second method, the pupil can use the cardinal value in the dividend, as in (n), dividing 7 by 3 to get 2 (rounded). This procedure determines that 7 tens can be separated into 2 groups of 3 tens, with 1 ten remaining. Since the quotient is a two-digit number, the 2 is written in the tens place. The second method may be easier for most pupils, since it enables them to deal with small numbers while still requiring a knowledge of multiplication and division facts. This procedure can also be used with divisors containing two or more digits.

The Use of Multiples

Although most pupils may find it time consuming, using multiples eliminates the need for estimation. When dividing by 15 by the multiple method, the pupils first write multiples of 15:

$1 \times 15 = 15$	$6 \times 15 = 90$
$2 \times 15 = 30$	$7 \times 15 = 105$
$3 \times 15 = 45$	$8 \times 15 = 120$
$4 \times 15 = 60$	$9 \times 15 = 135$
$5 \times 15 = 75$	

The pupil can now perform the division in (o) by recognizing that the quotient is a three-digit number, as 9480 is between 100 × 15 and 1000 × 15. The pupil then determines that 9 cannot contain 15, but 94 is between 6 × 15 and 7 × 15, so 6 must be the first quotient digit and is written over the hundreds place in the dividend. Next, the pupil determines that the tens digit is 3, since 48 is between 3 × 15 and 4 × 15. Finally, 2 × 15 = 30, so the ones digit is 2.

(o)
```
      H T O
      6 3 2
  15)9 4 8 0
     9 0
      4 8
      4 5
        3 0
        3 0
```

Some of the time lost in writing the multiples, which can be found by addition, can be regained by the elimination of estimation and the time spent to find partial products by multiplication.

Multiplying by a Two-Digit Number

Multiplication by a two-digit number involves three different types of examples:

1. Both factors are multiples of 10.

2. One factor is a multiple of 10.

3. Neither factor is a multiple of 10.

Exploratory work at this level is generally not productive unless pupils require remedial work with facts and multiplication with one-digit numbers. Exploratory activities can be used profitably in reviewing this material.

BOTH FACTORS A MULTIPLE OF 10

Multiplication by a two-digit number is usually introduced with examples using factors that are multiples of 10. Each factor is renamed as the product of 10 and a single-digit number. For example, in 20 × 30,

20 is renamed as 2 × 10 and 30 as 3 × 10. The solution is written as follows:

$$20 \times 30 = (2 \times 10) \times (3 \times 10)$$
$$= (2 \times 3) \times (10 \times 10)$$
$$= 6 \times 100, \text{ or } 600$$

By using both the associative and commutative properties, four factors can be rearranged in any manner without changing the product.

ONE FACTOR A MULTIPLE OF 10

If only one factor is a multiple of 10, as in 20 × 43, the 43 is renamed as 40 + 3. The multiplication is then performed as follows:

$$20 \times 43 = 20 \times (40 + 3)$$
$$= 20 \times 40 + 20 \times 3$$
$$= 800 + 60 \text{ or } 860$$

Example (a) illustrates the conventional way of writing the multiplication in the vertical form.

(a)
```
    43
  ×20
  860
```

NEITHER FACTOR A MULTIPLE OF 10

When neither factor is a multiple of 10, one factor can be renamed as was done when one factor was a multiple of 10. For example, in 34 :ts 12 = 34 × (10 + 2) = 34 × 10 + 34 × 2. The student can then complete the solution as shown in (b) or (c).

(b) 34 × 10 = 340   (c)
```
34        34
            +
34 × 2 =   68    ×10    ×2
34 × 12 = 408   340 +  68= 408
```

Example (d) shows a developmental method for multiplying 34 × 12.

(d)
```
    34
  × 12
    68   (2 × 34)
   340   (10 × 34)
   408
```

(e)
```
    34
  × 12
    68
    34
   408
```

Example (e) shows the mastery method for multiplying 34 × 12.

Example (f) can be sued profitably to stress the relationship between cardinal value and total value.

(f)	34	
	× 12	
	8	(2 × 4)
	60	(2 × 30)
	40	(10 × 4)
	300	(10 × 30)
	408	

Understanding the Algorism

In terms of the time they spend, pupils who perform the algorism by rote may be better off using a calculator. The following is a list of activities designed to help pupils recognize important concepts associated with the multiplication algorism.

1. Ask pupils to give cardinal, positional (or place), and total value for each digit in the multiplication.

2. Make sure pupils recognize the role of the distributive property when at least one factor has two or more digits.

3. Ask pupils to explain the sequence of steps in (d) or (e).

4. The commutative property of multiplication should be reinforced, as illustrated in (g). Some pupils may find it useful to write the zero, as in (g), when they begin to multiply with two-digit numbers.

(g)	12
	× 34
	48
	360
	408

Checking Multiplication

The following methods can be used to check multiplication.

1. Interchange factors, as illustrated in (g).

2. Go over the work by placing a piece of scrap paper over all but the original example so that previous computations are not seen.

3. Use a calculator, if one is available. Be careful when introducing this method, as pupils may wonder why they need to learn the algorism if they can use the calculator to find the answer with much less effort. Pupils should understand that learning the concepts associated with the algorism is at least as important as learning the algorism.

4. Use upper and lower limits with rounding. For example, the product of 12 × 34 must be between 300 (10 × 30) and 800 (20 × 40). Therefore, an answer of 408 is sensible. Pupils can also recognize that the answer should be closer to 300 than to 800 because 12 is closer to 10 than to 20, and 34 is closer to 30 than to 40.

5. Example (h) illustrates a common multiplication error, sometimes called a position error, that occurs when the multiplier contains a zero. The rounded product in (i) shows that the answer in (h) is not sensible.

(h)	736	(i)	700
	× 304		× 300
	2944		210,000
	2208		
	25024		

Dividing by a Two-Digit Number

Dividing by a two-digit number is one of the most difficult topics in computational arithmetic, and causes students a wide range of difficulties. In (a) the estimated quotient (6 ÷ 3 = 2) is the true quotient, and no regrouping is required in multiplication or subtraction. However, in (b), the estimated quotient (9 ÷ 2 = 4, rounded) is too small, and so regrouping is required for both multiplication and subtraction. The pupil should not begin dividing by a two-digit number by working examples presenting the difficulties of example (b).

```
(a)        21        (b)        56 r 14
     31)651               16)910
         62                   80
         31                  110
         31                   96
                              14
```

Repeat the Pattern

Using adult procedures to introduce a topic violates the principle of growth. We recommend that you use a less mature procedure, the same pattern used for a one-place divisor, to introduce division by a two-digit divisor. Have the pupils begin with the subtractive or pyramid method and refine it until they have mastered the conventional algorism.

The subtractive method enables the pupil to complete the algorism without revision when the estimated quotient is too small. As shown in (c), the pupil recognizes that there are at least ten 26s in 573, and subtracts as indicated. The difference of 313 indicates that there are at least 10 more 26s. Finally, two 26s are subtracted from 53 to obtain a remainder of 1.

The steps in the pyramid method, shown in (d), are identical to those in the subtractive method except that the partial quotients are written above the dividend to indicate place value.

```
(c) 26)573             (d)          22 r 1
        260   10                      2
        313                          10
        260   10                      10
         53                     26)573
         52    2                    260
          1   22 r 1                313
                                    260
                                     53
                                     52
                                      1
```

The subtractive or pyramid format often serves as a developmental or terminal form for pupils having difficulty with the standard algorism. There is no experimental evi-

dence to indicate that these developmental forms are more effective in helping a pupil to divide by the standard algorism than the direct introduction of that form. However, the use of these intermediate forms represents growth in dealing with a learning situation. Lang and Meyers[5] recommend that the use of transitional procedures, such as just described, should be curtailed in favor of a more direct introduction of the standard algorism.

Methods of Estimation

There are many ways for pupils to estimate the digits in a quotient. By knowing the multiplication facts, pupils may be able to find each quotient digit without learning a new procedure to estimate the quotient digit. There is no uniform method for teaching pupils to estimate each digit of the quotient. Most procedures can be classified as either a *one-rule* or *two-rule* method.

In the one-rule method, the divisor is rounded up or down to the nearest 10. If the divisor is rounded downward, the divisors 21 through 29 are rounded to 20 and the estimated quotient is either correct or too large. If the estimated quotient is too large, it is reduced by one; this procedure is repeated until the true quotient is found. To avoid erasures, the pupil can work trial multiplications on scrap paper to determine whether the estimated quotient is the true quotient. Fast learners may be able to make this determination mentally.

If the divisor is rounded upward, the estimated quotient will either be correct or too small. If the estimated quotient is too small, it may be increased by one and the procedure repeated until the true quotient is found. One problem with upward rounding is that pupils may not notice that the re-

5. Robert A. Lang and Ruth Ann Meyers, "Transitional Division Algorithms," *The Arithmetic Teacher*, May 1982, 29:10–12.

mainder is larger than the divisor and fail to complete the algorism correctly. On the other hand, if pupils see that the remainder is too large, the division can be completed with one or more additional subtractions, as illustrated in (e) and (f). Since the remainder of 32 in (e) is too large, the pupil performs an additional subtraction and changes the quotient, as shown in (f). This procedure is a variation of the pyramid method.

(e)
$$
\begin{array}{r}
14 \\
23\overline{)354} \\
\underline{23} \quad \text{trial: } 3 \div 3 = 1 \\
124 \\
\underline{92} \quad \text{trial: } 12 \div 3 = 4 \\
32 \quad \text{remainder too large}
\end{array}
$$

(f)
$$
\begin{array}{r}
15 \text{ r } 9 \\
14 \\
23\overline{)354} \\
\underline{23} \\
124 \\
\underline{92} \\
32 \\
\underline{23} \\
9
\end{array}
$$

TWO-RULE METHOD

In the two-rule method, the divisor can be rounded downward or upward, depending on its position in the decade. Divisors 21 and 24 are rounded downward to 20. Divisors 25 and 29 are rounded up to 30. Some textbooks advocate rounding down divisors 20 and 25. If divisors 20 through 24 are rounded down, the guide number is 2, or 20. If divisors 25 through 29 are rounded up, the guide number is 3, or 30. This pattern holds for divisors in all the different decades.

MERITS OF EACH METHOD

The advantages and disadvantages of the one-rule and two-rule methods have been debated for years, but experimental evidence has not proved any one method to be

superior. The multiple method illustrated on page 164 may be the only method that some pupils can use to complete the algorism successfully, while more advanced pupils may determine multiples mentally to find the true quotient digit.

Division is the only one of the four basic operations that requires estimation, and this is the main reason for its difficulty. Because no one method of estimation has been shown to be superior, teachers should rely on their experience in choosing the methods to be offered to pupils. Respect individual differences, and refrain from insisting that pupils use one particular method.

Three Types of Divisors

A two-place divisor occurs in three different situations:

1. The divisor is a multiple of 10.

2. The divisor is not a multiple of 10, but the estimated quotient is the true quotient.

3. The estimated quotient is not the true quotient. The second and third situations are the same, if the subtractive or pyramid method is used.

DIVISOR A MULTIPLE OF 10

A good way to introduce division by a multiple of 10 is to present a problem, such as "How many bundles of 20 tickets can be made from 60 tickets?" Help the pupils to rephrase the problem as "How many 20s are in 60?" Students should recognize the question "How many a's are there in b?" is a basic division situation. Ask them for a number sentence that describes the situation. Both of the following are correct:

$$n = 60 \div 20 \qquad 20n = 60$$

Writing both equations helps to stress the relationship between multiplication and division. The fact that the two sentences are equivalent arises out of the multiplication/division pattern, sometimes stated verbally as *factor × factor = product is equivalent to product divided by factor = factor.* This relationship is the basis for solving the equation $20n = 60$ at the elementary level. If factor (20) × factor *(n)* = product (60), then *n* (factor) = product (60) divided by factor (20). Once the students understand that they can find the answer to the problem by dividing 60 by 20, you should emphasize estimation of the quotient by means of activities such as the following:

1. Point out that the quotient is less than 10 × 20 and so is a one-digit number.

2. Show that the quotient 20 ÷ 10 can be found by dividing the tens digits. Emphasize this with additional examples:

$$30 \div 10 = 3 \div 1 = 3$$
$$40 \div 10 = 4 \div 1 = 4$$
$$40 \div 20 = 4 \div 2 = 2$$

Likewise, 60 ÷ 20 = 6 ÷ 2 = 3. Check by using the multiplication/division pattern.

3. Write multiples of 20 to show that 3 × 20 = 60.

4. Perform the division on the number line.

5. Record the result using the standard algorism: $20\overline{)60}$ with quotient 3 and $\underline{60}$

The procedure for a three-place dividend such as $20\overline{)120}$ is:

1. Determine that 120 is between 1 × 20 and 10 × 20, so that the divisor must be a one-place number.

2. Think 12 ÷ 2 = 6.

Similar activities should enable the pupils to think 15 ÷ 3 = 5 for the division $30\overline{)150}$, and so on. When the dividend is not a multiple of the divisor, as in $30\overline{)71}$, the procedure is essentially the same. Since 71 is less than 10 × 30, the quotient is a one-digit number. The estimated quotient (7 ÷ 3 = 2 rounded) is the true quotient. The work is written as follows:

$$30\overline{)71} \quad \text{check: } 2 \times 30 + 11 = 71$$

with 2 r 11 above, and $\underline{60}$, then 11.

Estimating the quotient digit is a vital part of the algorism but sheds little light on how or when to use division in problem-solving situations. Although it is an important process for students to learn, estimating must not become a focus and obscure the important concepts and applications of division.

Estimated Quotient Not True Quotient

When the divisor is not a multiple of 10 and the estimated quotient is the true quotient, pupils have no more difficulty than when handling a divisor that is a multiple of 10. For example, essentially the same procedure is used to solve $21\overline{)63}$ as for $20\overline{)60}$. Both have one-digit quotients, and in both cases the estimated quotient (6 ÷ 2 = 3) is the true quotient.

When the estimated quotient is not the true quotient, the estimated quotient must be adjusted. If the divisor is rounded down, the incorrect estimated quotient will be too large and must be reduced by 1 and a new partial product obtained. If the new estimated quotient digit is too large, the process is repeated. If the divisor is rounded up, the incorrect estimated quotient will be too small and must be increased by 1 until the true quotient is found. When the estimated quotient is too small, an alternate method is to subtract the divisor and proceed as described on page 167.

Quotients with Two or More Places

After mastering division with two-place divisors and one-place quotients, pupils should be able to find a quotient having two or more places. Regardless of the number of digits in the quotient, the procedure for finding each digit is the same. The steps are as follows:

1. Determine the number of digits in the quotient by multiplying the divisor by successive powers of 10. ·

2. Estimate the first digit in the quotient and revise it if necessary to find the true quotient digit.

3. Give the quotient digit its correct position or place value by writing it above the appropriate digit in the dividend. If the quotient is a one-place digit, it is written above the ones digit in the dividend. If it is a two-place quotient, the first digit is written above the tens place in the dividend, and so on.

4. Repeat steps 2 and 3 for each additional quotient digit.

5. Check by writing the appropriate number sentence.

For example, in 21)672 the quotient is a two-place number, as 672 falls between 10 × 21 and 100 × 21. The estimated quotient digit of 3 (6 ÷ 2 = 3) is the true quotient. Because the quotient is a two-place number, the 3 is written above the 7 in the dividend to give it a position or place value of 10.

The second estimated quotient digit is 2 (4 ÷ 2) and is also the true quotient, to be written to the right of the 3 in the ones place. If the first quotient digit is placed correctly, students should have little difficulty in writing the remaining digits unless a zero is involved. The work may be recorded as shown in (a). The frames for locating the position of the quotient digits are used in initial instruction of the topic and should be discontinued as soon as possible.

(a)

```
        T O
        3 2
 21)6 7 2
    6 3 0
      4 2      check: 32 × 21 = 672
      4 2
```

Correcting the Estimated Quotient

The quotient in 24)1776 is a two-digit number because 1776 is between 10 × 24 and 100 × 24. As shown in (b), the estimated quotient of 8 (17 ÷ 2, rounded) is not the true quotient. Since the divisor was rounded down, 8 is too large. Example (c) shows that the true quotient is 7, which is written above the second 7 in the dividend to indicate that it represents 7 tens. The second estimated quotient digit of 4 (9 ÷ 2, rounded) is the true quotient, also shown in (c). The sentence 24 × 74 = 1776 provides the check.

```
(b)         8      (c)         74
    24)1776          24)1776
       192               1680
                           96
                           96
```

In example (d), the rounding-up method for 26)1776 gives an estimated quotient of 5 (17 ÷ 3, rounded), which is not the true quotient. Because the divisor was rounded up, the estimated quotient of 5 is too small, and so a new estimated quotient of 6 must be chosen. Example (e) shows that 6 is the true quotient, which is written above the tens place in the dividend because the quotient is a two-digit number. Example (f) shows how example (d) can be completed by not changing the estimated quotient. This is the modified pyramid method shown on page 168.

```
(d)          5
    26)1776
       1300
         47
```

```
(e)         68 r 8
    26)1776
       1560
        216
        208
          8
```

(f)
$$
\begin{array}{r}
6 \\
58 \\
26)\overline{1776} \\
1300 \\
\hline
47 \\
26 \\
\hline
216 \\
208 \\
\hline
8
\end{array}
= 68 \text{ r } 8
$$

Check: $26 \times 68 + 8 = 1776$

(g)
$$
\begin{array}{r}
70 \text{ r } 28 \\
36)\overline{2548} \\
252 \\
\hline
28
\end{array}
$$

Aids in Estimation

1. Multiplying the divisor by 5 can help students in learning to estimate quotients. In example (g), $5 \times 36 = 180$. The first estimated quotient is 6 ($25 \div 4$, rounded). When they compare 254 with 180, many pupils recognize that the difference is more than twice 36 and so estimate the quotient as 7, rather than 6. Some teachers advocate using 1 times the divisor, 5 times the divisor, and 10 times the divisor as guides for estimation. As example (g) illustrates, there is value in estimating the number of digits in the quotient. If this were not done, some pupils would have written a quotient of 7 rather than 70.

2. Use *one* of the following methods of estimation:

Method I. Use the one-rule rounding-down method, remembering that an estimated quotient is either correct or too large. To adjust the estimation, reduce the quotient by one, continuing the process until the true quotient is found.

Method II. Use the one-rule rounding-up method and remember that the quotient is either correct or too small. To revise the incorrect estimate, increase the quotient by one, continuing until the true quotient is found. Because the divisor in this method is too small, an incorrect quotient can be corrected, without revision, using the modified pyramid method shown in (g).

Method III. Use the two-rule method, round-ing down divisor ending in 1 through 4 and rounding up divisor ending in 5 through 9. Pupils using this method may find it more difficult to remember when an incorrect quotient is too large or too small.

Method IV. Use the multiple method. Write a table of 1 through 9 times the divisor so that is is not necessary to estimate a quotient digit or multiply again to obtain partial products. This method is effective for slow learners.

MASTERY LEVEL

At the mastery level, the estimation process involves four basic steps:

1. Estimate.

2. Multiply.

3. Subtract.

4. Check to determine if difference is less than the divisor. If not, revise the estimate and repeat the process.

A Common Error

A mistake students often make when recording numbers is reversing digits. When students know an answer to be incorrect, it is standard practice to find the difference between the correct and incorrect answer. If the difference is divisible by 9, reversal of digits is likely. This procedure provides a useful application of the rule that a number is divisible by 9 if and only if the sum of digits is divisible by 9.

Verbal Problems in Multiplication and Division

A basic skill in problem solving is the ability to reword problems in simpler language. A typical one-step multiplication problem, such as asking the cost of 7 books when the cost of 1 book is $10, can be simplified as follows:

(a) 1 book $\longrightarrow$ $10
    7 books $\longrightarrow$?

"One book for $10" is a rate statement, and can also be expressed as "$10 per book." When pupils can reword as in (a), they understand what is given and what is wanted. This rewording is also an efficient way to write the solution, as shown in (b).

(b) 1 book$\longrightarrow$ $10
    7 books $\longrightarrow$ 7 $\times$ 10 = 70
    The cost of 7 books is $70.

The solution can also be written as in (c) and (d).

(c) n = 7 $\times$ 10   (d)   10
    n = 70 $\times 7$
    7 books cost $70.   ──────
                                   70
                              7 books cost $70.

The phrase "one-to-many" describes one-step multiplication problems. Each one-step multiplication problem starts with a rate that indicates to what 1 item corresponds. In (a), 1 item corresponds to $10. It may help some students to abbreviate the problem as "given 1, find 7."

Division Situations

Some one-step divison problems also begin with a rate statement. Problem 1 below begins by stating the rate as $12 per book, a situation that translates into "How many a's are there in b?"—in this case, how many 12s there are in 36.

Consider these four problems:

1. How many books, at $12 each, can be purchased for $36?

2. How many feet are there in 36 inches?

3. Bruce earns $36 in 12 days by doing odd jobs after school. What is his average earning per day?

4. What is the cost of 1 ticket if 12 tickets cost $36?

The answer to all four problems involves the division of 36 by 12 to obtain a numerical answer of 3. This answer is meaningless without the following interpretations:

Problem 1: 3 books for $36

Problem 2: 3 feet in 36 inches

Problem 3: $3 per day

Problem 4: $3 per ticket

Both problems 1 and 2 start with a rate, $12 per book and the implied 12 inches per foot, respectively. Pupils should recognize problems 1 and 2 as division situations when they are reworded as "How many 12s are there in 36?" There is one book for each $12 in the $36 in problem 1 and one foot for each 12 inches in the 36 inches in problem 2.

Problems 3 and 4 present "many-to-one" situations and can be viewed as "undoing" a multiplication of the type "given 1, find 12." Pupils should see them as division situations when they are reworded "given 12, find 1."

All four problems have the common property that if the unknown number is multiplied by 12, the product is 36. You can help students recognize this common property by rewording problems 1 and 2 as "n groups of 12 is a group of 36" and rewording problems 3 and 4 as "12 groups of n is a group of 36." The solution to all four problems, and their appropriate interpretations can be written as shown in (e).

(e) 12n = 36
    n = 3

As discussed on page 134, problems 1 and 2 involve measurement division and problems 3 and 4 represent partition division. It is more important that students recognize the common approach to the four problems, as illustrated in (e), than for them to focus on the difference. Pupils should not, however, be restricted to one specific way of recording the solution. It is important that the written solution indicate how the answer is determined. At this level the method is more important than the answer; a correct answer, found by an incorrect method, is not acceptable.

Here are some additional acceptable ways for recording the solutions to problems 1 through 4.

Problem 1: $12 \longrightarrow$ 1 book
$36 \longrightarrow 36 \div 12 = 3$
3 books for $36

Problem 2: If the pupil rewords the problem as "How many 12s are there in 36?" and recognizes it as division, the following is acceptable:

$$\overset{3}{12\overline{\smash{)}36}} \quad \text{3 feet in 36 inches}$$

Problem 3: 12 days $\longrightarrow$ $36
1 day $\longrightarrow 36 \div 12 = 3$
$3 per day

Problem 4: By rewording the problem as "given 12, find 1," the pupil may recognize it as division.

$$\overset{3}{12\overline{\smash{)}36}} \quad \text{\$3 per ticket}$$

It is not possible to list all the acceptable methods for writing solutions to verbal problems. The minimum requirements should include the algorism and an interpretation of the answer.

Summary

The multiplication and division algorisms must be introduced in their simplest form at the exploratory level, and gradually in-creased in difficulty at the symbolic and the mastery level. These algorisms should be introduced in conjunction with real-life problems and with emphasis on basic number properties. Multipliers and divisors should generally be restricted to two-digit numbers.

Division is the only one of the four operations that requires estimation, the major reason for its difficulty. Four common methods of estimation are the one-rule, round-ing-down method; the one-rule, rounding-up method; the two-rule method; and the multiple method.

Every one-step multiplication problem begins with a rate statement and can be described as a one-to-many problem or be reworded as "given 1, find many," where "many" is replaced by a number appropriate to the problem.

Some one-step division problems begin with a rate statement and can be reworded as "How many a's are there in b?" where a and b are replaced by numbers appropriate to the problem. Some one-step division problems can be described as "many-to-one" or reworded as "given many, find 1," where "many" is replaced by a number appropriate to the problem. Every one-step division problem can be described as a multiplication problem with a missing factor and solved by an equation of the type $12n = 36$, where 12 and 36 are replaced by numbers appropriate to the problem.

The individual differences of pupils must be recognized and respected. Students should not be forced to adhere to a specific method for solving problems.

Exercises

Give the thought pattern you would use to introduce problems 1 through 6 to a class in grades 4, 5, or 6. Discuss the remaining problems.

1. A diagram has 15 rows of 24 stars each. How many stars does the diagram contain?

2. A car averages 16 miles per gallon of fuel. At that rate, how many gallons of fuel would be needed for a trip of 560 miles?

3. Kathy bought a 5-pound roast at a shopping center for 78¢ a pound. She gave the cashier $5. How much change did she get?

4. The average temperature one day was the average of the highest and lowest temperatures on that day. The highest temperature was 69° and the lowest 43°. What was the average temperature that day?

5. A spool contained 36 yards of ribbon. After 15 yards were used, how many pieces 3 yards in length could be cut from the remaining ribbon?

6. When 10 is added to the product of two factors, the sum is 190. One of the factors is 12. What is the other factor?

7. Write 34 as 30 + 4 and 57 as 50 + 7 and multiply, using the distributive property.

8. Use upper and lower limits to estimate the product of 36 × 53.

9. Evaluate the multiple method of division.

10. Some teachers do not present methods for estimating quotients. Pupils multiply the divisor by the digits, beginning with 1. Evaluate this plan.

11. Refer to sets (a) and (b), and give all the examples that use the members of each set. (a) 12, 15, 180 (b) 912, 16, 57

12. Enumerate some of the procedures a teacher might use to help a slow learner succeed at division with a two-place divisor, as well as ways to challenge the quick learners.

13. Find the products in A and B. Write the generalization that applies to any set of products when one factor is constant.

A: 36	36	36	36
×4	×9	×15	×20

B: 12	14	23	45
×5	×5	×5	×5

14. Examine examples A and B, and find the quotients. Write the generalization pertaining to the quotient in A and in B.

A: 3)$\overline{60}$ 4)$\overline{60}$ 12)$\overline{60}$ 20)$\overline{60}$

B: 15)$\overline{30}$ 15)$\overline{75}$ 15)$\overline{120}$ 15)$\overline{450}$

15. In the example 9 × 48, it is necessary to add 7 to 36 to find the product. Write a two-place number that, when multiplied by a one-place number, it is necessary to add: a. 4 to 36 b. 5 to 32 c. 7 to 64

16. Reword each of the problems in one of the following ways: Given 1, find 4; Given 1, find 8; Given 4, find 1; Given 8, find 1; How many 4s are there in 32?; How many 8s are there in 32?

a. The cost of 4 books is $32. What does one book cost?

b. How many pounds of meat can be bought for $32 if one pound costs $4?

c. What is the cost of 8 items if one item costs $32?

d. Find the cost of 4 quarts of liquid if one quart costs $32.

e. How many books, at 8 dollars each, can be purchased for $32?

f. What is the cost of one item if 8 items cost $32?

Selected Readings

An Agenda for Action: Recommendations for School Mathematics for the 1980s. Reston, VA: National Council of Teachers of Mathematics, 1980.

Heddens, James W. *Today's Mathematics,* Fourth Edition. Chicago; Science Research Associates, 1980.

Marks, John L., C. Richard Purdy, Lucien B. Kinney, and Arthur A. Hiatt. *Teaching Elementary School Mathematics for Understanding.* New York: McGraw-Hill, 1975.

Reidesel, C. Alan, and Paul C. Burns. *Handbook for Exploratory and Systematic Teaching of Elementary Mathematics.* New York: Harper & Row, 1977.

Schminke, C. W., et al. *Teaching the Child Mathematics,* Second Edition. New York: Holt, Rinehart and Winston, 1978.

Topics in Mathematics for Elementary School Teachers, Twenty-ninth Yearbook. Reston, VA: National Council of Teachers of Mathematics, 1964.

Chapter 10
Problem Solving

In the 1960s, the theme of elementary mathematics programs was New Math, and in the 1970s, Back to Basics. The National Council of Teachers of Mathematics has designated "problem solving" as the theme for the 1980s.[1]

Achievement Goals

After studying the following chapter, you should be able to:

1. Understand the nature of a mathematical problem.
2. Know the essential steps in solving a problem.
3. Have a variety of problem-solving strategies that are suitable for elementary pupils.
4. Recognize that a wide variety of problems is suitable for the elementary mathematics program.
5. Become familiar with some basic research on problem solving.

1. *An Agenda for Action: Recommendations for School Mathematics for the 1980s* (Reston, VA: National Council of Teachers of Mathematics, 1980), p. 29.

6. Recognize the importance of estimation in solving and checking problems.

Vocabulary

Mastery of the following key terms will help you to understand this chapter. Each word is defined or illustrated in the Glossary at the end of the book.

Back to Basics	Key word
Deductive	Mathematical
reasoning	problem
Guess and test	New Math
Heuristic	Rate
Inductive	Strategy
reasoning	Variable

The Nature of Problems and Problem Solving

Polya, the master problem solver and teacher of problem solving, defines problem solving as: ". . . finding an unknown means to a distinctly conceived end. . . To find a way when no way is known offhand, to find a way out of a difficulty, to find a way around an obstacle. . . . There is no problem unless the individual has the desire to find a solution."[2] In other words, a mathematical problem, whether elementary or advanced, always involves finding an answer to a question that cannot be obtained by a habitual response. This definition of problem solving implies that what is a problem to one person (or at one grade level) will not be perceived as a problem by another.

For example, sixth-graders should be able to give the sum of 6 + 7 with a habitual response. However, this sum cannot be given as a habitual response by pupils who know only addition facts to the sum of 10. There are several ways in which pupils at this stage might solve such a problem:

1. Count out a set of 6 objects and a set of 7 objects. Combine them and determine that there are 13 objects.

2. Note that 3 of the objects from the first group can be combined with 7 objects in the second group to make a group of 10 objects; obtaining a group of 10 objects and a group of 3 objects gives a set of 13 objects.

3. Count on one's fingers to solve the problem.

4. Write 6 + 7 as (6 + 4) + 3, which is 10 + 3, or 13. The first three of these solutions are exploratory level. The fourth solution is a symbolic-level solution.

Computation and Mathematics

Many people erroneously equate computation with mathematics. Computation is definitely a part of methematics, but a full grasp of mathematics requires understanding—computation can be learned by rote with little understanding. The main thrust of a meaningful program in mathematics is enabling pupils to understand the work.

2. G. Polya, "On Solving Mathematical Problems in High School." In *Problem Solving in School Mathematics* (Reston, VA: National Council of Teachers of Mathematics, 1980), pp. 1–2.

This aim is not outmoded even in an age of calculators and computers: The main reason for teaching computation is to help pupils learn the ideas and concepts associated with the basic operations.

Problem Solving Is a Process

Problem solving is a process by which the choice of an appropriate strategy enables a pupil to proceed from what is given in a problem to its solution. Often, the answer is the least important part of the problem-solving process; few of the answers children obtain in school mathematics will have much value in their lives. The ideas used in the process are much more valuable than the answer. Thus, it is important for teachers to determine whether an incorrect answer is due to an error in process or in computation. Do not, however, infer from this discussion that errors in computation are acceptable; rather, keep in mind that overemphasis on answers may impede the pupil's understanding of the process. A pupil with poor computational ability who understands the process can use a calculator to get the answer. A pupil who can compute rapidly and accurately but does not understand the process is lost.

In the field of banking, a computational error that results in an inbalance of a single penny in an account may require as much time to correct as a computational error involving thousands of dollars.

National Assessment

The Second National Assessment of Mathematics was conducted in 1977. The results, which were released in 1978, indicated that pupils performed more poorly in problem solving than in any other major area in mathematics.[3]

3. Ibid., p. 1.

Table 10.1 Selected Results of the Second National Assessment, 1977

Type of Problem	Percent Correct	
	Age 9	Age 13
ADDITION		
Paul has 21 stamps in his collection. He buys 54 more from a dealer. How many does he have after he buys them?	82	96
SUBTRACTION		
Jim has 86 trading cards and Bill has 52. How many more cards does Jim have than Bill?	60	89
Mary's family took a car trip of 325 miles. The first day they traveled 158 miles. How much farther do they have to go?	38	82
MULTIPLICATION		
Kate rides her bike at an average rate of 10 miles per hour. At this rate, how far will she travel in 5 hours?	54	88
A rabbit eats 2 pounds of food per week. Given that there are 52 weeks in a year, how many pounds will 5 rabbits eat in a year?	47	56
DIVISION		
Jane is reading a book with 48 pages. If she reads 6 pages a day, how many days will it take her to finish the book?	46	——
Bill rode his bike 56 miles in 7 hours. What was his average speed?	22	82

Table 10.1 presents a selected sample of the 1977 assessment results. In response to the results of the second assessment, Carpenter and others concluded that ". . . Students appear to be learning mathematical skills at a rote manipulational level and do not understand the concepts underlying the computation. . . .

"In general, the respondents demonstrated a lack of even the most basic problem solving skills. Most respondents simply tried to apply a single arithmetic operation to the numbers in the problem. The results indicate that the students are not familiar with the most basic problem solving strategies as drawing a picture of the figure described in a problem, substituting a smaller number in a problem in an attempt to find a solution method, or checking the reasonableness of a result. . . ."[4]

The pupils involved in this assessment received the bulk of their education in the 1970s, at the height of the Back to Basics movement. Some educators claim that the assessment results are proof that Back to Basics overemphasized computation at the expense of problem solving. In its ten major recommendations for the 1980s, the National Council of Teachers of Mathematics included a definition of basic skills that en-

4. T. Carpenter, H. Kepner, M. Lindquist, and R. Rays, "Results and Implication of the Second NAEP Mathematics Assessment: Elementary Schools," *Arithmetic Teacher*, April 1980, 8:10–12, 44–47.

compassed more than computational facility. Their report states:

> There should be increased emphasis on such activities as
>
> Locating and processing quantitative information;
> Collecting and organizing data;
> Measuring with appropriate tools;
> Mentally estimating the results of calculations;
> Using technological aids to calculate;
> Using ratio and proportion to deal with rate problems in general and percent problems in particular.
>
> There should be decreased emphasis on such activities as
>
> Isolated drill with numbers apart from problem contexts;
> Performing paper-and-pencil computations with more than 2-digit numbers;
> Mastering highly specialized vocabularies not useful later in mathematics or in daily living.
>
> . . . common sense should dictate a reasonable balance among mental facility with simple problems done easily and rapidly and the use of the calculator for more complex problems or those in which problem analysis is the goal and cumbersome calculation is a distraction. . . .[5]

Strategies for Problem Solving

Some aspects of problem solving have been discussed and illustrated in our discussion of basic facts in Chapters 6–9, in which we saw that a correctly performed algorism guarantees success. However, there is no algorism for problem solving. To help pupils solve problems, general guidelines, sometimes called *heuristics*, must be used. If these guidelines are too specific, they will apply only to a very limited variety of problems. If the guidelines are too general, they will be difficult to apply to specific situations.

5. *An Agenda for Action*, p. 7.

Four Steps

The following four steps are widely recognized as the most helpful way to guide pupils in problem solving:

1. Understanding the problem.

2. Drawing up a plan.

3. Carrying out the plan and interpreting the result.

4. Checking or evaluating the solution.

However, unless these four steps are supplemented with additional information, they are too general. Strategies, or ideas and activities designed to help pupils implement these steps, are necessary. Before we list the strategies most commonly associated with each of the four steps, however, we must note that this list is not to be learned by rote. These strategies must be introduced gradually over the course of the elementary program. Few pupils, if any, will use all the strategies. The first activities given for each of the four steps should be introduced soon after the pupil has begun to solve problems on the symbolic level. Additional strategies are to be introduced as problem situations develop.

1. *Understanding the problem*
   a. Isolate the problem question. Determine what is wanted.
   b. Identify what is given.
   c. Ask if additional information, such as a formula, is needed.
   d. Picture the problem. Write each given number and identify things associated with it.
   e. Reword the problem using fewest words possible. Use the form:
      Given:
      Wanted:
   f. Look for relationships among the numbers, such as rates.

2. *Planning a solution*
   a. Visualize whether the quantities are

Solving problems with a calculator. (*Photo by Leland Perry*)

to be combined, compared, or separated. This visualization is an extension of the hands-on exploratory activity with objects in early number work.

b. Look for a familiar pattern to see if the problem is similar to one already solved. Problems sometimes appear to be similar when in fact they are quite different. The following questions contain the same words, but the transposing of "apples" and "dozen" completely changes the problem:

How many dozen are in 36 apples?

How many apples are in 36 dozen?

c. When large fractions or numbers are involved, rewrite the problem using small whole numbers. Pupils may be intimidated by the size of the numbers when asked, for example, to find the average daily output of a plant with an annual production of 14,510,350 items. It may be easy for these same pupils to determine the average output per day if they know that 40 items are produced in a five-day week.

A pupil may have difficulty finding the price per pound when a digital scale shows that the cost of 0.37 pounds is $1.47. Rewriting the problem so that it asks the cost of 1 pound when the cost of 3 pounds is $6 may enable the pupil to solve the original problem.

d. Use the "guess and test" method. For example, a pupil seeking to find the length of time it will take to travel 1000 kilometers at a speed of 75 kilometers per hour may first guess 10 hours, which will give a distance of 750 kilometers. The pupil can learn two things from making this guess. First, the correct answer is more than 10 hours; second, the product of the missing number and 75 must give 1000, leading to the equation $75n = 1000$. By guessing and testing, the pupil discerns that the answer is sensible and arrives at the correct operation.

e. Key words can be valuable, but they must be used with caution. For example, the word "sum" does not always indicate that addition must be used to solve a problem. To solve the problem question "What number, when added to 18, gives a sum of 31?" the student would obtain 13, the answer, by subtraction. The word "sum" suggests that 18 is to be added to an unknown addend. When the sum and one addend are known, the missing addend is determined by subtraction. Here, the problem question would be translated directly as the equation $18 + n = 31$.

If you are unclear about the limits of key-word use, meaningful learning may be inhibited. As the previous example illustrates, no word always indicates that one specific operation is required to solve a problem. However, if the word "sum" occurs in a one-step problem, addition or subtraction is required. The problem is then reduced to discovering whether all the addends are known and the sum is to be determined, or whether the sum and all addends but one are known. This discussion applies to words such as difference, product, and quotient.

The word "of" sometimes, but not always, indicates multiplication, as in "Find three-fourths of 40." But the question "Three-fourths of what number is 10?" is solved by division, rather than multiplication. When a situation suggests multiplication with a question containing "of," and the product and one factor are known, division is required for the solution.

An activity that helps strengthen the pupil's vocabulary of words associated with the four operations involves asking for oral or written answers to questions such as the following:

(1) What is the sum of 3 and 5?
(2) The product of what number and 8 is 40?
(3) Eight is 3 less than what number?
(4) Seventeen is how much more than 13?
(5) What is the difference between 9 and 4?
(6) What number is 3 less than 8?
(7) The difference of 8 and what number is 3?
(8) What number is the quotient of 10 divided by 2?
(9) The quotient of what number divided by 2 is 8?

Brief oral exercises performed frequently are more effective than a single extended session. Encourage pupils to write number sentences (equations) for questions of this type. If key words are to be of any value, it is essential that their limitations be understood.

f. A rate is one of the most common ways that numbers are related in problems included in elementary mathematics programs. Rates are common in everyday life—for example, in miles per hour, dollars per pound, and miles per gallon. When a rate is given in a one-step problem, the solution will require multiplication or division.

g. Look for a problem within a problem. Finding a simpler problem within a multipstep problem often helps to solve the original problem. Suppose that a problem asks for the cost of ten pounds but does not give the cost of one pound. The original problem can be solved by finding within it a problem that will result in the price per pound.

It is impractical to list every strategy that could be used in the elementary school. If you give the students too many strategies in too short a time, they may become as confused as if you have given them no help. *The background and attitudes of pupils must influence the choice and number of strategies introduced.*

3. *Carrying out the plan*

For most problems in elementary mathematics, carrying out the plan involves two steps. First, the computation is performed mentally, with paper and pencil or by calculator or computer; second, the numerical answer to the computation is interpreted, preferably with a simple sentence.

Some problems, such as those involving logic, may not require computation. Although such problems were not part of the traditional elementary curriculum, we recommend that they be included in programs of the 1980s.

4. *Checking*

The most important check is to determine whether an answer is sensible. Pupils should be taught to check their computations, but if they have chosen the wrong operation, such a check is useless. As pupils progress, they should be given more sophisticated methods of estimation to determine whether an answer is sensible.

One error that is common when equations or number sentences are used is thinking that the problem has been checked if the answer satisfies the equation. The computation is correct when the numerical answer satisfies the equation, but this is no guarantee that the correct equation has been used. Suppose that a problem asks the student: "Three less than what number is 8?" and the student writes the equation $n + 3 = 8$. The number 5 satisfies the equation but does not satisfy the problem condition, because 3 less than 5 is not 8. This example illustrates the importance of checking the problem conditions rather than the equation. If an answer does not meet the problem conditions, then there has been an error from one of two common sources: an error in computation or an incorrect choice of operation. Point out that the choice of equation leads to the choice of operation.

Multistep Problems

Early exploratory and symbolic work involves only single-step problems. Only one computation is required to solve single-step problems, which are sometimes called "choose-the-operation" problems. A problem is usually considered to be multistep if its solution requires at least two computations. For example, two computations are required to solve the equation $2n + 13 = 35$, and so a problem that includes this equation can be considered a two-step problem. There is no easy way to determine whether a problem involves one step or more than one step. The length of the problem and the numbers given or implied will give some indication. It is a good clue when a number usually given in a one-step problem is missing. For example, a problem may ask for the cost of ten books without giving the cost of one book. If the problem is to be solved, enough information must be given so that the cost of one book can be found either directly or indirectly. A proportion could be used to solve this problem without directly determining the cost of one book. Consider the following problem: If 7 books cost $21, what would be the cost of 10 books priced at the same rate?

Solution: Solve both of the following one-step problems:

Step 1: 7 books $\longrightarrow$ $21
         1 book $\longrightarrow$ $21 \div 7 = 3$
         The cost of one book is $3.

Step 2:   1 book $\longrightarrow$ $3
         10 books $\longrightarrow$ $10 \times 3 = 30$
         The cost of 10 books is $30.

By finding the cost of one book, one solves a problem within a problem, and then is led to the solution of the original problem. The original problem can be solved with a proportion, without specifically finding the cost of one book:

$$\frac{n}{21} = \frac{10}{7}$$

If $n \div 21 = \dfrac{10}{7}$, then, by the relationship between multiplication and division:

$$n = 21 \times \frac{10}{7} = 30$$

The cost of 10 books is $30.

By writing an equation, one can avoid breaking a problem into two one-step problems. For example, if Judy buys a head of cabbage for 89 cents and 3 cans of tomatoes at 30 cents per can, what is the total cost? This problem can be solved with two one-step problems. First, find the cost of 3 cans,

by multiplying 3×30, or 90 cents. Second, add 90 to 89 to get 179, for a total cost of 179 cents, or $1.79. Or the solution can be obtained with a single equation, as shown:

$$n = 3 \times 30 + 89$$
$$n = 179$$
Total cost is 179 cents, or $1.79.

Most problems at the elementary school level can be solved easily and accurately once the correct operation has been chosen. The equation indicates which operation has been chosen.

Additional Types of Problems

The key in solving one-step problems is choosing the correct operation. Often this step is easy for textbook problems, as it is common practice for all the problems in a section to require the same operation that was discussed on previous pages. Although this situation is fine when pupils are first exposed to new operations, it is important, as pupils progress, that they encounter problems that require a variety of operations. If the text does not include a mixture of problems, the teacher must provide the variety.

If problem solving is truely to be the major emphasis of the 1980s, then pupils must be exposed to a wider variety of problems than are found in traditional elementary programs. A wide variety of problems are suggested in the 1980 yearbook of the National Council, which is devoted to problem solving. Chapters 9, 10, and 11 deal specifically with the elementary program, with additional material of interest to elementary teachers included in other chapters.[6]

Most of the additional problems that are recommended are less structured than typical textbook problems, suggesting real-life problem situations that often have extra-

6. *Problem Solving in School Mathematics* (Reston, VA: National Council of Teachers of Mathematics, 1980).

neous or insufficient information. Formulating the problem is often a major step in solving problems of this type. In the next sections, we present some problems similar to those recommended for the elementary program.

Data Organization

If Anne has 3 pennies, 2 nickels, 4 dimes, and 3 quarters, how many different amounts can be formed by choosing one or more of these coins?

It is clear that the smallest amount is 1 cent and the largest is 128 cents. One approach to solving this problem is to make a table such as the following:

Total	Cents	Nickles	Dimes	Quarters
1	1	0	0	0
2	2	0	0	0
3	3	0	0	0
4	cannot be done			
5	0	1	0	0
6	1	1	0	0

This table, which includes a total of 128 lines, is not the most efficient way to solve the problem. A more concise solution would demonstrate that combinations of every number from 1 to 128, except 4, 9, 14, and so on, can be formed. Either approach will lead to the answer that there are 103 different amounts possible.

Another problem might ask for all the ways that a football team can score 20 points. The most likely method is to score 3 touchdowns and 2 points after touchdown. The least likely way is to score 10 safeties of 2 points each.

Pupils may be asked to gather information about different aspects of their school or community. Pupils can gain practice in measurement and experience in organizing data by recording the heights or weights of pupils in one or more classes. This experience in organizing and interpreting data can be valuable to them in the future, both in and out of school.

Logic Problems

The ability to draw logical conclusions is one of the most basic mathematical skills. On the elementary level, logic should be informal. It can involve *inductive* or *deductive* reasoning.

Inductive conclusions are based on experience. For example, a person watching the traffic on a freeway might conclude that all cars have 4 wheels, which is a false conclusion. Some cars have 3 wheels. An alert pupil might conclude that all numbers ending in 0 or 5 are divisible by 5, which is a correct conclusion.

A deductive conclusion follows an "if then" pattern. In other words, if something is true, then a certain fact must follow. Deductive reasoning is the basis of mathematical proof. In the appropriate mathematical setting, deductive reasoning can prove that every number ending in 0 or 5 is divisible by 5. Although there is little occasion to cover mathematical proof in the first six grades, and few educators recommend it, there is opportunity for informal deductive reasoning that provides readiness for proof.

Many problems contain no numbers but require logic for their solution. One such problem states that Joe will be sent to bed without supper or be spanked, depending on whether he makes a true or a false statement. If the statement is true, he will be spanked; if it is false, he will be sent to bed without supper. The problem question is: What statement can Joe make to escape punishment? The answer is: "I will be sent to bed without supper." If he is sent to bed, his statement is true, and so he should be spanked. If he is spanked, his statement becomes false and he should be sent to bed. Thus, no punishment is possible under the stated conditions. Although this problem bears little relation to reality, it does provide an opportunity to demonstrate that if one thing is true, then another must follow.

The logic of this problem is simple without being trivial. The National Council recommends problems involving logic for students studying to be elementary teachers. Such problems would appeal, if at all, to fast learners and are meant for enrichment, not general consumption.

Problems without Numbers

To solve problems without numbers, pupils must think more about the process than about the numbers. Here are some examples:

1. How can one find the cost of one pen by knowing the cost of many pens? Rephrasing the problem as a "many-to-one" or as a "given many, find one" situation can help the pupil identify it as a division problem.

2. How can one find the cost of many books if the cost of one is known? Rephrasing this problem as a "one-to-many" or as a "given one, find many" situation can help the pupil to recognize it as a multiplication problem.

3. How many neckties can be purchased for n dollars?

4. Sam went to the store with some money and bought several pounds of apples at a given price per pound. How much did he have left after the purchase? One way to solve the problem is to multiply the number of pounds times the price per pound and subtract this product from the original amount of money. Pupils can then be asked to substitute their own numbers and solve the problem.

A different type of problem that can be roughly described as without numbers is one that uses *variables* (letters) for numbers. Here are some examples:

1. Find the cost of one book if the cost of m books is n dollars.

2. Find the cost of n blouses if the cost of one blouse is m dollars.

3. Sam went to the store with n dollars and bought m pounds of apples at t dollars per pound. How much money did he have after the purchase?

Problems with variables are difficult for most pupils but are excellent enrichment material. If used judiciously, they can reinforce the pupil's understanding of letters in formulas and provide readiness for algebra.

Mental Arithmetic

Problem solving involves high-level mental activity, but the term "mental arithmetic" usually refers specifically to solving problems "in one's head" without using paper and pencil, except to record the answer. Computation in mental arithmetic should be so easy for elementary pupils that it can be done without recording the numbers. Mental arithmetic, popular in the early half of the century, was deemphasized in the days of New Math.

The emphasis in mental arithmetic should be on recognizing procedure and the relationships between numbers. If these problems are adapted to a given grade level, most pupils should be able to find the answer without using paper and pencil. The following examples are appropriate for grades 5 and 6:

1. How far will a car travel in 15 minutes if it travels 8 kilometers in 5 minutes?

2. The cost of 3 oranges is 40 cents. What is the cost of 6 oranges?

3. What is the (total) value of the numeral 5 in 3580?

4. What is the quotient of a number divided by itself?

5. How many centimeters are there in 2 meters?

6. What is the product of $8 \times 7 \times 0$?

7. With the numbers 4, 6, and 10, write a true number sentence using subtraction.

8. The product of two factors is 1. If one factor is 4, what is the other?

9. Thanksgiving day is the fourth Thursday in November. What is the earliest date for Thanksgiving? the latest date?

10. Give two ways a football team can score 16 points without scoring a safety or a 2-point after-touchdown conversion.

There are several types of problems in this sample set, including choice of operation, metrics, place value, number sentences, properties of 1 and 0, the calendar, and problems with multiple answers. Other types can also be included.

Applications

The National Council has published a useful book that stresses the value of applications to the student learning mathematics.[7]

Well-chosen applications will make mathematics more interesting to many pupils and help them to recognize it as a useful subject worth the effort required to learn it. It is unlikely, however, that any one application will interest every student in a class. A sports application, such as batting average, will interest many, while an automobile application may also interest several students, but not necessarily the same group. In order to interest most of the pupils in a class, a variety of applications must be available. The best guide for choosing appli-

cations for a given class and grade level is the teacher's experience. The teacher should be alert for new applications and continue to use those that have been successful in the past.

Textbooks contain many applications, but due to space limitations there is not the variety to interest the widest range of pupils. Many suggestions for the elementary level can also be found in the sourcebook of the National Council.

Below are two different types of problems that may interest a substantial number of pupils.

1. Car A travels 10 miles per gallon of gasoline; car B travels 15 miles per gallon. If the cost of gasoline is $1.50 a gallon, what is the difference in cost of driving each car 10,000 miles?

This is an excellent example of a multi-step problem that can be solved by a sequence of one-step problems. Direct pupils as follows: Find the cost per mile for car A and for car B. Find difference in cost for one mile, and then find the difference in cost for 10,000 miles.

Solution:

Car A 10 miles $\longrightarrow$ $1.50
         1 mile $\longrightarrow$ $150 \div 10 = 0.15$
         Cost per mile: $.15 or 15 cents

Car B 15 miles $\longrightarrow$ $1.50
         1 mile $\longrightarrow$ $1.50 \div 15 = 0.10$
         Cost per mile: $.10 or 10 cents

Difference in cost per mile: $.15 − $.10 = $.05

Difference for 10,000 miles: $10,000 \times .05 = 500$

Difference in cost for 10,000 miles is $500.

The same answer can be found by using the following formula, which uses the same plan with letters in place of numbers.

$$D = \frac{(m_1 - m_2) \times g \times d}{m_1 \times m_2}$$

D is difference in cost for d miles
m_1 is miles per gallon for car A

---

7. *A Sourcebook of Applications in School Mathematics* (Reston, VA: National Council of Teachers of Mathematics, 1980).

m_2 is miles per gallon for car B
g is cost of gasoline per gallon
d is number of miles

For this problem, D is to be determined: $m_1 = 15$; $m_2 = 10$; $g = 1.50$; $d = 10,000$.

$$D = \frac{(15 - 10) \times 1.50 \times 10,000}{15 \times 10} = 500$$

The difference in cost is $500.

The formula can be used to solve any problem in which all the variables except one are known.

2. The cost of electricity is now a much bigger factor in the household budget than ever before. Problems involving the cost of specific items, such as television sets, stereos, and toasters may interest a substantial number of pupils. By law, almost every electric appliance must carry a statement of its power consumption. This information is given in watts or amperes (usually abbreviated as amps). The power in watts (w) is the product of the electromotive force in volts (e) and the current in amps (a), or $w = ae$. If the current is 8 amperes and the electromotive force is 120 volts, then the power is 8 × 120, or 960 watts.

The quantity of electricity is measured in kilowatt-hours. A kilowatt, as the standard metric prefix indicates, is equal to 1000 watts. A kilowatt-hour is the quantity of electricity used by an appliance, rated at one kilowatt of power, in one hour. The formula for the cost of electricity is $C = ktc$ where:

C is the cost for t hours of use
k is the power rating in kilowatts
t is the number of hours in use
c is the cost per kilowatt-hour

Since most home devices list power in watts rather than kilowatts, the formula is usually more useful in the following form:

$$C = \frac{wtc}{1000} \qquad w = \text{power in watts}$$

For example, a 100-watt bulb burned for 24 hours at 10 cents per kilowatt-hour will cost:

$$C = \frac{100 \times 24 \times 10}{1000} = 24$$

The cost for 24 hours of use is 24 cents, or $.24.

The problem would probably interest more pupils if a television set or stereo were involved. Most television sets use about 100 watts of power.

Providing for Individual Differences

Every mathematics teacher faces the problem of how to provide for individual differences in learning, but the problem is especially acute in teaching problem solving. One plan that is often used is to have the slow learners solve a few problems, the average pupils a few more, and the fast learners still more. But unless the problems are carefully graded in difficulty, this plan will not effectively accommodate individual differences in problem solving.

Another effective plan that is easy to implement is to have pupils of varying ability give more than one solution for a problem. Have slow learners give one solution and the faster learners two or more solutions to a given problem. The following problem is an illustration of the plan.

Jim receives 12 cents for each box (quart) of strawberries he picks. One day he picked enough berries to fill 48 boxes. How much did he earn that day?

1. All members of the class would solve the problem in the usual fashion and obtain an answer of 576, which they would then interpret as $5.76. Have students see that in solving the problem the order of the factors can be interchanged, because of the com-

$$\begin{array}{cc} 48 & 12 \\ \times 12 & \times 48 \\ \hline 576 & 576 \end{array}$$

mutative property of multiplication. The faster learners will give other solutions, which may be the following. We shall not interpret the answer in these solutions.

2. Rename 12 as 10 + 2 and then apply the distributive property.

$$48 \times (10 + 2) = 480 + 96 = 576$$

3. Rename 48 as 50 − 2 and apply the distributive property.

$$12 \times (50 - 2) = 600 - 24 = 576$$

4. Factor 12 as 4 × 3 and apply the associative property.

$$4 \times 3 \times 48 = 4 \times (3 \times 48)$$
$$= 4 \times 144 = 576$$

5. Factor 48 as 12 × 4 and apply the associative property.

$$12 \times (12 \times 4) = (12 \times 12) \times 4$$
$$= 144 \times 4 = 576$$

Other factors of either 12 or 48 can be used to solve the problem. Enough solutions are given to demonstrate the plan.

After giving the class a fixed time to solve the problem, have the pupils describe the ways they solved it. Have a pupil who used a solution other than the first way show his or her method on the chalkboard. Make sure that as many different solutions as possible are given. Encouraging pupils to give as many solutions as possible challenges the fast learners and it becomes a game to see who can find the most solutions to a given problem. Finding a variety of ways to solve a problem leads to *power* in mathematics. (See Chapter 19.)

Research on Problem Solving

There is considerable research literature on the teaching and learning of problem solving. Many early studies focused on how computational skills could be improved

within the context of problem solving. Other studies attempted to determine the extent to which pupils followed a logical procedure. A few studies compared different approaches to problem solving so as to find the method that gave the best results.

During the 1970s and early 1980s, researchers devoted more time to problem solving than to any other topic in mathematics. Before 1970, research on problem solving in the elementary school was sparse and poorly done.

Research Regarding Young Children

Recent research has shown clearly that the approaches used by primary pupils in problem solving are quite different from those used by older children. Much recent research has involved pupils beyond the primary grades. Care must be taken to recognize the appropriate level for a given research project.

After an extensive review of the literature, F. K. Lester has concluded:

1. Young children need concrete problems, which are easier to solve than abstract problems.

2. The content and context of problems should be within the experience of the child.

3. Young children tend to focus on irrelevant aspects of a problem situation. Instruction should direct pupils to recognize the relevant facts in a problem.

4. During problem-solving activities, young children
  (a) take more time than older children.
  (b) make more errors.
  (c) rely more on trial-and-error methods.[8]

8. F. K. Lester, Jr. "Research on Mathematical Problem Solving." In *Research in Mathematics Education* (Reston, VA: National Council of Teachers of Mathematics, 1980), pp. 286–323.

It is generally accepted that young children are not ready for formal, logically ordered, sequential steps in problem solving. In the 1940s Piaget and Brownell agreed that young children were not yet mature enough to follow a sequence of steps in problem solving. Brownell questioned Dewey's classic formula for teaching children the logic of problem solving, a formula that included the following steps: (1) What is asked? (2) What is given? (3) What process should I use? (4) What is the probable answer? Computation was to follow the last question. On the basis of his research on young children, Brownell arrived at two conclusions. First, expert adult thinking may not follow this logical pattern, and children follow it even less; and second, this logical pattern is imposed on children before they are ready for it.[9]

According to Nelson and Kirkpatrick, young children learn to solve problems by seeing a relationship between a problem setting, "the event," and its mathematical model. They conclude that young children need problem-solving experience with problems that:

1. serve to develop mathematical ideas.

2. involve real objects.

3. are highly interesting to the children.

4. allow the children to take action on materials.

5. can be solved by various methods.

6. can be successfully solved.[10]

Teaching Children How to Solve Problems

As these remarks and suggestions indicate, the problem solving done by primary pupils should be largely on the exploratory level with little emphasis on logic. After the primary grades, there is more of a shift to symbolic learning, and more formal methods of problem solving can gradually be introduced.

In an article updating the research on problem solving, Suydam points out:

. . . research can't "tell anyone what to do"—it can only provide evidence and clues. . . . Research on problem solving has indicated that some broad generalizations appear true:

Problem solving strategies or heuristics can be specifically taught, and when they are, they are used more and students achieve correct solutions more frequently.

There is no one optimal strategy for solving all problems.

. . . Teachers can help pupils learn to solve problems with the following activities:

Expose children to many problems and to varied problems so that they develop flexibility in problem-solving behavior.

Teach children a variety of problem-solving strategies, plus an overall plan for how to go about problem solving.

Give children many opportunities to structure and analyze situations that really constitute a problem and not just a computational exercise.

. . . It would seem that one major conclusion is warranted from the research: teach problem-solving strategies! Take care that children do not come to regard them as they do algorithms—as rigid procedures to be followed. Problem solving demands flexibility, and strategies are one way to help pupils attain that flexibility.[11]

9. W. A. Brownell, "Problem Solving," *Psychology of Learning*, Forty-first Yearbook, Part 2 (Chicago: National Society for the Study of Education, 1942), p. 432.

10. D. Nelson and J. Kirkpatrick, "Problem Solving in Mathematics Learning in Early Childhood," *Thirty-seventh Yearbook of the National Council* (Reston, VA: National Council of Teachers of Mathematics, 1975), pp. 70–93.

11. M. N. Suydam, "Update on Research on Problem solving: Implications for Classroom Teaching," *Arithmetic Teacher*, February 1982, 6:56–57.

According to J. Worth:

> The first, most important, and most difficult (because it is attitudinal) idea to get across to students is what a problem is. Students must accept that a problem is a situation for which they do not know how to get an immediate answer. Too many students believe it is imperative that they find *the* single correct answer immediately, and if they *cannot find it immediately* they never will. . . . You the teacher have a "double-edged" commitment: you must provide explicit, carefully planned and structured problem-solving instruction, and you must provide the necessary time for solving a variety of problems during regularly scheduled class sessions.[12]

Summary

Problem solving is a process. In school learning situations, the process used to solve the problem is more important than the answer. Whereas the answers to most school problems will rarely be used again in daily life or in future learning, a sound problem-solving process will be used many times.

Some of the difficulty in problem solving comes from efforts to avoid relying on memory or rote processes. Pupils using this approach may become able to solve a limited number of problems, but they are helpless when confronted with minor variations in problems. Pupils should be given the opportunity to solve a wide variety of problems.

Every effort should be made to provide a substantial number of problems that are interesting to pupils. It is important, however, to attempt to instill in pupils the desire to solve a problem, interesting or not. Pupils should be reminded that mathematics that seems unimportant at one stage may be es-

sential at another. Pupils often fail to recognize that mathematics can be of value in a future career. Although many people have become successful without the aid of mathematics, pupils should recognize that it is necessary in order to enter many desirable fields, such as medicine, engineering, and data processing.

There is no algorism for problem solving. But there are procedures and strategies, sometimes called *heuristics*, which are often effective. Teachers must take care to introduce strategies gradually and judiciously, according to pupil attitudes and abilities. Keep in mind Suydam's remark: "It would seem that one major conclusion is warranted from the research: teach problem-solving strategies! Take care that children do not come to regard them as algorisms—as rigid procedures to be followed. Problem solving requires flexibility, and strategies are one way to help pupils attain that flexibility."

The following is an outline of the general plan for teaching problem solving and includes strategies that have proved to be successful.

I. *Understanding the Problem*
   1. Determine what is to be found by isolating the problem question.
   2. Determine what is given.
   3. Identify and supply any additional information that is required, such as 1000 grams per kilogram or the formula for the area of a rectangle.
   4. Picture the problem. If a figure is implied or required, draw and label it.
   5. Write each number in the problem and identify the items associated with it.
   6. Look for relationships among the numbers or quantities. Look for rates.
   7. Reword the problem. Use the few-

12. J. Worth, "Problem Solving in the Intermediate Grades: Helping Your Students Learn to Solve Problems," *Arithmetic Teacher*, April 1982, 6:16.

est words and simplest language possible.

II. *Drawing Up a Plan—Choosing a Strategy*

1. Visualize whether sets are combined, separated, or compared as an extension of the earlier work with objects.

2. Look for a familiar pattern. How is the problem similar to one already solved? How is it different?

3. To eliminate any confusion that can be caused by large numbers, fractional numbers, or variables (letters for numbers), rewrite the problem using small whole numbers.

4. Key words can be valuable but must be used with caution. For example, students should recognize that the word "sum" may indicate that the problem is to be solved with either subtraction or addition.

5. Guess and test. This procedure can often help students identify the correct operation (or operations) and determine the size of the answer and if it is sensible.

6. Identify rates. A one-step problem with a rate can be solved by multiplication if it is a one-to-many situation, and by division if it is a many-to-one situation.

7. Break the problem down into a sequence of simpler problems.

8. Write a simpler problem that will lead to the solution of the original problem.

III. *Carrying Out the Plan*

On the elementary level, the plan usually is carried out in two stages:
1. Perform the required computation.
2. Interpret the result of the computation.

If the scope of problems in the elementary program is broadened, carrying out the plan may involve organization of collected data or drawing one or more logical conclusions.

IV. *Checking the Problem Solution*

1. Check the solution against the conditions of the problem. Remember that checking the equation checks the computation but not the solution.

2. Estimate the answer in one or more ways to determine whether the answer is sensible.

3. Review the solution and look for alternate or more efficient ways to solve the problem.

Activities for Promoting Understanding in Problem Solving

1. Whenever possible, have pupils reword textbook problems by using the form: Given:
                    Wanted:

2. Write the numbers for each problem in a set of textbook problems on the chalkboard. Have pupils identify things associated with each number and show how numbers are related.

3. Ask pupils to make up their own problems for a specific operation.

4. Write an equation on the chalkboard. Ask pupils to write a problem for which the equation will lead to a solution.

5. Conduct frequent brief oral exercises to strengthen pupils' mathematical vocabulary.

6. Conduct frequent, brief oral exercises with, one-step problems that can be solved mentally. See page 185.

7. Encourage pupils to give a variety of solutions to a problem.

Exercises

1. Identify the four basic steps in problem solving.

2. Evaluate the "key word" approach to problem solving.

3. What are two advantages of the guess and test method?

4. What was the major conclusion drawn from the Second National Assessment in Mathematics?

5. Find the cost of 7 items if the cost of 3 items is $21.
   - A. Solve by using two one-step problems.
   - B. Solve with a proportion.

6. How much change will Sue receive from a ten-dollar bill if she buys two items at $3 each and another item for $2
   - (a) Solve by using a sequence of one-step problems.
   - (b) Solve by using a single equation.

7. Identify the rate, if there is one, in each of the following problems:
   - (a) Find the cost of 18 books if the cost of 1 book is $3.
   - (b) Find the number of books at $3 each that can be purchased for $18.
   - (c) Find the cost of 1 book if the cost of 3 books is $18.

8. Reword each problem in exercise 7 in one of the following ways: Given 1, find 18; given 3, find 1; how many 18s are there in 3?; how many 3s are there in 18?; given 18, find 1.

9. A problem requires the product of 3.28×7.92. Sam gets an answer of 19.81. Jim gets an answer of 26.98. Tina gets an answer of 33.2. None of the answers is correct. Which answer is sensible?

10. Discuss the value of a good memory in learning mathematics.

11. A bank teller cashed a customer's check for $280, giving the customer five bills. What was the value of each bill?

12. The customer in exercise 11 could have received six bills of only two different values. What would have been the value of each bill and how many of each would there have been?

Selected Readings

An Agenda for Action: Recommendations for School Mathematics for the 1980s. Reston, VA: National Council of Teachers of Mathematics, 1980. 30 pp.

Krulik, Steven, and Jesse A. Rudnick. *Problem Solving: A Handbook for Teachers.* Rockleigh, NJ: Allyn and Bacon, 1980.

Mathematical Applications, Selected Results from the Second Assessment of Mathematics. Denver: Education Commission of the United States, 1979.

Mathematics in Early Childhood, 37th Yearbook. Reston, VA: National Council of Teachers of Mathematics, 1975.

Problem Solving in School Mathematics. Reston, VA National Council of Teachers of Mathematics, 1980. 241 pp.

A Sourcebook of Applications in School Mathematics. Reston, VA: National Council of Teachers of Mathematics, 1980. 361 pp.

Chapter 11

Calculators and Computers

According to one leading company in the information-processing field, if the automobile industry had made as much progress and were as innovative in cost cutting as the electronics industry, a Rolls Royce would cost less than a dollar.

Achievement Goals

After studying this chapter, you should be able to:

1. Have a basic knowledge of some of the research on calculator use in the schools.
2. Understand the advantages and limitations of calculator use in teaching problem solving, basic facts, estimation, and number properties.
3. Recognize the motivational and recreational value of the calculator.
4. Understand that availability of software is as important in choosing a computer as is the choice of the computer (hardware).
5. Know that the microcomputer can be useful in teaching specific units, in providing remedial practice, and in testing.
6. Appreciate the value of microcomputers

in storing vast amounts of information, such as pupil records, which can be retrieved very quickly.

Vocabulary

Mastery of the following key terms will help you to understand this chapter. Each of these words is defined or illustrated in the Glossary at the back of the book.

Calculator logic	Disk drive
Cassette	Hardware
Computer-assisted	Kilobyte
instruction	Mainframe
Computer literacy	computer
Computer memory	Microcomputer
Computer program	Minicomputer
Courseware	Peripherals
Disk	Software

The Calculator Revolution

The advances in calculator technology in the past twenty years have been phenomenal. The first electronic desk calculators appeared in the mid-1960s. These devices, which cost more than $1000, had digital displays on a television-like screen and performed each of the four operations almost instantly. A mechanical calculator required a substantial amount of time to perform the simple division 2 ÷ 30. Today, a hand-held calculator that performs these operations and more can be purchased for less than $10. Programmable minicalculators that contain logarithmic and trigonometric functions are now available for less than $50.

The silicon chip, sometimes smaller than a thumbnail, has been the key element in this revolution. The space program, with its need for miniaturization, is responsible for producing this valuable tool. Silicon chips have also led to the development of electronic games, gasoline control systems, language translators, and much more.

Calculators in the School

The following problems can be used in a discussion of some of the uses of the calculator in the elementary school:

1. In seconds, Sue and Jim obtained answers to the following problem, which took the rest of the class several minutes to solve: Joe paid $351 for a television set after a 22 percent discount. What was the original price before the discount?

2. After studying decimals for only a few days, Anne used a calculator to multiply 2.345 by 10, 100, and 1000. By noting the change in the position of the decimal point, she discovered a faster way to multiply by powers of 10 without the calculator than with it.

3. The weight of each of Sam's six stamps is .01289 grams. What did he say to his brother when he came home that afternoon?

In problem 1, Sue and Jim used calculators. Sue got the correct answer of $450; she did this by interpreting the problem ques-

tion as: 22 percent less than what number is 351? Joe got an incorrect answer of $428.22 by taking 22 percent of 351 and adding it to 351. In problem 2, Anne used the calculator to discover a useful generalization that has often been taught by rote. In problem 3, if one finds the product 6 × .01289 on the calculator and turns it upside-down, the answer on the screen is "hello."

Using these situations, we can list some uses of the calculator in the elementary school:

1. The calculator reduces drudgery by keeping the time spent on computation to a minimum. However, the calculator will produce incorrect answers if pupils do not analyze problems correctly.

2. The calculator can help pupils discover important number properties.

3. The calculator has recreational value that can help to stimulate the interest and motivation of many pupils.

A Dramatic Drop

By the mid-1970s, there had been a dramatic drop in the price of minicalculators that made it possible for many pupils to own one. The use of calculators in the elementary school has aroused the interest and debate of educators, and has produced considerable research. The research on calculator use in the 1970s has been compiled by Suydam[1] in a valuable sourcebook that contains an exhaustive list of articles from popular magazines, books, dissertations, and research papers.

This compilation has a useful index that lists articles by category, such as testing, research, and games. Each article is usually summarized. The synopses of research articles generally include grade level, objectives, and results.

Thirty-five of the research articles con-

1. M. N. Suydam, *Calculators: A Categorized Compilation of References* (Columbus, OH: Eric, 1979).

cern the use of calculators in the elementary schools. About one-half of the studies focus on grade 5, 6, or both. Almost all of the work involved an experimental group and a control group. Many aspects of calculator use were studied, including effects on the understanding of mathematical concepts; value for slow learners; calculator use and motivation, attitudes, and the ability to compute.

In about 60 percent of the studies, the calculator group performed significantly better than the control group. The control group did better than the calculator group in only two studies. The remaining studies were inconclusive.

Wheatley[2] surveyed the results of thirteen studies on the use of calculators with elementary school children. In nine of the studies, the calculator group performed better than the control group; the control group performed better in only one study; and three of the studies were inconclusive.

It must be noted that most of these studies have taken place over one year, and, although no long-range studies have yet been done, substantial evidence has begun to accumulate that calculators can be useful in elementary education. More research and classroom experience are needed before we can maximize the use of calculators at each grade level.

The Calculator Debate

The use of calculators in the elementary school has generated considerable debate. The following is a list of the areas in which the use of calculators is being debated.

1. *The development of computational skills.* It is now generally agreed that the use of calculators does not eliminate the need

for pupils to acquire basic computational skills. On the other hand, pupils do not need to compute with the speed and accuracy that was needed in the early part of this century. Fifty years ago the ability to compute with speed and accuracy was a ticket to a good job. Today, calculators and computers do almost all the computation in the business world.

Wheatley concludes, ". . . evidence exists that calculators can facilitate mathematical performance with little risk of loss in computational proficiency."[3]

2. *The development of mathematical concepts.* Children develop mathematical concepts by engaging in a variety of activities. There is only limited evidence that calculators can contribute to that development. As we will discuss later, calculators can be used effectively to help pupils discover important number properties.

3. *The ability to solve verbal problems.* There are two advantages to the use of calculators in problem solving. First, using calculators greatly reduces computational time and thus allows more time for problem analysis. The vital thinking involved in solving a verbal problem consists of selecting the operation or operations rather than performing the computation.

Second, more realistic problems can be solved when a calculator is available. Most textbook problems are designed so that the computation is easy and the answer is usually a whole number. In real life, problems usually do not satisfy these conditions. The calculator is particularly effective in the "guess and test" method of solving verbal problems. (See page 181.)

4. *The use and study of mathematics.* The child initially reacts to the calculator with great interest that soon fades unless the instrument is effectively used in dealing with number and not as a novel toy. With teacher

2. C. Wheatley, "Calculator Use and Problem Solving Performance," *Journal for Research in Mathematics Education,* November 1980, 11:323.

3. Ibid., p. 324.

guidance, the learner can discover number patterns that lead to later insight and understanding.

The calculator can serve recreational purposes—a function that interests many pupils and improves their attitude toward mathematics. There are various books available that contain number games and recreational activities specifically designed for the calculator. (See page 198.)

5. *Learning basic facts in grades 1 and 2.* There has been little experimental evidence on the use of calculators in grades 1 and 2. Consequently, we recommend that calculators should not be used as learning aids before grade 3.

6. *The testing program.* Depending on the circumstance, calculators can sometimes be effectively used in testing. If the object of the test is to measure computational ability, calculators obviously will not be used. If the object is to measure problem-solving ability, calculators can be used, but any norm established with paper-and-pencil computation is invalid.

7. *The work in groups of different ability.* There is no experimental evidence to suggest that the use of calculators should depend on a pupil's ability. It is reasonable to assume that, with the proper guidance at the appropriate grade level, all pupils can benefit from calculator use.

In these days of high technology, the calculator is here to stay. Pupils will have them whether the school approves or not. Every effort should be made to use this new tool in the most effective manner possible.

Limitations of Calculator Use

Calculator use creates new problems as well as new opportunities. Some limitations of the calculator are:

1. The calculator cannot think. It does not tell the student which operation to perform,

the most basic decision in early problem solving.

2. Calculators can malfunction and their batteries run down. Performing the following calculation is a simple test to see whether the calculator is performing properly:

$$[(12 + 34 - 5.6) \times 7.8] \div 90$$
$$= 3.5013333 \ldots$$

The example uses the ten digits in order—except that zero is last rather than first—and the four operations. The problem and its answer can be written on tape and attached to the calculator, though the answer is rather easy to remember.

3. Pupils will press incorrect keys and fail to press correct ones hard enough. The ability to make reasonable estimates is the best safeguard against this type of error.

4. If a lesson requires calculators, spare calculators must be available for pupils who forget theirs or have one that malfunctions.

5. Calculators are a security risk.

6. Pupils who use calculators may encounter decimals before working formally with these numbers in school. Although this situation can cause confusion, proper handling of the students' natural curiosity can provide readiness for future work with decimals.

7. All calculators do not have the same logic. Different sequences of keys are required for the same operation on different calculators. The teacher must be aware of the types of calculator logic in use in the classroom. Caravella gives an excellent description of different types of calculator logic.[4]

It must be remembered that the calculator is only a tool. It can be very valuable when

4. J. R. Caravella, *Minicalculators in the Classroom* (Washington, D.C.: National Education Association, 1977).

its potential and its limitations are understood, but misuse can make it a liability.

Calculators above Grade 2

As pupils become more familiar with the four operations, a balance must be struck between computation with paper and pencil and with the calculator. One solution is to permit the use of calculators in problem solving, so as to place maximum emphasis on problem analysis. Pupils should practice without calculators, frequently but briefly, to maintain computational skills. Such practice can be oral or written.

In *An Agenda for Action*, the National Council recommends that teachers make the fullest use of the power of the calculator. It also recommends that paper-and-pencil computation be largely restricted to numbers less than three digits.[5]

The Use of Calculators in Problem Solving

After pupils have had ample experience in solving verbal problems with basic facts and algorisms, the calculator can be used to reduce computation time and enable the teacher to place more emphasis on problem analysis. Consider the following sample problems: (A.) Find the cost of 1 book if the cost of 8 books is $48. (B.) A company produces 1,321,000 cars in a 365-day year. What is the average daily production?

A pupil can solve problem B with a calculator in about as much time as is needed to solve problem A without one. By working and solving problems on the level of example B, the pupil will gain a better understanding of division situations by dealing with problems that have realistic numbers.

When solving a traditional problem with paper and pencil, a pupil might spend 90 percent of the solution time on computation and only 10 percent on problem analysis. The use of a calculator might reverse this situation.

Duea and Ockenga properly point out: "Because students can add, subtract, multiply and divide when they are using a calculator, computation does not stand in the way of writing or solving problems. The calculator puts emphasis on "what to do" rather than "how to do it.""[6]

The Calculator as Portable Answer Key

The calculator can be used as a portable answer key to check any computation almost instantaneously. However, pupils may ask why the calculator should not be used in the first place. There are a couple of reasons for this:

1. Pupils must understand that paper-and-pencil work is necessary in order to learn fundamental concepts associated with the computation.

2. Pupils cannot make effective use of the calculator until they understand the concepts associated with basic skills.

Using the Calculator to Discover Number Properties

The following activities show how a calculator can be used to discover important number properties:

1. Using a calculator, multiply a number, such as 17, by 10, 100, and 1000. Guide the pupils to discover how to multiply a whole number by a power of 10. Use the phrase "annexing zero" rather than "adding zero," since adding zero does not change the number. A similar activity involves dividing a number, such as 13,000, by 10, 100, and

5. *An Agenda for Action: Recommendations for School Mathematics of the 1980s* (Reston, VA: National Council of Teachers of Mathematics, 1980), pp. 7, 29.

6. J. Duea and E. Ockenga, "Classroom Problem Solving with Calculators," *Arithmetic Teacher*, February 1982, 6:50.

1000. The powers of 10 should be limited so that the quotient is a whole number and not a decimal. This activity can be expanded to include decimals.

2. To stress the special properties of one and zero, multiply numbers by 1 and 0 and add 0 to numbers, using the calculator. Note that $3 \times 0 = 0 + 0 + 0$.

3. To create readiness in dealing with equal fractions, divide 2 by 4, 4 by 8, and 8 by 16, and ask why the answers are the same.

4. Multiply $8 \times 11 \times 15$ on the calculator to get 1320. Next multiply only one factor by 2 such that: $16 \times 11 \times 15$; $8 \times 22 \times 15$; and $8 \times 11 \times 30$. Note that the product in all three cases is twice 1320, or 2640. This exercise demonstrates that multiplying one factor by a number multiplies the product by that number, a consequence of the associative property. Ask the class what would happen if every factor in the product were multiplied by 2. Show that $16 \times 22 \times 30$ is $8 \times (8 \times 11 \times 15)$, since the original product has been multiplied by 2 three times.

Estimation and the Calculator

Probably the most valuable use of estimation is in determining whether an answer is sensible. This includes checking the position of the decimal point, and determining whether a calculator is malfunctioning, or whether wrong keys have been pressed. The ability to estimate is one of the most valuable number skills that a person can acquire.

Because there is no standard algorism for estimation, it is a more difficult procedure to learn than standard computation. One of the most common procedures is rounding numbers to one or two nonzero digits, such as 432 to 400 or 1387 to 1400. Because it can provide instant information on how close the estimate is to the correct answer, the calculator is valuable to students learning to estimate.

It is useful for the teacher to present three to five problems in computation, at the level appropriate for the class, and ask for pupil estimates. The correct answers are then obtained by using the calculator and the methods of estimation discussed.

Basic methods of estimation are illustrated in the following examples:

1. Estimate 41×53. First round down to get $40 \times 50 = 2000$. Second, round up to get $50 \times 60 = 3000$. An estimate of 2500, halfway between the two, is useful for many purposes, including determining the position of the decimal point. A finer estimate can be made by noting that 41 is closer to 40 than 50 and 53 is closer to 50 than 60, so the answer should be closer to 2000 than 3000. If the students used this approach, estimates of 2100, 2200, or 2300 would be acceptable. The correct answer is 2173.

2. Estimate 41×47. The procedure outlined in example 1 will place the product between 1600 and 2500, leading to an estimate of 2050, halfway between the two. Multiplying 40×50 to get 2000 is also reasonable, but it is not obvious whether either estimate is too large or too small until one has more sophisticated methods. The correct answer is 1927.

Recreational Use

The recreational value of the calculator often helps to improve a pupil's attitude toward mathematics. Many books contain games and recreations designed specifically for the calculator. The books by Hartman[7] and Donner and Mateus[8] are completely devoted to games and recreations for the calculator. Below is a description of some typical recreational activities using the calculator.

7. A. Hartman, *The Calculator Game Book for Kids of All Ages* (New York: New American Library, 1977).

8. M. Donner and L. Mateus, *Calculator Games* (New York: Golden Press, 1977).

One simple game that can be played on the calculator involves only subtraction. The number 100 is keyed into the calculator and the first player subtracts from it any single-digit number except zero. The second player subtracts a nonzero single-digit number, and so on. When a player reaches the number 1, the only option remaining is to subtract 1 to obtain 0 and lose the game. This is a variation of an old Chinese game called *nim*.

A player can develop a winning strategy by recognizing that the person playing to 11 will lose the game if the opponent is knowledgeable. When a nonzero single-digit number is subtracted from 11, the result is a number from 2 through 10. A person playing to any one of these numbers can choose to subtract the single-digit number that will leave an answer of 1, forcing the opposing player to lose. It is logical that if the first player subtracts 9, the second player can be forced to lose by playing successively to 91, 81, 71, 61, and so on, until 1 is reached and the game lost. The initial number of 100 and the acceptable range of the number to be subtracted can be changed to give pupils the opportunity to make a new but similar analysis. The logic of this strategy is simple but not trivial.

In another game, a number, such as 125, is keyed into a calculator. The player is then asked to get an answer of zero with the fewest of the four operations possible on one-digit numbers. (Multiplication by zero is not permitted, as it would make the game trivial.) One solution would be to divide by 5 to get 25, divide 25 by 5 to get 5, and subtract 5 from 5 to get zero. Using larger numbers makes the game more interesting and difficult.

A different activity, more recreational than mathematical, is based on the fact that when a calculator is turned upside-down, the numbers on the screen can spell at least a dozen words. In the following examples, the numeral on the left spells the word on the right when a calculator is turned upside-down:

710	Oil
.07734	Hello
77345	Shell
55178	Bliss

An activity that was often engaged in when this property of the calculator was first discovered is as follows: Ask someone to use the calculator to find $250 \times 351 \times 810 - 155 = 71077345$ and then turn it upside down to find out who was responsible for the oil crisis. The answer is Shell Oil. Some people prefer a calculation that gives .0553 in order to blame Esso. If Texaco and others could be represented in this manner, they would take their share of the blame.

Another story involves a man with a plot of land that measured 142 meters by 5 meters. He thought the plot good only for gardening until he found its area on the calculator, which he then turned upside-down and read "oil."

A different type of activity asks the pupil to key in any three-digit number, such as 234. The pupil is then asked to obtain a six-digit number by repeating the original three digits, in this case, to get 234,234. The pupil then divides by 7, 11, and 13 to get 33462, 3042, and, finally, the original number 234. This procedure will work with any three-digit number: When a three-digit number is repeated to get a six-digit number and this number is divided successively by 7, 11, and 13, the final quotient will always be the original three-digit number. Pupils should be asked why this happens. The answer is that in the process the original three-digit number is multiplied by 1001 and then divided by 1001, illustrating the inverse relationship between multiplication and division—that is, multiplying by a number and dividing by it gives the original number. It also illustrates that successive division by 7, 11, and 13 is equivalent to dividing by $7 \times 11 \times 13$, or 1001. A pupil multiplying any three-digit number by 1001 will recognize that the product is a six-digit number whose second three digits are the same as the first three digits. This activity is worthwhile with paper and pencil but is much more time consuming than when using the calculator.

For another activity, ask the class to multiply 12345679 by multiples of 9. Then ask the pupils which digit is their favorite. If the answer is 6, the pupil is told to multiply 54×12345679 on the calculator. The answer will be 666,666,666. Note that 54 is 6×9. Multiplying $9 \times 12345679 = 111,111,111$. Therefore, multiplying $(6 \times 9) \times 12345679 = 6 \times 111,111,111$ or 666,666,666. Unfortunately, this will not work on a calculator with a capacity of only 8 digits.

These activities can also be performed on a computer.

Computers in the Elementary School

The advances in computer technology have been at least as spectacular as those in the calculator field. One manufacturer begins its advertisement as follows:

"Through the miracle of modern technology, a complete computer as powerful as the multimillion-dollar room-sized computers of a few years ago can be put into a package the size of a typewriter and sell for as little as a television set."

Technically, these typewriter-sized computers are known as *microcomputers,* though they are often called personal or home computers. The giant computers used by government and industry are called *mainframe* computers. There is also an intermediate class of computers called *minicomputers.*

The introduction of the microcomputer in the mid-1970s sparked the present computer revolution. It has been predicted that, by 1985, one out of every four homes will contain a personal computer. Having one or more computers in every classroom is no longer an impossible dream, though it is not yet an immediate reality. Microcomputers are now being introduced in many elementary schools. As they become more available, their immense impact on the elementary program will begin to be felt.

Home computers can be used to solve complicated mathematical programs, calculate tax returns, keep financial records and other types of information, analyze stock portfolios, play games, and perform a wide variety of additional tasks. Owners of home computers can subscribe to telephone networks and, at the touch of a few keys, can have access to a vast library of information, including plane and train schedules, news, financial reports, and more.[9]

Computer Hardware and Software

The term *hardware* refers to the computer and the many pieces of equipment, called *peripherals,* that can be attached to it. Common peripherals include video monitors or television sets, disks, cassette drive, and printers.

The computer is instructed in what to do by *computer programs,* which are also called *software.* The availability of appropriate software is just as important as the quality and flexibility of the hardware. Without software, computers are almost useless unless highly skilled programmers are available. Most pupils can learn to write a simple program in a short time but even a skilled programmer may need dozens or hundreds of hours to construct a useful educational program.

The quality and quantity of current educational software is at best barely adequate,

9. William J. Hawkins, "Info Banks," *Popular Science,* November 1980, 217:106–107.

Learning how to operate a computer. *(Photo by Leland Perry)*

but it is improving. As more elementary schools acquire computers, the availability of software will increase rapidly. In budgeting for one or more computers, a school system must include money for software. It is probably wise to start with the basic software requirements and add additional software as experience with the computer is gained. In general, software designed for one computer cannot be run on another.

Computer Memory

Computer memory (capacity) is measured in kilobytes (usually abbreviated as k). The memory of a computer determines the size of the program that can be run on it. A computer for the elementary schools would probably need at least a 48k memory to take advantage of desirable software. When purchasing a computer, a school system should be aware of the memory requirements of desirable software. Software requiring a 48k memory will not run on a 32k machine.

Storage and Retrieval of Information

The power of a computer depends largely on two factors:

1. Its ability to store and retrieve large amounts of information quickly.

2. Its ability to make decisions.

A high level of technical programming skill is required to take full advantage of the decision-making power of the computer. However, using relatively inexpensive software and with the basic technical knowledge, it is possible for a beginner to store and retrieve information.

Information fed into a computer is usually lost when the computer is turned off, but with proper peripheral equipment, information can be stored on cassette or disk. Although a disk drive costs almost half as much as a computer, it is almost essential for efficient school use. Storage and retrieval are nearly instantaneous with a disk drive, and are far more time consuming with cassette.

If a class of thirty pupils had a single computer, the amount of time for each pupil would be quite limited. Remember that the computer may be used for information storage and retrieval. The teacher can place a record of each pupil's grades and an anecdotal evaluation on a disk, to which the student would not have access. This record could be retrieved almost immediately for a conference with the pupil, parent, or administrator.

Almost unlimited information can be stored for ready retrieval—including formulas for mathematics and science, graphs for social studies, and so on. Review questions, sample quizzes, and similar information can also be stored. Encourage the students to bring in information they think is interesting or important. A collection of jokes and puzzles can provide a change of pace and stimulate interest. If a printer is available, printouts of any information on disk can be readily obtained. The variety and quantity of the information to be stored are limited only by the imagination and the number of disks available.

Computer-Assisted Instruction

Computer-assisted instruction, often abbreviated as CAI, is one of the most talked-about uses of computers in the schools. In this computer activity, the pupil interacts directly with the computer. The computer gives information and asks questions. The pupil types answers to which the computer then responds. To some extent, this program is similar to programmed learning, which was introduced in the late 1950s, but the power of the computer makes it far more flexible and effective. One of the major shortcomings of programmed learning was the lack of well-constructed programs. Similarly, computer-assisted instruction is no better than the program constructed for the subject matter under consideration.

The computer can administer tests for diagnosis, practice, or evaluation. A computer-administered test can tell the pupil immediately whether an answer is correct. Many computer tests allow the pupil to give two or three incorrect responses before giving the correct answer. A diagnostic computer test can indicate, for example, that difficulty with subtraction is the source of the pupil's difficulty with the division algorism. The effectiveness of computer-assisted instruction depends on the availability of computers and the quality of the software.

Courseware

Courseware refers to textbooks specifically designed to be used in conjunction with a computer. For example, a courseware text might enable a pupil to write a program for converting to and from the metric system. This program could be retrieved at will and used as the basis for estimating conversions and as a check on the accuracy of the estimate.

An algebra courseware text might enable the pupil to write a program for solving a quadratic equation. By solving many such equations in a short period of time, a pupil might develop a better understanding of the types of roots obtained from such equations.

The courseware teaches appropriate programming in connection with the course and enables the pupil to gain a fuller understanding of the programming and the subject matter. Currently, only limited courseware is available, but more will be produced as the number of computers in elementary schools increases.

Computer Literacy

The computer age is still in its infancy, even though almost everyone is affected directly or indirectly by the use of computers in government, banking, and many aspects of everyday commerce. It is commonly predicted that in the future our checking accounts will be handled by computer over the telephone and that we may read our morning newspaper over a computer's video monitor.

In the future, the ability to program a computer may be as fundamental a part of our education as reading and writing. Although today it is not necessary for everyone to learn computer programming, many educators argue that a person cannot be considered educated unless he or she possesses *computer literacy*, a basic knowledge of the capabilities and limitations of a computer. There is some controversy as to whether early computer education should focus on computer literacy or on the more technical aspects of computer use.

The International Council for Computers in Education publishes a journal, *The Computing Teacher*,[10] which deals with teaching about computers, teacher education in computers, and the impact of computers on the curriculum. The council also publishes a booklet[11] that discusses the use of computers in the elementary classroom.

Summary

Most households now have at least one calculator. The majority of elementary school pupils probably have access to a calculator, whether or not their school approves. Research evidence now indicates that calculators can be valuable in problem solving while posing no appreciable risk to computational ability. Calculators can reduce computation time to a minimum, but cannot tell pupils which operation to perform.

Calculators have recreational value and can help pupils to discover important number properties.

More than a half-million microcomputers can now be found in homes, schools, and business. It is estimated that by 1985 one out of every four homes will have a computer terminal. An important use of computers in the elementary school is storage

10. International Council for Computers in Education, *The Computing Teacher* (La Grande, Oregon: Eastern Oregon State College).

11. David Moursand, *Teacher's Guide to Computers in the Elementary School* (La Grande, Oregon: International Council for Computers in Education, 1980).

and retrieval of information. This includes keeping records of pupil achievement and building a library of useful and interesting information by the teacher and the class in a cooperative venture.

The computer can supply tests for remedial, diagnostic, and evaluative purposes. In addition to providing computer-assisted instruction (CAI), the computer can be used for remedial activities and enrichment.

Computer use in the elementary school is in its infancy. It is imperative for educators to keep abreast of the rapid expansion in this field.

Exercises

1. List three advantages of calculator use in the elementary schools.

2. List three disadvantages of calculator use in the elementary schools.

3. Estimate the following products by rounding to find the upper and lower limits. Check your results with a calculator.
   a. 34 × 61   b. 47 × 78   c. 23 × 49   d. 52 × 88

4. Use the relationship between multiplication and division to estimate the following quotients. Check your estimates with a calculator.
   a. 13 ÷ 62   b. 45 ÷ 148   c. 7 ÷ 231   d. 35 ÷ 437

5. The following examples contain correct digits, but without decimal points. Find the correct position of the decimal point by estimation.
   a. 2.43 × 51.5 = 125145
   b. .0134 × 876.8 = 1174912
   c. 14.1 ÷ 37.6 = 375
   d. 2548 ÷ 1456 = 175
   e. 421 ÷ .016 = 263125
   f. 1.2 ÷ 400 = 3

6. At what level does the calculator seem to be the least useful? Why?

7. Explain what is meant by each of the following terms: hardware, peripherals, software.

8. Discuss the relative value of hardware and software in purchasing a computer.

9. What two things are essential for a successful program in computer-assisted instruction?

10. What computer activity, with relatively inexpensive software, is one of the most useful?

In the following problems, use a calculator or a computer to check your computation.

11. Find the product of the first ten counting numbers; the first ten whole numbers.

12. Turn to Table 6.1 (p. 93) and find the sum of the numbers in the column headed by:
    a. 1
    b. 2
    c. 3

    d. From the answers you found, write the sum for each of the remaining six columns.

13. From problem 12 estimate the sum of the numbers in the nine columns. Check your estimation.

14. Refer to problems 18 and 19 on page 146. You found the sums of the numbers in the columns in Table 6.1 (p. 96). Estimate the total of these sums. Check your estimation.

15. The sum of the columns in problems 12 and 14 form an arithmetic series. In a series of this kind there is a common difference between any two consecutive numbers. The sum of an arithmetic series is equal to the average of the first and last numbers multiplied by the number of addends. If S equals sum, a equals first addend, l equals last addend, and n the number of addends, write the formula for writing the sum.

16. Use the formula you made in problem 15 and find the sum of the series in problem 13; in problem 14.

Selected Readings

An Agenda for Action: Recommendations for School Mathematics of the 1980s. Reston, VA: National Council of Teachers of Mathematics, 1980.

Caravella, Joseph R. *Minicalculators in the Classroom.* Washington, D.C.: National Education Association, 1977.

Doerr, Christine. *Microcomputers and the 3 R's.* Rochelle Park, NJ: Hayden Book Company, 1977.

Donner, Michael, and Lynn Mateus. *Calculator Games.* New York: Golden Press, 1977.

Hartman, Arlene. *The Calculator Game Book for Kids of All Ages.* New York: New American Library, 1977.

Moursand, David. *Teachers' Guide to Computers in the Elementary School.* La Grande, Oregon: International Council for Computers in Education, 1980.

Papert, Seymour. *Mindstorms: Children, Computers and Powerful Ideas.* New York: Basic Books, 1980.

Suydam, Marilyn N. *Calculators: A Categorized Compilation of References.* Columbus, OH: Eric, 1979.

Chapter 12

Primes, Composites, and Integers

The writer Clifton Fadiman[1] reports on the visit of the mathematician Littlewood to the self-taught Hindu scholar Ramanujan. When Littlewood mentioned that the number on his cab was an uninteresting 1729, the Hindu replied, "On the contrary, it has the very interesting property of being the smallest number which can be expressed as the sum of two cubes in two different ways." ($1729 = 1^3 + 12^3 = 9^3 + 10^3$.) This story contains an example from *number theory*, a branch of mathematics that deals with many properties of primes, composites, and integers.

Achievement Goals

After studying this chapter, you should be able to:

1. Understand the importance of the concept of multiples in elementary mathematics.

2. Understand how products, factors, divisors, and multiples are related.
3. Recognize the role of prime and composite numbers in the elementary program.
4. Have students grasp the importance of common multiples in working with fractions.
5. Introduce the concept of signed numbers to students in the upper elementary grades.

Vocabulary

Mastery of the following key terms will help you to understand this chapter. Each term is defined or illustrated in the Glossary at the back of the book.

Additive inverse	Lowest (least)
Casting out 9s	common
Common multiple	multiple
Composite number	Prime number
Counting number	Rational numbers
Divisor	Real numbers
Factor	Prime factorization
Integer	

1. Clifton Fadiman, "Meditations of a Mathematical Moron." In *Any Number Can Play* (Cleveland: World, 1953), p. 153.

Whole Numbers, Counting Numbers, and Zero

The term *whole numbers* is the everyday name for the set of numbers that mathematicians call *cardinal numbers,* or, more technically, nonnegative integers. The set is often represented as follows:

0, 1, 2, 3, 4, 5, 6, 7, 8, 9, . . .

The set of *integers* can be described as the set of positive and negative whole numbers and zero. Zero must be considered separately because it is neither positive nor negative. The set of integers can be represented as:

. . . ⁻3, ⁻2, ⁻1, 0, 1, 2, 3, . . .

Pupils should be made aware of the different properties of different sets of numbers. For example, elementary pupils sometimes are told that "6 cannot be subtracted from 5," which is a false statement in the set of integers. The correct statement "6 cannot be subtracted from 5 in the set of whole numbers" can arouse the students' curiosity and provide readiness for introducing the integers. The teacher should make every effort to avoid statements that must be corrected later.

Take the following quiz as an opportunity to review the sets of numbers under discussion. Match each term on the left with the set on the right that it describes.

I. Natural numbers
II. Cardinal numbers
III. Integers

A. 0, 1, 2, 3, . . .
B. Counting numbers
C. Whole numbers
D. Positive and negative whole numbers and zero
E. Positive integers
F. 1, 2, 3, 4, 5, . . .
G. Nonnegative integers (including zero)

Answers: I—B, E, F; II—A, C, G; III—D

Traditionally, negative 3 (not minus 3) is written as ⁻3. The minus sign in ⁻3 is a sign of direction, indicating that ⁻3 is a negative number. In 5 − 3, the minus sign is a sign of operation, indicating that 3 is to be subtracted from 5. Consistent use of this notation in early work with signed numbers keeps pupils from becoming confused.

Mathematicians refer to the *counting numbers* as *natural numbers,* or positive integers. This set can be represented as:

1, 2, 3, 4, 5, 6, 7, 8, 9, 10, . . .

New Math programs placed more emphasis on the names of sets of numbers than current programs do. Although teachers should use the correct names for these sets, pupils should not be required to use them.

Multiples of a Number

When students hear the term "even number," they should recognize that the numbers being discussed are whole numbers or integers. The number ½ is neither even nor odd. The word *multiple* restricts the discussion in the elementary program to the set of whole numbers.

The word *multiple* is derived from multiplication. When two or more numbers are multiplied, the product is a multiple of each factor and is a multiple of the product of two or more of these factors. For example, in the multiplication 24 = 2 × 3 × 4, 24 is a multiple of 2, 3, 4, 6, 8, 12, and 24. Every number is a multiple of itself.

The inverse relationship between multiplication and division requires that every true statement about multiples also be true of division, though rephrased in division terms, as long as division by zero is excluded. Because 15 = 5 × 3, it follows that 15 is divisible by 5 and 3. The statements "15 is a multiple of 3" and "15 is divisible by 3" are equivalent. It is sometimes more useful for pupils to recognize 15 as a multiple of 5 because it is divisible by 5 than to know that 15 = 5 × 3.

Because 0 = 0 × 5, 0 is both a multiple of 5 and divisible by 5. Therefore, zero is a multiple of every whole number and divisible by every whole number except zero.

The following sequence of activities illustrates how the concept of multiples can be introduced to a class:

1. Ask the class to write the multiples of 2 by successively multiplying each whole number by 2 to obtain: 0, 2, 4, 6, 8, . . .

2. Ask the class to write the first seven positive multiples of 5 on the chalkboard: 5, 10, 15, 20, 25, 30, 35. Ask the following questions:

  a. What multiple follows 5?
  b. Is 15 a multiple of 5?
  c. Is 5 a multiple of 15?
  d. Is 15 divisible by 5?
  e. Is 5 divisible by 15?
  f. Is it possible for *a* to be a multiple of *b* at the same time *b* is a multiple of *a*?
  g. Is 18 a multiple of 5?
  h. Is 20 a multiple of 30? of 10? of 3? of 20?

3. Use the number line below to do the following exercise:

  a. Circle the multiples of 2.
  b. What is another name for the multiples of 2?
  c. Place an x under each multiple of 3.
  d. What numbers are multiples of both 2 and 3?
  e. What numbers are divisible by both 2 and 3?

  f. What numbers are divisible by 6?
4. Is 6 a multiple of 3? Why?
5. Is 3 a multiple of 6? Why?
6. What is the smallest positive (greater than zero) multiple of 3?
7. Name the sequence: 0, 4, 8, 12, 16, 20, 24, 28, . . .

Factors, Products, Divisors, and Multiples

Factor and *product* are usually familiar terms when the multiple concept is introduced. The difference between a multiple and a product provides another example of a statement which is true in one set of numbers but not in another. The statement "Every product is a multiple" is true in the set of whole numbers, but not in any set that includes fractions (such as the rationals). For example, the sentence 6 = ½ × 12 does not imply that 6 is a multiple of ½.

The terms divisor and factor are synonymous as long as division by zero is not involved. The statement 6 × 0 = 0 indicates that 6 and 0 are factors of 0 and that 6 is a divisor of 0. However, 0 is not a divisor of 0. It would seem that 0 ÷ 0 should equal 1, leading to the true statement 0 = 0 × 1. However, the assumptions that 0 ÷ 0 = 2 and 0 ÷ 0 = 3 also lead to the true statements 0 = 0 × 2 and 0 = 0 × 3. This lack of uniqueness leads to the statement that 0 ÷ 0 is undefined. Do not initiate the difficult topic of division by zero on the elementary level but be prepared to give accurate answers to questions on this topic. For additional information, see page 61.

Prime Numbers

Every counting (natural) number greater than 1 is either a *prime number* or a *composite number*. The number 1 is called a unit and is neither prime nor composite. A prime number has only two unequal counting number factors—the number itself and 1. Every prime number is divisible only by itself and 1. Two is the first prime number and is the only even prime number.

A number cannot be prime if it is divisible by any number other than itself and 1. Therefore, every even number greater than 2 is composite, and 4 is the first composite number. Nine is the first odd composite number.

Since the number 1 is divisible only by itself and 1, some pupils may ask why it is not prime. It may seem arbitrary to them that 1 is not prime by definition. You should explain to them why it is defined as not prime. If 1 were a prime number, 6 could be factored into primes in many ways: $6 = 2 \times 3 = 2 \times 3 \times 1 = 2 \times 3 \times 1 \times 1$ and so on. Since 1 is not a prime number, every composite number factors uniquely into primes, except for the order in which the factors are written.

The Fundamental Theorem of Arithmetic

The *fundamental theorem of arithmetic* states that every composite number factors uniquely into prime factors, except for the order in which the factors are written. When the factors are written in the order of their magnitude, prime factorization can be done in only one way—that is, uniquely.

$$10 = 2 \times 5$$
$$12 = 2 \times 2 \times 3 = 2^2 \times 3$$
$$300 = 2 \times 2 \times 3 \times 5 \times 5$$
$$= 2^2 \times 3 \times 5^2$$

The Sieve of Eratosthenes

One well-known method for determining prime numbers is the sieve of Eratosthenes. This method involves the successive elimi-

nation of composites. Begin by constructing a table similar to the one below.

~~1~~	②	③	~~4~~	⑤	~~6~~
⑦	~~8~~	~~9~~	~~10~~	⑪	~~12~~
13	14	15	16	17	18
19	20	21	22	23	24
25	26	27	28	29	30
31	32	33	34	35	36

The number 1 is eliminated by definition. Circle 2, the first prime number. Now cross out every second number (4, 6, 8, and so on). This procedure eliminates all even composite numbers (multiples of 2 greater than 2). Now circle the number 3—(the first number not crossed out after 2)—and cross out every third number greater than 3 (9, 15, 21, and so on) that has not already been crossed out. This eliminates all multiples of 3 that are not multiples of 2. Now circle 5, the next number that has not been crossed out, and cross out every fifth number that has not already been crossed out. This eliminates all multiples of 5 that are not multiples of 3. Now circle 7 and cross out every seventh number that has not already been crossed out. Proceeding in this manner eliminates all composite numbers, and only primes are left.

Although traditionally the sieve is performed with a ten-column table, the advantage of using six columns is that all primes greater than 2 or 3 occur in the first or fifth column. Every natural number can be represented as $6n$, $6n + 1$, $6n + 2$, $6n + 3$, $6n + 4$, $6n + 5$ ($n = 0, 1, 2, 3, \ldots$). Because all the numbers except $6n + 1$ and $6n + 5$ have a factor of 2 or 3, none can be prime except when $n = 0$, then $6n + 2 = 2$, and also $6n + 3 = 3$. This leads to the generalization that all primes greater than 3 are of the form $6n + 1$ or $6n + 5$ ($n = 0, 1, 2, 3, \ldots$). Because numbers in the fifth column also are of the form $6n - 1$ ($n = 1, 2, 3, \ldots$), the generalization is sometimes stated that all primes greater than 3 are of the form 6n + 1 or 6n − 1, abbreviated as 6n ± 1 (n = 1, 2, 3, . . .).

Recently, in a project that took three years to complete, two high school students used a computer to find the largest prime ever discovered, $2^{21701} - 1$. This number, which contains 6533 digits, has no known practical value, but the methods used to find it may be useful in other situations.

Exercises 12.1

1. Give the first three primes that are of the form 6n + 1; the form 6n − 1.

2. If a number greater than 3 is divided by 6 with a remainder other than 1 or 5, it cannot be prime. Why?

3. Which of the following statements is true?
   a. If a number is of the form 6n + 1, it is prime.
   b. If a number is not of the form 6n + 1, it is not prime.
   c. If a number is of the form 6n + 1, it may be prime.

4. Divide each of the following numbers by 6 and determine whether (a) it is not a prime; or (b) it may be prime.
   a. 183   b. 1091   c. 1577   d. 811   e. 773   f. 1005

5. It is sometimes said that a prime number is divisible only by itself and 1. Is this statement true? Is it an adequate definition of a prime number? Why or why not?

6. How many even prime numbers are there?

7. Write prime factorizations for:
   a. 15   b. 8   c. 30   d. 126

8. Consider the expression A = 2 × 3 × 4 × 5 × 6 × 7 × 8 × 9 × 10.
   a. Why is A + 2 not a prime?
   b. Why is A + 3 composite?
   c. How many consecutive composite numbers are in the sequence: A + 2, A + 3, A + 4, A + 5, A + 6, A + 7, A + 8, A + 9, A + 10?

9. The set of counting numbers can be written in the form 4n, 4n + 1, 4n + 2, 4n + 3 (n = 0, 1, 2, 3, . . .). Which of these four representations cannot be prime? Complete the following statement: All prime numbers greater than 2 must be of the form _____ or _____ (n = 0, 1, 2, . . .).

Classroom Activities

The following activities suggest ways to familiarize pupils with prime numbers:

1. Ask pupils to rename 14 using only multiplication. The product ½ × 28 would be acceptable given these instructions. Now impose the additional restriction that only whole numbers can be used. Both 2 × 7 and 14 × 1 would be acceptable under these conditions. Now restrict the operation to multiplication with whole numbers

greater than 1. The only acceptable results would be 2 × 7 and 7 × 2. If the factors are written in order of magnitude, the only acceptable result is 2 × 7.

Now start with 11 and follow the same sequence to discover that 11 cannot be renamed using the operation of multiplication with whole numbers greater than 1. Here is another opportunity to discuss the relationship between multiplication and division. If 11 could be expressed as the product of two whole numbers greater than 1, it would be divisible by a whole number other than itself and 1, and could not be prime.

2. Have the class find prime numbers by using the sieve of Eratosthenes, as described on page 209. Help the class discover that numbers greater than 3 that have a remainder other than 1 or 5 when divided by 6 cannot be prime.

3. Use whatever rules of divisibility the class is familiar with to determine what numbers are not prime. For example, show that the number 111,111 cannot be prime because the sum of its digits is divisible by 3. (See page 215.)

4. Point out to the class that 1203 cannot be prime because it has a remainder of 3 when divided by 6. Examine other numbers in this manner to determine whether a number is not a prime or whether it can be a prime. For example, the number 1201 has a remainder of 1 when divided by 6, and is prime. The number 901 has a remainder of 1 when divided by 6, but is not prime, because 901 = 17 × 53.

5. Ask pupils to identify the prime numbers in a decade, such as from 40 through 49. Ask them why there cannot be more than four primes in a decade.

6. Ask the pupils to find twin primes. Twin primes, such as 11 and 13, are consecutive odd primes.

7. Have pupils name the one set of triple primes (3, 5, and 7) and the one pair of consecutive primes (2 and 3).

8. Students commonly guess the next number in a sequence, an activity that helps them to recognize patterns. If this is done in your class, write the following sequence on the chalkboard and ask for the next number:

2, 3, 5, 7, 11, 13

This exercise is difficult. You should hint that there is a common property, but no rule about getting from one number to the next, such as adding 2 in the set of even numbers. After three or four additional numbers have been named, ask for the common property and identify the set as prime numbers. This activity is probably best suited for above-average students.

Composite Numbers and Common Multiples

The set of counting (natural) numbers can be separated into the set of prime numbers, the set of composite numbers, and the unit 1. It is useful for students to rename composite numbers as products of primes. The tree diagram is a graphic illustration of this process. Figure 12.1 shows two forms of a tree diagram to find the prime factorization of 12.

In drawing a tree diagram, start with the original number and find any two factors. Place each factor at the end of a branch. Whenever a prime number occurs, no further branching takes place. The prime factorization is the product of the primes at the

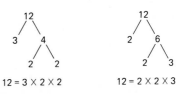

12 = 3 × 2 × 2   12 = 2 × 2 × 3

Figure 12.1

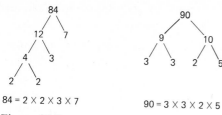

$84 = 2 \times 2 \times 3 \times 7$

$90 = 3 \times 3 \times 2 \times 5$

Figure 12.2

end of each branch. Figure 12.2 illustrates how a tree diagram can be used to find the prime factorization of 84 and 90.

A more common form of prime factorization is shown below. For pupils who are familiar with short division, the three divisions on the left can be abbreviated as shown on the right.

$$\frac{42}{2)84} \qquad \frac{21}{2)42} \qquad \frac{7}{3)21} \qquad \begin{array}{r} 2)84 \\ 2)42 \\ 3)21 \\ \hline 7 \end{array}$$

$$84 = 2 \times 2 \times 3 \times 7$$

The original number is divided by a prime, preferably the smallest such number. The quotient of this division is then divided by a prime, preferably the smallest such divisor. This procedure is continued until the quotient is a prime. The prime factorization consists of the product of the prime quotient and all the other prime divisors.

Common Multiples

The number 48 is both a multiple of 6 and of 8 and is therefore a *common multiple* of 6 and 8. It is not the *lowest (least) common multiple* of 6 and 8, as it is larger than 24, which is also a common multiple of 6 and 8. Note that 48 and 24 are divisible by 6 and 8. The lowest, or least, common multiple of a set of numbers is the smallest number (multiple) divisible by each number in the set.

Lowest common multiples are most often used in finding the lowest common denominator of a set of fractions. The lowest com-

mon denominator is the lowest common multiple of the denominators involved. The following activities are often used to introduce this procedure.

1. Have the class write the multiples of 6 and 8 as follows:

6, 12, 18, 24, 30, 36, 42, 48, 54
8, 16, 24, 32, 40, 48, 56, 64, 72

Have the class identify common multiples of 6 and 8 and to name the lowest common multiple.

2. Using the multiples of 6 from example 1, ask if 6 is a multiple of 9; if 12 is a multiple of 9; and if 18 is a multiple of 9. Help the students to recognize that 18 is the lowest common multiple of 6 and 9. Now ask if 9 is a multiple of 6, and if the next multiple of 9 (18) is a multiple of 6. Allow the students to discover that it took two steps using multiples of 9 and 3 steps using multiples of 6 to determine that 18 is the lowest common multiple of 6 and 9.

3. Ask the class to find the lowest common multiple of 9 and 12 by examining multiples of 9; by examining multiples of 12. Ask them which approach is faster; help them to recognize that using the multiples of the largest number requires fewer steps.

For most of the numbers that elementary pupils will encounter as denominators, examining multiples of the largest denominator may be the most efficient way to find the lowest common denominator. The pupil examines successive multiples of the largest denominator until finding one that is divisible by (is a multiple of) each of the other denominators. To find the lowest common denominator of 6, 10, and 15, for example, the pupil would note that 15 is not divisible by 6, but that 30 is divisible by 6 and 10, so that 30 is the lowest common multiple or denominator. Some pupils may prefer to write out both sets of multiples. This is perfectly acceptable but less efficient.

4. Have the class construct a table similar to the following:

Number Pair	Product	Lowest Common Multiple
6, 8	48	24
5, 7	35	35
4, 5	20	20
9, 15	135	45
8, 12	96	24
8, 9	72	72

By definition, the product of two numbers is a common multiple, which, as the table makes clear, is not always the lowest common multiple. If necessary, extend the table to give the pupils the opportunity to discover that the product is the lowest common multiple of two numbers only if they have no common factor other than 1.

Prime Factor Method

1. Have the class identify the lowest common multiple of 10 and 15 by noting that 30 is the first multiple of 15 divisible by 10. Now write the prime factorizations of 10 and 15:

$$10 = 2 \times 5 \qquad 15 = 3 \times 5$$

Allow them to discover that the lowest common multiple is the product of the different prime factors in 10 and 15, $2 \times 3 \times 5$. Note that even though 5 occurs as a prime factor in both 10 and 15, it occurs only once as a factor in the lowest common multiple, $2 \times 3 \times 5 = 30$.

2. Repeat the activity in example 1 using pairs of numbers having no prime factor oc-

curring more than once, such as 6 and 10, 6 and 15, 14 and 21, and so on.

3. By examining multiples of 15, determine that 60 is the lowest common multiple of 15 and 20. Now write the prime factorizations of 15 and 20.

$$15 = 3 \times 5 \qquad 20 = 2 \times 2 \times 5$$

Note that the different prime factors in the two numbers are 2, 3, and 5, but that 60 $(2 \times 2 \times 3 \times 5)$, and not 30, is the lowest common multiple. Ask them why 2 must be used twice.

Repeat this process with pairs of numbers, such as 4 and 6, 12 and 15, 12 and 18, and allow the class to discover the following rule about the prime factor method for finding the lowest common multiple:

The *lowest common multiple of two or more numbers is the product of the different prime factors occurring in the numbers with each factor used as many times as it occurs in any one number.* For example, find the lowest common multiple of 15, 20, and 36. The prime factorizations are:

$$15 = 3 \times 5$$
$$20 = 2 \times 2 \times 5$$
$$36 = 2 \times 2 \times 3 \times 3$$

The different prime factors are 2, 3, and 5. The lowest common multiple is 180, or $2 \times 2 \times 3 \times 3 \times 5$. The factor 2 is used twice because it occurs twice in 20, and 3 is used twice because it occurs twice in 36.

4. The following is an abbreviated and somewhat disguised form of the prime factor method, which is often taught by rote:

2)15	20	36
2)15	10	18
3)15	5	9
5) 5	5	3
1	1	3

This process of finding the lowest common multiple of 15, 20, and 36 consists of dividing out common prime factors. If the number does not contain the common factor being divided, it is brought down intact. The process continues until no two numbers (quotients) have a common factor. The lowest common multiple is the product of the divisors and the final quotients or $2 \times 2 \times 3 \times 5 \times 1 \times 1 \times 3 = 180$.

Exercises 12.2

1. Write the numbers of which 18 is a multiple.

2. Examine the multiples of 18 to find the lowest common multiple of 15 and 18.

3. Find the lowest common multiple of 15 and 18 by the prime factor method.

4. If one is available, use a calculator to find the lowest common multiple of 1001 and 385 by examining multiples of 1001. Proceed as follows: a. Divide 1001 by 385 and note a decimal quotient indicating that 1001 is not a multiple of 385. b. Divide 2×1001 by 385 and get a decimal quotient. Continue until the quotient of $5 \times 1001 \div 385 = 13$, indicating that 5005 is the lowest common multiple.

5. Use a calculator to find the lowest common multiple of 385 and 1001 by the prime factor method. To find the prime factorization of 1001, proceed as follows:

   a. Since 1001 is obviously not divisible by 2, divide by 3 and get a quotient with a decimal remainder, indicating that 1001 is not divisible by 3. If you are familiar with the rules of divisibility discussed in the next section, this step will be unnecessary, as a number is not divisible by 3 unless the sum of its digits is divisible by 3.

   b. Multiply by 3 to get the original 1001 and then divide by 7 to get to 143. Obviously, 1001 is not divisible by 5.

   c. Divide 143 by 7 to see whether 143 contains another factor of 7. Get a decimal quotient, which indicates that there is not a second factor of 7.

   d. Multiply by 7 to get back to 143 and divide by 11 to get 13. The prime factorization of 1001 is $7 \times 11 \times 13$.

   Note that if the number is odd, the first prime of 2 can be ignored. If the sum of the digits of the number is not divisible by 3, the second prime of 3 can be ignored. The next prime is 5 and can be ignored if the number does not end in 0 or 5. The primes 7, 11, 13, 17, and so on will be tried. It is worth noting that if there is no divisor less than the square root of the number, there cannot be a divisor larger than the square root. If a number factors into the product of two unequal numbers, one is larger than the square root and one is smaller.

   A similar procedure will reveal that the prime factors of 385 are $5 \times 7 \times 11$. Therefore, the lowest common multiple is $5 \times 7 \times 11 \times 13 = 5005$.

Some calculators make round-off errors that will give a quotient of 17.9999999 instead of 18. To check whether the decimal remainder reflects a round-off error or lack of divisibility, multiply the whole number by the divisor.

Rules of Divisibility

It is not practical to prove the rules of divisibility for students in the elementary grades.[2] Pupils should have the opportunity to discover them, with guidance, rather than being presented with them outright. For example, you might ask the class which of the numbers 11 through 19 are divisible by 3. You might then ask which of these numbers is the sum of the digits divisible by 3. You should test them with additional numbers until pupils recognize that a number is not divisible by 3 unless the sum of its digits is divisible by 3.

Although some of the rules may not be so obvious, it is almost always desirable to give pupils the opportunity to discover a mathematical rule or principle before formally presenting it. The most common rules can be stated as follows:

1. A number is divisible by 2 if and only if its last digit is divisible by 2.

2. A number is divisible by 3 if and only if the sum of the digits is divisible by 3.

3. A number is divisible by 4 if and only if the number represented by its last two digits is divisible by 4. For example, the number 11124 is divisible by 4 because 24 is divisible by 4.[3]

4. A number is divisible by 5 if and only if the last digit is 0 or 5.

5. A number is divisible by 6 if it is an even number with the sum of its digits divisible by 3. Under these conditions, the number is divisible by both 2 and 3, and therefore by 6.

6. A number is divisible by 9 if and only if the sum of its digits is divisible by 9.

Casting Out 9s

Casting out 9s is a useful check if its limitations are understood. Although a proof of the process is quite easy in *mod* 9, the process must be taught by rote on the elementary level.[4]

The key to the process involves finding the excess of nines (remainder when dividing by 9). It may be done as follows:

Excess of 9s in $231 = 2 + 3 + 1 = 6$
Excess of 9s in $472 = 4 + 7 + 2 = 13 = 1 + 3 = 4$
Excess of 9s in $234 = 2 + 3 + 4 = 9 = 0$
Excess of 9s in $9171 = 9 + 1 + 7 + 1 = 18 = 1 + 8 = 9 = 0$

The process is useful because the excess can be found quickly by adding the digits, rather than by dividing by 9 and finding the remainder. It should be made clear that the excess obtained by adding the digits, as shown here, is the same as the remainder obtained by dividing by 9. Note that when the sum of the digits is 9 or a multiple of 9, the excess is 0, rather than 9. A shortcut to find the excess in 472 is to note that $7 + 2 = 9$ and discard it, immediately leaving an excess of 4. Similarly, the 9 in 9171

---

2. Proofs of these rules can be found on page 239 of the sixth edition of this text.

3. We made no distinction between number and numeral in rule 1 because there was no possibility of confusion. We made the distinction in rule 3 because it would not be clear to state that the last 2 digits must be divisible by 4. This might imply that *each* digit must be divisible by 4, and this is not true.

[4]A proof can be found on page 255 of the sixth edition of this text.

can be discarded, illustrating the meaning of the term "casting out 9s."

Casting out 9s can be used to check multiplication, division, addition, and subtraction. Of the four operations, multiplication is checked most efficiently by this process, and addition and subtraction least efficiently. Its major limitation is that it does not reveal errors in place value or in the position of the decimal point. It will also fail to reveal random errors such that the difference between the correct and incorrect answer is a multiple of 9. Check the following multiplications by casting out 9s:

(a)   231 —   6   (b)   450 —   0
    × 41 — × 5   21 — × 3
    ───────────   ───────────
    231   30 — 3   450   0
    924   ═   900   ═
    ─────   ─────
    9471 — 3   9450 —   0
           ═   ═

(c)   123 —   6
     101 — × 2
     ───────────
     123   12 — 3
     123
     ─────
     1353 —   3
            ═

In (a), 6, or 2 + 3 + 1, is the excess of the multiplicand, and is multiplied by 5, or 4 + 1, which is the excess of the multiplier, to get 30, which has an excess of 3 + 0, or 3. The example checks because this 3 is equal to the excess of the product, 9 + 4 + 7 + 1 = 21 = 2 + 1, or 3. Note that if the 9 in 9471 is discarded, the excess is still 3, as 4 + 7 + 1 = 12 = 1 + 2 = 3. Because 9s and multiples of 9 can be discarded without changing the excess, the process is called casting out 9s.

Example (b) illustrates that if the sum of the digits is 9 or a multiple of 9, the excess is 0, indicating that the number is a multiple of 9 (with a remainder of 0 when divided by 9).

Example (c) shows that casting out 9s does not detect an error in place or position value. The second partial product is misplaced, but the multiplication checks by casting out 9s.

Exercises 12.3

1. Check each of the following numbers for divisibility by 3.
   a. 1111   b. 111   c. 11111   d. 111111   e. 14693

2. Check each of the following numbers for divisibility by 9.
   a. 451   b. 459   c. 782   d. 2222   e. 22221

3. Which of the following numbers are divisible by 6?
   a. 222   b. 333   c. 123456   d. 11112   e. 1423

4. Why is a number that is divisible by 9 also divisible by 3?

5. Change the last digit in 12321 so that it will be divisible by both 4 and 6.

6. Check the products in the following examples by casting out 9s. Then multiply the factors to see whether the check is correct.
   a. 24 × 75 = 180   b. 203 × 436 = 10,028   c. 42 × 57 = 2294

7. Examples (a) and (b) in problem 6 check by casting out 9s, but the answers are incorrect. Explain why this is so.

8. Example (c) in problem 6 does not check by casting out 9s. The product is incorrect. When a multiplication example does not check by casting out 9s, the solution is _____ .

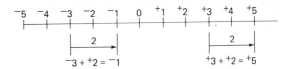

Figure 12.3

Integers

Although most elementary programs include some work with signed numbers, it is often restricted to readiness work in addition and subtraction of integers. Note that the term "signed numbers" includes rational and real numbers as well as integers. In this section, we discuss addition and subtraction of integers and how to introduce these topics on the upper elementary level.

Sign of Direction and Sign of Operation

The thermometer is often the best way to introduce signed numbers. Even in climates where temperatures do not drop below zero, newspapers and geography books will refer to subzero values. After discussing the thermometer, draw the following number line on the chalkboard and ask the class to name and label the first point to the left of zero.

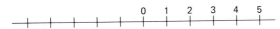

Pupils sometimes make interesting suggestions, such as "going away numbers." After listening to their suggestions, you should indicate the standard notation of $^-1$, $^-2$, $^-3$, and so on. The raised sign is called a sign of direction, as opposed to a sign of operation, as in the expression $5 - 3$. Signed numbers are often called directed numbers. Read the expression $^-3$ as "negative 3," and the expression $5 - 3$ as "5 minus 3." Similarly, read $^+5$ as "positive five" and $2 + 3$ as "2 plus 3." This practice helps to keep pupils from becoming confused about the two uses of the minus sign. Adults who were taught by the traditional programs will probably refer to $^-3$ as "minus 3" and $^+5$ as "plus 5."

Addition of Signed Numbers

Traditionally, addition of signed numbers is introduced on the number line. Because modern programs place more emphasis on the number line than traditional programs did, this approach is more useful than ever.

Figure 12.3 shows how the number line can be used to find the sums of $^+3 + {}^+2$ and $^-3 + {}^+2$.

In both cases, an arrow two units in length starts at a point representing the first addend, and the sum is indicated at the tip of the arrow. Since the pupil can see no difference in the behavior of $^+3$ and 3, you can state, after giving a brief introduction, that 3 is an abbreviation for $^+3$.

If the arrow for adding $^+2$ points to the right, then the arrow representing addition of $^-2$ should point to the left. Figure 12.4 shows how the number line can be used to find the sums of $^-2 + {}^+3$ and $^+3 + {}^-2$.

In the addition of $^-2 + {}^+3$, the arrow for $^+3$ starts at $^-2$ and points to the right. In the addition of $^+3 + {}^-2$, the arrow for $^-2$ starts at $^+3$ and points to the left. These two examples illustrate that addition of signed numbers is commutative, but this exercise should not be interpreted as a proof of this fact.

Subtraction of Signed Numbers

On the basis of previous experience, the pupil now knows that to add 2 ($^+2$) the arrow must point to the right; to subtract 2, the arrow must point to the left. After learning that adding $^-2$ involves an arrow point-

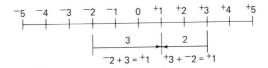

Figure 12.4

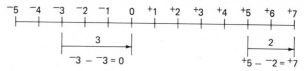

Figure 12.5

ing to the left, the student should be able to assume that to subtract ⁻2, the arrow should point to the right. Figure 12.5 shows how the number line can be used to find ⁺5 − ⁻2 and ⁻3 − ⁻3.

These subtractions are not learned as easily as the previous operations, although students are usually reassured to see that ⁻3 − ⁻3 = 0. It may be helpful to point out that just as 8 − 2 = 6 implies that 8 = 6 + 2, addition on the number line can verify that 5 − ⁻2 = 7 implies that 5 = 7 + ⁻2, which illustrates that the addition/subtraction pattern holds for signed numbers. This relation suggests another approach to subtraction: find 7 + ⁻2 = 5 on the number line and use the addition/subtraction pattern to determine that 5 − ⁻2 = 7.

There are some everyday analogies that can be readily grasped by many pupils. If a drop in temperature is eliminated, the temperature becomes higher. If Joe has $10 and owes $2, he has net assets of $8. If his mother pays (removes) his debt of $2, his net assets are $10, or 8 − ⁻2 = 10. Such analogies are of dubious value and should be used, if at all, with caution.

Negative numbers, such as ⁻3, are often referred to as opposites, such as the "opposite of 3." Although it is an important mathematical fact that the sum of any number and its opposite—*additive inverse*—is 0, little use can be made of this fact on the elementary level. At best, this fact can be used to make the analogy between division of fractions and subtraction of signed numbers. In division, instead of dividing by a number, one multiplies by its reciprocal—*multiplicative inverse*—while in subtraction, instead of subtracting a number, one

adds its opposite, or additive inverse. Also, just as the product of a number and its reciprocal is 1, the sum of a number and its opposite is 0 (the additive identity).

Summary

In the set of whole numbers but not necessarily in the set of rational numbers, which includes fractions, the product of two numbers is a multiple of each number. For example, the sentence 15 = 3 × 5 implies that 15 is a multiple of 3, 5, and 15, but the sentence 9 = ½ × 18 does not imply that 9 is a multiple either of 18 or ½. Pupils should be made aware of the different properties of different sets of numbers.

The concept of multiples is of major importance to students learning to add and subtract fractions.

Prime numbers are important in many phases of mathematics. On the elementary level, they can help pupils develop an understanding of the concept of lowest or least common multiple.

On the elementary level, work with signed numbers is largely confined to readiness activities, in preparation for more formal work later. Although fractions as well as integers are included in the set of signed numbers, early work is confined to integers.

Casting out 9s is a check that can be used with all four operations, but it is most functional when applied to multiplication. Casting out 9s will not reveal an error caused by misplacement of a digit in a numeral. For example, if the answer to an example is 348, the digits could be arranged in any order and the example would check by casting out 9s.

Exercises 12.4

1. Find the prime factorization of:
   a. 42   b. 120   c. 83

2. Use a number line to find three pairs of numbers whose sum is zero. Give two names for such pairs of numbers.

3. Use a tree diagram to find the prime factorization of 36.

4. If 20 is a multiple of 5, then 5 is a _____ of 20.

5. Examine multiples of 18 to find the lowest common denominator of 12, 15, and 18.

6. Use the prime factor method to find the lowest common multiple of 12, 15, and 18.

7. The sum of $^-4$ and 4 is 0. Use this fact to find the sum of $^-4 + 7$. Hint: Rename 7 as $4 + 3$.

8. Write the two addition sentences in the addition/subtraction pattern for $8 - {}^-3 = 11$.

9. Describe integers in terms of whole numbers.

10. What is the purpose of writing negative 3 as $^-3$, rather than the traditional -3?

11. What is the mathematical name for the set of whole numbers?

12. Give two other names for the set of counting numbers.

13. Outline a procedure that involves using a calculator to prove that 1729 can be expressed as the sum of two cubes in only two ways.

14. The answer to an example is 532. Why will the answer 523 check by casting out 9s?

Selected Readings

Danzig, Tobias. *Number, The Language of Science*, Fourth Edition. Garden City, NY: Doubleday/Anchor, 1957.

Heddens, James W. *Today's Mathematics*, Fourth Edition. Chicago: Science Research Associates, 1980, pp. 191–209.

Hooper, Alfred. *Makers of Mathematics*. New York: Random House, 1948, Chapter 1.

Ore, Oystein. *Number Theory and Its History*. New York: McGraw-Hill, 1948, Chapters 1–4.

Ried, Constance. *From Zero to Infinity*. New York: Crowell, 1961, Chapter 3.

Topics in Mathematics for Elementary School Teachers. Reston, VA: National Council of Teachers of Mathematics, 1964, Unit 5.

Chapter 13

Addition and Subtraction with Fractions

As the metric system gradually becomes more widely used in the United States, and as minicalculators gain widespread acceptance in the schools, there will be a shift in the emphasis placed on various aspects of the study of rational numbers named in common fraction form. In this chapter, we discuss addition and subtraction with *common fractions*. The terms "common fraction" and "fraction" usually refer to a rational number in the form $\frac{A}{B}$ where A (the numerator) is a whole number and B (the denominator) is a counting number (a whole number greater than zero).

Achievement Goals

After studying this chapter, you should be able to:

1. Discuss the changing nature of fractions in elementary mathematics programs.
2. Identify the materials used to teach the meanings of fractions.
3. Explain how to teach addition and subtraction of like fractions.
4. Demonstrate the steps involved in teaching pupils to rename fractions.
5. Describe the instructional sequence for adding and subtracting unlike fractions.
6. Illustrate ways to teach addition and subtraction of mixed numbers at the exploratory and symbolic levels.
7. Describe applications of fractions in problem solving at the mastery level.

Vocabulary

Mastery of the following key terms will help you to understand this chapter. Each term is defined or illustrated in the Glossary at the back of the book.

Common fraction	Least common
Congruent	multiple
Denominator	Like fractions
Equivalent (equal)	Lowest terms
fractions	Mixed number
Fraction	Numerator
Greatest common	Rational numbers
factor	Renaming fractions
Improper fractions	Unlike but related
Least common	fractions
denominator	Unlike fractions

Fractions in the Elementary Curriculum—Present and Future

The student's first experiences with fractions should be mainly "part of a whole" situations. As we discussed in Chapter 6, children learn to use fractions as names for various situations.

Elementary mathematics textbooks for grades K to 2 generally provide for a sequential development of the concepts and skills involved in working with fractions on the exploratory level. Primary pupils learn to name parts of objects, pictures, drawings, and geometric regions with fractions. They learn to use fractions in simple problem-solving activities.

During the 1970s, the treatment of fractions in elementary programs centered on a systematic development of the operations with fractions starting at the fourth-grade level. By the end of the fifth grade, most children had been taught addition and subtraction of fractions with unlike denominators. Emphasis was placed on renaming fractions to find least common denominators and on reducing fractions to lowest terms. The Back to Basics movement that dominated the era resulted in a tendency to teach operations on fractions "by the rules." Inadequate attention was paid to problem-solving activities and to exploratory experiences. Much of the instruction was from the children's textbook, and was at the symbolic level.

Student Achievement from the Second National Assessment[1]

The Second National Assessment of Educational Progress in Mathematics found that the achievement of pupils who had com-pleted the sixth grade was appallingly inadequate for addition and subtraction of common fractions. The error made most frequently for both addition and subtraction of fractions was adding or subtracting both the numerators and the denominators. One-third of the 13-year-olds tested would add numerators and denominators, such that $\frac{1}{2} + \frac{3}{4} = \frac{4}{6}$. Only one-third of the pupils performed the computation correctly. Other scores for the 13-year-olds who took the Second National Assessment are given in Table 13.1 on page 222.

Recommendations for Improvements

It is generally agreed that elementary school children need to learn to solve problems involving fractions.[2] To interpret situations in their daily life, students must be able to understand the meanings of fractions as parts of a whole. Even in an age of computers, pupils need to be able to add and subtract fractions with like and unlike denominators. They need to understand and be able to rename fractions so that they have common denominators and to reduce fractions to the lowest terms. With the growing use of minicalculators and metric measures, rational numbers written in common fractional form should be taught closer in sequence with decimals.

Trafton[3] has predicted that future programs, beginning with grade 4, will reduce the amount of work with fractions and place more emphasis on decimals, perhaps introducing tenths as early as grade 3. Addition and subtraction of unlike fractions at the fifth-grade level would be limited to proper

1. National Assessment of Educational Progress, *Mathematical Knowledge and Skills—Selected Results from the Second Assessment of Mathematics* (Denver: Education Commission of the States, August 1979), pp. 15–16.

2. Zalman P. Usiskin, "The Future of Fractions," *Arithmetic Teacher,* January 1979, 25:18–20.

3. Paul R. Trafton, "Assessing the Mathematics Curriculum Today." In *Selected Issues in Mathematics Education,* 1981 Yearbook of the National Society for the Study of Education (Berkeley, CA: McCutchan, 1980), pp. 24–25.

Table 13.1 Percent of Correct Answers by 13-year-olds on the Second National Assessment for Selected Topics on Fractions

Task	Percent Correct
Reducing to lowest terms:	
$\frac{3}{9}$	78
$\frac{14}{35}$	57
Renaming to a common denominator:	
$\frac{2}{3} = \frac{?}{6}$	71
$\frac{3}{8} = \frac{?}{32}$	65
Renaming improper fractions to mixed numbers:	
$\frac{7}{3}$	65
$\frac{14}{4}$	63
Addition of fractions:	
$\frac{4}{12} + \frac{3}{12}$	74
$\frac{3}{4} + \frac{1}{2}$	35
$4\frac{1}{4} + 3\frac{2}{5}$	26

fractions or mixed numbers requiring limited renaming.

Ellerbruch and Payne[4] recommend the instructional time lines (in the righthand column) leading to proficiency in adding fractions with unlike denominators for average to above-average classes:

Materials for Teaching Meanings of Fractions

Experience has shown that young children need to use manipulative materials and visual aids to solve problems involving fractions. The materials that are the most helpful in introducing the idea of a *part of a*

4. Lawrence W. Ellerbruch and Joseph N. Payne, "A Teaching Sequence from Initial Fraction Concepts through the Addition of Unlike Fractions." In *Developing Computational Skills*, 1978 Yearbook (Reston, VA: National Council of Teachers of Mathematics, 1978), pp. 129–147.

Grade-level	Topic	Days
Primary	Initial concepts and language (Includes work with concrete materials, oral language, and drawings.)	7–10
Fourth	Fraction concepts	5
	Adding like fractions	1
	Equivalent fractions	5
Fifth through Eighth	Fraction concepts	3
	Adding like fractions	1
	Equivalent fractions	3–5
	Adding unlike fractions	1

whole include (1) real objects that can be cut into parts, (2) a flannel board with various fractional parts of circular shapes and rectangular regions, (3) the pupil's fraction kit, and (4) a number line.

Real Objects

The kindergarten child's first contact with fractions usually comes as a part of a whole object. Typically, the teacher takes an orange or an apple and cuts it into two equal-sized parts and discusses the concept of "half an apple" and the fact that "two halves make a whole." Other objects, such as pies, cupcakes, sandwiches, candy bars, can be cut into equal-sized parts to demonstrate the concepts of ½, ⅓, and ¼ of a whole thing. Direct the pupils to name the number of equal-sized parts in the whole thing, the part considered, and the name of the fractional part of the whole.

Flannel Board

The flannel board is a useful aid in early work with fractions. The teacher's kit should include a set of congruent parts of circular and rectangular regions. The cutouts should be made or covered with flannel or some other material with a heavy nap so that they adhere to the flannel board. They should be large enough so that the parts can be seen easily by the pupils. The use of different colors on either side of a cutout, for example, red and green, clarifies a demonstration of fractional numbers on a flannel board. Figure 13.1 shows some sample flannel board demonstrations.

Pupil's Fraction Kit

Each pupil should have a *fraction kit* to work with while developing an understanding of the meanings of fractions. Student fraction kits should contain cutouts that are similar to, but smaller than the cutouts used for class demonstrations with the flannel

board. The children should store their cutouts in manila envelopes. As you show or illustrate various fraction parts with the demonstration kit on the flannel board, the pupils should perform the same activities with their fraction kits.

Number Lines

A *number line* is useful for illustrating the meanings of different fractions as parts of a line segment unit. A model of a line segment is easy to make both for demonstration purposes and for each pupil. It is versatile because (1) it can be drawn in different unit lengths, (2) it can be partitioned into many congruent parts, and (3) once

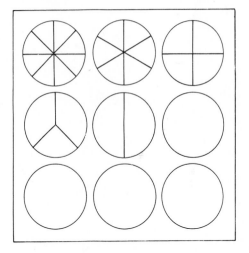

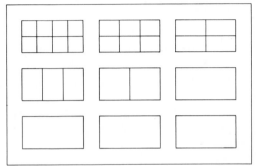

Figure 13.1
Flannel Board Cutouts

Pupils learn a new fraction game. *(Photo by Leland Perry)*

parts are shown, it is easy to consider one or more parts as a fractional part of the whole unit.

Beginning work with the number line should be on unit segments. Pupils should understand that a segment of any length can represent a unit segment as long as the left endpoint is labeled as 0, and the right endpoint is labeled as 1. The midpoint can then be named as one-half, and each of the two segments can be assigned a length of one-half. To avoid confusion in introductory work, you should emphasize fractions as the lengths of segments rather than as names for points. When you use congruent segments, you can compare different parts to illustrate the relationships of greater than, equal to, and less than.

Modeling Fractions

Pupils gain their first insights into fractional numbers by modeling with the various instructional aids discussed above. When a region on the flannel board is separated into two congruent parts, each is one-half of the original region. Fourths, sixths, and eighths can easily be modeled in this manner.

If a rectangular shape is folded along the line segment connecting the midpoints of opposite sides, the resulting rectangular area is one-half of the original shape. Likewise, if that area is folded again, each part is one-fourth of the original area. Pupils should model such fractions as halves, fourths, and eighths. They can represent these fractions by folding paper, by making drawings, or both.

An effective way to introduce eighths is to have pupils fold rectangular sheets of paper in eighths. The student should discover that an eighth is one-half of a fourth and that a fourth is equal to two eighths. Similarly, they should discover other relationships among halves, fourths, and eighths.

Next have the pupils model eighths by folding a square sheet of paper. Then encourage them to draw line segments in the square region so that eighths are shown. Encourage the class to demonstrate as many ways as possible of representing eighths in a square region. Most of the pupils will discover three of the six ways shown in Figure 13.2.

Modeling Parts of a Collection

Fractions can be used to describe parts of a collection. Two or more objects can represent a whole, just as line segments of different lengths can represent *one*. Thus, one object can be one-third of a collection of three objects, or one-fourth of a collection of four items.

One way to help children understand fractions as representing parts of a collection is to cut up egg cartons with various

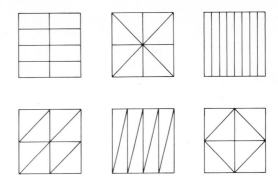

Figure 13.2
Showing Eighths of a Square Region

numbers of pockets in a single row. Put one item in each pocket of a two-pocket container, stating that each item is one-half of the two items in the container. Put two items in each pocket of the same container and note that two items are one-half of the four items in the container, and so on. Similar activities can be used with containers with three, four, and five pockets.

Use of Drawings

All of the aids we have described can be drawn on paper and discussed. One additional visual model to help understand different fractions is a *fraction strip,* such as:

Different patterns of geometric shapes can be drawn on heavy cardboard, and some can be colored. For each picture, raise the questions:

1. How many are shaded? → 3
2. How many in all? ⟶ 4
3. What part is shaded? ⟶ ¾

Problem-Solving Activities

Pupils enjoy using their fraction kits to solve oral story problems. Tell them a story about some part of a whole and have them solve the problem with manipulative materials. For example, "Charles bought a pizza that was cut into six pieces. If he ate one piece, what part of the whole pizza was this?"

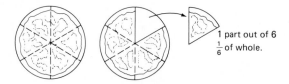

1 part out of 6
$\frac{1}{6}$ of whole.

The pupils will refer to the circular cutout in their fraction kits that is cut into six congruent pieces. Each piece can represent one-sixth of the whole pizza.

Have them use rectangular pieces to solve the following problem: "Jose's garden was divided into three equal-sized plots. If he planted tomatoes in one plot and carrots in another, what part of the garden was planted in tomatoes and carrots?" The solution to this problem involves the addition of the like fractions ⅓ and ⅓ at the exploratory level. Most pupils will readily discover the answer, that 2 plots out of 3 is ⅔ of the whole garden.

To represent what part of a collection a specific number of objects compose is more difficult than finding a part of a whole. Students find solutions by using manipulative materials. For example, "Mike brought five marbles to school. Two were black and three were white. What part of the marbles was black?" The pupils can solve this problem by using a "five-pocket" egg carton. By distributing one marble in each pocket in the order black, black, white, white, white as shown, pupils can readily find the answer to the problem as they also answer the following questions:

1. How many marbles are black?
2. How many marbles in the collection?
3. So that is "Two out of _____?"
4. Two out of five is what part?
5. How do we write that as a fraction?

Keep problems simple. Pupils like problems about everyday matters.

Comparing Fractions

In their initial work, pupils should use cutouts to compare fractions and then make a written record of the experience. They should discover, for example, that the denominator 4 in ¾ indicates the number of equal-sized parts into which the whole is divided, and the numerator 3 indicates how many of these parts are involved. The students should make two basic generalizations:

1. When the denominators are equal, the larger the numerator, the larger the fraction.
2. When the numerators are equal, the larger the denominator, the smaller the fraction.

The *number line* is an excellent way to demonstrate both of these generalizations, once pupils recognize that the closer the number is to zero, the smaller it is, or that if A is to the left of B, then A is smaller than B.

With the cutouts in their fraction kits, pupils can easily demonstrate the fact that a fraction with the largest denominator (assuming the same numerators) represents the smallest fraction.

Similarly, pupils should use their cutouts to compare like fractions (with equal denominators). They should discover that the value of like fractions changes as the numerator changes. If the pupils arrange cutouts in size from smaller to larger, they will obtain a symbolic record of the result such as that shown in (a). Once again, the pupils see that for like fractions, the larger the numerator the larger the fraction.

(a) $\dfrac{1}{8}$ $\dfrac{2}{8}$ $\dfrac{3}{8}$ $\dfrac{4}{8}$ $\dfrac{5}{8}$ $\dfrac{6}{8}$ $\dfrac{7}{8}$ $\dfrac{8}{8}$

Addition and Subtraction of Like Fractions

Early problem-solving work involving addition and subtraction of fractions with like denominators must be done on the exploratory level, using manipulative materials, drawings, and visual models. The exploratory aids used most often in beginning work with addition and subtraction of like fractions are (a) the pupils' fraction kits, (b) drawings, and (c) the number line. Experience shows that these aids should be used extensively when developing beginning concepts and skills. Based on their experience, individual teachers have their own preferences.

Start with a Problem Setting

Addition of like fractions can be introduced with the following problem:

Problem: Joe cut his apple into 4 equal-sized pieces. He gave 1 slice to Raymond and 2 slices to Mary. What part of his apple did he give away?

Solve Problems with Manipulatives

Pupils can easily solve the problem above by using an apple, but because it is difficult to cut an apple into equal-sized parts, a circular region cut into four congruent pieces is more effective. The pupils should participate in the discussion of each of the following steps:

1. Select a circular region and cut it into four congruent parts. Ask the pupils, "How many equal-sized parts are there?" "What part of the whole is each piece?"

2. Next, give a pupil one piece and note that this is one-fourth of the whole. Give another pupil two pieces and ask what part of the whole this is.

3. Next, join the one-fourth with the two-fourths and ask the pupils to identify what part of the whole this is. Pupils will easily see that one-fourth + two-fourths equals three-fourths.

Show Solutions with Drawings

If cutouts are not available, you may use a circle on the chalkboard and divide its interior region into fourths by drawing two diameters perpendicular to each other. You can then ask a pupil to use the chalk and shade in ¼ of the circular region. Another pupil can shade in another ²⁄₄ of the region, and the sentence ¼ + ²⁄₄ = ¾ can be written. The same procedure may be used with rectangular regions. Encourage pupils to use the materials in their fraction kits to solve addition and subtraction problems with fractions.

Record Solutions

As pupils use manipulative materials to solve problems involving like fractions, you should keep appropriate records of the thought process. A record of the solution of the above problem should be kept (a) in words, (b) with drawings, and (c) in symbolic notation, as follows:

(a) With words:

1 fourth
+2 fourths
3 fourths

(b) With drawings:

(c) With symbolic notation:

$$\frac{1}{4} + \frac{2}{4} = \frac{3}{4} \text{ or } \begin{array}{r} \frac{1}{4} \\ + \frac{2}{4} \\ \hline \frac{3}{4} \end{array}$$

Problem: David had his pizza cut into 6 equal-sized pieces. If he ate 4 pieces, what part of the pizza would be left?

Pupils can solve this problem by using a circular cutout in their fraction kits cut into six parts.

1. Use the circular region cut into six parts. Ask the pupils, "What is the size of each part?"

2. If David ate four pieces, what part of the pizza was this?

3. How many parts did David start with? Pupils should recognize that there are six parts and the whole region would be six sixths.

4. If David started with six sixths and removed four sixths, how many sixths were left?

Pupils who solve this problem with the use of manipulatives must be guided to operate at a higher level of abstraction. Pupils who feel comfortable in working with manipulatives should record their thinking symbolically.

Different Names for the Same Fraction

Pupils must learn that fractions, like whole numbers, can be renamed. For example, just as 16 can be renamed as 8 + 8, 2 × 8, 10 + 6, etc., ½ can be renamed as ¼, ⅛, etc. These fractions are often known as *equal* or *equivalent fractions.*

Some elementary textbooks use the term "equivalent fractions" to indicate that two fractional numerals name the same number. Although we prefer "equal fractions," both terms can be used to refer to the same idea.

Renaming Fractions to Lower Terms

The sum or difference that results from adding or subtracting fractions may not be expressed in *lowest terms.* A fraction in lowest terms is in *simplified form,* which is usually considered to be in the most acceptable form. A fraction is in lowest terms if the numerator and the denominator contain no common factors except 1.

Renaming a fraction means changing the terms of the fraction (numerator and denominator) without changing the value. By working with various instructional materials, young children learn that two-fourths of a circular region can also be named one-half, or that two-fourths make one-half. The fractions ¼ and ½ name the same rational number, and so we say that ¼ equals ½.

The fractions ⅝ and ¾ name the same number, but ¾ is in lowest terms, as the numerator and denominator have no common factors other than one. Traditionally, answers to problems are written in lowest terms. Replacing ⅝ with ¾ is often called "reducing to lowest terms."

Exploratory Level

The activities used to model fractions on the flannel board and with the pupil's fraction kit can be extended to renaming fractions.

USE OF FRACTION CUTOUTS

Have the class work with parts of circular regions to rename fractions that are equal. First, have the pupils represent the parts that are needed to make the whole unit. How many halves make one? How many fourths? How many sixths? How many eighths? The pupils will discover that the numerators and denominators for fractions that equal one are the same number. That is, $2/2 = 1$; $3/3 = 1$; $4/4 = 1$; $5/5 = 1$, etc.

Next, show the class a flannel board cutout of *one-half* of a circular region. Pupils should start with the corresponding one-half in their fraction kits and then try to discover other parts that equal one-half. Pupils will discover that $4/8 = 3/6 = 2/4 = 1/2$ by placing these parts over the one-half region.

USE OF A FRACTION CHART

Parts of congruent line segments can be used to represent equal fractions. Folding paper is a way to create congruent line segments and discover that several fractions can represent the same length. Have the pupils take an unlined piece of paper and, using a straight edge, draw five horizontal line segments across the page. Note that each line segment represents one unit segment. Have each pupil fold the sheet of paper down the center the long way to create two congruent rectangular regions. Now open up the paper and look at the parts of the segments that are formed. Note that the midpoint is named ½, which is the measure of the line segment from the left edge of the paper to the midpoint.

On the second horizontal line segment from the top, draw an arrow just under the segment from the left edge to the midpoint and label the midpoint ½. Continue to fold and label as illustrated in Figure 13.3 on page 230.

Encourage the pupils to think about what happens to the denominators each time in subsequent line segments. Each time there will be twice as many parts, but each part is one-half the size of the one in the previous line segment, and so the denominators double each time. Each pupil should then make a fraction chart similar to the one shown in Figure 13.3.

Once the pupils have their own fraction chart, they can use it to discover that some line segments can be named with equal fractions. Starting with the bottom line segment, it can be shown that $4/16$ can be named $2/8$ and $1/4$.

Renaming to Lowest Terms at the Symbolic Level

The most efficient way of renaming $8/12$ is to use the identity property of 1 for division. Thus, any nonzero number divided by one is the number. Also, any nonzero number divided by itself equals one. Thus, at the symbolic level:

$$\frac{8}{12} = \frac{2 \times 4}{3 \times 4} = \frac{2}{3} \longrightarrow \frac{8 \div 4}{12 \div 4} = \frac{2}{3}$$

Once pupils understand the algorism for multiplication with fractions, the following sequence can be helpful:

$$\frac{8}{12} = \frac{2}{3} \times \frac{4}{4} = \frac{2}{3} \times 1 = \frac{2}{3}$$

However, during the initial instruction on renaming to lowest terms, the correct procedure must be obtained on the basis of exploratory work.

Use exploratory materials to show the following:

$$\frac{1}{2} = \frac{2}{4} \qquad \frac{2}{3} = \frac{4}{6} \qquad \frac{3}{4} = \frac{6}{8}$$

Now use the above equalities and help the pupil discover:

$$\frac{2}{4} = \frac{2 \div 2}{4 \div 2} = \frac{1}{2} \longrightarrow \frac{1}{2} = \frac{1 \times \square}{2 \times 2} = \frac{2}{\square}$$

$$\frac{4}{6} = \frac{4 \div \square}{6 \div 2} = \frac{\square}{\square} \longrightarrow \frac{2}{3} = \frac{2 \times 2}{3 \times \square} = \frac{\square}{\square}$$

$$\frac{6}{8} = \frac{6 \div 2}{8 \div \square} = \frac{\square}{\square} \longrightarrow \frac{3}{4} = \frac{3 \times \square}{4 \times \square} = \frac{6}{\square}$$

The entire nonverbal sequence is the basis of the traditional verbalization: "Multiplying or dividing both terms (numerator and denominator) of a fraction by the same

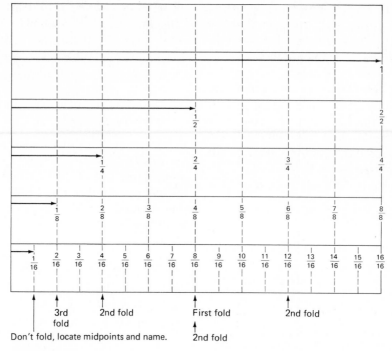

Figure 13.3
A Fraction Chart

Note: Each horizontal line segment is a number line. Thus, ⅛ is less than ⅜, since ⅛ is to the left of ⅜ (closer to zero), and so is less than ¼.

nonzero number does not change its value (changes the numeral without changing the number)."

The difficulty most pupils have when faced with a fraction that is not in lowest terms is to determine the *greatest common factor* (divisor) so that the fraction can be reduced to lowest terms. Three techniques can be used: (1) look for a *common divisor*; (2) write the *factors* of each term; and (3) *prime factor* each term.

The first approach is used by pupils who can immediately recognize a common divisor of the numerator and denominator to be renamed in lowest terms. For example, many pupils can identify 2 as a common factor of the terms 6 and 8 in ⅝. Then ⅝ can be reduced to lower terms as follows:

$$\frac{6}{8} = \frac{6 \div 2}{8 \div 2} = \frac{3}{4}$$

Pupils should recognize that if both the numerator and denominator of a fraction are even numbers, then 2 is a common factor (divisor). The difficulty here is that a common divisor may not be the *greatest* common factor, and so the resulting fraction will not be in *lowest terms*. For example, 2 is a common divisor of 8 and 12 in the fraction ⁸⁄₁₂. The fraction can be reduced to lower terms as follows:

$$\frac{8}{12} = \frac{8 \div 2}{12 \div 2} = \frac{4}{6}$$

Because 2 is not the greatest common factor of 8 and 12, the fraction ⁴⁄₆ is not in lowest terms, and so another step is needed. Most pupils recognize that 2 is a common factor of 4 and 6. Thus, each term would need to be divided by two:

$$\frac{4}{6} = \frac{4 \div 2}{6 \div 2} = \frac{2}{3}$$

If a pupil has difficulty in identifying the greatest common factor of the terms of a fraction, then we recommend using a more systematic approach.

A second technique for determining the greatest common factor (divisor) of two numbers is the *factor approach*. There are three steps to find the greatest common factor of 8 and 12:

1. Write the factors (divisors) of 8:
   1, 2, 4, 8

2. Write the factors (divisors) of 12:
   1, 2, 3, 4, 6, 12

3. Examine the factors (divisors) of 8 and 12 and determine the greatest common factor: It is 4.

Once the *greatest common factor* of 8 and 12 has been discovered, the fraction ⁸⁄₁₂ can be reduced to lowest terms as follows:

$$\frac{8}{12} = \frac{8 \div 4}{12 \div 4} = \frac{2}{3}$$

When the pupil renames a fraction by dividing both terms by the *greatest common factor* (divisor), the resulting equal fraction will be in *lowest terms*.

A third technique for identifying the greatest common factor (divisor) of the terms of a fraction is the *prime factor method*. This method is described on page 213.

Exercises 13.1

1. By an informal examination, identify the greatest common factor of each of the following pairs of numbers:

   a. 2, 4   c. 10, 15   e. 12, 36
   b. 6, 9   d. 8, 12   f. 6, 21

2. Find the greatest common factor of each of the following pairs of numbers by listing the factors (divisors) of each:

   a. 8, 24   c. 12, 15   e. 12, 20
   b. 9, 12   d. 8, 18   f. 16, 22

3. Find the greatest common factor of each of the following pairs of numbers by the prime factor approach:

   a. 18, 24   c. 24, 36   e. 30, 50
   b. 21, 28   d. 28, 52   f. 35, 42

4. Assume that each pair of numbers in exercises 1 through 3 is a fraction, and rename each to lowest terms.

Addition and Subtraction of Unlike Fractions

Mathematically, the statement of how to add and subtract fractions is deceptively simple:

(a) If the fractional numbers are represented by like denominators, use the basic patterns:

$$\frac{a}{c} + \frac{b}{c} = \frac{a + b}{c} \qquad \frac{a}{c} - \frac{b}{c} = \frac{a - b}{c}$$

(b) If the fractions have *unlike* denominators, rename so that the new numerals have like denominators, and use the basic pattern shown in (a).

Renaming fractions that have unlike denominators to fractions that have like denominators is very difficult for elementary school children. In an addition or subtraction example, what is involved is the renaming of one or both fractions to *higher terms*. This means that one or both of the denominators will be larger than the original denominator, assuming that the fractions are already in lowest terms.

Renaming Fractions to Higher Terms

EXPLORATORY LEVEL

As pupils explore renaming fractions to lower terms, they also gain insight into renaming fractions to higher terms. Work with fraction parts, a fraction chart, and the number line should build appropriate readiness for dealing with renaming to higher terms at the symbolic level.

SYMBOLIC LEVEL

At the symbolic level, pupils need a great deal of practice in renaming fractions. The following activities help to establish the pattern for renaming:

$$\frac{1}{2} = \frac{1 \times 2}{2 \times 2} = \frac{2}{4} \qquad \frac{1}{2} = \frac{1 \times 3}{2 \times 3} = \frac{3}{6}$$

$$\frac{2}{3} = \frac{2 \times 2}{3 \times 2} = \square \qquad \frac{2}{3} = \frac{2 \times 3}{3 \times 3} = \square$$

$$\frac{3}{4} = \frac{3 \times 2}{4 \times 2} = \square \qquad \frac{3}{4} = \frac{3 \times 3}{4 \times 3} = \square$$

Pupils can be helped to recognize the pattern in these sentences by means of open sentences like the following:

$$\frac{3}{8} = \frac{3 \times 2}{8 \times \square} = \frac{6}{\triangle} \qquad \frac{3}{5} = \frac{3 \times 4}{5 \times \triangle} = \frac{12}{\triangledown}$$

$$\frac{3}{4} = \frac{3 \times \square}{4 \times 5} = \frac{\triangledown}{20} \qquad \frac{5}{6} = \frac{5 \times \square}{6 \times \square} = \frac{10}{12}$$

Note that when a number is assigned to a frame, the same number must be assigned to that frame in a given sentence.

The following patterns can also be used to help pupils rename fractions:

$$\frac{1}{2}, \frac{2}{4}, \frac{3}{6}, \frac{4}{8}, \frac{5}{10}, \cdots$$

$$\frac{2}{3}, \frac{4}{6}, \frac{6}{9}, \frac{8}{12}, \frac{10}{15}, \cdots$$

$$\frac{3}{4}, \frac{6}{8}, \frac{9}{12}, \frac{12}{16}, \frac{15}{20}, \cdots$$

$$\frac{3}{5}, \frac{6}{10}, \frac{9}{15}, \frac{12}{20}, \frac{15}{25}, \cdots$$

The pattern is probably best stated by the open sentence in which the number that can be substituted for the frame is any non-zero number:

$$\frac{3}{5} = \frac{3 \times \square}{5 \times \square}$$

An excellent final exercise would involve the open sentence $\dfrac{2}{3} = \dfrac{2 \times \square}{3 \times \square}$. Have pupils rewrite it several times, placing a different numeral in the frames:

$$\frac{2}{3} = \frac{2 \times \boxed{3}}{3 \times \boxed{3}} = \frac{6}{9} \qquad \frac{2}{3} = \frac{2 \times \boxed{7}}{3 \times \boxed{7}} = \frac{14}{21}$$

$$\frac{2}{3} = \frac{2 \times \boxed{5}}{3 \times \boxed{5}} = \frac{10}{15} \qquad \frac{2}{3} = \frac{2 \times \boxed{10}}{3 \times \boxed{10}} = \frac{20}{30}$$

On the symbolic level, renaming ⅔ as ⁸⁄₁₂ is performed as follows:

$$\frac{2}{3} = \frac{8}{12} \quad \text{or} \quad \frac{2 \times \boxed{4}}{3 \times \boxed{4}} = \frac{8}{12}$$

The fraction ⅔ can be renamed as ⁸⁄₁₂ because both the numerator and the denominator are multiplied by the common factor, 4.

RENAMING FOR A SPECIFIC DENOMINATOR

Most renaming to higher terms is done so that addition and subtraction can be performed or two fractions can be compared. In example (b), the thought pattern for finding the unknown number in the given proportion (equation) would be as follows:

(b) $\dfrac{3}{4} = \dfrac{\square}{12}$

(1) $4 \times \square = 12$
$\square = 12 \div 4 = 3$

$\dfrac{3 \times \triangle}{4 \times \triangle} = \dfrac{\square}{12}$

(2) Now multiply both terms of the fraction ¾ by 3

$\dfrac{3 \times 3}{4 \times 3} = \dfrac{9}{12}$

(3) The new numerator = 9, and so
$\dfrac{3}{4} = \dfrac{9}{12}$

The pupil does not need to repeat the sentences as shown. The three sentences indicate the order in which the frames are to be filled.

Addition and Subtraction of Unlike but Related Fractions

Unlike but related fractions have unlike denominators, but one of the denominators is a common denominator, as in ½ + ⅜. By the time this topic is introduced at the symbolic level, the pupils should have had many experiences in finding equal fractions at the exploratory level. Manipulative and visual materials can be used to verify answers and assist pupils who need more experience at the exploratory level.

Since pupils have already learned that like fractions can be added and subtracted by adding or subtracting the numerators, the new element in adding or subtracting unlike fractions is to find a common denominator and express each fraction with that denominator.

For unlike but related fractions, one denominator is a multiple of the other. The pupil identifies the larger denominator of the example, such as 12 in ⅔ + ⁵⁄12, as the common denominator. Then ⅔ can be changed to twelfths by following the pattern in (b) in the previous section.

Common Denominator Is the Product of the Denominators

Pupils should discover that the product of two denominators is a common denominator but is not always the lowest or least common denominator.

Problem: Nan spent ⅓ of an hour working on her math homework and ¼ of an hour studying her spelling. What part of an hour did it take Nan to do her homework?

Although this problem can be solved at the exploratory level with manipulative materials and visual aids, at this point the pupils should be encouraged to solve the problem at the symbolic level.

1. Can we add ⅓ and ¼ in that form? (No. We need common denominators.)

2. Write some equal fractions for ⅓ and for ¼.

(a) $\dfrac{1}{3} = \dfrac{2}{6} = \dfrac{3}{9} = \dfrac{4}{12} = \dfrac{5}{15} \ldots$

(b) $\dfrac{1}{4} = \dfrac{2}{8} = \dfrac{3}{12} = \dfrac{4}{16} = \dfrac{5}{20} \ldots$

3. Examine the patterns in (a) and (b). Are there any fractions with the same denominators?
(Yes, ⁴⁄12 and ³⁄12.)

4. Now we can add the numerators: 4 twelfths + 3 twelfths = 7 twelfths, or ⁷⁄12.

Slow learners may need to verify the answer of ⁷⁄12 with manipulatives or visual models, for example, on a number line such as:

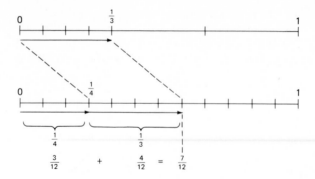

Fast learners should be challenged to find how many minutes it took Nan to do her homework by solving the following:

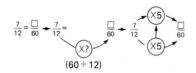

$(60 \div 12)$

$\frac{7}{12} = \frac{35}{60}$ of an hour or 35 minutes.

$\frac{1}{4}$ of an hour = 15 min.

$\frac{1}{3}$ of an hour = 20 min.

Total = 35 min.

Common Denominator Less Than Product of Denominators

Addition and subtraction of unlike and unrelated fractions involve finding a common denominator that may be less than the product of the denominators. This means that the denominators share a common factor. However, in finding a common denominator, pupils should make the following discovery: Look for the larger denominator. If it is not a common denominator, multiply the two denominators. The product will always be a common denominator, but not necessarily the lowest common denominator. One advantage of adding and subtracting fractions with lowest common denominators is that the numerators will involve smaller numbers.

There are three methods of finding a *least*

common denominator of two fractions, as discussed in Chapter 12. The following procedure is a summary of each method used to find a least common denominator for the example ¾ + ⅙ = _____.

(a) Write the multiples of each denominator; then find the common multiple that is the lowest:

Multiples of 4: 4, 8, 12, 16, 20, 24 . . .
Multiples of 6: 6, 12, 18, 24, 30, 36 . . .

In the series, there are two common multiples shown, 12 and 24. Either could be used as a common denominator for addition in the given example, but 12 is the *least common denominator*.

(b) Prime factor each denominator:

$6 = 2 \times 3$
$4 = 2 \times 2 \qquad \text{LCD} = 2 \times 2 \times 3 = 12$

(c) Write the two denominators horizontally and divide out the greatest common prime number:

$2)\overline{4,\ 6}$
$\quad 2,\ 3 \qquad \text{LCD} = 2 \times 2 \times 3 = 12$
(Note: LCD = ½ the product of 6 and 4)

All pupils should learn method (a). Pupils who have difficulty finding a lowest common multiple may be permitted to use a common denominator that is the product of the denominators.

Method (b) requires that pupils be able to find prime factors and then use each prime number as a factor as many times as it occurs in any one denominator. Many pupils find this technique difficult to understand.

Method (c) is an abbreviated form of (b) and can be an effective approach with larger denominators.

Elementary pupils should rarely have to deal with denominators larger than 32, except for fractions with denominators of 10, 100, 1000, etc. We recommend that pupils use the multiple approach to find the least common denominator for most fractions with denominators less than 50.

A notable technique for pupils to use as a modified version of the multiples approach is to write the multiples of the largest denominator and stop when such a multiple is divisible by the other denominator or denominators. For example, to find the least common denominator of 6, 8, and 12, write multiples of 12: 12, 24, 36, 48; stop at 48 because 48 is the least multiple of 12 that is divisible by 6 and 8, and so is the least common denominator.

A final method is to use a minicalculator to convert the common fractions to decimals and then perform the addition or subtraction.

Exercises 13.2
Find the least common multiple of the following:

(a) 12, 30   (c) 6, 45   (e) 6, 8, 15
(b) 8, 14   (d) 4, 6, 12   (f) 8, 12, 30

1. By using the multiples approach.

2. By using the prime factor method.

3. By dividing out common primes.

Addition and Subtraction of Mixed Numbers

Traditionally, expressions such as 2½ have been known as *mixed numbers*. In the 1960s, when the distinction between number and numeral was overemphasized, mixed numbers were sometimes called "fractional numbers represented by mixed numerals." Current opinion is that such precise terminology produces more confusion than understanding.

A mixed number is a rational number greater than one. It is the sum of a counting number and a fraction, such as 1 + ½, 2 + ¾, 5 + ⅛. After pupils understand this form, they can use the short form: 1½, 2¾, 5⅛.

Although pupils should have some exploratory work in addition and subtraction with mixed numbers, they should not need as much as with addition and subtraction of fractions less than one. Emphasize how this new work is related to previous work with fractions and with whole numbers.

Addition and Subtraction without Renaming

Addition and subtraction of mixed numbers without renaming is done simply, by adding the whole numbers and then adding the fractions.

EXPLORATORY LEVEL

At the exploratory level, addition and subtraction of mixed numbers can readily be shown on the flannel board or on the number line.

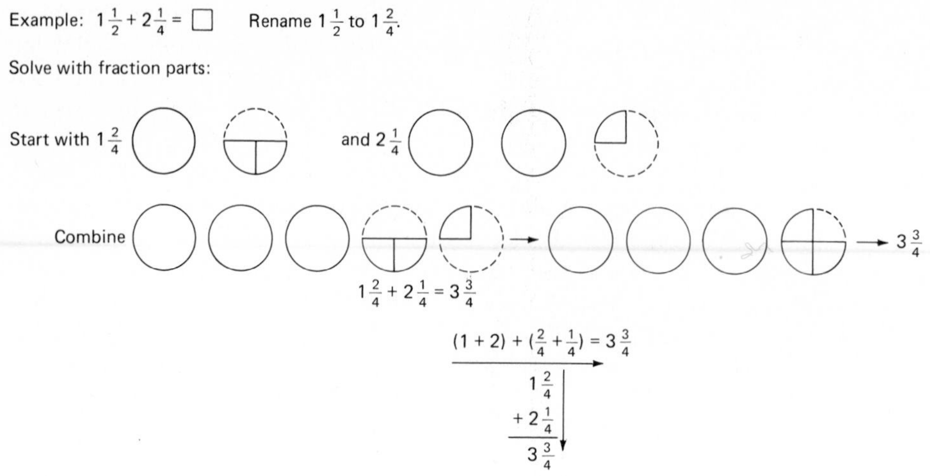

Example: $1\frac{1}{2} + 2\frac{1}{4} = \square$ Rename $1\frac{1}{2}$ to $1\frac{2}{4}$.

Solve with fraction parts:

Start with $1\frac{2}{4}$ and $2\frac{1}{4}$

Combine → $3\frac{3}{4}$

$$1\frac{2}{4} + 2\frac{1}{4} = 3\frac{3}{4}$$

$$(1 + 2) + \left(\frac{2}{4} + \frac{1}{4}\right) = 3\frac{3}{4}$$

$$\begin{array}{r} 1\frac{2}{4} \\ + 2\frac{1}{4} \\ \hline 3\frac{3}{4} \end{array}$$

Figure 13.4

Problem: Juan spent 1½ hours working on his math homework and 2¼ hours reading. How much time did he spend all together on school work? Figure 13.4 shows the solution to this problem on the flannel board.

Problem: Billie had to ride her bike 3¾ miles to a school picnic. After she rode 2¼ miles, how much farther did she have to go? Figure 13.5 shows the solution to this problem on a number line.

Improper Fractions

The sum of ¾ and ⅞ is ¹³⁄₈. The number as ¹³⁄₈ is an *improper fraction.* Improper fractions have numerators that are greater than or equal to the denominators. It is traditional in the elementary program to rename improper fractions, but this is not the case in many advanced mathematics programs. Also, when calculators are used, it is often more efficient *not* to change improper fractions to mixed numbers.

When you introduce renaming an improper fraction to a mixed number, we suggest the following sequence:

(a) $\dfrac{5}{4} = \dfrac{4}{4} + \dfrac{1}{4} = 1 + \dfrac{1}{4} = 1\dfrac{1}{4}$

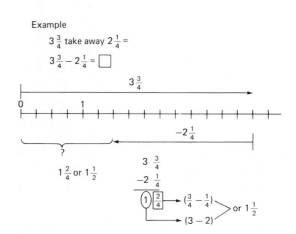

Example

$3\frac{3}{4}$ take away $2\frac{1}{4} =$

$3\frac{3}{4} - 2\frac{1}{4} = \square$

Figure 13.5

(b) $\dfrac{6}{5} = \dfrac{5}{5} + \dfrac{1}{5} = 1 + \dfrac{1}{5} = 1\dfrac{1}{5}$

(c) $\dfrac{8}{6} = \dfrac{6}{6} + \dfrac{2}{6} = 1 + \dfrac{2}{6} = 1\dfrac{1}{3}$

At the symbolic level, this sequence can be demonstrated on the flannel board with circular-area cutouts. Figure 13.6 shows how adding is done with mixed fractional numbers when the sum needs to be renamed.

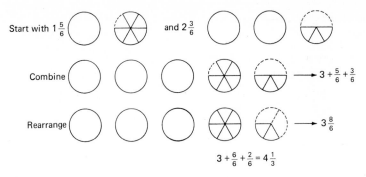

Figure 13.6

Subtraction of Mixed Numbers

The teacher should have the class discover the similarity of the procedures in subtracting whole numbers and mixed numbers. In each type renaming of numbers may be necessary. We shall rename a whole number and a mixed number by applying the associative property.

$$43 = 40 + 3 = (30 + 10) + 3$$
$$= (30 + 10) + 3 = 30 + (10 + 3)$$
$$= 30 + 13$$

$$6\frac{1}{3} = 6 + \frac{1}{3} = (5 + 1) + \frac{1}{3}$$
$$= (5 + \frac{3}{3}) + \frac{1}{3} = 5 + (\frac{3}{3} + \frac{1}{3}) = 5\frac{4}{3}$$

Practice exercises in renaming mixed numbers should be given before solving examples involving this operation.

Types of Mixed Numbers in Subtraction

There are four different types of examples in subtraction of mixed numbers. The types and the corresponding types in subtraction of whole numbers are as follows:

(a) $4\frac{1}{3}$ Subtracting a whole
        -2 number from a mixed
              number.

        41
      -20

(b) $6\frac{3}{4}$ No regrouping needed
        $-2\frac{1}{4}$ to subtract

        63
      -21

(c) 4 Interchange of types
        $-2\frac{1}{3}$ of numbers in (a)

        40
      -21

(d) $6\frac{1}{3}$ Regrouping needed
        $-2\frac{2}{3}$ to subtract

        51
      -22

Most pupils experience little difficulty in subtracting in examples (a) and (b). Many pupils encounter difficulty in solving examples (c) and (d). In (c) a mixed number is to be subtracted from a whole number. In the example $5 - 2\frac{1}{3}$, some pupils obtain the incorrect answer $3\frac{1}{3}$. In this type of example, the whole number must be renamed before the subtraction can be completed, as shown below:

$$5 = 4\frac{3}{3}$$
$$-2\frac{1}{3} = -2\frac{1}{3}$$
$$2\frac{2}{3}$$

Naturally the teacher must have the class learn to rename whole numbers as mixed numbers of the type $5 = 4\frac{3}{3}$.

Subtraction with Regrouping with Mixed Numbers

A positive difference will result only when the number being subtracted from a second number is smaller than the second number. Nevertheless, for mixed numbers, a positive difference could result and yet cause an impasse, if the fractions involved require renaming before the operation can be performed. For example, in $3\frac{1}{4} - 1\frac{3}{4}$, the difference will be positive because $3\frac{1}{4}$ is larger than $1\frac{3}{4}$. However, the fractional part $\frac{3}{4}$ cannot be subtracted from $\frac{1}{4}$ with a positive rational difference. So the $3\frac{1}{4}$ must be renamed for the subtraction of the fractions to be possible:

$$3\frac{1}{4} = 2\frac{5}{4}$$
$$-1\frac{3}{4} = -1\frac{3}{4}$$
$$\overline{}$$
$$1\frac{2}{4}$$
$$1\frac{2}{4}\qquad 1\frac{1}{2}$$

1. Cannot subtract $\frac{1}{4} - \frac{3}{4}$ so rename

$$3\frac{1}{4} = 2 + \frac{4}{4} + \frac{1}{4} =$$
$$2\frac{5}{4}$$

2. Subtract numerators $5 - 3$ and write over the denominator 4.
3. Subtract $2 - 1$.
4. Rename answer.

Figure 13.7 illustrates how to subtract with mixed numbers on the flannel board when renaming is required, as in $4\frac{1}{4} - 1\frac{3}{4}$.

Steps in Subtraction of Mixed Numbers

The following steps should be followed in subtraction of mixed numbers at the symbolic level.

1. Be sure that the fractional parts of a mixed number have the same denominator. If not, rename the fractions in like denominators.

2. If the fractional number in the minuend is equal to or greater than the fractional number in the subtrahend, subtract the numerators for the numerator of the fraction in the difference. Then subtract the whole numbers.

3. If the minuend is a whole number and the subtrahend a mixed number, reduce the whole number by one and rename the one as a fraction having the same denominator as the denominator in the subtrahend. Then subtract.

4. If the fraction in the minuend has a value less than the corresponding fraction in the other number, rename the number in the minuend so that subtraction is possible. The

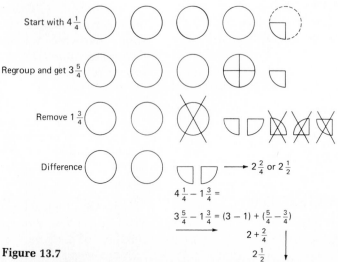

Start with $4\frac{1}{4}$

Regroup and get $3\frac{5}{4}$

Remove $1\frac{3}{4}$

Difference

$2\frac{2}{4}$ or $2\frac{1}{2}$

$4\frac{1}{4} - 1\frac{3}{4} =$

$3\frac{5}{4} - 1\frac{3}{4} = (3 - 1) + (\frac{5}{4} - \frac{3}{4})$

$2 + \frac{2}{4}$

$2\frac{1}{2}$

Figure 13.7

pattern for renaming is illustrated as, $7\frac{1}{4} = 6\frac{5}{4}$. Then subtract.

Addition and Subtraction of Fractions at the Mastery Level

At the mastery level, addition and subtraction of fractional numbers requires an ability to perform the operations at the symbolic level with understanding and in the most efficient way. Pupils should be able to find the sums and differences of fractions with and without renaming without resorting to manipulative or visual aids. To add two mixed numbers with renaming, the following steps are necessary:

$$(1) \quad 3\frac{1}{3} = \quad 3\frac{2}{6}$$
$$+2\frac{5}{6} = \quad +2\frac{5}{6}$$
$$(2) \qquad\qquad 5\frac{7}{6}$$
$$\downarrow$$
$$(3) \qquad\qquad 6\frac{1}{6}$$

1. Rename fractions with like denominators.
2. Add whole numbers; add fractions.
3. Rename to obtain proper fraction.

At the symbolic level, subtraction without renaming should lead naturally to the ability to perform this operation at the mastery level, in exercises such as the following:

$$3\frac{1}{4}$$
$$-2$$
$$1\frac{1}{4}$$

$$5\frac{7}{8}$$
$$-2\frac{3}{8}$$
$$3\frac{4}{8} = 3\frac{1}{2}$$

Pupils should need very little additional work in order to perform subtraction with unlike denominators, as long as no renaming is required:

$$5\frac{1}{2} = \quad 5\frac{3}{6}$$
$$-2\frac{1}{3} = \quad -2\frac{2}{6}$$
$$3\frac{1}{6}$$

Subtractions with mixed numbers that require renaming, such as $5\frac{1}{3} - 2\frac{2}{3}$, require considerable attention. The key to this operation is knowing how to rename $5\frac{1}{3}$ as $4\frac{4}{3}$. A renaming session may be very useful when you introduce subtraction with mixed numbers that require renaming. At the mastery level, pupils should make the following record of their thinking:

$$5\frac{1}{3} = \quad 4\frac{4}{3}$$
$$-2\frac{2}{3} = \quad -2\frac{2}{3}$$
$$2\frac{2}{3}$$

1. Rename $5\frac{1}{3}$ as $4\frac{4}{3}$.
2. Subtract whole numbers.
3. Subtract fractions.
4. Examine difference to make sure it is in lowest terms.

Mastery Involves Solving Verbal Problems

To achieve mastery, pupils need problem-solving experiences throughout the learning sequence of working with fractions. Pupils can solve verbal problems on the mastery level when they can write an appropriate equation for the problem, solve this equation without the use of manipulative aids, and interpret the answer correctly.

PROBLEMS FROM SENTENCES

A technique of problem solving that is often neglected is writing an equation and asking pupils to create a problem for which the equation will provide a solution.

For the equation $n = \frac{2}{12} + \frac{3}{12}$, the following problems are appropriate:

1. Joe had $12 and spent $2 in one store

and $3 in another store. What part of his original amount did he spend?

2. Joe had 12 km to walk. He walked 2 km and then rested. He then walked 3 km and rested again. What part of his journey had he finished by the time of his second rest?

3. Sally estimated that she needed 12 hours to finish sewing her fall outfit. She sewed for 2 hours on Friday night and for another 3 hours on Saturday. What part of her total job did she complete?

The following problems are appropriate for the sentence $n = \frac{3}{4} - \frac{1}{4}$ or $n + \frac{1}{4} = \frac{3}{4}$:

1. Nancy started the day with $\frac{3}{4}$ yards of ribbon and used $\frac{1}{4}$ yard. How much ribbon did she have left at the end of the day?

2. Sue started the day with a quarter in her purse. Her father gave her some money, which she put in her purse without looking. Later she discovered that she had 3 quarters in her purse. How much had her father given her?

You will find that this activity of stating an equation and asking for a problem helps pupils to recognize the relationship between a problem and its equation.

Remember that problems met in real life by engineers, mathematicians, and ordinary citizens are not written out nicely as problems in a text. These problems must first be formulated before they can be solved. An alert teacher should try to help pupils recognize such situations when they do occur in the classroom and proceed with formulating a problem as well as finding its solution. No text can supply a sufficient number and variety of problems to interest all pupils. A teacher familiar with the interests of the various pupils in the class can frequently find problems that are more appropriate than those given in the text.

Summary

In the future, as the use of calculators continues to increase, there will be less emphasis on the study of addition and subtraction of fractions. Furthermore, with the shift to the metric system, more problems will be presented in decimal form rather than as common fractions.

The level of pupil achievement on addition and subtraction of fractions has been relatively low in the past because basic concepts and procedures of working with fractions were not taught with adequate meaning and understanding. Pupils first discover the meanings essential for proficiency in working with fractions at the exploratory level of learning. Research and experience have shown that pupils need to use manipulative materials and visual aids to solve various problems involving fractions.

As pupils explore the meanings of fractions, appropriate records of the thought process should be kept. From these written records and language experiences pupils discover patterns and relationships at the symbolic level of learning.

The teaching–learning sequence for addition and subtraction of fractions is:

1. Start with a problem situation involving fractions.

2. Solve the problem with manipulatives.

3. Show solution with drawings.

4. Keep a symbolic record of the thought process.

5. Discover relationships and patterns at the symbolic level.

6. Reinforce through practice and drill for mastery.

At the mastery level, pupils will be able to add and subtract fractions with understanding and with efficiency. At this level, pupils should not use manipulative materials. Drawing may be helpful to verify the accuracy of an answer. At the mastery level, pupils are also able to solve verbal problems. Pupils achieve mastery when they can write an appropriate equation, solve it, and interpret the results correctly.

Exercises 13.3

1. Name three important aids for introducing fractions.
2. Use a rectangular area to show that $3/5$ can be renamed as $6/10$.
3. Use the number line to rename $3/5$ as $6/10$.
4. For symbolic addition of $2/3$ and $3/5$, rename as ______ and ______.
5. Use the factor method to determine the greatest common factor and reduce each of the following fractions to lowest terms:
   (a) $10/24$ (b) $12/30$ (c) $18/40$
6. Use the symbolic approach to rename the following fractions as indicated:
   (a) $\frac{5}{8} = \frac{\square}{40}$ (b) $\frac{7}{12} = \frac{\square}{60}$ (c) $\frac{3}{7} = \frac{\square}{28}$ (d) $\frac{4}{15} = \frac{\square}{45}$
7. Use the symbolic method to add the following:
   (a) $\frac{3}{8} + \frac{2}{8}$ (b) $\frac{2}{3} + \frac{5}{6}$ (c) $\frac{5}{6} + \frac{3}{8}$
8. Use the symbolic method to subtract the following:
   (a) $\frac{3}{4} - \frac{3}{8}$ (b) $\frac{5}{6} - \frac{2}{3}$ (c) $1\frac{3}{4} - \frac{5}{6}$ (d) $3\frac{5}{6} - 1\frac{3}{8}$
9. Find the least common denominator of 12 and 15 by the following methods:
   a. the "modified" or "abbreviated" multiples method
   b. by listing the multiples of 12 and 15
   c. by renaming 12 and 15 with prime factors
   d. by dividing out the greatest common prime factors
10. A teacher remarked: "If a pupil writes out all the steps involved in an operation, supplementary aids are not necessary." Evaluate this statement.
11. Evaluate the plans that may be used to find a least common denominator of fractions having unlike and unrelated denominators.
12. Use both the multiples approach and the prime factor approach to find the least common denominator of the following:
    a. 12 and 18
    b. 20 and 35
    c. 10, 15, and 18

13. Write a fraction having a numerator of 2 that names a fraction:
    a. less than ¾ but greater than ½
    b. less than ⅓ but greater than ⅕
    c. less than ¼ but greater than ⅛

14. A pupil notices that in adding ⅔ and ⁴⁄₁₁ he can get the correct sum by:
    a. obtaining the numerator of the sum by "cross-multiplying" and adding the two products $(2 \times 11) + (3 \times 4) = 34$.
    b. obtaining the denominator by multiplying denominators $3 \times 11 = 33$. Sum $= ³⁴⁄₃₃$. Will this method always give a correct answer? How should the teacher answer the pupil?

Selected Readings

Ellerbruch, Lawrence W., and Joseph N. Payne. "A Teaching Sequence from Initial Fraction Concepts through the Addition of Unlike Fractions." In *Developing Computational Skills,* 1978 Yearbook. Reston, VA: National Council of Teachers of Mathematics, 1978, Chapter 8.

Heddens, James W. *Today's Mathematics,* Fourth Edition. Chicago: Science Research Associates, 1980, Units 10 and 11.

Hlavaty, Julius H. (Ed.). *Mathematics for Elementary School Teachers, The Rational Numbers.* Reston, VA: National Council of Teachers of Mathematics, 1972, Chapters 1–4.

Marks, John L., C. Richard Purdy, Lucien B. Kinney, and Arthur A. Hiatt. *Teaching Elementary School Mathematics for Understanding.* New York: McGraw-Hill, 1975, Chapter 7.

Riedesel, C. Alan. *Teaching Elementary School Mathematics,* Third Edition. Englewood Cliffs, NJ: Prentice-Hall, 1980, Chapter 10.

Schminke, C.W., Norbert Maertens, and William Arnold. *Teaching the Child Mathematics,* Second Edition. New York: Holt, Rinehart and Winston, 1978, pp. 117–130.

Chapter 14

Multiplication and Division of Fractions

Chapter 13 indicated that calculators, computers, and metrics, will curtail the use of fractions, but the concepts of halves, thirds, fourths, will always have everyday applications. In Europe, where the metric system has been used for many years, meat is often sold by the half-kilogram.

Achievement Goals

After studying this chapter, you should be able to:

1. Know how to teach multiplication of fractions on the exploratory, symbolic, and mastery levels.
2. Know how to teach division of fractions on the exploratory, symbolic, and mastery levels.
3. Effectively stress the multiplication/division relation, the reciprocal (multiplicative inverse) concept, and the identity property of 1 in teaching division of fractions.
4. Relate multiplication and division of mixed numbers to the same operations with fractions.

5. Teach students to solve verbal problems involving fractions and mixed numbers.

Vocabulary

Mastery of the following key terms will help you to understand this chapter. Each word is defined or illustrated in the Glossary at the back of the book.

Denominator
Improper fraction
Mixed number
Multiplication/
　division relation
Multiplicative
　identity

Multiplicative
　inverse
Numerator
Proper fraction
Reciprocal
Unit fraction

Multiplication of Fractions

Multiplication of a Fraction and a Whole Number

EXPLORATORY LEVEL

The multiplication of a fraction by a mixed number, such as $3 \times \frac{1}{2}$, can be introduced with a problem such as the following: Jean picks 3 bags of grapes. If each bag weighs ½ pound, what is the combined weight of the 3 bags?

Students can solve this problem by using half-circles on the flannel board, where each half-circle represents half a pound of grapes, as shown in Figure 14.1.

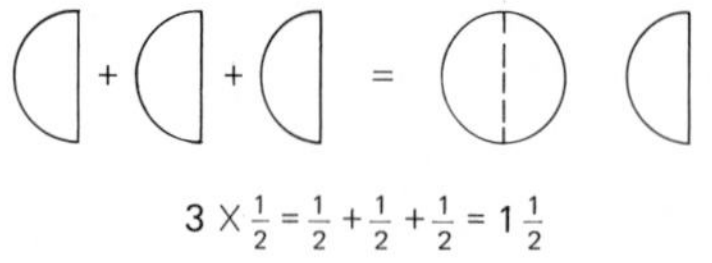

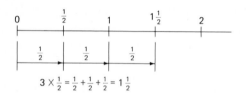

$$3 \times \tfrac{1}{2} = \tfrac{1}{2} + \tfrac{1}{2} + \tfrac{1}{2} = 1\tfrac{1}{2}$$

Figure 14.1

The number line can also be used, as shown in Figure 14.2.

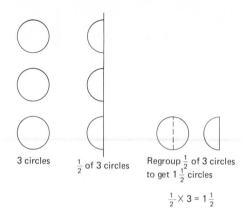

3 circles $\tfrac{1}{2}$ of 3 circles   Regroup $\tfrac{1}{2}$ of 3 circles to get $1\tfrac{1}{2}$ circles

$$\tfrac{1}{2} \times 3 = 1\tfrac{1}{2}$$

Figure 14.3

The number line can also be used, as shown in Figure 14.2.

$$3 \times \tfrac{1}{2} = \tfrac{1}{2} + \tfrac{1}{2} + \tfrac{1}{2} = 1\tfrac{1}{2}$$

Figure 14.2

Structurally, ½ × 3 = 3 × ½, but the two statements represent different situations. Consider the following problem: A ribbon is 3 feet long. What is the length of half of this ribbon? Students at the mastery level usually find ½ of a number by dividing by 2. On the exploratory level, this product is found by dividing something into two equal parts and taking one of them. The flannel board can be used to explore this problem. Place three circles, each formed by two half-circles, on the board. If individual kits are available, the pupils should perform the same activity at their seats. The three circles are separated into two equal parts (to obtain three half-circles). Allow the pupils to discover that the three half-circles can be rearranged to form one and one-half circles such that ½ × 3 = 1½, as shown in Figure 14.3.

The problem can also be solved using the number line, as shown in Figure 14.4.

Six rectangular blocks placed end to end, with each pair representing one, can readily be broken into two equal groups of three blocks, in which two of the blocks represent 1 and the remaining block represents ½, as shown in Figure 14.5. Similar activities can be performed to solve ¾ × 4 and ⅔ × 6.

SYMBOLIC LEVEL

Students at the early symbolic level find the product of a whole number and a fraction by using the identity 3 × n = n + n + n. Therefore, 3 × ½ = ½ + ½ + ½ = ³⁄₂ = 1½. The statement can also be written

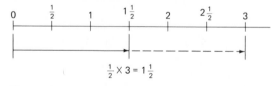

$$\tfrac{1}{2} \times 3 = 1\tfrac{1}{2}$$

Figure 14.4

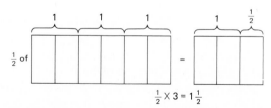

$$\tfrac{1}{2} \times 3 = 1\tfrac{1}{2}$$

Figure 14.5

as ½ + ½ + ½ = (½ + ½) + ½ = 1 + ½ = 1½. Although the product of ½ × 3 cannot be found in this way, it can be re-named as 3 × ½ by assuming the commutative property—a reasonable assumption on the basis of exploratory work. The following expansions illustrate this approach:

$$3 \times \frac{1}{4} = \frac{1}{4} + \frac{1}{4} + \frac{1}{4} = \frac{\Box}{4}$$

$$5 \times \frac{1}{2} = \frac{1}{2} + \frac{1}{2} + \frac{1}{2} + \frac{1}{2} + \frac{1}{2} = \frac{5}{\Box} = \triangle$$

$$4 \times \frac{1}{3} = \frac{1}{3} + \Box + \Box + \Box = \frac{4}{3} = \triangle$$

$$\frac{2}{3} \times 3 = 3 \times \frac{2}{3} = \frac{2}{3} + \Box + \Box = \frac{6}{3} = \triangle$$

$$3 \times \frac{3}{4} = \frac{3}{4} + \frac{3}{4} + \frac{3}{4} = \Box$$

$$\frac{3}{4} = \Box \times \frac{1}{4}$$

$$5 \times \frac{3}{4} = 5 \times (3 \times \frac{1}{4}) =$$

$$\Box \times \frac{1}{4} = \frac{15}{4} = \triangle$$

$$5 \times \frac{3}{4} = \frac{\Box \times 3}{4} = \triangle$$

Multiplication of Two Fractions

EXPLORATORY LEVEL

The following problem can be used to teach students how to find the product of two fractions.

A man owned a lot that was ⅘ of an acre in size. He used ⅔ of the lot for a garden. The garden measured what part of an acre?

To show ⅘ of an acre, draw a rectangle ABCD and draw verticals to divide it into five equal parts. Shade four of the parts to show ⅘ of an acre. The rectangle AFJD rep-represents $\frac{4}{\Box}$ of an acre.

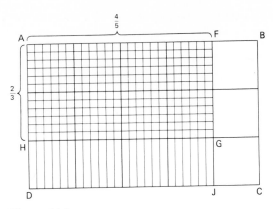

Figure 14.6

Next, divide the rectangle ABCD horizontally into 3 equal parts. Cross-hatch the squares in rectangle AFGH, which represents ⅔ of ¾ of an acre.

1. How many squares represent an acre? (15)

2. How many squares represent ⅘ of an acre? (12)

3. How many squares represent ⅔ of ⅘ of an acre? (8) The product of ⅔ × ⅘ = $\frac{\Box}{15}$.

The garden is $\frac{\Box}{15}$ of an acre. Is it more or less than ½ of an acre?

The product ⅔ × ⅘ can be found by using 15 objects or 15 pupils in the following activities:

1. Separate the 15 objects or pupils into 5 equal groups of 3. Take 4 of these groups to obtain 12 and show that ⅘ of 15 = 12.

2. Separate the 12 objects or pupils into 3 equal groups of 4. Take 2 of these groups to show that ⅔ of 12 (⅘ of 15) is 8.

3. Using the results of steps 1 and 2, help pupils discover that ⅔ of ⅘ of a group of 15 is ⁸⁄₁₅ of a group of 15, or that ⅔ × (⅘ × 15) = 8.

SYMBOLIC LEVEL

Activities such as those we have described should enable pupils to operate at the symbolic level and understand the work. Pupils at the symbolic level would be taught to find the product of ⅔ and ⅘ by proceeding as follows:

$$\frac{2}{3} \times \frac{4}{5} = \frac{2 \times 4}{3 \times 5} = \frac{8}{15}$$

The algorism for multiplication of two fractional numbers is the following:

$$\frac{a}{b} \times \frac{c}{d} = \frac{a \times c}{b \times d}$$

This algorism should also be stated verbally as: The *product of two fractions is the product of the numerators divided by the product of the denominators.*

Pupils should have no trouble recognizing that ⅔ of 15 is less than 15, and from this should see that ⅔ × ⅘ is less than ⅘ or ⅔. They should remember that the product of a *proper fraction* (between 0 and 1) and any number is less than that number, and that the product of two proper fractions is less than either of them. These generaliza-

tions enable students to estimate and recognize that an answer is sensible. A strong visual representation of this logic is the number line, as shown in Figure 14.7. The entire procedure can be done on a single number line, but the comparison between ⅔, ⅘, and ⅔ × ⅘ will not be as apparent, as when using 3 number lines, provided that the 3 number lines are properly aligned.

It is valuable for students to compare the size of fractions. Give them the following activity, asking them to fill in the blanks with "less than," "greater than," or "equal to."

1. ⅓ is _____ ⅔.

2. ⅓ is _____ ½.

3. ⅔ is _____ ½.

4. ²⁄₁₅ is _____ ½.

5. ⅜ is _____ ⅗.

6. ⅔ is _____ ¾.

The difference between ⅔ and ¾ is not obvious to beginning students. If the fractions are renamed as twelfths, then it becomes clear that ⅔ (⁸⁄₁₂) is less than ¾ (⁹⁄₁₂). Or you can compare ⅔ × 12 with ¾ × 12

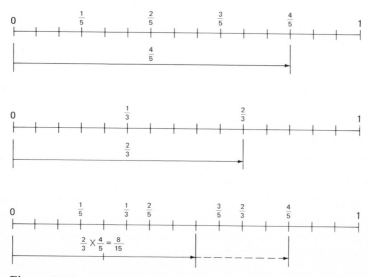

Figure 14.7

to show that 8, the product of the former, is less than 9. Note that by using the multiplication algorism:

$$\frac{2}{3} \times 12 = \frac{2}{3} \times \frac{12}{1} = \frac{2 \times 12}{3 \times 1} = 8.$$

The number line can also be used to compare fractions. It is a useful activity to draw a number line of length 1 on the chalkboard and ask pupils to estimate the size of a fraction, such as ⅖ or 4/7, by drawing an arrow of appropriate length. It is best to ask first whether the fraction to be estimated is more or less than ½. The students can check the accuracy of their estimate by measurement, making the exercise even more useful by providing motivation for measurement.

SYMBOLIC LEVEL

The four examples below are appropriate for students beginning work at the symbolic level:

1. $\dfrac{3}{5} \times \dfrac{4}{7} = \dfrac{\square \times 4}{5 \times 7} = \dfrac{\triangle}{35}$

2. $3 \times \dfrac{4}{5} = \dfrac{3 \times \square}{5} = \dfrac{\triangle}{5}$

3. $\dfrac{2}{3} \times \dfrac{5}{9} = \dfrac{10}{\square}$

4. $\dfrac{2}{7} \times \dfrac{4}{5} = \square$

The product 3 × ¼ = ¾ can be found by repeated addition or by using the multiplication algorism. By working this example, pupils should recognize that ¾ can be renamed as 3 × ¼. At this stage, the multiplication algorism can be reinforced with the following activity:

1. $\dfrac{2}{3} \times \dfrac{4}{5} = (2 \times \dfrac{1}{3}) \times (4 \times \dfrac{1}{5})$

$= (2 \times 4) \times (\dfrac{1}{3} \times \dfrac{1}{5})$

$= \square \times \dfrac{1}{15} = \dfrac{\square}{15}$

2. $4 \times \dfrac{3}{4} = 4 \times (3 \times \dfrac{1}{4})$

$= (4 \times 3) \times \dfrac{1}{4}$

$= \dfrac{\square}{4} = 3$

Fractions such as ⅓ and ⅕, with numerators of 1, are called *unit fractions*. There is little need in current elementary programs to take special notice of unit fractions. However, unit fractions are used in performing a mathematical proof of the multiplication algorism; to do this, begin with the proof that the product of two unit fractions is the product of the numerators (which is 1 for unit fractions) divided by the product of the denominators. The remainder of the proof follows the pattern in example 1 above.

Consider this problem: Diane withdrew ¾ of her savings and spent ⅔ of that amount for a radio. What fraction of the original amount in her savings account did she spend on the radio? Careful reading of the problem will enable the student to conclude that what is wanted is ⅔ of ¾ of Diane's savings. The symbolic solution would then follow, in the form of the equation:

$$n = \dfrac{2}{3} \times \dfrac{3}{4}$$

$$n = \dfrac{1}{2}$$

The radio cost ½ of her savings.

The answer is sensible because it is less than both ⅔ and ¾. For an additional check, the student might assume that the amount of original savings was $100. Diane would have withdrawn ¾ of 100, or 75 dollars, and spent ⅔ of this, or 50 dollars, which is ½ of the original $100. Point out that "of" in the phrase "⅔ of something" indicates multiplication.

Pupils have achieved mastery of problems such as ⅔ × ⅘ when they can give the answer ⁸⁄₁₅ as a habitual response. However, additional knowledge is required to achieve mastery of problems like ⅔ × ¾, which are usually performed as follows:

$$\overset{1}{\underset{1}{\frac{\overset{}{2}}{3}}} \times \overset{1}{\underset{2}{\frac{3}{\underset{}{4}}}} = \frac{1}{2}$$

The pupil must understand that dividing the numerator of the first fraction by 2 and the denominator of the second fraction by 2 divides both the numerator and denominator of the product by 2. Likewise, dividing the denominator of the first fraction by 3 and the numerator of the second fraction by 3 divides the numerator and the denominator of the product by 3.

A consequence of the associative and commutative properties is that in multiplying 3 × 7 by 2, either factor can be multiplied by 2: 2 × (3 × 7) = 6 × 7 = 3 × 14 = 42. As shown on page 251, division by 2 can be transformed into multiplication by ½, so that division of a product can be performed by dividing one factor, such as: (4 × 6) ÷ 2 = 2 × 6 = 4 × 3 = 12.

In the case of ⅔ × ¾, each numerator is a factor of the numerator of the product by the multiplication algorism. Similarly, the denominators are factors of the denominator of the product. Therefore, dividing one numerator by 2 divides the numerator of the product by 2. Dividing one denominator by 2 divides the denominator of the product by 2.

Many pupils will find the product as follows:

$$\frac{2}{3} \times \frac{3}{4} = \frac{2 \times 3}{3 \times 4} = \frac{6}{12} = \frac{1}{2}$$

This procedure is correct and acceptable,

but is not a mastery-level solution because it is very time consuming with large numbers. For example:

$$\overset{2}{\underset{9}{\frac{\cancel{26}}{\cancel{27}}}} \times \overset{5}{\underset{7}{\frac{\cancel{15}}{\cancel{91}}}} = \frac{2 \times 5}{9 \times 7} = \frac{10}{63}$$

Multiplying 26 × 15 and 27 × 91 and dividing out a common factor of 39 would be a much more time-consuming process.

Division of Fractions

A good way to introduce division of fractions is by working problems like the following:

How many pieces of ribbon ½ yard in length can be cut from a ribbon 3 yards long?

The question of how many ½'s there are in 3 should suggest to the students the operation of division and the number sentence:

$$n = 3 \div \frac{1}{2}$$

Use drawings on the chalkboard similar to those in Figure 14.8, or use a flannel board. Pupils should work at their seats

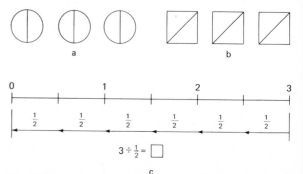

Figure 14.8

with fraction kits. Ask questions such as the following:

Refer to (a). How many half-circles are there in 3 circles?

Refer to (b). How many half-squares are there in 3 squares?

Refer to (c). How many ½'s are there in 3?

Ask the class how many half-dollars can be exchanged for 1 dollar; for 2 dollars; and for 3 dollars.

Write the solution to the original problem:

$$n = 3 \div \frac{1}{2}$$

$$n = 6$$

There are 6 ½-yard pieces of ribbon in 3 yards.

Help the class to recognize that if $n = 3 \div \frac{1}{2}$, then $\frac{1}{2}n = 3$. The students should have no trouble finding the answer to $\frac{1}{2}n = 3$ by the "guess and test" method to verify that $n = 6$. Every equation of the form $n = a \div b$ can be rewritten as $bn = a$, using the multiplication/division pattern. When the class has had more experience in dividing fractions, they should recognize that the answer is sensible, because dividing 3 by a number less than 1 should give a quotient greater than 3.

Exploratory work usually involves manipulative materials or drawings designed to help pupils visualize important procedures and concepts. It is essential that the result of the exploratory work be written symbolically whenever possible.

Take special care when choosing examples for exploratory work so that students do not find the work tedious. Make sure that there are suitable divisions on the number line. Similarly, work with geometric figures will not be effective unless the figures can be partitioned so as to illustrate the desired concept or operation.

SYMBOLIC LEVEL

The earliest symbolic work should draw on the pupils' previous experience with division as repeated subtraction, as shown in Figure 14.9. For example, you show that there are four ½'s in 2 by subtracting ½ four times, and so on.

The multiplication/division relation indicates that if $2 \times 3 = 6$, then $6 \div 2 = 3$ and $6 \div 3 = 2$. Do some exploratory work to show that this relation holds for fractions. For example, if $\frac{1}{2} \times 4 = 2$, then $2 \div \frac{1}{2} = 4$, which is verified by example (a) below. Similarly, if $\frac{2}{3} \times 3 = 2$, then $2 \div \frac{2}{3} = 3$, as verified by example (c).

(a)

$$\begin{array}{lr} & 2 \\ & -\frac{1}{2} \\ \hline (1) & 1\frac{1}{2} \\ & -\frac{1}{2} \\ \hline (2) & 1 \\ & -\frac{1}{2} \\ \hline (3) & \frac{1}{2} \\ & -\frac{1}{2} \\ \hline (4) & 0 \end{array}$$

$$2 \div \frac{1}{2} = \square$$

(b)

$$\begin{array}{lr} & 3 \\ & -1\frac{1}{2} \\ \hline (1) & 1\frac{1}{2} \\ & -1\frac{1}{2} \\ \hline (2) & 0 \end{array}$$

$$3 \div 1\frac{1}{2} = \square$$

(c)

$$\begin{array}{lr} & 2 \\ & -\frac{2}{3} \\ \hline (1) & 1\frac{1}{3} \\ & -\frac{2}{3} \\ \hline (2) & \frac{2}{3} \\ & -\frac{2}{3} \\ \hline (3) & 0 \end{array}$$

$$2 \div \frac{2}{3} = \square$$

Figure 14.9

Have each pupil perform the subtractions indicated in the given examples. Use manipulatives with the pupils who cannot yet operate at the symbolic level. Then give examples of the following type to help the class understand the relationship between multiplication and division with fractions.

1. If $\frac{1}{2} \times 2 = 1$, then $1 \div \frac{1}{2} = 2$. Note that either statement can be interpreted as: "There are 2 halves in 1."

2. If $\frac{1}{4} \times 4 = 1$, then $1 \div \frac{1}{4} = \square$. Interpret verbally.

3. If $\frac{1}{3} \times \frac{2}{5} = \frac{2}{15}$, then $\frac{2}{15} \div \frac{1}{3} = \square$.

4. If $\frac{2}{3} \times \frac{3}{5} = \frac{2}{5}$, then $\frac{2}{5} \div \frac{2}{3} = \square$ and $\frac{2}{5} \div \frac{3}{5} = \triangle$.

The Reciprocal and Multiplicative Inverse

Two numbers are *reciprocals* if and only if their product is 1. For example, the number $\frac{1}{2}$ is the reciprocal of 2, and 2 is the reciprocal of $\frac{1}{2}$. The terms "invert" and "inverse" are often used in connection with reciprocals. If $\frac{1}{2}$ is inverted, its reciprocal 2 is obtained. If 2—visualized as $\frac{2}{1}$—is inverted, its reciprocal $\frac{1}{2}$ is obtained. Although you should be aware that the mathematical name for reciprocal is "multiplicative inverse," you should not use this terminology on the elementary level. The following activities will help pupils to understand the concept of reciprocal:[1]

1. $\frac{1}{2} \times \square = 1$

2. $3 \times \square = 1$

3. $\frac{3}{5} \times \square = 1$

4. The reciprocal of 2 is _____ because the product of _____ and _____ is 1.

5. The reciprocal of $\frac{1}{5}$ is _____ because the product of _____ and _____ is 1.

6. The reciprocal of $\frac{3}{7}$ is _____ because the product of _____ and _____ is 1.

7. Two numbers are reciprocals if their product is _____.

The Division Algorism

In a sense, the division algorism ($\frac{a}{b} \div \frac{c}{d} = \frac{a}{b} \times \frac{d}{c}$) is misnamed because it indi-

cates not how to divide but how to transform an unfamiliar division into a familiar multiplication problem. Translating a new problem into a familiar one is a common and sound mathematical procedure. The following activities can give pupils the opportunity to discover the algorism. The key ideas involved are:

1. The multiplication/division relation.

2. The missing-factor form of division.

3. The multiplication property of one (multiplicative identity).

4. The concept of reciprocal (multiplicative identity).

I. a. Use the multiplication/division relation to complete the statement: If $\frac{1}{2} \times 4 = 2$, then $2 \div \frac{1}{2} = \square$.

   b. Multiply 2 by the reciprocal of $\frac{1}{2}$: $2 \times \square = 4$.

   c. Compare the results of (a) and (b) to complete the following sentence:
Rather than divide by $\frac{1}{2}$, one can multiply by the _____ of $\frac{1}{2}$, or _____.

II. a. Use the multiplication/division relation to complete the following sentence: If $\frac{3}{4} \times 8 = 6$, then $6 \div \frac{3}{4} = \square$.

   b. Multiply 6 by the reciprocal of $\frac{3}{4}$: $6 \times \square = 8$.

   c. Compare the results of (a) and (b) to complete the following sentence: Rather than divide by $\frac{3}{4}$, one can multiply by the reciprocal of _____, or _____.

III. a. If $\frac{2}{3} \times \frac{4}{5} = \frac{8}{15}$, then $\frac{8}{15} \div \frac{4}{5} = \square$.

   b. Multiply $\frac{8}{15}$ by the reciprocal of $\frac{4}{5}$: $\frac{8}{15} \times \square = \triangle$.

   c. Compare the results of (a) and (b) to complete the following sentence: Rather than divide by $\frac{4}{5}$, one can multiply by the _____ of $\frac{4}{5}$, or _____.

IV. Rather than divide by a number, one can multiply by its _____.

---

1. Zero has no reciprocal because there is no number that when multiplied by 0 will give 1. In other words, 0 has no reciprocal because it is not possible to divide by 0.

V. Use the pattern described in problem IV to complete the following statements:

    a. $4 \div \frac{1}{3} = 4 \times \square = \triangle$

    b. $2 \div \frac{2}{3} = 2 \times \square = \triangle$

    c. $\frac{3}{5} \div \frac{4}{3} = \frac{3}{5} \times \square = \triangle$

Complex Fractions (Enrichment)

At the introductory level, fractions were interpreted as parts of a whole. Pupils in the upper grades should be able to understand the mathematical interpretation of a fraction as an *indicated division*. Thus, $\frac{a}{b} = a \div b$. This interpretation leads to the following practice for verifying the division algorithm.

1. Write $4 \div \frac{1}{3}$ in fractional form and find the quotient.

$$4 \div \frac{1}{3} = \frac{4}{\frac{1}{3}}$$

To find the quotient of $4 \div \frac{1}{3}$ when written as $\frac{4}{\frac{1}{3}}$, multiply the fraction by 1 renamed as $\frac{3}{3}$. After 1 is renamed as $\frac{3}{3}$, the denominator of the given fraction ($\frac{1}{3}$) is multiplied by its reciprocal, or 3.

$$\frac{4}{\frac{1}{3}} = \frac{4}{\frac{1}{3}} \times \frac{3}{3} = \frac{4 \times 3}{\frac{1}{3} \times 3} = \frac{\square}{1} = \square$$

2. Find the quotient of $\frac{3}{5} \div \frac{3}{4}$ when written as $\frac{\frac{3}{5}}{\frac{3}{4}}$

    a. The denominator is $\frac{3}{4}$. To divide by $\frac{3}{4}$, one should multiply by $\frac{4}{\square}$.

    b. We can multiply the given fraction by 1 renamed as $\frac{\frac{4}{3}}{\frac{4}{3}}$

$$\frac{\frac{3}{5}}{\frac{3}{4}} = \frac{\frac{3}{5} \times \frac{4}{3}}{\frac{3}{4} \times \frac{4}{3}} = \frac{\frac{3}{5} \times \frac{4}{3}}{\square} = \frac{\frac{4}{\square}}{1} = \triangle$$

Therefore, $\frac{3}{5} \div \frac{3}{4} = \frac{3}{5} \times \square = \triangle$.

The fractions $\frac{4}{\frac{1}{3}}$ and $\frac{\frac{3}{5}}{\frac{3}{4}}$ are called *complex fractions*, or fractions within fractions. The procedure just illustrated, using complex fractions, was prevalent during the late 1960s and is still used in some current programs. This approach has two advantages. First, it provides an additional activity to help pupils understand the division algorism for fractions; second, it provides the mathematical basis for proving the division algorism for fractions:

$$\frac{a}{b} \div \frac{c}{d} = \frac{\frac{a}{b}}{\frac{c}{d}} \times \frac{\frac{d}{c}}{\frac{d}{c}} = \frac{\frac{a}{b} \times \frac{d}{c}}{1} = \frac{a}{b} \times \frac{d}{c}$$

The division algorism for fractions can be stated in the following three forms:

1. Algebraic form: $\dfrac{a}{b} \div \dfrac{c}{d} = \dfrac{a}{b} \times \dfrac{d}{c}$

2. Verbal form: Rather than divide by a fraction, one can multiply by its reciprocal.

3. Traditional form: Rather than divide by a fraction, invert the divisor and multiply. In the past, this rule was often taught by rote. Its major shortcoming is that it gives no hint of the mathematical structure involved in the process, which is identical with that of subtracting by adding the inverse.

The whole number 2 can be renamed as the fraction $\frac{2}{1}$ so that $3 \div 2 = 3$ multiplied by the reciprocal of 2, or $3 \times \frac{1}{2}$. Thus, the division algorism can be restated: *Rather than divide by a number, multiply by its reciprocal.* The division algorism applies to all numbers, not just to fractions.

Mastery Level

Pupils should acquire the habit of seeing whether answers for multiplication and division are sensible. The following generalizations, discovered by experience, can aid in this process:

1. When we multiply by a number less than 1, the product is less than the number multiplied (multiplicand). Therefore, the product of $\frac{2}{3} \times \frac{3}{4}$ must be less than $\frac{2}{3}$ and less than $\frac{3}{4}$.

2. When we multiply by a number greater than 1, the product is greater than the number being multiplied. Therefore, $\frac{1}{3} \times \frac{1}{2}$ must be greater than $\frac{1}{2}$, but by the first generalization must be less than $\frac{1}{3}$.

3. When we divide by a number less than 1, the quotient is larger than the number being divided (dividend). Therefore, $8 \div \frac{3}{4}$ must be greater than 8.

4. When we divide by a number greater than 1, the quotient is less than the dividend. Therefore, $7 \div \frac{4}{3}$ must be less than 7.

Enrichment

Beginning students can rationalize renaming fractions—for example, $\frac{1}{2}$ as $\frac{3}{6}$ by multiplying numerator and denominator by 3—on the basis of exploratory activities. The multiplication algorism for fractions is a more mathematical approach to this process:

$$\frac{1}{2} = \frac{1}{2} \times 1 = \frac{1}{2} \times \frac{3}{3} = \frac{1 \times 3}{2 \times 3} = \frac{3}{6}$$

Fractions can be reduced in a similar manner:

$$\frac{6}{8} = \frac{3 \times 2}{4 \times 2} = \frac{3}{4} \times \frac{2}{2} = \frac{3}{4} \times 1 = \frac{3}{4}$$

Both procedures illustrate the importance of 1 as the multiplicative identity. Activities such as the following will help strengthen this activity:

1. $\dfrac{2}{3} \times \dfrac{\square}{\square} = \dfrac{6}{9}$

2. $\dfrac{3}{5} \times \dfrac{\square}{4} = \dfrac{\triangle}{20}$

3. $\dfrac{3}{4} = \dfrac{3}{4} \times \dfrac{3}{\square} = \triangle$

4. $\dfrac{9}{12} = \dfrac{3 \times \square}{4 \times \square} = \dfrac{3}{4} \times \dfrac{\square}{\square} = \dfrac{3}{4} \times \triangle = \dfrac{3}{4}$

5. $\dfrac{a}{b} \times \dfrac{n}{n} = \dfrac{an}{bn}$ $(n \neq 0)$. Translate verbally.

6. $\dfrac{a}{b} = \dfrac{a \times \dfrac{1}{n}}{b \times \dfrac{1}{n}} = \dfrac{a \div n}{b \div n}$ $(n \neq 0)$. Translate verbally.

Note: According to the division algorism, to divide a by n, one multiplies a by $\frac{1}{n}$ the reciprocal of n: $a \div n = a \times \frac{1}{n}$. This mathematical sentence can be read either way and indicates that $a \times \frac{1}{n}$ is equivalent to $a \div n$, and that $a \div n$ can be renamed as $a \times \frac{1}{n}$. Since n is the reciprocal of $\frac{1}{n}$, it follows that instead of multiplying by a number, one can divide by its reciprocal; for example, divide by 2 rather than multiply by $\frac{1}{2}$.

Multiplication and Division with Mixed Numbers

Mixed numbers are rarely used in business and industry, as most computation is done with decimals on calculators and computers. One exception is the stock market, which lists stock prices on major exchanges as mixed numbers.

To multiply by a mixed number with the standard multiplication algorism, two mathematical skills are essential:

1. The ability to express a whole number as a fraction.

$$2 = \frac{2}{1} = \frac{4}{2} = \frac{6}{3} \qquad 3 = \frac{3}{1} = \frac{6}{2} = \frac{9}{3}$$

2. The ability to express a mixed number as a fraction:

$$2\frac{1}{2} = 2 + \frac{1}{2} = \frac{4}{2} + \frac{1}{2} = \frac{5}{2}$$

$$3\frac{2}{3} = 3 + \frac{2}{3} = \frac{9}{3} + \frac{2}{3} = \frac{11}{3}$$

Activities like the following strengthen the students' understanding:

1. $3\frac{1}{2} = 3 + \frac{\square}{2} = \frac{\triangle}{2} + \frac{1}{2} = \frac{7}{2}$

2. $2\frac{3}{4} = 2 + \square = \frac{\triangle}{4} + \frac{3}{4} = \frac{11}{4}$

3. $1\frac{1}{5} = \frac{\square}{5} + \frac{1}{5} = \triangle$

Improper Fractions

Any fraction equal to or greater than 1, such as ¼ or ⁷⁄₃, has traditionally been called an improper fraction. Multiplying and dividing by improper fractions are no different from performing these operations with fractions between 0 and 1 (proper fractions). In this text, we refer to both types simply as fractions.

When the final answer to a problem is a fraction greater than 1 (improper fraction), the result is often written as a mixed number:

$$\frac{5}{2} = \frac{4 + 1}{2} = \frac{4}{2} + \frac{1}{2} = 2\frac{1}{2}$$

$$\frac{7}{3} = \frac{6 + 1}{3} = \frac{6}{3} + \frac{1}{3} = \square$$

In the past, many pupils have had answers marked as incorrect when left as improper fractions, such as not changing ⁷⁄₃ to 2⅓. This is unfortunate, since both numerals represent the same number. If one answer is correct, then so must the other be. The problem ⁷⁄₃ × ⁴⁄₁₇ is performed on a cal-

culator as 7 × 4 ÷ 3 ÷ 17, and can be worked with far more ease than with mixed numbers. The calculator answer will be a decimal.

When pupils can express mixed numbers as fractions, they can perform multiplication and division by using the standard algorisms. Have them supply the missing numerals in the following sentences:

a. $5 \times 4\frac{2}{3} = \frac{5}{1} \times \frac{14}{3} = \frac{\square}{3}$, which is equal to mixed number _____.

b. Perform example (a) by renaming the product as $5 \times 4 + 5 \times \frac{2}{3}$; complete the process to show the answer is the same.

c. $2\frac{1}{3} \times 3\frac{1}{4} = \frac{\square}{3} \times \frac{\triangle}{4} = \frac{91}{12} = $ mixed number _____.

d. By rounding, the answer in (c) must be between _____ and _____.

e. $1\frac{1}{4} \times \frac{3}{4} = \frac{\square \times 3}{4 \times 4} = \frac{\square}{16} = $ mixed number _____.

f. The answer to (e) must be less than _____.

g. $2\frac{2}{3} \div 3 = 2\frac{2}{3} \times \frac{1}{3} = \frac{\square \times 1}{3 \times 3} = \frac{\triangle}{9} = $ mixed number _____.

h. The quotient in (g) must be less than _____.

i. $3\frac{3}{5} \div \frac{1}{2} = \frac{18}{5} \times \frac{\square}{1} = \frac{36}{\triangle} = $ mixed number _____.

j. $\frac{3}{4} \div 5\frac{1}{8} = \frac{3}{4} \div \frac{\square}{8} = \frac{3}{4} \times \triangle = \frac{24}{\triangledown} = $ in lowest terms _____.

k. In (j), the quotient must be less than _____.

The mastery-level solution to (j) can be written as:

$$\frac{3}{4} \div 5\frac{1}{8} = \frac{3}{4} \times \frac{\overset{2}{\cancel{8}}}{41} = \frac{6}{41}$$

Three Types of Problems

There are three basic types of one-step problems in multiplication and division, as illustrated by the following:

A. What number is three-fourths of 30?
$n = \frac{3}{4} \times 30$

B. What part of 20 is 15?
$20n = 15$ or $n = 15 \div 20$

C. Two-thirds of what number is 20?
$\frac{2}{3}a = 20$ or $a = 20 \div \frac{2}{3}$

The basic multiplication situation is n groups of $a = b$. In problem A, n and a are given and b is to be determined; in problem B, a and b are given and n is to be determined; in problem C, n and b are given and a is to be determined.

The three basic situations of percent are analogous to these three problems in fractions. We discuss these forms in the next chapter.

Verbal Problems

In teaching problems with fractional numbers, two techniques sometimes help pupils to find solutions:

1. Reword the problem. Use the simplest language and fewest words possible.

2. Replace fractions or mixed numbers with small whole numbers.

> *Problem A:* Jim walks at an average rate of 2½ miles per hour. What is the distance from his home to his office if he walks that distance in ¾ hours?

There are two ways to reword the problem:

I.   Given: 1 hour → 2½ miles
            Wanted: ¾ hours → ? miles

II. Given 1, find ¾. This is analogous to the pattern "given 1, find many," except that ¾ is not "many." The pupil should learn to

recognize this pattern as multiplication, regardless of whether the desired answer is more or less than 1. By changing ¾ to 3, the student would be expressing, "given 1, find 3," the standard multiplication pattern. It is important for pupils to recognize that changing numbers in this way does not change the required operation. If "given 1, find 3" implies multiplication by 3, then "given 1, find ¾" implies multiplication by ¾. Understanding this concept will help the pupils to recognize in algebra that "given 1, find x" implies multiplication by x.

The problem can now be solved:

(a) $n = \dfrac{3}{4} \times 2\dfrac{1}{2}$ (b) 1 hour → $2\dfrac{1}{2}$ miles

$n = 1\dfrac{7}{8}$ $\dfrac{3}{4}$ hours → $\dfrac{3}{4} \times 2\dfrac{1}{2} = 1\dfrac{7}{8}$

The answer, obtained by either approach, is interpreted as:

The distance is $1\dfrac{7}{8}$ miles.

This answer is sensible because it is between 1¼ (½ of 2½) and 2½ (1 × 2½).

> *Problem B:* Joe walks 1⅞ miles in ¾ of an hour. At this rate, how far will he walk in an hour?

I. The problem can be reworded as: ¾ of what number is 1⅞? This leads to the equation ¾n = 1⅞; n = 1⅞ ÷ ¾ = 2½.

II. The problem can be reworded as:

$\dfrac{3}{4}$ hour → $1\dfrac{7}{8}$ miles

1 hour → ? miles

Changing the numbers from ¾ hours for 1⅞ miles to 3 hours for 6 miles can help the student to recognize the problem as a division situation. Remember that changing the numbers in a one-step problem does not change the operation.

III. The problem can be reworded as "given ¾, find 1," which is similar to the "many-to-one" pattern—given 3, find 1—and indicates division by $\frac{3}{4}$.

Recognizing that $\frac{3}{4}$ of the required number must be $1\frac{7}{8}$ might suggest the "guess and test" approach to some pupils. A guess of 2 would give $\frac{3}{4} \times 2 = 1\frac{1}{2}$, indicating that 2 is too small. A guess of 3 would give $\frac{3}{4} \times 3 = 2\frac{1}{4}$, which is too large. A guess of $2\frac{1}{2}$ would give $1\frac{7}{8}$, indicating that $2\frac{1}{2}$ is the correct answer. The first two steps could be used to ascertain that the answer of $1\frac{7}{8}$, found from another approach, is sensible.

No matter which method the students use to find the answer, the interpretation "$2\frac{1}{2}$ miles in an hour" must be given.

Problem C: A grade of plywood is $\frac{3}{4}$ of an inch thick. How many sheets of this plywood are in a stack $10\frac{1}{2}$ inches high?

I. Rewording this as "How many $\frac{3}{4}$'s are there in $10\frac{1}{2}$?" should enable the pupils to recognize this as a division situation and to write the equation $n = 10\frac{1}{2} \div \frac{3}{4}$.

II. Rewording the problem as "$\frac{3}{4}$ of what number is $10\frac{1}{2}$?" leads to the equation $\frac{3}{4}n = 10\frac{1}{2}$, leading to $n = 10\frac{1}{2} \div \frac{3}{4}$.

III. Reword the problem as:

Given: $\frac{3}{4}$ inches → 1 board
$10\frac{1}{2}$ inches → ? boards

The solution $10\frac{1}{2} \div \frac{3}{4} = 14$ is interpreted as "There are 14 $\frac{3}{4}$-inch boards in a $10\frac{1}{2}$-inch stack."

A guess of 12 boards would lead to a stack of $\frac{3}{4} \times 12$, or a 9-inch stack, whereas a guess of 16 boards would lead to a stack of 12 inches. The answer 14 is sensible and could be obtained by the guess and test method without division. If a calculator were available and the pupil understood $\frac{3}{4} = 0.75$, then the answer could be obtained quickly by the guess and test method. Pupils should recognize that in both problems *B* and *C* the product and one factor are given with the missing factor to be determined.

Summary

To learn the multiplication and division algorisms, pupils should progress gradually from the exploratory to the symbolic to the mastery level. Two fractions are multiplied by finding the product of the numerators divided by the product of the denominators: $\frac{a}{b} \times \frac{c}{d} = \frac{ac}{bd}$.

The standard division algorism for fractions shows how to translate a division by $\frac{c}{d}$ into a multiplication by the reciprocal of $\frac{c}{d}$: $\frac{a}{b} \div \frac{c}{d} = \frac{a}{b} \times \frac{d}{c}$.

There are three key elements in understanding division of fractions:

a. The multiplication/division relation (the inverse relation between multiplication and division, often stated as factor × factor = product, is equivalent to product divided by factor = factor.

b. The product of a number and its reciprocal (multiplicative inverse) is 1.

c. The identity property of 1 is $a \times 1 = 1 \times a = a$ for all a. To use this property effectively, pupils must be able to rename 1 as $\frac{2}{2}$, $\frac{3}{3}$, and so on.

The three types of one-step problems involving fractions stem from the basic multiplication situation, "n groups of $a = b$." The three types are:

a. The numbers n and a are given and b is to be determined. $b = n \times a$

b. The numbers a and b are given and n is to be determined. $n = b \div a$

c. The numbers n and b are given and a is to be determined. $a = b \div n$

Rewording problems in simpler language and substituting whole numbers for fractions can help pupils understand problems involving fractions.

Exercises

1. If the product of a and b is 1, then a is the _____ of b and b is the _____ of a.

2. What number does not have a reciprocal?

3. Complete the following statement of the division algorism: Rather than divide by a number, _____.

4. In everyday language, rational numbers are called _____.

5. What is the cost of 2½ pounds of nuts at $4 per pound?

6. Which analysis is correct for problem 5: Given 2½, find 1, or given 1, find 2½?

7. A football halfback gained 108 yards in 24 carries. What is his average yardage per carry?

8. Which analysis is correct for problem 7: Given 1, find 24, or given 24, find 1?

9. Joe drinks ⅓ of a liter of milk. If his family drinks 10 liters of milk per week, how many liters does the rest of the family drink in a week? in a day?

10. Supply the missing numerals:

   a. $\dfrac{2}{3} \times \dfrac{4}{5} = \dfrac{\square \times \triangle}{15} = \triangledown$

   b. $\dfrac{3}{5} \div \dfrac{3}{4} = \dfrac{3}{5} \times \square = \triangle$

   c. Is the answer to (b) more or less than 1? Why?

   d. $4 \times \dfrac{5}{8} = \dfrac{\square \times 5}{8} = \triangle$ in lowest terms = _____.

   e. $3\dfrac{1}{2} \div 4\dfrac{1}{4} = \dfrac{\square}{2} \div \dfrac{\triangle}{4} = \dfrac{\square}{2} \times \dfrac{4}{\triangle} = \triangledown$

11. Gus runs the marathon at a rate of 5½ miles per hour. How long will it take him to finish the race if the total distance is 26⁷⁄₁₂ miles?

Selected Readings

Heddens, James W. *Today's Mathematics*, Fourth Edition. Chicago: Science Research Associates, 1980.

Marks, John L., C. Richard Purdy, and Arthur C. Hiatt. *Teaching Mathematics for Understanding*, Fourth Edition. New York: McGraw-Hill, 1975.

Riedesel, C. Alan. *Teaching Elementary School Mathematics*, Third Edition. Englewood Cliffs, NJ: Prentice-Hall, 1980.

Schminke, C.W., et al. *Teaching the Child Mathematics*, Second Edition. New York: Holt, Rinehart and Winston, 1978.

Twenty-ninth Yearbook of the National Council of Teachers of Mathematics. Reston, VA: National Council of Teachers of Mathematics, 1964.

Virginia Council of School Mathematics Teachers. *Practical Ways to Teach the Basic Skills*. Reston, VA: National Council of Teachers of Mathematics, 1979.

Chapter 15

Decimal Fractions and Percent

According to tradition, common fractions are taught before decimal fractions. But with the greater emphasis now on decimals, due to the rise of calculators, computers, and metrics, educators have begun to consider the possibility of teaching decimals before common fractions. Kidder[1] proposes that decimals can and should be taught before common fractions because of the parallel between decimals and whole numbers.

Although we follow the traditional pattern of introducing common fractions before decimals, we place less emphasis on common fractions than in earlier editions of this text.

Achievement Goals

After studying this chapter, you should be able to:

1. Acknowledge the increased use of decimals in everyday life.
2. Know how to introduce the important

phases of decimal knowledge and gradually proceed to the symbolic and mastery levels.
3. Stress effectively the common properties, differences, and relationships between common and decimal fractions.
4. Recognize the importance of the rounding process in dealing with terminating and nonterminating decimals.
5. Know how to introduce the concept of percent.
6. Recognize the value of estimation in work with decimals and percent.
7. Know how to help pupils solve problems involving decimals and percent.

Vocabulary

Mastery of the following key terms will help you to understand this chapter. Each term is defined or illustrated in the Glossary at the back of the book.

Base	Percentage
Decimal	Proportion
Nonterminating	Ragged decimal
decimal	Rate
Percent	Repetend
Percent formula	Symmetry

1. Richard F. Kidder, "Ditton's Dilemma, or What to Do about Decimals," *Arithmetic Teacher*, October 1980, 2:44–46.

Everyday Use of Percent

If pupils can perform the four basic operations with whole numbers, the only additional knowledge they need to compute with decimals is the ability to locate the decimal point in the answer. We add and subtract decimals without explicitly finding the common denominator. Recognizing that whole numbers are decimals with an unwritten decimal point helps students with these operations. Unfortunately, students often have more difficulty in locating the decimal point than might be expected, partly because they have often learned to do this by rote. The most reliable way to teach percent is to foster understanding and the ability to estimate.

Today's elementary pupils have more contact with decimals away from school than ever before. The use of the metric system, computerized scales in stores, and calculators all promote increased use of decimal fractions. Percentages have always been used by business and industry, but are more prevalent than ever in everyday conversation, as inflation, prime rates, sales tax, and discounts are among the many topics regularly being discussed.

Decimals are a relatively recent innovation. The Dutch mathematician Simon Stevin wrote the first systematic description in the late sixteenth century, but decimals were not in popular use until almost 200 years later.

Decimal symbolism is not universal. In some European countries, a comma is used in place of the decimal point. And in Britain, 3.14 is written with a raised decimal point, as 3·14.

Introducing the Decimal Concept

Materials

Each pupil should have a kit of squares and strips similar to the materials used in dealing with whole numbers. A large blank square represents 1. Another large square can be divided into 10 strips, with each strip representing one-tenth (.1). A third square can be divided into 100 small squares, each representing one-hundredth (.01). Figure 15.1 shows how these squares can be used to represent the number 1.35 (1 one, 3 tenths, and 5 hundredths).

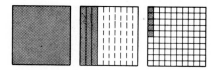

Figure 15.1

A number line is another effective aid for introducing decimals. As Figure 15.2 illustrates, fractional numerals are written above the line and decimal numerals below, enabling pupils to compare the new notation with a familiar one.

Your classroom should be equipped with a place-value chart (see Figure 15.3) to be used in demonstrations to represent ones, tenths, and hundredths.

Fraction charts are also effective teaching aids. These charts can be made of oaktag, or

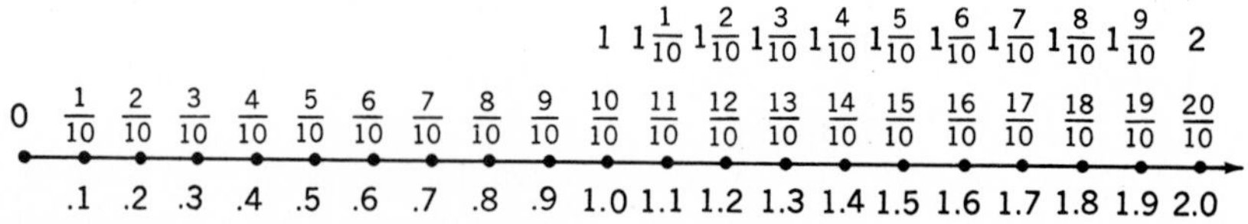

$$1 \quad 1\frac{1}{10} \ 1\frac{2}{10} \ 1\frac{3}{10} \ 1\frac{4}{10} \ 1\frac{5}{10} \ 1\frac{6}{10} \ 1\frac{7}{10} \ 1\frac{8}{10} \ 1\frac{9}{10} \quad 2$$

$$0 \quad \frac{1}{10} \ \frac{2}{10} \ \frac{3}{10} \ \frac{4}{10} \ \frac{5}{10} \ \frac{6}{10} \ \frac{7}{10} \ \frac{8}{10} \ \frac{9}{10} \ \frac{10}{10} \ \frac{11}{10} \ \frac{12}{10} \ \frac{13}{10} \ \frac{14}{10} \ \frac{15}{10} \ \frac{16}{10} \ \frac{17}{10} \ \frac{18}{10} \ \frac{19}{10} \ \frac{20}{10}$$

.1 .2 .3 .4 .5 .6 .7 .8 .9 1.0 1.1 1.2 1.3 1.4 1.5 1.6 1.7 1.8 1.9 2.0

Figure 15.2

Ones		Tenths	Hundredths

Figure 15.3

1									
$\frac{1}{2}$					.5				
$\frac{1}{10}$	.1	$\frac{1}{10}$	.1	$\frac{1}{10}$	.1	$\frac{1}{10}$	.1	$\frac{1}{10}$	.1

Figure 15.4

Fraction	Decimal
$\frac{1}{10}$	.1
$\frac{2}{10}$	.2
$\frac{3}{10}$	.3
.	.
.	.
.	.
$\frac{10}{10} = 1$	$1.0 = 1$

can consist of a frame with movable parts, as shown in Figure 15.4. The strips in the movable parts show equivalent numbers expressed as fractions and decimal numerals. On one strip a number is shown as a fraction, such as ½. On the adjacent strip the same number is expressed as a decimal.

Meaning of Tenths

EXPLORATORY LEVEL

At this level, pupils can identify the large square as 1 and each strip as ⅒, as they are able to see that the ten smaller strips make up the square representing 1. Have the pupils place one strip on a sheet of paper and write ⅒, the fractional numeral representing the value of the strip. Then show the decimal numeral representing the same number (.1). Next have the pupils place two strips on the paper and write 2/10; then write the corresponding decimal. Continue the demonstration until all ten strips are used, and you have completed the following table:

It is important for pupils to discover the relationship between decimal and fractional numerals. Stress the fact that 7/10 and .7 name the same number, using the number line in Figure 15.2. Point out that 10/10 can be interpreted as the decimal 1.0 or the whole number 1. Pupils should interpret whole numbers as decimals with an unwritten decimal point.

Next, have the class discover how to represent 11 tenths. Pupils should use their kits to show that this number can be represented in either grouped or ungrouped form by using both fractional and decimal numerals. By using fractions, the pupil finds that the ungrouped form is 11/10 and the grouped form is 1 1/10. The eleven strips in Figure 15.5 represent the ungrouped form, and the bundle of ten strips with one addi-

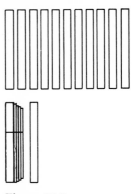

Figure 15.5

tional strip represents the grouped form. Because the tenths place is overloaded, 10 tenths (strips) are regrouped to make 1 to give 1¹⁄₁₀, or 1.1.

It is not necessary to use a marker to symbolize the decimal point when the pupils work with the kit to show a number. A break of approximately 2 inches should separate the square representing 1 and the strips representing tenths. Figure 15.6 shows how to represent the number 2.3.

Figure 15.6

Figure 15.7 shows how 2.3 is represented on the number line.

SYMBOLIC LEVEL

It is useful for students at the early symbolic level to practice renaming familiar common fractions in decimal notation. Here are some sample exercises:

a. Complete the following sequence by filling in the blanks with common fractions:

¹⁄₁₀, _____, ³⁄₁₀, _____, ⁵⁄₁₀, _____

b. The following sequence names the same numbers as sequence (a). Fill in the blanks with the appropriate decimal numerals.

.1, _____, .3, _____, .5, _____

c. Use mixed numbers to complete the following sequence:

2¹⁄₁₀, _____, 2³⁄₁₀, _____, 2⁵⁄₁₀ _____

d. The following sequence names the same numbers as sequence (c). Fill in the blanks with the appropriate decimal numerals.

2.1, _____, 2.3, _____, 2.5, _____

The activity just described stresses patterns as well as the relationship between common and decimal fractions. The next skill for you to emphasize is renaming decimals as common fractions. Pupils who have difficulty should be given additional exploratory work. Stress two key points in renaming decimals as common fractions:

1. The decimal point identifies the ones place immediately to its left and the tenths place immediately to its right.

2. The unwritten denominator is determined by the number of decimal places (the number of digits to the right of the ones place).

To rename a decimal as a common fraction, it is sufficient to eliminate the decimal point and write the correct denominator. The following illustrates early symbolic work of this nature:[2]

a. $0.3 = \dfrac{3}{\square}$

b. $3.2 = 3\dfrac{2}{\square}$

c. $.5 = \dfrac{\square}{10}$

The sum of 9 tenths, 8 tenths, and 4 tenths is 21 tenths, which can be regrouped as 2 ones and 1 tenth, or 2.1. To subtract .7 from 2.1, the student must regroup the latter as 21 tenths. The following activities illustrate this type of regrouping:

a. $2.1 = 2\dfrac{\square}{10} = \dfrac{\triangle}{10}$

2. Note that 0.5 and .5 are both acceptable and common notations for the decimal five-tenths.

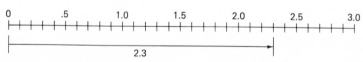

2.3

Figure 15.7

Pupils give names for the same number. *(Photo by Leland Perry)*

b. $3.2 = \dfrac{\square}{10}$

c. $\dfrac{17}{10} = 1\dfrac{\square}{10} =$ _____ (decimal)

d. $\dfrac{31}{10} =$ _____ (decimal)

Meaning of Hundredths

EXPLORATORY LEVEL

Review an exercise showing the value of the large square and the rectangular strips in the pupil's kit. A large square represents

1. Ten rectangular strips also represent 1, so one strip represents one-tenth, or .1. Each rectangular strip contains ten small squares, and so one small square is equal to one-tenth of one-tenth, or one-hundredth, or .01. Help pupils discover that just as 10 ones make a ten and 10 tens make a hundred, 10 tenths make a one and 10 hundredths make a tenth. This is the key to the structure of the place system: ten items in any place make one item in the place immediately to the left.

Figure 15.8 shows how one-hundredth can be represented on a place-value chart. Both the empty pocket in the tenths place and the zero in the numeral indicate that there are no tenths.

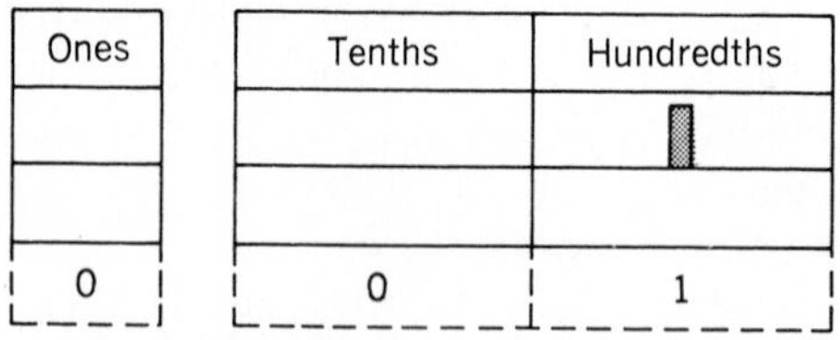

Figure 15.8

SYMBOLIC LEVEL FOR HUNDREDTHS

The following activity is suitable for early symbolic learning:

a. The decimal 0.1, or .1, is a one-place decimal because it has one digit to the right of the ones place (immediately to the left of the decimal point), and thus has an unwritten denominator of _____.

b. The decimal 0.14, or .14, is a _____-place decimal because it has _____ digits to the right of the ones place.

c. The decimal .14 has an unwritten denominator of _____.

d. The two-place decimal .03 has an unwritten denominator of _____.

e. The one-place decimal 21.3 has an unwritten denominator of _____.

f. $37/100$ = _____ (decimal)

g. The common fraction for .75 is _____.

h. A two-place decimal has an unwritten denominator of _____. Complete the following sequences:

i. .01, .02, _____, .04, _____, _____

j. 1.02, 1.04, _____, 1.08, _____, _____

k. .25, .30, _____, _____, .45, _____

MASTERY LEVEL FOR TENTHS AND HUNDREDTHS

Pupils achieve mastery of tenths and hundredths when they become able to change notation from decimal to common fractions and from common fractions to decimal on a habitual basis.

Identifying the Denominator

Figure 15.9 shows how the ones place is used as the reference for separating tens and tenths, hundreds and hundredths, thousands and thousandths. The ones place can be regarded as the center of symmetry, with the tenths place a reflection of tens, and so on. For example, in the numeral 321.23, the 2 one place to the left of the ones place is in the tens place, while the 2 one place to

Thousands	Hundreds	Tens	Ones	Tenths	Hundredths	Thousandths
10^3	10^2	10	10^0	10^{-1}	10^{-2}	10^{-3}
1000	100	10	1	.1	.01	.001
1000	100	10	1	$1/10$	$1/100$	$1/1000$

Figure 15.9

the right of the ones place is in the tenths place, and so on.

A series of questions such as these can give students the opportunity to discover this symmetry:

1. The 4 in 641.35 is one place to the left of the ones place, and therefore is in the _____ place.

2. The 3 in 642.35 is _____ place to the right of the ones place, and therefore is in the _____ place.

3. The 6 in 641.35 is two places to the left of the ones place, and therefore is in the _____ place.

4. The 5 in 641.35 is _____ place(s) to the _____ of the ones place, and therefore is in the _____ place.

It is important to use the ones place rather than the decimal point as the reference. Stress the fact that the decimal point identifies the ones place immediately to its left.

It is sometimes stated incorrectly that a decimal has no denominator. Every decimal has an unwritten denominator that is determined by the number of places to the right of the ones place. By completing a table like the following, pupils will gain an understanding of the pattern for identifying the denominator:

After examining the completed table, students should be able to conclude: The unwritten denominator of a decimal is 10, 100, 1000, and so on, such that the number of zeros following 1 is equal to the number of decimal places. Recognizing the denominator of a decimal fraction should enable pupils to regroup 21 tenths as 2.1 and 2.1 as 21 tenths.

Introducing Thousandths

Thousandths should not be introduced at the exploratory level, for two reasons. First, there are too many pieces involved to show relationships; second, pupils should discover the *pattern* for naming 3 places to the right of the ones place. If they understand the work in the preceding section, they should quickly recognize the pattern for thousandths. For example, they should see that the decimal .234 has three decimal places, so its denominator is 1000 (1 followed by a zero for each decimal place). It can also be named as 234 thousandths, or $234/1000$. Activities such as the following can be helpful:

1. The 5 in 5431.789 is 3 places to the left of the ones place and is in the thousands place, and so the 9 that is 3 places to the right of the ones place is in the _____ place.

Decimal	Denominator	Number of decimal places	Number of zeros in denominator
.2	10	1	1
0.3	☐	1	☐
.23	100	2	2
1.4	10	☐	☐
2.34	☐	2	☐
0.35	☐	☐	☐
123.13		☐	☐
.10	☐	☐	☐
1243.8	☐	☐	☐

2. The 7 in 5431.789 is in the tenths place, the 8 is in the hundredths place, and the 9 is in the _____ place.

3. The place immediately to the right of the ones place is the _____ place; the second place to the right of the ones place is the _____ place, and the third place to the right of the ones place is the _____ place.

4. Since ten items in any place equal one item in the place immediately to the left, ten items in the third place to the right of the ones place must equal 1 hundredth. If $10n = \frac{1}{100}$, then $n = \frac{1}{100} \div 10 = \triangle$.

Pupils at the mastery level can deal with this material habitually.

Decimals and the Calculator

If calculators are available, they can help pupils understand some fundamental facts about decimals.

a. To verify that 10 tenths = 1, 10 hundredths = .1, and 10 thousandths = .01, have pupils use the calculator to perform the following multiplications: $10 \times .1$, $10 \times .01$, $10 \times .001$.

b. Remind pupils that $\frac{1}{10}$ can be renamed as $1 \div 10$. Use the calculator to show:

$$\frac{1}{10} = 1 \div 10 = .1$$

$$\frac{1}{100} = 1 \div 100 = .01$$

$$\frac{1}{1000} = 1 \div 1000 = .001$$

c. Have pupils use the calculator to divide $1 \div 5$ to get .2. Rename .2 as $\frac{2}{10}$ and reduce to lowest terms to get $\frac{1}{5} = 1 \div 5$.

d. Have pupils find the quotient $4 \div 25$ by following the pattern in example (c). Additional examples of this type can be helpful, but early work should not include nonterminating decimals. See page 275 for a discussion of nonterminating decimals.

e. Multiply $.1 \times 25$, $.10 \times 25$ and $.100 \times$ 25 and then show that $.10 = \frac{10}{100} = \frac{1}{10} = .1$ and that $.100 = .1$. Activities like this can help pupils discover that annexing a zero to a decimal does not change its value. When you discuss this point, emphasize that measurements of .1 and .10 indicate different levels of acceptable error in the measurement.

f. Have pupils use the calculator to find the following quotients:

$$4 \div 25 \qquad 60 \div 375 \qquad 180 \div 1125$$

Ask why all the answers are the same.

Pupils can discover the relationship between adjacent places by comparing the total value of a digit when it occupies different places. For example, in the number 222.22, the total value of each 2 from left to right is 200, 20, 2, .2, .02.

Have the class solve the following number sentences to find the ratio of the total value of a digit to the value of the same digit in the place immediately to the left.

$$\frac{20}{200} = \square$$

$$\frac{2}{20} = \square$$

$$\frac{.2}{2} = \frac{2}{10} \div 2 = \square$$

$$\frac{.02}{.2} = \frac{2}{100} \div \frac{2}{10} = \square$$

Have them solve the following number sentences to find the ratio in the opposite order:

$$\frac{.2}{.02} = \frac{2}{10} \div \frac{2}{100} = \square$$

$$\frac{2}{.2} = 2 \div \frac{2}{10} = \square$$

$$\frac{20}{2} = 20 \div 2 = \square$$

$$\frac{200}{20} = 200 \div 20 = \square$$

The point the pupils should understand is that if the total value of any digit is multiplied by 10, the product is equal to the total value of that digit in the place immediately to its left. If the total value of a digit is divided by 10, the quotient is equal to the total value of that digit in the place immediately to its right. It is important that pupils discover that moving in opposite directions in a numeral involves opposite operations, namely, multiplication when moving to the left and division when moving to the right.

Writing Decimals from Dictation

You should spend a minimum of class time dictating decimals, for several reasons. First, it is difficult for pupils to write dictated decimals because of the promiscuous use of the word "and" in reading a whole number, such as "four hundred and fifty." Second, it is difficult to distinguish between the spoken endings of corresponding places on each side of the ones place, such as hundreds and hundred*ths*. Third, business practices do not follow this plan. In everyday business, each digit is read by giving its face value. The number 2.375 is read as 2 point 3, 7, 5. A familiar usage is the conventional reading of the approximate value of π as 3 point 1, 4, 1, 6. Fourth, writing decimals from dictation does not increase the students' understanding of them. A pupil should, however, be able to write a decimal expressed as tenths, hundredths, and perhaps as thousandths from dictation.

Learning Goals

To develop an adequate understanding of decimals, pupils must

1. Be able to identify one decimal place as tenths and two decimal places as hundredths.

2. Know that the decimal point identifies the ones place.

3. Be able to locate a digit in a numeral with reference to the ones place. Figure 15.9 gives the pattern for identifying a place in a numeral either to the left or right of the ones place.

4. Know that the number of decimal places in a numeral is the same as the number of zeros in the denominator of an equivalent fractional numeral in which the denominator is a power of 10.

Give illustrations like the following to allow pupils to discover the relationship between the two types of numerals described in item 4.

$$\frac{3}{10} = .3$$

$$\frac{27}{100} = .27$$

$$\frac{125}{1000} = .125$$

Addition and Subtraction of Decimals

EXPLORATORY LEVEL

Have the pupils use rectangular strips to find the sum of the pair of decimals .4 + .8, as shown in Figure 15.10.

The pupils write the answers in horizon-

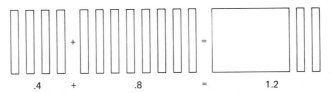

.4   +   .8   =   1.2

Figure 15.10

tal and vertical form. Exploratory work loses much of its value if pupils do not record it.

$$
\begin{array}{cc}
.4 & .8 \\
+\ .8 & .4 \\
\hline
1.2 & 1.2
\end{array}
\qquad
\begin{array}{l}
.4 + .8 = 1.2 \\
\\
.8 + .4 = 1.2
\end{array}
$$

As written, these examples illustrate the commutative property of addition.

NUMBER LINE

The number line is useful for early exploratory work in addition and subtraction as well as to illustrate the inverse relationship between the two operations. To find the sum of .5 and .4, start with an arrow of length .5 beginning at zero and pointing to the right. Place the second arrow of length .4 as indicated in Figure 15.11 and read the sum of .9 at the tip of the second arrow.

To subtract .5 from .9, start with an arrow of length .5 beginning at .9 and pointing left. The difference of .4 is read at the tip of the arrow.

These two examples illustrate that addition of .5 can be "undone" by subtracting .5 and that the addition/subtraction relation holds in this case. Because common fractions and decimals are different ways of naming the same numbers, they should be expected to have the same properties.

SYMBOLIC LEVEL

Early work with decimal addition and subtraction can be related to what is already known about addition and subtraction of common fractions.

$$
.2 + .3 = \frac{2}{10} + \frac{3}{10} = \frac{\square}{10} = .5
\qquad
\begin{array}{r}
.2 \\
+\ .3 \\
\hline
.5
\end{array}
$$

$$
.8 + .9 = \frac{8}{10} + \frac{9}{10} + \frac{17}{\square} = 1.7
\qquad
\begin{array}{r}
.8 \\
+\ .9 \\
\hline
1.7
\end{array}
$$

$$
.9 - .6 = \frac{9}{10} - \frac{6}{10} = \frac{\square}{10} = .3
\qquad
\begin{array}{r}
.9 \\
-\ .6 \\
\hline
.3
\end{array}
$$

$$
1.2 + 4.5 = \frac{12}{10} + \frac{\square}{10} = \frac{57}{\triangle} = 5.7
\qquad
\begin{array}{r}
1.2 \\
+\ 4.5 \\
\hline
5.7
\end{array}
$$

$$
.23 + .35 = \frac{\square}{100} + \frac{\triangle}{100} = \triangledown
\qquad
\begin{array}{r}
.23 \\
+\ .35 \\
\hline
.58
\end{array}
$$

These examples can also be used to demonstrate how addition and subtraction of decimals relate to whole numbers.

Concrete verbal problems can make early symbolic work more meaningful. For example:

1. Joan saved $13.27 and earned $2.25 more. How much does she now have?

2. Sylvia went to the store with $5.00 and spent $3.89. How much change should she receive?

3. Joe played golf and hit his first chip shot 81.3 meters and his second 68.6 yards. What was the total distance of his first two shots?

Column Addition of Decimals

The traditional rule for adding decimals in vertical form is to keep the decimal points in a column. Unfortunately, this rule has often been taught by rote rather than by providing activities that give pupils the opportunity to discover it. One way to guide their discovery is to ask the pupils why the addition in (a) is incorrect.

$$
\text{(a)} \quad
\begin{array}{r}
2345 \\
+\ 123 \\
\hline
3575
\end{array}
$$

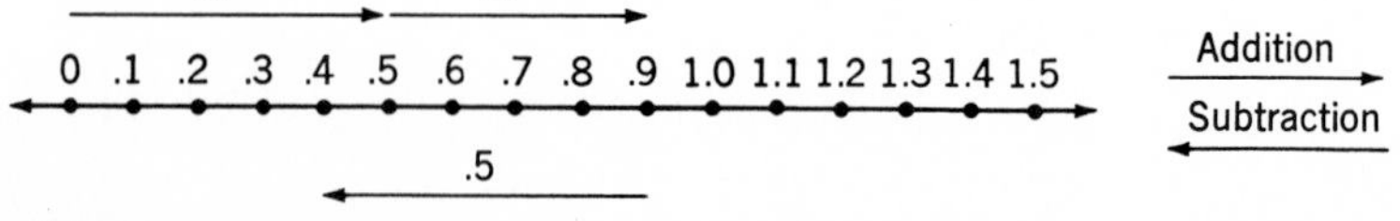

Figure 15.11

The pupils should recognize that the way the example above is written, 3 ones are to be added to 4 tens. The sum of 7 here has no reasonable interpretation.

The pupils can then be asked to write the addends for the sum 1.23 + 3.45 in vertical form so that ones are added to ones, tenths are added to tenths, and so on. Activities such as this give pupils the opportunity to discover and understand the "decimal points in a column" rule for addition and subtraction of decimals. Help pupils to recognize whole numbers as decimals with an unwritten decimal point, and to see that they have been using the "vertical column" rule in addition and subtraction of whole numbers without realizing it.

Example (b) illustrates addition of *ragged decimals*. This addition is "ragged" because the two addends do not have the same number of decimal places.

$$(b) \quad \begin{array}{r} 1.232 \\ + \ 21.43 \\ \hline 22.662 \end{array}$$

Many educators have objected to the teaching of ragged decimal addition because most practical applications of addition and subtraction involve decimals rounded to the same number of places. However, the following example shows how ragged decimals can occur, even with the increased emphasis on changing common fractions to decimals:

(c) Add ¼ and ⅛ as common fractions. Check by changing to decimals to show that the same number is obtained using either notation.

$$\frac{1}{4} + \frac{1}{8} = \frac{2}{8} + \frac{1}{8} = \frac{3}{8} = 3 \div 8 = .375$$

$$\frac{1}{4} + \frac{1}{8} = .25 + .125 = .375$$

$$\begin{array}{r} .125 \\ + .25 \\ \hline .375 \end{array}$$

Some educators advocate annexing one or more zeros when ragged decimals occur so that all addends have the same number of decimal places.

MASTERY LEVEL

Pupils who have achieved mastery of addition and subtraction of whole numbers should have little difficulty mastering addition and subtraction of decimals. These pupils should be able to add and subtract both whole numbers and decimals efficiently with very few errors, automatically recognizing basic facts in both operations.

Decimal Addition and the Calculator

Calculators can be used to verify addition with decimals, but some pupils should be able to perform many additions faster mentally than they can be keyed into the calculator. One very useful application of the calculator is to add common fractions by converting them to decimals, as illustrated in example (d).

$$(d) \quad \frac{1}{13} + \frac{2}{17} = .077 + .118 = .195$$

The sum in (d) is probably more useful as .195 than as ⁴³/₂₂₁. This activity is too time consuming without using a calculator. Point out to students the discrepancy when rounding to hundredths.

$$.08 + .12 = .20 \qquad \frac{43}{221} = .194 \text{ or } .19$$

Such discrepancies are common but can be eliminated by using the appropriate number of decimal places. Many people have avoided decimals in the past because of the need for rounding.

Introducing Percent

At this point, pupils know that fractional numbers can be renamed as decimals. Percent can now be introduced as another way of naming numbers that the pupil has met in the form of common fractions and decimals. For example, if a baseball team wins 70 out of 100 games, it has won 70 percent of its games. The word *percent* means "per hundred"; 70% indicates a ratio of $^{70}/_{100}$.

EXPLORATORY LEVEL

A hundred board (see Figure 15.12) is an effective instructional aid for introducing percent. A hundred board contains a square array with 10 disks on a side. Each pupil determines the number of disks on the board by counting the number in a row and the number of rows. Take a disk from the board and have the class describe the disk in terms of the total number of disks. The class should state that it is "1 out of 100." Then have the class write this fact using numerals:

Fraction: $\dfrac{1}{100}$

Decimal: 0.01

Percent: 1%

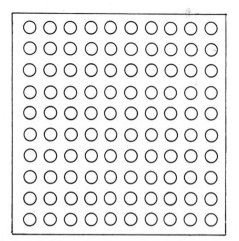

Figure 15.12

You will have to supply the third answer, since the class does not yet know this notation. Repeat the same procedure for other representations, such as 2 disks, 3 disks, 7 disks, and 10 disks. The class should give five numerals that represent the 10 disks in a row. These numerals are .1, .10, $^1/_{10}$, $^{10}/_{100}$, and 10%. Encourage the class to give as many different numerals as possible to express a number. The collection of 50 disks can be expressed with the numerals $^1/_2$, $^5/_{10}$, $^{50}/_{100}$, .5, .50, and 50%. A group of 25 disks can be represented as $^1/_4$, $^{25}/_{100}$, .25, and 25%. All the disks on a hundred board can be represented as 1, 1.0, 1.00, $^{10}/_{10}$, $^{100}/_{100}$, and 100%.

For numerals such as 3%, 15%, 25%, or 40%, have the pupils use decimal and fractional numerals to express the same number as represented by each given numeral. The same plan is followed for both fractional and decimal numerals. The pupils give at least one numeral in each of the two remaining ways to represent the given number.

Renaming to and from Percent

The key to renaming a percent as a decimal or common fraction or vice versa is recognizing that "percent" and "hundredths" are interchangeable.

a. $1\% = 1 \text{ hundredth} = .01 = \dfrac{1}{100}$

b. $4\% = 4 \text{ hundredths} = .04 = \dfrac{4}{100}$

c. $\dfrac{2}{5} = \dfrac{2}{5} \times 1 = \dfrac{2}{5} \times \dfrac{20}{20} = \dfrac{40}{100}$
$\qquad = 40 \text{ hundredths} = \Box\%$

d. $\dfrac{2}{3} = \dfrac{2}{3} \times \dfrac{33^1/_3}{33^1/_3} = \dfrac{66^2/_3}{100}$
$\qquad = 66^2/_3 \text{ hundredths} = \Box\%$
$66^2/_3\%$ is often approximated as 66.7%.

Multiplying by $\dfrac{20}{20}$ or $\dfrac{33^1/_3}{33^1/_3}$ illustrates one of the many ways to apply the identity element for multiplication.

Exercises 15.1

1. Complete the following:

a. $\frac{1}{5} \times \frac{\square}{20} = \frac{\triangle}{100} = \triangle$ hundredths $= \triangle$ %

b. $.23 = \frac{\square}{100} = \square$ hundredths $= \square$ %

c. $\frac{3}{8} = 3 \div 8 = .375 = \frac{375}{1000} = \frac{37.5}{\square} = \triangle$ %

2. Rename as percents: a. ¹⁄₁₀ b. ³⁄₅ c. ³⁄₄ d. ¹⁄₃

3. Rename as common fractions: a. 7% b. 13% c. 75% d. 10%

4. Rename as decimals: a. 11% b. 10% c. 75% d. 112%

Multiplication of Decimals

Multiplying a Whole Number and a Decimal

EXPLORATORY LEVEL

The product of 2 and .3 may be found on the exploratory level as follows:

1. Use 2 sets of 3 strips (from student kits) to obtain a set of 6 strips and show that 2 × .3 = .6.

2. Use the number line as illustrated:

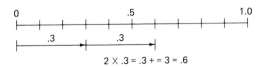

SYMBOLIC LEVEL

After the students have done sufficient work with exploratory materials, they can be taught to find products such as 2 × .3 in the following ways:

1. Using common fractions, such as 2 × ³⁄₁₀ = ⁶⁄₁₀ = .6

2. Using repeated addition, such that 2 × .3 = .3 + .3 = .6

3. Help pupils recognize that both 2 × 3 and 2 × .3 give a product with the single numeral 6 but that the position of the deci-

mal point differs in each. Note that .3 is between 0 and 1 so that the product 2 × .3 must be between 0 × 2 and 1 × 2 or between 0 and 2. Since .6 is between 0 and 2, the answer is sensible.

Products Involving Renaming

The methods outlined above also apply to products involving renaming, such as 2 × 1.6.

1. 2 × 1.6 = 1.6 + 1.6 = 3.2

2. 2 × 1.6 = 2 × ¹⁶⁄₁₀ = ³²⁄₁₀ = 3.2

3. Apply the distributive property:

2 × 1.6 = 2 × (1 + .6) = 2 + 1.2 = 3.2

Note that 1.6 is between 1 and 2, so that 2 × 1.6 is between 2 × 1 and 2 × 2, or between 2 and 4. The answer 2.8 is sensible because it is between 2 and 4.

The following equations (open sentences) contain a whole number factor and a one-place decimal factor:

a. 2 × .3 = □
   □ × .4 = .8
   .3 + .3 = 2 × □
   .4 + .4 = □ × .4
   2 × □ = 1.0
   .5 × □ = 1.5
   □ × .7 = 7
   □ × 1.3 = 1.3

Pupils should solve equations like those shown in (a) until they understand the pattern. They should discover this generalization: *The product of a whole number and a one-place decimal is a one-place decimal.*

Multiplying Ones and Hundredths

Initial work with multiplication of a whole number and a decimal begins with tenths and is extended to hundredths. Use as many of the procedures described for multiplying ones and tenths as the class needs to discover how to find the product of ones and hundredths. Most pupils who understand how to deal with ones and tenths quickly discover how to deal with ones and hundredths, or ones and any other decimal. Pupils should discover that the product of ones and hundredths is hundredths. Similarly, the product of ones and thousandths is thousandths. Thousandths represent three decimal places.

The class can approximate to find the position of the decimal point in the product or apply the rule that the product of ones and tenths is tenths, ones and hundredths is hundredths, and so on.

MASTERY LEVEL

Pupils achieve mastery level in multiplying a whole number and a decimal when they no longer rely on place value to determine the position of the decimal point in the product. Pupils discover that the product contains as many decimal places as the decimal factor. Thus, the product 7 × .345 will contain three decimal places because the decimal factor .345 contains three decimal places. It is important that the *class* discover this rule for finding the position of the point in the product. You should not give the rule and then have the class demonstrate its application in a mechanical way. When pupils use this shortcut to locate the point in the product, they should check the

answer either by approximation to see if it is sensible or by use of place value. Advanced pupils should be encouraged to use both methods.

The Product of Two Decimals

SYMBOLIC LEVEL

Multiplication of two decimals begins at the symbolic level because the activities outlined for the product of whole numbers do not apply. It is difficult to demonstrate how to take .2 of a group of .3, except perhaps by using the number line. We feel that if pupils have an understanding of the product of a whole number and a decimal, it is more efficient to introduce multiplication of two decimals at the symbolic level. If students need more exploratory work, it should be with the product of a whole number and a decimal.

The pupils use previous experience with whole numbers and common fractions to find the product of two decimals. For example, to find the product of .2 and .3, the students would rename each decimal as a common fraction and multiply:

a. $.2 \times .3 = \frac{2}{10} \times \frac{3}{10} = \frac{6}{\square} = .06$

b. $.2 \times .3 = 2$ tenths $\times 3$ tenths $= (2 \times 3) \times$ (tenths $\times$ tenths) $= 6 \times (\frac{1}{10} \times \frac{1}{10}) = 6 \times \frac{1}{\square} = \frac{6}{\square} = .06$

Example (b) can help pupils discover that tenths × tenths = hundredths, a statement that is analogous to tens × tens = hundreds.

c. $.3 \times .4 = \frac{3}{\square} \times \frac{4}{\square} = \frac{12}{\triangle} = .12$

d. $.3 \times .4 = 3$ tenths $\times 4$ tenths $= (3 \times 4) \times$ (tenths $\times$ tenths) $= 12$ hundredths $= .12$

e. $1.2 \times .23 = \frac{12}{10} \times \frac{\square}{100} = \frac{276}{\triangle} = .276$

f. $1.2 \times .23 = 12$ tenths $\times 23$ hundredths $= (12 \times 23) \times$ (tenths $\times$ hundredths) $= 276$ thousandths $= \square$. This example leads students to draw the conclusion that tenths × hundredths = thousandths, a useful generalization. Point out that 1.2 × .23 is between 1 × 0 and 2 × 1 or between 0 and 2, and that therefore the answer .276 is sensible.

By working examples like this, pupils discover that the number of decimal places in the product is equal to the sum of the number of places in the two factors. After the pupils make this discovery, they no longer rely on place value for locating the decimal point in the product.

The Multiplication Algorism

Have the students multiply two decimals containing two or more digits. Use the multiplication algorism as shown in (a) and (b) and determine the decimal point by estimation.

$$
\begin{array}{r}
\text{(a)} \quad 4.5 \\
\times \ 1.5 \\
\hline
225 \\
45 \\
\hline
6.75
\end{array}
\qquad
\begin{array}{r}
\text{(b)} \quad 35 \\
\times \ .23 \\
\hline
105 \\
70 \\
\hline
8.05
\end{array}
$$

To multiply two decimals, the students should proceed as follows:

1. Multiply as with whole numbers.

2. Find the sum of the number of decimal places in the two factors.

3. Counting from the right, mark off as many places in the product as are found in step 2.

4. Estimate to determine if the answer is sensible.

The pupils now operate at the mastery level, because they are applying a rule that does not require the use of place value. The pupils now understand the mathematical basis of the shortcuts; hence use of the rule does not constitute rote learning.

Often pupils do not understand why the product of two decimals, such as .2 × .4 = .08, is less than either factor. The solution with fractional numbers will show clearly that the product is smaller than either factor. In dealing with fractional numbers, the class learned how multiplying by a number less than 1 affects the product. Since both factors, .2 and .4, are less than 1, the product will be less than either factor.

Problems Involving Multiplication of Decimals

A typical real-life problem might be encountered at the meat counter of the supermarket, where a computerized scale states the price of 1.35 pounds of meat at $1.89 per pound. The solution may be written:

1 pound $\rightarrow$ $1.89
1.35 pounds $\rightarrow$ 1.35 × 1.89 = 2.5515
The cost of 1.35 pounds is $2.55.

The $2.55 is obtained by standard rounding procedures, although some stores may round up and charge $2.56.

Pupils should obtain supermarket tags that have the price per pound, the number of pounds, and the total price. The total should be verified by paper and pencil computation. Calculators can be used after pupils have achieved reasonable competence at paper-and-pencil computation. This activity provides a practical application of decimal multiplication as well as experience in rounding.

Finding a Percent of a Number

Paying sales tax can be a pupil's first experience with percent. A typical problem might ask the student to find the sales tax and total price of an $8.00 item when the tax rate is 5%.

5% of 8 = .05 × 8 = .40
Tax is $.40 or 40 cents.
The total cost is $8.00 + $.40 = $8.40.

The total cost can also be found by taking 105% of $8.00. The total is 100% of the cost plus 5% of the cost or 105% of the cost: 105% of 8 = 1.05 × 8 = 8.40, or $8.40. This approach can be used with a calculator.

Ask pupils to bring in sales slips with the tax listed separately. Verify the results using both paper and pencil and a calculator.

Discount is another common percent situation that involves multiplication of decimals. A typical problem might ask the student to determine the amount saved if a $60 item is purchased at a 20% discount.

20% of 60 = .20 × 60 = 12.
The amount saved is $12.

The problem may also ask for the new price, which is $60 − $12, or $48. Because the new price is 100% of $60 − 20% of $60, it is 80% of 60 or .80 × 60 = 48, or $48.

Interest rates and many other everyday situations involve percent. Pupils should be encouraged to bring in newspaper clippings that use the language of percent.

Exercises 15.2

1. Find the cost of .35 pounds of meat if the cost per pound is $2.45.

2. Find the money saved if a $25 camera is purchased at a discount of 10%.

3. In problem 2, find the actual amount paid in two different ways.

4. If the sales tax is 6%, find the tax on a $7000 car.

5. In problem 4, find the total cost of the car in 2 ways.

Decimal Multiplication and the Calculator

Pupils can use the calculator to verify and reinforce symbolic work in multiplication of decimals. Make sure, though, that calculator use does not keep pupils from learning basic skills and concepts with decimals.

Students can discover the procedure for multiplying and dividing by 10, 100, 1000, and other powers of 10 in a brief calculator session conducted shortly after multiplication of decimals has been introduced. By performing these operations with a calculator, the pupil discovers the movement of the decimal point almost instantly, and can make this generalization:

Multiplying by a power of 10 moves the decimal point one place to the right for each zero in the numeral; dividing by a power of 10 moves the decimal point one place to the left for each zero in the numeral (power of 10). Without the calculator, this generalization is often not discovered

until junior high school, and it is not unusual to find college students using the standard algorisms to multiply and divide by powers of 10.

Estimation

The calculator should be used to help pupils learn to estimate because it can give immediate information about the accuracy of the estimate. The following activities are useful for this purpose. Answers are given in (a), (d), and (f) to illustrate the procedure.

a. The number .341 is between 0 and 1. Therefore, the product .341 × 27 is between 0 × 27 and 1 × 27, or 0 and 27. The product is closer to zero because .341 is closer to 0 than to 27. Either 9 or 10 is a good estimate, since the correct answer is 9.207. Because .341 is close to .333 (the decimal approximation for ⅓), multiplying 27 by ⅓ to get 9 is also sound procedure.

b. The number 3.87 is between consecutive integers ____ and ____. Therefore, the

product 3.87 × 17 is between ____ and
____. A reasonable estimate is ____.
c. The product 5.12 × 21 is between ____
× 21 and ____ × 21 or ____ and ____. A
reasonable estimate is ____.

Examples (d) and (e) require the student
to know that tenths × tenths = hundredths.
d. The product .327 × .432 is between
.3 × .3 and .4 × .5 or between 9 hundredths and 20 hundredths. Knowledgeable
pupils should recognize that the answer is
between .1 and .2. Either .13, .14, or .15 is
a good estimate. The correct answer is
.141264.
e. Follow the pattern in (d) to estimate
.561 × .882.
f. Because tenths × hundredths = thousandths, .352 × .027 is between 6 thousandths (.3 × .02) and 12 thousandths (.4 ×
.03). Either .009 or .010 is a good estimate.
The correct answer is .009504.
g. Follow the pattern in (f) to estimate
.0773 × .389.

Division of Decimals

Types of Examples

There are four major types of examples in
the division of decimals, illustrated as follows:

1. 2)6.2: Dividing a decimal by a whole
number.

2. 4)3: Dividing two whole numbers with a
decimal in the quotient.

3. .2)6: Dividing a whole number by a decimal.

4. .2).14: Dividing a decimal by a decimal.

If pupils understand all phases of the division of decimals, probably no one type of
example is more difficult than another. On
the other hand, pupils who have an incom-
plete understanding of the procedure make
more errors finding the quotient in the third

type of example than in any of the other
three. It is possible for pupils to solve examples of these three types very skillfully
but with a limited understanding of the
work. This is not true of examples of the
type .3)5.[3]

Two Types of Examples

The four types of examples in the division of decimals can be reduced to two
types if the divisor is changed to a whole
number by multiplying by a power of 10. If
the divisor is a whole number, a decimal
can occur only in the quotient or in both the
dividend and the quotient, as follows:

(a) 4)1 with .25   Decimal in the quotient only

(b) 2).6 with .3   Decimal in dividend and quotient

In fact, these two types can be considered
one. To complete the division in example
(a), the dividend 1 must be renamed as 1.00.
Then example (a) is of the same type as example (b).

Dividing a Decimal by a Whole Number

EXPLORATORY LEVEL

Have the pupils use their kits to discover
how to divide a decimal by a whole number. To divide 2)2.6, the pupils represent
2.6 as shown in Figure 15.13 and separate
the markers into two matching groups. The

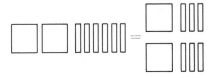

Figure 15.13

3. See F. E. Grossnickle, "Types of Errors in Division
of Decimals," *Elementary School Journal*, November
1941, 42:184–194.

students then represent the experience symbolically.

Students will have little difficulty in dividing examples that involve no renaming. When regrouping is necessary, as in 2)1.4 or 2).14, the work becomes more difficult to understand. To make sure that the class understands how to divide in an example such as 2).14, have the pupils perform the following activities:

1. Use kit material to find the answer. Emphasize the renaming necessary to make the representation.

2. Give a visual representation at the chalkboard with pocket charts. Have the class explain the steps in the model shown in Figure 15.14. (A) shows .14 expressed as .1 and .04; (B) shows .1 renamed as .10 to form 14 hundredths; (C) shows .14 separated into two groups of .07 each.

SYMBOLIC LEVEL

1. Relate division to multiplication by working the following examples:

$$2 \times .07 = .14 \qquad .14 \div 2 = .07$$
$$.07 \times 2 = .14 \qquad .14 \div .07 = 2$$

2. Rename .14 as .10 + .04 and apply the distributive property of division over addition:

$$\frac{.14}{2} = \frac{.10}{2} + \frac{.04}{2} = .05 + .02 = .07$$

3. Rename .14 as $14 \times \frac{1}{100}$ and apply the associative property of multiplication:

$$.14 \div 2 = \frac{1}{2} \times \left(14 \times \frac{1}{100}\right)$$
$$= \left(\frac{1}{2} \times 14\right) \times \frac{1}{100} = 7 \times \frac{1}{100}$$
$$= \frac{7}{100}, \text{ or } .07.$$

4. Tell why the quotient must be less than one-tenth.

MASTERY LEVEL

At the mastery level, the pupil can divide a decimal by a whole number without having to rely on any one method of locating the decimal point in the quotient. The pupil now approximates the quotient, or discovers that the number of decimal places in the quotient is the same as the number of such places in the dividend when the divisor is a whole number. He or she knows that the answer is sensible and can verify it in several different ways.

Renaming Fractional Numbers as Decimals

The following activities help pupils to gain understanding of how to express a fractional number as a decimal. Begin with the fractional number named by ½.

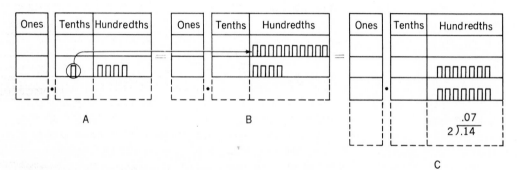

A   B

C

Figure 15.14

EXPLORATORY LEVEL

1. Using a number line, show that ½ and .5 name the same number.

2. To show the renaming or dividing of 1 by 2, demonstrate with a pocket chart or make a drawing on the chalkboard (Figure 15.15). In Figure 15.15, (A) shows 1 one, (B) shows 1 renamed as 10 tenths, and (C) shows 1.0 divided into two groups of .5.

SYMBOLIC LEVEL

Pupils learn to rename fractions as decimals by using the multiplicative identity as follows:

$$\frac{1}{2} = \frac{1}{2} \times \frac{5}{5} = \frac{5}{10} = .5$$

Once the pupils have learned to divide and obtain a decimal quotient, they can interpret the fraction ½ as $1 \div 2$, which they convert to decimals as follows:

$$2\overline{)1.0} \quad .5$$

If calculators are available, the division concept of a fraction can be introduced earlier.

Converting common fractions to decimals by the division process strengthens both the pupil's ability to divide and grasp the concept of a fraction as an indicated division. You should confine the early work on converting common fractions to decimals to terminating decimals. Work with nonterminating decimals and the rounding process is among the more difficult aspects of decimal use. The calculator is particularly valuable for helping pupils to understand this topic because it eliminates the drudgery of performing division and allows practically all the time involved to be spent on stressing concepts rather than on the mechanics of division.

Terminating and Nonterminating Decimals

When the numerator of a fraction is divided by its denominator, there are two possible outcomes:

1. The resulting decimal terminates, such as $\frac{3}{8} = .375$

2. The resulting decimal is repeating and nonterminating, such as

$$\frac{1}{3} = .33333333 \ldots$$

$$\frac{123}{999} = .123123123 \ldots$$

The following activity can be used to help pupils understand terminating and nonterminating decimals. Write a dozen fractions on the chalkboard, half of which terminate. Have the class use calculators to find decimal equivalents. Then have them find the prime factors of each denominator. This process can lead them to discover that if the denominator of a fraction in its lowest terms contains only factors of 2 or 5 or both, the corresponding decimal terminates. Thus, ⅕,

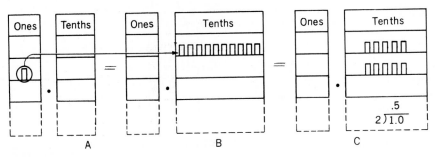

Figure 15.15

3/8, and 7/20 are expressed as terminating decimals.

If the denominator of a fraction in lowest terms contains any factor other than 2 or 5, the corresponding decimal will be nonterminating and repeating.

$$\frac{1}{11} = .090909\ldots = .\overline{09}$$

$$\frac{1}{7} = .\overline{142857}142857\ldots = .\overline{142857}$$

The .09 and .142857 are called *repetends.* A bar over the repetend indicates that the decimal repeats and does not terminate, as given above for the fraction 1/7.

The greatest number of places that can occur in a repetend is one less than the denominator, as illustrated in (c). The only possible remainders are 0, 1, 2, 3, 4, 5, and 6. The decimal terminates when there is a remainder of zero. Thus, at most there are 6 different remainders for a divisor of 7 before there is a repeat.

```
c.      .1 4 2 8 5 7
     7)1.0 0 0 0 0 0
        7
       (3)0
        2 8
          20
          1 4
          (6)0
           5 6
            (4)0
             3 5
             (5)0
              4 9
              (1)
```

Rounding the Quotient

A common way of expressing 1/3 is .33 1/3, which combines decimal and common fractional notation. The notation .33 1/3 can still be used as the final answer, as in 33 1/3%, but is used much less often today than in the past, because it is not convenient when using calculator or computer.

It is almost universal in science, business, and industry to express a nonterminating decimal, such as 1/6, in the rounded form .17 or .167 rather than as .16 2/3. No fixed number of decimal places can be chosen arbitrarily. The appropriate number of places depends on the application. It may be reasonable for instructional purposes to have pupils round decimals to two places unless instructed otherwise, but make sure that this practice does not keep pupils from recognizing that the situation determines the appropriate number of decimal places.

Pupils should realize that .33 is an approximation for 1/3 and that no matter how many decimal places are used, the decimal representation for 1/3 does not equal 1/3. However, the appropriate number of decimal places will make the error negligible for the given application. The following multiplications will help pupils recognize that the more decimal places used, the less the error: $\frac{1}{3} \times 6 = 2$; $.3 \times 6 = 1.8$; $.33 \times 6 = 1.98$; $.333 \times 6 = 1.998$; $.3333 \times 6 = 1.9998$.

Many pupils have had limited experience with nonterminating decimals because of the time-consuming divisions required. Use of the calculator will enable the pupil to deal with many such problems in the time that it would take to perform one division on paper with pencil.

Some calculators will give an answer of 1.999999999 rather than 2 because of internal round-off errors, but will not usually do so with numbers of 5 digits or less for the four operations.

A Decimal Divisor

Introduce division by a decimal divisor with a problem of the following type:

How many pieces of ribbon 1.5 yards long can be cut from a ribbon 6 yards long?

Write the following number sentence on the chalkboard: $n \times 1.5 = 6$. The activities for finding the value of n include:

EXPLORATORY LEVEL

1. Take a string 6 yards long and measure a length 1.5 yards. Then apply this length to the string to see how many pieces can be formed.

2. Use a number line to find the answer (see Figure 15.16).

Figure 15.16

SYMBOLIC LEVEL

3. Divide 6 by 1½.

$$6 \div 1\frac{1}{2} = 6 \div \frac{3}{2} = 6 \times \frac{2}{3} = 4$$

4. The class will find that the answer to the problem is 4. Now have them apply the multiplication/division relation for the numbers 4, 1.5, and 6:

$$4 \times 1.5 = 6 \qquad 6 \div 1.5 = 4$$
$$1.5 \times 4 = 6 \qquad 6 \div 4 = 1.5$$

5. Apply the identity element for multiplication. The example $1.5\overline{)6}$ can be written in fractional form as $^6/_{1.5}$. Now multiply the fractional number by 1, named as $^{10}/_{10}$:

$$1 \times \frac{6}{1.5} = \frac{10}{10} \times \frac{6}{1.5} = \frac{60}{15} = 15\overline{)60}^{\,4}$$

The identity element applies equally well when the conventional notation for division is used. Multiplying both divisor and dividend by 10, as in $1.5\overline{)6} = 15\overline{)60}$, is the equivalent of multiplying the example by 1.

Thus, there are 4 pieces of ribbon.

Follow these steps to introduce division by a decimal divisor:

1. Write the dividend as a numerator and the divisor as a denominator in fractional form.

2. Multiply both terms of the fractional nu-

meral by a power of 10 to make the divisor (denominator) a whole number.

3. Divide the numerator by the denominator.

4. Check the quotient by one or more of the following methods:

a. Rename the decimals with fractional numerals and then divide.

b. Multiply the decimal divisor and the quotient to see if the product is equal to the number divided.

c. Approximate the answer to see if it is sensible.

The Dividend Is a Decimal

Once the pupils understand how to divide a whole number by a decimal, they will have no particular difficulty understanding how to divide a decimal by a decimal, as in the example $.4\overline{)}.36$. In each case, they transform the example so that the divisor is a whole number. Clearly, the pupil must know by what power of 10 both divisor and dividend must be multiplied to effect this transformation. The number of decimal places in the divisor indicates this power of 10.

The chief difficulties pupils will have in the division of decimals are:

1. The division operation.

2. Placement of the first digit in the quotient.

3. Location of the decimal point in the quotient.

The ability to locate the decimal point is the chief factor determining the pupil's success in this phase of division. Therefore, you should use a test consisting of easy division examples in order to measure a pupil's ability in the division of decimals.

Place Point in Product or Quotient

Since the main problem in the division of decimals is placement of the point in the quotient and not the division operation itself, a very effective learning exercise has the pupil place the point in the quotient when the quotient digits are given. Similarly, a multiplication example should have the product expressed with the decimal point missing. The following examples should be adapted for exercises in learning to locate the position of the point in the answer in multiplication and division of decimals.

Supply the decimal point in each product or quotient:

$$.3 \times .8 = 24 \qquad .2\overline{)\,1.3}^{\,65}$$

$$2.5 \times .25 = 625 \qquad 6\overline{)\,.42}^{\,7}$$

MASTERY LEVEL

Pupils achieve mastery in dealing with a decimal divisor when they no longer follow a fixed procedure. They will make the divisor a whole number by applying the identity element of multiplication until they discover a shorter method of computation. Then they discover that it is not necessary to transform an example so that the divisor will be a whole number. In examples (a) and (b), the pupil may discover that multiplying both divisor and dividend by 10 shifts the decimal point one place to the right in each numeral.

a. $.3\overline{)\,12}$

b. $.4\overline{)\,.72}$

c. $.3_\wedge\overline{)\,12.0_\wedge}$

d. $.4_\wedge\overline{)\,.7_\wedge2}$

They indicate this fact as shown in (c) and (d). The pupil who understands the mathematical basis of the procedure should be allowed to use a caret as shown in (d) to indicate the position of the decimal point in the transformed example. Pupils have achieved mastery when they use a shortcut that they understand.

Approximate the Quotient

At the mastery level, the pupil not only understands the mathematical basis involved in dealing with a decimal divisor, but also is able to approximate the quotient. In the example $.3\overline{)\,12}$, the pupil should be able to approximate the answer to determine if it is sensible by a thought pattern such as the following:

"The divisor is approximately ⅓; hence the quotient should be about 3 × 12, or 36.

"The divisor is less than ½; hence the quotient should be more than 2 × 12, or 24."

It is very important for more advanced pupils to be able to verify an answer by approximation.

Finding What Percent One Number Is of Another

Previous problems involving division with whole numbers and with common fractions can now be solved by using decimals. The use of decimals often makes the problems more realistic. However, certain aspects of percent cannot be treated effectively until the pupil understands division involving decimals. Use problems whose answers are readily apparent to introduce how to find what percent one number is of another. Do oral work. Have each pupil identify the number to be compared and the number with which it is compared. Then have them write a number sentence for the situation. The following problems illustrate the procedure:

1. 5 is what percent of 100?
   5 = n% of 100
   5 is compared with 100, or $\frac{5}{100}$ = 5%

2. 3 is what percent of 10?
   3 = n% of 10
   3 is compared with 10, or $\frac{3}{10}$ = $\frac{30}{100}$ = 30%

3. What percent of 10 is 7?

  7 = n% of 10

  7 is compared with 10, or $\frac{7}{10} = \frac{70}{100} = 70\%$

Solving such easy problems enables the pupils to discover the pattern for writing the number sentence in problems of this type. Then they are ready for problems in which the ratio is not so readily determined as a percent.

For example, the class knows how to express ⅝ as the decimal .625. To find what percent 5 is of 8, rename .625 as 62.5%. To find what percent one number is of another, one simply divides one number by another (or writes a common fraction) and expresses the quotient as a percent. Because division is not commutative, it is vital to know which number to use as the divisor (denominator). This process compares two numbers. One of them, the base, represents 100%. The number compared with the base is the percentage. There is no single rule that will always identify the base. In the standard form, r% of b = p, the base follows "of."

The terms "percent" and "percentage" often confuse pupils. The percent is a *rate*. The percentage is a *number* obtained by multiplying the base by the rate.

Exercises 15.3

1. What percent of 12 is 3?

2. What percent of 3 is 12?

3. What percent of 7 is 4? Give the answer in the closest whole percent.

4. Give the answer to problem 3 in the nearest tenth of a percent by rounding the division to 3 decimal places and expressing as a percent.

5. Jim has 7 of 10 answers correct on a test. What percent of his answers are correct?

6. Express what percent 2 is of 3 to the nearest hundredth of a percent.

7. The calculator says that 7 ÷ 41 = .1707317. What percent of 41 is 7? Give the answer in:
   a. the closest whole percent.
   b. the closest tenth of a percent.
   c. the closest hundredth of a percent.

8. A man pays a tax of $1 on an article that costs $20. What is the rate of the sales tax in percent?

Standard Percent Situations

Page 254 shows the three types of problems involving multiplication and division of fractions related to the basic multiplication situation "n groups of a = b."

a. Find a fractional part of a number, such as ½ of 10 (a and n are given and b is to be determined).

b. Find what part one number is of another (a and b are given and n is to be determined).

c. Find a number when a fractional part of it is known, such as ¼ of what number is 10 (n and b are given and a is to be determined).

Because percents are another way of naming fractional (rational) numbers, the three types of percent problems correspond to the three types just listed for multiplication and division of fractions. The three types of percent problems are derived from the basic percent statement r% of b = p where r is the rate, b the base, and p the percentage. The three types are:

a. Find the percent of a number, such as 5% of 40 (the rate and base are given and the percentage is to be determined).

b. Find what percent one number is of another, such as what percent 3 is of 4 (the base and percentage are given and the rate is to be determined).

c. Find a number when a percent of it is given, such as 2% of what number is 4 (the rate and percentage are given and the base is to be determined).

The following table identifies the rate, base, and percentage and gives the percent statement in its standard form.

The percentage is obtained by multiplying the base by the rate, or $r \times b = p$. This relation is called the *percent formula* and is usually written as $p = br$ where p is the percentage (a number), b the base, and r the rate (percentage divided by the base). When using the formula, the rate is expressed as a common or decimal fraction.

When the base and rate are known, the formula indicates that the rate is to be multiplied by the base. For problem (a) in the preceding table, $p = br = 40 \times .05 = 2$.

When the base and percentage are known, the rate is a missing factor that can be determined by dividing the percentage by the base. For problem (b) in the preceding table, $b = 4$ and $p = 3$, so $r \times 4 = 3$ or $r = 3 \div 4 = .75 = 75$%.

When the percentage and rate are known, the base is a missing factor and can be found by dividing the percentage by the rate. For (c) in the preceding table, $r \times b = p$ becomes $.02 \times b = 4$, so that $b = 4 \div .02 = 200$.

Point out that when using the formula, and any two items are known, the third is found by direct multiplication or by finding a missing factor with the multiplication/division relation.

Estimation and Percent

Because percent is a common occurrence in everyday affairs, the ability to estimate percent is valuable. Pupils should know how to find 1%, 10%, and 50% of a number almost instantaneously by dividing by 100, 10, or 2: 1% of 167 = 1.67; 1% of 4.8 is .048; 10% of 35 = 3.5; 10% of 48.3 is 4.83; 50% of 467 = 233.5. The ability to find these percents mentally in conjunction with the "guess and test" approach will enable a pupil to estimate all three types of problems.

For example, to estimate 17% of 381, a pupil would think: 10% of 381 is 38.1 so 20% is 2 × 38.1 or approximately 76. The answer is clearly closer to 76 than to 38, so

Type	Rate	Base	Percentage	Standard Sentence
(a)	5%	40	p	5% of 40 = p
(b)	r	4	3	r% of 4 = 3
(c)	2%	b	4	2% of b = 4

any guess between 60 and 70 is reasonable. A more accurate estimate can be found by noting that 1% is about 4, so 17% is 3% less than 20%, or 76 − 12 = 64. The correct answer is 64.77.

When estimating what percent 23 is of 61, one sees clearly that it is less than 50% ($\frac{1}{2}$ × 61 = 30.5). 40% is 50% less 10% or 30 − 6 (rounded), or 24. Therefore, an estimate of 38% or 39% is indicated. The correct answer is 37.7% (rounded). Note that 40% is also 4 × 10%, or in this case, 4 × 6.1, or 24.4.

To estimate 13% of what number is 119, find 10% of 100 = 10, 10% of 1000 = 100, 13% of 1000 = 100 + 30 or 130 (10% + 3 × 1%). Therefore, 1000 is too large. Similarly, 13% of 900 = 90 + 27, or 117, so the correct answer is just over 900. Any estimate between 910 and 920 is excellent. The correct answer is 915.4 (rounded).

The Proportion Method

The percent formula, as described in the previous section, has been the traditional method for solving problems in percent. In the 1960s, the proportion method became popular, and is still widely used. A proportion has two equal quotients.[4]

The formula $p = br$ can be restated, by applying the multiplication/division relation, as the proportion $\frac{r}{1} = \frac{p}{b}$. Therefore, the three problems discussed in the previous section can now be restated as proportions:

4. Traditionally, a proportion in geometry has been defined as having two or more equal ratios. A ratio is often interpreted as a quotient for numbers representing similar things, whereas a rate is a quotient of numbers representing different types of things. We make no such distinction for this topic, but the use of rate in problem-solving discussions does imply a quotient of numbers representing unlike quantities.

Formula Sentence	Proportion
$b = p$	$\frac{r}{100} = \frac{p}{b}$
5% of 40 = p	$\frac{5}{100} = \frac{p}{40}$
r% of 4 = 3	$\frac{r}{100} = \frac{3}{4}$
2% of what = 4	$\frac{2}{100} = \frac{4}{b}$

Note that r in the proportion is 100 times r in the formula.

Traditionally, these problems have been solved by "cross-multiplying," learned by rote, and then solving the resulting equation. This approach is objectionable in a program that stresses meaningful learning. The following solutions use the multiplicative identity to stress meaning.

a. $\dfrac{5}{100} = \dfrac{p}{40}$

$\dfrac{p}{40} = \dfrac{1}{20}$ Reduce $\dfrac{5}{100}$ to $\dfrac{1}{20}$

$\dfrac{p}{40} = \dfrac{1}{20} \times \dfrac{2}{2} = \dfrac{2}{40}$

Therefore: p = 2

b. $\dfrac{r}{100} = \dfrac{3}{4}$

$\dfrac{r}{100} = \dfrac{3}{4} \times \dfrac{25}{25} = \dfrac{75}{100}$

Therefore: r = 75%

c. $\dfrac{2}{100} = \dfrac{4}{b}$

$\dfrac{4}{b} = \dfrac{2}{100} \times \dfrac{2}{2} = \dfrac{4}{200}$

Therefore: b = 200

In the previous examples the proportion method seems deceptively simple because the numbers have been chosen to simplify the computation. Solving an apparently simple proportion can require complex fractions, as follows:

$$\frac{h}{7} = \frac{13}{11} \qquad \frac{h}{7} = \frac{13}{11} \times \frac{\frac{7}{11}}{\frac{7}{11}}$$

$$\frac{h}{7} = \frac{\frac{91}{11}}{7} \qquad h = \frac{91}{11} = 8\frac{3}{11}$$

The following equations illustrate the solution by the "cross-multiplication" method:

$$\frac{h}{7} = \frac{13}{11} \qquad 11n = 7 \times 13$$

$$n = \frac{91}{11} = 8\frac{3}{11}$$

If pupils learn to solve proportions by using the multiplicative identity, as previously illustrated, it is easy to understand why the "cross-multiplication" method works:

$$\text{If } \frac{a}{b} = \frac{c}{d}, \text{ then } \frac{a}{b} \times \frac{d}{d} = \frac{c}{d} \times \frac{b}{b}$$

$$\text{or } \frac{a \times d}{b \times d} = \frac{b \times c}{b \times d}.$$

Therefore: $a \times d = c \times b$.

This process is often stated as "the product of the means $(b \times c)$ is equal to the product of the extremes $(a \times d)$.

Comparison of the Formula and Proportion Methods

In the formula method, when the rate is known, it must be changed to a decimal or common fraction before it is substituted in the formula for computational purposes. If the rate is determined by dividing the percentage by the base, it must be converted from the common or decimal fraction, obtained from the division, to a percent. Changing to and from percent is often a source of difficulty for students learning to use the formula.

The proportion method requires that a rate of $r\%$ be expressed as the fraction $r/100$. This method does not require the pupil to make the decision as to whether to change the rate to a common or decimal fraction. The proportion method can make the pupil more aware of the fact that the base corresponds to 100%.

Both methods require two computations. The formula method requires the computation of changing to or from percent and the multiplication or division required by the formula. In its most efficient form, the proportion method requires "cross-multiplication" and the multiplication or division required to solve the resulting equation.

Both methods require the correct identification of rate, base, and percentage. It is important to emphasize identifying the base represents 100%. If the base is identified correctly, students rarely have difficulty in identifying the rate and percentage.

Summary

Although the everyday use of decimals has increased substantially, the traditional sequence of introducing common fractions and then decimals is still accepted procedure.

A decimal fraction has an unwritten denominator of the form 10^n where n is equal to the number of decimal places.

If a student can compute with whole numbers, the ability to position the decimal point correctly will enable him or her to compute with decimals.

To use decimals efficiently, a pupil must know how to round off terminating and nonterminating decimals.

Common fractions are converted to decimals by dividing numerator by denominator. Decimals are converted to common fractions by eliminating the decimal point and writing the denominator.

The language of percent is common in everyday affairs as well as in business and industry. The percent sign is equivalent to one-hundredth, the basis for changing to and from percent. The percent sign is used mainly for descriptive purposes and rarely in computation.

There are three basic percent situations corresponding to the three basic one-step problems in fractions. Percent problems can be solved by use of the formula or by use of proportions. Both methods are in common use.

Exercises 15.4

Give the pattern you would use to teach these problems to a class of average achievers at the grade 6 level:

1. The length of a bookshelf is 2.75 feet. What is the length of three of these shelves?

2. A gardener planted 60 rose bushes. If 90% of them grew, how many did not grow?

3. How many pieces of ribbon 1.5 yards in length can be cut from a roll of ribbon containing 24 yards?

4. A team won 13 of the 20 games it played. What percent of the games played did that team win?

5. A team won 12 games and lost 13 games. What percent of the games played did that team win?

6. A tank contains 48 gallons of fuel oil when it is 30% filled. How many gallons will the tank hold when completely filled?

7. A manufacturer advertises that the cutting edge of a razor blade is 17 millionths of an inch thick. Write the decimal for this number.

8. What is the largest possible number of digits in the repetend of the decimal representation of the fraction $1/n$? Check your answer by finding the repetend for $1/17$.

9. If two numbers (not zero) are equal, their reciprocals are equal. Show this to be true by multiplying both sides of the equation $1/n = 1/m$ by mn.

10. Show how the statement in problem 9 applies to $3/4 = 12/n$.

11. A teacher introduced division by a decimal divisor using a caret to shift the decimal point, as illustrated in the example: $.3_\wedge)\overline{.1_\wedge 8}$ Evaluate this technique.

12. Solve by formula: 30% of what number is 48?

13. Solve problem 12 by the proportion method.

14. What is the cost of a book selling for $9 if it is sold at 20% above cost? A student gave the following solution:

    20% of $9 = $1.80. The cost is $9 − $1.80 or $7.20.

    As a teacher, how would you evaluate this solution?

15. The total prize money in a golf tournament is $300,000. The first prize is $54,000; the second is $32,400; the third prize is $24,000. Each prize is what percent of the total?

Selected Readings

Bell, Fredrick. *Teaching Elementary School Mathematics, Methods and Content for Grades K–8.* Dubuque, IA: William C. Brown, 1980.

Fass, Arnold L., and Claire M. Fass. *Mathematics: Content, Methods, Materials for Elementary School Teachers.* New York: Heath, 1975.

Heddens, James W. *Today's Mathematics,* Fourth Edition. Chicago: Science Research Associates, 1980.

Marks, John L., C. Richard Purdy, and Arthur C. Hiatt. *Teaching Mathematics for Understanding,* Fourth Edition. New York: McGraw-Hill, 1975.

Twenty-ninth Yearbook of the National Council of Teachers of Mathematics. Reston, VA: National Council of Teachers of Mathematics, 1964.

Virginia Council of Teaching Mathematics, *Practical Ways to Teach the Basic Mathematical Skills.* Reston, VA: National Council of Teachers of Mathematics, 1979.

Chapter 16

Measurement: Metric and English Systems

"Metric System Gaining—Meters and Liters Becoming Common": So read the headline of an Associated Press news release of May 11, 1981, which reported that ". . . Americans are slowly making the switch. At the gasoline pump and the supermarket, in auto plants and liquor stores, the system of grams, meters and liters is slowly replacing pounds, feet and gallons . . . a little here and a little there, metrics are coming. They are being taught in more detail in the schools now—sometimes as the primary method of measurement. . . ."

Today metric measures are being introduced to school children across the United States. Ninety-five percent of the countries in the world now use the metric system, and the United States is moving slowly toward conversion. Most states require that public school children be instructed in metric measures, and some states require that metric measures be taught as the primary measuring system. Teaching metrics to children who daily come in contact with English units is a monumental undertaking for American education. Teachers must know and understand the metric system and be able to teach metrics to children in a meaningful, interesting, and effective way.

Achievement Goals

After studying this chapter, you should be able to:
1. Discuss the origins of measurement systems.
2. Outline the early development of the metric system.
3. Describe the evolution of metric measures in the United States.
4. Enumerate the essential features of the metric system, including SI units.
5. List major objectives for teaching measurement in the primary and upper grades.
6. Describe various approaches to teaching measurement in the elementary school.
7. Draw up plans to provide measurement activities, particularly for (a) length, (b) mass, (c) capacity, and (d) temperature.*

* For topics of money and time, see Chapter 5.

Vocabulary

Mastery of the following key terms will help you to understand this chapter. Each term is defined or illustrated in the Glossary at the back of the book.

Accuracy in measurement	Liter
	Mass
Centi-	Meter
Degree Celsius	Milli-
Density	Nonstandard units
English units	Precision
Gram	SI metric units
Kilo-	Standard units

Origins of Measurement Systems

In early times, measurement was indefinite and crude. Just as the decimal system of numeration grew out of the use of the fingers of the hand, measures of various kinds were derived from natural events, parts of the body, and units that were easy to manage and understand. The movements of the stars and planets provided an easy way to *reckon time*. A day was the time that elapsed from sunrise to sunrise; a month, the time between a certain phase of the moon and its recurrence; and a year, the time it took the sun to pass through successive changes from one position in the heavens back to the same position.

The length of objects was first measured by using parts of the human body. A *cubit* was equal to the length of the arm from the middle finger to the bend of the elbow. A *foot* was the length of a real foot—in eighth century Rome, Charlemagne's foot. In the eleventh century, King Henry I of England established the *yard* as the distance from his nose to the end of his outstretched hand.

The human stride was a convenient way of measuring distances. People measured short distances by the number of steps taken to cover them. Longer distances were de-

scribed by the number of days it took to make a journey.

Capacity was measured with bowls and cups, and mass was determined by balancing with grains of wheat or barley. For thousands of years, barter was the means of exchange, and so definite units of value were not needed.

Development of Standard Units

Measurement is the process by which a *unit of measure* is compared with the thing being measured. A *standard unit* of measure is needed to make measurements consistent that are done by different individuals. The first uniform standards of measurement were established centuries ago by rulers, priests, and merchants. Later, standard units of measure were established by law by governments throughout the world. In the United States, the U. S. Bureau of Standards is the official agency that regulates and maintains standard units of measure.

Before trade and industry were widespread, there was little concern that methods and units of measure were not uniform. However, when people began forming groups to conduct business, industry, and construction, and began to trade, there came a need for *standard units* with a common meaning. The English System of Weights and Measures, adopted by the United States during the eighteenth century, had evolved in Britain and was used throughout the world.[1]

In 1817, Congress appointed Secretary of State John Quincy Adams to study weights and measures and recommend a way to unify standards throughout the country. After four years of study, Adams endorsed the metric system, but was reluctant to rec-

---

1. Ronald Edward Zupke, *British Weights and Measures—A History from Antiquity to the Seventeenth Century* (Madison: University of Wisconsin Press, 1977).

ommend its adoption because of the extensive trade the United States conducted with countries using the English system. In 1830, Congress ordered the Secretary of the Treasury to study standards used in custom-houses throughout the country. The Secretary then proceeded to create a complete set of standards based on a standardization of *English units*. This system was adopted by Congress in 1839.

After that, the metric system's use became more and more widespread throughout Europe, and trade with nations that were using metric units became more and more difficult for countries using the English system. In 1866, Congress passed a law making the metric system *legal*, but not the established system of weights and measures for the United States.[2]

The use of English units has been customary or standard in the United States for many years, and people feel comfortable with inches, feet, miles, quarts, gallons, ounces, and pounds. Clearly, these units will continue to be used in everyday life in American society for some time to come.

Origins of the Metric System[3]

A scientific report made in 1790 to the French National Assembly proposed a decimal system of money, weights, and measures. The report was approved by the king, who named the French Academy of Sciences responsible for development. In 1791, the Academy of Sciences designated the standard of length as one ten-millionth of the distance from the equator to the North Pole, running through Paris. This distance

was to be determined by first measuring the meridian arc from near Dunkirk on the English Channel to Barcelona, on the Mediterranean, in Spain. From this measured distance the distance of one ten-millionth a quarter meridian could be calculated.

In addition to the standard *meter*, the French Academy created a standard unit of *mass* equal to a cubic decimeter (1000 cubic centimeters) of distilled water lowered to the temperature of melting ice. The new standard was called a *kilogram*, and a platinum–iridium cylindrical bar was constructed with a height and a diameter of 3.9 centimeters. The standard for capacity later became the cubic decimeter, which was named *liter*.[4] The metric system was designed specifically to make measurement easier by creating a system, rather than a collection, of units of measure.

Evolution of Metric Measures in the United States

Between 1900 and 1935, conditions in America were conducive to conversion to metric measures. Unfortunately, the antimetric forces, led by American manufacturers, convinced Congress that the cost of conversion would be enormous. From 1948 to 1960, four significant events took place in the United States with regard to the metric system:[5]

1. In 1948, the National Council of the Teachers of Mathematics published its 20th Yearbook, which was devoted to the topic of *metrics*.

2. Frank Donovan, *Prepare Now for a Metric Future* (New York: Weybright and Talley, 1970), pp. 26–33.

3. For one of the most comprehensive treatments of the "Evolution of Measurement Systems," see the 1978 edition of *Metric System Guide*, Volume V, Part I (Neenah, WI: J.J. Keller, 1978), pp. 1–79.

4. Ann M. Wilderman, Harold S. Resnick, and David E. Kapel, *Metric Measure Simplified* (Boston: Prindle, Weber & Schmidt, 1974), pp. 1–5.

5. "Evolution of Measurement Systems," *Metric System Guide*, Volume V, Part I (Neenah, WI: J.J. Keller, 1978), pp. 63–66.

2. In 1950, Congress approved metric measures for electrical and photometric enterprises.

3. In 1957, the U.S. Army authorized metric linear measures for weapons.

4. The United States defined English measures in terms of metric equivalents:

1 yard = 0.9144 meter
1 pound = 0.453 592 37 kilogram

Of course, the metric system has been used in the United States for many years in scientific fields, such as photography, pharmaceuticals, and electrical engineering.

In 1968, Congress enacted the Metric Study Act, which directed the National Bureau of Standards of the Department of Commerce to conduct a study of the impact on the United States of increasing worldwide use of the metric system. The three-year study was presented to Congress by the Secretary of Commerce in July 1971. The Secretary's recommendation was "that the United States change to the International Metric System deliberately and carefully through a ten-year coordinated national program."[6]

On December 23, 1975, President Ford signed into law the Metric Conversion Act of 1975 (PL 94-168), which pronounced the conversion to metric measures as national policy. It established a seventeen-member U.S. metric board to set overall policy for converting to metric units. It charged the Secretary of Commerce with the responsibility of interpreting or modifying metric standards.

As of the early 1980s, of the four major economic trading groups of the world—the United States, the European Economic Community, the Council for Mutual Economic Assistance, and Japan—the United States is the only one not legally requiring metric measuring units.[7]

From Water Clock to Atomic Clock

Time was originally measured in natural units, such as day, month, or year. The day was of obvious length, while the month was based on the time it took the moon to revolve around the earth—about twenty-nine days—and the year lasted 365¼ days. Later, mechanical devices, such as the water clock, were used to find the number of intervals of time that had elapsed. The discovery of the laws of the pendulum led to the development of highly efficient clocks and watches.

In our modern age, a high degree of accuracy is required in measuring time, including measurement to the nearest millionth or billionth of a given unit. The most accurate instrument available for measuring time is the atomic clock, which is governed by the natural rhythm of an isotope of the cesium atom, which vibrates 9 192 631 700 times per second. It is calculated that the atomic clock will neither gain nor lose more than one second in 6000 years. In 1967, the General Conference of Weights and Measures adopted the atomic clock as the standard for measuring time.

A New Standard for the Meter

In 1960, a new standard for the meter was established, for two reasons: The distance of one ten-millionth of a quadrant of a meridian was difficult to measure, and the standard meter prototype marked on a platinum–iridium alloy bar was not as accurate as scientists desired. Consequently, the International General Conference defined the meter as 1 650 763.73 wavelengths of the orange-red light emitted by excited atoms of

6. U.S. Department of Commerce, *A Metric America, A Decision Whose Time Has Come* (Washington, D.C.: National Bureau of Standards, 1971).

7. Louis F. Sokol, "The Case for Metrication." In *The Metric Debate* (Boulder: Colorado Associated University Press, 1980), p. 7.

the krypton-86 in a vacuum. Soon, however, this was not considered accurate enough. In 1979 the U.S. Metric Association reported that "scientists at the U.S. National Bureau of Standards and the Canadian National Research Council have accomplished the highest direct frequency measurement ever made on an electromagnetic wave. . . ."[8] Measurements based on the spectroscopic (visual spectrum) frequency of light are potentially a thousand times more accurate than current measurements of wavelength. The proposed new standard is to be presented to the General Conference of Weights and Measures.

Essential Features of the Metric System

The metric system is superior to all other previous systems of weights and measures for several reasons. First, the system has a

8. *U.S. Metric Association Newsletter,* November–December 1979, 14:5.

base of ten. That is, each basic unit is subdivided into powers of ten. Thus, the ratio between consecutive units of the metric system is the same as the decimal ratio of consecutive places in our number system. Computation with metric units is much easier because decimals are used rather than "denominate" numbers and common fractions.

Second, the basic units of length, mass, and capacity are consistently related to each other. Once the meter was standardized, it was subdivided into ten parts (each called a decimeter), 100 parts (centimeters), and 1000 parts (millimeters). The basic unit of mass is the kilogram, which is the mass of a decimeter cube (10 centimeters on each edge) filled with distilled water at a temperature of melting ice. Capacity is the amount of substance it takes to fill a decimeter cube, and its basic unit is the *liter.*

Third, the names of the consecutive units are consistent for all of the units of metric measure. The same prefixes are used for subdivisions of every unit and for the multiples of ten of every unit. (For purposes of

Table 16.1 SI Prefixes Commonly Taught in the Elementary School

Factor	Prefix	Symbol	Pronunciation
$1\,000\,000 = 10^6$	mega	M	*meg-a-*
$1\,000 = 10^3$	kilo	k	*kill-o-*
$100 = 10^2$	hecto	h	*hec-toe-*
$10 = 10^1$	deka	da	*deck-a-*
$1 = 10^0$	(basic unit)		
$0.1 = 10^{-1}$	deci	d	*dess-ie-*
$0.01 = 10^{-2}$	centi	c	*sen-ta-*
$0.001 = 10^{-3}$	milli	m	*mill-ie-*
$0.000\,001 = 10^{-6}$	micro	μ	*mi-cro*

Note: Prefixes 10^1 to 10^6 are derived from Greek words; prefixes 10^{-1} to 10^{-6} are derived from Latin words.

discussing prefixes, the gram will be used as the basic name of mass, even though the basic standard is the kilogram.) The prefix for any subdivision of a metric unit that is divided into 1000 parts is *milli*—as in millimeter, milliliter, and milligram. Each metric unit multiplied times 1000 has the prefix *kilo*, as in kilometer, kiloliter, and kilogram. See Table 16.1 for the prefixes commonly taught in the elementary school.

Fourth, the standards of the metric system are uniform throughout the world, a uniformity that is made possible by the International Bureau of Weights and Measures under the aegis of the General Conference on Weights and Measures, with delegates from forty-three nations. All countries that use the metric system are able to trade manufactured articles with consistent measurements.

International System of Metric Units (SI)

Metric measurement refers to the *International System of Units* (SI), known as the modernized metric system, as approved by

the General Conference on Weights and Measures held in Paris in 1960. This system includes seven basic SI units—meter, kilogram, second, ampere, kelvin, mole, and candela—two supplementary SI units—radian, steradian—and almost sixty derived SI units with special names.[9] Figure 16.1 lists the units taught to pupils in the elementary school.

Metric Rules

There are precise rules for using SI metric symbols. Metric words for units of measure start with lower-case letters, except when the unit is taken from the name of a person, such as Celsius. The prefixes are pronounced with the accent on the first syllable, as in ki-lo-gram. The units for length and capacity are metre and litre, by the French spelling, which is preferred by the International General Conference and the U.S. Metric Association. The "er" spelling, however, is used by the Department of Com-

9. *ASTM Standard for Metric Practice*, E 380-79 (Philadelphia; American Society for Testing and Materials, 1980), pp. 3–4.

Table 16.2 International System of Units (SI)

SI BASE UNITS

Physical Quantity	Unit	Symbol
length	meter	m
mass	kilogram	kg
time	second	s
electric current	ampere	A
thermodynamic temperature	kelvin	K
amount of substance	mole	mol
luminous intensity	candela	cd

Source: *Metric Units of Measure and Study Guide—SI* (Boulder, CO: U.S. Metric Association, 1976), pp. 10–11.

merce, as published in the *Federal Register,* December 10, 1976. The Metric Conversion Act of 1975 designated the Department of Commerce as legally responsible for interpreting SI standards for the United States. Both spellings are found in the literature and in elementary textbooks, so either should be considered acceptable.

Word names for SI basic units all begin with lower-case letters, and the letter symbol for each is a lower-case letter, except for two units—K (kelvin) and A (ampere), as shown in Table 16.2.

When used as words, the prefixes to metric SI units are all lower-case letters. The letter designations are capitalized for pre-

fixes denoting a million or more, and those less than a million are lower-case letters. Prefixes can be used only in combination with names of units; it is correct to say 13 kilograms, but not 13 kilos.

The letter designations for metric units are not followed by a period except at the end of a sentence. The symbols for units are never pluralized; for example, 250 meters = 250 m, not 250 ms.

Large numbers should be divided into groups of three digits counting to the left or right of the decimal position, and these periods should be separated by a space, and not with a comma. A group of four digits may or may not be grouped. The numeral

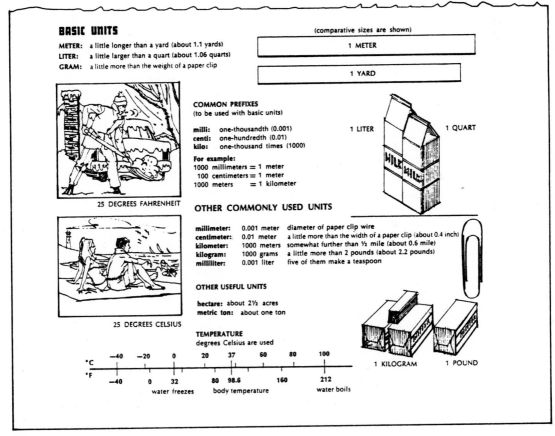

Figure 16.1
Metric Units Taught to Elementary School Pupils (See inside back cover.).
Source: U.S. Department of Commerce, Letter Circular 1052, February 1974.

for "forty-six thousand two hundred thirty-five" is written as 46 235, rather than 46,235. For numbers less than one, a zero is written before the decimal point, such as 0.637, not .637. An exception is the case in which amounts of money are written on legal documents and checks. In these situations, each number period should be separated by a comma to avoid a space that can be filled with a digit.

Common fraction notation is not used in metric measurements. A measure of 25 centimeters, for example, should be in terms of meters, as 0.25 m, not as ¼ meter.

A space is left between the numeral and the metric letter symbol, as in 23 cm, not 23cm. In names or symbols for units with prefixes, no space is left between the letter for the prefix and the letter for the metric unit; for example, 46 milliliters is written as 46 mL, not 46 m L. The symbol for degree Celsius is °C with no space between ° and C. Temperature should be written as 22 °C not 22°C.

Metric measurements can be expressed in different degrees of precision. The smaller the measuring unit used, the more precise the measurement. The greatest possible error in a measure is ± 0.5 of the smallest unit used on the measuring instrument.

Changing Prefixes for a Metric Measurement

Because metric prefixes are ordered by powers of ten, it is very easy to change from one prefix to another for the same unit of measure. For example, it would be easy to report the height of a basketball player as 2.10 meters, rather than 210 centimeters, because 100 cm = 1 m and 210 divided by 100 = 2.10. The zero is still needed in the hundredths place to show that the measurement is accurate to the nearest centimeter.

After pupils have learned about decimals and what happens to a number when the decimal point is moved to the left or to the right, you can show them a simple technique of changing from one prefix to another. First, make a relationship chart as shown below:

1000	100	10	Basic unit	$\frac{1}{10}$	$\frac{1}{100}$	$\frac{1}{1000}$
kilo	hecto	deka	meter	deci	centi	milli
k	h	da	liter	d	c	m
			gram			

In this chart, each prefix to the left of another is ten times the one to the right. But for a particular measure expressed with a particular prefix, to change the prefix to any one to the left, the number must be *divided* by ten for each successive prefix. Say, for example, that a measure of 1256 mm is to be changed to centimeters. Centimeters is one place to the left of millimeters, so divide by ten. Thus, 1256 mm = 125.6 cm = 12.56 dm = 1.256 m = 0.1256 dam = 0.012 56 hm = 0.001 256 km. This technique disregards the concept of accuracy of measurement, which should be considered.

To change from a larger prefix to a smaller one, each prefix to the right on the chart is ten times larger than the preceding one, so the number is multiplied by ten for each place moving to the right. For example, 4.125 km = 41.25 hm = 412.5 dam = 4125 m = 41 250 dm.

Approaches to Teaching Measurement in the Elementary School

There are three possible approaches to teaching measurement in the elementary school. First, teach the English system as currently used in society, and then discuss the metric system as a secondary system. Second, teach the metric system as the primary system, and then cover the English system. And third, teach only the metric system. State and local policies determine how a local district decides which approach is to be used. We recommend that elementary pupils be instructed in the measurement process using nonstandard, English, and metric units. Reference should be made to English measures in terms of how these units are used in daily life. Students in the upper grades should learn the metric system as the primary system of measurement, along with a study of how metric units and measurements relate to the most common English units.

In the elementary school, there should be little emphasis on conversion from English to metric units. Conversion is so time consuming for most pupils to learn that it is nonproductive. To be able to convert within any system or from one system to another, a pupil must know two things: whether to divide or multiply, and the conversion factor. Common sense should dictate that one needs more smaller units to measure a given quantity than larger units, meaning that multiplication is required. For example, most pupils know that 4 ft. = 4 × 12, or 48 inches. They can use this example as a guide telling them whether to multiply or divide in converting in other situations.

Calculators minimize computation, and so make conversion a practical and useful activity, provided that pupils are not required to memorize conversion factors. Also, this activity, when supplemented by conversion in the metric system, helps pupils recognize why the metric system is desirable. If calculators are not available, conversion should be done mostly by estimation, except where conversion factors are small whole numbers.

Exercises 16.1

1. The edges of three cubes are 1 cm, 10 cm, and 100 cm, respectively. Find the capacity of each cube.

2. Supply the missing numbers for linear measure:
   a. 3000 m = _____ km
   b. 200 dam = _____ m
   c. 500 m = _____ km
   d. 50 km = _____ m
   e. 825 cm = _____ m
   f. 221 mm = _____ cm
   g. 216 km = _____ m
   h. 3240 m = _____ km
   i. 32 m = _____ mm
   j. 264 mm = _____ m

3. Supply the missing numbers for measure of capacity:
   a. 32 L = _____ mL
   b. 32 mL = _____ L
   c. 1000 mL = _____ L
   d. 150 L = _____ cL
   e. 355 mL = _____ L
   f. 1345 L = _____ mL

4. Supply the missing numbers for weight (mass):
   a. 240 g = _____ kg
   b. 562 mg = _____ g
   c. 86 g = _____ dag
   d. 7321 kg = _____ t
   e. 2350 mg = _____ kg
   f. 2.75 t = _____ kg

5. Write =, >, or < in the blanks to make each statement true:
   a. 100 cm^3 _____ 1 L
   b. 1 t _____ 1000 kg
   c. 100 g _____ 0.1 kg
   d. 25 cm _____ 1 ft
   e. 40 mph _____ 60 km/h
   f. 100 lb _____ 50 kg

Measurement in the Primary Grades

Children learn about measurement by doing measurements. Their first contact with measurement is in everyday life, with regard to time, length, capacity, weight (mass), and so on. Beginning at an early age, the English system of measurement becomes part of their language—they drink a cupful of orange juice, weigh 46 pounds, walk a half-mile to school, and have recess at quarter past ten. These and many other measurement terms are incidental but necessary aspects of a child's life.

The first contact most pupils have with the metric system is in school activities—often, in the development of concepts and skills in metric measurements. Any English or conventional units of measurement that are included in the instructional program

The teacher demonstrates liters and milliters.
(*Photo by Leland Perry*)

should be treated as *informational*, to show pupils that the units are present in daily life, but that they are being replaced by metric units.

Piaget found that the stages of development for measurement concepts were generally the same as those he described for the development of number concepts. Piaget and his co-workers, Inhelder and Szeminska, investigated the ways that children dealt with space in measurement and geometry. Their conclusions are summarized as follows:[10]

1. *Ages 2 to 7.* The child focuses on a single attribute of an object or situation, a process known as "centering" on one feature at a time. Children at this stage cannot *conserve* length—that is, they do not recognize that the same rod has the same length regardless of its position in space. Also, their thought is not *reversible* in measurement situations. That is, a child does not perceive the distance from a desk to the door as the same length as the distance from the door to the desk. Nor are children at this stage capable of understanding *transitivity*. That is, when given three rods A, B, and C, they do not comprehend that if B is longer than A and if C is longer than B, C must be longer than A.

2. *Ages 7 and 8.* The child is able to compare different units of measure and use nonstandard units of measure to describe length, capacity, and mass.

3. *Ages 9 to 11.* The child is able to measure with a specified degree of accuracy (to the nearest centimeter) and can calculate perimeters, areas, and volumes.

The following is a list of the most common objectives in measurement for pupils

in the primary grades (K to 3). Children should be able:

1. To use nonstandard units of measure to estimate and verify length, mass, capacity, and time.

2. To identify typical parts of the body, objects, and containers that measure approximately a meter, a centimeter, a gram, a kilogram, a liter, and so on.

3. To know and understand the relationships between units of measure, such as 100 cm = 1 m; 1000 g = 1 kg; and 1000 L = 1 kL.

4. To measure objects using standard metric units to a specified degree of accuracy, such as measuring a pencil to the nearest centimeter.

5. To tell time on the hour and half hour and know the days of the week and months of the year. The child should know how to read a digital clock.

6. To use words to describe variations of hot or cold and be able to read and record temperature readings in degree Celsius.

Measurement in the Upper Grades

Pupils in the grades 4 to 6 should have had a variety of measurement experiences. They still need exploratory activities of actually measuring length and distance, capacity and volume, mass, and time. They should be expected to estimate measures and then measure to a certain degree of accuracy. Pupils at this level are introduced to structural aspects of metric measures at the symbolic level and can be expected to perform computations with metric measurements. They should be expected to investigate the history and science of both the metric and English systems of measurement.

We recommend that metric measures be treated as the primary system of measure-

10. Dorothy G. Singer and Tracey A. Revenson, *A Piaget Primer: How a Child Thinks* (New York: International Universities Press, 1978), pp. 75–98.

ment in the upper grades. Because pupils will still come in contact with various aspects of the English system, we suggest that these units be presented informationally, and pupils be given the opportunity to build charts of relationships. They should not be expected to convert from metric to English units except to build a relationships chart and then only with the use of a mini-calculator. Encourage pupils to find uses of metric measures in everyday life, and in newspapers and magazines.

The following is a list of the most common objectives for teaching measurement to pupils in grades 4 to 6.[11] Pupils should be able to:

1. Given specific things to measure (length, capacity, mass), (a) select the appropriate unit of measure, (b) estimate the measurement, (c) measure to a specified degree of accuracy, and (d) calculate the difference between the estimate and the measure.

2. Given the basic units of meter, liter, and gram, understand the structure and relationships between the various prefixes for each unit and change a particular measure from one designation to another, such as from centimeters to meters, meters to kilometers, milliliters to liters, grams to kilograms, and grams to milligrams.

3. Understand and use metric symbols in writing metric measures.

4. Become proficient in calculating with metric units in problem-solving situations.

5. Be able to relate metric measures to English measures by building and using an equivalents chart.

6. Become aware of the uses of metric mea-

---

11. See James E. Inskeep, Jr., "Teaching Measurement to Elementary School Children," in *Measurement in School Mathematics*, 1976 Yearbook (Reston, VA: National Council of Teachers of Mathematics, 1976), Chapter 4, pp. 60–86.

sures in business and industry and in everyday life, and in other school subjects.

Measurement Activities through the Grades

Measuring Length with Nonstandard Units

In the primary grades, pupils begin to measure, using nonstandard units, by a process of comparing and counting. Measuring units should be introduced through everyday usage that can be demonstrated with concrete materials. Let pupils choose their unit of measure—such as a paper clip, the width of a hand, or a drinking straw. Once the unit has been selected, various things can be measured by counting how many times the unit is contained in the thing being measured.

One of the basic problems in measurement that a child faces is to discover that the length of an object does not change regardless of its position in space. Piaget called this property *conservation of length*. The unit of measure selected also must be constant.

Pupils also must learn to use the measuring unit. The unit must be placed at the end of the object to be measured and moved end to end until it reaches the other end of the object. Each move must be counted.

In addition, pupils must learn that the object measured may not contain the unit of measure an exact number of times. Young children will call this phenomenon "coming out uneven." The child will need to be directed first to count the whole number of times, and if the object measures a little bit but not a whole unit more, then just to report the measure the whole number of times plus "a little bit more."

Finally, pupils who measure the same object with different units of measure obviously will obtain different answers. The length of a table may be 29 straw lengths, or 35 hands wide, or 5 steps. This situation will lead pupils to conclude that to get the same number of units, the unit of measure being used needs to be the same length.

Laboratory Activities

To teach measurement with nonstandard units, you should provide laboratory activities and have the pupils measure different lengths with different units. Set up a table with several lengths of doweling (unmarked) measuring from 1 centimeter to 1 meter. Pick one piece of about average length and paint it a color, perhaps red. This rod is the *comparison unit.* On the left-hand side of the table, put a sign reading "Shorter than Red Rod," and on the right-hand side a sign "Longer than Red Rod." The task for each child is to take each piece of doweling, compare it with the red rod, and place it on the appropriate side of the table. Children can work together in pairs, with one child estimating those that are shorter and the other estimating those that are longer. Then they can measure to find out if their guesses were correct.

A variation of this laboratory activity is to fill the table with various objects of different length, such as chalk, pencils, erasers, string, sticks, paper strips, and so on. The reference unit could be something picked by the child, such as the "width of a hand," or "distance between tips of two outstretched adjacent fingers."

Measuring Length with Standard Units

Beginning at the third-grade level, children learn to measure with *standard units* "to the nearest unit." Upper-grade pupils need to learn to select appropriate units to measure different lengths; they need to learn to make estimates before measuring; and they need to develop a sense of length. They should measure and label various

things in the classroom, such as tabletops, books, and desks.

Beginning experiences with measuring long distances around the school should include measuring distances from one place to another and putting up signs. For example, put up a sign to indicate a point *"52 meters to cafeteria,"* or *"Principal's Office—35 meters"* (or, as a joke, 3500 cm). Distances along a length of the playground could be marked off in lengths of 10 meters from 0 to 1000 meters or 1 kilometer, if the school yard is large enough. Pupils should be aware that metric measures are used in the Olympic games. The distance between bases on a baseball diamond should be marked in meters. You might mark off other distances for games and races in meters, or measure the "ball throw" in meters, and so on.

Upper-grade pupils should collect model objects that measure certain measures:

A dime measures 1 millimeter thick.
The diameter of a nickel is 2 centimeters.
A large paper clip is 1 centimeter wide.
A meter is the height of the teacher's chair.

To measure length, the classroom should be equipped with: (a) 30-cm rulers (about a foot long), (b) meter sticks, and (c) trundle wheels for measuring longer distances. Rulers should also be marked in millimeters for measuring very small objects.

Have pupils fill out a special chart, "My measurements in metrics." Have them record their height in centimeters, mass (weight) in kilograms, head size in millimeters, length of foot in centimeters, and so on. (See Exercises 16.2, p. 299.)

TEACHING THE MEANING OF PREFIXES

The prefixes used most often to measure length and distances are, for very short lengths, the millimeter and centimeter, and for long distances, the meter and kilometer. Upper-grade children should frequently be asked to show the relationship among these prefixes.

RELATION OF METRIC UNITS TO ENGLISH
UNITS

For some time to come, pupils will continue to have contact with distances in English units. Road signs, mileage on road maps, dimensions printed on models, and the like will continue to be printed in English units.

Students and adults who have learned to measure with English units often need to have on hand a reference of equivalents to metric units. With a minicalculator and an equivalent table, it is easy to convert individual measures from English to metric units. We do not recommend mathematical conversion from one system to another for elementary pupils. Instead, prepare a visual chart showing patterns and relationships that can be used when English units are given and metric units are desired, or vice versa. However, in many cases precise conversions are not necessary. When this happens, pupils should be able to approximate equivalents for comparison purposes. For example, they should know that a quart is a little less than a liter, a yard is a little less than a meter, and a pound is a little less than one-half of a kilogram. The chart format shown in Table 16.3 can be used to show the approximate relationship between miles and kilometers. Suppose that a map of a country is marked in miles. For a class project, have students convert distances from one city to another. The chart shows that for every 5 miles there are approximately 8 kilometers. To determine the number of kilometers for 85 miles, the pupil would divide by 5 ($85 \div 5 = 17$) and multiply by 8 ($17 \times 8 = 136$). Therefore, 85 mi. $\approx$ 136 km. (The symbol $\approx$ means that the two measures are approximately equal.) An-

Table 16.3 Approximate Relationships between Miles and Kilometers

Miles	Kilometers
5	8
10	16
15	24
20	32
25	40
30	48
35	56
40	64
45	72
50	80

other method is to find two numbers under miles that have a sum of 85—for example, 50 and 35. Write the corresponding kilometers for each—80 and 56—and then find the sum of 136 km. With the aid of a calculator, miles can be converted to kilometers by multiplying the number of miles by 1.6093 and rounding off to the nearest tenth.

Children in the upper grades enjoy taking different things that are marked in English units and translating them into metric units. They can do this by using standard conversion tables, such as shown below, and minicalculators to prepare charts of equivalent measures.

Measuring Mass

The unit for mass in the metric system is the *kilogram*. This unit is the only basic unit in SI that has a prefix. Prefixes are applied to the unit *gram*, which is a very light measure, about equal to the mass of a small paper clip. To find the mass of a very light object, the unit gram would be appropriate.

English to Metric	Metric to English
1 inch = 2.54 centimeters	1 centimeter = 0.3937 inch
1 foot = 30.48 centimeters	1 meter = 3.2808 feet
1 yard = 0.9144 meter	1 meter = 1.0936 yards
1 mile = 1609.33 meters	1 kilometer = 0.6214 mile
1 mile = 1.609 kilometers	

Exercises 16.2

1. Estimate metric measurements, then use a metric tape and find actual dimensions:

	Estimate	Measured
a. My height	———— cm	———— cm
b. My head size	———— mm	———— mm
c. The length of one of my shoes	———— cm	———— cm
d. My waist size	———— cm	———— cm
e. The length of my arm	———— cm	———— cm
f. My arm span	———— m	———— m
g. My chest size	———— mm	———— mm

2. First estimate the length of each of the following line segments to the nearest millimeter. Then use a ruler graduated in millimeters to measure each to the nearest centimeter:

	Estimate	Measured
a. ————	———— mm	———— cm
b. ————————	———— mm	———— cm
c. ————————————	———— mm	———— cm
d. ————————————————	———— mm	———— cm
e. ————————————————————	———— mm	———— cm

3. Obtain a road map for your state. Select four major cities. Ask students to find the distance in miles between each pair of major cities and use a minicalculator to convert these distances to kilometers.

A four-ounce candy bar has a mass of 113.4 grams. A one-pound box of candy has a mass of 453.6 grams. One thousand grams equal one kilogram. The one-pound box of candy would have a mass of 0.45 kilograms.

Most people do not like to use the word *mass* to describe an object. The term *weight* is so well established in our vocabulary that for practical purposes it would be useless to try to change it to mass. What did the baby weigh? How much does that roast weigh? Will you weigh this package to find out the amount of postage required? Mass and weight are equal at the equator, at sea level, or in a vacuum. A person's weight varies very little from one place on earth to another. The two measures are approximately the same on earth. But on the moon, a person's mass would remain the same, but his weight would be much less than on earth.

A child's first experiences with weight involve finding his or her own weight. Beyond that, young children do not often refer to weight. Provide experiences with balance scales to determine which objects weigh more or less than the comparison unit. Set up a table with a type of "pan balance." Have on the table several different objects. Pick one as the *reference unit* and have students compare each of the other things to this unit in order to sort the objects into groups of "heavier than," "lighter than," or "same as" the reference unit. As in other lab activities, the children should be encouraged to estimate before they make their comparisons and keep some written record of their work to share later with other members of the class.

Measuring Mass Activities in Grades 4 to 6

Pupils should engage in some of the same activities suggested for primary-grade pupils. In addition, activities such as the following should be provided.

1. Encourage pupils to find things that weigh 1 gram, 5 grams, 10 grams, 20 grams, 28 grams (about an ounce), 100 grams, 500 grams, and 1 kilogram.

2. Have pupils weigh and label common objects in the classroom, such as books, chalk, erasers, notebooks, and blocks.

3. Have pupils weigh cubes of the same size but made from different materials. Do they weigh the same? Is this why a kilogram is defined as the mass of a cubic decimeter of distilled water at sea level at the temperature of melting ice?

Converting from English to Metric

Pupils will find that many of the articles in stores are now double-labeled, that is, with both English and metric units. For objects that are labeled only in English units, pupils can use the table of equivalents at the bottom of the page and, with a minicalculator, prepare their own equivalents charts for conversion purposes.

Measuring Capacity

One cubic decimeter of distilled water at the temperature of melting ice at sea level would weigh one *kilogram* and would be equal to one *liter* of liquid. Under these conditions, one cubic centimeter would weigh one *gram*. Because different types of liquid have different *densities* (the mass of a substance per unit volume), a cubic decimeter of milk will not weigh exactly one kilogram, although it will be one *liter* of milk.

The unit *liter* was most probably named after Claude Émile Jean-Baptiste Litre (1716–1778). In 1736, Mr. Litre was alleged to have gone to Sandwich, where he met Josiah Barrel, who wanted to design a vessel in which to measure his cranberry crop. To-

English to Metric	Metric to English
1 ounce = 28.35 grams[12]	1 gram = 0.0353 ounce
1 pound = 0.4536 kilogram	1 kilogram = 2.2046 pounds
1 ton = 0.9072 metric ton	1 metric ton = 1.102 tons (2000 lb)

12. This is the *avoirdupois* ounce, which is equal to 28.35 grams. The *troy* ounce, which is equal to 31.103 48 grams, is 10 percent larger than the avoirdupois ounce. Gold is sold on the international market by the troy ounce. A *fluid* ounce equals 29.6 mL.

Exercises 16.3

1. Have pupils first estimate the weight (mass) of each of the following personal things. Then have them use a metric scale graduated in grams to measure each.

	Estimate	Measured
a. My weight	_____ kg	_____ kg
b. Both of my shoes	_____ g	_____ g
c. My textbook	_____ g	_____ g
d. My pencil or pen	_____ g	_____ g
e. My wallet or purse	_____ g	_____ g
f. A nickel	_____ g	_____ g

2. Ask pupils to visit their local grocery store and find five articles that are marked in both ounces and grams. Have them make a record:

	ounces	grams
Article _____	_____	_____
_____	_____	_____
_____	_____	_____
_____	_____	_____
_____	_____	_____

gether they created a "cranberry barrel." Later Mr. Litre made a fortune with the graduated cylinders he designed and sold throughout Europe during the 1770s.[13]

Pupils learn about liters and milliliters by pouring activities. Provide a variety of different containers, both small and large, such as juice cans, pop bottles, distilled-water jugs, milk cartons, plastic containers, and coffee cans, to use for measuring capacity. The child's first experience with capacity should be with nonstandard units.

Set up a table with containers of different shapes and sizes. Select a small juice can as the measuring unit. Fill a large container with some material, such as sand. (Water is good, but makes a mess.) Have children work in pairs to answer the question "How many cans does it take to fill each container?" For activities like this, we suggest that you label each container with some symbol and prepare a sheet for children to use in recording their answers.

Have pupils find containers that hold about one liter. Collect plastic containers and have the pupils mark them in milliliters and liters.

Figure 16.2 (p. 302) illustrates cardboard models of a 125 mL and a 1000 mL (1 liter) container that pupils can make from patterns. The 125 mL container measures 5 cm on each edge and the 1000 mL container measures 10 cm on each edge. Children will find that it takes eight 125 mL containers to fill the 1000 mL container.[14]

Graduated beakers up to one liter should be available for upper-grade pupils to use in measuring various materials. Instead of water, lima beans, sand, corn, rice, and the like

---

13. *U.S. Metric Association Newsletter*, January–February 1980, 15:3.

14. The original symbol for liter was the script "l" or ℓ. This was changed by the General Conference on Weights and Measures to a capital "L" to avoid confusion with other symbols.

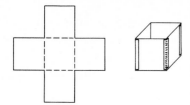

Figure 16.2
Model of a 125 mL container—5 cm per edge; and a 1000 mL container—10 cm per edge. The volume of a 125 mL container is 125 cm³, and the volume of a 1000 mL container is 1000 cm³.

can be used for different measuring activities.

Have the pupils pick different containers—various sizes of bottles and cans—and fill each with some type of material that will pour. Then have each pupil transfer the material from one container to a graduated beaker and record the measure in milliliters. Have them record the measures in the following way:

A coffee cup of rice = _____ mL
A glass of corn   = _____ mL
A can of beans   = _____ mL
A quart of milk   = _____ mL

CONVERTING FROM ENGLISH TO METRIC MEASURES

Pupils may notice that some containers in the grocery store are marked in English

Table 16.4 A Chart of Equivalents of Gallons to Liters

Gal to L		10	20	30
		37.8	75.7	113.6
1	3.785			
2	7.6		83.3	
3	11.4			124.9
4	15.1			
5	18.9	56.8		
6	22.7			
7	26.5			
8	30.3			
9	34.1	71.9		

(Gallons)

units with the metric equivalent given. For example, a quart of milk may be marked 0.9463 liter. At gas stations, a sign may read "1 gallon = 3.785 liters." Have pupils look for different items that are "double-labeled" and make a list, writing the measure in both English and metric units for each item.

Have capable pupils use a minicalculator and the table of equivalents at the bottom of the page to make a chart of liquid measure equivalents similar to that in Table 16.4.

Measuring Temperature

For many years, the unit for measuring temperature in the United States was degree

English to Metric[15]	**Metric to English**
1 ounce = 0.0296 liter	1 liter = 33.815 ounces
1 pint (16 oz) = 0.4732 liter	1 liter = 2.1134 pints
1 quart (32 oz) = 0.9463 liter	1 liter = 1.0567 quart
1 gallon = 3.785 liters	1 liter = 0.2642 gallons

15. 1 barrel (of petroleum) = 159 L
1 metric ton (tonne) of petroleum = 7.32 barrels, or 1.164 m³

Exercises 16.4

1. With a minicalculator complete the equivalents chart shown in Table 16.4.

2. Given: One fluid ounce = 29.574 mL in volume. Make a chart of equivalents to fit the pattern below, rounding off to the nearest tenths place.

Ounces 20 mL		10	20	30
		295.7		
1	29.57			
2				946.4
3				
4				
5				
6		473.2		
7				
8	236.6			
9				

(a) 8 fl oz = _____ mL
(b) 16 fl oz = _____ mL
(c) 32 fl oz = _____ mL
(d) 12 fl oz = _____ mL
(e) 18 fl oz = _____ mL

3. The public may dislike purchasing gasoline by the liter because distances are still measured in miles and people will want to know how many miles per gallon they are getting. Complete the table below to convert miles per gallon to kilometers per liter.

Mi/gal to km/L		10	20	30
		4.25	8.5	12.75
1	0.425			
2				
3				
4				
5	2.12	6.38	10.62	14.88
6				
7				
8				
9				

(a) 10 mi/gal = _____ km/L
(b) 15 mi/gal = _____ km/L
(c) 20 mi/gal = _____ km/L
(d) 22 mi/gal = _____ km/L
(e) 32 mi/gal = _____ km/L

Fahrenheit. On this scale, water freezes at 32°F and boils at 212°F. One degree of Celsius = 5/9 Fahrenheit. That is, every 5 degrees Celsius represent 9 degrees Fahrenheit.

The 100-unit scale thermometer invented by Anders Celsius set the melting point of snow as 100 °C and the point of boiling water as 0 °C. After Celsius died, the points were reversed.

For practical reasons, elementary school children should not be expected to convert from one scale to another by the formula: C = 5/9 (F − 32) and F = (9/5 × C) + 32. Using a calculator, one would convert from Fahrenheit to Celsius by the formula: °F − 32 × 5 ÷ 9 = °C. To convert from Celsius to Fahrenheit, the formula is: °C × 1.8 + 32 = °F.

Teaching Temperature

Many weather reports give temperatures in degrees Fahrenheit and then in degrees Celsius. Very soon, most temperatures will be given in degrees Celsius, without the conversion to degrees Fahrenheit. In the elementary school, pupils should become accustomed to what different temperatures *feel* like.

100 °C	Water boils. Boil some water and measure the temperature with a cooking thermometer.
37 °C	Body temperature. Use a clinical thermometer and take the temperature of at least six children.
22 °C	Comfortable room temperature. Have an outdoor–indoor thermometer and have pupils keep a record of hourly temperatures.
0 °C	Water freezes. Bring in a bucket of ice and measure the temperature.

You can set up a weather station center to keep records of temperatures in degrees Celsius, rainfall in millimeters, and wind velocity in km/h (kilometers per hour).

Exercises 16.5

Here is a simple technique for developing a table of equivalents for Fahrenheit to Celsius:

1. On a sheet of lined paper, start near the bottom and record 32°F = 0 °C.

2. For each increase or decrease of 9°F, there will be a corresponding 5 °C increase or decrease. Fill in a table such as the one below:

3. For each increase or decrease of 4.5°F, there will be a corresponding 2.5 °C increase or decrease. Fill in these values on your table.

4. For every 2°F, there is approximately 1 °C.

5. A rule for quick estimation for changing from C to F is double C and add 30; to change from F to C subtract 30 from F and divide by two. This gives satisfactory approximations for most normal temperatures. Try this rule on the values in the table in exercise 2 above and observe the differences.

Summary

As the United States changes from the English to the metric system, it is necessary to teach metric units, even though English measures are still predominant. As a result, teachers must instruct pupils in both systems of measures.

The best way to teach measurement to pupils in the elementary school is to emphasize measurement activities designed to develop both concepts and skills, such as the following:

1. Have pupils actually measure various things using nonstandard units. Discuss variations. Laboratory activities are essential to learning to measure.

2. Introduce only the most commonly used English and metric units. Have pupils learn to select the appropriate units and measure the same things with both systems. Discuss historical points of interest about how measurement units were discovered and used by our ancestors.

3. Have pupils estimate a measure before measuring an object. Pupils who can make a close guess at a measurement demonstrate their understanding of the process.

4. Discuss the approximate nature of measurement results. Develop the idea of accuracy of a measurement to one-half of the smallest unit represented on the measurement instrument.

5. Have pupils discover the advantages of the metric system over the English system by having them change from smaller to larger units, or the reverse. They will see that all that is required in the metric system is to move the decimal point, whereas the English system requires division or multiplication.

6. Have pupils discover that in daily life, only a limited number of units in a metric table are used, such as centimeters, meters, and kilometers for linear measure. The other units are included to show that the ratio between any two consecutive places is ten.

7. Have students develop a "feel" for approximate equivalents of both English and metric measures. For the next several years, pupils will be using both the English and metric systems. They need to understand the approximate relationships between corresponding units of measurement.

8. Enrichment may include converting from one system to the other with a table of equivalents and a minicalculator. Otherwise, this activity should not be used for drill purposes.

Exercises 16.6

1. Examine the scope and sequence chart of a recently published series of elementary mathematics textbooks and determine the sequence and grade placement of metric topics.

2. Make a list of the measuring devices and aids needed in typical primary and upper-grade classrooms.

3. Prepare a learning-center project for one or more aspects of metric measures: (a) Design worksheets for pupils to use; (b) Have available required materials; and (c) Provide for discussion and evaluation.

4. Outline the advantages and disadvantages of the United States' conversion to the metric system by 1990.

5. List the advantages and disadvantages of teaching only metric measures in the elementary schools.

Selected Readings

Donovan, Frank. *Prepare Now for a Metric Future.* New York: Weybright and Talley, 1970.

Goldbecker, Sheralyn S. *Metric Education.* Washington, D.C.: National Education Association, 1976.

Higgins, Jon L. (Ed.). *A Metric Handbook for Teachers.* Reston, VA: National Council of Teachers of Mathematics (no date).

Kurtz, Ray V. *Metrics for Elementary and Middle Schools.* Washington D.C.: National Education Association, 1978.

Leffin, Walter W. *Going Metric, Grades K–8.* Reston, VA: National Council of Teachers of Mathematics, 1975.

Metric Units of Measure and Style Guide—SI. Boulder, CO: U.S. Metric Association, Inc., 1976.

Nelson, Doyal (Ed.). *Measurement in School Mathematics,* 1976 Yearbook. Reston, VA: National Council of Teachers of Mathematics, 1976.

Youngpeter, John M. and Dennis P. Davan. *Meter—Suggested Activities to Motivate the Teaching of the Metric System,* Spice Series. Stevensville, MI: Educational Service, 1975.

Agencies to Contact for Up-to-Date Metric Information

United States Metric Board
1600 Wilson Boulevard
Arlington, VA 22209

U.S. Metric Association
10245 Andasol Avenue
Northridge, CA 91325

American National Metric Council
1625 Massachusetts Avenue NW
Washington, DC 20036

Chapter 17
Geometry

The word "geometry" is derived from the Greek words *gaia*, from the root *gé*, which means "earth," and *metrein*, which means "to measure." Not surprisingly, the original purpose of geometry was to take measurements of the earth. The ancient Egyptians used geometry extensively in building the great pyramids and in taking the land measurements required by the overflow of the Nile River each year. Later, geometry became an abstract study of the elements of space—points, lines, and planes—and their relationships to one another. The oldest and best-known work on geometric theory is *Elements*, a thirteen-volume series written by the Greek mathematician Euclid (300 BC). For years, Euclidean geometry with formal proofs was the geometry taught in secondary schools around the world.

Achievement Goals

After studying this chapter, you should be able to:

1. Justify the inclusion of geometry in the elementary curriculum.
2. Summarize the objectives for teaching geometry to primary and upper-grade pupils in the elementary school.
3. Describe and illustrate the meaning of various concepts and terms of geometry. (See vocabulary words.)
4. Identify and illustrate one-dimensional figures, two-dimensional figures, and three-dimensional figures.
5. Describe common properties of geometric figures.
6. Outline activities for teaching concepts and skills for dealing with one-dimensional figures, such as lines, segments, rays, and angles.
7. Design activities to teach concepts and skills for working with two-dimensional figures, such as circles and various polygons, such as triangles, squares, rectangles, trapezoids, and parallelograms.
8. Design activities to teach concepts and skills for dealing with three-dimensional figures, such as prisms, pyramids, cylinders, cones, and spheres.

Vocabulary

Mastery of the following key terms will help you to understand this chapter. Each term is defined or illustrated in the Glossary at the back of the book.

Acute angle	Polyhedron
Adjacent angles	Protractor
Angle	Quadrilateral
Area	Ray
Circumference	Region
Cylinder	Rhombus
Equilateral triangle	Scalene triangle
Isosceles triangle	Segment (line)
Obtuse angle	Similar figures
Parallel lines	Solid
Parallelogram	Symmetry
Perimeter	Tetrahedron
Perpendicular	Trapezoid
Pi (π)	Volume
Polygon	

Geometry in the Elementary School

The study of geometry at the elementary school level is quite different from high school and college geometry, which emphasizes definitions and formal proofs. At the elementary school level, pupils are informally taught concepts and general notions about geometric figures, without formal definitions and proofs. Both the nonmetric and metric aspects of geometry are included at the elementary school level. Nonmetric geometry deals with the concepts and representations of sets of points in space, whereas metric geometry uses numbers to measure and describe the various properties of geometric figures.

Most elementary mathematics programs include a systematic study of geometry. By and large, the study of geometry for young children should be informal and intuitive, and should use a variety of physical and visual models for demonstration and discussion. The work of Piaget and others has shown that before age nine, children recognize geometric figures in global terms but cannot yet deal with the various properties of different shapes. Young children tend to

focus on one attribute of a geometric shape at a time. Although they can recognize the difference between a circle and a triangle, they cannot explain why the two shapes are different, except in very general ways.[1]

Children encounter many geometric shapes in their everyday environment. The elementary school pupil begins to learn geometry by developing concepts at the exploratory level with manipulative materials, such as logic blocks, geoboards, and models of geometric shapes. Students first learn to recognize different figures and their names. Then they learn to work with drawings of geometric shapes as they use the number line and rectangular and circular regions in working with number operations and with fractions. Then pupils learn to draw geometric figures to represent geometric concepts and to assist them in problem solving.

The major objectives of teaching geometry in the primary grades are to enable pupils:

1. To identify various geometric figures from physical models, including the square, rectangle, circle, triangle, cube, cylinder, pyramid, cone, and sphere.

2. To recognize certain properties of shapes from physical models and drawings, with some attention to type of regions, edges, angles, sides, and so on.

3. To sort, compare, measure, and draw various geometric plane figures.

Research in mathematics education supports the teaching of geometry in the elementary school.[2] Pupils in the upper grades

1. Thomas P. Carpenter, "Research in Cognitive Development." In *Research in Mathematics Education* (Reston, VA: National Council of Teachers of Mathematics, 1980), pp. 172–175.

2. Phares G. O'Daffer, "Geometry: What Shape for a Comprehensive, Balanced Curriculum?" In *Selected Issues in Mathematics Education*, 1981 Yearbook of the National Society for the Study of Education (Berkeley, CA: McCutchan, 1981), pp. 90–105.

A young child learning about size and shape. *(Photo by Leland Perry)*

study geometry at the exploratory and symbolic levels. They are able to examine models of geometric figures and identify properties and relationships. They form generalizations about the relationships of geo-metric figures to one another. Upper-grade pupils use the instruments of geometry—compass, straight edge, protractor—to measure and draw simple geometric figures. These learners become proficient in finding

study of special properties of polygons should be delayed until the upper grades. Pupils must rely entirely on shape for their earliest identification of geometric figures, based on general perceptions of characteristic features. For example, in the early stages, pupils should be able to distinguish between triangles and squares on the basis of the number of sides: triangles have three sides and squares have four. The special features of the square are that the sides must be *congruent* (equal in measure) and the angles *right angles* (measure 90°). Children learn to name geometric figures that are squares long before they are able to understand these two properties.

Current textbooks provide numerous opportunities to identify geometric figures. Sometimes it helps to supplement the textbook work with the following laboratory activities. These laboratory activities require readiness, which you can achieve by first showing and discussing models of the various figures, before you ask pupils to draw them.

1. Give each child a piece of blank, unlined paper, a sharp pencil, and a straight edge.

2. Have each child place three different dots on the paper, not in a straight line.

3. Then have each child use the straight edge to connect the three points with line segments.

4. Let each child show and tell about his drawing. Make note of the fact that each drawing is a triangle.

5. Have precut cardboard models of different-sized square regions, and give each child a different one.

6. Have each child trace around the edges of his or her own square region on a blank, unlined piece of paper.

7. Let each child show and tell about his or her drawing. Remind students of the fact that each drawing is a square, and talk about various features of squares.

Triangles

Elementary textbooks generally refer to six different kinds of triangles. Figure 17.6 depicts these different kinds of triangles, and lists their names and special features. Elementary school pupils are usually able to identify only a few of these types of triangles. In general, students can be expected to distinguish between right triangles and nonright triangles. Nonright triangles are either *acute* or *obtuse*.

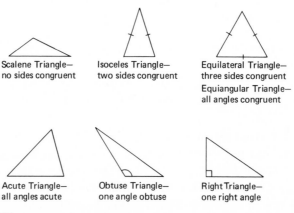

Scalene Triangle—
no sides congruent

Isoceles Triangle—
two sides congruent

Equilateral Triangle—
three sides congruent
Equiangular Triangle—
all angles congruent

Acute Triangle—
all angles acute

Obtuse Triangle—
one angle obtuse

Right Triangle—
one right angle

Figure 17.6
Types of Triangles

Quadrilaterals

Quadrilaterals are polygons that have four sides, four angles, and four vertexes. Textbooks refer to several different kinds of quadrilaterals. The different kinds, and their names and special features, are shown in Figure 17.7.

A good activity for teaching the various appropriate names for different quadrilaterals is to furnish patterns and from them have each student cut out of cardboard the following quadrilaterals:

1. Two different-sized trapezoids

2. Two different-sized parallelograms (not rhombuses or squares)

3. Two different-sized rectangles (not squares)

4. Two different-sized rhombuses (not squares)

5. Two different-sized squares

In addition, you should prepare a "classification board" using Figure 17.7 as a pattern.

Have each pupil pick a quadrilateral region at random and place it on the classification board with its appropriate name. Then ask pupils to give the distinguishing characteristics of each figure. If pupils can answer questions such as the following, they will understand the concept of the measures of the sides and angles of these polygons:

1. How many sides are there in a quadrilateral?

2. How many sides are there in (a) a square? (b) a rectangle? (c) a trapezoid? (d) a parallelogram? (e) a rhombus?

3. Are opposite sides congruent in (a) a square? (b) a rectangle? (c) a trapezoid? (d) a parallelogram? (e) a rhombus?

4. What kind of angle is formed by the adjacent sides of (a) a square, (b) a rectangle?

5. Is a square a rectangle?

6. Is a rectangle a square?

7. How can a parallelogram differ from a rectangle?

8. Is a rectangle a parallelogram?

9. Is a parallelogram a rectangle?

Activities with Tangrams

Tangrams are valuable in helping children visualize spatial relationships with polygons. Tangram pieces are made up of seven regions cut from a square region of heavy cardboard, as shown in Figure 17.8.

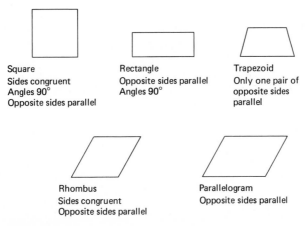

Square
Sides congruent
Angles 90°
Opposite sides parallel

Rectangle
Opposite sides parallel
Angles 90°

Trapezoid
Only one pair of opposite sides parallel

Rhombus
Sides congruent
Opposite sides parallel

Parallelogram
Opposite sides parallel

Figure 17.7
Some Properties of Five Quadrilaterals

You should provide young children with the pieces, but encourage upper-grade pupils to make their own tangrams.

If you are teaching young children, you should draw the boundary of a polygon to be created on the front of a brown envelope containing the needed pieces. In the beginning phases, kindergarten children need to have an outline of each piece.

Upper-grade pupils should make their own tangram pieces by following the pattern shown in Figure 17.8. Square ABCD can be any size. We recommend a square with sides of 10 cm for primary pupils. The pieces should be numbered from 1 to 7 for identification purposes, as shown in Figure

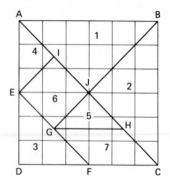

Figure 17.8
Pattern for Tangram Pieces

17.8. The cut-out pieces should be stored in an envelope.

Exercises 17.3

Make a set of tangrams and number the pieces as shown in Figure 17.8.
1. Make a *triangle* with the following set of pieces:
   (a) 1, 2 (b) 4, 5, 7 (c) 1, 4, 5, 7 (d) 3, 4, 5, 6, 7 (e) all seven pieces
2. Make a *square* with the following set of pieces:
   (a) 4, 5 (b) 3, 4, 5 (c) 1, 3, 4, 5 (d) 3, 4, 5, 6, 7 (e) all seven pieces
3. Make a *parallelogram* or a *rectangle* with the following set of pieces:
   (a) 1, 2 (b) 4, 5, 6 (c) 1, 4, 5, 7 (d) 4, 5, 6, 7 (e) 1, 2, 4, 5, 6 (f) 1, 2, 3, 4, 5 (g) 1, 3, 4, 5, 6, 7 (h) all seven pieces
4. Make a *trapezoid* with the following set of pieces:
   (a) 5, 6, 7 (b) 4, 5, 6, 7 (c) 1, 2, 4, 5, 6 (d) 1, 2, 3, 4, 5, 6 (e) all seven pieces

Activities on a Geoboard

The geoboard is an excellent instructional aid to help children understand different characteristics of polygons. Geoboards can be purchased commercially or made from a piece of plywood and nails. As we discussed in Chapter 3, a 25-nail board is recommended. Here are some beginning activities with the geoboard. Have pupils:

1. Make a three-sided figure with one right angle and describe the figure.

2. Make a three-sided figure with two sides of equal length. Describe the figure.

3. Make a four-sided figure with four equal sides. Describe the figure.

4. Make a four-sided figure that has all right angles. Describe.

5. Make a four-sided figure with no right angles. Describe.

6. Make a four-sided figure that has only two parallel sides. Describe.

7. Make the smallest square you can using only one rubber band. This is 1 square unit.

8. Make a quadrilateral (four-sided figure) that contains 8 square units. Describe.

9. Make a rectangle that has 4 square units (not a square).

10. Make a square that has 16 square units.

Describe. How many units are there around the square (perimeter)?

11. Make a rectangle that has 6 square units. Describe. What is its perimeter?

12. Make a square with an area of one. What is its perimeter?

13. Make a four-sided square that has a perimeter of 12 units. What is its area?

14. Make a four-sided square whose perimeter measures the same as its area. Describe the figure.

Symmetry

A geometric figure can have either point or line *symmetry*. A geometric shape has point symmetry if every line segment through the point of symmetry connecting two points on the shape is bisected[2] by the point of symmetry. A circle has point symmetry with respect to its center. Line symmetry exists if a line can be located such that all line segments perpendicular to the given line connecting two points on the shape are bisected by the given line. A circle has line symmetry with respect to any diameter. Figure 17.9 presents examples of geometric figures that have line symmetry. The geoboard and geobands can be used to illustrate symmetry.

An interesting project for children is to have them collect pictures from old magazines. Then have them cut each picture along a line of symmetry and paste it onto a piece of construction paper. The task is for the child to draw the "other half" of the picture.

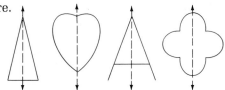

Figure 17.9
Figures with Line Symmetry

2. A point *bisects* a line segment if it separated the segment into two congruent parts.

SIMILAR GEOMETRIC FIGURES

Two geometric figures are *similar* if they have the same shape. All circles are similar. Two triangles are similar if their corresponding angles are congruent or if their corresponding sides are in the same proportion. Figure 17.10 presents examples of similar geometric shapes.

CIRCLES

A *circle* is a one-dimensional plane figure that is a simple, closed curve. It is not a polygon because it is not made up of line segments. It has an *interior* region and an *exterior* region. The distance from the center of the interior region to the circle is called the *radius*. A circle is a set of points equidistant from a point in the center. The circle and its interior region are a two-dimensional figure.

A circle can be drawn by tracing a circular surface, such as a coin or the base of a bottle. A circle of any given radius can be drawn by using a compass, as shown in Figure 17.11.

Figure 17.10
Similar Geometric Shapes

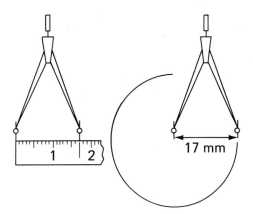

Figure 17.11
Drawing a Circle with a Compass

Perimeters and Areas

Finding Perimeters

The *perimeter* of a polygon (measure[3] of the "rim") is the sum of the measures of the sides of the figure.

A textbook problem may ask the student to find a perimeter, either giving the dimensions of the figure, or requiring the student to measure the sides. The length of a side can be found by direct measurement with a ruler or by using a compass and a ruler.

Figure 17.12 shows how to find the perimeter of a polygon by using a compass. Lay off in succession the measures of the sides *a*, *b*, and *c* of the triangle as illustrated. The sum of these measures is the perimeter of the triangle. Open the compass to the length of these line segments and find the distance between the points of the compass with a ruler.

Students begin dealing with perimeters of polygons at the exploratory level and continue at the symbolic level.

EXPLORATORY LEVEL

Pupils at the exploratory level perform activities such as the following in dealing with perimeters:

1. Find the perimeter in centimeters of each of the polygons in Figure 17.13.

2. Draw figures having the same shape as those in problem 1. Then measure the sides with a ruler and find the perimeter.

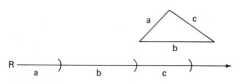

Figure 17.12

---

3. A *measure* is a number and a *length* contains a label such as inches or cm. We add numbers and not inches. This distinction is not usually made in current elmentary programs.

3. Find the perimeter of triangle DEF in Figure 17.14, by using the method illustrated in Figure 17.12 and used in Figure 17.13.

SYMBOLIC LEVEL

At the symbolic level, pupils in the upper grades find perimeters of polygons by developing and using formulas.

4. Find the perimeters of the polygons in Figure 17.15. From demonstrations of the type given at the exploratory level, have the class explain the sequence of steps in finding a perimeter, such as the triangle in Figure 17.14. Have the class tell how a letter can be used to represent each side of a tri-

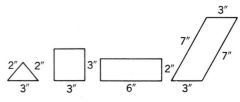

Figure 17.13

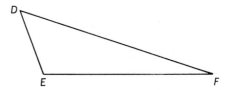

Figure 17.14

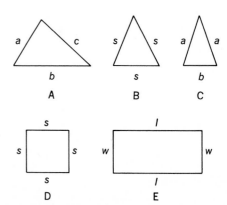

Figure 17.15

angle. Then have the students develop a rule and a formula for finding the perimeter of a triangle.

a. The perimeter of any triangle is equal to the sum of the measures of the three sides. The formula is:

p = a + b + c

b. The perimeter of an equilateral triangle is equal to three times the measure of one side. The formula is:

p = 3s

The formula for the perimeter of an equilateral triangle is an application of the distributive property and the identity property for multiplication:

p = s + s + s
= (1 × s) + (1 × s) + (1 × s)
= (1 + 1 + 1)s
p = 3s

c. The formula for the perimeter of an isosceles triangle is:

p = 2a + b

d. The perimeter of a square is equal to four times the measure of one side. The formula is:

p = s + s + s + s, or p = 4s

The formula for the perimeter of a square follows the pattern given in (b):

p = s + s + s + s
= (1 × s) + (1 × s) + (1 × s)
+ (1 × s)
= (1 + 1 + 1 + 1)s
p = 4s

e. The perimeter of a rectangle is equal to the sum of the measures of the four sides. The formula is:

p = l + w + l + w
p = 2l + 2w
p = 2(l + w)

The students demonstrate that all three formulas for the perimeter of a rectangle are equivalent by replacing *l* and *w* with numerals and then doing the indicated operations. They also identify the formula *p = 2(l + w)* as an application of the distributive property of multiplication over addition.

Unit of Measure for Area

Finding the area of a plane surface is the same as measuring its *region*. For example, the rectangle ABCD in Figure 17.16 encloses a region. The rectangle itself has no area, as it consists of line segments. When we say "Find the area of a rectangle," we mean "Find the area of the region enclosed by a rectangle."

The unit of measure for a region is another region that is used to cover the enclosed space. The standard unit of measure for a plane surface is a unit square (having a side of one). One standard unit of area is a square centimeter (cm^2), as shown in B, Figure 17.17.

Rectangle A of Figure 17.17 is divided into four squares, each of which is congruent to square B. The area of square B is 1 cm^2, and so the area of rectangle A is 4 cm^2.

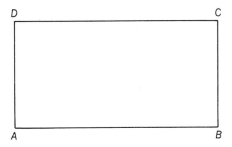

Figure 17.16

Figure 17.17

Finding the Area of a Rectangle

EXPLORATORY LEVEL

In the rectangular region shown in Figure 17.18, each of the square regions is equal to 1 cm², the unit of measure. You should direct pupils to see that they use the square regions to cover the rectangular surface—for example, as one "tiles" the floor. Allow them to discover that each row has the same number of square units. The total number of square units is the number in each row times the number of rows.

Students begin work on finding the area of a rectangular region at the exploratory level. The class should participate in the following kinds of activities:

1. Divide several rectangular surfaces drawn on the chalkboard into square regions and have the pupils find the area of each by finding the number of squares in one row times the number of rows. Each area is represented by the number of squares plus the symbol for the unit of measure (square units).

2. Show the class a picture in which a rectangular surface is divided into square units. Ask the class to find the area, expressed in square units, of the entire region.

3. Have each pupil draw a rectangle having measures expressed as whole numbers, such as 2 cm by 4 cm, and divide the figure into 1-cm squares. Then have each student find the number of squares by multiplying the number in a row by the number of rows.

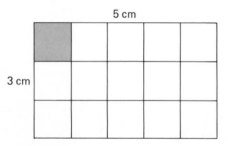

5 cm

3 cm

Figure 17.18

4. On the chalkboard, draw several rectangular regions labeled in whole-number dimensions. Have the class find the area, expressed in square units, of each figure.

SYMBOLIC LEVEL

Pupils at the symbolic level can derive a rule and a formula for finding the area of a rectangular region. The rule for the area of a rectangular region is: *The number of square units in the area of a rectangular surface is the product of the number of units in length and width.* Both dimensions must be expressed in the same linear unit. The area must be expressed in square units. The formula for the area of a rectangle is: $A = l \times w$.

The *square* is a special kind of rectangle whose sides are of equal measure. The letter s is generally used to represent the side of a square; hence, the formula for the area of a square becomes $A = s \times s$, or $A = s^2$. The measure of the area of a 4-cm square is 4×4, or 16, and the area is 16 cm².

The class should apply the rule or formula for finding the area of a square and other rectangular regions that is given in the textbook.

MASTERY LEVEL

The pupils have achieved mastery when they can apply the formula for finding the area of a rectangle with skill and understanding. The amount of time spent on a topic helps to determine how fast elementary students achieve mastery.

Finding the Area of Other Plane Figures

The elementary school curriculum may or may not include finding the area of plane figures such as triangles, parallelograms, trapezoids, or circles. If you introduce this topic for any or all of these figures, you should follow the same pattern as is given for finding the area of a rectangle. The introductory work is at the exploratory level. Have pupils cut parallelograms or triangles from paper and arrange or transform them so as to form rectangles. Then have them compare the area of the triangle or the parallelogram with the area of the rectangle. Have them use a picture or make a drawing of a figure and transform it so that they can find the area of the enclosed region.

At the symbolic level, the class can derive a rule or formula for finding the area of a figure. The formulas for finding the area of four figures using a minicalculator are:

Area of a triangle = base × height ÷ 2 or
$A = b \times h \div 2 = \frac{1}{2} \times b \times h$
Area of a parallelogram = base × height or
$A = b \times h$
Area of a trapezoid = the sum of the measures of the parallel bases (b_1 and b_2) divided by 2 and multiplied by the height or
$A = b_1 + b_2 \div 2 \times b$.
Area of a circle = pi times radius squared, or $3.14 \times r \times r$ or $A = \pi r^2$.

Height

The height of a triangle is a perpendicular segment from a vertex of the triangle to the line containing the opposite side. In Figure 17.19, the height of triangle ABC is $\overline{BD}$. Name the height of each of the other triangles in the figure. If there is more than one height, name all of them. Height is sometimes called altitude.

The height in a parallelogram is a perpendicular segment from a point on one side to the line containing the opposite side. More than one height is drawn in each of the parallelograms shown in Figure 17.20.

The Circumference and Diameter of a Circle

Each student, or each small group of students, should use a cylindrical can or a wheel to find the ratio of the circumference

of a circle to the diameter. The class should compare the ratios of different size cans or wheels. The value of each ratio should be a little more than 3. Then the teacher should have a class demonstration with a 7-inch wooden disk to show how to find the ratio of the circumference to the diameter. A student should mark a point on the circumference and then roll the disk along a yardstick until the marked point touches the stick. The scaled value of this point should be approximately 22 inches. This distance divided by the diameter would give a quotient of $^{22}/_7$, or $3\frac{1}{7}$, which may be expressed approximately as 3.14

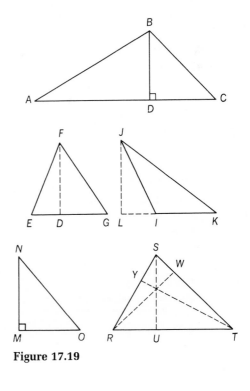

Figure 17.19

Rectangle   Parallelogram   Square

Figure 17.20

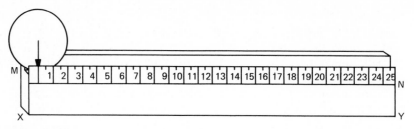

Figure 17.21
Coordinate Axes

The diagram in Figure 17.21 shows an effective instructional aid for demonstrating the method of finding the ratio of the circumference to the diameter. In the diagram, XY is a board about 24 inches long and MN is part of a yardstick or a cloth tape fastened to the side of the board. At the base of XY there is a groove about ⅜ inch wide in which circular disks of plywood about ¼ inch thick can be rolled. If the teacher has disks of 3″, 4″, and 7″ in diameter, a student can give a demonstration to show the circumference of each circular disk. Then the class can find the ratio of the circumference to the diameter for each disk. The experiment should show that the circumference is about 3.1 times the diameter.

The teacher should have the students compare the results of their experiments with the ratio 3⅐. Most of the results

should be approximately 3.1. The ratio of the circumference to the diameter is π and its value is approximately 3⅐, or 3.14. The exact value of π cannot be determined, but in beginning work with this symbol, π is usually given the value of 3⅐, or 3.14. The more precise value, 3.1416, is used when greater accuracy is demanded than that used at the junior high school level.

The pupils should discover that the circumference of any circle is equal to π times its diameter, or π times twice the radius. The formula for the circumference of a circle is

$$C = \pi d \text{ or } C = 2\pi r$$

The teacher should have the students make a graph, similar to the graph shown in Figure 17.22, to display on the bulletin board. If the radius is 3½ inches, the diam-

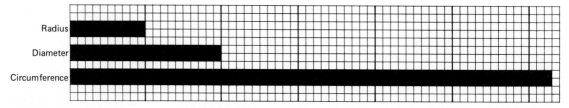

Figure 17.22

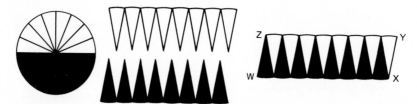

Figure 17.23

eter will be 7 inches, and the circumference will be 22 inches. Metric units should also be used. The superior students should discover that the circumference of a circle is a function of its diameter.

The Area of a Circular Region

The formula for the area of a circular region can be derived or verified by transforming a circle so as to approximate a parallelogram and showing that the formula, $A = \pi r^2$, gives the area of the circular region.

The teacher should have a circular disk, cut from heavy cardboard, about 6 inches in diameter and cut into at least 8 equal sectors, preferably 12 or 16 equal sectors. The sectors should be arranged as shown. The resulting figure will approximate a parallelogram as represented by *WXYZ* in Figure 17.23. The greater the number of equal sectors into which the disk is cut, the closer will the figure formed by these sectors approximate a parallelogram. The altitude of the parallelogram is equal to the radius of the circle. The base of the parallelogram is approximately half of the circumference, or $\frac{2\pi r}{2}$, or πr. Substituting r for h and πr for b in the formula, $A = bh$, the formula for the area of a circular region is shown to be:

$$A = \pi r \times r, \text{ or } A = \pi r^2$$

This method is not satisfactory as a strict mathematical proof but is appropriate for this grade level.

The circle inscribed in the square in Figure 17.24 provides a method for verifying the approximate value of π as 3.14.

By inspection there are approximately 78½ square units in one quadrant of the circular region. Four times 78.5 equals 314 square units, the area of the circular region. In the corresponding quadrant, the square region has a side of 10, which is also the radius of the circle. The area of the square region equals 100 square units. If we multi-

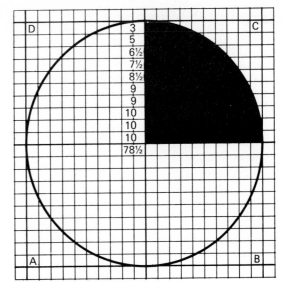

Figure 17.24

ple 100 (which is r^2) times 3.14 (the approximate value of π), the result is 314 square units.

Locating Points on a Grid

Elementary school pupils can be taught to make various kinds of graphs—bar, circle, and line graphs. Both bar and broken-line graphs involve a form of coordinate graphing. As pupils become capable of constructing these graphs, it is essential that they gain an understanding of coordinate graphing.

One type of graphing involves locating points on a plane grid. The plane grid is formed out of a horizontal and a vertical line that intersect to form right angles. The point of intersection is zero. To the right of the point of intersection, several other points are marked off at equal distances from one another and numbered from left to right 1, 2. . . . On the vertical line above zero points are marked off at equal distances from one another and numbered 1, 2, . . . In geometry, the two number lines are called the *coordinate axes,* as shown in Figure 17.25.

To locate a point with the *coordinates* of (2,4) means to move to the right along the horizontal axis 2 units and up the vertical axis 4 spaces. Point A in Figure 17.25 has the coordinates of (2,4). Many interesting activities can be devised for upper-grade children by using the techniques of coordinate geometry.

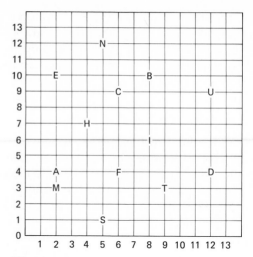

Figure 17.25

Exercises 17.4

Use Figure 17.21 and decode the following message:

(2,3) (2,4) (9,3) (4,7) (8,6) (5,1) (6,4) (12,9) (5,12)

LETTERS:_____ _____ _____ _____ _____ _____ _____ _____ _____

Three-Dimensional Figures

A three-dimensional geometric figure is a *solid.* Some solids are bounded by faces (flat surfaces) that are polygonal regions, such as cubes, prisms, and pyramids. Other solids are bounded by "curved surfaces," such as cylinders, cones, and spheres. Pupils at the elementary level should hear few formal statements of the properties of each of these solids. However, pupils *should* be expected to identify each of the kinds of solids listed above.

ACTIVITIES

1. Discuss with the class the number of line segments needed to enclose a region and help them to discover that at least three line segments are needed. Ask them for the smallest number of sides needed to form a polygon and help them recognize that this is the same as the previous question.

2. Discuss with the class the number of plane surfaces necessary to enclose a portion of space. Have some physical models of solids or some pictures of them on hand for reference and help the class discover that at least four surfaces are needed, or that the fewest possible faces that a solid may have is four. Have pupils give answers before they refer to the physical models so that they have the opportunity to visualize geometric situations mentally.

3. A triangular piece of paper (with all angles less than 90°) can be used to make a solid of four sides (a *tetrahedron*). Start with triangle *ABC*, as is illustrated in Figure 17.26. Determine the three midpoints of the three sides, *X, Y,* and *Z*. Fold firmly along the line segments $\overline{XY}$, $\overline{XZ}$, and $\overline{YZ}$. With careful and proper folding, the three vertexes of the triangle—*A, B,* and *C*—will then meet to form the fourth vertex of a tetrahedron whose other vertexes are *X, Y,* and *Z*.

If you use triangles of different shapes (all

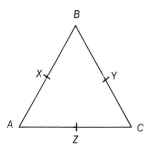

Figure 17.26

Table 17.1

	Faces	Edges	Vertexes
Tetrahedron	4	6	4
Cube	6	12	8
Pyramid with square bases	5	8	5

acute triangles), tetrahedrons of different shapes will result. If you use a right triangle, two of the faces will fold over to equal the third and form a rectangle. If an obtuse triangle is used, a tetrahedron cannot be formed. If an equilateral triangle is used, a regular tetrahedron will result (with all edges equal and all faces with the same size and shape).

4. Have the class make other solids by folding on the basis of patterns drawn on paper (see Figure 17.27 for patterns for familiar figures).

5. Use soda straws, toothpicks, pipe cleaners, or similar materials to construct models of polyhedrons.

6. Have the class count the faces, vertexes, and edges of a tetrahedron and other polyhedrons and make a table (see Table 17.1).

When the table has been completed for all the polyhedrons that are available, ask pupils if they can discover a pattern or relationship among the number of faces, vertexes, and edges. This relationship was first formulated more than two hundred years ago by the Swiss mathematician Euler as $F + V = E + 2$, where F represents the number of faces, V the number of vertexes, and E the number of edges.

Surface Area of a Solid

Each geometric solid has a *surface* measured in square units. The surface area of a solid is the sum of the areas of its faces. For example, a cube with 2-cm edges has an area of 4 cm^2 for each face. A cube has 6

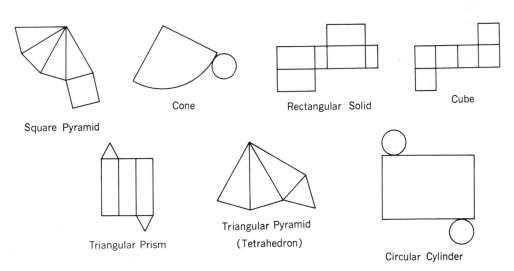

Square Pyramid

Cone

Rectangular Solid

Cube

Triangular Prism

Triangular Pyramid
(Tetrahedron)

Circular Cylinder

Figure 17.27

faces. The surface area of this cube is 6 × 4 cm² = 24 cm². Although there is a formula for finding the surface of each of the regular space figures called solids, pupils at the elementary school level should not be expected to find the surface of solids other than for a cube and a rectangular prism. We recommend that pupils find the surface of these solids by calculating the area of each face of the square or prism and taking the sum of the area of the faces.

Volume of a Solid

When we find the *volume* of a solid, we measure its interior. A solid is a figure that has dimensions of length, width, and height. Just as we used a square region to measure the area of plane figures, we use a cubic unit to measure the volume of a solid. For example, a standard metric unit for finding volume is the cubic centimeter (cm³). For any given solid, the volume is the number of cubic centimeters it contains.

Finding the volume of a solid will be restricted to a rectangular prism because most curriculums do not deal with other solids in the elementary school.

FINDING THE VOLUME OF A RECTANGULAR PRISM

Each face and base of a rectangular prism is a rectangle, as shown in Figure 17.28. At the elementary school level, students find the volume of solids at both the exploratory and symbolic levels. The classroom should be equipped with approximately 125 1-cm cubes and several small rectangular boxes having unlike dimensions. The inside dimensions of each box should be a whole number of centimeters. The class should participate in activities such as the following to gain the background needed to formulate a rule for finding the volume of a rectangular solid.

EXPLORATORY LEVEL

1. Have the class select a box and find the number of 1-cm cubes needed to fill it. The dimensions of the box in centimeters may be 2 × 5 × 3. A member of the class puts one layer of cubes in the box, as shown in Figure 17.29. The teacher has the class note that there are 10 cubes in 1 layer (5 cubes in each row and 2 rows = 10 cubes). Since there will be 3 layers, it will take 3 times 10 cubes, or 30 cubes, to fill the box. The volume is 30 cm³. Repeat this activity with other boxes of different size.

2. Draw figures of rectangular prisms on the chalkboard or show pictures of them. Have the class find the number of cubic units in a layer of a prism and then multiply by the number of layers. Be sure the pupils discover that the number of cubic units in a layer is equal to the product of the number of linear units in length and width. Also, the number of layers is the same as the number of linear units in the height.

3. Have the class derive a rule for finding the volume of a rectangular prism. The rule

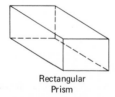

Rectangular
Prism

Figure 17.28

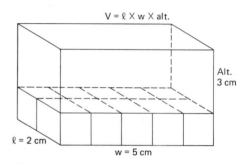

$V = \ell \times w \times$ alt.

Alt.
3 cm

$\ell = 2$ cm

$w = 5$ cm

Figure 17.29

can be stated as: The number of cubic units in the measure of a rectangular prism is equal to the product of the dimensions (expressed in the same units of linear measure), and the volume is that number with the cubic unit used.

4. Have the class derive a formula for the rule: $V = l \times w \times h$ where l = length, w = width, and h = height.

5. Have the pupils substitute numbers in the formula and calculate the product. Point out that the calculation of $l \times w \times h$ will result in a number, whereas the volume is that number along with the symbol for the cubic unit used. For example, if l = 6 cm, w = 4 cm, and h = 3 cm, the number of cubes is 6 × 4 × 3, or 72, and the volume of the prism is 72 cm^3.

Summary

A study of geometry gives pupils the opportunity to explore their environment. It is an interesting subject that pupils in the elementary school study eagerly. You can foster this enthusiasm by relating geometry to everyday experiences and by providing activities designed to develop each child's interest. Teaching geometry at the elementary level should take an informal, activity-oriented approach. Pupils need not be bombarded with formal definitions of many geometric terms. The language of geometry is important, but it should be developed gradually and with reference to geometric models made from concrete materials and shown with drawings. It is essential that pupils studying geometry be allowed the time to discover basic concepts from exploratory activities.

Primary grade children should learn to identify various geometric figures from physical models. They should be able to sort, compare, measure, describe, and draw various geometric figures. Upper-grade pupils study more advanced concepts of geometry, such as perpendicularity, parallelism, congruency, and symmetry. At this level pupils also learn to measure and calculate perimeters and areas of common polygons and circles. They study various solids, such as cones, cylinders, spheres, prisms, pyramids, and rectangular solids, including the cube. They learn to find the surface area and volume of a rectangular solid.

Exercises 17.5

1. What is a geometric figure?
2. What is the simplest geometric figure?
3. Identify the 10 line segments in the figure below:

4. How many "curved" lines can be drawn from point A to point B?
5. How many line segments can be drawn from point A to point B?

6. Name each of the geometric figures below:

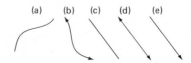

(a) (b) (c) (d) (e)

7. Differentiate between a figure and its region; between the area of a figure and its volume.

8. Illustrate the difference between drawing and constructing an equilateral triangle.

9. Use a carpenter's rule to illustrate different kinds of triangles; different kinds of quadrilaterals.

10. Draw a circle having a radius of 6 centimeters. With that radius, mark off in succession 6 arcs on the circle. Connect these points to form a hexagon. What is the perimeter of the hexagon?

11. The measure of an acute angle is between what two numbers? The measure of an obtuse angle is between what two numbers?

12. Under what conditions will a height of a triangle fall without the triangle? Coincide with a side of the triangle?

13. The perimeter of an isosceles triangle is 21 centimeters. If the length of the base is 5 centimeters, what is the length of each congruent side?

Selected Readings

Aichele, Douglas B., and Melfried Olson. *Geometric Selections for Middle School Teachers (5–9).* Washington, D.C.: National Education Association, 1981.

Brydegaard, Marguerite, and James E. Inskeep, Jr. (Eds.). *Readings in Geometry from the Arithmetic Teacher.* Reston, VA: National Council of Teachers of Mathematics, 1970.

Glenn, J. A. (Ed.). *Children Learning Geometry.* New York: Harper & Row, 1979.

Kespohl, Ruth Carwell. *Geometry Problems My Students Have Written.* Reston, VA: National Council of Teachers of Mathematics, 1979.

Lesh, Richard (Ed.). *Recent Research Concerning the Development of Spatial and Geometric Concepts.* Columbus, OH: ERIC Science, Mathematics and Environmental Education Clearinghouse, May 1978.

O'Daffer, Phares. "Geometry: What Shape for a Comprehensive, Balanced Curriculum?" In *Selected Issues in Mathematics Education,* 1981 Yearbook of the National Society for the Study of Education. Berkeley, CA: McCutchan, 1981, Chapter 7.

Young, John E., and Grace A. Bush. *Geometry for Elementary Teachers.* San Francisco: Holden-Day, 1971.

Chapter 18

Evaluation and Diagnosis

Evaluation and diagnosis are integral to the process of teaching elementary mathematics. *Evaluation* is the process of periodically identifying and assessing needed improvements, in this case, in the instruction of children. Reliable *diagnosis* will point out the areas in which individual pupils have difficulty. When sources of difficulty are located, proper remedial measures can be taken to enable learners to make satisfactory progress. Thus, appraisal, diagnosis, and guidance are intimately connected parts of a continuous process of directed learning.

Achievement Goals

After studying this chapter, you should be able to:

1. Identify the functions of evaluation in elementary mathematics.

2. List the essential steps in the evaluation process.

3. Discuss the role of educational goals and objectives in evaluation.

4. Enumerate various techniques for assessing mathematical achievement.

5. Outline the advantages and disadvantages of objective tests.

6. Summarize the most important characteristics of standardized norm-referenced and criterion-referenced tests.

7. Prepare different types of objective test items for measuring selected objectives in mathematics.

8. Describe the elements and techniques of effective diagnosis in mathematics.

9. Name ways to interpret and utilize the results of appraisals.

10. Identify ways to evaluate (a) the curriculum, (b) methods of teaching, and (c) instructional materials.

Vocabulary

Mastery of the following key terms will help you to understand this chapter. Each term is defined or illustrated in the Glossary at the back of the book.

Assessment	Norm-referenced
Continuum	test
Criterion-referenced	Reliability
test	Standardized tests

Diagnosis

Formative
evaluation

Summative
evaluation

Validity

Functions of Evaluation

Two types of evaluation processes are commonly used in elementary mathematics programs.[1] These are *summative* and *formative* evaluation. *Summative* evaluation is used by teachers to measure the achievement of different groups or classes, and by administrators to compare the achievement of different groups or classes. Many schools use standardized tests for this type of evaluation. Well-constructed standardized achievement tests provide valuable information as to where each pupil stands in comparison with other children of about the same age and grade. These tests can also be used to measure a pupil's growth over a given period of time and offer valuable insights into the child's level of achievement.

Formative evaluation measures the extent to which children have mastered specific learning tasks. This type of evaluation provides feedback to both the teacher and the pupil, enabling each to make the necessary adjustments for continued progress. This process identifies specific areas in which mastery is lacking so that the teacher can arrange to provide needed additional instruction.

One way to determine how well a student is learning the subject is by giving frequent short tests or quizzes, not designed for purposes of assigning grades. The results of a well-constructed test for a cluster of mathematical concepts and/or skills provide valuable information about each child's specific strengths and weaknesses.

1. Benjamin S. Bloom et al., *Handbook on Formative and Summative Evaluation of Student Learning* (New York: McGraw-Hill, 1971).

The Evaluation Process

There are four essential steps in the evaluation process:

1. formulating the educational goals and objectives

2. selecting and constructing measuring instruments

3. securing a record of achievement

4. interpreting assessment results

Formulating the Educational Goals and Objectives

The first essential step of any instructional program is to define and clarify the program's goals and objectives. Likewise, the first essential step of any evaluation program is to identify the goals and objectives toward which the children have been working. In Chapter 2 we list the major goals and objectives for teaching elementary mathematics.

Broad objectives help to lend general direction to a program. Evaluation of a program's effectiveness for groups of children can be done in terms of these general objectives. More specific objectives are necessary for lesson planning and for appraising progress on a particular concept, skill, or application in elementary mathematics.

The effectiveness of the evaluation depends largely on how closely the objectives measured match the accepted objectives. When objectives to be evaluated are stated too narrowly, a teacher may direct class activities to specific test items. There is evidence that the Back to Basics movement encouraged teachers to stress computation at the expense of the concepts involved and problem-solving abilities.

One major objective of elementary mathematics is to enable students to apply the tools of mathematics to solve problems both in the classroom and in everyday life. Outcomes are most effective when they form the background for quantitative thinking. To deal effectively with number in quantitative problem situations, many specific objectives must be attained. Learning to compute with reasonable speed and accuracy is certainly essential in problem solving. A child may demonstrate mastery of computational skills and yet be unable to solve problems successfully.

The Many Types of Objectives

Objectives can take various forms. They can emphasize *final* outcomes or concentrate on the *process* of learning. They can be stated in *broad* terms or state very specific *narrow* tasks to be performed.

Objectives of daily lessons need to deal with specific outcomes. For example, one of the major objectives of a mathematics program is understanding the number system. This understanding implies that the learner can demonstrate:

1. the meaning of base ten.

2. place value of a digit to the left or right of the ones place.

3. what happens to the total value of a digit when it is moved a certain number of places to the left or right in a numeral.

Another major objective in elementary mathematics is for children to understand the meanings involved in computational algorisms. To analyze this objective, a task analysis process is needed to determine the types of skills and understandings that are required for any particular algorism. For example, the child's understanding of multiplication facts can be analyzed and delineated to include the following specific tasks:

1. Using objects to model basic multiplication facts.

2. Modeling basic facts on a number line.

3. Using arrays as a model.

4. Recognizing the sign "×" and the words "factor" and "product."

5. Writing multiples of a given one-digit number.

6. Understanding the commutative property of multiplication.

7. Generalizing facts with a factor of zero or one.

8. Using multiplication in solving one-step problems.

All Objectives Need to Be Appraised

Evaluations of mathematics achievement should include an assessment of all of the program's goals and objectives, including knowledge, skills, problem solving, problem-solving processes, and student attitudes toward mathematics. Hoepfner et al.[2] have listed four major *categories* of goals for elementary mathematics for the purpose of evaluating standardized tests of mathematics content.

I. Understanding mathematical concepts
   a. Knowledge of numbers
   b. Knowledge of numeral systems and number properties
   c. Knowledge basic to algebra
II. Performing arithmetic operations
   a. Whole-number computation
   b. Computation with fractions
   c. Decimal and percentage computation
III. Applying and valuing mathematics
   a. Solution of word problems
   b. Personal use and appreciation of mathematics
IV. Geometry and measurement skills
   a. Knowledge of geometric figures and relations
   b. Measurement knowledge and skills
   c. Use of tables, graphs, and statistical concepts

In this chapter, we place major emphasis on evaluating and diagnosing children's

2. Ralph Hoepfner et al., *CSE Elementary School Test Evaluations* (Los Angeles: Center for the Study of Evaluation, 1976).

achievement within a classroom situation at a particular grade level. The following is a list of some sources of objectives that the classroom teacher should have available.

Goals and Objectives of the National Assessment of Educational Progress, 700 Lincoln Tower, 1800 Lincoln Street, Denver, CO 80203.

Goals and objectives at the state level, in terms of curriculum frameworks in mathematics and statements of various commissions. Information about state-level goals and objectives is given in state Department of Education publications, found in most district administrative offices.

District-level statement of goals and objectives for mathematics. Every district should have a document that lists the goals and objectives in mathematics, usually at each grade level and in terms of priorities.

Grade-level objectives for a particular school. Each school faculty should have an agreed-upon list of major goals and objectives in mathematics at each grade level in the school.

Selecting and Constructing Measurement Instruments

After goals and objectives have been determined, the second step in evaluation is to select and construct measurement instruments.

Methods of Evaluation

Just as there are many different objectives in elementary mathematics, there are many different techniques for assessing outcomes of learning. The most valuable methods are:

I. Standardized, norm-referenced tests
  1. Survey achievement tests
     (a) Group tests
     (b) Individualized tests

2. Mathematics achievement tests
     (a) Readiness
     (b) Diagnostic
     (c) Survey
II. Criterion-reference tests
  1. Standardized
  2. Nonstandardized
III. Tests within an instructional program
  1. Textbook tests
     (a) Readiness, pretests
     (b) Placement tests
     (c) End-of-unit tests
  2. Teacher-made tests
IV. Teacher assessments of how children learn
  1. Observations of daily work
  2. Clinical interviews with the pupils
  3. Demonstrations by the learners
  4. Analysis of daily written work
  5. Approaches to problem-situation activities
V. Affective assessments
  1. Interest inventories
  2. Rating scales and questionnaires
  3. Behavior checklists and sociometric procedures

In *An Agenda for Action* (1980), the National Council of Teachers of Mathematics recommends that "the success of mathematics programs and student learning must be evaluated by a wider range of measures than conventional testing."[3] It must be emphasized that the NCTM's definition of *basic skills* encompasses much more than traditional computational skills. Although test scores are useful in evaluating achievement in mathematics, there are goals that are not adequately measured by conventional tests. For example, the thinking involved in problem solving cannot be evaluated by test scores alone. For the most part, the thinking approaches in problem solving are assessed

3. *An Agenda for Action—Recommendations for School Mathematics for the 1980s* (Reston, VA: National Council of Teachers of Mathematics, 1980), p. 13.

by the classroom teacher by observing how children solve problems, through clinical interviews, and by examining a child's written record of problem-solving activities.

Values of Objective Tests

A teacher's major task is to facilitate learning by each child. Objective tests verify and document that specific knowledge has been acquired and that certain learning objectives have been achieved.

An *objective test* is systematically constructed, administered, and scored such that the judgment of the scorer does not affect the results. Objective tests help to focus attention on selected important learning outcomes and provide a written record of the performance of each pupil. When pupils expect to be tested, their motivation to learn tends to increase. Although it is difficult to construct meaningful objective test questions, objective tests are relatively easy to administer and to score. An analysis of the

Using the Key Math Diagnostic Arithmetic Test to diagnose learning difficulties. *(Photo by Billie Perry)*

results of a test should become a written record of a child's degree of mastery of certain objectives.

As they progress through school, pupils take many different objective tests for a variety of purposes. They need to develop a "test wiseness" in order to score well on objective tests. The tests that are included in the instructional program should provide valuable experiences for learning how to take a test. This experience in turn should help reduce test anxiety, which afflicts many students.

Shortcomings of Objective Tests

Objective tests have many shortcomings. They are sometimes used only to measure memorized responses. Memorization is the lowest level of cognitive functioning. As well, tests can fail to indicate a full understanding of mathematical concepts. When a test score represents the number of correct answers, there is no attention given to the *thought process* that went into finding the answers. One cannot assume from a test score, found merely by counting the number of correct answers, that a child has a full understanding of and a positive attitude toward the material that has been tested.

Values of Teacher Assessments

One of the most important methods of evaluating learning in mathematics occurs as part of the ongoing activity of the class. The teacher who is a good observer, a perceptive listener, and an insightful interviewer will know a great deal about how and what the children are learning.[4]

Selection of Norm-Referenced Standardized Tests

Many excellent standardized tests in elementary mathematics are available for survey purposes. Table 18.1 lists some of the most widely used tests in the United States. Although they are very much alike in outward appearance and content, the tests differ widely in their emphasis on different objectives and on content. For example, Hoepfner[5] studied thirteen nonoverlapping objectives selected for analysis on eight standardized norm-referenced tests, and found that the percentage of items in a test that measured a given objective differed by at least 10 percent from test to test in 68 out of 156 cases.

Characteristics of Norm-Referenced Standardized Tests

A norm-referenced standardized test is primarily concerned with cognitive tasks that can be measured objectively with pencil and paper. Achievement is defined in terms of the number of correct items, translated for comparison purposes into various tables called *norm tables*. The items on a norm-referenced test are selected and arranged systematically in order to rank the pupils from high to low scores. The procedures for administering and scoring the test are uniform. (See page 335.)

VALIDITY

A test is *valid* if it measures accurately what it is designed to measure. There are several methods for determining the validity of the results. One approach is if the results of a test closely match the objectives

---

4. Marilyn N. Suydam, *Evaluation in the Mathematics Classroom, from What and Why to How and Where* (Columbus, OH: ERIC Information Center for Science, Mathematics and Environmental Education, Ohio State University, 1974).

5. R. Hoepfner, "Achievement Test Selection for Program Evaluation." In J. J. Wargo and D. R. Green (Eds.), *Achievement Testing of Disadvantaged and Minority Students for Educational Program Evaluation* (Monterey, CA: CTB/McGraw-Hill, 1978).

of the program, then the results of the test should be considered a valid indication of each pupil's achievement.

Table 18.1 Norm-Referenced Standardized Tests[6]

California Achievement Test, 1978. Grades K–12.

Comprehensive Test of Basic Skills, Form U, 1981, Grades K–12. CTB/McGraw-Hill, Del Monte Research Park, Monterey, CA 93904.

Iowa Test of Basic Skills, 1979. Grades 3–9, multilevel battery. Houghton Mifflin, Test Department, Box 1970, Iowa City, IA 52240.

Key Math Diagnostic Arithmetic Test, 1971; Metric Supplement, 1978. Individualized in test book, continuous by strands.

Peabody Individual Achievement Test, 1970. Individualized in test book, math section continuous K–12. American Guidance Service, Publisher's Building, Circle Pines, MN 55014.

Sequential Test of Educational Progress, III–1979. Grades 4–12. Addison-Wesley Testing Service, 2725 Sand Hill Road, Menlo Park, CA 94025.

SRA Achievement Series, 1978. Grades K–12. Science Research Associates, 155 North Wacker Drive, Chicago, IL 60606.

Metropolitan Achievement Test, 1978. Grades K–12.

Stanford Achievement Test, 1973, Grades 2–9.

Stanford Diagnostic Mathematics Test, 1976. Grades 2–12. Psychological Corporation, 757 Third Avenue, New York, NY 10017.

6. Oscar Krisen Buros, *The Eighth Mental Measurements Yearbook*, Volume I (Highland Park, NJ: Gryphon Press, 1978). An excellent reference for listings, descriptions, and critical reviews of tests in many different subjects, including elementary mathematics.

RELIABILITY

A test is *reliable* if it measures accurately and consistently. In other words, the children get approximately the same scores if measured again. For example, a watch is a reliable timepiece if it measures 60 minutes per hour. It is a valid measure if it gives the correct time. A watch set to give the correct time in the eastern time zone will not give a valid time in another zone. A test can be reliable and not valid, but a valid test must be reliable.

A test is only a sample of a pupil's knowledge of a subject. The true measure would be derived from an unlimited sampling of a subject. Since tests of unlimited sampling are impossible, limited sampling is used. The test scores are corrected for *error of measurement*. Statistical procedures beyond the scope of this text are used to correct such errors.

EASE OF ADMINISTRATION AND SCORING

The test should have clear directions for administering and scoring. This is the case for most tests, which are constructed for machine scoring by a computer. The computer will do a complete detailed analysis of the test results for each pupil.

NORMS

To establish norms for a given test, standardized tests are given to a large sample of pupils of the same chronological age or grade level. A norm can be expressed in different ways: as a mean, median, grade equivalent, or percentile rank.

The *mean* is another name for the arithmetic average. The sum of the raw scores on a test divided by the number of scores is the mean.

The *median* is the middle number, or the mean of two middle numbers, of a set of numbers arranged in order of size.

The *grade equivalent* is the most frequently used statistic derived from a norm-reference test. For children who score within the "average range," the grade-equivalent derived score is fairly accurate and useful in determining the general performance expected for each pupil in the typical mathematics program. Grade equivalents that are two years or more above or below grade level are subject to gross misinterpretation.

A grade-equivalent score on a standardized test should not be used as an indicator of mastery of the subject matter at a particular grade level. For example, if a second-grade pupil scores at the 4.0 grade level in mathematics, this does not mean that he or she has mastered average fourth-grade work. The pupil has scored well above average second-graders in mathematics, but if he or she were given a test designed for fourth-graders, it is very unlikely that he or she would score equal to 4.0 grade equivalent. Consequently, grade equivalents are not appropriate for placing children in the grade levels that match their scores. Many other factors must be considered before a child is placed in a grade level with children a year or more older or younger.[7]

Another frequently used score derived from a standardized test is *percentile rank*. Again, percentile is a statistical, but relatively simple, concept. The raw scores of a particular group of children who take the same test at the same time under similar conditions can be arranged from highest to lowest and percentile ranks calculated. By percentile rank, we mean that for a particular score the percentile equivalent represents the percent of children who took the test that scored at or below that point. Percentiles range from 1 to 99. A percentile rank of 50th means that 50 percent of the children scored at or below the score associated with this ranking. A raw score of 62

may assign a pupil to the 50th percentile. There may be 15 pupils who have the same score.

Nonstandardized Objective Tests

Nonstandardized objective tests are used by teachers and school administrators for a variety of purposes. They can be used for both summative and formative evaluation. In summative evaluation, pupils' scores are ranked from highest to lowest, and various statistics are used to describe the relative position of a child in terms of the mean, median, standard deviation, quarters of the distribution, and so on. Summative evaluation provides information about the top, middle, and lowest students at a particular grade level. Standardized tests are more reliable and valid for this purpose than other kinds of nonstandardized assessments.

If a nonstandardized objective test is used for formative evaluation, the results should indicate what children have learned in each unit of the instructional program. The results of a nonstandardized objective test should indicate the extent to which each pupil has mastered the specific learning objectives.

The most frequently used type of teacher-made test in mathematics is one in which pupils are given a series of examples to work, problems to solve, and/or exercises to complete. Pupils are asked to show their work and circle their answers. The teacher not only counts the correct answers, but also tries to determine why the pupils obtained incorrect answers. Tests of this type are valuable as daily, weekly, and/or monthly quizzes. They are closely related to the instructional program and provide both the pupil and the teacher with evidence of the pupil's achievement on topics currently being studied.

In addition to the types of exercises we have mentioned, the most widely used types of items for nonstandardized objective

---

7. See the *Test Coordinator's Handbook, Forms C and D, California Achievement Tests* (Monterey, CA: CTB/McGraw-Hill, 1978), p. 53.

tests are: (a) simple recall, (b) multiple-choice, (c) alternate response, and (d) matching. In the next sections, we present a sample of each type of test, with directions for the pupil. For summative evaluation of these items, the number of correct answers would be needed. For formative evaluation, an item-by-item analysis of rights and wrongs for each pupil would be needed.

SIMPLE RECALL ITEMS

To complete simple recall items, the pupil is instructed to write the correct answer in the blank. The pupil's score is the number of correct answers. Here are some simple recall items on the topic of place value.

1. The total value of the 2 in 325 is _____.

2. The cardinal value of the 4 in 347 is _____.

3. The digit that names the number of greatest value in the numeral 149 is _____.

4. The value of the place two places to the left of the ones place is _____.

For ease of scoring, you can have pupils record their answers in a space to the left of each item or on a separate answer sheet. The answers to the above items are 20, 4, 1, and 100, respectively.

MULTIPLE-CHOICE ITEMS

Multiple-choice items are used most often on standardized tests. Although these questions are difficult to write, they are relatively easy to score. The pupils should be instructed to write the letter of the answer that makes the statement true. The score for each pupil is the number of correct answers. Here are some multiple-choice items on the topic of fractions.

_____ **1.** The fraction ⅔ can be renamed:
(a) ⁴⁄₉   (b) ³⁄₂   (c) ⁹⁄₁₂   (d) ¹²⁄₁₈

_____ **2.** The fraction ¾ can be renamed:
(a) $\dfrac{3 + 1}{4 + 1}$ (b) $\dfrac{3 - 1}{4 - 1}$

(c) $\dfrac{3 \times 2}{4 \times 2}$ (d) $\dfrac{3 \times 3}{4 \times 4}$

_____ **3.** The sum of ½ + ⅓ is:
(a) ⅚   (b) ⅕   (c) ⅖   (d) ⅙

_____ **4.** To divide a fraction by 2:
(a) divide the denominator by 2.
(b) divide both the numerator and denominator by 2.
(c) multiply the denominator by 2.
(d) multiply either the numerator or the denominator by 2.

The answers to the above items are d, c, a, c, respectively.

ALTERNATE-CHOICE ITEMS

To answer alternate-choice items, the pupil must select one of two responses (a) or (b), mark a statement as true (T) or false (O), or answer a question either yes or no. The pupil should be instructed to fill in the blank with a T if a statement is true or an O if a statement is false. Here are some alternate-choice items on the topic of basic operations.

_____ **1.** Addition and subtraction are opposite operations.

_____ **2.** Multiplication will "undo" addition.

_____ **3.** The commutative property holds for both addition and subtraction.

_____ **4.** The sum of zero and a number is that number.

The answers to the above items are T, O, O, T.

Since there is a 50 percent chance that a pupil will answer an alternate-choice item correctly, we recommend a correction for guessing. For quick hand scoring of a true/false test, circle each wrong answer and mark each omission with a dash. Do not mark the correct answers. A pupil's score is the total number of items *attempted*, minus twice the number of items missed. To find the number of items attempted, subtract the number of omissions from the total number of questions on the test. A pupil's score (S) equals the total number attempted (T) minus twice the number of wrong items $(2W)$:

$$S = T - 2W.$$

MATCHING TESTS

A matching test consists of a list of five to ten statements in a left-hand column and a corresponding list of possible answers in a right-hand column. Usually, the right-hand column contains one or two more items than the left-hand column. The pupil is instructed to fill in the blank with the letter from column II that matches the statement (or question) in column I. The score is the number of correct matchings. Here is a sample matching test on the topic of number properties.

I

_____ 1. Associative property
_____ 2. Commutative property
_____ 3. Distributive property
_____ 4. Identity element for addition
_____ 5. Identity element for multiplication

II

(a) $2 \times 3 = 3 \times 2$
(b) $2 (3 + 4) = (2 \times 3) \times (2 \times 4)$
(c) $(3 + 2) + 4 = 3 + (2 + 4)$
(d) one
(e) $3 \times (2 + 4) = (3 \times 2) + 4$
(f) zero
(g) $2 (1 + w) = (2 \times 1) + (2 \times w)$

The answers to the above matching test are as follows: c, a, g, f, and d, respectively.

Sources of Test Items

There are several sources of test items in mathematics. In addition to items contained in standardized and criterion-reference tests, almost every textbook series in elementary mathematics now includes several different

Table 18.2 Criterion-Referenced Tests*

Analysis of Skills, 1974.
Seven levels, grades 1–8, with 44–58 objectives per level and three multiple-choice items per objective. Scholastic Testing Service, 480 Meyer Road, Bensenville, IL 60106

Diagnosis: An Instructional Aid in Mathematics, 1973.
Two levels, grades 1–6, with a survey test plus a series of diagnostic probe tests for each level. All items are multiple choice. Science Research Associates, 259 East Erie Street, Chicago, IL 60611

Diagnostic Mathematics Inventory, 1975.
Seven levels, grades 1.5–7.5 with 37–179 multiple-choice items per level and 5–10 items per objective. CTB/McGraw Hill, Del Monte Research Park, Monterey, CA 93940

Individual Pupil Monitoring System, 1974.
Eight levels, grades 1–8, with three assessment modules and 48–64 objectives per level and 5–10 items per objective. Houghton Mifflin, 777 California Avenue, Palo Alto, CA 94304

Mastery: An Evaluation Tool in Mathematics, 1975.
Nine levels, K–8, with 15–40 objectives per level, and three multiple-choice items per objective. Science Research Associates, 259 East Erie Street, Chicago, IL 60611

Tests of Achievement in Basic Skills, 1974.
Seven levels, survey tests, K–12, with one item per objective grouped in clusters. Educational Industrial Testing Service, P.O. Box 7234, San Diego, CA 92107

---

*For an evaluation of criterion-referenced tests, see Clinton B. Walker, *CSE Criterion-Referenced Test Handbook* (Los Angeles: Center for the Study of Evaluation, University of California, 1979).

kinds of test items. Table 18.2 presents a list of selected criterion-reference tests, with the publisher from whom they can be obtained.

Assessing Attitudes toward Mathematics

In Chapter 2, we stated that one of the major objectives of elementary school education is behavioristic. One part of the behavioristic objective is the pupil's attitude toward the subject. A favorable attitude toward aspects of mathematics cannot be measured directly, but can be inferred from a variety of observational techniques, which show that the pupil:

1. willingly participates in learning activities.

2. enjoys working with mathematics.

3. is interested in learning.

4. appreciates the value of mathematics for future study and for activities outside of school.

The most common way of measuring attitudes toward mathematics has been to use some type of questionnaire. The attitudes of pupils in the primary grades can be measured best by observational techniques and personal interviews. If a written response from each child is needed, you can read the questions to the pupils and have them mark, on the form with "faces," the face that best describes their answers (p. 340). Pupils in the upper grades can use a checklist such as that shown in Table 18.3. Attitude scales are relatively easy to create and administer, but are difficult to interpret.

Table 18.3 Inventory of Attitudes toward Mathematics

Directions: Put a checkmark in the column that best describes your answer for each statement below.

Attitude	Always	Sometimes	Never
I like mathematics.			
I enjoy working problems and puzzles in mathematics.			
I think mathematics is useful.			
I make good grades in mathematics.			
I want to continue my study in mathematics			
I complete mathematics assignments on time.			
I use mathematics outside of school.			
I work hard in mathematics.			
I find mathematics easy.			
I do well on tests on mathematics.			

Note: Score "Always" 3 points, "Sometimes" 2 points, and "Never" 1 point. Maximum score is 30, minimum score is 10.

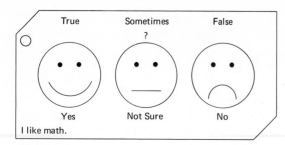

Two major difficulties of using a test to measure attitudes is the reliability and validity of the instrument. It is difficult to judge the extent to which a score on an attitude scale is a true picture of a pupil's attitude toward mathematics.

Kulm[8] has reviewed the many research studies that have dealt with various aspects of attitude toward mathematics. Generally, research has shown that there is a positive relationship between attitude and achievement in mathematics. This does not mean that one has been shown to *cause* the other, but rather that they tend to go together. So when a child's attitude or achievement improves, this does not necessarily mean that the other will improve as a result. Both are important outcomes in mathematics education.

Diagnosis Using a Continuum

There are four phases to diagnosis:

1. Determining what children are expected to understand, be able to do, and how they feel about mathematics.

2. Collecting data about the child's attitudes and interests, and the extent to which he or she performs identified tasks, and demonstrates understanding.

3. Analyzing the data to determine specific weaknesses and the probable causes of deficiencies.

4. Setting in motion appropriate prescriptions for improved learning.

One way to carry out diagnosis is to use a *mathematics continuum* for each level of instruction. The mathematics continuum should be created at the local school level by teachers at each grade level following these steps:

1. Record all the achievements expected in terms of behavioral objectives.
   a. Identify items that should have been mastered.
   b. Determine what knowledge is essential to the instructional program.
   c. Specify objectives that will provide readiness experiences for the next level of instruction.
2. Group objectives into categories such as
   a. Concepts (understanding desired).
   b. Operations (skills developed).
   c. Measurement/applications/problem solving.
3. Prepare a record sheet listing objectives in the left-hand column and leaving space for recording observations on the right.[9]
4. For each child, use information from a variety of sources to code performances in terms of level of achievement.
   a. Performs at the readiness stage. (R)
   b. In the development level, ready for directed instruction. (D)
   c. Has mastered the objective and needs reinforcement and enrichment. (M)
5. Analyze data for all students and set up the instructional program to meet the needs of the children.

---

8. Gerald Kulm, "Research on Mathematics Attitude." In *Research in Mathmatics Education* (Reston, VA: National Council of Teachers of Mathematics, 1980), Chapter 12, pp. 356–387.

9. See Bob Underhill et al., *Diagnosing Mathematical Difficulties* (Columbus, OH: Charles E. Merrill, 1980), Appendix B—Task Model Checklist, pp. 271–297.

Diagnostic Techniques

The techniques one should use to diagnose difficulties in learning elementary school mathematics depend on the kind of diagnosis to be made. There are three levels of diagnosis: general diagnosis, analytical diagnosis, and case study procedures.

General Diagnosis

General diagnosis implies the use of systematic and comprehensive tests and other types of evaluation procedures. The results of standarized tests are the most efficient means of measuring pupils' general level of achievement. To be of maximum value, the tests should be administered early in the school year.

When standardized achievement tests are not available, informal inventory tests of the work done in previous grades should be administered early in the year. These tests are available in most mathematics textbooks, or can be prepared by individual teachers. The inventory test can be constructed so that a quick analysis of total scores and those for each section of the test will not only give a fairly satisfactory measure of the individual pupil's general level of ability but will also indicate to both teacher and pupil the areas in which the pupil is strong and those in which carefully planned review, even reteaching, may be necessary.

Analytical Diagnosis

Analytical diagnosis is designed to identify a pupil's specific weakness in mathematics achievement. The results of a survey test will show how a pupil's achievement compares with the norm for his or her age group. A low score on a survey test does not indicate the specific phase or cause of the low achievement. Analytical diagnostic tests are used for this purpose.

A survey test covers a wide range of subject matter in a given area, such as multiplication of whole numbers or fractional numbers. There is only a limited sampling of specific types of examples. On the other hand, a diagnostic test deals with a small segment of subject matter with intensive sampling of a given topic. This feature of the test enables one to reliably diagnose the point at which the pupil has difficulty with a topic.

Sample of a Diagnostic Test

A diagnostic test in addition of fractions should contain subunits, such as a unit dealing with fractions expressed with like denominators, with unlike denominators when one is a common denominator, and with unlike denominators when a common denominator is not given.

The subunit of a diagnostic test, on page 342, in addition of fractions covers unlike but related denominators. The three examples in each set contain the same difficulty. In order to make a reliable diagnosis one would need at least three samples of the same difficulty so as to distinguish between a *chance* error and a *constant* error. A chance error occurs at random and is not repeated in a similar number situation. A constant, or systematic, error recurs in similar number situations because the pupil has faulty or limited knowledge of the number involved. If only one of the responses to the three similar examples is incorrect, the error is due to chance. If at least two of the three responses are incorrect, the error is systematic.

The test can be expanded to include examples involving mixed fractions, in order to sample all the types of examples involving adding fractions with unlike but related denominators. If a pupil gets at least two examples incorrect within a set, the new step in the solution is the source of the difficulty. The teacher is now able to apply the correct remedial measures, which enable the pupil to deal with that particular type of fraction example.

Diagnostic Test in Addition of Fractions

(Denominators are unlike but related)

I.	$\dfrac{1}{2}$	$\dfrac{1}{4}$	$\dfrac{2}{5}$	The sum is in the simplest form.
	$\dfrac{1}{4}$	$\dfrac{3}{8}$	$\dfrac{3}{10}$	

II.	$\dfrac{7}{8}$	$\dfrac{5}{6}$	$\dfrac{3}{4}$	Same as Set I except the sum is greater than 1.
	$\dfrac{1}{2}$	$\dfrac{1}{3}$	$\dfrac{1}{2}$	

III.	$\dfrac{1}{3}$	$\dfrac{1}{2}$	$\dfrac{1}{5}$	The sum must be renamed to be in the simplest form.
	$\dfrac{1}{6}$	$\dfrac{1}{6}$	$\dfrac{3}{10}$	

IV.	$\dfrac{1}{2}$	$\dfrac{7}{10}$	$\dfrac{5}{6}$	Same as Set III except the sum is greater than 1.
	$\dfrac{5}{6}$	$\dfrac{1}{2}$	$\dfrac{2}{3}$	

Effective diagnosis requires assessments of various subskills within a particular operation. For example, to determine the extent to which children have mastered division by one-place divisors, one would need a test consisting of several examples of this type. If a student solved most of the examples correctly with reasonable speed, it could be assumed that he or she can also deal effectively with all the subskills involved. On the other hand, if a student misses several examples, then one would need to administer a diagnostic test made up of the subskills of division by a one-place divisor.

So many skills are involved in division by a one-place divisor that it is difficult to find a reliable diagnostic test to point out the source of most errors in the operation. The errors made with a one-place divisor stem from a deficiency in one or more of the following abilities:

1. Identification of the number of places in the quotient

2. Knowledge of division facts

3. Knowledge of multiplication facts

4. Renaming in subtraction

5. Repeating the operation (bringing down the next dividend digit)

A pupil should be able to estimate that the quotient of $3\overline{)452}$ will be a three-place number. He or she should have no difficulty in dealing with the zero in the quotient. The most frequent incorrect answer to the example is 15 r 2.

The teacher should give an example with a divisor ranging from 6 to 9 to sample a pupil's ability to deal with other knowledge needed for division by a one-place divisor. Consider the example $8\overline{)543}$. The solution involves renaming in subtraction, a difficult fact in both division and multiplication, and a repetition of the procedure after bringing down the digit in the ones place in the dividend.

A diagnostic test must have in-depth sampling of a given skill. For division by a one-place divisor, such a test should include a good sampling of both division and multiplication facts, as well as a sampling of renaming in subtraction with a final remainder, and several examples. An analysis of the child's work, along with an interview, should effectively locate various difficulties that need to be remediated. Success in dividing by one-place divisors depends largely on proficiency in the required subskills. If a child is not proficient in working examples of this type, he or she cannot be expected to solve problems that involve division.

Case Study Procedures

Case study procedures apply diagnostic techniques that enable you to analyze in detail the performance or achievement of a pupil having learning difficulties. These procedures are clinical, and are best adapted to the study of the work of individual pupils or groups of pupils. Case study diagnosis of learning difficulties in elementary school mathematics includes the following procedures:

1. Analysis of written work to discover faulty responses, such as:

a. Numerals written incorrectly, such as reversal in the primary grades.

b. Types of examples worked incorrectly.[10]

c. Nature of computational errors made in tests and in regular daily written work.

2. Analysis of oral statements:

a. Faulty thought processes are revealed by having each pupil "say aloud" the steps in working difficult examples or problems.

b. Reading difficulties are revealed by having each pupil read the problem aloud.

c. Faulty thinking is revealed by having each pupil tell how he or she would solve a problem.

3. Personal interview to secure information by asking the pupils:

a. About their thought processes in working an example.

b. To test their understanding of a number operation.

c. About methods of solving a problem.

d. About interests, attitudes, and methods of work.

10. Robert B. Ashlock, *Error Patterns in Computation,* Second Edition (Columbus, OH: Charles E. Merrill, 1976).

4. Questionnaires and inquiry blanks:

a. Securing interest ratings of topics in mathematics.

b. Reports from classmates, parents, and teachers.

c. Study habits and methods of work.

5. Observation in the course of daily work provides evidence of:

a. The use of counting and other inefficient methods.

b. Rate of work.

c. Study habits; use of reference books.

d. Factors affecting performance, such as health and vision.

e. Methods of using a measuring device.

6. Analysis of available records:

a. Anecdotal records.

b. School cumulative records.

7. Administration of diagnostic tests given in textbooks or workbooks or prepared by the teacher.

Interpreting the Results of Appraisal

The interpretation of evaluation data should be done with caution, even when standardized procedures are used and when agreed-upon norms and standards are available. In the absence of standards, as in the case of informal procedures, special care must be taken in interpreting the results. You must take into consideration the background and experience of the pupils when you interpret the scores made on standardized tests.

Three groups that should be involved in interpreting the results of survey tests in elementary school mathematics:

1. The superintendent and the central staff.

2. Staffs of individual schools and consultants.

3. Individual teachers with principal or consultant.

Superintendent and Central Staff

The analysis of survey tests for the superintendent of schools and central staff should include:

1. Analysis of district-wide results grade by grade, compared with expected performance.

2. Comparison with results of previous years.

3. Consideration of the consolidated distributions of class results.

4. Overview of results for various schools.

5. Consideration of possible causes of variations in results among the different schools.

6. Planning next steps for improving the educational program.

School Staffs

The analysis of test scores for staffs of individual schools should include:

1. Comparison of overall results for the school with district-wide scores and with standard scores at various grade levels.

2. General trends or progress from grade to grade, compared with results for previous years.

3. The deviation of each grade and class from expected levels of achievement in relation to the ability of the children, their social backgrounds, and health.

4. Consistency of levels of achievement in the various areas tested.

5. The range of test results for each area within individual classes.

6. The overlapping of test scores at consecutive grade levels.

7. Identifying strengths and weaknesses of the school's program on the basis of the test results.

8. Considering possible next steps.

Individual Teachers

The analysis of test scores for individual teachers in cooperation with principal or consultant should include:

1. Overview of the results for the class as a whole; sharing the information with the pupils.

2. Analysis of the progress made by individual pupils, based on comparison with previous tests, preferably summarized in graphic profile form.

3. Critical comparison of educational levels achieved in relation to the mental ability of individuals.

4. Consideration of factors that might shed light on variations in individual achievement and deviations from levels of expectancy.

5. Consideration of discrepancies between test results for individual pupils and teacher's estimates.

6. Analysis of the test items that have possible diagnostic value.

7. Planning ways to use the data more effectively in the public relations program.

Evaluating the Instructional Program

There are three aspects of an instructional program that should be evaluated as part of a comprehensive appraisal program:

1. The curriculum.

2. Methods of classroom instruction.

3. Materials and equipment available.

The Curriculum

The curriculum should be evaluated according to criteria that grow out of group discussion and study of modern trends in elementary mathematics. Some of the questions or topics to be considered in evaluating the curriculum are:

1. Are the objectives well defined?

2. Is the subject matter well organized?

3. Does the content agree with modern elementary school mathematics?

4. Are the standards of achievement flexible?

5. Is the material so constructed as to provide for individual differences?

6. Is the curriculum restricted to the textbook, or are the resources of the community explored?

Classroom Instruction

The evaluation of methods of teaching used in classrooms should be a cooperative undertaking in which teachers take an active part. Criteria such as the following should be set up cooperatively by the group and applied in appraising instruction:

1. Procedures should be used that will make number and number operations meaningful to the children, with emphasis on understanding structure and problem solving.

2. The procedures should stress the understanding of number and efficiency in quantitative thinking.

3. The work in elementary mathematics should be associated with the activities of the entire school day, not just with a particular class period.

4. Instruction should provide adequate time in school for the systematic practice needed to develop competence and skill in the use of number and quantitative procedures.

5. The discovery method should hold a dominant place in the instructional program.

6. The instruction should allow for differences in rate and capacity to learn by recognizing the exploratory, symbolic, and mastery levels of maturity.

7. There should be a continuous program of evaluating learning that informs the child, teacher, and parents about the individual's growth in mathematics.

Materials

The adequacy of instructional materials can be evaluated by applying the following criteria:

1. Manipulative and exploratory materials, objects, and visual aids can make mathematical concepts meaningful to children.

2. Supplementary reading materials can be used to explore and extend the vocabulary and background of mathematics.

3. A mathematics laboratory equipped with many types of materials serves a twofold purpose:

    a. To arouse interest in mathematics.

    b. To provide for individual differences in achievement.

4. Scientific testing and practice materials can be used to measure and maintain the basic skills in the program.

You may find that the instructional materials and equipment are fully adequate to meet the needs of a learning laboratory as described in Chapters 3 and 5. Or you may feel the quality and variety of what is available are severely limited.

Sometimes, limited supplementary material and few visual aids are available, and little use is made of places of business, museums, libraries, and other civic centers to enrich and broaden learning. These situations arise partly because these agencies may be indifferent, even unwilling, to permit the schools to use them, and partly because the school has not integrated them into learning experiences.

Improving the Mathematics Program

After the existing program has been evaluated and points of weakness have been identified, the task is to institute an improvement program. Through group discussion, you should select a particular phase of the program for improvement, such as the ability to write number sentences for verbal problems. The improvement program should be flexible and adapted to the needs of particular classes or groups. The program may involve a number of techniques such as:

1. A series of study groups made up of administrators, teachers, and perhaps parents.

2. Special teachers' meetings on improving mathematics instruction.

3. Bulletins, idea sheets, and study guides developed by teachers.

4. Study groups to examine student interests, attitudes, problems, and needs.

5. Visit to other schools, attendance at conferences, and enrollment in university courses in mathematics education.

6. Committees to examine new textbooks and instructional materials.

7. Study groups to organize a resource file of current tests in mathematics education.

8. An evaluation committee to analyze information collected from tests, scales, and inventories and to suggest improvements.

One major technological advancement that will lead to improved testing procedures is a computerized system of grading tests and reporting results. Many school districts have installed computer terminals with automatic test-scoring systems that, in a matter of minutes, can process a set of test papers and provide, for each pupil, a detailed analysis of strengths, weaknesses, and suggested remediation.[11]

The need for good evaluation and diagnosis in the elementary mathematics program is paramount. The frequency with which tests are used as part of the evaluation process is likely to increase during the 1980s. There will be a continued effort not only to improve testing, but also to make better uses of test data for improvement of instruction. As Ebel has said, "Critics who urge that testing be limited or abandoned advise our schools and society badly. . . . Educators should work to improve, not to destroy testing."[12]

Clearly, schools will move toward more competency testing at more grade levels and educators will begin to use the scores to make promotion or nonpromotion decisions. As a result, teachers will need to exert a great deal of leadership to make sure that there is more to evaluation than testing and that a decision about a child's future rests on more than a test score.

Summary

The major purpose of evaluation and diagnosis is to improve instruction. Evaluation can be summative or formative. Summative evaluation describes a pupil's overall performance, such as with a grade on a unit of work or in a course. Formative evaluation indicates the extent to which each pupil has achieved specific learning objectives.

The stages in the evaluation process include: (1) establishing goals and objectives, (2) selecting and/or constructing assessment instruments, (3) securing a record of achievement, and (4) interpreting assessment results.

Standardized tests can be norm-reference or criterion-reference. Norm-reference tests are designed to rank-order pupils' achieve-

11. John W. Noble, "Computerized Testing: More Learning for Less Drudgery," *Phi Delta Kappan*, March 1980, 61:485–486.

12. Robert L. Ebel, "Using Tests to Improve Learning," *Arithmetic Teacher*, November 1969, 27:12.

ment. Criterion-reference tests determine the pupils' mastery of various learning objectives.

Tests used to measure achievement must be valid, or represent accurately the pupils' true performance. Tests also must be reliable, meaning that they need to measure concepts and skills consistently.

The test that is the most useful and frequently used in elementary mathematics is that which is an integral part of the day-to-day instructional program. Teacher-made tests provide valuable information on how well each pupil is learning mathematics. They also provide diagnostic data that can assist the teacher in planning for proper re-

mediation, as well as appropriate enrichment.

Diagnosis involves four components: (a) setting individual learning objectives, (b) assessing the child's status in terms of the objectives, (c) analyzing the child's strengths and weaknesses, and (d) providing appropriate remediation and/or enrichment. An effective teacher diagnoses pupil progress daily and suggests to each child, in individual conferences, ways to improve performance.

When interpreted properly, evaluation data should lead to improvements in the mathematics curriculum, methods of teaching, and materials available.

Exercises

1. What are several purposes for evaluating mathematics achievement in the elementary school?

2. Explain the difference between summative and formative evaluation. Under what conditions should each be used?

3. Why is it necessary to establish a set of accepted objectives in mathematics as a first step in evaluation?

4. What are the values and limitations of norm-reference standardized tests? of criterion-reference tests?

5. Examine the types of tests that are included in a mathematics textbook. Evaluate the tests.

6. Identify several ways a teacher can assess a pupil's ability to solve word problems in mathematics.

7. Why may the results of a standardized test for a given school be considerably above or below the norm published by the testing company?

8. How could the fact that a pupil operates at the exploratory level affect his or her score on a standardized test?

9. Explain the difference between evaluation and testing. What is the teacher's role in each?

10. Explain the difference between testing and diagnosing. What is the teacher's role in each?

11. Give an illustration of general diagnosis, analytical diagnosis, and case study procedures.

12. Obtain the results of a mathematics test for some class. Analyze the errors and indicate the type of remedial measures you would apply.

13. Evaluate a widely used standardized test in elementary school mathematics, as reported in the *Eighth Mental Measurements Yearbook, Volume I* (Highland Park, NJ: Gryphon Press, 1978).

Selected Readings

Anderson, Lorin W. *Assessing Affective Characteristics in the Schools.* Boston; Allyn and Bacon, 1981.

Fennell, Francis M. *Elementary Mathematics Diagnosis and Correction Kit.* West Nyack, NY: Center for Applied Research in Education, 1981.

Gronlund, Norman E. *Measurement and Evaluation in Teaching,* Fourth Edition. New York: Macmillan, 1981.

Hopkins, Charles D., and Richard L. Antes. *Classroom Testing—Construction.* Itasca, IL: F. E. Peacock, 1979.

Hopkins, Kenneth D., and Julian C. Stanley. *Educational and Psychological Measurement and Evaluation.* Englewood Cliffs, NJ: Prentice-Hall, 1981.

Mehrens, William A., and Irvin J. Lehmann. *Standardized Tests in Education,* Third Edition. New York: Holt, Rinehart and Winston, 1978.

Reisman, Fredricka K. *Diagnostic Teaching of Elementary School Mathematics.* Chicago: Rand McNally, 1977.

Suydam, Marilyn N. *Evaluation in the Mathematics Classroom.* Columbus, OH: ERIC Science, Mathematics and Environmental Education Clearinghouse, January 1974.

Tyler, Ralph W., and Richard M. Wolf (Eds). *Crucial Issues in Testing.* 1973 Yearbook of the National Society for the Study of Education. Berkeley, CA: McCutchan, 1973.

Underhill, Bob, Ed Uprichard, and Jim Heddens. *Diagnosing Mathematical Difficulties.* Columbus, OH: Charles E. Merrill, 1980.

Chapter 19

Accommodating Individual Differences

Pupils on the same grade level are alike in many ways. They are about the same age, dress alike, watch the same television programs, and have similar interests and behavior patterns. There are, however, some significant differences. Children vary in intellectual, emotional, and social maturity; in language fluency and physical appearance, as well as family background, motivation and so on. Every effort should be made to adjust the instructional program to take account of these differences and encourage all pupils to maximize their potential and achieve optimum learning.

One of the greatest challenges a teacher faces is the complex task of working with and accommodating differences among individual pupils in the classroom.

Achievement Goals

After studying this chapter, you should be able to:

1. Summarize the many ways that children at the same grade level can differ from one another.
2. Discuss several techniques to deal with individual differences within the self-contained classroom.

3. Describe the features of individualized, self-paced learning and the ungraded approach to dealing with individual differences.
4. Identify the characteristics of slow learners and rapid learners.
5. Suggest ways to provide instruction that is appropriate for slow learners and rapid learners.
6. Explain the differences between horizontal and vertical enrichment and how each can be used effectively to adjust for individual differences.

Vocabulary

Mastery of the following key terms will help you to understand this chapter. Each term is defined or illustrated in the Glossary at the back of the book.

Academic acceleration	Horizontal enrichment
Correlation	Individualized instruction
Heterogeneous class	Ungraded class
Homogeneous class	Vertical enrichment

349

How Children Differ

Children differ from one another in many ways. Some of these differences fall within the normal range, and so no special adjustments in the instructional program are needed. On the other hand, other differences are so pronounced that provisions must be made in order for optimum learning to take place.

According to recent estimates, at least 20 percent of the pupils in a typical classroom deviate so much from the norm that drastic measures must be taken to create successful educational experiences and appropriate personal–social development.[1]

Intellectual Differences

Children differ in levels of intellectual functioning. The intellectual capacity of children has traditionally been measured using an IQ (Intelligence Quotient) test. The IQ of a 5-year-old child who has a mental age of 6, as measured by the test, would be $(6 \div 5) \times 100 = 120$, or stated in general terms, 100 times the quotient of mental age divided by the chronological age. According to the Wechsler Intelligence Scales for children, approximately 16 percent of elementary school children have IQs of 115 or higher and are classified as rapid learners. Less than 3 percent have IQs of 130 or more and are classified as gifted. Approximately 16 percent have IQs of 85 or less and are classified as slow learners.

The validity of the IQ test is the subject of continuing intense debate, and some critics claim that the test discriminates against children from lower socioeconomic backgrounds. At best, the test measures only one dimension of a child's ability.[2]

Achievement Differences

One obvious way to see how children differ is to examine the results of a standardized achievement test in mathematics.

In one self-contained fifth-grade class, there may be children who score all the way from the second-grade level to the seventh-grade level. The achievement level is a function of the pupil's rate of learning. Pupils in the top quarter of the norm group are among the rapid learners in mathematics, whereas the pupils who score in the lowest quarter are among the slow learners. The middle 50 percent are relatively homogeneous in their abilities to achieve in mathematics. The pupils in a class who have about the same IQ are considered to be homogeneous for that trait. If IQ is not considered a factor in selecting a class, then the pupils are considered to be heterogeneous for that trait.

Different Family Environments

Children come from very different home environments. Children from affluent homes who have well-educated parents usually come to school with a rich background of experiences and tend to be average or rapid learners. In contrast, children of parents who are economically poor and uneducated usually tend to be slow learners.

The home also influences the child's attitudes toward mathematics. Research has shown a positive correlation between the child's attitude toward mathematics and the

1. William I. Gardner, *Learning and Behavior Characteristics of Exceptional Children and Youth* (Boston: Allyn and Bacon, 1977), p. 3.

2. Julian C. Stanley, "The Study and Facilitation of Talent for Mathematics," in *The Gifted and the Talented*, 78th Yearbook of the National Society of the Study of Education (Chicago: University of Chicago Press, 1979), pp. 169–171.

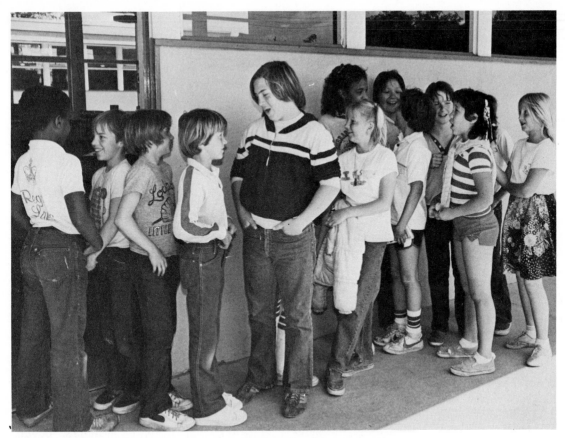

Physical differences within a group of fifth-grade pupils. *(Photo by Leland Perry)*

parents' attitude toward this subject. Wilhelm and Brooks found that mothers have considerable influence on their daughters' anxiety about mathematics, and fathers influence their sons' attitudes. The mother influences both the son and daughter's self-concept.[3]

Cultural and Ethnic Backgrounds

Children also differ in their cultural and ethnic backgrounds. Motivation to learn varies from culture to culture, as do children's interests and the value placed on educational achievement.

Educational Factors

Educational factors influence levels of academic achievement. Children who have progressed through an effective, meaningful, sequential mathematics program such as that advocated here, tend to be average and rapid learners. Pupils who have experienced a minimum, drill-type program limited to learning computational techniques and memorizing basic facts usually have difficulty at the upper levels of elementary mathematics.

3. Sharon Wilhelm and Douglas M. Brooks, "The Relationship between Pupil Attitudes toward Mathematics and Parental Attitudes toward Mathematics," *Educational Research Quarterly*, Summer 1980, 5:14–15.

Dealing with Individual Differences within the Self-Contained Classroom

There are a variety of ways to adjust for individual differences within a typical self-contained classroom in elementary mathematics. Two easily administered approaches are varying the difficulty of the subject matter, and varying the level of maturity of operation.

Pupils of average ability will be able to complete the adopted textbook. Slow learners cannot be expected to master all the topics treated in a regular program, whereas fast learners need in-depth enrichment of the subject matter in such areas as problem solving.

One of the most effective ways to adjust for individual differences in a heterogeneous class is to vary the amount of time pupils operate at different levels of maturity. The slow learners operate at the exploratory level with concrete materials, while the fast learners operate at the mastery level. Most of the pupils participate in appropriate learning experiences at the symbolic level.

There are two advantages to having students operate at different levels of maturity. First, the program is relatively easy to administer. All the pupils start each unit of the mathematics program together, as a group. Introductory exploratory experiences are provided to all children. The teacher divides the class into subgroups, based on the particular needs of each child. The groupings are kept flexible so if a pupil in the exploratory group working with concrete materials moves to the stage of working with numerals and symbols, he or she then joins the subgroup that operates at the symbolic level. In the same way, a pupil can advance or fall back to the next higher or lower subgroup.

The second advantage of having pupils operate at different levels of maturity is its effectiveness within the framework of class organization. The conventional curriculum is geared to the pupil of average ability. Most mathematics textbooks include a series of ten or more units or chapters to be completed in blocks of two or three weeks each during the school year. The time is constant for each unit, and the variables are the subject matter and the degree of mastery. Average pupils devote some time to exploratory activities. Laboratory materials are useful for all children, but some pupils need to spend more time with them than others. All children at the symbolic level need some systematic instruction by the teacher.

The most able pupils need fewer exploratory experiences. They can easily grasp structural aspects of various topics at the symbolic level.

The slow learners spend much of their time in each unit at the exploratory level. They are able to progress to the simple aspects of the symbolic level during the time spent on each unit. These children generally need reinforcement and practice with additional learning experiences beyond those covered in the normal class period.

Children learning mathematics will have different needs at different times. You should consider making the following adjustments for individuals and for groups.

1. *Vary the time.* Some pupils may need extra time to complete the following activities:
   a. Work with laboratory materials.
   b. Practice on basic facts and computational exercises.
   c. A learning-center task.
   d. Work on a measurement project.
   e. A problem-solving assignment.
2. *Vary the space.* Not every pupil can learn mathematics successfully out of a book and by just watching the teacher show and tell. Special spaces need to be created for small-group work, areas such

as practice centers, laboratory stations, demonstration materials, and listening posts. In addition, many schools provide a learning laboratory outside the classroom so that exceptional children who have special needs receive special assistance.

3. *Vary the people.* Learning is fostered by having different individuals present and work with the material. As well, it is impossible for you to be with every child for every moment they are studying mathematics. There are many ways to arrange having other people be of assistance to children as they learn mathematics.

   a. Work in small study groups, not homogeneously arranged. Rapid learners can serve as leaders.
   b. Work in small study groups, arranged homogeneously. Children tend to learn from one another as they discuss their work.
   c. Use older pupils to assist younger pupils who need extra help (cross-age tutors).
   d. Instructional aides help to direct pupils and meet their special needs.
   e. Parents can assist as volunteers in the classroom and as tutors at home.

4. *Vary the curriculum.* Some topics can be presented to the whole class. Other special topics can be selected by individual students. Some aspects of the mathematics curriculum should be adjusted to the individual interests of each pupil.

5. *Vary the instructional materials.* Instructional materials should be varied and adjusted to individual needs. Special learning centers, practice materials, calculators and computers, and multiple textbooks can be varied as is appropriate to the students' individual needs.

6. *Vary the methods of teaching.* Vary your teaching approaches by providing some balance among the following techniques.

   a. Self-discovery, guided discovery, and teacher presentations.
   b. Self-paced, individualized work, small group discussions, and whole-class, teacher-directed demonstrations.
   c. Teacher-controlled developmental activities, independent assigned seatwork.

Mastery Learning—A Group-Based Approach

The traditional assumption has been that in order to adjust adequately for individual differences in learning mathematics, teachers must group children into three ability groups for instruction. Research has not supported this contention. As Callahan and Glennon report, ". . . simply narrowing the ability range does not necessarily result in better adjustment of method or content and does not necessarily result in increased achievement."[4]

The mastery-learning approach has been proposed as a way to give all students an opportunity to achieve at a higher level of mastery. It is an effective way to organize instruction not only to reach students who lack basic mathematical skills, but also to promote rapid learners to go beyond the minimum requirements.

The premise of mastery learning is that a student can master a subject if he or she spends enough time in learning it. The time that each pupil needs is determined by three factors: (1) the pupil's aptitude, (2) the quality of instruction, and (3) the capacity of the student to understand.[5] With the mas-

4. Leroy G. Callahan and Vincent J. Glennon, *Elementary School Mathematics—A Guide to Current Research* (Washington, D.C.: Association for Supervision and Curriculum Development, 1975), pp. 94–95.

5. Judith Harle Hector, "Organizing for Mastery Learning: A Group-based Approach." In *Organizing for Mathematics Instruction*, 1977 Yearbook (Reston, VA: National Council of Teachers of Mathematics, 1977), Chapter 8, pp. 131–145.

tery-learning approach, virtually all pupils can learn well and master most of what they are taught. Instruction is organized according to the following sequence.

1. Specific learning objectives that all students are expected to master are established.

2. A comprehensive unit test is prepared.

3. After an initial period of instruction with the whole class, taking perhaps 50 to 75 percent of the total time allotted for completion of the unit, a unit test is given to all pupils. The results will show how each pupil has progressed toward mastery of the objectives.

4. Then a set of alternative approaches is developed, to reteach the items on the test missed by each pupil. These approaches may include one or more of the following situations:
    a. Small-group study sessions, with or without a leader.
    b. Individual tutoring by peers, by cross-age tutors, by an instructional aide, or by a rapid learner in the class.
    c. Learning centers including laboratory materials, audiovisual tapes, filmstrips, and the like.
    d. Alternative learning aids including different text materials, workbooks, and various practice materials.
    e. Computers and minicalculators with directed instruction and individualized approaches.
    Pupils who have mastered all of the learning objectives of the unit are given opportunities to serve as tutors of slower students and are given the option of working on a variety of enrichment activities. (The topic of teaching the rapid learner is discussed in a later section of this chapter.)

5. A specific length of time is set aside for alternative approaches; and every student is expected to complete his or her assignment, even if out-of-class time is necessary.

6. At the end of the unit, a final test is administered and graded. It is likely that at least 80 percent of the pupils will have mastered the objectives of the unit. With mastery, the pupils will have developed a complete understanding of a concept or operation and be able to use it out of habit. Occasional chance errors will occur, however.

Individualized, Self-Paced Learning

Individualized, self-paced learning is essential to any good instructional program. Some authorities advocate the exclusive use of this approach in teaching and learning elementary mathematics. Individualized, self-paced instruction includes the following basic components:

1. *Learning objectives.* Objectives to be achieved by each pupil are identified and written in a hierarchy from simple to complex, with a summary achievement profile sheet for each learner.

2. *Tests.* A variety of tests are used. Placement tests are used to determine readiness for each block of instruction so that each pupil can be placed at the proper level on the continuum. Progress tests are administered individually, as the child progresses through the learning materials. Mastery tests are used to determine required levels of achievement.

3. *Learning prescriptions.* Based on diagnostic data, each child is given appropriate learning materials, usually a programmed workbook. Pupils are expected to try to progress through the materials on their own, asking for help only when necessary. The rate of learning is set by the pupil.

4. *Record-keeping system.* Progress records are kept for each pupil. A system of recording the objectives that have been mastered is maintained.

To make individualized instruction more

personal, you should confer with each pupil about personal objectives, with regard to both content and time. Encourage the pupils to use different kinds of learning materials as they proceed through the content.

Individualized learning has been used successfully by many teachers to adapt instruction to the very slow and the very rapid learners. However, it has doubtful value as an approach for all the students in a class.

The Ungraded Approach to Accommodating Individual Differences

There is a growing concern in American education with regard to social promotion policies. By social promotions, we mean the practice of making sure that pupils are kept with their own age group as they progress through a typical elementary school program. There have been several plans to break this tradition such as ability grouping, nonpromotion practices, and departmentalized teaching. Ability grouping puts all the slow learners together, and the result tends to be that they are unable to break out of the "low track." Nonpromotion forces the child to repeat a grade, with no different results than occurred initially. Departmentalized teaching is not widely practiced at the elementary school level because this approach works no better than learning in the self-contained classroom. One innovative approach to adjusting for uneven growth patterns and differences in learning achievement among young children is the "ungraded primary."

When pupils enter an ungraded primary program they are not enrolled in a particular grade level but are simply registered into a particular classroom and assigned to a particular teacher. Operating within the classroom structure, the teacher diagnoses the levels of development of each child for each subject and groups the children according to their levels of achievement. Regrouping may be necessary when the children in a given group show such a disparity of development that they no longer derive equal benefit from the instructional program provided in that group. Regrouping can occur between two classes, as well as within a class. Grouping in mathematics depends on the level and rate of development of each pupil's mathematical understanding and skills.

To accommodate individual differences within the self-contained classroom, you should develop and use whatever approaches seem to work for different children. By and large, teaching exceptional children merely requires applying good teaching practices.

1. Establish learning objectives and adjust to meet individual needs.

2. Be flexible and provide a variety of learning activities with a variety of materials.

3. Accept and respect each child. Give praise and encouragement.

4. Foster independence and self-discipline.

5. Be positive about mathematics; make learning fun and exciting.

Characteristics of Slow Learners

Children become slow learners of elementary mathematics for many different reasons. To treat the causes of slow learning adequately, you need to understand the characteristics of each slow learner. Slow learners are most often found to possess the following characteristics.

1. *Below average in intelligence.* Slow learners are usually low in intellectual functioning, although this is not always true. Some low achievers have normal intelligence, but are slow for other reasons.

Children of very low intelligence generally have limited vocabularies, use faulty grammar, and have low functional reading skills. They usually have difficulty in drawing conclusions, in making generalizations, and in seeing relationships. They have trouble remembering things, and find it difficult to solve word problems.

2. *Poor adjustment to school.* Slow learners typically do not like school very much. They have a short attention span, and are distracted easily. Most slow learners are poor test takers, and are low achievers in several subjects. Many times they cause discipline problems in the classroom and in the school.

3. *Physical deficiencies.* Slow learners are usually not as well developed physically as normal learners. Some have poor diets. They are ill a lot, and miss more school than the average pupil. Many slow learners have problems with their eyes and ears.

4. *Psychological and emotional problems.* Slow learners generally lack interest in learning-related tasks. They have a low level of motivation to learn.

5. *Poverty-level homes.* It is estimated that at least 20 percent of the families in the United States live at the poverty level. In some urban areas, this figure can exceed 50 percent.

   Poverty often produces low educational achievement. Many children of poverty are handicapped by:
   a. limited language development.
   b. lack of balanced meals; generally poor nutrition.
   c. inadequate medical care.
   d. less family stability; many broken homes.
   e. negative attitudes toward school.
   f. lack of parental encouragement to try in school or to help at home.

6. *Handicapped.* Slow learners sometimes have serious physical and/or intellectual handicaps. In the past, these pupils were assigned to special education classes.

But, since the passage of Public Law 94-142 in 1975, many handicapped children are being "mainstreamed" into the normal self-contained classroom. Often, the handicapped child needs to make some type of adjustment to the instructional program in order to learn successfully. Generally, the teacher deals individually with the slow learners in this group of children, and includes them in other aspects of the instructional program as it becomes appropriate.

Providing Appropriate Instruction for Slow Learners

A great many children are unsuccessful in achieving adequate levels of performance in elementary mathematics. A child's lack of success can be the result of a variety of causes. To improve a child's learning of mathematics, you must be able to diagnose each child's exact deficiencies and identify the specific reasons for the lack of appropriate achievement. Effective instruction for the slow learner requires two major efforts:

1. Treatment needs to be directed toward the causes for poor achievement.

2. Instruction should concentrate on specific diagnosed difficulties in mathematics.

The methods by which slow learners master the concepts and skills of mathematics are not unique or very different from those used by children of greater ability. A large number of slow learners function successfully within the typical self-contained classroom by applying the approaches discussed in a previous section, "Dealing with Individual Differences within the Self-contained Classroom."

There are, however, a few slow learners who become so retarded that special adjustments in the instructional approaches are needed for them to make any kind of progress in mathematics.

Recommended Adjustments for the Slow Learner

Here are some of the most useful ways to adjust instruction for slow learners:

1. Select content that involves personal survival skills, such as work with money, time, and measurement. Avoid limiting the curriculum to computation. Content of mathematics for the slow learner should be the kind that pupils will want and be able to learn naturally.

2. Present material at a level and pace that will ensure success. Begin at a point slightly below the child's deficiency. Do not repeat a procedure that has already resulted in failure. Pupils should never participate in learning situations in which they face repeated failure. Teach for success and proceed slowly.

3. Provide extensive opportunities for the pupil to work with laboratory materials at the exploratory level. Have pupils use concrete objects as they solve practical problems. Much of the current effort to accommodate slow learners has centered on the laboratory approach. (See Chapter 3.)

Use a wide variety of visual aids—such as pictures and diagrams—so that the learner can visualize the situation involved and grasp the meaning of steps to be taken in the new operation. Supplemental readers, pictures, and illustrations of mathematics in daily life are all valuable ways to visualize learning experiences.

4. Give diagnostic tests systematically to locate weak areas at the early stages of learning. Reteach in a simpler way, if this is necessary. Link skills to concepts, for understanding is important to slow learners. Keep each child informed of his or her progress, and provide immediate positive reinforcement.

5. Insist on an understanding and mastery of each step before presenting new work to avoid the practicing of errors and faulty procedures.

6. Spread the presentation of a new process or topic over a longer period of time than average learners would require.

7. Allow slow learners more time and variety to practice exercises than are required by average learners to develop skills. To avoid monotony, vary the exercises by using games in social situations.

8. Give frequent, short practice exercises, rather than a few long ones, to allow for the short attention span of slow learners.

9. Delay introduction of a new topic until you are clear that the pupil has acquired the basic skills and concepts needed for success in the new work.

10. If possible, assign to slow learners only those textbook activities and problems that are not likely to create frustration. Most publishers of elementary textbooks provide suggestions about materials that can be used in a laboratory setting for slow learners.

11. Conduct frequent observational checks of children's work habits. Use individual interviews to uncover evidences of difficulty, faulty methods, and lack of comprehension.

12. Have pupils tell their thought pattern as they solve a problem or perform a computation. This is one of the best ways to diagnose a pupil's difficulty in mathematics.

13. Give considerable guidance to reading activities so that children develop reading skills connected with the use of the textbook and supplementary materials.

14. Work to change the attitudes of slow learners toward school and mathematics. Since most slow learners are not highly motivated toward school work, a reward system helps to stress the value of learning.

15. Involve the parents in the plan to improve learning. When parents are willing to cooperate and limit the time the child spends watching television and require that assigned homework be completed, progress is almost always improved.

16. Avoid isolating slow learners from other children. They need to learn not only from pupils who serve as good models but also from those who serve as individual tutors.

Characteristics of Rapid Learners

In a typical self-contained classroom of heterogeneous pupils, there should be approximately as many rapid learners as slow learners. As we stated earlier, the average class will consist of approximately 16 percent slow learners and 16 percent rapid learners. The middle two-thirds of the group are classified as average learners. Among the group of about one-sixth rapid learners, perhaps 2 or 3 percent will be among the academically gifted of the total population. Thus, in any one classroom, there will certainly be rapid learners of mathematics and even one or more gifted pupils.

Rapid learners have some of the same characteristics as gifted pupils, but not in the same intensity. Most rapid learners are found to possess the following characteristics.

1. *Above average in intelligence.* Rapid learners are usually above average in general intelligence. Most have well-developed language patterns, which tend to help them score higher than average on IQ tests that place an emphasis on verbal ability.

Rapid learners:
  a. are alert, curious, and observant.
  b. have good memories and reason well.
  c. enjoy asking and answering questions.
  d. are good problem solvers.
  e. discover patterns and relationships among numbers.

2. *High achievement in mathematical reasoning.* Ability in mathematics does not necessarily go hand in hand with measured intelligence, although there is a high positive correlation between the two. An effective and simple way to identify fast learners of mathematics is to select those pupils who achieve one or more grade levels above average in mathematics. High achievers in mathematics are the rapid learners.

3. *Well adjusted to school.* Fast learners are well adjusted and self-sufficient. They have wide interests and enjoy mathematics activities, especially games and applications.

4. *High socioeconomic status.* Pupils who are fast learners usually come from home environments that enjoy a relatively high socioeconomic status.

5. *Task commitment.* Fast learners are often very task oriented. They approach problems and learning in mathematics with considerable zeal and determination.[6]

6. *Creativity.* Many times fast learners are also highly creative. Rapid learners are usually versatile and flexible in their thinking. They are willing to take chances, or run the risk of being wrong. They seem to have an intuition about how ideas fit into the right order and structure in problem-solving activities. They show confidence and are inventive in their approaches to problem-solving and mathematics situations.[7]

7. *Social adjustment.* Rapid learners are typically well accepted socially. They are usually competitive and forceful in their behavior. They exhibit a great deal of independence in their work in mathematics, and work well both in group and individualized situations.[8]

6. H. Laurence Ridge and Joseph S. Renzulli, "Teaching Mathematics to the Talented and Gifted." In *The Mathematical Education of Exceptional Children and Youth* (Reston, VA: National Council of Teachers of Mathematics, 1981), pp. 200–201.

7. Ibid., pp. 208–209.

8. James J. Gallagher, "Mathematics for the Gifted." In *Teaching the Gifted Child*, Second Edition (Boston: Allyn and Bacon, 1975), pp. 95–118.

Providing Appropriate Instruction for Rapid Learners

A great many children in the self-contained classrooms of American schools are not being challenged sufficiently in elementary mathematics. In the typical learning environment, a child who is a rapid learner in mathematics often completes only the standard program provided in the adopted textbook.

A well-planned program for pupils of average ability is inadequate for the fast learner for the following reasons:

1. Fast learners can achieve at a more rapid rate than the average pupil.

2. Fast learners can achieve at a higher level of content than the average learner.

3. Fast learners can generalize and discover different solutions to problems that pupils of average ability are unable to solve.

Organizational Patterns for Rapid Learners

Many rapid learners perform up to their potential within the organizational patterns discussed in the section "Providing for Individual Differences within the Self-contained Classroom." All these plans involve some type of grouping, which is necessary for effective mathematics programs at all levels. After he examined the research evidence on grouping, Begle concluded: ". . . The evidence is quite clear that most able students should be grouped together, separate from the rest of the student population. . . ."[9]

This is not to imply that rapid learners should be isolated and segregated from other pupils at all times as they learn mathematics. Often, you will want to group stu-

dents in ways other than by level of achievement. Nevertheless, there must be some basis for the groups, which also must be kept flexible. Sometimes, you will want to instruct the class as a group, as when you present a new topic or game, or demonstrate a measurement activity. At other times, you may form subgroups for special purposes, such as: (1) laboratory activities, (2) practice on skills, (3) learning-center tasks, and (4) problem-solving activities. At times, you may guide a small-group discussion of a mathematics topic, or work with an individual pupil who needs help.

In addition to the organizational plans we have discussed, there are two other basic plans for the self-contained classroom: (1) use of specialist teachers, and (2) creation of special classes.[10]

Use of Specialist Teachers

Many educators believe that there is a need for teachers who are specialists in mathematics to strengthen the program for mathematically talented children.

In some schools, mathematically talented pupils are sent to special mathematics rooms where they work for periods of time with a teacher who has a rich mathematical background in a variety of very challenging topics.

Some states provide funding so that schools may establish programs taught by teachers trained to deal with gifted and talented children.

Creation of Special Classes

Some communities provide special classes for talented and gifted children. These pupils work with a special teacher—sometimes full time, sometimes part time. Some-

9. E. G. Begle, *Critical Variables in Mathematics Education* (Washington, DC: Mathematics Association of America and the National Council of Teachers of Mathematics, 1979), p. 106.

10. James Hersberger and Grayson Wheatley, "A Proposed Model for a Gifted Elementary School Mathematics Program," *Gifted Child Quarterly*, Winter 1980, 24:37–40.

times, classes are recruited from several schools, and in some areas classes contain children of several age levels, for economic reasons. There also is grouping in extracurricular activities, such as math clubs.

Adjusting the Curriculum for Fast Learners

Acceleration and *enrichment* are two widely used means of adjusting the curriculum for the rapid learners in mathematics. Acceleration enables the talented pupil to progress through the mathematics program at a faster than normal rate. Enrichment provides the talented child with an opportunity to participate in the basic mathematics program, plus extension activities in both the breadth and depth of mathematics.

ACCELERATION

Acceleration can be achieved by means of: (1) academic acceleration, (2) the ungraded classroom, and (3) skipping a grade.

1. *Academic acceleration.* Academic acceleration permits a talented child to progress through the graded textbooks in mathematics at a pace faster than normal. Thus, when a third-grade rapid learner finishes the mathematics textbook for grade 3, he or she is given a grade 4 textbook. When the child completes the grade 4 textbook, he or she moves on to the grade 5 textbook and continues in this manner, even though that pupil is still in the third grade.

2. *The ungraded classroom.* The organizational approach of the ungraded classroom, as we have discussed previously, provides for acceleration by two different procedures. First, it premits a talented child to enter kindergarten or grade 1 at an earlier age than the standard age. Second, the child is permitted to complete three grades of work in two years, by progressing according to his or her ability to achieve. The major difference between the ungraded plan and ac-

ademic acceleration is the instructional approaches that are used. In the ungraded classroom, the child has opportunities to work with other pupils in a variety of activities, but this is not so in an academic acceleration program.

3. *Skipping a grade.* Skipping a grade is based on two assumptions that often prove to be false:

a. A talented learner is talented in all subject areas.

b. A talented learner can acquire the skills and concepts achieved in the grade skipped at the next grade level.

Children often have a given talent or aptitude and are not equally talented in all subject areas. It is possible that a specific skill or concept necessary for progress in a sequential subject, such as mathematics, may not be acquired when a grade is skipped. For this reason, we do not recommend skipping a grade unless there is no other way to provide enrichment.

ENRICHMENT

Enrichment is a widely accepted means of providing appropriate learning experiences for children who are talented in elementary mathematics. Enrichment for the rapid learner implies that the material covered will be broader and deeper than that which is normally included in the basic mathematics program, but will be related to and grow out of this standard program. There are two kinds of enrichment: horizontal enrichment, and vertical enrichment.

1. *Horizontal enrichment.* Horizontal enrichment includes *more* learning experiences on the level of the pupil's present achievement status. With horizontal enrichment, the content being studied is broader in scope than that which occurs in textbooks at that grade level. Often this type of enrichment is interpreted to mean "more of the same." That is, when a fast learner completes his or her assigned textbook work, the teacher merely assigns the same type of exercises from another book or hands out a ditto to work on the same materials. Talented learners are not challenged by this sort of busy work. Most elementary school mathematics textbooks suggest horizontal enrichment activities of the following types:

a. Performing a laboratory activity and keeping a record of steps.

b. Picking a topic for further study, such as a study of ways that primitive cultures used number, measured, or used money.

c. Creating a bulletin board display about the topic under study.

d. Playing games.

e. Working with the minicalculator.

f. Completing a puzzle or other type of recreational activity.

g. Writing word problems.

h. Completing problems a second time with a minicalculator.

i. Viewing a film or filmstrip on the topic being studied.

2. *Vertical enrichment.* Vertical enrichment provides advanced work or further specialization in the same area of learning. This type of enrichment increases the quality of the work being offered so as to widen and deepen understanding in a given area. Vertical enrichment leads to *power* in mathematics. Among the experiences that can be used to develop mathematical power are:

a. Discovering varied methods of solving examples that involve number operations.

b. Discovering varied methods of solving verbal problems.

c. Identifying mathematical properties applied in operations.

d. Developing an understanding of how the basic properties of mathematics are applied in shortcut procedures.

e. Independent study of the operational procedures in available reference materials.

f. Independent study of topics related to the applications of mathematics.

g. Studying topics without class instruction. The learner confers with the teacher for guidance in the assignment.

h. Independent study of subject matter through the use of adequate programmed materials and other textbooks.

i. Studying the newer kinds of computational devices and machines.

j. Verbalizing generalizations, rules, and conclusions in concise language.

k. Solving and making puzzles requiring the application of basic mathematical properties.

Mathematics textbooks suggest a wide variety of activities that enrich the learning of mathematics for the more able children in grades 1 through 6. Some of the more widely used methods are:

a. Exploration of the uses of mathematics in all curriculum areas, especially science, health, music, and social studies.

b. Starred problems within instructional units that require independent research, reading, and logical inquiry.

c. Lists of topics and problems for special investigation and report.

d. Challenges for the more capable learners.

e. Solving equations and formulas.

f. Mathematical puzzles and recreations.

g. Geometrical constructions and proofs.

h. Activities leading to the discovery of principles, generalizations, and relationships.

i. Field work requiring the application of mathematical procedures, especially geometry.

j. Mathematics scrapbooks—individual or class.

k. "Brain twisters."

l. The preparation of exhibits, displays, and collections.

m. Excursions and field trips.

n. Mathematics clubs.

o. Sections of the textbook labeled

"Challenges" or "Extensions," in which the material is keyed to the main body of the text. Extensions are designed to create power in dealing with number.

p. Supplementary books dealing with programming and electronic computers. If the school has a microcomputer, students should learn how to operate it.

THE SCHOOL LIBRARY

Library resources should be used continually to enrich the work in mathematics. The library is the heart of an enrichment program for superior learners with special interest in mathematics. These students are likely to browse widely among all kinds of available printed materials, seeking information on matters of interest. Independent reading and study are a high-level type of learning that you should encourage and facilitate by having available a well-selected variety of printed materials, including general books, reference books, magazines, bulletins, schedules, and the like.

Motivating Superior Learners

How can you help pupils to set goals that will challenge them? What can be done to motivate them? To what extent should external inducements and artificial stimuli—such as grades, examinations, rewards, and punishments—be used to stimulate them to greater efforts?

Ideally, motivation should help pupils to develop purposes, interests, and expectations that will direct their efforts and activities toward the fulfillment of long-range ambitions and goals. Some children reveal at an early age a marked aptitude in mathematics that should be guided and developed by the school. The experiences of young children in the home and elsewhere may have stimulated them to explore a variety of everyday uses of mathematics. This impetus should be expanded and encouraged by the whole staff of the school. It is unfortunate

that lack of motivation accounts for the failure of a large number of talented youths to complete mathematics courses within their secondary education or continue the study of mathematics at the college level.

Some of the motivational techniques used by schools are:

1. Honor rolls.

2. Invitations to membership in mathematics clubs.

3. Student interviews with counselors and teachers.

4. Letters to parents praising unusual achievements.

5. Scholarship luncheons and banquets.

6. Mathematics contests.

7. The availability of a wide variety of books and mathematical devices and instruments. Some elementary schools have set up mathematics workrooms in which children can work when they wish. (For mathematics laboratories, see Chapter 3.)

8. Centers of interest in classrooms.

Summary

Children are alike as well as different in many ways. For the teacher, the challenge is to know when children should learn mathematics as a group, all performing similar activities, and when to differentiate the curriculum and methods of teaching.

Each individual child has strengths and weaknesses. To accommodate individual differences, you must adjust the program so that each child lives up to his potential. Adjustments can be made in content difficulty, in levels of maturity, in time, in space, in materials used, and in teaching approaches.

The mastery-learning approach is a wholeclass approach that provides small-group and individualized instruction. The ungraded approach helps to ensure continuous growth for all pupils. There should be some type of grouping according to achievement in mathematics and the needs of the pupils.

There are many reasons why pupils become low achievers. You should treat the causes, if possible. Use diagnostic techniques and remediate weaknesses. Slow learners need more time at the exploratory level with laboratory activities than average pupils. Time is an important factor in achievement for slow learners.

The pupil who is talented at mathematics needs to be challenged with the structural aspects of mathematics. Emphasize patterns, relationships, properties, and alternative algorisms. Fast learners need to study advanced topics in mathematics not normally found in a typical program. They need a variety of problem-solving experiences that involve estimating, alternative solutions, and more abstract thinking at the symbolic level. They need extensive appli-cations of mathematics. Limited accelera-tion is desirable for the gifted child who is outstanding in most aspects of the curri-culum.

Both slow and fast learners need various forms of enrichment. We recommend hori-zontal enrichment for slow learners, while the fast learner needs activities that will lead to the development of power in math-ematics.

As a teacher, you need to maintain an at-titude of experimentation—a willingness to be flexible and adaptable—trying different approaches with different groupings of chil-dren, and systematically studying results.

There is no one best approach to accom-modate individual differences. Both the teacher and the pupils need to create ap-proaches to learning that will produce optimum growth in mathematics for each child.

Exercises

1. How does grouping a class according to levels of maturity adjust for differences in ability in elementary school mathematics?

2. A year-long course of study is planned for a given grade. Is subject matter or time a variable or a constant? Or are both time and subject matter constants? If time is a constant and subject matter is a variable, how would that affect the course of study?

3. List at least five characteristics of slow learners; of fast learners.

4. Evaluate the following statement: Slow learners and fast learners should be taught in segregated groups.

5. What is meant by the ungraded elementary school? Tell why you do or do not approve of it.

6. What is the difference between a slow learner and a slow achiever?

7. If homogeneous groups are formed, enumerate at least three factors that should be considered in the formation of the groups.

8. Under what conditions would you approve of acceleration as an acceptable means of adjusting the program for fast learners in mathematics?

9. Give five different solutions for finding the product of 15 and 45. Do not include the standard algorithm for multiplication of two two-digit numbers.

Selected Readings

Bartkovich, Kevin G., and William C. George. *Teaching the Gifted and Talented in the Mathematics Classroom.* Washington, D.C.: National Education Association, 1980.

Bloom, Benjamin S. *All Our Children Learning.* New York: McGraw-Hill, 1980.

Callahan, Leroy G., and Vincent J. Glennon. *Elementary School Mathematics—A Guide to Current Research.* Washington, D.C.: Association for Supervision and Curriculum Development, 1975.

Fox, Lynn. *Programs for the Gifted and Talented.* Part I, 78th Yearbook of the National Society for the Study of Education. Chicago: University of Chicago Press, 1979.

Gallagher, James J. "Mathematics for the Gifted." In *Teaching the Gifted Child,* Second Edition. Boston: Allyn and Bacon, 1975, pp. 95–118.

Glennon, Vincent J. (Ed.). *The Mathematical Education of Exceptional Children and Youth—An Interdisciplinary Approach.* Reston, VA: National Council of Teachers of Mathematics, 1981.

Hector, Judith Harle. "Organizing for Mastery Learning: A Grouped-based Approach." In *Organizing for Mathematics Instruction,* 1977 Yearbook. Reston, VA: National Council of Teachers of Mathematics, 1977, pp. 131–145.

Howell, Daisy, et al. *Activities for Teaching Mathematics to Low Achievers.* Jackson: University of Mississippi Press, 1974.

Hurwitz, Abraham B., et al. *Number Games to Improve Your Child's Arithmetic.* New York: Funk and Wagnalls, 1975.

Hurwitz, Abraham B., et al. *More Number Games—Mathematics Made Easy through Play.* New York: Funk and Wagnalls, 1976.

Kennedy, Leonard M., and Ruth L. Michon, *Games for Individualizing Mathematics Learning.* Columbus, OH: Charles E. Merrill, 1973.

Smith, Seaton E., Jr., and Carl A. Backman (Ed.). *Games and Puzzles for Elementary and Middle School Mathematics.* Reston, VA: National Council of Teachers of Mathematics, 1975.

Sobel, Max A., and Evan M. Maletsky, *Teaching Mathematics: A Sourcebook of Aids, Activities, and Strategies.* Englewood Cliffs, NJ: Prentice-Hall, 1975.

Appendix A

How to Prepare Essential Materials and Learning Aids

The teacher may equip the mathematics classroom with either commercial or home-made materials. The directions that follow cover the essential materials for classroom use as described in this text.

Flannel Board

A flannel board can be made by covering a piece of masonite or similar material (24 by 30 inches) with flannel having a good nap (Figure. A.1). Make fractional disks lined with flannel about 10 inches in diameter. Cut these disks into halves, thirds, fourths, sixths, and eighths. Keep two disks whole.

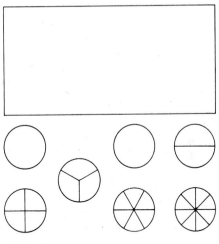

Figure A.1

Place-Value Charts

A place-value chart may be made of wood or oaktag. For the primary grades the teacher may find it helpful to use a place-value chart consisting of three separate sections, each made of oaktag. Each section is used to represent a place in the number system, such as ones, tens, and hundreds. For grades 4–6 one chart can be subdivided into three sections or parts to show the given places. Since the same teacher will seldom be teaching at all six grade levels, directions for making each type of pocket chart follow.

THREE POCKET CHARTS FOR PRIMARY GRADES

Use three sheets of oaktag, each 20 by 26 inches, to make the pocket charts.

The steps in making the card holders are (see also Figure A.2):

1. Place the paper on a table with the short edges at top and bottom. Measure down 5 inches from the top along each side and place dots. Join the dots with a line, as in Figure A.2(A).

2. Fold the top back and under along this line and crease firmly, as in Figure A.2(B).

3. Measure down 2 inches from the crease along each side and join the dots with a line, as in Figure A.2(C).

4. Fold the top back and under along this line and crease firmly, as in Figure A.2(D).

5. Open up flat on the table. Lift the lower creased fold up over the upper crease. The upper crease will slide down under the fold and you will have the first pocket. Crease firmly and staple each edge of the pocket together so that it stays in place, as is shown in Figure A.2(E).

6. To make the second pocket, measure down 5 inches from the top edge of the first pocket on each side of the chart and place two dots. Join the dots with a line, as in Figure A.2(F). Form the next pocket by repeating the process described above.

7. Repeat direction (6) until you have three pockets on the card holder.

8. Make two more card holders of the same kind, following directions (1–7) above, so as to have a total of three pocket charts.

9. Each card holder now needs a stiff backing. Three sides of a packing carton, each side at least as large as a card holder, are needed for this purpose.

Lay the back of the card holder on the cardboard backing and cut the cardboard to the size of the pocket chart. Then staple the cardboard and the chart together. You may choose to bind the edges of the chart with masking tape to improve its appearance.

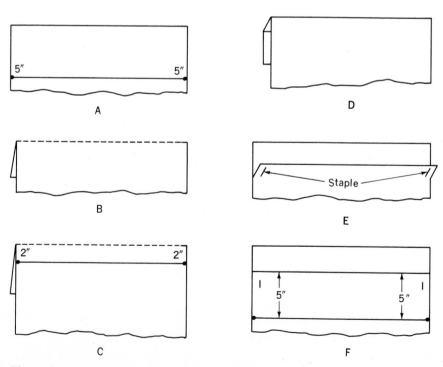

Figure A.2

10. Finally, use a white crayon or a small brush with white poster paint to print the name of each card holder above the top pocket, as is shown in Figure A.3.

CARDS FOR CARD HOLDERS

You need 20 sheets of 9″ × 12″ red construction paper to make the cards for the pocket charts, and a supply of rubber bands to make bundles of cards. Use miniature rubber bands for the tens bundles.

1. On your paper cutter you can cut five sheets at a time.

2. Using the 9-inch edge of the paper, measure and cut three 3-inch strips, as is shown in Figure A.4(A).

3. From each 3″ × 4″ strip you can cut eight 3″ × 1½″ cards, as is shown in Figure A.4(B).

4. Since you get 24 cards from each 9″ × 12″ sheet, you will have 480 cards, an adequate supply for the operations needed in the primary grades.

5. Cut five 3″ × 12″ strips at a time into 1½″ × 3″ cards, cutting off 1½-inch strips from the 12-inch edge. Pick up the cut cards in groups of five. Then make bundles of 10 cards, or tens bundles. Have the children help make 45 bundles of 10 cards each.

6. To make a hundreds bundle, pick up 10 tens and wrap them together with a rubber band. Make 2 hundreds bundles, keeping the bands on the tens.

7. Keep the 2 hundreds bundles, 25 tens bundles, and 30 single cards you now have in a box.

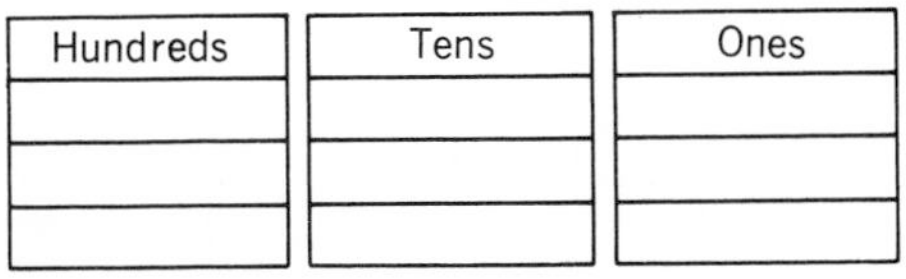

ONE-PIECE POCKET CHART

The pocket chart for the intermediate grades should be in one piece, divided into three sections. The teacher of the lower grades may prefer to use a pocket chart of this kind. The chart may be made of wood or of oaktag, 20″ × 26″. The steps in making the chart are:

1. Place the paper on a table with one of the 26-inch edges nearest you. Measure down 5 inches from the top edge of the paper and draw a line parallel to this edge. Fold the top along this edge and crease firmly.

2. Repeat steps (2–4) listed for the primary grades pocket chart.

3. Divide the sheet longitudinally to form three equal pockets in each row. Staple at the points of intersection with the rows of pockets.

4. Beginning on the right, label the sections *ones, tens, hundreds* to show whole numbers. Beginning on the left, label the pockets *ones, tenths, hundredths* to show decimals. The same pockets may be used for both whole numbers and decimals provided different labels are given.

5. Fasten the top of the chart to a wire coat hanger.

Use cards approximately 1½″ × 2½″ to

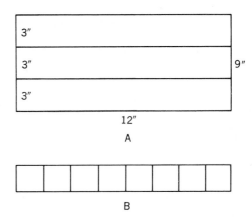

Figure A.3

Figure A.4

insert in the pockets to represent numbers. Tongue depressors or splints may be substituted for cards.

At the level of grade 4 or above it should not be necessary to use a bundle of 10 cards to represent each digit one place to the left of a given place. Cards of different colors may be used to show the values represented in the respective places. Thus, a red card may represent 1 one in the ones place, a blue card may represent 1 ten in the tens place, and a green card may represent 1 hundred in the hundreds place. Similarly, different-colored cards may be used to represent the places to the right of the ones place.

At the next higher level of understanding of place value, a card of the same color should be used to represent a digit in a given pocket. If all of the cards are red, three of these cards in the ones pocket represent 3; in the tens place, 30; and in the hundreds place, 300. The pupil who reaches this stage in understanding place value is ready to interpret the value of a digit in a numeral. He or she then knows that a 3 two places to the left of the ones place represents 300, as in the numeral 347.

Fraction Kit for Pupils

Each pupil in grades 5 and 6 should have a kit of circular cutouts for demonstrating fractional numbers. Have these cutouts made of oaktag or construction paper. Supply each pupil with 12 circular disks approximately 5 inches in diameter. He should use two of these to represent wholes. He should cut two other disks to represent halves and then cut the rest of the disks in pairs to represent thirds, fourths, sixths, and eighths.

In grade 5 it may not be necessary to have cutouts to represent thirds and sixths. In that case 8 circular disks are needed. The teacher should remember that it is necessary to supply a pupil with a model cutout equal to a third. Then he can fold a third so

as to form two equal parts, each of which is equal to a sixth.

The radius of a circle may be used in dividing the circle into sixths. Draw a circle and mark a point on it. Open compasses to equal the radius. From the given point mark in succession five other points on the circle. Connect the six points with the center of the circle. Each sector now marked is a sixth of the circular region. Cut along the radii you drew to represent sixths.

Rectangular Squares and Strips

Supply each pupil in grades 3–6 with squares and rectangular strips to be used to objectify the work with whole numbers and decimals. A piece of construction paper 15″ × 21″ can be ruled into ¾-inch squares to provide the necessary squares and rectangular strips. A paper of this size will provide 20 rows and 28 columns, each ¾-inch wide, making a total of 560 ¾-inch squares (20 by 28). Cut these squares to form large squares and rectangular strips as follows:

1. 3 large squares containing 100 ¾-inch squares

2. 20 strips of 10 ¾-inch squares

3. 60 ¾-inch squares cut as:
(a) 15 single squares
(b) 5 strips of 2 squares
(c) 5 strips of 3 squares
(d) 5 strips of 4 squares

The pupil should use the ruled side of the squares and the strips to represent whole numbers. Figure A.5 shows the number 138. The 8 ones may be represented by

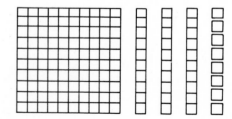

Figure A.5

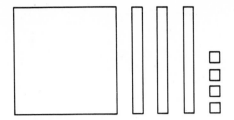

Figure A.6

8 small squares, two groups of 4 squares, or any other combination of squares having a sum of 8.

The pupil should use the unruled side of the squares and the strips to represent decimals. The unruled side of a large square represents a whole; a full single strip represents a tenth; and a small square represents a hundredth.

Figure A.6 shows how to represent the number 1.34.

Have the pupil keep the cutouts, squares, and rectangular strips in two manila envelopes. Be certain that he or she has a flat-top desk on which to manipulate these exploratory materials when they are used in class.

Pattern Block Sequence Cards

Pattern block sequence cards may be made by cutting strips of poster board approximately 18 in. in length and 4 in. in width. Mark the center of the strip. On the left side, produce a pattern by using commercially available colored pattern block stickers, or use actual blocks to trace around, or pattern block commercially available templates. If the stickers are not used, color the pattern the same as the actual blocks. The right side of the poster

board strip should remain blank for the child to use to extend the pattern. Be creative in designing the patterns. Make a set of approximately ten cards. Ask pupils to first use actual blocks to cover the existing pattern and then to extend the pattern without clues.

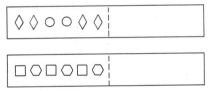

Bean Sticks

Bean sticks, useful for base 10 models, can be made using common dried beans, wooden popsicle sticks or tongue depressor sticks, nontoxic paint, cardboard, and plastic bags. Paint the beans to make them more visible because beans and the sticks may be similar in color. To paint the beans, place them on newsprint and spray them with a bright-color paint.

A single bean is equivalent to 1. For a model of 10, first coat a stick with glue. When the glue becomes "tacky" place 10 beans on a stick in a row. It may be desirable to allow for extra space between 2 groups of 5 when showing 10. Coat the tops of the beans and stick with glue and allow to dry thoroughly. White wood glue that dries clear is suitable. For a model of 100, glue 10 prepared sticks to a cardboard square. For a model of 1000, place 10 of the 100 models in a plastic bag and secure the opening or tie the bundle of 10 together with a string. (See Figure A.7)

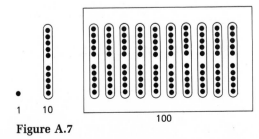

1   10

100

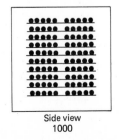

Side view
1000

Figure A.7

Show-Me Cards

Show-me cards are made by writing the ten digits 0, 1, 2 . . . 9 on individual rectangular cardboards approximately 3 in. × 5 in. An extra card containing 1 is needed in order to show the sum of a number pair of the type 5 + 6. A pupil shows the answer to a number pair by selecting the answer from the cards arranged in sequence on his or her desk. To give the answer to the number pair 4 × 8, he or she would hold up the cards containing 3 and 2 or place them in a card holder.

The digits should be large and made near the top of the card so that a child's hand does not cover part of the digit when he or she is holding a card or when the card(s) are used with a "show-me card holder." For extra durability, laminate the cards.

Show-Me Card Holder

To make a show-me card holder, cut construction paper in a rectangle approximately 4 in. × 6 in. in size. See A in the diagram. Fold 1¼ in. of the bottom edge of the rectangle and staple as shown in B and C. The holders are used with show-me cards as a pupil places the appropriate cards in the holder to answer a basic fact.

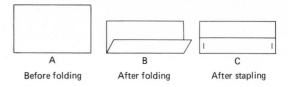

A
Before folding

B
After folding

C
After stapling

Appendix B
Probability

An individual may look at the sky and predict the probability of rain. This prediction is usually a guess. The weather bureau, however, predicts the probability of rain on a much more scientific basis by using such factors as humidity, atmospheric pressure, dew point, and wind patterns. When the weather bureau states that there is a 30 percent probability of rain, it means that on three of ten days in the past rain has occurred when the measurable conditions were about the same as the day of the prediction.

Public opinion polls provide a well-known example of the use of probability. A pollster discovers the view of a limited sample of people on a given topic, and uses the results to predict the opinions of the entire population. The size of the sample and the manner of choice are dictated by the mathematical theory of probability.

Industry spends much time and effort in testing samples of products turned out by its production lines in order to determine the quality of the total production. This process, called quality control, is guided by the mathematical theory of probability.

The simplest elements of probability have been introduced on the elementary school level by many recent series of textbooks.

Vocabulary

And (as used in probability)
Equally likely events
Or (as used in probability)
Probability formula
Random event or choice

Probability Formula

Readiness for Probability

Use a pair of black marbles and a pair of red marbles. Checkers or other markers may also be used. Place a black marble and a red one in a container (a bag or box). Place the other black and red marbles in a second container. It is important that it be impossible to see what color of marble is drawn from the container.

Have one pupil draw a marble from the first container at about the same time that a second pupil draws a marble from the second container. Note the color for each drawing and then have each marble returned to its own container. Repeat the drawing with the same or different pupils and record the result of each drawing as is illustrated in the following table showing the results of seven drawings:

not necessarily the same, but that they tend to be approximately equal as the number of trials increases.

Drawing marbles from a container is essentially equivalent to tossing two coins and determining when there will be two heads, two tails, or one of each.

Black (1)-Black (2)	Red (1)-Red (2)	Black (1)-Red (2)	Red (1)-Black (2)
I		II	IIII

Before a trend has developed, pupils should be asked to predict the outcome in terms of frequency. Then the probability concept can be introduced, and pupils can restate their estimates in terms of probability. Pupils should estimate where the probabilities for the three situations in the table are the same or different.

When the drawing process is repeated often enough so as to make it clear that the probability of obtaining opposite colors is greater than that of obtaining two black or two red, a discussion should follow to see if an explanation for this difference can be found.

If the class discussion does not lead to the discovery of such a reason, it may be helpful to identify the containers as 1 and 2 and make a new table to record the results of a new set of drawings.

The activity just described has many variations. Some teachers may prefer to present it as a game, where each team or individual gets a point depending on the result of the drawing. The main point of the activity is to demonstrate the relationship between experimental probability and mathematical probability. The activity also demonstrates the importance of identifying the number of equally likely possibilities for calculating mathematical probabilities. This procedure will help pupils understand that a mathematical probability of ¼ and the corresponding experimental probability are

Activities similar to these provide excellent readiness for understanding the probability formula.

Formula

Five markers of the same size and shape are numbered from 1 to 5 and placed in a container. If a marker is removed from the container at random, the chance of drawing marker number 1 is 1 out of 5. There are five possibilities for drawing a marker but there is only one chance of obtaining the marker with 1 written on it. Because there is one chance for success out of 5 equally likely possibilities, we say that the probability of drawing a marker with a 1 written on it is one-fifth (⅕).

If we know the total number of ways in which an event can happen *(H)* out of a total number of equally likely possibilities *(N)*, then we can write the formula for probability *(P)*.

$$P = \frac{H}{N}$$

Applying the Probability Formula

There are 999 counting numbers less than 100, and 333 of them are divisible by 3. Therefore, the probability that a counting number less than 1000, selected at random, is divisible by 3 is $^{333}/_{999}$ or $^1/_3$.

If a manufacturer discovers that there are 100 defective items in a run of 10,000 of these items, the probability of obtaining a defective item from that run is 100 ÷ 10,000 or .01, assuming the items are chosen at random.

Equally Likely Choices

The probability formula demands that the total number of possibilities (N) be equally likely. One may argue that the probability of becoming a millionaire is ½ as there are only two possibilities—being a millionaire or not being a millionaire. This argument fails because the two possibilities are not equally likely. This illustration should make it clear that the probability formula is meaningless unless all the possibilities under consideration are equally likely.

Random Choices

A random choice is one in which no other factor than chance can affect the selection. Random choice is as fundamental in probability as the concept of equally likely possibilities. Industry rarely tests every item it manufactures to identify rejects. Instead, companies rely on random sampling. Experience has shown that by testing an appropriate number of random samples, the number of defective items in a given production can be predicted within narrow limits. It is essential, however, that the selection be totally random. A famous case of lack of randomness involved a magazine poll in the 1936 election which proved to be very inaccurate. It was discovered that only people with telephones had been polled, but during the Depression many people did not have telephones. Thus, a subset of the population which was not random had been selected and it was not representative of the entire population. If one wanted to estimate the probability of finding a pupil in a partic-

ular school who was able to swim, it would not be a random choice to ask only members of the swimming team. A sample poll at a political rally for one party would be of little value in predicting the outcome of an election.

Counting and Probability

Counting various possible situations is an important mathematical activity in computing theoretical probabilities. The counting process varies from simple to very complex. Many beginners will count incorrectly in the situation where a coin is tossed twice. A superficial count indicates three possibilities: both heads, both tails, and one head and one tail. The correct count, as indicated by the following tree diagram, is two heads, two tails, one head and one tail, and one tail and one head.

As the tree diagram indicates, there are four possibilities and the probability of getting a head and a tail is 2 ÷ 4 or ½ because two of the four situations have a head and a tail. The probability of tossing twice and obtaining a head on the first toss and a tail on the second is ¼.

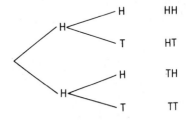

Situations Involving "And" and "Or"

Two of the most fundamental problems in elementary probability are:

1. *Given:* The probability of A and the probability of B.
Find: The probability of "A or B."

2. *Given:* The probability of A and the probability of B.
Find: The probability of "A *and* B."

If a problem asks for the probability of "A or B," the following condition is implied:

If A occurs B cannot occur or if B occurs A cannot occur. This situation is often described as *mutually exclusive.*

Probability theory states the following result:

P(A *or* B) = P(A) + P(B)

where P(A *or* B) is the probability of "A or B" and P(A) is the probability of A and P(B) is the probability of B. For example, the probability of obtaining a head *or* tail on the single toss of a coin is the probability of obtaining a head *plus* the probability of obtaining a tail or ½ + ½ = 1. A probability of 1 indicates that an event is certain to happen. When a coin is tossed once, either a head or tail must occur and in this situation, are mutually exclusive.

When a problem asks for the probability of "A *and* B" it is implied that if A occurs, B may or may not occur and if B occurs A may or may not occur. The following holds for "and" situations:

P(A and B) = P(A) × P(B)

where P(A *and* B) is the probability of "A *and* B" and P(A) and P(B) represent the probabilities of A and B respectively. For example, the probability of obtaining two heads (a head *and* a head) on two successive tosses of a coin is the probability of obtaining a head on the first toss multiplied by the probability of obtaining a head on the second toss or ½ × ½ = ¼. In the same manner, the probability of obtaining two tails would also be ¼.

Problems may involve "and" and "or" without specifically stating them, such as finding the probability that two successive tosses will produce the same result. This problem asks indirectly for the probability of obtaining two heads *or* two tails or ¼ + ¼ = ½. Note that the problem also involves "and" in determining the probability of two heads and the probability of two tails. The tree diagram on page 000 will verify these results.

The probability of getting heads on three successive coin tosses is ½ × ½ × ½ = ⅛ and is the same for obtaining three successive tails. Therefore, the probability of obtaining the coin to produce the same result on all three tosses is the probability of obtaining three heads *plus* the probability of obtaining three tails or ⅛ + ⅛ or ¼.

Pupils should be reminded that the probability of "A *and* B" must be less than the probability of A or the probability of B. This statement assumes that neither A nor B is certain to happen and must therefore have a probability less than 1, and is therefore a consequence of the fact that the product of two proper fractions is less than either.

Applications of Probability

The following examples illustrate the application of fundamental principles in "and" and "or" situations:

A box contains 3 white, 4 yellow, and 5 red tees. The probability of drawing a white tee is ³⁄₁₂ or ¼; a yellow tee ⁴⁄₁₂ or ⅓; and a red tee ⁵⁄₁₂.

1. What is the probability of drawing a white *or* a yellow tee in one drawing? This is an "or" situation. Since either a white or yellow tee is acceptable, the probability for the event is the sum of the probability for drawing a white and a yellow tee. This probability is ¼ + ⅓ or ⁷⁄₁₂.

2. What is the probability of drawing a white *and* a yellow tee in two consecutive drawings? (Assume the tee on the first drawing was replaced before the second drawing.)

This is an "and" situation. The required probability is the product of the probability of drawing, which is ¼ × ⅓, or ¹⁄₁₂.

3. What is the probability of drawing a white *and* a red tee if the tee is not replaced after the first drawing?

The probability of drawing a white tee is ¼, as before. Now the conditions are different from those in Problem 2 because there are only eleven tees in the box. Hence the probability of drawing a red tee is ⁵⁄₁₁ and not ⁵⁄₁₂. The probability of drawing a white and a red tee is the product of the two probabilities, which is ¼ × ⁵⁄₁₁, or ⁵⁄₄₄.[1]

Fallacies

Probably the most common fallacy in probability is the belief that if five heads are obtained in five consecutive tosses of the coin that the probability for obtaining a tail on the sixth toss will be increased. This belief is false. Coins have no memories. The probability of obtaining heads on a given toss is ½, no matter what has happened previously.

The probability of tossing five consecutive heads in five tosses is ¹⁄₃₂. This may be verified by extending the tree diagram shown on p. 373, or using the fact that obtaining 5 heads is obtaining a head *and* a head *and* a head *and* a head *and* a head. The probability of obtaining five consecutive heads is therefore the product ½ × ½ × ½ × ½ × ½ = ¹⁄₃₂.

The second fallacy is the belief that if a coin is tossed 50 times that exactly 25 of the tosses will result in tails, since the probabil-

ity of obtaining a tail on a single toss is ½. Experimental probability, as determined by tossing coins, usually differs from mathematical probability. The difference between them approaches zero as the number of trials increases.

ACTIVITIES

1. Have every member of the class place a book on his desk. Have each pupil open the book at random and give the page number. Keep track of how many of these numbers are even and how many are odd. This procedure may not give approximately 50 percent odd numbers if pupils have a tendency to choose the number on the right-hand page when they open the book. The numbers of all the right-hand pages are odd and the left-hand pages are even. If, in place of giving the page number, the number represented by the sum of the digits is given, the ratio of odd numbers (or even) to the total will approach 50 percent.

2. Lack of randomness can be illustrated by using the book opening activity and having pupils record only the right-hand page numbers until they discover that this procedure gives only odd numbers.

3. Obtain a spinner used in connection with board games. Spin the pointer and record the results. If this activity is carried out over a period of time, each number should occur about the same number of times or with the same probability.

4. Place marbles of two different colors in a jar or can. Black and white checkers or other markers may also be used. Place twice as many of one color as the other and mix thoroughly. Then have each pupil remove a marble or marker without looking, identify its color, and return it. Keep a record of the colors obtained in this manner. If the marbles or markers are thoroughly mixed, the ratio of the colors chosen should approach two to one. The activity may be repeated

---

1. In problem 2, the events are called independent as replacing the ball means that the result of the first drawing has no influence on the second drawing. In problem 3, the events are called dependent since the first ball is not replaced and the result of the second drawing is affected by the result of the first. In dependent events, the second probability is computed on the assumption that the first event has occurred.

with different ratios of marbles or markers in the container.

5. Lack of randomness may be demonstrated by deliberately placing all marbles of one color together in the container.

6. Give pupils an introduction to sampling techniques by having them attempt to predict the ratio of colors in the container by choosing a limited sample at random. It is an important mathematical problem to determine the size of the smallest sample which will have approximately the same ratio as the entire collection in the container.

7. Toss thumbtacks into a container and keep a record of the positions in which the tacks land. Do this over a period of time, keeping a record, and estimate the probability of the thumbtack coming to rest in each position.

8. Toss 4 pennies at a time 16 times. Count the number of heads and tails each time. Compare your results with the theoret-

ical probability, as is shown in the following table.

Heads	Tails	Frequency
4	0	1
3	1	4
2	2	6
1	3	4
0	4	1

9. Have every pupil in the class write a number. Determine how many pupils have chosen multiplies of 3. Compare the actual ratio of the number of multiplies of 3 to total number of pupils with the theoretical probability of $\frac{1}{3}$. For one such trial the difference may be substantial. If cumulative totals are kept, the ratio will approach $\frac{1}{3}$ providing that pupils write random choices.

Glossary

The following terms are defined or described. Descriptions are used when precise definitions are too technical.

Abacus An ancient counting frame or device consisting of movable beads on parallel rods. Each rod represents a place in a numeral. An empty rod performs the same function that zero performs in holding a place in a numeral.

Academic acceleration The process which makes it possible for a pupil to advance in a subject faster than usual and complete a school program or grade in less than the usual allotted time.

Accountability The degree that specified goals or objectives have been attained in a given subject.

Accuracy in measurement If M and N represent two measurements, M is more accurate than N when the relative error in M is less than in N.

Acute angle An angle having a measure between $0°$ and $90°$.

Addend A number to be added to find a sum. The addends in $4 + 7 + 9$ are 4, 7, and 9.

Adding by endings Involves the addition of a two-digit number and a one-digit number in one mental operation.

Additive inverse The sum of any number and its additive inverse is zero.

Adjacent angles Two angles having the same vertex and a ray (side) in common.

Affective objectives Desired ends to be attained pertaining to the learner's attitude toward the subject studied.

Algorism (Algorithm) A method of writing and performing any of the four basic operations.

And (probability) The probability of "A and B" is the probability of A multiplied by the probability of B. In symbolic form: P(A and B) = P(A) × P(B)

Angle A geometric figure formed by two rays with a common beginning point (vertex).

Approximation. A number which is nearly correct, often arrived at by estimation.

Area The number of square units representing the measure of the interior region of a plane figure.

Arithmetic expression Consists of one or more symbols to represent numbers. If two or more numbers are represented, they are connected by conventional signs to indicate the operations to be performed. Examples of arithmetic expressions are 5, 3 + 7, 2 × 6, 18 ÷ 3 (*see Numeral*).

Array An orderly arrangement of the elements of a set in rows, with the same number of elements in each row.

Assessment The process of collecting comprehensive information for the purpose of evaluating a pupil's performance.

Associative picture A picture that is related to a topic, as a car for a problem dealing with mileage.

Associative property for addition According to this property, the way in which three addends are grouped does not affect the sum, as in $(a + b) + c = a + (b + c)$.

Associative property for multiplication According to this property, the way in which three factors are grouped does not affect the product, as in $(a \times b) \times c = a \times (b \times c)$.

Attribute blocks Sets of concrete learning aids including circles, triangles, squares, rectangles, and hexagons, all in three colors, two sizes, and two thicknesses.

Back to Basics The name frequently given to the mathematics program of the 1970s.

Base (percentage formula) The number used for applying the rate to find the percentage. In the equation 3% of 80 = n, the base is 80 $(p = br)$.

Base (system of numeration) The number of digits in a place system. Our system is base 10 because it uses the digits 0,1,2,3,4,5,6,7,8,9. The base also indicates the number of units in any place required to make one unit in the place immediately to the left (in a place system).

Base 10 blocks Manipulative models of the base 10 numeration system. Components consist of units, tens, hundreds, and thousands blocks. The unit cube is often 1 cm³. The ten, hundred, and thousand blocks increase in value by powers of 10, as in our base 10 system.

Base 10 type materials Any manipulatives used to help pupils understand our base 10 system, such as "bean sticks" and sets of pennies, dimes, and dollars.

Basic fact Any combination in addition or multiplication of a pair of one-digit numbers with the sum or product. The corresponding fact in subtraction or division is derived from the opposite operation, excluding division by 0.

Basic number pair Two one-digit numbers that may be used to form a basic fact in addition and multiplication.

Behavioral objective A type of behavior, such as the ability to divide by a two-place divisor. Many educators specify that an acceptable

means of determining this behavior be included.

Binary (operation) Involves only two numbers. All four basic operations are binary.

Brain hemisphere The brain is divided into a left and right hemisphere. Current research is investigating which functions are controlled by each hemisphere.

Bridging the decade A term used in adding by endings. When 5 is added to 18, the sum of 23 is in a new decade and bridging is said to occur.

Calculator logic The logic for a calculator determines the order in which keys must be pressed to perform a given operation.

Cardinal number A number that answers the question How many?

Cassette Contains magnetic tape which may be used to store microcomputer programs.

Casting out 9s The process of finding the remainder when a number is divided by 9, usually by the shortcut of adding the digits, for the purpose of checking computation.

Centi A metric prefix which indicates one-hundredth ($\frac{1}{100}$).

Circle The set of all points in a plane with a given distance from a fixed point called its center.

Circumference The distance "around" or length of a circle.

Closure A set of numbers is closed with respect to an operation if the answer obtained by applying that operation is an element in that set.

Cognitive The process of knowing based on perception, introspection, and/or memory.

Column impasse A place in subtraction in which numbers cannot be subtracted without regrouping.

Common fraction A rational number expressed in the form a/b where a, the numerator, and b, the denominator, are integers and b is not 0.

Common multiple A number divisible by two or more numbers. A common multiple may or may not be the least (lowest) common multiple.

Commutative property for addition The order of adding two numbers does not affect the sum, as in $a + b = b + a$.

Commutative property for multiplication The order of multiplying two factors does not affect the product, as in $a \times b = b \times a$.

Comparative subtraction A subtraction problem situation in which two numbers are compared to determine how much more or less one number is than the other.

Complex fraction Contains a fraction in the numerator, the denominator, or in both terms.

Complex number A number of the form $a + ib$ where a and b are real numbers and $i = \sqrt{-1}$ (square root of negative 1).

Composite number Has other whole-number factors besides itself and 1, for example, 6, which has factors of 2 and 3.

Computer-assisted instruction A process in which a computer helps a pupil to learn a topic by conducting a dialogue with the pupil, correcting errors, and reinforcing correct responses.

Computer literacy Understanding the nature and capabilities of a computer, including what it cannot do as well as what it can.

Computer memory The part of a computer that enables it to store information. This information may be alphabetic or numeric.

Computer program A set of instructions that enables the computer to perform a desired task.

Conceptual Associated with understanding basic ideas. A mental image of an action or thing.

Congruent Two geometric figures are congruent when they have the same size and shape.

Continuum A set of sequential skills from simple to more difficult in an uninterrupted progression.

Correlation A measure of the relationship between two sets of measurements. A high correlation indicates a close relationship between sets of measurements but not necessarily between sets being measured. It is not a causal relationship.

Counting board A manipulative device for early elementary work.

Counting numbers Whole numbers greater than 0 (1, 2, 3, 4, . . .); sometimes called natural numbers or positive integers.

Courseware Textbooks designed to be used in conjunction with a computer.

Criterion-reference test A test designed to determine the degree of mastery for specific objectives.

Decade A set of ten consecutive whole numbers beginning with a multiple of 10.

Decimal A fractional numeral in which the denominator is not written because it is indicated by the position of the decimal point.

Decimal fraction Usually abbreviated as "decimal."

Decomposition A method of subtraction that requires regrouping in order to complete the subtraction.

Deductive method A logical procedure that requires an "if-then" pattern.

Degree Celsius A metric unit for measuring temperature (0°C is freezing and 100°C is boiling).

Denominator In the fraction $\frac{a}{b}$, b is the denominator.

Density The mass of an object divided by its volume.

Diagnosis A process that enables a teacher to identify the step in an operation which causes a pupil error.

Diagnostic testing Giving tests to determine the place in which a learner has difficulty with a given operation or procedure.

Difference The answer obtained by subtracting two numbers.

Digit Any one of the 10 symbols used in the decimal system of numeration.

Direct measurement The measuring instrument is applied directly to the object that is being measured.

Directed numbers *See* Signed Numbers.

Discovery method of learning The way by which the learner finds out for himself or herself the thing to be learned. The teacher usually provides the types of activities that enable the learner to make discoveries.

Disk A magnetic-coated circular object on which computer programs are stored.

Disk drive A mechanism that stores and retrieves programs on disks.

Distributive property According to this property, if an indicated sum is to be multiplied by a number, each addend must be multiplied by that number and these products added. Thus, $a(b + c) = ab + ac$.

Dividend In a division example the dividend is the number to be divided, as 34 in the example $2\overline{)34}$. The dividend corresponds to the product in multiplication when one factor is missing.

Divisible One number, n, is divisible by another number, p, if p is a factor of n. Thus, 12 is divisible by 2, 3, 4, and 6 because each number is a factor of 12.

Divisor In a division example the divisor is the number by which the dividend is to be divided, as ⅔ in the example 6 ÷ ⅔. The product of the divisor and the quotient is equal to the dividend.

Egocentric behavior Concerned with only one's own activities or needs.

English units Common units, such as feet and inches, derived from the English system of measurement.

Equal additions method A method of subtraction in which the same power of 10 is added to each of the numbers involved.

Equally likely events Probability is based on the assumption that any event in a given set is as likely to occur as any other.

Equality See Equation.

Equation A mathematical statement indicating that two expressions name the same number. The equation $3 = 2 + 1$ is true; but the equation $3 = 2$ is false.

Equilateral triangle A triangle with congruent sides.

Equivalent fractions Another name for equal fractions. Two fractions are equal if they name the same number.

Error pattern Computational errors that follow the same pattern.

Exploratory level of maturity Pupils operate at the exploratory level of maturity when they deal with manipulative or visual materials.

Exponent The exponent "3" in 4^3 shows that the base 4 is to be used as a factor three times. The expression 4^3 is read "4 to the third power," and it means $4 \times 4 \times 4$.

Expository method A student uses a rule or a statement given by the teacher or some other authoritative source for learning. This method is a telling procedure that is the opposite of the discovery method.

Expressive vocabulary The vocabulary used in speaking and writing.

Face value (digit) The cardinal value of a digit in a numeral. The face value of 2 in 27 is cardinal value two.

Fact finder A set of movable beads on a rod to be used to model the basic facts in an operation, especially addition and subtraction.

Factor If two or more whole numbers are multiplied, each number is a factor of the product. In the expression $9 \times 24 = 216$, 9 and 24 are factors of 216.

Fine motor control The ability to handle and manipulate small materials with precision.

Formative evaluation Evaluation a teacher uses in the instruction process that is designed to direct and develop learning.

Fraction Usually used as an abbreviation for common fraction but may be used to refer to a decimal fraction.

Frame A frame holds a place for a numeral as in $\square + 3 = 8$. (See Variable.)

Functional picture A picture that provides data or information necessary to solve a problem or helps to clarify a given concept.

Geoboard A board, usually 25 cm by 25 cm (10″ by 10″), with a 5×5 array of pegs securely fastened to the board for stretching geobands (rubber bands) around the pegs to represent geometric shapes and number patterns.

Geometric figure One or more points in space.

Gram A metric unit of mass (weight) equal to the weight of a cubic centimeter of water (distilled) at 4°C.

Greatest common factor The largest factor (divisor) of two or more given numbers.

Guess and test A strategy for problem solving. The name describes the process.

Guided discovery A procedure in which the teacher provides carefully chosen activities that will enable pupils to make desired discoveries.

Hardware The computer and any physical device attached to it, such as a printer.

Heterogeneous class A class in which pupils have substantially different traits such as achievement, aptitude, attitude, and the like.

Heuristic A problem-solving procedure, frequently called a *strategy*, which often enables a pupil to solve a problem, as opposed to an algorism which guarantees success.

Higher-decade addition Adding by endings when the sums are in the 20s or beyond.

Higher-decade multiplication Multiplication in which the products are in the higher decades, usually above the 30s, as are certain products when multiplying by 6, 7, 8, or 9.

Homogeneous class A class in which pupils have similar traits such as age, aptitude, achievement, and the like.

Horizontal enrichment Activities for pupils beyond the normal offerings for the purpose of broadening their experiences by working in areas not ordinarily explored in a typical textbook.

Identity element for addition The identity element for addition is 0. Zero added to any number is that number.

Identity element for multiplication The identity element for multiplication is 1. Any number multiplied by 1 is that number.

Improper fraction A fraction greater than or equal to 1.

Indirect measurement When the measuring instrument is not applied directly to the object measured.

Individualized instruction An approach in which the teacher gives attention to individual needs of pupils and makes assignments on the basis of these needs.

Inductive method A logical procedure that draws conclusions on the basis of observations.

Inequality A number sentence showing that two expressions are names for different numbers; for example, $3 \neq 5$, or $n - 5 < 2$.

Integer The set of integers includes the set of positive whole numbers, negative whole numbers, and 0.

Interpretive vocabulary The vocabulary used in listening and reading.

Inverse operation An operation that "undoes" a given operation, as addition undoes subtraction or vice versa.

Irrational number A real number which cannot be expressed as the quotient of two integers.

Isosceles triangle A triangle with two congruent sides.

Key word A word that helps a pupil to recognize the operation required to solve a problem such as "difference," which often indicates subtraction. Such words must be used with caution as "difference" may require addition for the problem solution.

Kilo A metric prefix indicating 1000 times the base unit.

Kilobyte The basic unit of computer memory consisting of 1024 bytes (2^{10}) rather than 1000 because of the binary nature of computers.

Learning laboratory (center) A place where children can handle materials, perform mathematical experiments, practice skills, and become involved in the process of learning mathematics while developing an attitude of inquiry.

Least (lowest) common denominator The smallest number divisible by each denominator in a set of denominators; the lowest common multiple of a set of denominators.

Least (lowest) common multiple The smallest number divisible by each whole number in a given set of whole numbers.

Like fractions Fractions with a common denominator.

Line segment The shortest path between two points.

Liter The basic metric measure of capacity, equal to 1000 cm^3 and approximately 1.1 quarts.

Lowest terms A fraction is in lowest terms if numerator and denominator have no common factor greater than 1.

Mainframe computers The largest class of computers used in government and industry.

Manipulative materials Materials used in exploratory activities.

Mapping The pairing of members of one set with those of another. Two basic types are (1) one-to-one relationships and (2) many-to-one relationships.

Mastery level of maturity A pupil performs at the mastery level of maturity when the response is habitual with understanding.

Mathematical problem A problem that cannot be solved with a habitual response.

Mathematical sentence An equation or inequality.

Mathematical structure A set of properties that characterize a mathematical system.

Measurement The process of finding the number of standard units there are in an object or thing.

Measurement division The process of finding how many groups of a specific size are in a given group. The numbers involved represent like quantities. The quotient is a ratio.

Meter The standard metric measure of length (1 meter is 39.37 inches, rounded).

Microcomputers The smallest class of computers; often called *personal computers*.

Milli A metric prefix indicating one-thousandth of the standard unit.

Minicomputers A class of intermediate-sized computers.

Minuend The number from which another number is subtracted.

Mixed number   A number expressed in the form 2½ or 3¼, with a numeral containing a whole number and a fraction.

Motivation   An inner urge that causes students to willingly learn about a topic or subject.

Multiple   The product of any integer and a whole number is a multiple of that number.

Multiplicand   The number that is being multiplied.

Multiplication-division pattern   In verbal form: factor times factor = product is equivalent to product divided by factor = factor. The following four sentences illustrate the pattern: $3 \times 4 = 12$; $4 \times 3 = 12$; $12 \div 3 = 4$; $12 \div 4 = 3$.

Multiplicative identity   The number 1 is the multiplicative identity because $1 \times n = n \times 1 = n$ for all n.

Multiplicative inverse   *See* Reciprocal.

Multiplier   The number which multiplies the multiplicand.

Natural number   *See* Counting number.

Negative number   A number that is less than zero.

New Math   A term often applied to the mathematics curriculum of the 1960s because it involved many changes from the curriculum of the 1950s.

Nonstandard unit   An arbitrary unit selected to introduce the concept of measurement.

Nonterminating decimal   A decimal with an indeterminate number of decimal places, such as the decimal representation for ⅓.

Norm-referenced test   A standardized test that has statistical information available that may be used to interpret the score of a particular individual.

Number family   A set of basic facts with the same sum.

Number line   A line having numbers corresponding to points on the line.

Number pattern   An arrangement of numbers to illustrate a mathematical concept.

Number period   The system of grouping places in a numeral to facilitate the reading of the number represented.

Number property   A fundamental characteristic of a number or number operation.

Number system   A set of numbers and one or more operations.

Numeral   A symbol that represents a number.

Numeration system   A set of symbols for numbers such as the base 10 system or the Roman system.

Numerator   In the fraction ⅚, a is the numerator.

Objectives   Specific goals to be attained.

Obtuse angle   An angle having a measure between 90° and 180°.

Open sentence   A sentence that contains one or more variables.

Or (probability)   The probability of "A or B" is the probability of A plus the probability of B or: $P(A \text{ or } B) = P(A) + P(B)$.

Ordinal number   Answers the question, "Which one?" in a set of numbers, such as first or third.

Overloaded place   A place is overloaded when the number of items in that place cannot be expressed by a single digit.

Parallel   Two lines in the same plane are parallel if they do not intersect.

Parallelogram   A four-sided plane figure with opposite sides parallel.

Partial dividend   The dividend used to determine each quotient figure when the quotient contains more than one digit.

Partitive division   The separation of a collection into a given number of equal parts, involving numbers representing unlike objects. The quotient is a rate.

Pattern blocks   Versatile hardwood geometric shapes, usually in six colors, useful for counting, sorting, matching, linear and area measurement, and problem solving.

Percent   Another word for hundredths, as 11 percent = 11% = 11 hundredths = .11.

Percentage   The result obtained from finding the percent of a number. In 3 percent of 80 = 2.4, the percentage is 2.4.

Percentage formula $p = b \times r$ where p is the percentage b the base, and r the rate.

Perimeter   The sum of the measures of the sides of a polygon.

Peripherals   Devices that are attached to a computer, such as a printer.

Personal attributes   The visible characteristics of a person.

Pi (π)   The ratio of circumference divided by diameter of any circle, often approximated as 3.14, 3.1416, or 3 ½.

Perpendicular   Perpendicular lines intersect at right angles.

Place value The property of our numeration system which gives a digit a value that depends on its position in a numeral.

Polygon A plane closed figure formed by line segments.

Polyhedron A closed three-dimensional figure having four or more faces. Each face is a polygon and its interior.

Positional value Another name for place value. The positional or place value of 7 in 173 is 10.

Positive number Any number which is greater than zero.

Power of 10 Any number in the form 10^n. In elementary work, n is restricted to a whole number.

Precision The measurement M is more precise than the measurement N if the absolute error in M is smaller than the absolute error in N. Smaller units usually produce more precise measurement.

Preoperational A period in a child's cognitive development identified by Piaget as occurring from ages two to seven.

Prime factorization Consists in expressing a number as the product of its prime factors, as $12 = 2 \times 2 \times 3$.

Prime number A whole number greater than 1 which is divisible only by itself and 1.

Probability The ratio of the number of ways an event can succeed to the total number of ways it can succeed or fail.

Probability formula If H is the total number of ways in which an event can happen out of a total number of equally likely ways (N), the probability (P) is defined: $P = H/N$.

Product The result obtained by multiplying two numbers.

Proper fraction A fraction between 0 and 1.

Proportion In its most elementary form, a proportion consists of two equal rates or ratios, such as $\%$ = $\%$.

Protractor An instrument for measuring angles, usually semicircular for measuring angles from $0°$ to $180°$.

Psychomotor Muscular activity directly related to mental processes.

Pupil kit A set of materials for individual use in exploratory work. Primary and intermediate kits may differ.

Quadrilateral A four-sided polygon.

Quantitative thinking The ability to understand and interpret an amount or quantity when expressed in verbal or written form.

Quotient The answer obtained by dividing one number by another.

Ragged decimals Term usually applied to addition or subtraction of decimals containing different numbers of decimal places.

Random event A random event or choice is one in which no other factor than chance can affect its occurrence or selection.

Rate (percent) The rate times the base equals the percentage. The rate is often called the percent and is expressed with the percent sign or as a common or decimal fraction.

Rate A quotient, sometimes used interchangeably with ratio, but usually indicating division with numbers representing unlike quantities (partition division).

Ratio A quotient, sometimes used interchangeably with rate, but more often indicating division by numbers representing like quantities (measurement division).

Rational number The quotient of two integers with the divisor not zero.

Ray A part of a line beginning at a point and extending indefinitely in one direction.

Real numbers The set of numbers composed of the set of rational and irrational numbers. These numbers can be placed in a one-to-one correspondence with the points on a line.

Reciprocal The reciprocal of n is $1/n$ where n is not 0. The product of a number and its reciprocal is 1.

Region A part of a plane in two dimensions. A portion of space in three dimensions.

Regrouping The process of exchanging items in adjacent places for a base ten numeral on a 10 for 1 or 1 for 10 basis.

Reinforcement An activity designed to strengthen a concept or skill.

Reliability The reliability of a test reflects the consistency of results when the test is repeated.

Remainder The difference between the dividend and the largest multiple of the divisor contained in the dividend.

Renaming The process of replacing one numeral by another without changing the number.

Repeating decimal Usually applied only to nonterminating decimals. When a fraction with a factor other than 2 or 5 in its denominator is expressed as a decimal, the result is a nonterminating, repeating decimal as $\frac{1}{3} = .333 \ldots$ and $\frac{1}{11} = .0909 \ldots$

Repetend   The repetend in the repeating decimal $.09090909 \ldots$ is "09," the sequence of digits that repeat. A bar is sometimes used to indicate the repetend as $\frac{1}{11} = .\overline{09}$.

Rhombus   An equilateral quadrilateral.

Right angle   An angle having a measure of 90°.

Scalene triangle   Has no two sides that are congruent.

Scope and sequence   Reference to the amount of material to be covered (scope) at a given grade level and the order in which the material is to be taught (sequence).

Sensorimotor   The development of mental processes due to impulses carried from the brain and main nerves to produce a response to the sensory organs.

Sequence   A set of numbers such as 2, 3, 4 . . . Will usually have a common difference, ratio, or recognizable pattern for elementary grades.

Sequence cards   Individual cards, each containing a numeral that may be arranged in consecutive order.

Seriation   The process of placing numbers in order of magnitude.

Signed numbers   The set of numbers including positive numbers, negative numbers, and zero.

SI metrics   A modernized metric system known as the international system of units.

Similar figures   Figures having the same shape. Similar polygons have corresponding angles equal and corresponding sides proportional.

Social promotion   Pupils are promoted to the next grade in order to remain with their age group even though their academic achievement does not warrant promotion.

Software   A computer program or set of programs.

Solid   A three-dimensional figure and its interior.

Sorting board   A cardboard or wood surface with specifically marked areas to assist a child when placing objects from a collection in a category.

Standard algorism   The most common form of the procedure for performing basic operations.

Standard units   Officially designated units of measure with standards established and kept by a government.

Standardized test   A test carefully prepared and administered to large groups to establish norms.

Strand   Refers to the content of mathematics being taught, as addition, multiplication, estimation, and geometry.

Strategy   A problem-solving procedure. In most problems for the elementary program, a correct strategy enables the pupil to choose the operation or operations required for the solution.

Summative evaluation   Evaluation made at the end of a unit or course of study as a representation of a pupil's overall achievement.

Symbolic level of learning   Pupils operate at the symbolic level of learning when they deal with symbols, without the need for manipulative materials, and are guided by patterns and properties of numbers.

Symmetry   Correspondence in relative size, shape, and position with respect to a dividing point, line, or plane.

System of numeration   See Numeration system.

Tactile experiences   Learning experiences involving the sense of touch.

Terms of a fraction   The numerator and denominator of a fraction.

Tetrahedron   A polyhedron with four faces.

Tolerance   The allowable error in a measurement.

Total value (digit)   The product of the cardinal value of a digit and its place value. The total value of 2 in 325 is 20.

Trapezoid   A quadrilateral with one pair of parallel sides.

Twin primes   Two consecutive odd prime numbers, such as 3 and 5.

Ungraded class   A class composed of pupils chosen without reference to age, ability, achievement, or standard-grade classifications.

Unifix cubes   Plastic interlocking cubes for building rods of any length so that number values may be depicted to show operations with whole numbers, place value, estimation, measurement, graphing, and problem-solving situations.

Unit fraction   A fraction with a numerator of 1.

Unlike fractions   Fractions with unlike denominators.

Unlike but related fractions   Fractions such that the denominator of one is a multiple of the denominators of the others in the set.

Validity The validity of a test refers to its ability to measure what it was designed to measure (comparison of its result to initial criteria). Different types of validity are *concurrent, construct, content, face,* and *predictive.* Validity indicates the extent to which the results of a test agree with true achievement.

Variable A variable holds the place for a numeral. In the equation $x + 3 = 10$, x is a variable. A frame is a particular type of variable used in elementary programs.

Venn diagram A diagram that shows how sets are related.

Vertical enrichment The practice of providing more advanced content than is typical for a given class.

Volume The measure of the interior of a closed three-dimensional figure, usually expressed in cubic units.

Whole numbers The common name for cardinal numbers: 0, 1, 2, 3. . . .

Answers to Selected Exercises

CHAPTER 4

Exercises 4.1 (p. 54)

1. (a) 20,310 (b) 2,240 (c) 300,030 (d) 468 (e) 2,020,060
2. (a) ∩∩∩ | | (b) ℓℓℓ ∩∩

   (c) ℓℓ | | | (d) 𝆠 ℓℓ ∩∩∩
                        ℓℓℓ ∩∩∩

   (e) 𝆠 𝆠 |

Exercises 4.2 (p. 55)

1. (a) 245 (b) 440 (c) 2645 (d) 1,001,600 (e) 584 (f) 100,149 (g) 2,000,000 (h) 704 (i) 600,000 (j) 500,100
2. (a) CV (b) MMCCL (c) MCDXL (d) MI (e) $\overline{\text{M}}$ (f) $\overline{\text{CC}}$

Exercises 4.3 (pp. 59–60)

1. (a) 7356 (b) 5165 (c) 735 (d) 209 (e) 3026 2. (a) 3 thousands + 7 hundreds + 8 tens + 2 ones (b) 4 thousands + 2 tens + 5 ones 3. (a) $(4 \times 10^3) + (7 \times 10^2) + (3 \times 10^1) + 8$ (b) $(2 \times 10^4) + (9 \times 10^3) + (1 \times 10^2)$ 4. 732 = 7 hundreds + 3 tens + 2 ones; 73 tens + 2 ones; 732 ones. 5. (a) 378 = 3 hundreds + 7 tens + 8 ones; 37 tens + 8 ones; 378 ones (b) 2235 = 2 thousands + 2 hundreds + 3 tens + 5 ones; 22 hundreds + 3 tens + 5 ones; 223 tens + 5 ones; 2235 ones 6. (a) 3000 (b) 500 (c) 1 (d) 203

Exercises 4.4 (p. 62)

1. Identity 2. n + 0 = 0 + n = n; n × 1 = 1 × n = n for all n 3. 5 + 0; 0 + 5; 1 × 5; 5 × 1; many other answers 4. ¾ × ½ = ⅜ 5. 1 − 0 ≠ 0 − 1 6. (a) 0 (b) 1 (c) ¼ (d) 2, 10 (e) 3 (f) 3 (g) 0 (h) 1 (i) ⅔ (j) ⅚ (k) 1 (l) n

Exercises 4.5 (p. 63)

1. 4 + 3 2. (4 − 1) + 3 3. (4 + 1) + 3; 3 + (1 + 4); (1 + 4) + 3 4. Reduce the number almost by half.

Exercises 4.6 (pp. 64–65)

1. b 2. (2 + 8) + 7 3. (a) A (b) A (c) B (d) A (e) C 4. (a) 5, A (b) 0, A (c) 3, B (d) 7, C

Exercises 4.7 (pp. 67–68)

1 and 2. Two operations are needed to apply the distributive property 3. (a) (3 × 4) + (3 × 5) (b) 4 (5 + 15) (c) ½ (2 + 3) (d) X (2 + 3) 4. ½ (18 − 4) = ½ ×

14 = 2 5. 3 + (4 × 5) ≠ (3 + 4) × (3 + 5) 6. (8 − 4) ÷ 2 = (8 ÷ 2) − (4 ÷ 2); 2 ÷ (8 − 4) ≠ (8 ÷ 2) − (4 ÷ 2) 7. (a) 4 (b) 3 (c) 3 8. (a) × (b) + (c) × (d) − 9. (a) (3 × 5) + 2 (b) 4 + (3 × 4) (c) 9 − (2 × 3) (d) (8 ÷ 4) + 2 (e) (2 × 3) + (2 × 4) (f) 5 × 7) − (5 × 2) (g) 7 − (4 ÷ 2) (h) (6 ÷ 2) + (6 ÷ 3) (i) (6 × 2) − (6 ÷ 3) (j) (12 × 3) − 8 + 5

Exercises 4.8 (p. 71)

1. (a) whole numbers or cardinal numbers (b) counting or natural numbers, positive integers (c) integers (d) rationals 2. (a) N, C, I, Ra, R (b) C, I, Ra, R (c) Ra, R (d) I, Ra, R (e) N, C, I, Ra, R (f) Ir, R

Exercises 4.9 (p. 72)

1. (a) commutative (b) identity (c) commutative (d) identity (e) commutative (f) inverse (g) distributive (h) commutative (i) associative (j) associative (k) inverse 2. (a), (b), (d), (h) 3. (a) associative (b) distributive (d) associative (h) commutative 4. (a) ⅓ (b) ⁴⁄₃ (c) 2 (d) 2 (e) ⁻2 (f) ⁻2

CHAPTER 7 (p. 131)

7. (a) 100 − 55 = n; 45¢ (b) 25 + 42 = n; 67 papers (c) 54 − 15 = n; 39 (d) 56 − (21 + 18) = n; 17 cm 8. Dec.: "9 from 12, 3; 0 from 9, 9; 3 from 9, 6; 1 from 4, 3" EA: "9 from 12, 3; 1 from 10, 9; 4 from 10, 6; 2 from 5, 3"

CHAPTER 8

Exercises 8.1 (p. 140)

1. (a) 6 + 9; 8 + 7 (b) 5 + 5 + 5; 3 + 3 + 3 + 3 + 3 (c) 3 × 5 = 15; 5 × 3 = 15; (d) 15 ÷ 3 = 5; 15 ÷ 5 = 3 ÷ 2 2. (a) M, 4 × 8 = n (b) D-M, 35 ÷ 5 = n (c) M, 2 × 8 = n (d) D-M, 12 ÷ 4 = n (e) D-P, 10 ÷ 5 = n (f) D-P, 25 ÷ 5 = n

Exercises 8.2 (pp. 153–154)

1. 4 × 5 = n; 20 players 2. 3 × 8 = n; 24 yds. 3. 18 ÷ 6 = n; 3 hrs. 4. 35 ÷ 5 = n; 7 packages 5. 5 × 8 = n; 40 trees 6. 48 ÷ 8 = n; 6 stamps 7. commutative and associative; both addition and multiplication used in distributive 8. 3 × (30 + 2) 9. see page 61 11. (a) measurement (b) measurement (c) measurement (d) partition (e) partition 13. 10, 100; 10 = (9 + 1)

CHAPTER 9 (pp. 173–175)

1. 360 stars 2. 35 gallons 3. $1.10 change 4. 56° average temperature 5. 7 pieces 6. 15 7. (30 + 4) × (50 + 7) = (30 + 4) × 50 + (30 + 4) × 7 = 30 × 50 + 4 × 50 + 30 × 7 + 4 × 7 = 1500 + 200 + 210 + 28 = 1938 8. lower limit 1500; upper limit

2400   **9.** It eliminates estimation; usually takes longer; requires more space; useful for slow learners. **10.** Similar to multiple method but need not require all multiples to be written. For a quotient of 12, at most the first 3 multiples would be required.   **11.** (a) 12 × 15 = 180; 15 × 12 = 180; 180 ÷ 15 = 12; 180 ÷ 12 = 15 (b) 57 × 16 = 912; 16 × 57 = 912; 912 ÷ 16 = 57; 912 ÷ 57 = 12   **12.** Slow learners: use the multiple method; use the pyramid or subtractive method; write 1 × divisor, 5 × divisor and 10 × divisor as guides in estimation. Fast learners: Stress mental estimation with as little paper and pencil work as possible.   **13.** (a) For a given multiplicand, the larger the multiplier the larger the product. (b) For a given multiplier, the larger the multiplicand, the larger the product.   **14.** (a) For a given dividend, the larger the divisor the smaller the quotient. (b) For a given divisor, the larger the dividend the larger the quotient.   **15.** (a) 6 × 68 or 9 × 45 (b) 8 × 47 (c) 8 × 89   **16.** (a) given 4, find 1 (b) how many 4s are in 32 (c) given 1, find 8 (d) given 1, find 4 (e) how many 8s are in 32 (f) given 8, find 1

CHAPTER 10 (p. 194)

1. see page 179   **2.** see page 181   **3.** see page 181 **4.** see page 179   **5.** (a) 21 − 3 = 7; 1 item costs $7; 7 × 7 = 49; 7 items cost $49 (b) $^{n}/_{21}$ = $^{7}/_{3}$; n = 49; 7 items cost $49   **6.** (a) 2 × 3 = 6; 6 + 2 = 8; 10 − 8 = 2; $2 remain (b) n = 10 − 2 × 3 − 2; n = 2; $2 remain   **7.** (a) $3 per book (b) $3 per book (c) rate in answer: $6 per book   **8.** (a) given 1, find 18 (b) how many 3s are in 18 (c) given 3, find 1   **9.** $26.98   **11.** 2 hundreds, 1 fifty, 1 twenty, and one ten   **12.** 2 hundreds and 4 twenties

CHAPTER 11 (p. 204)

1. see page 194   **2.** see page 196   **3.** (a) 1800, 2800; closer to 1800; any number from 2000 to 2200 is a good estimate (b) 2800, 4000; closer to 4000; any number from 3600 to 3800 is a good estimate (c) 800, 1500; closer to 1500; any number from 1050 to 1250 is a good estimate (d) 4000, 5400; about in middle; 4700 is good estimate   **4.** (a) .2 (b) .3 (c) .03 (d) .08, .09, or .1 **5.** (a) 125.145 (b) 11.74912 (c) .0375 (d) 1.75 (e) 26312.5 (f) .00003   **6.** see page 196   **7.** see page 200   **8.** see page 200   **9.** appropriate software and availability of computers   **10.** storage and retrieval of information **11.** 3,628,800; and zero   **12.** (a) 55 (b) 65 (c) 75 (d) 85, 95, 105, 115, 125, and 135   **13.** 855   **14.** 2050   **15.** s = ½n(a + 1)

CHAPTER 12

Exercises 12.1 (p. 210)

1. 7, 13, 19; 5, 11, 17   **2.** The number is divisible by 2 or 3.   **3.** (a) false (b) false (c) true   **4.** (a) not prime

(b) may be prime (c) may be prime (d) may be prime (e) may be prime (f) not prime   **5.** see page 209   **6.** one (2)   **7.** (a) 15 = 3 × 5 (b) 8 = 2 × 2 × 2 or 2^3 (c) 30 = 2 × 3 × 5 (d) 2 × 3 × 3 × 7   **8.** (a) divisible by 2 (distributive property) (b) divisible by 3 (distributive property) (c) 9   **9.** 4n and 4n + 2; 4n + 1 or 4n + 3

Exercises 12.2 (pp. 214–215)

1. 1, 2, 3, 6, 9, 18   **2.** 18, 36, 54, 72, 90. 90 is LCM as it is first multiple of 18 which is divisible by 15. **3.** 15 = 3 × 5; 18 = 2 × 3 × 3; LCM = 2 × 3 × 3 × 5 = 90

Exercises 12.3 (p. 216)

1. 111 and 111111 are divisible by 3   **2.** 459 and 22221 are divisible by 9   **3.** 222, 123456, and 11112 are divisible by 6.   **4.** because 9 is divisible by 3   **5.** 12324   **7.** the error is a multiple of 9   **8.** incorrect

Exercises 12.4 (p. 219)

1. (a) 42 = 2 × 3 × 7 (b) 120 = 2 × 2 × 2 × 3 × 5 (c) prime   **4.** factor   **5.** LCM = 180; it is first multiple of 18 divisible by 12 and 15   **6.** 12 = 2 × 2 × 3; 15 = 3 × 5; 18 = 2 × 3 × 3; LCM = 2 × 2 × 3 × 3 × 5.   **7.** (⁻4 + 4) + 3 = 3   **8.** 8 − 11 = ⁻3; 8 = 11 + ⁻3   **9.** positive and negative whole numbers and zero   **10.** to distinguish between sign of direction and operation   **11.** Cardinal numbers   **12.** Natural numbers and positive integers   **14.** Error is multiple of 9

CHAPTER 13

Exercises 13.1 (p. 231)

1. (a) 2 (b) 3 (c) 5 (d) 4 (e) 12 (f) 3   **2.** (a) 8 = 2, 4, 8; 24 = 2, 3, 4, 6, 8, 12, 24; gcf = 8 (b) 9 = 3, 9; 12 = 2, 3, 4, 6, 12; gcf = 3 (c) 12 = 2, 3, 4, 6, 12; 15 = 3, 5, 15; gcf = 3 (d) 8 = 2, 4, 8; 18 = 2, 3, 6, 9, 18; gcf = 2 (e) 16 = 2, 4, 8, 16; 22 = 2, 11; gcf = 2   **3.** (a) 18 = 2 × 3 × 3; 24 = 2 × 2 × 2 × 3; gcf = 2 × 3 = 6 (b) 21 = 3 × 7; 28 = 2 × 2 × 7; gcf = 7 (c) 24 = 2 × 2 × 2 × 3; 26 = 2 × 13; gcf = 2 (d) 28 = 2 × 2 × 7; 52 = 2 × 2 × 13; gcf = 4 (e) 30 = 2 × 3 × 5; 50 = 2 × 5 × 5; gcf = 2 × 5 = 10 (f) 35 = 5 × 7; 42 = 2 × 3 × 7; gcf = 7   **4.** 3.   (a) ¾ (b) ¾ (c) $^{12}/_{13}$ (d) $^{7}/_{13}$ (e) ⅗ (f) ⅚

Exercises 13.2 (p. 235)

1. (a) 12, 24, 36, 48, 60 . . . ; 30, 60 . . . LCM = 60 **2.** 12 = 2 × 2 × 3; 30 = 2 × 3 × 5; LCM = 2 × 2 × 3 × 5 = 60
3. 2 | 12   30
     3 | 6   15
          2   5 = 2 × 3 × 2 × 5 = 60

(d) **1.** 4, 8, 12 . . . ; 6, 12 . . . ; 12 . . . ; LCM = 12 **2.** 4 = 2 × 2; 6 = 2 × 3; 12 = 2 × 2 × 3; LCM = 2 × 2 × 3 = 12

3.

$$\begin{array}{c|ccc} 2 & 4 & 6 & 12 \\ 2 & 2 & 3 & 6 \\ 3 & 1 & 3 & 3 \\ \hline & 1 & 1 & 1 \end{array} = 2 \times 2 \times 3 = 12.$$

Exercises 13.3 (p. 241)

4. $^{10}\!/_{15}$ and $^{9}\!/_{15}$ **5.** (a) $^{5}\!/_{12}$ (b) $^{2}\!/_{\varepsilon}$ (c) $^{9}\!/_{20}$ **6.** (a) $^{25}\!/_{40}$ (b) $^{35}\!/_{60}$ (c) $^{12}\!/_{28}$ (d) $^{12}\!/_{45}$ **6.** (a) 25 (b) 35 (c) 12 (d) 12 **7.** (a) $^{5}\!/_{8}$ (b) $^{4}\!/_{6} + ^{5}\!/_{6} = ^{11}\!/_{6}$ or $1^{5}\!/_{6}$ (c) $^{20}\!/_{24} + ^{9}\!/_{24} = ^{29}\!/_{24} = 1^{5}\!/_{24}$ **8.** (a) $^{3}\!/_{8}$ (b) $^{1}\!/_{6}$ (c) $^{11}\!/_{12}$ (d) $2^{11}\!/_{24}$ **9.** (a) 15, 30, 45, 60. GCD is 60, first multiple of 15 divisible by 12 (b) 12, 24, 36, 48, 60; 15, 30, 45, 60; LCM is 60 (c) 12 = 2 × 2 × 3; 15 = 3 × 5; LCM = 2 × 2 × 3 × 5 = 60 (d)

$$3 \begin{array}{|cc} 2 & 15 \\ 4 & 5 \end{array}$$

GCD = 3 × 4 × 5 = 60 **12.** (a) 18, 24, 36; 36 is divisible by 12; LCM = 36; 12 = 2 × 2 × 3; 18 = 2 × 3 × 3; LCM = 2 × 2 × 3 × 3 = 36 (b) 35, 70, 105, 140; 140 is divisible by 20; LCM = 140; 20 = 2 × 2 × 5; 35 = 5 × 7; LCM = 2 × 2 × 5 × 7 = 140 (c) 18, 36, 54, 72, 90; 90 is divisible by 10 and 15; LCM = 90; 10 = 2 × 5, 15 = 3 × 5, 18 = 2 × 3 × 3; LCM = 2 × 2 × 3 × 3 × 5 = 90 **13** (a) $^{2}\!/_{3}$ (b) $^{2}\!/_{7}$ (c) $^{2}\!/_{9}$ **14.** yes, but the answer will not always be in lowest terms.

CHAPTER 14 (p. 256)

1. reciprocal (multiplicative inverse); reciprocal **2.** zero **3.** multiply by its reciprocal **4.** fractions **5.** n = 2½ × 4 = 10; total is $10 **6.** given 1, find 2½ **7.** 4.5 yards per carry. **8.** given 24, find 1. **9.** 7⅔ gallons **10.** (a) $\dfrac{2 \times 4}{15} = ^{8}\!/_{15}$ (b) $^{3}\!/_{5} \times ^{1}\!/_{3} = ^{1}\!/_{5}$ (c) less than 1; divisor greater than dividend (d) $\dfrac{4 \times 5}{8} = 2\frac{1}{2}$ (e) $^{7}\!/_{2} \times ^{4}\!/_{17} = ^{14}\!/_{17}$ **11.** 4⅚ hours or 5 hours and 50 minutes

CHAPTER 15

Exercises 15.1 (p. 269)

1. (a) $^{1}\!/_{5} \times ^{20}\!/_{20} = ^{20}\!/_{100} = 20$ hundredths = 20%

(b) .23 = $^{23}\!/_{100}$ = 23 hundredths = 23% (c) $^{3}\!/_{8} = 3 \div 8 = .375 = ^{375}\!/_{1000} = ^{37.5}\!/_{100} = 37.5\%$ **2.** (a) 10% (b) 60% (c) 75% (d) 33⅓% or 33.3% **3.** (a) $^{7}\!/_{100}$ (b) $^{13}\!/_{100}$ (c) $^{75}\!/_{100}$ or $^{3}\!/_{4}$ (d) $^{1}\!/_{10}$ **4.** (a) .11 (b) .1 or .10 (c) .75 (e) 1.12

Exercises 12.2 (p. 272)

1. $.86 or 86¢ **2.** $2.50 **3.** $25 − $2.5 = $22.50; 90% of 25 = 22.50; $22.50 paid **4.** $420 **5.** $7000 + $420 = $7420; 106% of 7000 = 7240 or $7420 paid

Exercises 15.3 (p. 279)

1. 25% **2.** 400% **3.** 57% **4.** 57.1% **5.** 70% **6.** 66.67% **7.** (a) 17% (b) 17.1% (c) 17.07% **8.** 5%

Exercises 15.4 (p. 283)

1. 8.25 ft. **2.** 6 roses **3.** 16 pieces **4.** 65% **5.** 48% **6.** 160 gallons (30% of n = 48) **7.** .000017 **8.** n − 1 **10.** $^{12}\!/_{12} = ^{4}\!/_{3} = ^{16}\!/_{12}$; n = 16 **12.** .3 × n = 48; n = 48 ÷ .3; n = 160 **13.** $^{30}\!/_{100} = ^{48}\!/_{n}$; 30n = 4800; n = 160 **14.** Solution is incorrect as 9 is used for base instead of cost. Correct answer comes from 120% of n = 9; cost is $7.50 **15.** 18%; 10.8%; 8%.

CHAPTER 16

Exercises 16.1 (p. 293)

1. 1 cm³ = 1 mL; 1000 cm³ = 1 L; 1,000,000 cm³ = 1 kL **2.** (a) 3 km (b) 2000 m (c) 0.5 km (d) 50,000 m (e) 8.25 m (f) 22.1 cm (g) 216,000 m (h) 3.240 km (i) 32,000 mm (j) 0.264 **3.** (a) 32,000 mL (b) 0.032 L (c) 1 L (d) 15,000 cL (e) 0.355 L (f) 1,345,000 mL **4.** (a) 0.240 kg (b) 0.562 g (c) 8.6 dag (d) 7.321 t (e) 0.002350 kg (f) 2750 kg **5.** (a) < (b) = (c) = (d) < (e) > (f) <

Exercises 16.4 (p. 303)

2. (a) 236.6 (b) 473.2 (c) 946.4 (d) 354.8 (e) 532.3 **3.** (a) 4.25 (b) 6.38 (c) 8.5 (d) 9.35 (e) 13.6

Index